MyBCommLab.com

Use MyBCommLab.com to test your understanding of the concepts presented in every chapter and explore additional materials that will bring the ideas to life in video, activities, and an online multimedia ebook.

Get the latest information and advice with Real-Time Updates

A unique integration of print and electronic media, the Real-Time Updates service provides fresh content throughout the course to reinforce your learning.

Discover a proven writing process that will help you for the rest of your life

The time-tested three-step writing process helps you craft a variety of messages for print and electronic media quickly and easily. (See examples on pp. 49, 146, and 311.)

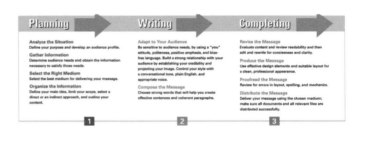

Find answers quickly with the Handbook of Grammar, Mechanics, and Usage

This handy reference offers summaries of essential points of grammar, mechanics, and usage—plus helpful lists of frequently confused, misused, and misspelled words. (See p. H-1.)

1.2 Pronouns

A **pronoun** is a word that stands for a noun; it saves repeating the noun:

> Employees have some choice of weeks for vacation, but *they* must notify the HR office of *their* preference by March 1.

The pronouns *they* and *their* stand in for the noun *employees*. The noun that a pronoun stands for is called the **antecedent** of the pronoun; *employees* is the antecedent of *they* and *their*.

When the antecedent is plural, the pronoun that stands in for it has to be plural; *they* and *their* are plural pronouns because *employees* is plural. Likewise, when the antecedent is singular, the pronoun has to be singular:

> We thought the contract had expired, but we soon learned that *it* had not.

1.2.1 Multiple Antecedents

Sometimes a pronoun has a double (or even a triple) antecedent:

Simplify and accelerate learning with MyBcommLab.com

Use MyBCommLab.com to test your understanding of the concepts presented in the text and explore additional materials that will bring the ideas to life in video, activities, and an online multimedia ebook.

PEARSON
mybcommlab™

Business Communication Essentials

Business Communication Essentials

FOURTH EDITION

Courtland L. Bovée

Professor of Business Communication
C. Allen Paul Distinguished Chair
Grossmont College

John V. Thill

Chairman and Chief Executive Officer
Global Communication Strategies

Upper Saddle River, New Jersey

Library of Congress Cataloging-in-Publication Data
Bovée, Courtland L.
   Business communication essentials/Courtland L. Bovée, John V. Thill.—4th ed.
   p. cm.
   ISBN 978-0-13-608441-9 (alk. paper)
   I. Business communication. 2. Business writing. 3. Business presentations. I. Thill,
   HF5718.B659 2010
   658.4'5--dc22   2008043322

Acquisitions Editor: James Heine
Editorial Director: Sally Yagan
Product Development Manager: Ashley Santora
Editorial Assistant: Karin Williams
Marketing Manager: Nikki Jones
Marketing Assistant: Ian Gold
Permissions Project Manager: Charles Morris
Senior Managing Editor: Judy Leale
Associate Managing Editor: Suzanne DeWorken
Production Project Manager: Karalyn Holland
Senior Operations Specialist: Arnold Vila
Operations Specialist: Carol O'Rourke
Creative Director: Christy Mahon
Senior Art Director: Janet Slowik
Cover Designer: Kristine Carney
Interior Designer: Ilze Lemesis
Art Director: Ilze Lemesis
Director, Image Resource Center: Melinda Patelli
Manager, Rights and Permissions: Zina Arabia
Manager, Visual Research: Beth Brenzel
Image Permission Coordinator: Nancy Seise
Manager, Cover Visual Research & Permissions: Karen Sanatar
Composition: GGS Higher Education Resources, A Division of Premedia Global, Inc.
Full-Service Project Management: Jeanine Furino/GGS Higher Education Resources,
A Division of Premedia Global, Inc.
Printer/Binder: Courier Companies - Kendallville
Typeface: 10.5/12 Minion

Credits and acknowledgments for materials borrowed from other sources and reproduced, with permission, in this textbook appear on page AC-1.

Pearson Education Ltd., London
Pearson Education Singapore, Pte. Ltd
Pearson Education, Canada, Inc.
Pearson Education–Japan
Pearson Education Australia PTY, Limited

Pearson Education North Asia, Ltd., Hong Kong
Pearson Educación de México, S.A. de C.V.
Pearson Education Malaysia, Pte. Ltd
Pearson Education Upper Saddle River,
New Jersey

Prentice Hall
is an imprint of

PEARSON

10 9 8 7 6 5 4 3
ISBN-13: 978-0-13-608441-9
ISBN-10:   0-13-608441-9

www.pearsonhighered.com

Contents in Brief

Preface xv
Prologue P-1

[unit 1] BUSINESS COMMUNICATION FOUNDATIONS 3

CHAPTER 1   Understanding Business Communication in Today's
             Workplace 4
CHAPTER 2   Mastering Interpersonal Communication 28

[unit 2] THE THREE-STEP WRITING PROCESS 47

CHAPTER 3   Planning Business Messages 48
CHAPTER 4   Writing Business Messages 68
CHAPTER 5   Completing Business Messages 92

[unit 3] BRIEF BUSINESS MESSAGES 115

CHAPTER 6   Crafting Messages for Electronic Media 116
CHAPTER 7   Writing Routine and Positive Messages 143
CHAPTER 8   Writing Negative Messages 172
CHAPTER 9   Writing Persuasive Messages 200

[unit 4] LONGER BUSINESS MESSAGES 231

CHAPTER 10   Understanding and Planning Reports and Proposals 232
CHAPTER 11   Writing and Completing Reports and Proposals 260
CHAPTER 12   Developing Oral and Online Presentations 310

[unit 5] EMPLOYMENT MESSAGES AND JOB
            INTERVIEWS 337

CHAPTER 13   Building Careers and Writing Résumés 338
CHAPTER 14   Applying and Interviewing for Employment 365

APPENDIX A   Format and Layout of Business Documents A-1
APPENDIX B   Documentation of Report Sources A-20
APPENDIX C   Correction Symbols A-26

Video Guide VG-1
Handbook of Grammar, Mechanics, and Usage H-1
Answer Key AK-1
References R-1
Acknowledgments AC-1
Index I-1

Contents

Preface xv

Prologue P-1

[unit 1]　BUSINESS COMMUNICATION FOUNDATIONS 3

CHAPTER 1　**Understanding Business Communication in Today's Workplace 4**

Communicating in Today's Global Business Environment 4
Recognizing Effective Communication 5
Understanding What Employers Expect from You 5

Understanding the Communication Process 7

Developing Your Business Communication Skills 8
Committing to Ethical Communication 8
Adopting an Audience-Centered Approach 9
Improving Your Intercultural Sensitivity 10
Giving—and Responding to—Constructive Feedback 15
Being Sensitive to Business Etiquette 20
Using Communication Technology Effectively 20

Document Makeover 21

Chapter Review and Activities 21
Test Your Knowledge 22
Apply Your Knowledge 22
Practice Your Knowledge 23
Expand Your Knowledge 25
MyBCommLab.com 25
Improve Your Grammar, Mechanics, and Usage 25

CHAPTER 2　**Mastering Interpersonal Communication 28**

Improving Your Performance in Teams 28
Advantages and Disadvantages of Teams 29
Collaborative Writing 29

Developing Your Business Etiquette 30
Etiquette in the Workplace 30
Etiquette in Social Settings 31

Making Your Meetings More Productive 32
Preparing for Meetings 32
Leading and Participating in Meetings 33
Using Meeting Technologies 35

Improving Your Listening Skills 36
Recognizing Various Types of Listening 36
Understanding the Listening Process 36
Overcoming Barriers to Effective Listening 37

Improving Your Nonverbal Communication Skills 38

Document Makeover 40

Chapter Review and Activities 40
Test Your Knowledge 41
Apply Your Knowledge 41
Practice Your Knowledge 42
Expand Your Knowledge 44

MyBCommLab.com 44

Improve Your Grammar, Mechanics, and Usage 44

 THE THREE-STEP WRITING PROCESS 47

CHAPTER 3   **Planning Business Messages 48**

Understanding the Three-Step Writing Process 48

Analyzing Your Situation 49
Defining Your Purpose 50
Developing an Audience Profile 50

Gathering Information 51
Uncovering Audience Needs 52
Providing Required Information 52

Selecting the Right Medium 52
Oral Media 52
Written Media 53
Visual Media 53
Electronic Media 53
Factors to Consider When Choosing Media 55

Organizing Your Message 56
Defining Your Main Idea 58
Limiting Your Scope 58
Choosing Between Direct and Indirect Approaches 59
Outlining Your Content 60

Document Makeover 61

Chapter Review and Activities 61

Test Your Knowledge 62

Apply Your Knowledge 62

Practice Your Knowledge 62

Expand Your Knowledge 65

MyBCommLab.com 66

Improve Your Grammar, Mechanics, and Usage 66

CHAPTER 4   **Writing Business Messages 68**

Adapting to Your Audience 68
Being Sensitive to Your Audience's Needs 69
Building Strong Relationships with Your Audience 72
Controlling Your Style and Tone 74

Composing Your Message 76
Choosing Strong Words 77
Creating Effective Sentences 80
Crafting Coherent Paragraphs 81

Using Technology to Compose and Shape Your Messages 84

Document Makeover 84

Chapter Review and Activities 85

Test Your Knowledge 85

Apply Your Knowledge 85

Practice Your Knowledge 86

Expand Your Knowledge 89

MyBCommLab.com 90

Improve Your Grammar, Mechanics, and Usage 90

CHAPTER 5   **Completing Business Messages 92**

Revising Your Message 92
Evaluating Your Content, Organization, Style, and Tone 92
Reviewing for Readability 93
Editing for Clarity 95
Editing for Conciseness 97
Evaluating, Editing, and Revising the Work of Others 99
Using Technology to Revise Your Message 99

Producing Your Message 102
Adding Graphics, Sound, Video, and Hypertext 102
Designing for Readability 102
Using Technology to Produce Your Message 105

Proofreading Your Message 106

Distributing Your Message 106

Document Makeover 107

Chapter Review and Activities 108

Test Your Knowledge 108

Apply Your Knowledge 108

Practice Your Knowledge 109

Expand Your Knowledge 112

MyBCommLab.com 112

Improve Your Grammar, Mechanics, and Usage 112

[unit 3]   BRIEF BUSINESS MESSAGES 115

CHAPTER 6   **Crafting Messages for Electronic Media 116**

Choosing Electronic Media for Brief Messages 116

Creating Effective E-Mail Messages 117
Adapting the Three-Step Process for Successful E-Mail 117

Creating Effective Instant Messages and Text Messages 120
Understanding the Benefits and Risks of IM 121
Adapting the Three-Step Process for Successful IM 121

Creating Effective Business Blogs 123
Understanding the Business Applications of Blogging 123
Adapting the Three-Step Process for Successful Blogging 124

Creating Effective Podcasts 126
Adapting the Three-Step Process for Successful Podcasting 126
Assembling a Podcasting System 128

Collaborating on Wikis 128
Understanding the Wiki Philosophy 129
Adapting the Three-Step Process for Successful Wiki Writing 129

Document Makeover 130

Chapter Review and Activities 130

Test Your Knowledge 131

Apply Your Knowledge 131

Practice Your Knowledge 132

Expand Your Knowledge 136

MyBCommLab.com 136

Improve Your Grammar, Mechanics, and Usage 140

CHAPTER 7   Writing Routine and Positive Messages 143

Using the Three-Step Writing Process for Routine and Positive Messages 143

Making Routine Requests 144
Strategy for Routine Requests 144
Common Examples of Routine Requests 145

Sending Routine Replies and Positive Messages 148
Strategy for Routine Replies and Positive Messages 148
Common Examples of Routine Replies and Positive Messages 150

Document Makeover 157

Chapter Review and Activities 157
Test Your Knowledge 158
Apply Your Knowledge 158
Practice Your Knowledge 158
Expand Your Knowledge 164
MyBCommLab.com 164
Improve Your Grammar, Mechanics, and Usage 169

CHAPTER 8   Writing Negative Messages 172

Using the Three-Step Writing Process for Negative Messages 172
Step 1: Planning Negative Messages 172
Step 2: Writing Negative Messages 173
Step 3: Completing Negative Messages 173

Developing Negative Messages 173
Using the Direct Approach Effectively 174
Using the Indirect Approach Effectively 176

Exploring Common Examples of Negative Messages 178
Sending Negative Messages on Routine Business Matters 178
Sending Negative Employment Messages 183
Sending Negative Organizational News 186

Document Makeover 187

Chapter Review and Activities 188
Test Your Knowledge 188
Apply Your Knowledge 188
Practice Your Knowledge 189
Expand Your Knowledge 192
MyBCommLab.com 192
Improve Your Grammar, Mechanics, and Usage 197

CHAPTER 9   Writing Persuasive Messages 200

Using the Three-Step Writing Process for Persuasive Messages 200
Planning Persuasive Messages 200
Writing Persuasive Messages 202
Completing Persuasive Business Messages 203

Developing Persuasive Business Messages 203
Strategies for Persuasive Business Messages 203
Common Examples of Persuasive Business Messages 207

Developing Marketing and Sales Messages 208
Strategies for Marketing and Sales Messages 209

Document Makeover 215

Chapter Review and Activities 215

Test Your Knowledge 216

Apply Your Knowledge 216

Practice Your Knowledge 217

Expand Your Knowledge 222

MyBCommLab.com 222

Improve Your Grammar, Mechanics, and Usage 227

[unit 4]   LONGER BUSINESS MESSAGES 231

CHAPTER 10 **Understanding and Planning Reports and Proposals 232**

Applying the Three-Step Writing Process to Reports and Proposals 232
Analyzing the Situation 233
Gathering Information 234
Selecting the Right Medium 235
Organizing Your Information 236

Supporting Your Messages with Reliable Information 236
Planning Your Research 237
Locating Data and Information 237
Using Your Research Results 240

Planning Informational Reports 242
Organizing Informational Reports 242
Organizing Website Content 242

Planning Analytical Reports 244
Focusing on Conclusions 244
Focusing on Recommendations 244
Focusing on Logical Arguments 245

Planning Proposals 246

Document Makeover 249

Chapter Review and Activities 250

Test Your Knowledge 250

Apply Your Knowledge 250

Practice Your Knowledge 251

Expand Your Knowledge 253

MyBCommLab.com 254

Improve Your Grammar, Mechanics, and Usage 257

CHAPTER 11 **Writing and Completing Reports and Proposals 260**

Writing Reports and Proposals 260
Adapting to Your Audience 260
Composing Reports and Proposals 261

Illustrating Your Reports with Effective Visuals 269
Choosing the Right Visual for the Job 269
Designing Effective Visuals 276

Completing Reports and Proposals 277
Revising Reports and Proposals 277
Producing a Formal Report 277
Producing a Formal Proposal 293
Proofreading Your Reports and Proposals 294
Distributing Your Reports and Proposals 296

Document Makeover 297

Chapter Review and Activities 298

Test Your Knowledge 299

Apply Your Knowledge 299

Practice Your Knowledge 300

Expand Your Knowledge 301

MyBCommLab.com 302

Improve Your Grammar, Mechanics, and Usage 307

CHAPTER 12 **Developing Oral and Online Presentations 310**

Building Your Career with Oral Presentations 310

Planning Your Presentation 311
Analyzing the Situation 311
Selecting the Right Medium 312
Organizing Your Presentation 313

Writing Your Presentation 316
Adapting to Your Audience 317
Composing Your Presentation 317
Enhancing Your Presentation with Effective Visuals 320

Completing Your Presentation 325
Finalizing Slides and Support Materials 325
Preparing to Speak 327
Practicing Your Delivery 327
Overcoming Anxiety 328
Handling Questions Responsively 328

Document Makeover 329

Chapter Review and Activities 329

Test Your Knowledge 330

Apply Your Knowledge 330

Practice Your Knowledge 331

Expand Your Knowledge 333

MyBCommLab.com 334

Improve Your Grammar, Mechanics, and Usage 335

[unit 5]   EMPLOYMENT MESSAGES AND JOB
                INTERVIEWS 337

CHAPTER 13 **Building Careers and Writing Résumés 338**

Securing Employment in Today's Job Market 338
Understanding Employers' Approach to the Employment Process 338
Organizing Your Approach to the Employment Process 340

Preparing Résumés 342
Planning Your Résumé 342
Writing Your Résumé 348
Completing Your Résumé 352

Document Makeover 357

Chapter Review and Activities 358

Test Your Knowledge 358

Apply Your Knowledge 358

Practice Your Knowledge 359

Expand Your Knowledge 361

MyBCommLab.com 361

Improve Your Grammar, Mechanics, and Usage 362

CHAPTER 14 Applying and Interviewing for Employment 365

Writing Application Letters and Other Employment Messages 365
Application Letters 365
Application Follow-Ups 369

Understanding the Interviewing Process 370
The Typical Sequence of Interviews 370
Common Types of Interviews 370
Interview Media 371
What Employers Look For in an Interview 372
Preemplyment Testing and Background Checks 372

Preparing for a Job Interview 373
Learning About the Organization 373
Thinking Ahead About Questions 373
Bolstering Your Confidence 376
Polishing Your Interview Style 376
Planning to Look Good 377
Being Ready When You Arrive 378

Interviewing for Success 378
The Warm-Up 378
The Question-and-Answer Stage 379
The Close 380
Interview Notes 381

Following Up After an Interview 381
Thank-You Message 381
Message of Inquiry 381
Request for a Time Extension 382
Letter of Acceptance 382
Letter Declining a Job Offer 383
Letter of Resignation 383

Document Makeover 384

Chapter Review and Activities 384
Test Your Knowledge 385

Apply Your Knowledge 385

Practice Your Knowledge 386

Expand Your Knowledge 388

MyBCommLab.com 388

Improve Your Grammar, Mechanics, and Usage 390

APPENDIX A Format and Layout of Business Documents A-1
APPENDIX B Documentation of Report Sources A-20
APPENDIX C Correction Symbols A-26

Video Guide VG-1
Handbook of Grammar, Mechanics, and Usage H-1
Answer Key AK-1
References R-1
Acknowledgments AC-1
Index I-1

LOOKING FOR A COMPETITIVE ADVANTAGE THAT WILL HELP YOU AT EVERY STAGE OF YOUR CAREER?

Communication is one the most fundamental elements of business, whether it's a research team gathering clues about market trends or an inspirational leader guiding a company in pursuit of shared goals. Effective communication is essential to success for both organizations and individuals, and ineffective communication is often the cause of minor mistakes, major strategic blunders, and catastrophic failures. No matter what profession you want to pursue, the ability to communicate will be an essential skill—and a skill that employers expect you to have when you enter the workforce.

This course introduces you to the fundamental principles of business communication and gives you the opportunity to develop your communication skills. You'll discover how business communication differs from personal and social communication, and you'll see how today's companies are using blogging, podcasting, video, wikis, and other innovative technologies. You'll learn a simple three-step writing process that works for all types of writing and speaking projects, both in college and on the job. Along the way, you'll gain valuable insights into ethics, etiquette, listening, teamwork, and nonverbal communication. Plus, you'll learn effective strategies for the many different types of communication challenges you'll face on the job, from routine messages about transactions to complex reports and websites.

Colleges and universities vary in the prerequisites established for the business communication course, but we advise taking at least one course in English composition before taking this class. Having completed some coursework in business studies will also give you a better perspective on communication challenges in the workplace. However, we have taken special care not to assume any in-depth business experience, so you can use *Business Communication Essentials* successfully even if you have limited on-the-job experience or business coursework.

HOW THIS COURSE WILL HELP YOU

Few courses can offer the three-for-the-price-of-one value you get from a business communication class. Check out these benefits:

- **In your other classes.** The communication skills you learn in this class can help you in virtually every other course you will take in college. From simple homework assignments to complicated team projects to oral presentations, you'll be able to communicate more effectively with less time and effort.

- **During your job search.** You can reduce the stress of searching for a job and stand out from the competition. As you'll see in Chapters 13 and 14, every activity in the job search process relies on communication. The better you can communicate, the more successful you'll be in landing interesting and rewarding work.

- **On the job.** After you get that great job, the time and energy you have invested in this course will continue to yield benefits year after year. As you tackle each project and every new challenge, influential company leaders—the people who largely determine how quickly you'll get promoted and how much you'll earn—will be paying close attention to how well you communicate. They will observe your interactions with colleagues, customers, and business partners. They'll take note of how well you can collect data, find the essential ideas buried under mountains of information, and convey those points to other people. They'll observe your ability to adapt to different audiences and circumstances. They'll be watching when you encounter tough situations that require careful attention to ethics and etiquette. All this may sound daunting, but every insight you gain and every skill you develop in this course will help you shine in your future career.

HOW TO SUCCEED IN THIS COURSE

Although this course explores a wide range of message types and appears to cover quite a lot of territory, the underlying structure of the course is actually rather simple. You'll learn a few basic concepts, identify some key skills to use and procedures to follow, and then practice, practice, practice. Whether you're writing a blog posting in response to one of the real-company cases or drafting a copy of your own résumé, you'll be practicing the same skills again and again. With feedback and reinforcement from your instructor and your class-mates, your confidence will grow, and the work will become easier and more enjoyable.

The following sections offer advice on approaching each assignment, using your text-book, and taking advantage of some other helpful resources.

Approaching Each Assignment

In the spirit of practice and improvement, you will have a number of writing (and possibly speaking) assignments throughout this course. These suggestions will help you produce better results with less effort:

- **First, don't panic!** If the thought of writing a report or giving a speech sends a chill up your spine, you're not alone. Everybody feels that way when they are first learning busi-ness communication skills, and even experienced professionals can feel nervous about major projects. Keeping three points in mind will help. First, every project can be broken down into a series of small, manageable tasks. Don't let a big project overwhelm you; it's nothing more than a bunch of smaller tasks. Second, remind yourself that you have the skills you need to accomplish each task. As you move through the course, the assign-ments are carefully designed to match the skills you've developed up to that point. Third, if you feel panic creeping up on you, take a break and regain your perspective.

- **Focus on one task at a time.** A common mistake is trying to organize and express your ideas while simultaneously worrying about audience reactions, grammar, spelling, format-ting, page design, print quality, and a dozen other factors. You must fight the temptation to do everything at once; otherwise, your frustration will soar, and your productivity will plummet. In particular, don't worry about grammar, spelling, and word choices during your first draft. Concentrate on the organization of your ideas first, then the way you express those ideas, and then the presentation and production of your messages. Following the three-step writing process is an ideal way to focus on one task at a time in a logical sequence.

- **Give yourself plenty of time.** As with every other school project, putting things off to the last minute creates unnecessary stress. Writing and speaking projects in particular are much easier if you tackle them in small stages, with breaks in between, rather than try to get everything done in one frantic blast. Moreover, there will be instances when you simply get stuck on a project; the best thing to do in such a situation is walk away and give your mind a break. If you allow room for this in your schedule, you'll minimize the frustration and spend less time overall on your homework, too.

- **Step back and assess each project before you start.** The writing and speaking projects you'll have in this course cover a wide range of communication scenarios, and it's essen-tial that you adapt your approach to each new challenge. Resist the urge to dive in and start writing without a plan. Ponder an assignment for a while, consider the various approaches you might take, and think carefully about your objectives before you start writing. Nothing is more frustrating than getting stuck halfway through because you're not sure what you're trying to say or you've wandered off track. Spend a little time plan-ning, and you'll spend a lot less time writing.

- **Use the three-step writing process.** The essential planning tasks are the first step in the three-step writing process, which you'll learn about in Chapter 3 and use throughout the course. This process has been developed and refined by professional writers with decades of experience and thousands of projects, ranging from simple e-mail messages to 600-page textbooks. It works; take advantage of it.

- **Learn from the examples and model documents.** This textbook offers dozens of real-istic examples of business messages, many with notes along the sides that explain strong and weak points. Study these and any other examples that your instructor provides. Learn what works and what doesn't work and then apply these lessons to your own writing.

- **Learn from experience.** Finally, learn from the feedback you get from your instructor and from other students. Don't take the criticism personally; your instructor and your classmates are commenting about the work, not about you. View every piece of feedback as an opportunity to improve.

Using This Textbook Package

This book and its accompanying online resources introduce you to the key concepts and skills in business communication while helping you develop essential English skills. As you read each chapter, start by studying the learning objectives and the "From the Real World" quotation. These will help you identify the most important concepts in the chapter and give you a feel for what you'll be learning. As you work your way through the chapter, compare the advice given with the various examples, both brief in-text examples and the standalone model documents. At the end of each chapter, read the "Chapter Summary" section carefully to make sure you grasp essential information. (This section reflects the learning objectives at the beginning of the chapter, so it provides an easy way to check your learning.) Each chapter includes a variety of questions and exercises that help you gauge how well you've learned the material and are able to apply it to realistic business scenarios. Several chapters also have downloadable exercises; if your instructor assigns these, follow the instructions in the text to locate the correct files.

In addition to the 14 chapters of the text itself, here are some special features that will help you succeed in the course and on the job:

- **Prologue: Building a Career with Your Communication Skills.** This brief section (immediately following this Preface) helps you understand today's dynamic workplace, the steps you can take to adapt to the job market, and the importance of creating an employment portfolio.

- **Workbook.** The integrated workbook "Improve Your Grammar, Mechanics, and Usage" appears at the end of every chapter, with three levels of assessment and skill building in workplace applications and document critiques.

- **Handbook.** The "Handbook of Grammar, Mechanics, and Usage" (see page H-1) serves as a convenient reference of essential business English.

- **MyBCommLab.com.** Use MyBCommLab.com to test your understanding of the concepts presented in every chapter and explore additional materials that will bring the ideas to life in video, activities, and an online multimedia e-book.

- **Real-Time Updates.** You can use this unique newsfeed service to make sure you're always kept up to date on important topics. Plus, at strategic points in every chapter, you will be directed to the Real-Time Updates website to get the latest information about specific subjects. To sign up for automatic updates via RSS, visit http://real-timeupdates.com/bce.

- **Business Communication Web Search.** With this revolutionary approach to searching, which was developed by the authors, you can quickly access more than 325 search engines. The tool uses a simple and intuitive interface engineered to help you find precisely what you want, whether it's PowerPoint files, Adobe Acrobat PDFs, Microsoft Word documents, Excel files, videos, or podcasts.

- **Companion Website.** This text's Companion Website, at www.pearsonhighered.com/bovee, offers free access to practice Document Makeovers, a student version of the PowerPoint package, an updated list of featured websites, the "English–Spanish Audio Glossary of Business Terms," and an online version of the "Handbook of Grammar, Mechanics, and Usage." In addition, the "Business Communication Study Hall" helps you brush up on several aspects of business communication—grammar, writing skills, critical thinking, report writing, résumés, and PowerPoint development.

Taking Advantage of Other Resources

Supplement your learning efforts with these helpful resources.

CourseSmart eTextbooks Online

CourseSmart is an exciting new choice for students looking to save money. As an alternative to purchasing the print textbook, you can purchase an electronic version of the same content and save up to 50% off the suggested list price of the print text. With a CourseSmart eTextbook, you can search the text, make notes online, print out reading assignments that incorporate lecture notes, and bookmark important passages for later review. For more information or to purchase access to the CourseSmart eTextbook, visit www.coursesmart.com.

FEEDBACK

The authors and the product team would appreciate hearing from you! Let us know what you think about this textbook by writing to college_marketing@prenhall.com. Please include "Feedback about Bovee/Thill BCE 4e" in the subject line.

ABOUT THE AUTHORS

Courtland L. Bovée and John V. Thill have been leading textbook authors for more than two decades, introducing millions of students to the fields of business and business communication. Their award-winning texts are distinguished by proven pedagogical features, extensive selections of contemporary case studies, hundreds of real-life examples, engaging writing, thorough research, and a unique integration of print and electronic resources. Each new edition reflects the authors' commitment to continuous refinement and improvement, particularly in terms of modeling the latest practices in business and the use of technology.

Professor Bovée has 22 years of teaching experience at Grossmont College in San Diego, where he has received teaching honors and was accorded that institution's C. Allen Paul Distinguished Chair. Mr. Thill is a prominent communications consultant who has worked with organizations ranging from Fortune 500 multinationals to entrepreneurial start-ups. He formerly held positions with Pacific Bell and Texaco.

ACKNOWLEDGMENTS

The fourth edition of *Business Communication Essentials* reflects the professional experience of a large team of contributors and advisors. We express our thanks to the many individuals whose valuable suggestions and constructive comments influenced the success of this book.

Reviewers of Previous Editions

Thank you to the following professors: Victoria Austin, Las Positas College; Faridah Awang, Eastern Kentucky University; Jeanette Baldridge, University of Maine at Augusta; Diana Baran, Henry Ford Community College; JoAnne Barbieri, Atlantic Cape Community College; Kristina Beckman, John Jay College; Judy Bello, Lander University; Carol Bibly, Triton College; Nancy Bizal, University of Southern Indiana; Yvonne Block, College of Lake County; Edna Boroski, Trident Technical College; Nelvia M. Brady, Trinity Christian College; Arlene Broeker, Lincoln University; David Brooks, Indiana University Southeast; Carol Brown, South Puget Sound Community College; Domenic Bruni, University of Wisconsin; Jeff Bruns, Bacone College; Gertrude L. Burge, University of Nebraska; Sharon Burton, Brookhaven College; Robert Cabral, Oxnard College; Dorothy Campbell, Brevard Community College; Linda Carr, University of West Alabama; Sharon Carson, St. Philip's

College; Rick Carter, Seattle University; Dacia Charlesworth, Indiana University–Purdue University Fort Wayne; Jean Chenu, Genesee Community College; Connie Clark, Lane Community College; Jerrie Cleaver, Central Texas College; Clare Coleman, Temple University; M. Cotton, North Central Missouri College; Pat Cowherd, Campbellsville University; Pat Cuchens, University of Houston–Clear Lake; Walt Dabek, Post University; Cathy Daly, California State University–Sacramento; Linda Davis, Copiah–Lincoln Community College; Harjit Dosanjh, North Seattle Community College; Amy Drees, Defiance College; Lou Dunham, Spokane Falls Community College; Donna Everett, Morehead State University; Donna Falconer, Anoka–Ramsey Community College; Kate Ferguson Marsters, Gannon University; Darlynn Fink, Clarion University of Pennsylvania; Bobbi Fisher, University of Nebraska–Omaha; Laura Fitzwater, Community College of Philadelphia; Matthew Gainous, Ogeechee Technical College; Yolande Gardner, Lawson State Community College; Gina Genova, University of California–Santa Barbara; Lonny Gilbert, Central State University; Nancy Goehring, Monterey Peninsula College; Dawn Goellner, Bethel College; Robert Goldberg, Prince George's Community College; Jeffrey Goldberg, MassBay Community College; Helen Grattan, Des Moines Area Community College; Barbara Grayson, University of Arkansas at Pine Bluff; Deborah Griffin, University of Houston–Clear Lake; Alice Griswold, Clarke College; Bonnie Grossman, College of Charleston; Lisa Gueldenzoph, North Carolina A&T State University; Wally Guyot, Fort Hays State University; Valerie Harrison, Cuyamaca College; Tim Hartge, The University of Michigan–Dearborn; Richard Heiens, University of South Carolina–Aiken; Maureece Heinert, Sinte Gleska University; Leighanne Heisel, University of Missouri–St. Louis; Gary Helfand, University of Hawaii–West Oahu; Cynthia Herrera, Orlando Culinary Academy; Kathy Hill, Sam Houston State University; Pashia Hogan, Northeast State Tech Community College; Sarah Holmes, New England Institute of Technology; Ruth Hopkins Zajdel, Ohio University–Chillicothe; Michael Hricik, Westmoreland County Community College; Rebecca Hsiao, East Los Angeles College; Mary Ann Hurd, Sauk Valley Community College; Pat Hurley, Leeward Community College; Harold Hurry, Sam Houston State University; Marcia James, University of Wisconsin–Whitewater; Frank Jaster, Tulane University; Jonatan Jelen, Parsons The New School For Design; Irene Joanette Gallio, Western Nevada Community College; Mark Johnson, Rhodes State College; Joanne Kapp, Siena College; Jeanette A. Karjala, Winona State University; Christy L. Kinnion, Lenior Community College; Deborah Kitchin, City College of San Francisco; Lisa Kirby, North Carolina Wesleyan College; Claudia Kirkpatrick, Carnegie Mellon University; Betty Kleen, Nicholls State University; Fran Kranz, Oakland University; Jana Langemach, University of Nebraska–Lincoln; Joan Lantry, Jefferson Community College; Kim Laux, Saginaw Valley State University; Ruth Levy, Westchester Community College; Nancy Linger, Moraine Park Technical College; Jere Littlejohn, University of Mississippi; Dana Loewy, California State University–Fullerton; Jennifer Loney, Portland State University; Susan Long, Portland Community College; Sue Loomis, Maine Maritime Academy; Thomas Lowderbaugh, University of Maryland–College Park; Jayne Lowery, Jackson State Community College; Lloyd Matzner, University of Houston–Downtown; Ron McNeel, New Mexico State University at Alamogordo; Dr. Bill McPherson, Indiana University of Pennsylvania; Phyllis Mercer, Texas Woman's University; Donna Meyerholz, Trinidad State Junior College; Annie Laurie I. Meyers, Northampton Community College; Catherine "Kay" Michael, St. Edward's University; Kathleen Miller, University of Delaware; Gay Mills, Amarillo College; Julie Mullis, Wilkes Community College; Pamela Mulvey, Olney Central College; Jimidene Murphey, Clarendon College; Cindy Murphy, Southeastern Community College; Dipali Murti-Hali, California State University–Stanislaus; Shelley Myatt, University of Central Oklahoma; Cora Newcomb, Technical College of the Lowcountry; Ron Newman, Crafton Hills College; Linda Nitsch, Chadron State College; Leah Noonan, Laramie County Community College; Mabry O'Donnell, Marietta College; Diana Oltman, Central Washington University; Ranu Paik, Santa Monica College; Lauren Paisley, Genesee Community College; Patricia Palermo, Drew University; John Parrish, Tarrant County College; Diane Paul, TVI Community College; John T. Pauli, University of Alaska–Anchorage; Michael Pennell, University of Rhode Island; Melinda Phillabaum, Indiana University; Ralph Phillips, Geneva College; Laura Pohopien, Cal Poly Pomona; Diane Powell, Utah Valley State College; Christine Pye, California Lutheran University;

Norma Pygon, Triton College; Dave Rambow, Wayland Baptist University; Richard David Ramsey, Southeastern Louisiana University; Charles Riley, Tarrant County College–Northwest Campus; Jim Rucker, Fort Hays State University; Dr. Suzan Russell, Lehman College; Calvin Scheidt, Tidewater Community College; Nancy Schneider, University of Maine at Augusta; Brian Sheridan, Mercyhurst College; Bob Shirilla, Colorado State University; Joyce Simmons, Florida State University; Gordon J. Simpson, SUNY Cobleskill; Jeff Smith, University of Southern California; Eunice Smith, Bismarck State College; Harvey Solganick, LeTourneau University–Dallas campus; Stephen Soucy, Santa Monica College; Linda Spargo, University of Mississippi; W. Dees Stallings, Park University; Angelique Stevens, Monroe Community College; Steven Stovall, Wilmington College; Alden Talbot, Weber State University; Michele Taylor, Ogeechee Technical College; Wilma Thomason, Mid-South Community College; Ed Thompson, Jefferson Community College; Lori Townsend, Niagara County Community College; Lani Uyeno, Leeward Community College; Wendy VanHatten, Western Iowa Tech Community College; Jay Wagers, Richmond Community College; Jie Wang, University of Illinois at Chicago; Chris Ward, The University of Findlay; Dorothy Warren, Middle Tennessee State University; Glenda Waterman, Concordia University; Kellie Welch, Jefferson Community College; Mathew Williams, Clover Park Technical College; Beth Williams, Stark State College of Technology; Brian Wilson, College of Marin; Sandra D. Young, Orangeburg–Calhoun Technical College.

Reviewers of "Document Makeover" Feature

We sincerely thank the following reviewers for their assistance with the Document Makeover feature: Lisa Barley, Eastern Michigan University; Marcia Bordman, Gallaudet University; Jean Bush-Bacelis, Eastern Michigan University; Bobbye Davis, Southern Louisiana University; Cynthia Drexel, Western State College; Kenneth Gibbs, Worcester State College; Ellen Leathers, Bradley University; Diana McKowen, Indiana University; Bobbie Nicholson, Mars Hill College; Andrew Smith, Holyoke Community College; Jay Stubblefield, North Carolina Wesleyan College; Dawn Wallace, Southeastern Louisiana University.

Reviewers of Model Documents

The many model documents in the text and their accompanying annotations received invaluable review from Dacia Charlesworth, Indiana University–Purdue University Fort Wayne; Diane Todd Bucci, Robert Morris University; Estelle Kochis, Suffolk County Community College; Sherry Robertson, Arizona State University; Nancy Goehring, Monterey Peninsula College; James Hatfield, Florida Community College at Jacksonville; Avon Crismore, Indiana University.

Personal Acknowledgments

We wish to extend a heartfelt thanks to our many friends, acquaintances, and business associates who provided materials or agreed to be interviewed so that we could bring the real world into the classroom.

A very special acknowledgment goes to George Dovel, whose superb editorial skills, distinguished background, and wealth of business experience assured this project of clarity and completeness. Also, recognition and thanks to Jackie Estrada for her outstanding skills and excellent attention to details. Her creation of the "Peak Performance Grammar and Mechanics" material is especially noteworthy. Paul Straley's professionalism and keen eye for quality were invaluable.

We also feel it is important to acknowledge and thank the Association for Business Communication, an organization whose meetings and publications provide a valuable forum for the exchange of ideas and for professional growth.

Additionally, we would like to thank the supplement authors who prepared material for this new edition. They include: Dacia Charlesworth, Indiana University–Purdue University Fort Wayne; Myles Hassell, University of New Orleans; and Jay Stubblefield, North Carolina Wesleyan College.

We want to extend our warmest appreciation to the devoted professionals at Prentice Hall. They include Jerome Grant, president; Sally Yagan, editorial director; James Heine, acquisitions editor; Nikki Jones, marketing manager; Ashley Santora, product development manager; Karin Williams, editorial assistant; all of Prentice Hall Business Publishing; and the outstanding Prentice Hall sales representatives. Finally, we thank Suzanne DeWorken, associate managing editor of production, and Karalyn Holland, production project manager, for their dedication; and we are grateful to Jeanine Furino, senior production editor at GGS Higher Education Resources, A Division of Premedia Global, Inc.; Janet Slowik, senior art director; and Ilze Lemisis, interior designer, for their superb work.

Courtland L. Bovée
John V. Thill

This book is dedicated to you and the many thousands of other students who have used this book in years past. We appreciate the opportunity to play a role in your education and we wish you success and satisfaction in your studies and in your career.

Courtland L. Bovée
John V. Thill

Take advantage of this FREE online service that extends the value of your textbook with fresh multimedia content every week

http://real-timeupdates.com/bce

Business Communication Essentials' Real-Time Updates feature makes it easy to learn from the pros, get great ideas for class projects, and stay up to date with the world of business communication.

This unique service provides weekly content updates that keep your textbook current and reinforce the concepts you learn in class. Simply visit the website to find podcasts, PowerPoint presentations, online videos, PDFs, and articles—or get new items delivered to your desktop automatically via RSS newsreader.

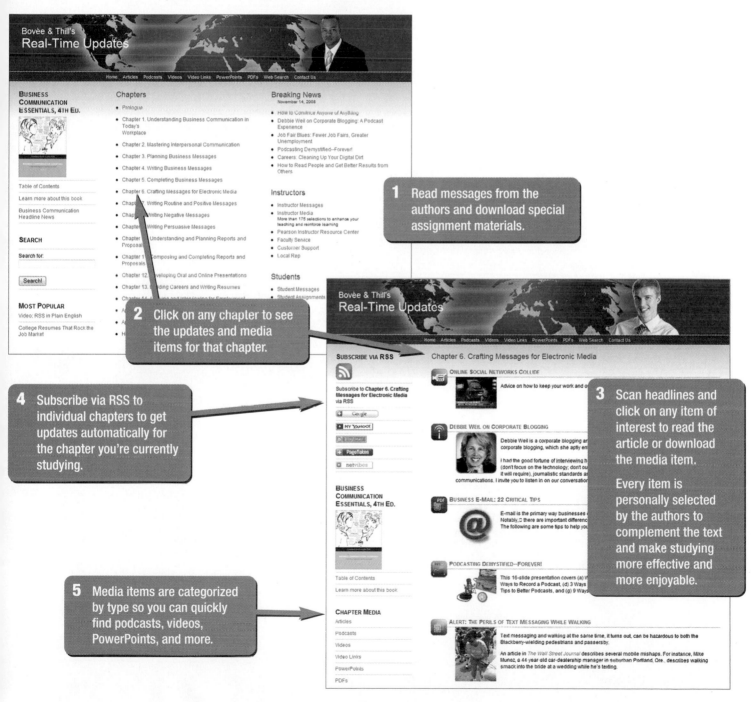

1 Read messages from the authors and download special assignment materials.

2 Click on any chapter to see the updates and media items for that chapter.

3 Scan headlines and click on any item of interest to read the article or download the media item.

Every item is personally selected by the authors to complement the text and make studying more effective and more enjoyable.

4 Subscribe via RSS to individual chapters to get updates automatically for the chapter you're currently studying.

5 Media items are categorized by type so you can quickly find podcasts, videos, PowerPoints, and more.

Building a Career with Your Communication Skills

USING THIS COURSE TO HELP LAUNCH YOUR CAREER

This course will help you develop vital communication skills that you'll use throughout your career—and those skills can help you launch an interesting and rewarding career, too. This brief prologue sets the stage by helping you understand today's dynamic workplace, the steps you can take to adapt to the job market, and the importance of creating an employment portfolio. Take a few minutes to read it while you think about the career you hope to create for yourself.

UNDERSTANDING TODAY'S DYNAMIC WORKPLACE

Social, political, and financial events continue to change workplace conditions from year to year, so the job market you read about this year might not be the same market you try to enter a year or two from now. However, you can count on a few forces that are likely to affect your entry into the job market and your career success in years to come:[1]

- **Stability.** Your career probably won't be as stable as careers were in your parents' generation. In today's business world, your career will likely be affected by globalization, mergers and acquisitions, short-term mentality driven by the demands of stockholders, ethical upheavals, and the relentless quest for lower costs. On the plus side, new opportunities, new companies, and even entire industries can appear almost overnight. So while your career might not be as predictable as careers used to be, it could well be more of an adventure. In fact, trying to make a long-term career plan might not be a wise use of your time anyway. As retired Lockheed Martin CEO Norman Augustine puts it, "There are just too many changes ahead, too many things that are going to happen that you can't anticipate."[2]

- **Lifetime employment.** The idea of lifetime employment, in which employees spend their entire working lives with a single firm that takes care of them throughout their careers, is all but gone in many industries. Boeing, the Chicago-based aerospace giant, speaks of lifetime *employability*, rather than lifetime employment, putting the responsibility on employees to track market needs and keep their skills up to date—even changing careers if necessary. In fact, many U.S. employees will not only change employers multiple times but will even change careers three to five times over their working lives.

- **Growth of small business.** Small businesses employ about half of the private-sector workforce in this country and create somewhere between two-thirds and three-quarters of new jobs, so chances are good that you'll work for a small firm at some point. One expert predicts that before long, 80 percent of the U.S. labor force will be working for firms that employ fewer than 200 people.

- **Increase in independent contractors.** The nature of employment is changing for many people. As companies try to become more flexible, more employees are going solo and setting up shop as independent contractors, sometimes selling their services back to the very companies they just left.

- **Changing view of job-hopping.** Given all the changes, job-hopping doesn't have quite the negative connotation it once had. Even so, you still need to be careful about "jumping ship" at every new opportunity. Recruiting and integrating new employees takes time and costs money, and most employers are reluctant to invest in someone who has a history of switching jobs numerous times without good reason.

Would you like to pursue a career in business but have the flexibility to work from home? Many professionals now do so, as either independent contractors or corporate employees who telecommute.

What do all these forces mean to you? First, take charge of your career—and stay in charge of it. Understand your options, have a plan, and don't count on others to watch out for your future. Second, as you will learn throughout this course, understanding your audience is key to successful communication, starting with understanding how employers view today's job market.

How Employers View Today's Job Market

From an employer's perspective, the employment process is always a question of balance. Maintaining a stable workforce can improve practically every aspect of business performance, yet many employers want the flexibility to shrink and expand payrolls as business conditions change. Employers obviously want to attract the best talent, but the best talent is more expensive and more vulnerable to offers from competitors, so there are always financial trade-offs to consider.

Employers also struggle with the ups and downs of the economy. When unemployment is low, the balance of power shifts to employees, and employers have to compete in order to attract and keep top talent. When unemployment is high, the power shifts back to employers, who can afford to be more selective and less accommodating. In other words, pay attention to the economy; at times you can be more aggressive in your demands, but at other times you should be more accommodating.

Many employers now fill some labor needs by hiring temporary workers or engaging contractors on a project-by-project basis. Many U.S. employers are now also more willing to move jobs to cheaper labor markets outside the country and to recruit globally to fill positions in the United States. Both trends have stirred controversy, especially in the technology sector, as U.S. firms recruit top engineers and scientists from other countries while shifting mid- and low-range jobs to India, China, Russia, the Philippines, and other countries with lower wage structures.[3]

What Employers Look For in Job Applicants

Given the forces in the contemporary workplace, employers are looking for people who can adapt to the new dynamics of the business world, survive and thrive in fluid and uncertain situations, and continue to learn throughout their careers. Companies want team players with strong work records, leaders who are versatile, and employees with diversified skills and varied job experience.[4] In addition, most employers expect college graduates to be sensitive to cultural differences and to have a sound understanding of international affairs.[5] In some cases, your chances of being hired are better if you've studied abroad, learned another language, or can otherwise demonstrate an appreciation of other cultures.

Adapting to Today's Job Market

Adapting to the workplace is a lifelong process of seeking the best fit between what you want to do and what employers are willing to pay you to do. For instance, if money is more important to you than anything else, you can certainly pursue jobs that promise high pay; just be aware that most of these jobs require years of experience, and many produce a lot of stress, require frequent travel, or have other drawbacks you'll want to consider. In contrast, if location, lifestyle, intriguing work, or other factors are more important to you, you may well have to sacrifice some level of pay to achieve them. It's important to know what you want to do, what you have to offer, and how to make yourself more attractive to employers.

What Do You Want to Do?

Economic necessities and the vagaries of the marketplace will influence much of what happens in your career, of course; nevertheless, it's wise to start your employment search by examining your values and interests. Identify what you want to do first and then see whether you can find a position that satisfies you at a personal level while also meeting your financial needs. Consider these questions:

- **What would you like to do every day?** Research occupations that interest you. Find out what people really do every day. Ask friends, relatives, or alumni from your school. Read interviews with people in various professions to get a sense of what their careers are like.

- **How would you like to work?** Consider how much independence you want on the job, how much variety you like, and whether you prefer to work with products, machines, people, ideas, figures, or some combination thereof. Do you prefer constant change or a predictable role?

- **What specific compensation do you expect?** What do you hope to earn in your first year? What's your ultimate earnings goal? Are you willing to settle for less money in order to do something you really love?

- **Can you establish some general career goals?** Consider where you'd like to start, where you'd like to go from there, and the ultimate position you'd like to attain.

- **What size company would you prefer?** Do you like the idea of working for a small, entrepreneurial operation or a large corporation?

- **What sort of corporate culture are you most comfortable with?** Would you be happy in a formal hierarchy with clear reporting relationships? Or do you prefer less structure? Teamwork or individualism? Do you like a competitive environment?

- **What location would you like?** Would you like to work in a city, a suburb, a small town, an industrial area, or an uptown setting? Do you favor a particular part of the country? Another country?

Filling out the assessment in Table 1 might help you get a clearer picture of the nature of work you would like to pursue in your career.

What Do You Have to Offer?

Knowing what you *want* to do is one thing. Knowing what you *can* do is another. You may already have a good idea of what you can offer employers. If not, some brainstorming can help you identify your skills, interests, and characteristics. Start by jotting down 10 achievements you're proud of, such as learning to ski, taking a prize-winning photo, tutoring a child, or editing your school paper. Think carefully about what specific skills these achievements demanded of you. For example, leadership skills, speaking ability, and artistic talent may have helped you coordinate a winning presentation to your school's administration. As you analyze your achievements, you'll begin to recognize a pattern of skills. Which of them might be valuable to potential employers?

TABLE 1 Career Self-Assessment

What work-related activities and situations do you prefer? Evaluate your preferences in each of the areas listed here and use the results to help guide your job search.

Activity or Situation	Strongly Agree	Agree	Disagree	No Preference
1. I want to work independently.				
2. I want variety in my work.				
3. I want to work with people.				
4. I want to work with technology.				
5. I want physical work.				
6. I want mental work.				
7. I want to work for a large organization.				
8. I want to work for a not-for-profit organization.				
9. I want to work for a small family business.				
10. I want to work for a service business.				
11. I want to start or buy a business someday.				
12. I want regular, predictable work hours.				
13. I want to work in a city location.				
14. I want to work in a small town or suburb.				
15. I want to work in another country.				
16. I want to work outdoors.				
17. I want to work in a structured environment.				
18. I want to avoid risk as much as possible.				
19. I want to enjoy my work, even if that means making less money.				
20. I want to become a high-level corporate manager.				

Next, look at your educational preparation, work experience, and extracurricular activities. What do your knowledge and experience qualify you to do? What have you learned from volunteer work or class projects that could benefit you on the job? Have you held any offices, won any awards or scholarships, mastered a second language?

Take stock of your personal characteristics. Are you aggressive, a born leader? Or would you rather follow? Are you outgoing, articulate, great with people? Or do you prefer working alone? Make a list of what you believe are your four or five most important qualities. Ask a relative or friend to rate your traits as well.

If you're having difficulty figuring out your interests, characteristics, or capabilities, consult your college placement office. Many campuses administer a variety of tests that can help you identify interests, aptitudes, and personality traits. These tests won't reveal your "perfect" job, but they'll help you focus on the types of work best suited to your personality.

How Can You Make Yourself More Valuable?

While you're figuring out what you want from a job and what you can offer an employer, you can take positive steps now toward building your career. First, look for volunteer projects, temporary jobs, freelance work, or internships that will help expand your experience base and skill set. These temporary assignments not only help you gain valuable experience and relevant contacts but also provide you with important references and with items for your employment portfolio (see the following section).[6]

Second, consider applying your talents to *crowdsourcing* projects, in which companies and nonprofit organizations invite the public to contribute solutions to various challenges. For example, Fellowforce (www.fellowforce.com) posts projects involving advertising, business writing, photography, graphic design, programming, strategy development, and other skills.[7] Even if your contributions aren't chosen, you still have solutions to real business problems that you can show to potential employers as examples of your work.

Third, learn more about the industry or industries in which you want to work and stay on top of new developments. Join networks of professional colleagues and friends who can help you keep up with trends and events. Many professional societies have student chapters or offer students discounted memberships. Take courses and pursue other educational or life experiences that would be difficult while working full time.

Even after an employer hires you, it's a good idea to continue improving your skills, in order to distinguish yourself from your peers and to make yourself more valuable to current and potential employers. Acquire as much technical knowledge as you can, build broad-based life experience, and develop your social skills. Learn to respond to change in positive, constructive ways; doing so will help you adapt if your "perfect" career path eludes your grasp. Learn to see each job, even so-called entry-level jobs, as an opportunity to learn more and to expand your knowledge, experience, and social skills. Share what you know with others instead of hoarding knowledge in the hope of becoming indispensable; helping others excel is a skill, too.[8]

Building an Employment Portfolio

Employers want proof that you have the skills to succeed on the job, but even if you don't have much relevant work experience, you can use your college classes to assemble that proof. Simply create and maintain an *employment portfolio*, which is a collection of projects that demonstrate your skills and knowledge. You can create both a *print portfolio* and an *e-portfolio*; both can help with your career effort. A print portfolio gives you something tangible to bring to interviews, and it lets you collect project results that might not be easy to show online, such as a handsomely bound report.

An e-portfolio is a multimedia presentation of your skills and experiences.[9] Think of it as a website that contains your résumé, work samples, letters of recommendation, articles you have written, and other information about you and your skills. Be creative. For example, a student who was pursuing a degree in meteorology added a video clip of himself delivering a weather forecast.[10] The portfolio can be burned on a CD-ROM for physical distribution or, more commonly, posted online—whether it's a personal website, your college's site (if student pages are available), or a networking site such as www.collegegrad.com or www.creativeshake.com. To see a selection of student e-portfolios from colleges around the United States, go to http://real-timeupdates.com/bce, click on "Student Assignments," then click on "Prologue" to see Student E-Portfolios.

Throughout the course, pay close attention to the activities and cases marked "Portfolio Builder" (beginning in Chapter 6). These items will make particularly good examples of not only your communication skills but your ability to understand and solve business-related challenges. By combining these projects with samples from your other courses, you can create a compelling portfolio by the time you're ready to start interviewing. Your portfolio is also a great resource for writing your résumé because it reminds you of all the great work you've done over the years. Moreover, you can continue to refine and expand your portfolio throughout your career; many professionals use e-portfolios to advertise their services, for instance (see Figure 1).

As you assemble your portfolio, collect anything that shows your ability to perform, whether it's in school, on the job, or in other venues. However, you *must* check with an employer before including any items that you created while you were an employee. Many business documents contain confidential information that companies don't want distributed to outside audiences.

For each item you add to your portfolio, write a brief description that helps other people understand the meaning and significance of the project. Include items such as these:

- **Background.** Why did you undertake this project? Was it a school project, an article you wrote on your own initiative, or something else?
- **Project objectives.** Explain the project's goals, if relevant.
- **Collaborators.** If you worked with others, be sure to mention that and discuss team dynamics, if appropriate. For instance, if you led the team or worked with others long distance as a *virtual team*, point that out.

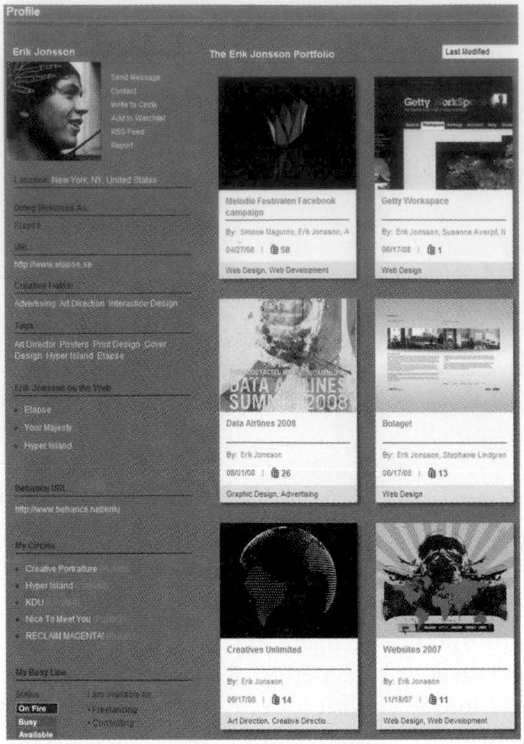

Figure 1 Professional E-Portfolio
Erik Jonsson, a digital media designer, uses e-portfolio services such as Behance.net (www.behance.net/erikj) to display samples of his work. Potential clients or business partners can click on the images shown here to learn more about each project. No matter what your intended profession or level of experience may be, you can use an e-portfolio to help potential employers learn more about your skills and qualifications.

- **Constraints.** Sometimes the most impressive thing about a project is the time or budget constraints under which it was created. If such constraints apply to a project, consider mentioning them in a way that doesn't sound like an excuse for poor quality. If you had only one week to create a website, for example, you might say that "One of the intriguing challenges of this project was the deadline; I had only one week to design, compose, test, and publish this material."

- **Outcomes.** If the project's goals were measurable, what was the result? For example, if you wrote a letter soliciting donations for a charitable cause, how much money did you raise?

- **Learning experience.** If appropriate, describe what you learned during the course of the project.

Keep in mind that the portfolio itself is a communication project, so be sure to apply everything you'll learn in this course about effective communication and good design. Assume that every potential employer will find your e-portfolio site (even if you don't tell them about it), so don't include anything that could come back to haunt you. Also, if you have anything embarrassing on Facebook, MySpace, or any other social networking site, remove it immediately.

To get started, first check with the career center at your college; many schools now offer e-portfolio systems for their students. (Some schools now require e-portfolios, so you may already be building one.) You can also find plenty of advice online; search for "e-portfolio" or "student portfolio." Finally, consider reading a book such as *Portfolios for Technical and Professional Communicators*, by Herb J. Smith and Kim Haimes-Korn. This book is intended for communication specialists, but it offers great advice for anyone who wants to create a compelling employment portfolio.

Best wishes for success in this course and in your career!

Business Communication Essentials

Business Communication Foundations

CHAPTER 1: Understanding Business Communication in Today's Workplace

CHAPTER 2: Mastering Interpersonal Communication

Understanding Business Communication in Today's Workplace

LEARNING OBJECTIVES

After studying this chapter, you will be able to

1. Explain why effective communication is important to your success in today's business environment

2. Describe the five characteristics of effective business communication

3. Identify 10 communication skills that today's employers expect from their employees

4. List and briefly define the eight phases of the communication process

5. Identify six important ways to improve your business communication skills

6. Differentiate between an ethical dilemma and an ethical lapse

[from the real world]

"Conversation marketing . . . means creating a dialog with customers in which useful information is exchanged so that both parties benefit from the relationship."
—*Paul Gillin,*
Author, The New
Influencers:
A Marketer's Guide to
New Social Media
www.paulgillin.com

In talking about "conversation marketing," Paul Gillin is referring to the use of *social media*—blogs, social networking websites, wikis, and other electronic tools with which all participants can contribute to the discussion. Beyond the specific tools involved, however, the notion of a two-way conversation is one of the most profound changes in business communication today. Today's audiences are not willing to be passive recipients; they want and demand to be active participants in the communication process.[1]

COMMUNICATING IN TODAY'S GLOBAL BUSINESS ENVIRONMENT

Every business organization needs effective communication, both internally and externally.

Successful professionals such as Paul Gillin understand that achieving success in today's workplace requires the ability to communicate effectively with a wide variety of audiences. **Communication** is the process of transferring information and meaning between *senders* and *receivers*, using one or more written, oral, visual, or electronic channels. During your career, you'll communicate with a wide range of audiences. **Internal communication** refers to the exchange of information and ideas within an organization. In contrast, **external communication** carries information into and out of an organization. Companies constantly exchange messages with customers, suppliers, distributors, competitors, investors, journalists, and community representatives.

Effective communication delivers a variety of important benefits.

For any audience, communication is *effective* only when the intended message is understood and when it stimulates desired actions or encourages the audience to think in new ways. Effective communication yields a number of important benefits for both you and your company:

- Faster problem solving
- Stronger decision making
- Increased productivity
- Steadier work flow
- Stronger business relationships

- More compelling promotional messages
- Enhanced professional images and stronger brands
- Improved response from colleagues, employees, supervisors, investors, customers, and other important audiences

In fact, companies that communicate well exhibit significantly higher financial performance than companies that communicate poorly.[2] Because communication is clearly a huge advantage in business, you might expect that most professionals in most companies communicate well most of the time. Unfortunately, the reality is far from this ideal. For example, the Conference Board, a leading business organization, found that nearly two-thirds of U.S. employees are dissatisfied with the manner in which their companies communicate with them.[3] Communication efforts can fail for many reasons, from overworked staff to "office politics" to a simple lack of skills.[4] View this challenge as an opportunity: You can use your communication skills to succeed as an employee, to lead people more effectively as a manager, and to help your company connect with all its audiences.

This course teaches you how to create effective messages and helps you improve your communication skills through practice in an environment that provides honest, constructive criticism. You will discover how to collaborate in teams, listen well, master nonverbal communication, and participate in productive meetings. You'll learn about communicating across cultural boundaries. You'll learn a three-step process that makes it easier to write effective business messages, and you'll get specific tips for writing a wide variety of messages, from e-mail and instant messages to blogs to online presentations. With these skills, you'll start your business career with a competitive advantage.

Recognizing Effective Communication

You can have the greatest ideas in the world, but they're no good to your company or your career if you can't express them clearly and persuasively. For your messages to be effective, make them practical, factual, concise, clear, and persuasive:

Effective messages are practical, factual, concise, clear, and persuasive.

- **Provide practical information.** Give recipients useful information, whether it's to help them perform a desired action or understand a new company policy.
- **Give facts rather than vague impressions.** Use concrete language, specific detail, and information that is clear, convincing, accurate, and ethical. Even when an opinion is called for, present compelling evidence to support your conclusion.
- **Present information in a concise, efficient manner.** Audiences respond more positively when you provide only the information they need. Also, take care not to send unnecessary messages. Being inundated with messages can result in **information overload**, which not only makes it difficult to discriminate between useful and useless information but also amplifies workplace stress.[5]
- **Clarify expectations and responsibilities.** Write messages to generate a specific response from a specific audience. Clearly state what you expect from audience members or what you can do for them.
- **Offer compelling, persuasive arguments and recommendations.** Show your readers precisely how they will benefit from responding to your message the way you want them to.

Keep these five important characteristics in mind as you review Figure 1.1. You might notice that it is more formal and "professional sounding" than many of the e-mail messages you send now. Employers expect you to be able to communicate with a similar style.

Understanding What Employers Expect from You

No matter how good you are at accounting, engineering, law, or whatever professional specialty you pursue, employers expect you to be competent at a wide range of communication tasks. In fact, employers start judging your ability to communicate before you even show

Your ability to communicate will influence your success at every stage of your career.

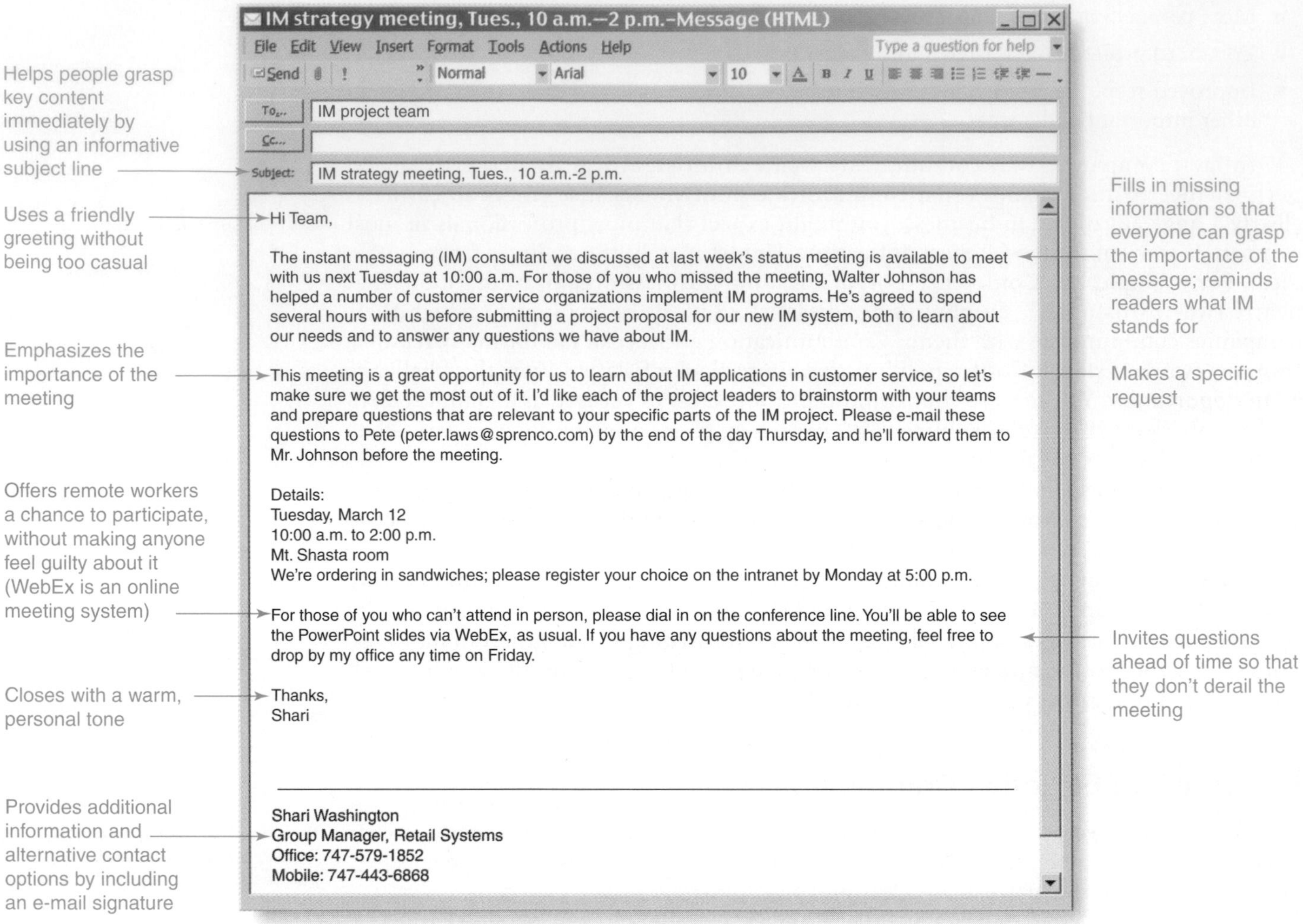

Helps people grasp key content immediately by using an informative subject line

Uses a friendly greeting without being too casual

Emphasizes the importance of the meeting

Offers remote workers a chance to participate, without making anyone feel guilty about it (WebEx is an online meeting system)

Closes with a warm, personal tone

Provides additional information and alternative contact options by including an e-mail signature

Fills in missing information so that everyone can grasp the importance of the message; reminds readers what IM stands for

Makes a specific request

Invites questions ahead of time so that they don't derail the meeting

> **IM strategy meeting, Tues., 10 a.m.–2 p.m.–Message (HTML)**
>
> File Edit View Insert Format Tools Actions Help   Type a question for help
>
> Send | ! | Normal ▼ Arial ▼ 10 ▼ A B I U ≡ ≡ ≡ ≡ ≡ ≡ ≡ — ▼
>
> To... | IM project team
> Cc... |
> Subject: | IM strategy meeting, Tues., 10 a.m.-2 p.m.
>
> Hi Team,
>
> The instant messaging (IM) consultant we discussed at last week's status meeting is available to meet with us next Tuesday at 10:00 a.m. For those of you who missed the meeting, Walter Johnson has helped a number of customer service organizations implement IM programs. He's agreed to spend several hours with us before submitting a project proposal for our new IM system, both to learn about our needs and to answer any questions we have about IM.
>
> This meeting is a great opportunity for us to learn about IM applications in customer service, so let's make sure we get the most out of it. I'd like each of the project leaders to brainstorm with your teams and prepare questions that are relevant to your specific parts of the IM project. Please e-mail these questions to Pete (peter.laws@sprenco.com) by the end of the day Thursday, and he'll forward them to Mr. Johnson before the meeting.
>
> Details:
> Tuesday, March 12
> 10:00 a.m. to 2:00 p.m.
> Mt. Shasta room
> We're ordering in sandwiches; please register your choice on the intranet by Monday at 5:00 p.m.
>
> For those of you who can't attend in person, please dial in on the conference line. You'll be able to see the PowerPoint slides via WebEx, as usual. If you have any questions about the meeting, feel free to drop by my office any time on Friday.
>
> Thanks,
> Shari
>
> _____
>
> Shari Washington
> Group Manager, Retail Systems
> Office: 747-579-1852
> Mobile: 747-443-6868

Figure 1.1   Technology and Communication: Effective E-Mail
Notice how this message is more formal and "professional sounding" than the e-mail messages you probably send to your friends and family. Except for short messages between close colleagues and team members, most businesses will expect you to communicate with a style that is more formal than the style to which you are currently accustomed.

up for your first interview, and the process of evaluation never really stops. Fortunately, the skills that employers expect from you are the same skills that will help you advance in your career:

- Organizing ideas and information logically and completely
- Expressing ideas and information coherently and persuasively
- Reading and listening to extract the intended meaning from other people's messages
- Communicating effectively with people from diverse backgrounds and experiences
- Using communication technologies effectively and efficiently
- Following accepted standards of grammar, spelling, and other aspects of high-quality writing and speaking
- Communicating in a civilized manner that reflects contemporary expectations of business etiquette
- Communicating ethically, even when choices aren't crystal clear
- Adhering to applicable government regulations and guidelines (In accounting and finance, for instance, executives say that communication skills are more important today than they've ever been.[6])
- Using your time productively

You'll have the opportunity to practice all these skills throughout this course—but don't stop there. Successful professionals continue to hone communication skills throughout their careers.

UNDERSTANDING THE COMMUNICATION PROCESS

By viewing communication as a process (see Figure 1.2), you can identify and improve the skills you need in order to be more successful—and you can recognize the many places and ways in which communication can fail. Any model is a simplification of the complex reality of human communication, of course, but these eight steps provide a practical overview:

The communication process starts with a sender having an idea and then encoding the idea into a message that can be transferred to a receiver.

1. **The sender has an idea.** You conceive an idea and want to share it. Whether a communication effort will ultimately be effective starts right here, depending on the nature of the idea, the composition of the audience and your relationship to these people, and your motivation for wanting to share the idea.

2. **The sender encodes the idea in a message.** When you put your idea into a message (words, images, or both) that your receiver will understand, you are **encoding** it. Much of the focus of this course is on developing the skills needed to successfully encode your ideas into effective messages.

3. **The sender produces the message in a transmittable medium.** With the appropriate message to express your idea, you now need a **communication medium** to present that message to your intended audience. As you'll read in Chapter 3, media for transmitting messages can be divided into *oral*, *written*, and *visual*, as well as various *electronic* forms of the other three.

4. **The sender transmits the message through a channel.** The distinction between communication media and channels can get a bit murky, but think of a medium as the *form* a message takes (such as an e-mail message) and a **communication channel** as the system used to *deliver* the message (such as a computer network).

5. **The audience receives the message.** If all goes well, your message survives the trip through the channel and arrives at your intended audience. However, arrival at the destination is no guarantee that the message will be noticed or understood correctly.

6. **The audience decodes the message.** The audience now needs to extract your idea from the message, a step known as **decoding**. For the message to be successful, your receiver must decode from your message the same meaning that you encoded into it.

7. **The audience responds to the message.** By crafting your messages in ways that show the benefits of responding, you can increase the chances that your audiences will respond as you'd like them to.

8. **The audience provides feedback to the sender.** Aside from responding (or not responding) to the message, audience members may also give **feedback** that helps you evaluate the effectiveness of your communication effort. Feedback can range from

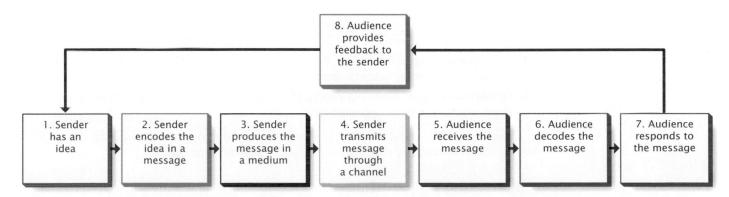

Figure 1.2 The Communication Process
While this eight-step model is a simplified representation of how communication works in real life, understanding this basic model is vital to improving your communication skills.

subtle facial expressions to blunt statements such as "I don't understand you." Use feedback to measure the effectiveness of your communication efforts and as a guideline for improving your skills.

As noted on the first page of this chapter, social media are changing the relationship between senders and receivers in the business world. In the past, business communication was often a one-way process, with little or no opportunity for receivers to respond in any meaningful way. For example, social media are creating new opportunities for customers to "talk back" to companies—and to talk with one another.

DEVELOPING YOUR BUSINESS COMMUNICATION SKILLS

In the coming chapters, you'll find real-life examples of both effective and ineffective communication, with clear explanations to help you recognize what is good or bad about them. You'll notice that six themes keep surfacing as keys to good communication: (1) committing to ethical communication, (2) adopting an audience-centered approach, (3) improving your intercultural sensitivity, (4) giving—and responding to—constructive feedback, (5) being sensitive to business etiquette, and (6) using communication technology effectively. Close attention to these themes will help you improve your business communication skills.

Committing to Ethical Communication

Ethics are the accepted principles of conduct that govern behavior within a society. Put another way, ethical principles define the boundary between right and wrong. Former Supreme Court Justice Potter Stewart defined *ethics* as "knowing the difference between what you have a right to do and what is the right thing to do."[7] To make the right choices as a business communicator, you have a responsibility to think through not only what you say but also the consequences of saying it.

Of course, people in a society don't always agree on what constitutes ethical behavior. For instance, the emergence of *stealth marketing*, in which customers don't know they're being marketed to, has raised new concerns about ethics. A common stealth marketing technique is paying or otherwise rewarding consumers to promote products to their friends without telling them it's a form of advertising. Critics—including the U.S. Federal Trade Commission and the Word of Mouth Marketing Association—assert that such techniques are deceptive because they don't give their targets the opportunity to raise their instinctive defenses against the persuasive powers of marketing messages.[8]

Ethical communication includes all relevant information, is true in every sense, and is not deceptive in any way. By contrast, unethical communication can include falsehoods and misleading information (or exclude important information). Unfortunately, unethical communication seems to be on the rise. In a 2005 survey, 19 percent of U.S. employees claimed to have observed dishonest communication by their colleagues or employers. By 2007, the number had jumped to 25 percent.[9] Examples of unethical communication include:[10]

- **Plagiarizing.** Stealing someone else's words or work and claiming it as your own
- **Selectively misquoting.** Deliberately omitting damaging or unflattering comments to paint a better (but untruthful) picture of you or your company
- **Misrepresenting numbers.** Increasing or decreasing numbers, exaggerating, altering statistics, or omitting numeric data
- **Distorting visuals.** Making a product look bigger or changing the scale of graphs and charts to exaggerate or conceal differences

On the surface, ethical practices appear fairly easy to recognize, but deciding what is ethical can be a considerable challenge in complex business situations.

Recognizing Ethical Choices

Every company has responsibilities to multiple groups of people inside and outside the firm, and those various groups often have competing interests. For instance, employees generally want higher wages and more benefits, but investors who have risked their money in the

---

Margin notes:

You can improve your business communication by

- Committing to ethical communication
- Adopting an audience-centered approach
- Improving your intercultural sensitivity
- Giving and receiving constructive feedback
- Being sensitive to business etiquette
- Using technology effectively

Ethical communication avoids deception and provides the information audiences need.

Unethical practices to avoid include plagiarizing, selectively misquoting, misrepresenting numbers, and distorting visuals.

company want management to keep costs low so that profits are strong enough to drive up the stock price. Both sides have a valid position; neither one is "right" or "wrong."

An **ethical dilemma** involves choosing among alternatives that aren't clear-cut. Perhaps two conflicting alternatives are both ethical and valid, or perhaps the alternatives lie somewhere in the gray area between clearly right and clearly wrong. Suppose you are president of a company that's losing money. You have a duty to your shareholders to try to reduce your losses and a duty to your employees to be fair and honest. After looking at various options, you conclude that you'll have to lay off 500 people immediately. You suspect that you may have to lay off another 100 people later on, but right now you need those 100 workers to finish a project. What do you tell them? If you confess that their jobs are shaky, many of them may quit just when you need them most. However, if you tell them that the future is rosy, you'll be stretching the truth.

If you must choose between two ethical alternatives, you are facing an ethical dilemma.

Unlike a dilemma, an **ethical lapse** is a clearly unethical (and frequently illegal) choice. For example, eight auto dealers in Massachusetts were recently fined for displaying deceptively low prices in their advertising headlines. The "fine print" at the bottom of the ads explained that to get these prices, buyers had to either trade in another car or make a cash payment.[11]

If you choose an alternative that is unethical or illegal, you have committed an ethical lapse.

Making Ethical Choices

Employers have a responsibility to establish clear guidelines for ethical behavior, including business communication. In a recent global survey by the International Association of Business Communicators, 70 percent of communication professionals said their companies clearly define what is considered ethical and unethical behavior.[12] Ensuring ethical business communications requires three elements: ethical individuals, ethical company leadership, and the appropriate policies and structures to support ethical decision making.[13] Many companies establish an explicit ethics policy by using a written **code of ethics** to help employees determine what is acceptable. A code is often part of a larger program of employee training and communication channels that allows employees to ask questions and report instances of questionable ethics. Showing employees that the company is serious about ethical behavior is also vital. As Sharon Allen, chairman of the board of the financial services firm Deloitte LLP, put it, "Management and leadership have a huge responsibility in setting examples for their organizations and living the values they preach if they want to sustain a culture of ethics."[14]

Responsible employers establish clear ethical guidelines for their employees to follow.

If you find yourself in a situation in which the law or a code of ethics can't guide you, answer the following questions:[15]

If company ethics policies don't cover a specific situation, you can ask yourself a number of questions in order to make an ethical choice.

- Have you defined the situation fairly and accurately?
- What is your intention in communicating this message?
- What impact will this message have on the people who receive it, or who might be affected by it?
- Will the message achieve the greatest possible good while doing the least possible harm?
- Will the assumptions you've made change over time? That is, will a decision that seems ethical now seem unethical in the future?
- Are you comfortable with your decision? Would you be embarrassed if it were printed in tomorrow's newspaper or spread across the Internet? Would you be proud to describe your choice to someone you admire and respect?

One helpful way to make sure your messages are ethical is to consider your audience: What does your audience need? What will help your audience the most?

Adopting an Audience-Centered Approach

Adopting an **audience-centered approach** means focusing on and caring about the members of your audience—making every effort to get your message across in a way that is meaningful and respectful to them (see Figure 1.3). In business communication, this is often referred to as the *"you" attitude*, as in making your messages about "you" rather than "me." You'll read more about this in Chapter 3.

Focus on the needs of your audience to make your messages more effective.

January 16, 2008

Shiny new icon for the iPhone and iPod Touch

Have an iPhone or iPod Touch? If you add the TypePad for iPhone web app as a webclip to your iPhone's home screen, you'll now get a bright icon that will look great alongside your other favorite iPhone apps and websites.

Adding it is easy. After you've updated your iPhone to version 1.1.3, visit i.typepad.com in Safari and click on the "+" button in the toolbar at the bottom of the screen. Now you'll have a quick and easy way to sign in to TypePad from your iPhone, and a great-looking TypePad icon on your home screen!

Update: And here's a tip on how you can add your own custom icon for your blog, in case any of your readers add your blog to their iPhone's home screen as a webclip.

1. Create your own custom 57x57 icon, and save it in PNG format.
2. Name that file "apple-touch-icon.png"
3. Upload it to the main folder of your account by signing into TypePad and visiting Control Panel > Files.

It's that easy! The next time someone saves your blog as a webclip on their iPhone, they'll get your pretty icon instead of an automatically generated screenshot.

Posted by Michael Sippey on January 16, 2008 at 04:41 PM in Mobile | Permalink

Offers links to additional information

Provides technical instructions in an easy-to-follow numbered list

Supports quick reading with an open, uncluttered design

TrackBack

TrackBack URL for this entry:
http://www.typepad.com/t/trackback/174921/25201430
Listed below are links to weblogs that reference Shiny new icon for the iPhone and iPod Touch:

Comments

Great. Now back to work on better stats:-)

Posted by: Petur Jonsson | January 16, 2008 at 05:50 PM

Offers a commenting feature so that readers can join the conversation (notice the friendly but firm tone of this reader's comments as he asks for a product improvement)

Figure 1.3   Audience-Centered Communication
This blog post from the developers of the popular TypePad blogging system demonstrates concern for the audience in several ways, including content that addresses audience interests, a design that makes the content easy to absorb, and the opportunity for readers to participate in the conversation.

Improving Your Intercultural Sensitivity

Cultural symbols, beliefs, attitudes, values, expectations, and norms for behavior influence communication.

Culture is a shared system of symbols, beliefs, attitudes, values, expectations, and norms for behavior. Today's workforce is composed of people from many cultures, people who differ in race, gender, age, national and regional attitudes and beliefs, family structure, religion, native language, and educational background. The interaction of culture and communication is so pervasive that separating the two is virtually impossible. To a large degree, your culture influences the way you think, which naturally affects the way you communicate as both a sender and a receiver.[16] In any cross-cultural situation, whether it's within your own office or with an audience halfway around the world, you can communicate more effectively if you heed the following tips:[17]

You can take a number of easy steps to improve your cultural sensitivity.

- **Assume differences until similarity is proved.** Don't automatically assume that others think, believe, or behave as you do.
- **Withhold judgment.** Accept differences in others without judging them.

- **Show respect.** Learn how respect is communicated in various cultures (through gestures, eye contact, and so on).
- **Tolerate ambiguity.** Learn to control your frustration when placed in an unfamiliar or confusing situation.
- **Look beyond the superficial.** Don't be distracted by things such as dress, appearance, or environmental discomforts.
- **Recognize your own cultural biases.** Learn to identify when your assumptions are different from those of another person.
- **Be flexible.** Be prepared to change your habits and attitudes when communicating with someone from another culture.
- **Emphasize common ground.** Look for similarities from which to work.
- **Deal with the individual.** Communicate with each person as an individual, not as a stereotypical representative of another group.
- **Learn when to be direct.** Investigate each culture so that you'll know when to send a message in a straightforward manner and when to be indirect.
- **Observe and learn.** The more you learn, the more effective you'll be.

Travel guidebooks are a great source of information about norms and customs in other countries. Check to see if your library has online access to the CultureGram database or review the country profiles at www.kwintessential.co.uk.

Recognizing Cultural Differences

Problems often arise when we assume that other people's attitudes and lives are like our own. Start by unlearning the "Golden Rule" you were probably taught as a child, to treat others as you would want them to treat you. Instead of treating others the way *you* want to be treated, treat them the way *they* want to be treated. You don't need to become an expert in the details of every culture in which you do business, but you do need to attain a basic level of cultural proficiency to ensure successful communication.[18] Start by recognizing and accommodating differences in such areas as context, law and ethics, social customs, and nonverbal communication.

> Cultural differences exist in areas such as context, ethics, social custom, and nonverbal communication.

Cultural Context   Every attempt at communication occurs within a **cultural context**, the mixture of traditions, expectations, and unwritten social rules that help convey meaning between members of the same culture. Cultures vary widely in the role that context plays in communication (see Figure 1.4).

> Cultural context includes physical cues, environmental stimuli, and varying degrees of implicit understanding.

In a **high-context culture** people rely less on the explicit content of the message and more on the context of nonverbal actions and environmental setting to convey meaning. For instance, a Chinese speaker expects the receiver to discover the essence of a message and uses indirectness and metaphor to provide a web of meaning.[19] In high-context cultures, the rules of everyday life are rarely explicit; instead, as individuals grow up, they learn how to recognize situational cues (such as gestures and tone of voice) and how to respond as expected.[20] Also, in a high-context culture, the primary role of communication is building relationships, not exchanging information.[21]

> In high-context cultures, communication relies less on the explicit content of a message than on the context of the message.

In a **low-context culture** people rely more on the explicit content of the message and less on circumstances and cues to convey meaning. In other words, compared to high-context cultures, in low-context cultures, more of the conveyed meaning is encoded into the actual message itself.[22] For example, an English speaker feels responsible for transmitting the meaning of a message and often places sentences in strict chronological sequence to establish a clear cause-and-effect pattern.[23] In a low-context culture, rules and expectations are usually spelled out through explicit statements such as "Please wait until I'm finished."[24] Exchanging information is the primary task of communication in low-context cultures.[25]

> In low-context cultures, communication relies more on message content than on message context.

The different expectations of low- and high-context cultures can create friction and misunderstanding when people try to communicate across cultural boundaries. For example, people from a low-context culture might view the high-context emphasis on building relationships as a waste of time. Conversely, people from a high-context culture might view the low-context emphasis on information exchange and task completion as being insensitive to group harmony.[26]

IN LOW-CONTEXT CULTURES	IN HIGH-CONTEXT CULTURES
Executive offices are separate with controlled access.	Executive offices are shared and open to all.
Workers rely on detailed background information.	Workers do not expect or want detailed information.
Information is highly centralized and controlled.	Information is shared with everyone.
Objective data are valued over subjective relationships.	Subjective relationships are valued over objective data.
Business and social relationships are separate.	Business and social relationships overlap.
Competence is valued as much as position and status.	Position and status are valued more than competence.
Meetings have fixed agendas and plenty of advance notice.	Meetings are often called on short notice, and key people always accept.

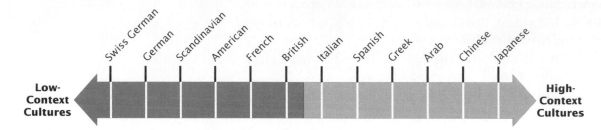

Figure 1.4   How Cultural Context Affects Business Communication
Cultural differences can have a profound effect on business communication. Bear in mind that this is a simplified model; individuals and companies within a given culture can vary widely along the high-context to low-context continuum. However, this model is a good starting point whenever you're preparing to interact with a new culture for the first time.

Members of different cultures sometimes have different views of what is ethical or even legal.

Legal and Ethical Differences Between Cultures   Legal and ethical behaviors are affected by cultural context. For example, because members of low-context cultures value the written word, they consider written agreements binding. They also tend to view laws as being flexible. However, members of high-context cultures put less emphasis on the written word and consider personal pledges more important than contracts. Plus, they tend to adhere more strictly to the law.[27]

Legal systems differ from culture to culture. In the United Kingdom and the United States, accused parties are presumed innocent until proven guilty, a principle rooted in English common law. On the other hand, in Mexico and Turkey, accused parties are presumed guilty until proven innocent, a principle rooted in the *Napoleonic Code*.[28] These distinctions are particularly important if your firm must communicate about a legal dispute in another country.

Making ethical choices can be difficult within your own culture. But trying to make ethical choices across cultures can be incredibly complicated. When communicating across cultures, keep your messages ethical by applying four basic principles:[29]

Learn the four principles that will help you keep your intercultural messages ethical.

- **Actively seek mutual ground.** Both parties must be flexible and avoid insisting that an interaction take place strictly in terms of one culture or another.
- **Send and receive messages without judgment.** Both parties must recognize that values vary from culture to culture, and they must find a way to trust each other.
- **Send messages that are honest.** Both parties must see a situation as it is—not as they would like it to be. They must be fully aware of their personal and cultural biases.
- **Show respect for cultural differences.** Both parties must understand and acknowledge the other's needs and preserve each other's dignity by communicating without deception.

Whether formal or informal, the rules governing social customs differ from culture to culture.

Social Customs   Social behavior varies among cultures, sometimes dramatically. Such behavior is guided by numerous rules, some of them formal and specifically articulated (table manners are a good example) and others more informal and learned over time (such as the comfortable standing distance between two speakers in an office or the acceptability of male and female employees socializing outside work). The combination of formal and informal rules influences the overall behavior of everyone in a society, or at least most of the people most of the time, in such areas as manners, attitudes toward time, individual versus community values, attitudes toward status and wealth, and respect for authority.

For example, in the United States and many other Western cultures, employees are often encouraged to speak up when they see problems or opportunities for improvement. However, W.R. Grace, a multinational manufacturing company based in Columbia, Maryland, encountered resistance from both workers and managers when it tried to instill this behavior in some of its facilities in Asia. In some cultures, a strong tradition of showing respect for authority discourages people in the lower ranks from saying anything that might imply criticism of company management. "In a lot of Asian cultures it's very hard for an employee to do something that could in any way embarrass the leader, and we needed to train our leaders to encourage this form of reporting," noted one Grace executive.[30]

Nonverbal Communication   Nonverbal communication is a vital part of the communication process. Factors ranging from facial expressions to style of dress can influence the way receivers decode messages, and the interpretation of nonverbal signals can vary widely from culture to culture. Wal-Mart learned this lesson the hard way when the giant retailer tried to expand into Germany. Store clerks resisted the company requirement of always smiling at customers—a cornerstone of customer relationship strategies in the United States—because customers sometimes misinterpreted the smiling as flirting. Wal-Mart dropped the requirement but after a number of other cultural and strategic missteps eventually left the German market.[31] You'll learn more about nonverbal communication in Chapter 2.

Overcoming Ethnocentrism and Stereotyping

Ethnocentrism is the tendency to judge all other groups according to the standards, behaviors, and customs of one's own group. When making such comparisons, people too often decide that their own group is superior.[32] An even more extreme reaction is **xenophobia**, a fear of strangers and foreigners. Clearly, businesspeople who take these views will not interpret messages from other cultures correctly, nor are they likely to send successful messages.

Distorted views of other cultures or groups also result from **stereotyping**, assigning a wide range of generalized—and often inaccurate—attributes to an individual on the basis of membership in a particular culture or social group, without considering the individual's unique characteristics. For instance, assuming that an older colleague will be out of touch with the youth market or that a younger colleague can't be an inspiring leader is an example of stereotyping age groups.

Those who want to show respect for other people and to communicate effectively in business need to adopt a more positive viewpoint, in the form of **cultural pluralism**—the practice of accepting multiple cultures on their own terms. When crossing cultural boundaries, you'll be even more effective if you move beyond simple acceptance and adapt your own communication style to that of the new cultures you encounter—even integrating aspects of those cultures into your own.[33] A few simple habits can help you avoid both the negativity of ethnocentrism and the oversimplification of stereotyping:

- **Avoid assumptions.** Don't assume that others will act the same way you do, that they will operate from the same values and beliefs, or that they will use language and symbols the same way you do. For instance, in a comparison of the 10 most important values in three cultures, people from the United States had no values in common with people from Japanese or Arab cultures.[34]
- **Avoid judgments.** When people act differently from you, don't conclude that they are in error, that their way is invalid, or that their customs are inferior to your own.
- **Acknowledge distinctions.** Don't ignore the differences between another person's culture and your own.

Writing for Intercultural and International Audiences

The letter in Figure 1.5 communicates across cultures quite effectively. To help you prepare effective written communications for multicultural audiences, remember these tips:[35]

- **Use plain English.** Use short, precise words that say exactly what you mean.
- **Be clear.** Rely on specific terms and concrete examples to explain your points.

Ethnocentrism is the tendency to judge all other groups according to the standards, behaviors, and customs of one's own group.

Stereotyping is assigning generalized attributes to an individual on the basis of his or her membership in a particular group.

Cultural pluralism is the acceptance of multiple cultures on their own terms.

Important tips for improving your intercultural writing include using plain English, avoiding slang, and using short sentences and short paragraphs.

La Cristallerie

Troy Halford, U.S. Sales Representative
163 Pico Boulevard
Los Angeles, CA 90032
Voice: (213) 975-8924
Fax: (213) 860-3489
hallford@comcast.net

5 April 2009

M. Pierre Coll
Commissaire aux Comptes
La Cristallerie
22, Boulevard de la Marne
21200 Beaune
FRANCE

Dear Monsieur Coll:

Enclosed are my expense statement and receipts for March 2009. My expenses are higher than usual this month because an unexpected snowstorm that closed the airport in Chicago left me stranded for nearly five days. I was able to get a hotel for the duration of the storm, although the only room available was far more expensive than my usual accommodations.

In addition to the regular expenses identified in the enclosed report, here are the additional expenditures caused by the weather delay:

Three nights at the Carlton-O'Hare Hotel	$ 877
Meals over four days	175
Transportation between hotel and terminal	72
Phone calls to reschedule meetings	38
Total extra expenses	**$1,162**

If you have any questions or need any more information about these expenses, please contact me.

Sincerely,

Troy Halford

Troy Halford
U.S. Sales Rep

Enclosures: Expense statement and receipts

Annotations (left margin):
- Follows French preferences for title and address format
- Addresses the reader more formally in the salutation, as is expected in most French correspondence
- Uses clear and precise language that is easy for non-native English speakers to read
- Provides a total of the extra expenses
- Indicates that additional materials are enclosed with the letter

Annotations (right margin):
- Uses the international date format, which is preferred in French correspondence
- States the main idea directly and clearly in the opening, leaving no room for confusion about the letter's purpose
- Clearly identifies the extra expenses in a list that is easy to read
- Closes with an offer to help the reader with any further needs

Figure 1.5   Effective Intercultural Letter
This letter from a U.S. sales representative to an accounting manager in a French company is a good example of successfully adapting to an audience in another culture.

- **Address international correspondence properly.** The order and layout of address information vary from country to country, so follow the conventions that appear in the company's letterhead.
- **Cite numbers carefully.** Use figures (such as *27*) instead of spelling them out (*twenty-seven*).
- **Avoid slang and be careful with jargon and abbreviations.** Words and phrases that you consider to be everyday language may in fact be nonstandard usage and difficult for your audience to translate. However, when writing to audiences in the same field, *jargon* (terminology used in a particular profession) and abbreviations can be effective if you're sure the audience understands them.
- **Be brief.** Construct sentences that are short and simple.
- **Use short paragraphs.** Each paragraph should stick to one topic.
- **Use transitions.** Help readers follow your train of thought; you'll learn more about transitions in Chapter 4.

Speaking with Intercultural and International Audiences

When speaking in English to people whose native language is not English, you may find these tips helpful:

- **Speak clearly, simply, and relatively slowly.** Pronounce words clearly, stop at distinct punctuation points, and make one point at a time.

- **Look for feedback.** Be alert to signs of confusion in your listener. Realize that nods and smiles don't necessarily mean understanding.

- **Rephrase if necessary.** If someone doesn't seem to understand you, rephrase using simpler words.

- **Clarify your meaning with repetition and examples.** Use concrete and specific examples to illustrate difficult or vague ideas.

- **Don't talk down to the other person.** Try not to overenunciate and don't "blame" the listener for not understanding. Say, "Am I going too fast?" rather than "Is this too difficult for you?"

- **Learn important phrases in your audience's language.** Learn common greetings and a few simple phrases in the other person's native language; this not only makes initial contact easier, but it shows respect as well.

- **Listen carefully and respectfully.** If you do not understand a comment, ask the person to repeat it.

- **Adapt your conversation style to the other person's.** For instance, if the other person appears to be direct and straightforward, follow suit.

- **Check frequently for comprehension.** After you make each point, pause to gauge the other person's comprehension before moving on.

- **Clarify what will happen next.** At the end of a conversation, be sure that you and the other person agree on what has been said and decided.

In short, take advantage of the other person's presence to make sure that your message is getting across and that you understand his or her message, too.

Important tips for improving your oral intercultural skills include speaking clearly and slowly, looking for feedback, and listening carefully.

Giving—and Responding to—Constructive Feedback

You will encounter many situations in which you are expected to give and receive feedback regarding communication efforts. Be sure you do so in a constructive way. **Constructive feedback**, sometimes called *constructive criticism*, focuses on the process and outcomes of communication, not on the people involved (see Table 1.1). In contrast, **destructive**

Constructive feedback focuses on opportunities to improve, not on mistakes or personal shortcomings.

(continued on page 20)

TABLE 1.1 Giving Constructive Feedback

How to Be Constructive	Explanation
Think through your suggested changes carefully.	Because many business documents must illustrate complex relationships between ideas and other information, isolated and superficial edits can do more harm than good.
Discuss improvements rather than flaws.	Instead of saying "this is confusing," explain how the writing can be improved to make it clearer.
Focus on controllable behavior.	Because the writer may not have control over every variable that affected the quality of the message, focus on those aspects the writer can control.
Be specific.	Comments such as "I don't get this" or "Make this clearer" don't identify what the writer needs to fix.
Keep feedback impersonal.	Focus comments on the message, not on the person who created it.
Verify understanding.	Ask for confirmation from the recipient to make sure the person understood your feedback.
Time your feedback carefully.	Make sure the writer will have sufficient time to implement the changes you suggest.
Highlight any limitations your feedback may have.	If you didn't have time to give the document a thorough edit, or if you're not an expert in some aspect of the content, let the writer know so that he or she can handle your comments appropriately.

Powerful Tools for Communicating Effectively

The tools of business communication evolve with every new generation of digital technology. Selecting the right tool for each situation can enhance your business communication in many ways. In today's flexible office settings, communication technology helps people keep in touch and stay productive. When co-workers in different cities need to collaborate, they can meet and share ideas without costly travel. Manufacturers use communication technology to keep track of parts, orders, and shipments—and to keep customers well-Informed. Those same customers can also communicate with companies in many ways at any time of day or night.

Electronic Presentations

Combining a color projector with a laptop or personal digital assistant (PDA) running the right software lets people give business presentations that are enhanced with sound, animation, and website hyperlinks.

Wireless Networks

Wireless access lets workers with laptop PCs and other devices stay connected from just about anywhere—around the corporate campus and from coffee shops, airports, hotels, and other remote locations.

REDEFINING THE OFFICE

Technology makes it easier for people to stay connected with co-workers and retrieve needed information. Some maintain that connection without having a permanent office, a desktop PC, or even a big filing cabinet. For example, Sun Microsystems lets staff members choose to work either at the main office or at remote offices called "drop-in centers." Many Sun facilities have specially equipped "iWork" areas where phone and computer connections can be quickly reconfigured to meet individual requirements.

Virtual Meeting Spaces

A number of companies (such as Cranial Tap, whose virtual headquarters is shown here) are experimenting with meeting spaces in virtual worlds such as Second Life. Advantages include being able to explore three-dimensional product models and data visualization displays.

Electronic Whiteboards

Electronic whiteboards can capture, store, and e-mail the results of brainstorming sessions and other meetings. The newest versions work with electronic presentations, too, letting users write and draw directly on displayed slides.

Unified Communications

Many workers can now access all their voice and e-mail communication through a single portal. *Follow-me phone service* automatically forwards incoming calls to remote sites, home offices, or mobile phones. Integrated systems can retrieve voice-mail messages via computer or read e-mail messages over the phone.

Wikis

Wikis promote collaboration by simplifying the process of creating and editing online content. Anyone with access (some wikis are private, while some are public) can add and modify pages as new information becomes available.

Web-Based Meetings

Web-based meetings allow team members from all over the world to collaborate online. Various systems support instant messaging, live video, real-time editing tools, and more.

COLLABORATING

Working in teams is essential in almost every business. Teamwork can become complicated, however, when team members work in different parts of the company, in different time zones, or even for different companies. Technology helps bridge the distance by making it possible to brainstorm, attend virtual meetings, and share files from widely separated locations. Communication technology also helps companies save money on costly business travel without losing most of the benefits of face-to-face collaboration.

Shared Workspaces

Online workspaces such as eRoom and Groove make it easy for far-flung team members to access shared files anywhere, anytime. Accessible through a browser, the workspace contains a collection of folders and has built-in intelligence to control which team members can read, edit, and save specific files.

Videoconferencing and Telepresence

Videoconferencing provides many of the same benefits as in-person meetings at a fraction of the cost. Advanced systems feature *telepresence*, in which the video images are life sized and extremely realistic.

Voice Technologies

The human voice is being supplemented by a variety of technologies. *Voice synthesis* regenerates a human speaking voice from computer files. *Voice recognition* converts human speech to computer-compatible data.

RSS Newsfeeds and Aggregators

Aggregators, sometimes called *newsreaders*, automatically collect information about new blog postings and podcasts via Really Simple Syndication (RSS) newsfeeds. They give audiences more control over the content they receive from businesses. Businesses are now sending some messages to internal and external audiences via RSS newsfeeds instead of e-mail.

Extranets

Extranets are secure, private websites and networks that share information with suppliers, business partners, and customers. Think of an extranet as an extension of a company intranet that is available to people outside the organization by invitation only.

Social Tagging and Bookmarking

Audiences become part of the communication channel when they find and recommend online content through tagging and bookmarking sites such as Delicious.com.

Location and Tracking Technologies

Location and tracking technologies can replace manual reporting. Radio-frequency identification (RFID) tags enable automated tracking of goods and containers. Geographic data from the Global Positioning System (GPS) enables new forms of communication, such as location-based advertising (getting an ad on your mobile phone from a store you're walking past, for instance) and remote monitoring of medical patients and trucking fleets.

SHARING THE LATEST INFORMATION

Companies use a variety of communication technologies to create products and services and deliver them to customers. The ability to easily access and share the latest information improves the flow and timing of supplies, lowers operating costs, and boosts financial performance. Easy information access also helps companies respond to customer needs by providing them timely, accurate information and service and by delivering the right products to them at the right time.

Supply Chain Management Software

Manufacturers, distributors, and retailers now automatically share information that used to require labor-intensive manual reporting. Improved information flow increases report accuracy and helps each company in the *supply chain* manage stock levels.

Online Customer Support

For online shoppers who need instant help, many retail websites make it easy to connect with a live sales rep via phone or instant messaging. In addition, software tools known as *virtual agents* or *bots* can perform a variety of communication tasks, such as answering simple questions and responding to requests for electronic documents.

Podcasts

With the portability and convenience of downloadable audio and video recordings, podcasts have quickly become a popular means of delivering everything from college lectures to marketing messages. Podcasts are also used for internal communication, replacing conference calls, newsletters, and other media.

INTERACTING WITH CUSTOMERS

Maintaining an open dialog with customers is a great way to gain a better understanding of their likes and dislikes. Today's communication technologies make it easier for customers to interact with a company whenever, wherever, and however they wish. A well-coordinated approach to phone, web, and in-store communication helps a company build stronger relationships with its existing customers, which increases the chances of doing more business with each one.

Help Lines

Some people prefer the personal touch of contact by phone. Moreover, some companies assign preferred customers special ID numbers that let them jump to the front of the calling queue. Many companies offer multilingual support as well.

In-Store Kiosks

Staples is among the retailers that let shoppers buy from the web while they're still in the store. Web-connected kiosks give customers quick access to thousands of in-store items and many more that are available online.

Blogs

Blogs let companies connect with customers and other audiences in a fast and informal way. Commenting features let audiences participate in the conversation, too.

feedback delivers criticism with no effort to stimulate improvement.[36] For example, "This proposal is a confusing mess, and you failed to convince me of anything" is destructive feedback. Your goal is to be more constructive: "Your proposal could be more effective with a clearer description of the construction process and a well-organized explanation of why the positives outweigh the negatives." When giving feedback, avoid personal attacks and give the person clear guidelines for improvement.

When you receive constructive feedback, resist the immediate urge to defend your work or deny the validity of the feedback. Remaining open to criticism isn't easy when you've poured your heart and soul into a project, but feedback provides a valuable opportunity to learn and improve. Try to disconnect your emotions from the work and view it simply as something you can improve.

Being Sensitive to Business Etiquette

An important element of audience-centered communication is **etiquette**, the expected norms of behavior in a particular situation. In today's hectic, competitive world, the notion of etiquette might seem outdated and unimportant. However, the way you conduct yourself can have a profound influence on your company's success and your career. When executives hire and promote you, they expect your behavior to protect the company's reputation. The more you understand such expectations, the better chance you have of avoiding career-damaging mistakes.

> Respect, courtesy, and common sense will help you avoid etiquette mistakes.

Long lists of etiquette "rules" can be overwhelming, and you'll never be able to memorize all of them. Fortunately, you can count on three principles to get you through just about any situation: respect, courtesy, and common sense. Moreover, these principles will encourage forgiveness if you do happen to make a mistake. As you encounter new situations, take a few minutes to learn the expectations of the other people involved. Don't be afraid to ask questions, either. People will respect your concern and curiosity. You'll gradually accumulate considerable knowledge, which will help you feel comfortable and be effective in a wide range of business situations. Chapter 2 offers more information about business etiquette.

Using Communication Technology Effectively

> Communicating in today's business environment nearly always requires some level of technical competence.

Today's businesses rely heavily on technology to improve the communication process, and you'll be expected to use a variety of these tools on the job. The four-page photo essay "Powerful Tools for Communicating Efficiently" (pages 16–19) offers an overview of the technologies that connect people in offices, factories, and other business settings. Even as technologies continue to advance, anyone who has used a computer knows that the benefits of technology are not automatic. To communicate effectively, you need to keep technology in perspective, use technological tools productively, and disengage from the computer frequently to communicate in person.

Keeping Technology in Perspective

> Don't let technology overwhelm the communication process.

Technology is an aid to communication, not a replacement for it. Technology can't think for you, communicate for you, or make up for a lack of essential skills. The spell checker in your word processor is a great example. It's happy to run all your words through the dictionary, but it doesn't know whether you're using the correct words or the best words possible.

The sheer number of possibilities offered by many technological tools can also get in the way of successful communication. For example, both senders and receivers may be distracted if they're having trouble configuring their computers to participate in an online meeting. Or the content of a message may be obscured if an electronic presentation is overloaded with amateurish visual effects. By focusing on your message and your audience, you can avoid falling into the trap of letting technology get in the way of successful communication.

Using Tools Wisely

You don't have to become an expert to use most communication technologies effectively, but you do need to be familiar with the basic features and functions of the tools your employer expects you to use. For instance, if you don't know the basic functions of your word processor, you could spend hours trying to format a document that a skilled user could format in minutes. Whatever the tool, if you learn the basics, your work will be less frustrating and far more productive.

Employers who are comfortable using communication technologies have a competitive advantage in today's marketplace.

Reconnecting with People Frequently

Even the best technologies can hinder communication if they are overused. A recent survey of U.S. and Canadian companies uncovered widespread employee frustration with the communication efforts of senior managers; the most common complaint was that managers rely too heavily on e-mail and don't communicate face-to-face often enough.[37]

No matter how much technology is involved, communication will always be about people connecting with people.

Moreover, even the best communication technologies can't show people who you really are. You can create stunning documents and compelling presentations without ever leaving your desk or meeting anyone in person. You might be funny, bright, and helpful, but you're just a voice on the phone or a name on a screen until people can interact with you in person. Remember to step out from behind the technology frequently to learn more about the people you work with—and to let them learn more about you.

For the latest information on business communication technologies, visit http://real-timeupdates.com/bce and click on Chapter 1. ■

DOCUMENT MAKEOVER

Improve This Memo

To practice correcting drafts of actual documents, visit the "Document Makeovers" section in either MyBCommLab.com or the Companion Website for this text.

If MyBCommLab.com is being used in your class, see your User Guide for specific instructions on how to access the content for this chapter.

If you are accessing this feature through the Companion Website, click on "Document Makeovers" and then select Chapter 1. You will find a memo that contains problems and errors related to what you've learned in this chapter about improving business communication. Use the Final Draft decision tool to create an improved version of this memo. Check the message for ethical communication, an audience-centered approach, and intercultural sensitivity. ●

" CHAPTER REVIEW AND ACTIVITIES

Chapter Summary

The ability to communicate well will play a key role in your success as a business professional. Not only will you be more effective in your own job, but you will also be able to influence and lead others and make significant contributions to your company's success. To be effective, your communication efforts need to provide practical information, give facts rather than vague impressions or unsupported opinions, present information efficiently to minimize information overload, clearly define expectations and responsibilities, and offer persuasive arguments and recommendations.

Developing your communication abilities promises a double payoff because the skills that will help you advance in your career will also help your company succeed in today's competitive global marketplace. These skills include organizing ideas and information logically and completely; expressing ideas and information coherently and persuasively; reading and listening to extract intended meaning from messages; communicating effectively with people from diverse backgrounds and experiences; using communication technologies effectively and efficiently; following accepted standards of grammar, spelling, and other aspects of high-quality writing and speaking; meeting contemporary expectations of business etiquette; communicating ethically; adhering to applicable government regulations and guidelines; and using your time productively.

Communication can be modeled as an eight-step process: (1) the sender has an idea, (2) the sender encodes that idea in a message, (3) the sender produces the message in a transmittable medium, (4) the sender transmits the message through a channel, (5) the audience receives the message, (6) the audience decodes the message, (7) the audience responds to the message, and (8) the audience provides feedback to the sender.

Six ways you can improve your communication are committing to ethical communication, which involves knowing the difference between an ethical dilemma and an ethical lapse; adopting an audience-centered approach; improving your intercultural sensitivity; giving and responding to constructive feedback; being sensitive to business etiquette; and using communication technology effectively.

Test Your Knowledge

1. What benefits does effective communication give you and your organization?

2. How does cultural context affect communication?

3. Define *ethics* and explain what ethical communication encompasses.

4. Why should communicators take an audience-centered approach to communication?

5. Why is it important to also connect in person when using technology to communicate?

Apply Your Knowledge

1. Why do you think communication is vital to the success of every business organization? Explain briefly.

2. How does your understanding of the communication process help you conduct business more effectively?

3. Your company has relocated to a U.S. city that has a strong Vietnamese subculture. Many employees will be from this subculture. As a member of the human resources department, what suggestions can you make to improve communication between management and the Vietnamese Americans your company is hiring?

4. How does the presence of a reader comments feature on a corporate blog reflect audience-centered communication?

5. **Ethical Choices**   Because of your excellent communication skills, your boss always asks you to write his reports for him. But when the CEO compliments him on his logical organization and clear writing style, your boss responds as if he'd written all those reports himself. What kind of ethical choice does this represent? What can you do in this situation? Briefly explain your solution and your reasoning.

Practice Your Knowledge

Activities

Active links for all websites in this chapter can be found online. If MyBCommLab.com is being used in your class, see your User Guide for instructions on accessing the content for this chapter. Otherwise, visit www.pearsonhighered.com/bovee, locate *Business Communication Essentials*, Fourth Edition, click the Companion Website link, select Chapter 1, and then click on "Featured Websites." Please note that links to sites that become inactive after publication of the book will be removed from the Featured Websites section.

1. **Analyze This Message**   Your boss wants to send a brief e-mail message to welcome employees recently transferred to your department from your Hong Kong branch. They all speak English, but your boss asks you to review her message for clarity. What would you suggest your boss change in the following e-mail message—and why? Would you consider this message to be audience centered? Why or why not?

   I wanted to welcome you ASAP to our little family here in the states. It's high time we shook hands in person and not just across the sea. I'm pleased as punch about getting to know you all, and I for one will do my level best to sell you on America.

2. **Ethical Choices**   In less than a page, explain why you think each of the following is or is not ethical:

   a. Deemphasizing negative test results in a report on your product idea

   b. Taking a computer home to finish a work-related assignment

   c. Telling an associate and close friend that she should pay more attention to her work responsibilities, or management will fire her

   d. Recommending the purchase of excess equipment to use up your allocated funds before the end of the fiscal year so that your budget won't be cut next year

3. **The Changing Workplace: Personal Expression at Work**   Blogging has become a popular way for employees to communicate with customers and other parties outside the company. In some cases, employee blogs have been quite beneficial for both companies and their customers, providing helpful information and "putting a human face" on otherwise formal and imposing corporations. However, in some cases, employees have been fired for posting information that their employers said was inappropriate. One particular area of concern is criticism of the company or individual managers. Should employees be allowed to criticize their employers in a public forum such as a blog? In a brief e-mail message, argue for or against company policies that prohibit any critical information in employee blogs.

4. **Internet**   Cisco is a leading manufacturer of equipment for the Internet and corporate networks and has developed a code of ethics that it expects employees to abide by. Visit the company's website at www.cisco.com and find the *Code of Conduct*. In a brief paragraph, describe three specific examples of things you could do that would violate these provisions; then list at least three opportunities that Cisco provides its employees to report ethics violations or ask questions regarding ethical dilemmas.

5. **Communication Etiquette**   Potential customers often visit your production facility before making purchase decisions. You and the people who report to you in the sales department have received extensive training in etiquette issues because you frequently deal with high-profile clients. However, the rest of the workforce has not received such training, and you worry that someone might inadvertently say or do something that would offend one of these potential customers. In a two-paragraph e-mail, explain to the general manager why you think anyone who might come in contact with customers should receive basic etiquette training.

6. **Self-Introduction**   Write a paragraph or prepare a two-minute oral presentation, introducing yourself to your instructor and your class. Include such things as your background, interests, achievements, and goals.

7. **Teamwork**   Your boss has asked your work group to research and report on corporate child-care facilities. Of course, you'll want to know who (besides your boss) will be reading your report. Working with two team members, list four or five other things you'll want to know about the situation and about your audience before starting your research. Briefly explain why each of the items on your list is important.

8. **Communication Process: Analyzing Miscommunication**   Use the eight phases of the communication process to analyze a miscommunication you've recently had with a co-worker, supervisor, classmate, teacher, friend, or family member. What idea were you trying to share? How did you encode and transmit it? Did the receiver get the message? Did the receiver correctly decode the message? How do you know? Based on your analysis, what do you think prevented your successful communication in this instance?

9. **Ethical Choices**   Knowing that you have numerous friends throughout the company, your boss relies on you for feedback concerning employee morale and other issues affecting the staff. She recently approached you and asked you to start reporting any behavior that might violate company polices, from taking office supplies home to making personal long-distance calls. List the issues you'd like to discuss with her before you respond to her request.

10. **Intercultural Sensitivity: Recognizing Differences**   Your boss represents a Canadian toy company that's negotiating to buy miniature truck wheels from a manufacturer in Osaka, Japan. In the first meeting, your boss explains that your company expects to control the design of the wheels as well as the materials that are used to make them. The manufacturer's representative looks down and says softly, "Perhaps that will be difficult." Your boss presses for agreement, and to emphasize your company's willingness to buy, he shows the prepared contract he's brought with him. However, the manufacturer seems increasingly vague and uninterested.

    Your task: What cultural differences may be interfering with effective communication in this situation? Explain briefly in an e-mail message to your instructor.

11. **Teamwork**   Working with two other students, prepare a list of 10 examples of slang (in your own language) that would probably be misinterpreted or misunderstood during a business conversation with someone from another culture. Next to each example, suggest other words you might use to convey the same message. Do the alternatives mean *exactly* the same as the original slang or idiom?

12. **Intercultural Communication: Studying Cultures**   Choose a specific country, such as India, Portugal, Bolivia, Thailand, or Nigeria, with which you are not familiar. Research the culture and write a brief summary of what a U.S. businessperson would need to know about concepts of personal space and rules of social behavior in order to conduct business successfully in that country.

13. **Workforce Diversity: Bridging Differences**   Differences in gender, age, and physical abilities contribute to the diversity of today's workforce. Working with a classmate, role-play a conversation in which

    a. A woman is being interviewed for a job by a male human resources manager

    b. An older person is being interviewed for a job by a younger human resources manager

    c. A person using a wheelchair is being interviewed for a job by a person who can walk

    How did differences between the applicant and the interviewer shape the communication? What can you do to improve communication in such situations?

14. **Intercultural Sensitivity: Understanding Attitudes**   You are the assistant to the director of marketing for a telecommunications firm based in Germany. You're accompanying your boss to negotiate with an official in Guangzhou, China, who's in charge of selecting a new telephone system for the city. Your boss insists that the

specifications be spelled out in detail in the contract. However, the Chinese negotiator argues that in developing a long-term business relationship, such minor details are unimportant.

Your task: What can you suggest that your boss do or say to break this intercultural deadlock and obtain the contract so that both parties are comfortable? Outline your ideas in a brief e-mail message to your instructor.

Expand Your Knowledge

Exploring the Best of the Web

Check Out These Free Resources   The Business Writer's Free Library, www.managementhelp.org/commskls/cmm_writ.htm, is an excellent resource for business communication material. Categories of information include basic composition skills, basic writing skills, correspondence, reference material, and general resources and advice. Log on and read about the most common errors in English, become a word detective, ask Miss Grammar, review samples of common forms of correspondence, fine-tune your interpersonal skills, join a newsgroup, and more. Follow the links and improve your effectiveness as a business communicator. (Note that the formatting of some of the samples shown on this website may differ from document formats in this textbook.)

Exercises

1. What are some strategies for communicating with an uncooperative audience?

2. What is the value of diversity in the workplace?

3. Why is bad etiquette bad for business?

Surfing Your Way to Career Success

Bovée and Thill's Business Communication Headline News offers links to hundreds of online resources that can help you with this course, your other college courses, and your career. Visit http://businesscommunicationblog.com and click on "Web Directory." The Business Communication and Communication sections connect you to a variety of websites and articles on basic communication skills and intriguing topics such as communication ethics and disinformation. Identify three websites from these sections that could be useful in your business career. For each site, write a two-sentence summary of what the site offers and how it could help you launch and build your career.

MyBCommLab.com

Use MyBCommLab.com to test your understanding of the concepts presented in this chapter and explore additional materials that will bring the ideas to life in video, activities, and an online multimedia e-book. Additionally, you can improve your skill with nouns and pronouns by using the "Peak Performance Grammar and Mechanics" module within the lab. Take the Pretest to determine whether you have any weak areas. Then review those areas in the Refresher Course. Take the Follow-Up Test to check your grasp of nouns and pronouns. For an extra challenge, take the Advanced Test. Finally, for even more reinforcement, go to the "Improve Your Grammar, Mechanics, and Usage" section that follows, and complete the "Level 1: Self-Assessment" exercises.

Improve Your Grammar, Mechanics, and Usage

Level 1: Self-Assessment—Nouns

Use the following self-assessment exercises to improve your knowledge of and power over English grammar, mechanics, and usage. Review all of Section 1.1 in the Handbook of Grammar, Mechanics, and Usage that appears at the end of this book. Answers to these exercises appear on page AK-1.

In items 1–5, underline the common nouns and circle the proper nouns.

1. Give the balance sheet to Melissa.

2. We'd like to order 50 more satchels for Craigmont Stores and 3 each for the other stores on our list.

3. Tarnower Corporation donates a portion of its profits to charity every year.

4. Which aluminum bolts are packaged?

5. Please send the Joneses a dozen of each of the following: stopwatches, canteens, headbands, and wristbands.

In items 6–10, underline the subjects and circle the objects.

6. The technician has already repaired the machine for the client.

7. An attorney will talk to the group about incorporation.

8. After her vacation, the buyer prepared a third-quarter budget.

9. The new flat monitors are serving our department very well.

10. Accuracy overrides speed in importance.

In items 11–15, underline inappropriate noun plurals and possessives and write the correct form in the space provided.

11. _____ Make sure that all copys include the new addresses.

12. _____ Ask Jennings to collect all employee's donations for the Red Cross drive.

13. _____ Charlie now has two son-in-laws to help him with his two online business's.

14. _____ Avoid using too many parenthesises when writing your reports.

15. _____ Follow President Nesses rules about what constitutes a weeks work.

Level 2: Workplace Applications

The following items contain numerous errors in grammar, capitalization, punctuation, abbreviation, number style, word division, and vocabulary. Rewrite each sentence, correcting all errors. Write *C* for any sentence that is already correct.

1. If a broken down unproductive guy like Carl can get a raise; why can't a take charge guy like me get one?

2. Visit our website and sign up for "On Your Toes", our free newsletter that keeps you informed of promotions, discounts and about Internet-only specials.

3. As of March, 2007, the Board of Directors have 9 members including: three women, one African-American, and one American of Hispanic descent.

4. As one of the nearly 3,000,000 New York Life policyholders eligible to vote, we urge you to approve the new investment advisory agreement.

5. Gerrald Higgins, vice president for marketing, told us reporters that Capital One provides financial services to one-fourth of homes in the United States.

6. Our Customer Relations associates work with people everyday to answer questions, provide assistance, and helping solve problems.

7. If anyone breaches the lease, its likely that the landlord will file legal action against them to collect on the remainder of they're lease.

8. A IRA is one of the most common plans for the self-employed because of it's ease of setting up and administering.

9. My advise to you is, to put you're mission statement on your web cite.

10. According to Karen Smiths' report small-business owners do'nt recognize the full effect that layoffs and terminations are liable to have on the motivation of surviving employees'.

11. To exacerbate the processing of your US tax return, use the mailing label and bar coded envelope that comes with your tax package.

12. The NASE have implemented a exciting array of programs that make it more easy for legislative opinions and concerns to be voiced by you.

13. Keep in mind the old saying "When we laugh the world laugh with us, when you cry you cry alone."

14. Albert Edmunds and me are Owners of the real estate firm of Edmunds & Cale, which have recently opened a new office in San Diego co.

15. The memo inferred that the economic downturn will have a greater affect on the company's bottom line then we previously assumed, this was the worse news we could of gotten.

Level 3: Document Critique

The following document may contain errors in grammar, capitalization, punctuation, abbreviation, number style, word division, and vocabulary. Correct all errors using standard proofreading marks (see Appendix C).

Memo

TO:	All Employees
FROM:	Roberta Smith, Personnel Director
DATE:	December 28, 2009
SUBJECT:	time Cards

After reviewing our Current Method of keeping track of employee hours; we have concluded that time cards leave a lot to be desired. So starting Monday, we have a new system, a time clock. You just have to punch in and punch out; when-ever you will come and go from your work area's.

The new system may take a little while to get used to, but should be helpful to those of us who are making a new years resolution to be more punctual.

Happy New Year to all!

Mastering Interpersonal Communication

[from the real world]

"The only way that people feel really, really a part of something is if they know everything."
—*Kip Tindell,*
Co-founder, The
Container Store
www.containerstore.com

When Kip Tindell and his partner Garrett Boone set out to create the "best retail store in the United States," they built teamwork and team communication into the very fabric of The Container Store's culture. Tindell and Boone believe so strongly in sharing information and listening to employees that every store location begins and ends the day with a team meeting known as a "huddle." Similar to a huddle in football, it helps give everyone a common purpose: to set goals, share information, boost morale, and bond as a team. The Container Store has rapidly become one of the most respected retail chains in the country, and its commitment to teamwork and open communication is a vital part of this ongoing success.[1] This chapter focuses on the skills you need in order to work well in teams and on other interpersonal communication skills that will help you on the job: business etiquette, productive meetings, listening, and nonverbal communication.

IMPROVING YOUR PERFORMANCE IN TEAMS

Team members have a shared mission and are collectively responsible for the team's performance.

A **team** is a unit of two or more people who share a mission and the responsibility for working to achieve their goal.[2] Teams are a popular form of organization in business today, and when they are successful, they improve productivity, creativity, employee involvement, and even job security.[3] In fact, many companies now base pay raises and promotions on employees' effectiveness as team players.

Effective teams

- Understand their purpose
- Communicate openly and honestly
- Build consensus
- Think creatively
- Stay focused
- Resolve conflict

Communication plays a key role in team performance, and the best teams have a clear communication strategy that overcomes the challenges of geographic distance and organizational boundaries.[4] Good team collaborators are willing to exchange information, examine issues, and work through conflicts that arise. They trust each other, working toward the greater good of the team and organization rather than focusing on personal goals.[5] The most effective teams have a clear sense of purpose, communicate openly and honestly, reach decisions by consensus, think creatively, and know how to resolve conflict.[6] Learning these team skills takes time and practice, and U.S. companies now teach teamwork more frequently than any other aspect of business.[7]

Communication problems can greatly reduce team effectiveness. For instance, trust can be eroded when team members are suspicious of one another's motives or ability to contribute.[8] Teams that operate across cultures, countries, and time zones can suffer from communication breakdowns.[9] Poor communication can also result from basic differences in conversational styles. For example, some people expect conversation to follow an orderly pattern in which team members wait their turns to speak. Others view conversation as more spontaneous and are comfortable with an overlapping, interactive style.[10]

Advantages and Disadvantages of Teams

A successful team can provide a number of advantages:[11]

- **Increased information and knowledge.** By pooling the resources of several individuals, a team has access to more information in the decision-making process.
- **Increased diversity of views.** Team members bring a variety of perspectives to the decision-making process. Keep in mind, however, that unless these diverse viewpoints are guided by a shared goal, the multiple perspectives can actually hamper a team's efforts.[12]
- **Increased acceptance of a solution.** Those who participate in making a decision are more likely to support the decision enthusiastically and encourage others to accept it.
- **Higher performance levels.** Working in teams can unleash new amounts of creativity and energy, and effective teams can be better than top-performing individuals at solving complex problems.[13]

On the other hand, unsuccessful teamwork can waste time and money, generate lower-quality work, and frustrate both managers and employees. Teams need to be aware of and work to counter the following potential disadvantages:

- **Groupthink. Groupthink** occurs when peer pressure causes team members to withhold contrary or unpopular opinions. The result can be decisions that are worse than ones the team members might have made individually.
- **Hidden agendas.** Some team members may have a **hidden agenda**—private motives that affect the group's interaction.
- **Free riders.** Some team members may be **free riders**—those who don't contribute their fair share to the group's activities.
- **Cost.** Another drawback to teamwork is the cost of coordinating group activities, such as aligning schedules, arranging meetings, and coordinating individual parts of a project.

> Teams are unproductive when
> - Members feel pressured to conform and agree to unwise decisions
> - Group members' personal motives interfere with the group's efforts
> - Some team members don't contribute
> - The cost of coordinating a team outweighs the benefits of teamwork

Collaborative Writing

Teams are often expected to collaborate on reports, websites, presentations, and other communication projects. The following guidelines will help you work together more successfully:[14]

- **Select collaborators carefully.** Choose a combination of people who have the experience, information, and talent needed for each project.
- **Agree on project goals before you start.** Starting without a clear idea of what you hope to accomplish inevitably leads to frustration and wasted time.
- **Give your team time to bond before diving in.** Make sure people can get to know each other before being asked to collaborate.
- **Clarify individual responsibilities.** Because team members will be depending on each other, make sure individual responsibilities are clear.
- **Establish clear processes.** Make sure everyone knows how the work will be done, including checkpoints and decisions to be made along the way.
- **Avoid writing as a group.** Group writing can be a slow, painful process, so assign the actual writing to one person or divide larger projects among multiple writers.
- **Verify tools and techniques.** If you plan to use technology for sharing or presenting materials, test the system before work begins.

> Successful collaboration requires a number of steps, from selecting the right partners and agreeing on project goals to establishing clear processes and avoiding writing as a group.

Collaboration tools include multiauthor blogs, content management systems, and wikis.

A variety of writing collaboration tools exist, including group review and commenting features in word processors, multiauthor blogs, and **content management systems** that organize and control the content for websites. Each of these tools addresses specific needs, but none offers quite the level of direct collaboration as the wiki. A **wiki**, from the Hawaiian word for *quick*, is a website that allows anyone who has access to add new material and edit existing material. For instance, Yahoo! uses private wikis to facilitate communication among hundreds of team members around the world who are involved in creating and documenting new services.[15] Chapter 6 offers some great tips for writing using wikis.

Shared workspaces give team members instant access to shared resources and information.

Shared workspaces are "virtual offices" that give everyone on a team access to the same set of resources and information: databases, calendars, project plans, pertinent IM and e-mail exchanges, shared reference materials, and team-created documents. Workspaces such as Documentum eRoom, Microsoft SharePoint, and IBM Lotus Team Workspace create a seamless environment for collaboration. Such workspaces, which are part of a larger class of software know as **groupware**, make it easy for geographically dispersed team members to access shared files anytime, anywhere.

Most systems have built-in intelligence to control which team members can read, edit, and save specific files. *Revision control* goes one step further: It allows only one person at a time to check out a given file or document and records all the changes each person makes. This feature prevents two people from independently editing the same report at the same time, thus avoiding the messy situation in which a team ends up with two versions of the same document.[16]

DEVELOPING YOUR BUSINESS ETIQUETTE

As Chapter 1 pointed out, etiquette is now widely considered to be an important business skill. Nobody wants to work with someone who is rude to colleagues or an embarrassment to the company. Moreover, shabby treatment of others in the workplace can be a huge drain on morale and productivity.[17] Here are some key etiquette points to remember when you're in the workplace and out in public.

Etiquette in the Workplace

If you want to appear polished, professional, and confident in business settings, learn the behavioral expectations in your workplace.

Knowing how to behave and how to interact with people in business will help you appear polished, professional, and confident.[18] Understanding business etiquette also helps you put others at ease so that they are comfortable enough to do business with you.[19]

For instance, rightly or wrongly, your personal appearance often has considerable impact on your career success. Pay attention to the style of dress where you work and adjust your style to match. If you're not sure, dress moderately and simply—earn a reputation for what you can *do*, not for what you can wear. Expectations vary widely, so adapt your wardrobe for your specific job, company, and industry. Don't be afraid to ask for advice if you're not sure.

In addition to your clothing, personal grooming affects the impression you give others in the workplace. Pay close attention to cleanliness and avoid using products with powerful scents, such as perfumed soaps, colognes, shampoos, and aftershave lotions (many people are bothered by these products, and some are allergic to them). Shampoo frequently, keep hands and nails neatly manicured, use mouthwash and deodorant, and make regular trips to a hair stylist or barber.[20]

Your smile also affects the way people do business with you. When you smile, do so genuinely. A fake smile is obvious because the timing is frequently off and the expression fails to involve all the facial muscles that a genuine smile would.[21] However, certain occasions require smiling, such as when you're introduced to someone, when you give or receive a compliment, and when you applaud someone's efforts.[22]

Even with the growth of instant messaging, blogs, and other new media, your telephone skills will be vital to your business success.

Much of your interaction with team members, other colleagues, and customers will take place over the telephone, and phone skills will have a definite impact on your career success. Because phone calls lack the visual richness of face-to-face conversations, you have to rely on your attitude and tone of voice to convey confidence and professionalism. See Table 2.1 for helpful phone tips.

TABLE 2.1 Quick Tips for Improving Your Phone Skills

General Tips	Placing Calls	Receiving Calls	Using Voice Mail
Use frequent verbal responses that show you're listening ("Oh yes," "I see," "That's right").	Be ready before you call so that you don't waste the other person's time.	Answer promptly and with a smile so that you sound friendly and positive.	When recording your outgoing message, make it brief and professional.
Increase your volume just slightly to convey your confidence.	Minimize the noise level in your environment as much as possible to avoid distracting the other party.	Identify yourself and your company. (Some companies have specific instructions for what to say when you answer.)	If you can, record temporary greetings on days when you are unavailable all day so that callers will know you're gone for the day.
Don't speak in a monotone; vary your pitch and inflection so people know you're interested.	Identify yourself and your organization, briefly describe why you're calling, and verify that you've called at a good time.	Establish the needs of your caller by asking, "How may I help you?" If you know the caller's name, use it.	Check your voice-mail messages regularly and return all necessary calls within 24 hours.
Slow down when conversing with people whose native language isn't the same as yours.	Don't take up too much time. Speak quickly and clearly and get right to the point of the call.	If you can, answer questions promptly and efficiently; if you can't help, tell the caller what you can do.	Leave simple, clear messages with your name, number, purpose for calling, and times when you can be reached.
Stay focused on the call throughout; others can easily tell when you're not paying attention.	Close in a friendly, positive manner and double-check all vital information, such as meeting times and dates.	If you must forward a call or put someone on hold, explain what you are doing first.	State your name and telephone number slowly so that the other person can easily write them down; repeat both if the other person doesn't know you.
		If you forward a call to someone else, try to speak with that person first to verify that he or she is available and to introduce the caller.	Be careful what you say; most voice-mail systems allow users to forward messages to anyone else in the system.
		If you take a message for someone else, be complete and accurate, including the caller's name, number, and organization.	Replay your message before leaving the system to make sure it is clear and complete.

If you're accustomed to using your mobile phone anywhere, everywhere, and any time day or night, get ready to change your habits. Mobile phones are causing so much disruption in the workplace that some senior executives now ban their use in meetings, for example.[23] In any setting, show respect for others by choosing ringtones that are appropriate for a professional environment, refraining from using your phone whenever doing so will disrupt others, and speaking in a normal voice when you do need to use your phone—there's no need to shout with today's phones.[24]

Etiquette in Social Settings

You often represent your company when you're out in public, so make sure your appearance and actions are appropriate to the situation. Get to know the customs of the culture when you meet new people. In North America, a firm handshake is expected when two people meet, whereas in Japan a respectful bow of the head is more appropriate. If you are expected to shake hands, be aware that the passive "dead fish" handshake creates an extremely negative impression. If you are physically able, always stand when shaking someone's hand.

When introducing yourself, include a brief description of your role in the company. When introducing two other people, speak both their first and last names clearly and then try to offer some information (perhaps a shared professional interest) to help the two people ease into a conversation.[25] Generally speaking, the lower-ranking person is introduced to the senior-ranking person, without regard to gender.[26] When you're introduced to someone, repeat the person's name as soon as possible. Doing so is both a compliment and a good way to remember the name.[27]

You represent your company when you're out in public—or communicating online under your own name—so etiquette continues to be important even after you leave the office.

Business is often conducted over meals, and knowing the basics of dining etiquette will make you more effective in these situations.[28] Choose foods that are easy to eat; you may not want to wrestle with a lobster while trying to carry on a conversation. If an alcoholic drink is appropriate, save it for the end of the meal so that you can stay clear and composed. Leave business papers under your chair until entrée plates have been removed; the business aspect of the meal doesn't usually begin until then.

Remember that business meals are about business. Don't bring up politics, religion, or any other topic that's likely to stir up emotions. Avoid complaining about work, refrain from using profanity, and be careful with humor—a joke that might entertain some people could offend others. In general, learn from co-workers who are respected by customers and colleagues. You'll find that they choose topics carefully, listen with respect, and leave a positive impression with everyone they meet.

As with your phone behavior in the office, practice courtesy and common sense when using your mobile phone in public places. When you make or take calls in public, you send the message that people around you aren't as important as your call and that you don't respect your caller's privacy.[29] If it's not a matter of life and death—literally—wait to have the conversation until you're back in the office or away from your colleagues.

Finally, remember that you also represent your company when you are online, even when you're posting information about yourself on social networking websites or leaving comments on blogs. Online etiquette blunders can come back to haunt you, so act professionally.

> Poor mobile phone etiquette is a common source of complaints in both the workplace and social settings.

MAKING YOUR MEETINGS MORE PRODUCTIVE

Much of your workplace communication will occur in meetings, so to a large degree, your ability to contribute to the company and to be recognized for your contributions will depend on your meeting participation skills.

> Much of the communication you'll participate in will take place in meetings.

> A poorly planned or poorly run meeting can waste thousands of dollars.

Unfortunately, many meetings are unproductive. In one study, senior and middle managers reported that only 56 percent of their meetings were actually productive and that 25 percent of them could have been replaced by a phone call or a memo.[30] You'll help your company make better use of meetings by preparing carefully, conducting meetings efficiently, and using meeting technologies wisely.

Preparing for Meetings

Careful preparation helps you avoid two of the biggest meeting mistakes: (1) holding a meeting when distributing a message would do the job and (2) holding a meeting without a specific goal. Before you even begin preparing for a meeting, make sure the meeting is truly necessary. Once you're sure, proceed with these four preparation tasks:

> To ensure a successful meeting, decide on your purpose ahead of time, select the right participants, choose the time and facility carefully, and set a clear agenda.

- **Identify your purpose.** Although many meetings have multiple purposes, most meetings are one of two types: *Informational meetings* involve sharing information and perhaps coordinating action. *Decision-making meetings* involve persuasion, analysis, and problem solving. Whatever your purpose, make sure it is clear—and clearly communicated to all participants.

- **Select participants for the meeting.** With a clear purpose in mind, it's easier to identify the right participants. If the session is purely informational and one person will do most of the talking, you can invite a large group. *Webcasts* (see Chapter 12) are an increasingly popular tool for such meetings; they enable you to reach large or geographically widespread audiences. For decision-making meetings, invite only those people who are in a direct position to help the meeting reach its objective. The more participants, the more comments and confusion you're likely to get, and the longer the meeting will take.

- **Choose the time and the facility.** Morning meetings are often more productive than afternoon sessions because people tend to slow down after lunch. As you choose the facility, consider the seating arrangements: Are rows of chairs suitable, or do you need a conference table or some other setting? Plus, give some attention to details such as room temperature, lighting, ventilation, acoustics, and refreshments; these details can make or break a meeting.

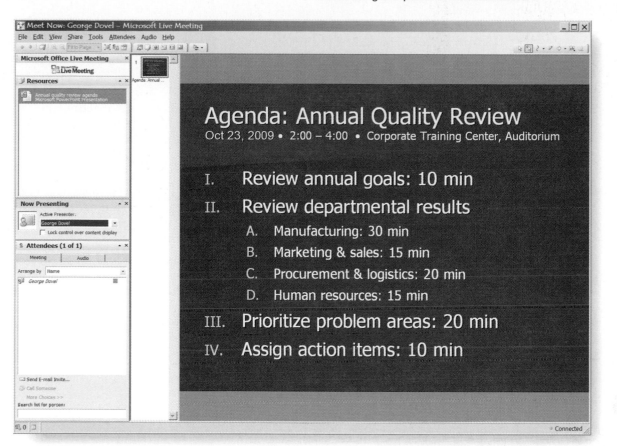

Figure 2.1   Typical Meeting Agenda
Agenda formats vary widely, depending on the complexity of the meeting and the presentation technologies used. For an online meeting, for instance, a good approach is to first send a detailed planning agenda in advance of the meeting so that presenters know what they need to prepare; then you can create a simpler display agenda such as this one to guide the progress of the meeting.

- **Set the agenda.** The success of any meeting depends on the preparation of the participants. People who will be presenting information need to know what is expected of them, non-presenters need to know what will be presented so they can prepare questions, and everyone needs to know how long the meeting will last. In addition, the agenda is an important tool for guiding the progress of the meeting (see Figure 2.1). A productive agenda answers three key questions: (1) What do we need to do in this meeting to accomplish our goals? (2) What issues will be of greatest importance to all participants? (3) What information must be available in order to discuss these issues?[31] In addition to improving productivity, this level of agenda detail shows respect for participants and the other demands on their time.

Leading and Participating in Meetings

Everyone in a meeting shares the responsibility for keeping the meeting productive and making it successful. If you're the designated leader of a meeting, however, you have an extra degree of responsibility and accountability. To ensure productive meetings, be sure to do the following:

Everyone shares the responsibility for successful meetings.

- **Keep the meeting on track.** A good meeting draws out the best ideas and information the group has to offer. Good leaders occasionally guide, mediate, probe, stimulate, summarize, and encourage all participants to contribute.
- **Follow agreed-upon rules.** Business meetings run the gamut from informal to extremely formal, complete with detailed rules for speaking, proposing new items to discuss, voting on proposals, and so on. The larger the meeting, the more formal you'll need to be to maintain order. Formal meetings use **parliamentary procedure**, a time-tested method for planning and running effective meetings. The best-known guide to this procedure is *Robert's Rules of Order* (www.robertsrules.com). Whatever system of rules you employ, make sure everyone is clear about the expectations.

- **Encourage participation.** As a meeting gets under way, you may discover that some participants are too quiet and others are too talkative. The quiet participants might be shy, they might be expressing disagreement or resistance, or they may simply not be paying attention. Draw them out by asking for their input. For the overly talkative, you can say that time is limited and others need to be heard.
- **Participate actively.** Try to contribute to both the subject of the meeting and the smooth interaction of the participants. Use your listening skills and powers of observation to size up the interpersonal dynamics of the group and then adapt your behavior to help the group achieve its goals. Speak up if you have something useful to say but don't monopolize the discussion.
- **Close effectively.** At the conclusion of a meeting, verify that the objectives have been met; if they have not, arrange for follow-up work as needed. Either summarize the general conclusion or list the actions to be taken. Make sure all participants understand and agree on the outcome.

For formal meetings, it's good practice to appoint one person to record the *minutes,* a summary of the important information presented and the decisions made during a meeting. If your company doesn't have a specific format for minutes, follow the generic format shown in Figure 2.2. Key elements include a list of those present and a list of those who were invited

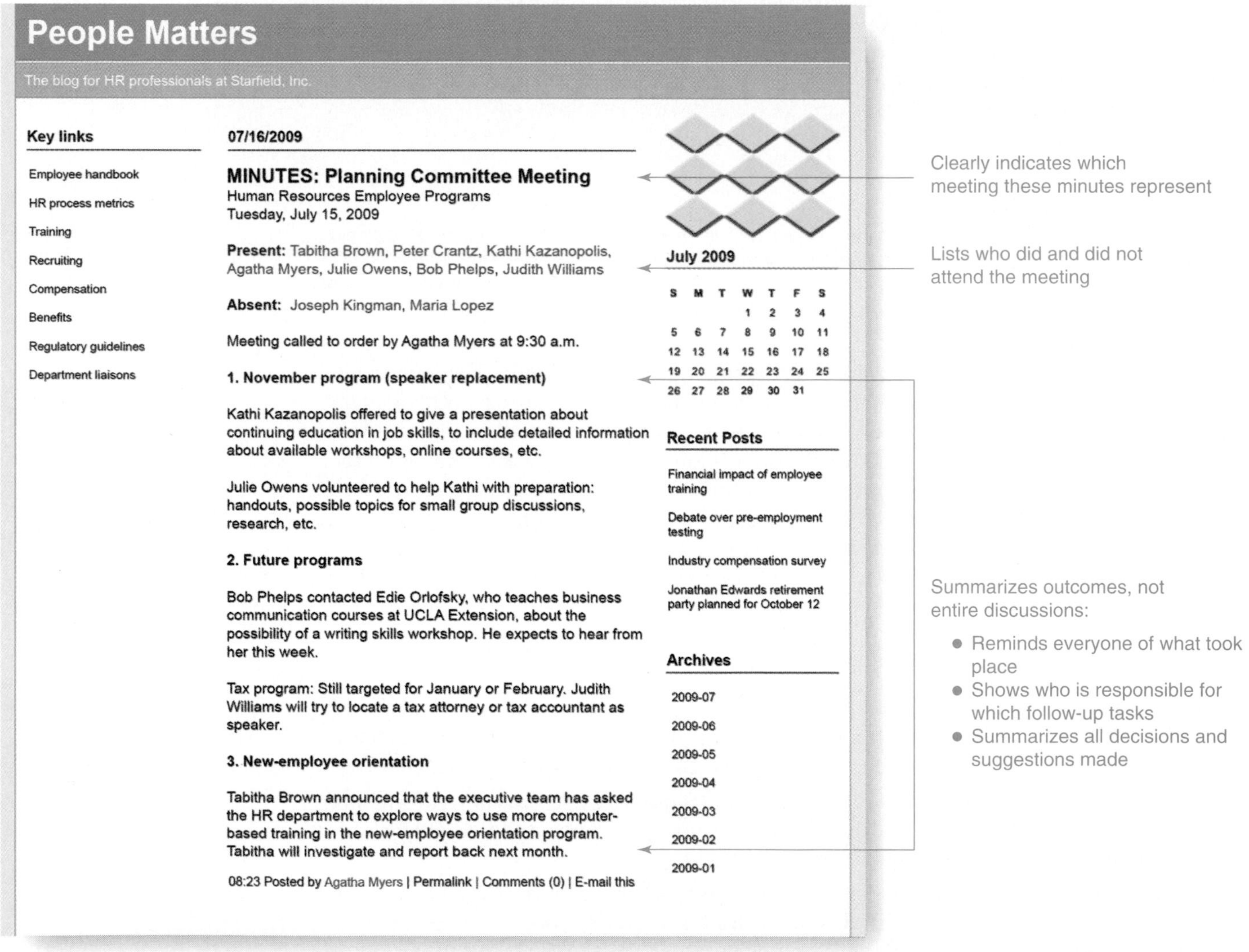

People Matters

The blog for HR professionals at Starfield, Inc.

Key links
Employee handbook
HR process metrics
Training
Recruiting
Compensation
Benefits
Regulatory guidelines
Department liaisons

07/16/2009

MINUTES: Planning Committee Meeting
Human Resources Employee Programs
Tuesday, July 15, 2009

Present: Tabitha Brown, Peter Crantz, Kathi Kazanopolis, Agatha Myers, Julie Owens, Bob Phelps, Judith Williams

Absent: Joseph Kingman, Maria Lopez

Meeting called to order by Agatha Myers at 9:30 a.m.

1. November program (speaker replacement)

Kathi Kazanopolis offered to give a presentation about continuing education in job skills, to include detailed information about available workshops, online courses, etc.

Julie Owens volunteered to help Kathi with preparation: handouts, possible topics for small group discussions, research, etc.

2. Future programs

Bob Phelps contacted Edie Orlofsky, who teaches business communication courses at UCLA Extension, about the possibility of a writing skills workshop. He expects to hear from her this week.

Tax program: Still targeted for January or February. Judith Williams will try to locate a tax attorney or tax accountant as speaker.

3. New-employee orientation

Tabitha Brown announced that the executive team has asked the HR department to explore ways to use more computer-based training in the new-employee orientation program. Tabitha will investigate and report back next month.

08:23 Posted by Agatha Myers | Permalink | Comments (0) | E-mail this

July 2009

S	M	T	W	T	F	S
			1	2	3	4
5	6	7	8	9	10	11
12	13	14	15	16	17	18
19	20	21	22	23	24	25
26	27	28	29	30	31	

Recent Posts
Financial impact of employee training
Debate over pre-employment testing
Industry compensation survey
Jonathan Edwards retirement party planned for October 12

Archives
2009-07
2009-06
2009-05
2009-04
2009-03
2009-02
2009-01

Figure 2.2 Typical Meeting Minutes
Intranet and blog postings are common tools for distributing meeting minutes. The specific format of the minutes is less important than making sure you record all the key information, particularly regarding responsibilities that were assigned during the meeting.

but didn't attend, followed by the times the meeting started and ended, all major decisions reached at the meeting, all assignments of tasks to meeting participants, and all subjects that were deferred to a later meeting. In addition, the minutes objectively summarize important discussions, noting the names of those who contributed major points. Outlines, subheadings, and lists help organize the minutes; additional documentation (such as tables or charts submitted by meeting participants) is noted in the minutes and attached.

Using Meeting Technologies

You can expect to use a variety of meeting-related technologies throughout your career. These technologies have spurred the emergence of **virtual teams**, whose members work in different locations and interact electronically through **virtual meetings**. Instant messaging and **teleconferencing**, in which three or more people are connected by phone simultaneously, are the simplest forms of virtual meetings. **Videoconferencing** lets participants see and hear each other, demonstrate products, and transmit other visual information. The latest videoconferencing technologies enable realistic conferences in which participants thousands of miles away almost seem to be in the same room.[32] The most sophisticated **web-based meeting systems** combine the best of instant messaging, shared workspaces, and videoconferencing with other tools, such as *virtual whiteboards,* that let teams collaborate in real time. Such systems are used for everything from spontaneous discussions among small groups to carefully planned, formal events such as customer training seminars or press conferences.[33]

> Virtual meeting technologies connect people spread around the country or around the world.

Technology continues to create intriguing opportunities for online interaction. For instance, one of the newest virtual tools is *online brainstorming,* in which a company can conduct "idea campaigns" to generate new ideas from people across the organization. These range from small team meetings to huge events such as IBM's giant InnovationJam, in which 100,000 IBM employees, family members, and customers from 160 countries were invited to brainstorm online for three days.[34]

> Recent innovations in meeting technology include online brainstorming systems and virtual worlds.

Companies are also beginning to experiment with virtual meetings and other communication activities in *virtual worlds* such as Second Life (www.secondlife.com). In much the same way that gamers can create and control characters (often known as *avatars*) in a multiplayer video game, professionals can create online versions of themselves to participate in meetings, training sessions, sales presentations, and even casual conversations with customers they happen to bump into (see Figure 2.3). For example, the computer company Sun Microsystems created the Sun Pavilion in Second Life, a virtual arena where Sun executives and invited guests present information and share ideas.[35]

Conducting successful meetings over the phone or online requires extra planning before the meeting and more diligence during the meeting. Because virtual meetings offer much

Figure 2.3   Meeting in a Virtual World
Cranial Tap, whose online headquarters is shown here, is one of a growing number of firms that use Second Life as a virtual meeting place.

less visual contact and nonverbal communication than in-person meetings, leaders need to make sure everyone stays engaged and has the opportunity to contribute. Paying attention during online meetings takes greater effort as well. Participants need to stay committed to the meeting and resist the temptation to work on unrelated tasks.[36]

For the latest information on meeting technologies, visit http://real-timeupdates.com/bce and click on Chapter 2.

IMPROVING YOUR LISTENING SKILLS

Listening is a vital skill, no matter what career path you choose.

Your long-term career prospects are closely tied to your ability to listen effectively. In fact, some 80 percent of top executives say that listening is the most important skill needed to get things done in the workplace.[37] Plus, today's younger employees place a high premium on being heard, so listening is becoming even more vital for managers.[38]

Effective listening strengthens organizational relationships, alerts the organization to opportunities for innovation, and allows the organization to manage growing diversity both in the workforce and in the customers it serves.[39] Companies whose employees and managers listen effectively are able to stay informed, up-to-date, and out of trouble. Conversely, poor listening skills can cost companies millions of dollars per year as a result of lost opportunities, legal mistakes, and other errors. Effective listening is also vital to the process of building trust between organizations and between individuals.[40]

Recognizing Various Types of Listening

To be a good listener, adapt the way you listen to suit each situation.

Effective listeners adapt their listening approaches to different situations. The primary goal of **content listening** is to understand and retain the information in the speaker's message. With this type of listening, you ask questions to clarify the material but don't argue or judge. Try to overlook the speaker's style and any limitations in the presentation; just focus on the information.[41] In contrast, the goal of **critical listening** is to understand and evaluate the meaning of the speaker's message on several levels: the logic of the argument, the strength of the evidence, the validity of the conclusions, the implications of the message for you and your organization, the speaker's intentions and motives, and the omission of any important or relevant points. If you're skeptical, ask questions to explore the speaker's point of view and credibility. Be on the lookout for bias that might color the way the information is presented and be careful to separate opinions from facts.[42]

The goal of **empathic listening** is to understand the speaker's feelings, needs, and wants so that you can appreciate his or her point of view, regardless of whether you share that perspective. By listening in an empathic way, you help the individual vent emotions that prevent a calm, clear-headed approach to the subject. Avoid the temptation to jump in with advice unless the person specifically asks for it; don't judge the speaker's feelings, and don't try to tell people they shouldn't feel this or that emotion. Instead, let the speaker know that you appreciate his or her feelings and understand the situation. Once you establish that connection, you can then help the speaker search for a solution.[43]

No matter what mode they are using at any given time, effective listeners try to engage in **active listening**, making a conscious effort to turn off their own filters and biases to truly hear and understand what the other party is saying. They ask questions or summarize the speaker's message to verify key points and encourage the speaker through positive body language and supportive feedback.[44]

Understanding the Listening Process

Listening seems like a simple procedure. After all, you've been doing it all your life. However, most of us aren't terribly good at it. Most people listen at or below a 25 percent efficiency rate, remember only about half of what's said during a 10-minute conversation, and forget half of that within 48 hours.[45] Furthermore, when questioned about material they've just heard, they are likely to get the facts mixed up.[46]

Why is such a seemingly simple activity so difficult? The reason is that listening is not a simple process, by any means. Listening follows the same sequence as the general communication process model you explored in Chapter 1 (page 7), with the added difficulty that it happens in real time. To listen effectively, you need to successfully complete five steps:[47]

1. **Receiving.** Start by physically hearing the message and recognizing it as incoming information.

2. **Decoding.** Assign meaning to sounds, according to your own values, beliefs, ideas, expectations, roles, needs, and personal history.

3. **Remembering.** Store the information for future processing.

4. **Evaluating.** Evaluate the quality of the information.

5. **Responding.** React based on the situation and the nature of the information.

If any one of these steps breaks down, the listening process becomes less effective or even fails entirely. As both a sender and a receiver, you can reduce the failure rate by recognizing and overcoming a variety of physical and mental barriers to effective listening.

Listening involves five steps: receiving, decoding, remembering, evaluating, and responding.

Overcoming Barriers to Effective Listening

In today's hectic business environment, good listeners look for ways to overcome the many potential barriers to successful listening (see Table 2.2). Some factors you may not be able to control, such as conference room acoustics, poor phone reception, and so on. However, you can certainly control other factors, such as not interrupting speakers and not creating distractions that make it difficult for others to pay attention. If you have questions, wait until the speaker has finished talking. And don't think that you're not interrupting just because you're not talking. Such actions as rustling papers or checking your watch can interrupt a speaker and lead to communication breakdowns.

Selective listening is one of the most common barriers to effective listening. If your mind wanders, you may stay tuned out until you hear a word or phrase that gets your attention

Good listeners actively try to overcome the barriers to successful listening.

TABLE 2.2 What Makes an Effective Listener?

Effective Listeners	Ineffective Listeners
Listen actively	Listen passively
Take careful and complete notes	Take no notes or take ineffective notes
Make frequent eye contact with the speaker (depends on culture to some extent)	Make little or no eye contact or make inappropriate eye contact
Stay focused on the speaker and the content	Allow their minds to wander, are easily distracted, work on unrelated tasks
Mentally paraphrase key points to maintain attention level and ensure comprehension	Fail to paraphrase
Adjust listening style to the situation	Listen with the same style, regardless of the situation
Give the speaker nonverbal cues (such as nodding to show agreement or raising eyebrows to show surprise or skepticism)	Fail to give the speaker nonverbal feedback
Save questions or points of disagreement until an appropriate time	Interrupt whenever they disagree or don't understand
Overlook stylistic differences and focus on the speaker's message	Are distracted by or unduly influenced by stylistic differences; are judgmental
Make distinctions between main points and supporting details	Are unable to distinguish main points from details
Look for opportunities to learn	Assume that they already know everything that's important to know

once more. But by that time, you'll be unable to recall what the speaker *actually* said; instead, you'll remember what you *think* the speaker probably said.[48]

Your mind can process information much faster than most speakers talk, which makes you vulnerable to distractions.

One reason listeners' minds tend to wander is that people think faster than they speak. Most people speak at about 120 to 150 words per minute. However, humans can process audio information at up to 500 words per minute or more.[49] In other words, your brain has a lot of free time whenever you're listening, and if left unsupervised, it will find a thousand other things to think about. Make a conscious effort to focus on the speaker and use the extra time to analyze what you hear, prepare questions you might need to ask, and engage in other relevant thinking.

Selective perception distorts incoming messages by shaping the information to fit what you already believe about the subject.

Another common barrier to successful interpretation is prejudgment—making up your mind before truly hearing what another person has to say. Similarly, *selective perception* leads listeners to mold a message to fit what they already believe about a given subject. If you believe you've done an excellent job writing a report but the people reading it try to give you negative feedback, you may not even "hear" what they're saying. Listening with an open mind isn't always easy, but it's the only way to make sure you really hear what people are telling you.

Even when your intentions are the best, you can still misinterpret incoming messages if you and the speaker don't share enough language or experience. Lack of common ground is the reason misinterpretation occurs so frequently between speakers of different native languages, even when they're trying to speak the same language. When listening to a speaker whose native language or life experience is different from yours, try to paraphrase that person's ideas. Give the speaker a chance to confirm what you think you heard or to correct any misinterpretation.

When information is crucial, don't count on your memory.

After you've successfully avoided all these barriers, you need to retain the information in order to act on it. One simple rule: Don't count on your memory if the information is crucial. Record it, write it down, or capture it in some other physical way. However, if you do need to memorize something, you can capture information in *short-term memory* for a few seconds or a few minutes by repeating it to yourself (silently, if need be), by organizing it into patterns (perhaps in alphabetical order or as steps in a process), and by breaking a long list of items into several shorter lists. To store information in *long-term memory,* four techniques can help:

- Associate new information with something closely related (such as the restaurant in which you met a new client).
- Categorize the new information into logical groups (for example, alphabetize the names of products you're trying to remember).
- Visualize words and ideas as pictures.
- Create *mnemonics* such as acronyms or rhymes.

Note that these four techniques have an important factor in common, and that's action: You have to *do* something to make the information stick.

IMPROVING YOUR NONVERBAL COMMUNICATION SKILLS

Nonverbal communication supplements spoken language.

Nonverbal communication is the process of sending and receiving information, both intentionally and unintentionally, without using written or spoken language. Nonverbal signals play two important roles in communication. The first is complementing verbal language. Nonverbal signals can strengthen a verbal message (when nonverbal signals match words), weaken a verbal message (when nonverbal signals don't match words), or replace words entirely.

Nonverbal clues help you ascertain the truth of spoken information.

The second role for nonverbal signals is revealing truth. Nonverbal communication often conveys more to listeners than the words you speak—particularly when they're trying to decide how you really feel about a situation or when they're trying to judge your credibility and aptitude for leadership.[50] However, even the power of nonverbal cues is not infallible when it comes to detecting truth. In one study, most people failed to detect dishonest speech roughly half the time; only a tiny fraction of the population are able to consistently detect when people are lying to them.[51]

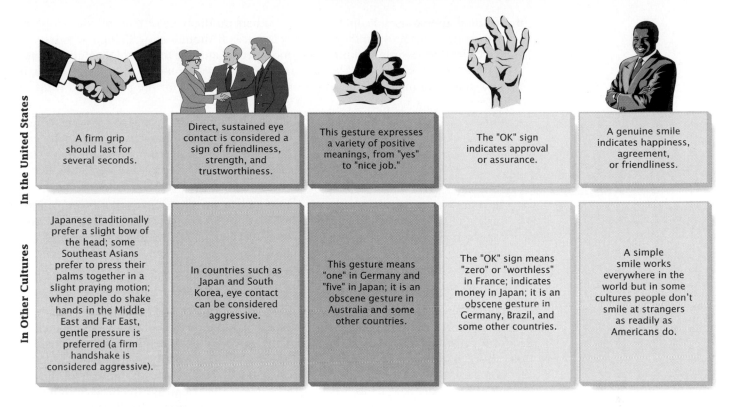

Figure 2.4   Avoiding Nonverbal Mishaps
These examples demonstrate some of the many complexities of nonverbal communication across cultures. Be sure to learn the basic nonverbal signals of any culture in which you need to communicate.

You've been tuned in to nonverbal communication since your first contact with other human beings. Paying special attention to these signals in the workplace will enhance your ability to communicate successfully. Moreover, as you work with a diverse range of people both inside and outside your company, you'll also need to grasp the different meaning of common gestures in various cultures (see Figure 2.4).

The range and variety of nonverbal signals is almost endless, but you can grasp the basics by studying six general categories:

- **Facial expressions.** Your face is the primary site for expressing your emotions; it reveals both the type and the intensity of your feelings.[52] Your eyes are especially effective for indicating attention and interest, influencing others, regulating interaction, and establishing dominance.[53] As with other areas of nonverbal expressions, however, facial signals can vary widely from culture to culture. For instance, maintaining eye contact is usually viewed as a sign of sincerity and openness in the United States, but it can be viewed as rude in Japan.[54]

- **Gestures and postures.** Many gestures—a wave of the hand, for example—have a specific and intentional meaning. Other types of body movement are unintentional and express more general messages. Slouching, leaning forward, fidgeting, and walking briskly are all unconscious signals that reveal whether you feel confident or nervous, friendly or hostile, assertive or passive, powerful or powerless.

- **Vocal characteristics.** Your voice carries both intentional and unintentional messages. Consider the sentence "What have you been up to?" If you repeat that question, changing your tone of voice and stressing various words, you can consciously convey quite different messages. However, your voice can also reveal things of which you are unaware. Your tone and volume, your accent and speaking pace, and all the little *um's* and *ah's* that creep into your speech say a lot about who you are, your relationship with the audience, and the emotions underlying your words.

- **Personal appearance.** People respond to others on the basis of their physical appearance, sometimes fairly and other times unfairly. Although an individual's body type and facial features impose limitations, most people are able to control their appearance to some degree. Grooming, clothing, accessories, style—you can control all of these. If your goal is to make a good impression, adopt the style of the people you want to impress.

- **Touch.** Touch is an important way to convey warmth, comfort, and reassurance. Touch is so powerful, in fact, that it is governed by cultural customs that establish who can touch whom and how in various circumstances. You can learn more about these customs at websites such as www.businessoftouch.com. In general, remember that touch is a complex subject. When in doubt, don't touch.

- **Time and space.** Like touch, time and space can be used to assert authority, imply intimacy, and send other nonverbal messages. For instance, some people try to demonstrate their own importance or disregard for others by making other people wait; others show respect by being on time. Similarly, taking care not to invade private space, such as standing too closely when talking, is a way to show respect for others. Keep in mind that expectations regarding both time and space vary by culture.

When you listen, be sure to pay attention to nonverbal clues. Do these signals amplify the spoken words or contradict them? Is the speaker intentionally using nonverbal signals to send you a message that he or she can't put into words? Be observant but don't assume that you can "read someone like a book." Nonverbal signals are powerful, but they aren't infallible. Contrary to popular belief, just because someone doesn't look you squarely in the eye doesn't mean he or she is lying.[55] If something doesn't feel right, ask the speaker an honest and respectful question; doing so might clear everything up, or it might uncover issues you need to explore further. ∎

DOCUMENT MAKEOVER

Improve This E-Mail Message

To practice correcting drafts of actual documents, visit the "Document Makeovers" section in either MyBCommLab.com or the Companion Website for this text.

If MyBCommLab.com is being used in your class, see your User Guide for specific instructions on how to access the content for this chapter.

If you are accessing this feature through the Companion Website, click on "Document Makeovers" and then select Chapter 2. You will find an e-mail message that contains problems and errors related to what you've learned in this chapter about communicating in teams. Use the Final Draft decision tool to create an improved version of this e-mail message. Check the message for clarity, relevance of topics to meeting participants, and a collaborative tone. ●

" CHAPTER REVIEW AND ACTIVITIES

Chapter Summary

The advantages of successful teamwork include improved productivity, creativity, and employee involvement; increased information and knowledge; greater diversity of views; and increased acceptance of new solutions and ideas. The potential disadvantages of working in teams include groupthink (the tendency to let peer pressure overcome one's better judgment), the pursuit of hidden agendas, free riders who contribute little or nothing, and the cost (in money and time) of planning and conducting team activities.

Etiquette is an essential business skill because the impression you make on others and your ability to help others feel comfortable will be major contributors to your career success. Personal appearance and interpersonal gestures such as smiles and handshakes all send signals—positive or negative—and you need to be aware of the signals you are sending. The need for etiquette extends to the telephone as well, particularly mobile phone usage. In social settings, whether a business lunch or online interaction, remember that you represent your company. Make a positive impression by learning how to introduce yourself and others in a professional manner and by conducting yourself gracefully at dinners and other social gatherings.

Meetings are an essential business activity, but they can waste considerable time and money if conducted poorly. Help your company make better use of meetings by preparing carefully, conducting meetings efficiently, and using meeting technologies wisely. Make sure your meetings are necessary, are carefully planned, include only the necessary participants, and follow clear agendas.

A variety of meeting technologies are available to help teams and other groups communicate more successfully. The primary advantage of these tools is the ability to conduct virtual meetings that don't require everyone to be in the same place at the same time. The tools range from simple instant messaging sessions and teleconferences to videoconferencing and web-based meetings to specialized capabilities such as online brainstorming systems and virtual reality simulators.

The listening process involves five steps: receiving, decoding, remembering, evaluating, and responding. At any stage, barriers can disrupt the process, so good listeners practice active listening, avoid disrupting the speaker or other people, work hard to see past superficial differences and distractions, and take care to memorize important information.

Nonverbal communication, the process of sending and receiving information without using written or spoken language, plays two important roles in communication. The first role is complementing verbal language. Nonverbal signals can strengthen a verbal message (when nonverbal signals match words), weaken a verbal message (when nonverbal signals don't match words), or replace words entirely. The second role is revealing truth; nonverbal signals help audiences decide how much trust to put in the speaker's message. The six major categories of nonverbal expression are facial expressions, gestures and posture, vocal characteristics, personal appearance, touch, and use of time and personal space.

Test Your Knowledge

1. What are five characteristics of effective teams?

2. What four things must effective teams avoid?

3. What activities make up the listening process?

4. Name the three main barriers to effective listening.

5. In what six ways can an individual communicate nonverbally?

Apply Your Knowledge

1. Whenever your boss asks for feedback, she blasts anyone who offers criticism, so people tend to agree with everything she says. You want to talk to her about it, but what should you say? List some of the points you want to make when you discuss this issue with your boss.

2. Several members of your sales team are protesting the company's "business casual" dress code, claiming that dressing nicely makes them feel awkward and overly formal in front of customers. You have to admit that most of the company's customers dress like they've just walked in from a picnic or a motorcycle ride, but that doesn't change the fact that

you want your company to be seen as conscientious and professional. How will you explain the policy to these employees in a way that will help them understand and accept it?

3. Chester never seems to be paying attention during weekly team meetings. He has never contributed to the discussion, and you've never even seen him take notes. He says he wants to support the team but that he finds it difficult to focus during routine meetings. List some ideas you could give him that might improve his listening skills.

4. Considering what you've learned about nonverbal communication, what are some of the ways in which communication might break down during an online meeting in which the participants can see video images of only the person presenting at any given time—and then only his or her head?

5. **Ethical Choices**   As team leader, you've just received a voice-mail message from Tanya Moore, asking if she can lead next week's meeting. She's been with the company for six weeks and with your team for three. From what you've already observed, she's opinionated (a bit of a know-it-all), and her approach discourages the more reserved team members from speaking up.

    You can't allow her to run next week's meeting, and without improvement in her attitude toward others, she may never be ready to lead. You consider three options for explaining your view of her position: (1) leaving her a voice-mail message, (2) meeting with her in person, or (3) sending her an e-mail message. What should you do? Explain your choice.

Practice Your Knowledge

Activities

Active links for all websites in this chapter can be found online. If MyBCommLab.com is being used in your class, see your User Guide for instructions on accessing the content for this chapter. Otherwise, visit www.pearsonhighered.com/bovee, locate *Business Communication Essentials*, Fourth Edition, click the Companion Website link, select Chapter 2, and then click on "Featured Websites." Please note that links to sites that become inactive after publication of the book will be removed from the Featured Websites section.

1. **Analyze This Message**   A project leader has made notes about covering the following items at the quarterly budget meeting. Prepare an agenda by putting these items into a logical order and rewriting them, where necessary, to give phrases a more consistent sound.

    Budget Committee Meeting to be held on December 12, 2009, at 9:30 a.m.

    - I will call the meeting to order.
    - Site director's report: A closer look at cost overruns on Greentree site.
    - The group will review and approve the minutes from last quarter's meeting.
    - I will ask the finance director to report on actual vs. projected quarterly revenues and expenses.
    - I will distribute copies of the overall divisional budget and announce the date of the next budget meeting.
    - Discussion: How can we do a better job of anticipating and preventing cost overruns?
    - Meeting will take place in Conference Room 3.
    - What additional budget issues must be considered during this quarter?

2. **Teamwork**   With a classmate, attend a local community or campus meeting where you can observe group discussion. Take notes individually during the meeting and then work together to answer the following questions.

   a. What is your evaluation of this meeting? In your answer, consider (1) the leader's ability to clearly state the meeting's goals, (2) the leader's ability to engage members in a meaningful discussion, and (3) the group's listening skills.

   b. How well did the individual participants listen? How could you tell?

   c. Compare the notes you took during the meeting with those of your classmate. What differences do you notice? How do you account for these differences?

3. **Team Communication**   Every month, each employee in your department is expected to give a brief oral presentation on the status of his or her project. However, your department has recently hired an employee who has a severe speech impediment that prevents people from understanding most of what he has to say.

   Your task: As assistant department manager, how will you resolve this dilemma? Please explain.

4. **Meeting Productivity: Analyzing Agendas**   Obtain a copy of the agenda from a recent campus or work meeting. Does this agenda show a start time or an end time? Is it specific enough that you, as an outsider, would be able to understand what was to be discussed? If not, how would you improve the agenda?

5. **Listening Skills: Overcoming Barriers**   Identify some of your bad listening habits and make a list of some ways you could correct them. For the next 30 days, review your list and jot down any improvements you've noticed as a result of your effort.

6. **Telephones and Voice Mail**   Late on a Friday afternoon, you learn that the facilities department is going to move you—and your computer, your desk, and all your files—to another office first thing Monday morning. However, you have an important client meeting scheduled in your office for Monday afternoon, and you need to finalize some contract details on Monday morning. You simply can't lose access to your office at that point, and you're more than a little annoyed that your boss didn't ask you before approving the move. He has already left for the day, but you know he usually checks his voice mail over the weekend, so you decide to leave a voice-mail message, asking him to cancel the move or at least call you at home as soon as possible. Using the voice-mail guidelines listed in Table 2.1, plan your message (use an imaginary phone number as your contact number and make up any other details you need for the call). As directed by your instructor, submit either a written script of the message or a podcast recording of the actual message.

7. **Nonverbal Communication: Analyzing Written Messages**   Select a business letter and envelope that you have received at work or at home. Analyze their appearance. What nonverbal messages do they send? Are these messages consistent with the content of the letter? If not, what could the sender have done to make the nonverbal communication consistent with the verbal communication?

8. **Nonverbal Communication: Analyzing Body Language**   Describe what the following body movements suggest when they are exhibited by someone during a conversation. How do such movements influence your interpretation of spoken words?

   a. Shifting one's body continuously while seated

   b. Twirling and playing with one's hair

   c. Sitting in a sprawled position

   d. Rolling one's eyes

   e. Extending a weak handshake

9. **Listening Skills: Self-Assessment**   How good are your listening skills? Rate yourself on each of the following elements of good listening and then examine your ratings to identify where you are strongest and where you can improve, using the tips in this chapter.

Elements of Listening	Always	Frequently	Occasionally	Never
1. I look for areas of interest when people speak.	_____	_____	_____	_____
2. I focus on content rather than delivery.	_____	_____	_____	_____
3. I wait to respond until I understand the content.	_____	_____	_____	_____
4. I listen for ideas and themes, not isolated facts.	_____	_____	_____	_____
5. I take notes only when needed.	_____	_____	_____	_____
6. I really concentrate on what speakers are saying.	_____	_____	_____	_____
7. I stay focused even when the ideas are complex.	_____	_____	_____	_____
8. I keep an open mind despite emotionally charged language.	_____	_____	_____	_____

Expand Your Knowledge

Exploring the Best of the Web

Cultural Savvy for Competitive Advantage   Want to be more competitive when doing business across borders? Executive Planet offers quick introductions to expected business practices in a number of countries, from setting up appointments to giving gifts to negotiating deals. Visit www.executiveplanet.com and browse the country reports to answer the following questions.

Exercises

1. What sort of clothes should you pack for a business trip to Mexico that will include both meetings and social events?

2. You've been trying to sell your products to a Saudi Arabian company whose executives treat you to an extravagant evening of dining and entertainment. Can you take this as a positive sign that they're likely to buy from you?

3. You collect antique clocks as a hobby, and you plan to give one of your favorites to the president of a Chinese company you plan to visit. Would such a gift likely help or hurt your relationship with this person?

Surfing Your Way to Career Success

Bovée and Thill's Business Communication Headline News offers links to hundreds of online resources that can help you with this course, your other college courses, and your career. Visit http://businesscommunicationblog.com and click on "Web Directory." The Intercultural Communication section connects you to a variety of websites and articles on intercultural communication, international business etiquette, English as a second language, and language barriers. Identify three websites from this section that could be useful in your business career. For each site, write a two-sentence summary of what the site offers and how it could help you launch and build your career.

MyBCommLab.com

Use MyBCommLab.com to test your understanding of the concepts presented in this chapter and explore additional materials that will bring the ideas to life in video, activities, and an online multimedia e-book. Additionally, you can continue to improve your skill with nouns and pronouns by using the "Peak Performance Grammar and Mechanics" module within the lab. Take the Pretest to determine whether you have any weak areas. Then review those areas in the Refresher Course. Take the Follow-Up Test to check your grasp of nouns and pronouns. For an extra challenge, take the Advanced Test. Finally, for even more reinforcement, go to the "Improve Your Grammar, Mechanics, and Usage" section that follows, and complete the "Level 1: Self-Assessment" exercises.

Improve Your Grammar, Mechanics, and Usage

Level 1: Self-Assessment—Pronouns

Review Section 1.2 in the Handbook of Grammar, Mechanics, and Usage and then complete the following 15 items.

In items 1–5, replace the underlined nouns with the correct pronouns.

1. _____ To <u>which retailer</u> will you send your merchandise?

2. _____ Have you given <u>John and Nancy</u> a list of parts?

3. _____ The main office sent the invoice to <u>Mr. and Mrs. Litvak</u> on December 5.

4. _____ The company settled <u>the company's</u> accounts before the end of the year.

5. _____ <u>Which person's</u> umbrella is this?

In items 6–15, circle the correct pronoun form provided in parentheses.

6. The sales staff is preparing guidelines for (*their, its*) clients.

7. Few of the sales representatives turn in (*their, its*) reports on time.

8. The board of directors has chosen (*their, its*) officers.

9. Gomez and Archer have told (*his, their*) clients about the new program.

10. Each manager plans to expand (*his, their, his or her*) sphere of control next year.

11. Has everyone supplied (*his, their, his or her*) Social Security number?

12. After giving every employee (*his, their, a*) raise, George told (*them, they, all*) about the increased workload.

13. Bob and Tim have opposite ideas about how to achieve company goals. (*Who, Whom*) do you think will win the debate?

14. City Securities has just announced (*who, whom*) it will hire as CEO.

15. Either of the new products would readily find (*their, its*) niche in the marketplace.

Level 2: Workplace Applications

The following items contain numerous errors in grammar, capitalization, punctuation, abbreviation, number style, word division, and vocabulary. Rewrite each sentence, correcting all errors. Write *C* for any sentence that is already correct.

1. Anita Doig from Data Providers will outline their data interpretations as it relates to industry trends, additionally Miss Doig will be asked to comment on how their data should be ulililzed.

2. You're order for 2000 mylar bags has been received by us; please be advised that orders of less than 5000 bags only get a 20 percent discount.

3. Just between you and I, the new 'customer centric' philosophy seems pretty confusing.

4. Podcasting can be an effective way to distribute messages to a widespread audience, but you need to pay close attention to the demands of an audio medium.

5. Among the specialties of Product Marketers International is promotional efforts for clients, including presence on the Internet, radio, and on television.

6. An overview of a typical marketing plan will be covered in the introduction to this report, to give you an idea of what's in it.

7. Subsidiary rights sales can be a discreet source of income and compliment your overall sales.

8. Special events ranging from author breakfasts and luncheons to awards programs and reception's offers a great way to make industry contacts.

9. We will show you how not only to meet the challenges of information rich material but also the challenges of electronic distance learning.

10. To site just one problem, the reason that the market is in such a state of confusion is the appalling lack of standards whether for hardware, software or for metadata.

11. Two leading business consultants Doug Smith and Carla McNeil will share their insights on how specialty stores can effectively compete in a world of Corporate Superstores.

12. One of the big questions we need to address are "How does buying effect inventory levels"?

13. The closing of many industry digital entities have greatly affected the perception of e-books as a viable platform.

14. A competent, motivated, and enthusiastic staff can be a managers' most important asset in a competitive marketplace.

15. Come by the Technology Lounge where you can log on to computers and plug into laptops and check out demos of sponsor's websites.

Level 3: Document Critique

The following document may contain errors in grammar, capitalization, punctuation, abbreviation, number style, and vocabulary. Correct all errors using standard proofreading marks (see Appendix C).

DATE: Thurs, 14 November 2009 11:07:33 -0800
FROM: rick glissmeyer <rickg@aol.com>
TO: richard herman <rcherman@ddc.com>
SUBJECT: Please supply shipping costs

Dear Richard:

As you requested heres the complete order for seed mixes required by Roberta Mcdonald in

Vancouver:

- Fifty-lb. 80/20 canary seed mix @ $15.45
- 50 lbs. soak seed @ $20.25
- Total order: $305.70

The seeds are to be shipped to:

Roberta C. McDonald

1725 w. Third Av.

Vancuover, BC, V5M-5R6

We will mail our check, as soon as you reply with the amount of shipping costs. Roberta says "her flock's getting ready for breeding," and she needs the soak seed by the end of this month.

Thanks for your Quick Srevice

Rick Glissmeyer

The Three-Step Writing Process

CHAPTER 3: Planning Business Messages

CHAPTER 4: Writing Business Messages

CHAPTER 5: Completing Business Messages

"Planning Business Messages

LEARNING OBJECTIVES

After studying this chapter, you will be able to

1. Describe the three-step writing process
2. List four questions that can help you test the purpose of a message
3. Describe the importance of analyzing your audience and identify the six factors you should consider when developing an audience profile
4. Discuss gathering information for simple messages and identify three attributes of quality information
5. List factors to consider when choosing the most appropriate medium for a message
6. Explain why good organization is important to both you and your audience
7. Summarize the process for organizing business messages effectively

After launching a breakthrough podcasting series called "IBM and the Future of . . ." as a way of letting IBM experts share knowledge on a wide range of topics with customers and investors, the company made podcasting tools available to all its employees and then sat back to see how they might take advantage of this exciting new medium. Not surprisingly for a company full of bright, creative people, IBM staffers began distributing a wide variety of messages via podcast. One gained an instant following by podcasting about the daily challenges and rewards of being a mobile information worker. Another saved hundreds of thousands of dollars a year in telephone charges simply by replacing a massive weekly teleconference with podcasts. IBM employees now create podcasts for a wide variety of internal and external communication needs. No matter what the technology, innovators such as IBM are constantly looking for new ways to reach their audiences with effective messages.[1]

UNDERSTANDING THE THREE-STEP WRITING PROCESS

Whether you're creating a conventional printed report or a message in the latest digital format such as podcasting, your goal is to create messages that have a clear purpose, meet the needs of your audience, and communicate efficiently and effectively. For every message you send, you can reduce the time and energy required to achieve this goal by following a clear and proven three-step process (see Figure 3.1):

The three-step writing process consists of planning, writing, and completing your messages.

- **Planning business messages.** To plan any message, first *analyze the situation* by defining your purpose and developing a profile of your audience. With that in mind, you can *gather information* that will meet your audience's needs. Next, *select the right medium* (oral, written, visual, or electronic) to deliver your message. With those three factors in

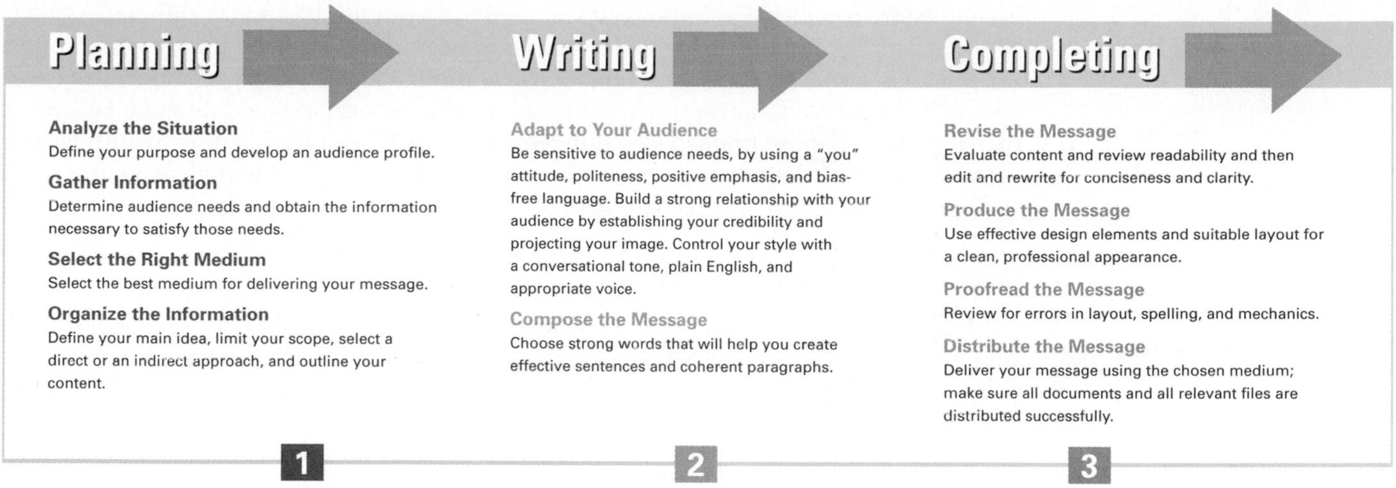

Planning →	Writing →	Completing →
Analyze the Situation Define your purpose and develop an audience profile. **Gather Information** Determine audience needs and obtain the information necessary to satisfy those needs. **Select the Right Medium** Select the best medium for delivering your message. **Organize the Information** Define your main idea, limit your scope, select a direct or an indirect approach, and outline your content.	**Adapt to Your Audience** Be sensitive to audience needs, by using a "you" attitude, politeness, positive emphasis, and bias-free language. Build a strong relationship with your audience by establishing your credibility and projecting your image. Control your style with a conversational tone, plain English, and appropriate voice. **Compose the Message** Choose strong words that will help you create effective sentences and coherent paragraphs.	**Revise the Message** Evaluate content and review readability and then edit and rewrite for conciseness and clarity. **Produce the Message** Use effective design elements and suitable layout for a clean, professional appearance. **Proofread the Message** Review for errors in layout, spelling, and mechanics. **Distribute the Message** Deliver your message using the chosen medium; make sure all documents and all relevant files are distributed successfully.
1	**2**	**3**

Figure 3.1 **The Three-Step Writing Process**
This three-step process will help you create more effective messages in any medium. As you get more practice with the process, it will become easier and more automatic.

place, you're ready to *organize the information* by defining your main idea, limiting your scope, selecting an approach, and outlining your content. Planning messages is the focus of this chapter.

- **Writing business messages.** Once you've planned your message, *adapt to your audience* with sensitivity, relationship skills, and style. Then you're ready to *compose your message* by choosing strong words, creating effective sentences, and developing coherent paragraphs. Writing business messages is discussed in Chapter 4.

- **Completing business messages.** After writing your first draft, *revise your message* to make sure it is clear, concise, and correct. Next *produce your message*, giving it an attractive, professional appearance. *Proofread* the final product for typos, spelling errors, and other mechanical problems. Finally, *distribute your message* using an appropriate combination of personal and technological tools. Completing business messages is discussed in Chapter 5.

Throughout this book, you'll see the three steps in this process applied to a wide variety of business messages: basic tasks for short messages (Chapters 6 through 9), additional tasks for longer messages (Chapters 10 and 11), special tasks for oral presentations (Chapter 12), and distinct tasks for employment messages (Chapter 14).

The more you use the three-step writing process, the easier and faster it will become. You'll also get better at allotting your time for each step. As a general rule, try using roughly half your time for planning, one-quarter of your time for writing, and the remaining quarter for completing the project. Of course, you don't need to undertake an elaborate process to create simple messages, but approaching your writing projects with the three steps in mind always helps. Even for small writing projects, resist the temptation to skip the planning step. For instance, spending even just a minute or two thinking through the purpose of an e-mail message can help you write much faster because you'll know in advance what you want to say. And leave plenty of time to complete your documents, too; you don't want to compromise the quality of a good message by shortchanging the important steps of revising, producing, proofreading, and distributing.[2]

> As a general rule, try to use half your time for planning, one-quarter for writing, and one-quarter for completing your messages.

ANALYZING YOUR SITUATION

A successful message starts with a clear purpose that connects the sender's needs with the audience's needs. Identifying your purpose and your audience is usually a straightforward task for simple, routine messages. However, this task can be more demanding as situations

49

become more complex. For instance, if you need to communicate about a shipping problem between your Beijing and Los Angeles factories, your purpose might be simply to alert upper management to the situation, or it might involve asking the two factory managers to explore and solve the problem. These two scenarios have different purposes and different audiences; therefore, they require dramatically different messages. If you launch directly into writing without clarifying both your purpose and your audience, you'll waste time and energy, and you'll probably generate a less effective message.

Defining Your Purpose

Business messages have both general and specific purposes.

All business messages have a **general purpose**: to inform, to persuade, or to collaborate with your audience. This purpose helps define the overall approach you'll need to take, from gathering information to organizing your message. Within the scope of that general purpose, each message also has a **specific purpose**, which identifies what you hope to accomplish with your message. You need to state your specific purpose as precisely as possible, even identifying which audience members should respond, how they should respond, and when.

Once you have defined your specific purpose, make sure it merits the time and effort required for you to prepare and send the message. Ask these four questions:

After defining your purpose, verify that the message will be worth the time and effort required to create, send, and receive it.

- **Will anything change as a result of your message?** Make sure you don't contribute to information overload by sending messages that won't change anything. Complaining about things that you have no influence over is a good example of a message that probably shouldn't be sent.

- **Is your purpose realistic?** If your purpose involves a radical shift in action or attitude, proceed carefully. Consider proposing a first step so that your message acts as the beginning of a learning process.

- **Is the time right?** People who are busy or distracted when they receive your message are less likely to pay attention to it.

- **Is your purpose acceptable to your organization?** Your company's business objectives and policies, and even laws that apply to your particular industry, may dictate whether a given purpose is acceptable.

Once you are satisfied that you have a clear and meaningful purpose and that now is a smart time to proceed, your next step is to understand the members of your audience and their needs.

Developing an Audience Profile

Before audiences will bother to pay attention to your messages, they need to be interested in what you're saying. They need to see what's in it for them—which of their needs will be met or problems will be solved by listening to your advice or doing what you ask. The more you know about your audience members, their needs, and their expectations, the more effectively you'll be able to communicate with them. The planning sheet in Figure 3.2 shows an example of the kind of information you need to compile in an audience analysis. Conducting an audience analysis involves the following steps:

Ask yourself some key questions about your audience members:
- Who are they?
- How many people do you need to reach?
- How much do they already know about the subject?
- What is their probable reaction to your message?

- **Identify your primary audience.** For some messages, certain audience members might be more important than others. Don't ignore the needs of less influential members but make sure you address the concerns of the key decision makers.

- **Determine audience size and geographic distribution.** A message aimed at 10,000 people spread around the globe will likely require a different approach than one aimed at a dozen people down the hall.

- **Determine audience composition.** Look for both similarities and differences in culture, language, age, education, organizational rank and status, attitudes, experience, motivations, and any other factors that might affect the success of your message.

If audience members have different levels of understanding of the topic, aim your message at the most influential decision makers.

- **Gauge audience members' level of understanding.** If audience members share your general background, they'll probably understand your material without difficulty. If not, your message will need an element of education, and deciding how much information to include can be a challenge. Try to include only enough information to accomplish the

Audience analysis notes

Project: A report recommending that we close down the on-site exercise facility and subsidize private memberships at local health clubs.

- **Primary audience:** Nicole Perazzo, vice president of operations, and her supervisory team.

- **Size and geographic distribution:** Nine managers total; Nicole and five of her staff are here on site; three other supervisors are based in Hong Kong.

- **Composition:** All have experience in operations management, but several are new to the company.

- **Level of understanding:** All will no doubt understand the financial considerations, but the newer managers may not understand the importance of the on-site exercise facility to many of our employees.

- **Expectations and preferences.** They're expecting a firm recommendation, backed up with well-thought-out financial rationale and suggestions for communicating the bad news to employees. For a decision of this magnitude, a formal report is appropriate; e-mail distribution is expected.

- **Probable reaction.** From one-on-one discussions, I know that several of the managers receiving this report are active users of the on-site facility and won't welcome the suggestion that we should shut it down. However, some nonexercisers generally think it's a luxury the company can't afford. Audience reactions will range from highly positive to highly negative; the report should focus on overcoming the highly negative reactions since they're the ones I need to convince.

Figure 3.2   Using Audience Analysis to Plan a Message
For simple, routine messages, you usually don't need to analyze your audience in depth. However, for complex messages or messages for indifferent or hostile audiences, take the time to study their information needs and potential reactions to your message.

specific purpose of your message. If the members of your audience have various levels of understanding, gear your coverage to your primary audience (the key decision makers).

- **Understand audience expectations and preferences.** Will members of your audience expect complete details or just a summary of the main points? Do they want an e-mail or will they expect a formal memo? In general, the higher up the organization your message goes, the fewer details people want to see.

- **Forecast probable audience reaction.** As you'll read later in the chapter, audience reaction affects the organization of a message. If you expect a favorable response, you can state conclusions and recommendations up front and offer minimal supporting evidence. If you expect skepticism, you'll probably want to introduce conclusions gradually, with more proof along the way.

A gradual approach and plenty of evidence are required to win over a skeptical audience.

GATHERING INFORMATION

With a clear picture of your audience, your next step is to assemble the information that you will include in your message. For simple messages, you may already have all the information at hand, but for more complex messages, you may need to do considerable research and analysis before you're ready to begin writing. Chapter 10 describes formal techniques for finding, evaluating, and processing information. Meanwhile, you can often use a variety of informal techniques to gather insights and help focus your research efforts:

- **Consider other viewpoints.** Putting yourself in someone else's position helps you consider what that person might be thinking, feeling, or planning.

- **Read reports and other company documents.** Your company's various resources may be a rich source of information. Seek out annual reports, financial statements, news releases, memos, marketing reports, web content, blogs, wikis, and customer surveys for helpful information. Find out whether your company has a *knowledge management system*, a centralized database that collects the experiences and insights of employees throughout the organization.

- **Talk with supervisors, colleagues, or customers.** Co-workers and customers may have information you need, or they may know what your audience will be interested in.
- **Ask your audience for input.** If you're unsure of what audience members need from your message, ask them. Admitting you don't know but want to meet their needs will impress an audience more than guessing and getting it wrong.

Uncovering Audience Needs

If you're given a vague request, ask questions to clarify it before you plan a response.

In many situations, your audience's information needs are readily apparent, such as when a consumer sends an e-mail asking a specific question. In other cases, your audience might be unable to articulate exactly what is needed. If someone makes a vague or broad request, ask questions to narrow the focus. Asking a question or two often forces the person to think through the request and define more precisely what is required.

Include any additional information that might be helpful, even though the requester didn't specifically ask for it.

In some cases, you may need to do some detective work to find out what information is needed. If you're asked to suggest steps a company can take to improve employee morale, for example, you'll need to investigate the underlying reasons for low morale. By including this information in your report—even though it wasn't specifically requested—you demonstrate to your audience that you've thoroughly investigated the problem.

Providing Required Information

Test the completeness of your document by making sure it answers all the important questions: who, what, when, where, why, and how.

Once you've defined your audience's information needs, your next step is to satisfy those needs completely. In addition to delivering the right *quantity* of required information, you are responsible for verifying the *quality* of that information. Ask yourself these three questions:

- **Is the information accurate?** Inaccuracies can cause a host of problems, from embarrassment and lost productivity to serious safety and legal issues. Be sure to review any mathematical or financial calculations. Check all dates and schedules. Examine your own assumptions and conclusions to be certain they are valid.
- **Is the information ethical?** By working hard to ensure the accuracy of the information you gather, you'll also avoid many ethical problems in your messages. However, messages can also be unethical if important information is omitted or obscured.
- **Is the information pertinent?** Remember that some points will be more important to your audience than others. Moreover, by focusing on the information that concerns your audience the most, you increase your chances of sending an effective message.

SELECTING THE RIGHT MEDIUM

Selecting the best medium for your message can make the difference between effective and ineffective communication.[3] As Chapter 1 notes, a communication medium is the form through which you choose to communicate your message. You may choose to talk with someone face-to-face, write a letter, send an e-mail message, or record a podcast. With today's ever-expanding technology, you often have a variety of media options to choose from.

Although media categories have become increasingly blurred in recent years, for the sake of discussion, you can think of media as being oral, written, visual, or electronic (which often combines several media types).

Oral Media

Oral communication is best when you need to encourage interaction, express emotions, or monitor emotional responses.

Primary oral media include face-to-face conversations, interviews, speeches, and in-person presentations and meetings. By giving communicators the ability to see, hear, and react to each other, traditional oral media are useful for encouraging people to ask questions, make comments, and work together to reach a consensus or decision. In particular, experts recommend that managers engage in frequent "walk-arounds," chatting with employees to get input, answer their questions, and interpret important business events and trends.[4]

Of course, if you don't want a lot of questions or interaction, oral media can be an unwise choice. However, consider your audience carefully before deciding to limit interaction by choosing a different medium. As a manager, you will encounter unpleasant situations (declining an employee's request for a raise, for example) in which sending an e-mail message or otherwise avoiding personal contact will seem appealing. However, in many such cases, you owe the other party the opportunity to ask questions or express concerns. Moreover, facing the tough situations in person will earn you a reputation as an honest, caring manager.

> Oral media limit participation to those who are present, reduce your control over the message, and make it difficult to revise or edit your message.

Written Media

Written media take many forms, from traditional memos to glossy reports that rival magazines in production quality. Written messages increase your control, help you reach dispersed audiences, and minimize distortion. The disadvantages of written media include the difficulty of feedback, lack of nonverbal cues, and extra time and skill sometimes required to prepare written messages.

> Written media increase your control, help you reach dispersed audiences, and minimize distortion.

Most letters and memos are relatively brief documents, generally one or two pages, although some run much longer. **Memos** are used for routine, day-to-day exchange of information within an organization. Because of their open construction and informal method of delivery (such as being placed in in-boxes), memos are less private than letters. In many organizations, e-mail messages, blogs, and other electronic media have largely replaced paper memos.

Letters are brief written messages sent to recipients, often those outside the organization. In addition to conveying a particular message, letters perform an important public relations function in fostering good working relationships with customers, suppliers, and others. Many organizations rely on form letters to save time and money on routine communication. Form letters are particularly handy for such one-time mass mailings as sales messages about products, information about organizational activities, and goodwill messages such as seasonal greetings.

Reports and proposals are usually longer than memos and letters, although both can be created in memo or letter format. These documents can be a variety of lengths, ranging from a few pages to several hundred, and are usually fairly formal in tone. Chapters 11 and 12 discuss reports and proposals in detail.

Visual Media

Although you probably won't work with many messages that are purely visual (with no text), the importance of visual elements in business communication continues to grow. Traditional business messages rely primarily on text, with occasional support from graphical elements such as charts, graphs, or diagrams to help illustrate points discussed in the text. However, many business communicators are discovering the power of messages in which the visual element is dominant and supported by small amounts of text. For the purposes of this discussion, you can think of *visual media* as formats in which one or more visual elements play a central role in conveying the message content (see Figure 3.3).

> In some situations, a message that is predominantly visual, with text used to support the illustration, can be more effective than a message that relies primarily on text.

Messages that combine powerful visuals with supporting text can be effective for a number of reasons. Today's audiences are pressed for time and bombarded with messages, so anything that communicates quickly is welcome. Visuals are also effective at describing complex ideas and processes because they can reduce the work required for an audience to identify the parts and relationships that make up the whole. Also, in a multilingual business world, diagrams, symbols, and other images can lower communication barriers by requiring less language processing. Finally, visual images can be easier to remember than purely textual descriptions or explanations.

Electronic Media

The range of electronic media is broad and continues to grow even broader, from telephones and podcasts to blogs and wikis to e-mails and text messages. When you want to make a powerful impression, using electronic media can increase the excitement and visual appeal with computer animation, video, and music.

Why should I care about CRM?

XPLANATIONS® by XPLANE®

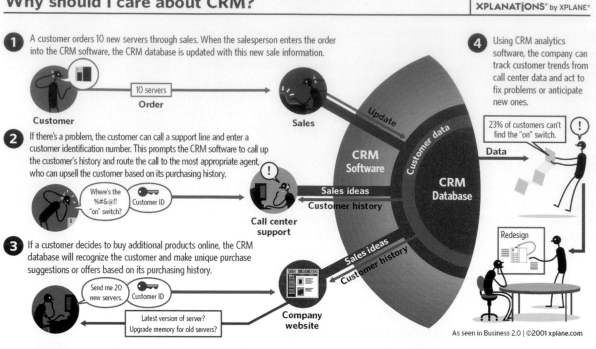

1 A customer orders 10 new servers through sales. When the salesperson enters the order into the CRM software, the CRM database is updated with this new sale information.

4 Using CRM analytics software, the company can track customer trends from call center data and act to fix problems or anticipate new ones.

2 If there's a problem, the customer can call a support line and enter a customer identification number. This prompts the CRM software to call up the customer's history and route the call to the most appropriate agent, who can upsell the customer based on its purchasing history.

3 If a customer decides to buy additional products online, the CRM database will recognize the customer and make unique purchase suggestions or offers based on its purchasing history.

As seen in Business 2.0 | ©2001 xplane.com

Figure 3.3 Visual Media
In traditional business messages, visual elements usually support the text. However, in some instances, the message can be presented more effectively by reversing that relationship—basing the message on a dominant visual and using text to support that image. (In this figure, *CRM* stands for *customer relationship management*, a category of software that helps companies manage their interactions with customers.)

To use many electronic media options successfully, you must have at least some degree of technical skill.

The growth of electronic communication options is both a blessing and a curse for business communicators. On the one hand, you have more tools than ever before to choose from, with more ways to deliver rational and emotional content. On the other hand, the sheer range of choices can complicate your job because you often need to choose among multiple media, and you need to know how to use each medium successfully. You'll learn more about using electronic media throughout this book (and in Chapter 6 in particular); for now, here is a quick overview of the major electronic media used in business today:

- **Electronic versions of oral media.** These include telephone calls, teleconferencing (when three or more people participate in the same call), voice-mail messages, audio recordings such as compact discs and podcasts, and even animated customer service *avatars* on websites. The simple telephone call is still a vital communication link for many organizations, but even it has joined the Internet age, thanks to *Internet telephony*, also known by the technical term VoIP (which stands for *Voice over Internet Protocol*). More than 10 million people worldwide now use Skype, which offers free basic phone service over the Internet.[5] Although telephone calls can't convey all the nonverbal signals of an in-person conversation, they can convey quite a few, including tone of voice, laughter, pauses, and so on. Voice mail is a handy way to send brief messages when an immediate response isn't crucial, but it's a poor choice for lengthy messages because the information is difficult to retrieve. You'll learn about podcasts, perhaps the most significant business audio advancement of recent years, in Chapter 6.

Electronic written media have largely replaced traditional written media in many companies.

- **Electronic versions of written media.** These media range from e-mail and instant messages to blogs, websites, and wikis. Instant messaging (IM) is rapidly overtaking e-mail in some companies. At IBM, for instance, employees send more than 5 million instant messages each month.[6] *Text messaging*, a phone-based medium that has long been popular with consumers in Asia and Europe, is finally catching on in the United States.[7] Even documents that were once distributed on paper are now easily transferred electronically, thanks to Adobe's portable document format (PDF). Faxes have been replaced by other electronic options in many cases, although they still have a role in business communication. Internet-based fax services, such as eFax, lower the cost of faxing by eliminating the need for a dedicated fax line and fax machine.

- **Electronic versions of visual media.** These media can include electronic presentations (using Microsoft PowerPoint and other software), computer animation (using software such as Adobe Flash to create animated sequences for websites), and video. Businesses have made extensive use of video (particularly for training, new product promotions, and executive announcements) for years—first on tape, then on DVD, and now online. Video is also incorporated in podcasting, creating *vidcasts*, and in blogging, including *video blogs* (*vlogs*) and *mobile blogs* (*moblogs*).[8] **Multimedia** refers to the use of two or more media to craft a single message, typically some combination of audio, video, text, and visual graphics.

As you'll read in Chapter 6, many recent innovations in electronic media have spurred the development of *social media*—Internet-based media that enable and encourage audience participation. For many companies, this changing role of the audience is transforming the nature of business communication. For the latest innovations in electronic media, visit http://real-timeupdates.com/bce and click on Chapter 3.

Factors to Consider When Choosing Media

Choosing the right medium for each message is a question of balancing your needs with your audience's needs (see Table 3.1). Be sure to consider how your message is affected by the following factors:

- **Media richness.** Richness is a medium's ability to (1) convey a message through more than one *informational cue* (visual, verbal, vocal), (2) facilitate feedback, and (3) establish personal focus. The richest medium is face-to-face communication; it's personal, it provides immediate feedback (verbal and nonverbal), and it conveys the emotion behind a message.[9] Multimedia presentations and multimedia webpages are also quite rich, with the ability to presents images, animation, text, music, sound effects, and other elements. Many electronic media are also *interactive*, in that they enable audiences to participate in the communication process. At the other extreme are the leanest media—those that communicate in the simplest ways, provide no opportunity for audience feedback, and aren't personalized.

  > The more complicated the message, the richer the medium required.

- **Message formality.** Your choice of medium affects the style and tone of your message. For instance, to share simple information with employees, you would probably send an e-mail message or post an announcement on a blog rather than write a formal printed memo or make a face-to-face presentation.

- **Media limitations.** Every medium has limitations. For example, IM is perfect for communicating simple, straightforward messages, but it is ineffective for sending complex ones.

- **Sender intentions.** Your choice of medium influences your audience's perception of your intentions. If you want to emphasize the formality of your message, use a more formal medium such as a memo or a letter. To convey emotion, consider a visual medium such as a personal speech or a videoconference. For immediate feedback, meet face-to-face, make a phone call, or use IM.[10]

  > Your intentions heavily influence your choice of medium.

- **Urgency and cost.** Electronic media have lowered the cost of transmitting messages, but in some instances (usually involving printed messages), you need to weigh cost versus delivery time.

  > Time and cost affect medium selection.

- **Audience preferences.** Make sure to consider which medium or media your audience expects or prefers.[11] What would you think if your college tried to deliver your diploma by fax? You'd expect the college to hand the diploma to you at graduation or mail it to you.

  > When choosing the appropriate medium, don't forget to consider your audience's expectations.

After you select the best medium for your purpose, situation, and audience, you are ready to start thinking about the organization of your message.

TABLE 3.1   Media Advantages and Disadvantages

Media	Advantages	Disadvantages
Oral	• Provide opportunity for immediate feedback • Allow a certain ease of interaction • Involve rich nonverbal cues (both physical gesture and vocal inflection) • Allow you to express the emotion behind your message	• Restrict participation to those physically present • Unless recorded, provide no permanent, verifiable record of the communication • Reduce communicator's control over the message • Other than for messages that are prewritten and rehearsed, offer no opportunity to revise or edit your spoken words
Written	• Allow you to plan and control your message • Reach geographically dispersed audiences • Offer a permanent, verifiable record • Minimize the distortion that can accompany oral messages • Can be used to avoid immediate interactions • Deemphasize any inappropriate emotional components	• Are usually not conducive to speedy feedback • Lack the rich nonverbal cues provided by oral media • Often take more time and more resources to create and distribute • Can require special skills in preparation and production if document is elaborate
Visual	• Can convey complex ideas and relationships quickly • Are often less intimidating than long blocks of text • Can reduce the burden on the audience to figure out how the pieces fit	• Can require artistic skills to design • Require some technical skills to create • Can require more time to create than an equivalent amount of text • Are more difficult to transmit and store than simple textual messages
Electronic	• Deliver messages quickly • Reach geographically dispersed audiences • Offer the persuasive power of multimedia formats • Can increase accessibility and openness in an organization • Enable audience interaction through social media features	• Are easy to overuse (sending too many messages to too many recipients) • Create privacy risks and concerns (exposing confidential data; employer monitoring of e-mail and IM; accidental forwarding) • Entail security risks (viruses, spyware) • Create productivity concerns (frequent interruptions; non-business websurfing)

ORGANIZING YOUR MESSAGE

Organizing your message well saves time for both you and your audience (see Figure 3.4). Your draft goes more quickly because you're not putting ideas in the wrong places or composing material you don't need. In addition, you can use your organizational plan to get some advance input from your audience, making sure you're on the right track before spending hours working on your draft. And, if your project is large and complex, you can even use your organization plan to divide the writing job among co-workers.

In addition to helping you, good organization helps your audience:

■ **It helps your audience understand your message.** By making your main point clear at the outset, and by stating your needs precisely, your well-organized message will satisfy your audience's need for information.

■ **It helps your audience accept your message.** Even when your message is logical, you need to select and organize your points in a diplomatic way. Softening refusals and leaving a good impression enhances credibility and adds authority to your messages.

Good message organization helps you by reducing the time and energy needed to create messages and by making your messages more effective.

Good organization helps your audiences by helping them understand and accept your message in less time.

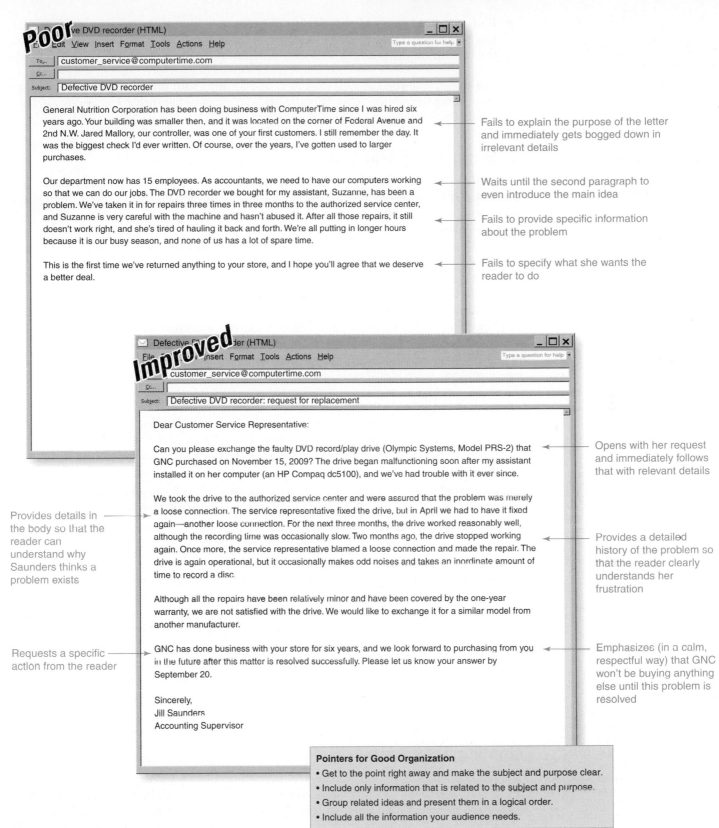

Figure 3.4 Improving the Organization of a Message
The poorly written draft displays weak organization, while the organization is much improved in the revised version. Before you begin to write, think about what you're going to say and how you're going to say it.

- **It saves your audience time.** Audience members receive only the information they need, and because that information is relevant, brief, and logically placed, your audience can follow your thought pattern without a struggle.

You can achieve good organization by clearly defining your main idea, limiting the scope of your message, grouping supporting points, and establishing their sequence by selecting either a direct or an indirect approach.

Defining Your Main Idea

The **topic** of your message is the overall subject, such as employee insurance claims. Your **main idea** is a specific statement about the topic of your message, such as your belief that a new web-based claim filing system would reduce costs for the company and reduce reimbursement delays for employees.

Your main idea may be obvious when you're preparing a brief message with simple facts that have little emotional impact on your audience. If you're responding to a request for information, your main idea may be simply "Here is what you wanted." However, defining your main idea is more complicated when you're trying to persuade someone or when you have disappointing information to convey. In these situations, try to define a main idea that will help you establish a good relationship with your audience. In longer documents and presentations, you often need to unify a mass of material, so you'll need to define a main idea that encompasses all the individual points you want to make. Sometimes you won't even be sure what your main idea is until you sort through the information. For tough assignments like these, consider a variety of techniques to generate creative ideas:

- **Brainstorming.** Working alone or with others, generate as many ideas and questions as you can, without stopping to criticize or organize. After you capture all these pieces, look for patterns and connections to help identify the main idea and the groups of supporting ideas.
- **Journalistic approach.** The **journalistic approach** asks *who, what, when, where, why,* and *how* questions to distill major ideas from unorganized information.
- **Question-and-answer chain.** Start with a key question, from the audience's perspective, and work back toward your message. In most cases, you'll find that each answer generates new questions, until you identify the information that needs to be in your message.
- **Storyteller's tour.** Some writers find it best to talk through a communication challenge before they try to write. Record yourself as you describe what you intend to write. Then listen to the playback, identify ways to tighten and clarify the message, and repeat the process until you distill the main idea down to a single, concise message.
- **Mind mapping.** You can generate and organize ideas by using a graphic method called *mind mapping*. Start with a main idea and then branch out to connect every other related idea that comes to mind. You can learn more about mind mapping from the Mind Mapping Software Weblog at http://mindmapping.typepad.com and try a free online tool at http://bubbl.us.[12]

Limiting Your Scope

The **scope** of your message is the range of information you present, the overall length, and the level of detail—all of which need to correspond to your main idea. Some business messages have a preset length limit, whether from a boss's instructions, the technology you're using, or a time frame such as individual speaker slots during a seminar. Even if you don't have a preset length, it's vital to limit yourself to the scope needed to convey your message—and no more.

Whatever the length of your message, keep the number of major supporting points to half a dozen or so—and if you can get your idea across with fewer points, all the better. Listing 20 or 30 supporting points might feel as though you're being thorough, but your audience is likely to view such detail as rambling and mind numbing. Instead, look for ways to group supporting points under major headings, such as finance, customers, competitors,

---

To organize a message
- Define your main idea
- Limit the scope
- Choose the direct or indirect approach
- Group your points

The topic is the broad subject; the main idea makes a statement about the topic.

Defining your main idea is more difficult when you're trying to persuade someone or convey disappointing information.

Limit the scope of your message so that you can convey your main idea as briefly as possible.

employees, or whatever is appropriate for your subject. You may need to refine your major supporting points so that you have a smaller number with greater impact.

If your message needs to be brief, your main idea will have to be easy to understand and easy to accept. However, if your message is long, you can develop the major points in more detail. How much space you need to communicate and support your main idea depends on your subject, your audience members' familiarity with the material and their receptivity to your conclusions, and your credibility. You'll need fewer words to present routine information to a knowledgeable audience that already knows and respects you. You'll need more words to build a consensus about a complex and controversial subject, especially if the members of your audience are skeptical or hostile strangers.

Choosing Between Direct and Indirect Approaches

After you've defined your ideas, you're ready to decide on the sequence you will use to present your points. You have two basic options:

- **Direct approach.** When you know your audience will be receptive to your message, use the **direct approach**: Start with the main idea (such as a recommendation, conclusion, or request) and follow that with your supporting evidence.

- **Indirect approach.** When your audience will be skeptical about or even resistant to your message, use the **indirect approach**: Start with the evidence first and build your case before presenting the main idea.

Use a direct approach if the audience's reaction is likely to be positive and the indirect approach if the reaction is likely to be negative.

To choose between these two alternatives, analyze your audience's likely reaction to your purpose and message. Bear in mind, however, that each message is unique. No simple formula will solve all your communication problems. For example, although an indirect approach may be best when you're sending bad news to outsiders, if you're writing a memo to an associate, you may want to get directly to the point, even if your message is unpleasant. The direct approach might also be a good choice for long messages, regardless of your audience's attitude, because delaying the main idea could cause confusion and frustration. Figure 3.5 summarizes how your approach may differ, depending on the likely audience reaction. The

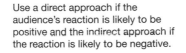

	Direct approach	**Indirect approach**	
Audience Reaction	Eager/interested/ pleased/neutral	Displeased	Uninterested/unwilling
Message Opening	Start with the main idea, the request, or the good news.	Start with a neutral statement that acts as a transition to the reasons for the bad news.	Start with a statement or question that captures attention.
Message Body	Provide necessary details.	Give reasons to justify a negative answer. State or imply the bad news, and make a positive suggestion.	Arouse the audience's interest in the subject. Build the audience's desire to comply.
Message Close	Close with a cordial comment, a reference to the good news, or a statement about the specific action desired.	Close cordially.	Request action.

Figure 3.5   Choosing Between Direct and Indirect Approaches
Think about the way your audience is likely to respond before choosing your approach.

type of message also influences the choice of a direct or indirect approach. In the coming chapters, you'll get specific advice on choosing the best approach for a variety of different communication challenges.

Outlining Your Content

Once you have chosen the right approach, it's time to figure out the most logical and effective way to provide your supporting details. For anything beyond simple projects, get into the habit of outlining: You'll save time and get better results. Whether you use specialized outlining and idea-mapping software, use the outlining features provided with word-processing software, or simply jot down three or four points on paper, making a plan and sticking to it will help you cover the important details.

You're no doubt familiar with the basic outline formats that identify each point with a number or letter and that indent certain points to show their relationships. A good outline divides a topic into at least two parts, restricts each subdivision to one category, and ensures that each subdivision is separate and distinct (see Figure 3.6).

Whichever outlining or organizing scheme you use, start your message with the main idea, follow that with major supporting points, and then illustrate those points with evidence:

- **Start with the main idea.** The main idea helps you establish the goals and general strategy of the message, and it summarizes two things: (1) what you want your audience members to do or think and (2) why they should do so. Everything in your message should either support the main idea or explain its implications.

- **State the major points.** Now it's time to support your main idea with the major points that clarify and explain your ideas in more concrete terms. If your purpose is to inform, your major points might be based on something physical or financial, for instance. When you're describing a process, the major points are almost inevitably steps in the process. When you're describing an object, the major points correspond to the components of the object. When you're giving a historical account, major points represent events in the chronological chain. If your purpose is to persuade or to collaborate, select major points that develop a line of reasoning or a logical argument that proves your central message and motivates your audience to act.

- **Illustrate with evidence.** After you've defined the main idea and identified supporting points, you're ready to illustrate each point with specific evidence that helps audience members understand and remember the more abstract concepts you're presenting.

Alphanumeric Outline	Decimal Outline
I. First major point	1.0 First major point
A. First subpoint	1.1 First subpoint
B. Second subpoint	1.2 Second subpoint
1. Evidence	1.2.1 Evidence
2. Evidence	1.2.2 Evidence
a. Detail	1.2.2.1 Detail
b. Detail	1.2.2.2 Detail
3. Evidence	1.2.3 Evidence
C. Third subpoint	1.3 Third subpoint
II. Second major point	2.0 Second major point
A. First subpoint	2.1 First subpoint
1. Evidence	2.1.1 Evidence
2. Evidence	2.1.2 Evidence
B. Second subpoint	2.2 Second subpoint

Figure 3.6 Two Common Outline Formats
Your company may have a tradition of using a particular outline form for formal reports and other documents. If not, either of these two approaches will work for almost any writing project.

Up to a point, the more evidence you provide, the more conclusive your case will be. If your subject is complex and unfamiliar, or if your audience is skeptical, you'll need a lot of facts and figures to demonstrate your points. On the other hand, if your subject is routine and your audience is positively inclined, you can be more sparing with the evidence. You want to provide enough support to be convincing but not so much that your message becomes boring or difficult to read. ■

Provide enough evidence to make your message convincing but don't overload the audience with too many minor supporting points.

DOCUMENT MAKEOVER

Improve This Letter

To practice correcting drafts of actual documents, visit the "Document Makeovers" section in either MyBCommLab.com or the Companion Website for this text.

If MyBCommLab.com is being used in your class, see your User Guide for specific instructions on how to access the content for this chapter.

If you are accessing this feature through the Companion Website, click on "Document Makeovers" and then select Chapter 3. You will find a letter that contains problems and errors related to what you've learned in this chapter about planning and organizing business messages. Use the Final Draft decision tool to create an improved version of this letter. Check the document for audience focus, the right choice of medium, and the proper choice of direct and indirect approach. ●

CHAPTER REVIEW AND ACTIVITIES

Chapter Summary

The three-step writing process is built around planning, writing, and completing business messages. This chapter focuses on planning, which involves four tasks: (1) analyzing your situation, which includes defining both general and specific purposes and developing a profile of your audience by identifying the primary audience, determining audience size, determining audience composition, gauging your audience's level of understanding, projecting your audience's expectations and preferences, and estimating your audience's probable reaction; (2) gathering necessary information by exploring audience needs and then collecting information that will meet those needs; (3) selecting the right medium (oral, written, visual, or electronic); and (4) organizing your message by defining the main idea, limiting the scope, grouping your points, choosing the direct or indirect approach, and crafting an outline.

To test the purpose of your message, ask yourself whether anything will change as a result of sending the message, whether your purpose is realistic, whether the timing is right, and whether the purpose is acceptable to your organization. Analyzing your audience is a vital part of planning because the more you know about your audience members, their needs, and their expectations, the more effectively you'll be able to communicate with them. To create an audience profile, identify the primary audience, its size and geographic distribution, the composition of the audience (language, education, experience, and so on), and its level of understanding, expectations and preferences, and probable reaction to your message.

Simple messages usually don't require extensive information gathering, but to acquire useful insights, consider other viewpoints; read reports and other company documents; talk with supervisors, colleagues, or customers; and ask your audience for input. Judge the quality of any information you include by making sure it is accurate, ethical, and pertinent.

To choose the most appropriate medium for every message, consider media richness, message formality, media limitations, your intentions, urgency and cost, and audience preferences.

Good organization is important to both you and your audience. It saves you time when preparing messages, and it saves time and reduces frustration for your audience—which benefits you in return because it increases the odds that audiences will respond favorably to your messages.

Test Your Knowledge

1. What are the three steps in the writing process?

2. What two types of purposes do all business messages have?

3. What do you need to know in order to develop an audience profile?

4. When including information in your message, what three conditions must you satisfy?

5. What are the main advantages of oral media? Of written media? Of visual media?

Apply Your Knowledge

1. Some writers argue that planning messages wastes time because they inevitably change their plans as they go along. How would you respond to this argument? Briefly explain.

2. As a member of the public relations department, which medium (or media) would you recommend using to inform the local community that your toxic-waste cleanup program has been successful? Justify your choice.

3. Would you use a direct or an indirect approach to ask employees to work overtime to meet an important deadline? Please explain.

4. Considering how fast, easy, and inexpensive they are, should e-mail messages, instant messages, blogs, and podcasts completely replace meetings and other face-to-face communication in your company? Why or why not?

5. **Ethical Choices**   Your company president has asked you to draft a memo for her signature to the board of directors, informing them that sales in your new line of gourmet fruit jams have far exceeded anyone's expectations. As a member of the purchasing department, you happen to know that sales of moderately priced jams have declined quite a bit (many customers have switched to the more expensive jams). You were not directed to add that tidbit of information. Should you write the memo and limit your information to the expensive gourmet jams? Or should you include the information about the decline in moderately priced jams? Please explain.

Practice Your Knowledge

Exercises for Perfecting Your Writing

Specific Purpose   For each of the following communication tasks, state a specific purpose (if you have trouble, try beginning with "I want to . . .").

1. A report to your boss, the store manager, about the outdated items in the warehouse

2. A blog posting (on your external website) to customers and the news media about your company's plans to acquire a competitor

3. A letter to a customer who hasn't made a payment for three months

4. An e-mail message to employees about the office's high water bills

5. A phone call to a supplier to check on an overdue parts shipment

6. A podcast to new users of the company's online content management system

Audience Profile   For each communication task below, write brief answers to three questions: (1) Who is my audience? (2) What is my audience's general attitude toward my subject? (3) What does my audience need to know?

7. A final-notice collection letter from an appliance manufacturer to an appliance dealer, sent 10 days before initiation of legal collection procedures

8. A promotional message on your company's e-retailing website, announcing a temporary price reduction on high-definition television sets

9. An advertisement for peanut butter

10. A letter to the property management company responsible for maintaining your office building, complaining about persistent problems with the heating and air conditioning

11. A cover letter sent along with your résumé to a potential employer

12. A request (to the seller) for a price adjustment on a piano that incurred $150 in damage during delivery to a banquet room in the hotel you manage

Media and Purpose   List three messages you have read, viewed, or listened to lately (such as direct-mail promotions, letters, e-mail or instant messages, phone solicitations, podcasts, and lectures). For each message, determine the general and the specific purpose, then answer the questions listed.

Message #1:

13. General purpose:

14. Specific purpose:

15. Was the message well timed?

16. Did the sender choose an appropriate medium for the message?

17. Was the sender's purpose realistic?

Message #2:

18. General purpose:

19. Specific purpose:

20. Was the message well timed?

21. Did the sender choose an appropriate medium for the message?

22. Was the sender's purpose, realistic?

Message #3:

23. General purpose:

24. Specific purpose:

25. Was the message well timed?

26. Did the sender choose an appropriate medium for the message?

27. Was the sender's purpose realistic?

Message Organization: Choosing the Approach   Indicate whether the direct or the indirect approach would be best in each of the following situations. Write *direct* or *indirect* in the space provided.

28. _____ An e-mail message to a car dealer, asking about the availability of a specific make and model of car

29. _____ A letter from a recent college graduate, requesting a letter of recommendation from a former instructor

30. _____ A letter turning down a job applicant

31. _____ A blog posting explaining that because of high air-conditioning costs, the plant temperature will be held at 78 degrees during the summer

32. _____ A final request to settle a delinquent debt

Message Organization: Drafting Persuasive Messages If you were trying to persuade people to take the following actions, how would you organize your argument? Write *direct* or *indirect* in the space provided.

33. _____ You want your boss to approve your plan for hiring two new people.

34. _____ You want to be hired for a job.

35. _____ You want to be granted a business loan.

36. _____ You want to collect a small amount from a regular customer whose account is slightly past due.

37. _____ You want to collect a large amount from a customer whose account is seriously past due.

Activities

Active links for all websites in this chapter can be found online. If MyBCommLab.com is being used in your class, see your User Guide for instructions on accessing the content for this chapter. Otherwise, visit www.pearsonhighered.com/bovee, locate *Business Communication Essentials*, Fourth Edition, click the Companion Website link, select Chapter 3, and then click on "Featured Websites." Please note that links to sites that become inactive after publication of the book will be removed from the Featured Websites section.

1. **Analyze This Message** A writer is working on an insurance information brochure and is having trouble grouping the ideas logically into an outline. Prepare the outline, paying attention to appropriate subordination of ideas. If necessary, rewrite phrases to give them a more consistent sound.

Accident Protection Insurance Plan

- Coverage is only pennies a day
- Benefit is $100,000 for accidental death on common carrier
- Benefit is $100 a day for hospitalization as result of motor vehicle or common carrier accident
- Benefit is $20,000 for accidental death in motor vehicle accident
- Individual coverage is only $17.85 per quarter; family coverage is just $26.85 per quarter
- No physical exam or health questions
- Convenient payment—billed quarterly
- Guaranteed acceptance for all applicants
- No individual rate increases
- Free, no-obligation examination period
- Cash paid in addition to any other insurance carried
- Covers accidental death when riding as fare-paying passenger on public transportation, including buses, trains, jets, ships, trolleys, subways, or any other common carrier
- Covers accidental death in motor vehicle accidents occurring while driving or riding in or on automobile, truck, camper, motor home, or nonmotorized bicycle

2. **Ethical Choices: Providing Information** Your supervisor has asked you to withhold important information that you think should be included in a report you are preparing. Obeying him could save the company serious public embarrassment, but it would also violate your personal code of ethics. What should you do? On the basis of the discussion in Chapter 1, would you consider this situation to be an ethical dilemma or an ethical lapse? Please explain.

3. Message Planning Skills: Self-Assessment   How good are you at planning business messages? Use the following chart to rate yourself on each of the following elements of planning an audience-centered business message. Then examine your ratings to identify where you are strongest and where you can improve.

Element of Planning	Always	Frequently	Occasionally	Never
1. I start by defining my purpose.	_____	_____	_____	_____
2. I analyze my audience before writing a message.	_____	_____	_____	_____
3. I investigate what my audience wants to know.	_____	_____	_____	_____
4. I check that my information is accurate, ethical, and pertinent.	_____	_____	_____	_____
5. I consider my audience and purpose when selecting media.	_____	_____	_____	_____
6. I consider the audience's likely reaction to my message before deciding on a direct or indirect approach.	_____	_____	_____	_____
7. I plan carefully, particularly for longer or complex messages, to make sure I use my time wisely.	_____	_____	_____	_____
8. I limit the scope of my messages to the extent of information needed to accomplish my specific purpose.	_____	_____	_____	_____

Expand Your Knowledge

Exploring the Best of the Web

Learn from the Best in the Business   See how some of today's brightest entrepreneurs and business managers are using blogging to reach their target markets. *Forbes* regularly highlights business-oriented blogs that the magazine's editors believe make effective use of the unique benefits of blogging. At the www.forbes.com/bow page, click "Blogs" under the "Departments" heading (look below the Web Site Reviews icon) and then check out the Career, Marketing, and Small Business blogging sections.

Exercises

1. What are some of the reasons *Forbes* selected these particular blogs as being among the best on the web?

2. What weaknesses does the magazine see in some of these blogs?

3. What can you learn from these blogs that you could apply to your own future as an entrepreneur or a business manager?

Surfing Your Way to Career Success

Bovée and Thill's Business Communication Headline News offers links to hundreds of online resources that can help you with this course, your other college courses, and your career. Visit http://businesscommunicationblog.com and click on "Web Directory." The Writing Process section connects you to a variety of websites and articles on planning, writing, revision, audience analysis, and brainstorming. Identify three websites from this section that could be useful in your business career. For each site, write a two-sentence summary of what the site offers and how it could help you launch and build your career.

MyBCommLab.com

Use MyBCommLab.com to test your understanding of the concepts presented in this chapter and explore additional materials that will bring the ideas to life in video, activities, and an online multimedia e-book. Additionally, you can improve your skill with verbs by using the "Peak Performance Grammar and Mechanics" module within the lab. Take the Pretest to determine whether you have any weak areas. Then review those areas in the Refresher Course. Take the Follow-Up Test to check your grasp of verbs. For an extra challenge, take the Advanced Test. Finally, for even more reinforcement, go to the "Improve Your Grammar, Mechanics, and Usage" section that follows, and complete the "Level 1: Self-Assessment" exercises.

Improve Your Grammar, Mechanics, and Usage

Level 1: Self-Assessment—Verbs

Review Section 1.3 in the Handbook of Grammar, Mechanics, and Usage and then complete the following 15 items.

In items 1–5, provide the verb form called for in the following exercises.

1. I _____ (present perfect, *become*) the resident expert on repairing the copy machine.
2. She _____ (past, *know*) how to conduct an audit when she came to work for us.
3. Since Joan was promoted, she _____ (past perfect, *move*) all the files to her office.
4. Next week, call John to tell him what you _____ (future, *do*) to help him set up the seminar.
5. By the time you finish the analysis, he _____ (future perfect, *return*) from his vacation.

For items 6–10, rewrite the sentences so that they use active voice instead of passive.

6. The report will be written by Leslie Cartwright.
7. The failure to record the transaction was mine.
8. Have you been notified by the claims department of your rights?
9. We are dependent on their services for our operation.
10. The damaged equipment was returned by the customer before we even located a repair facility.

In items 11–15, circle the correct verb form provided in parentheses.

11. Everyone upstairs (*receive, receives*) mail before we do.
12. Neither the main office nor the branches (*is, are*) blameless.
13. C&B Sales (*is, are*) listed in the directory.
14. When measuring shelves, 7 inches (*is, are*) significant.
15. About 90 percent of the employees (*plan, plans*) to come to the company picnic.

Level 2: Workplace Applications

The following items contain numerous errors in grammar, capitalization, punctuation, abbreviation, number style, word division, and vocabulary. Rewrite each sentence, correcting all errors. Write *C* for any sentence that is already correct.

1. Cut two inches off trunk and place in a water stand, and fill with water.
2. The newly-elected officers of the Board are: John Rogers, president, Robin Doig, vice-president, and Mary Sturhann, secretary.
3. Employees were stunned when they are notified that the trainee got promoted to Manager only after her 4th week with the company.
4. Seeking reliable data on U.S. publishers, *Literary Marketplace* is by far the best source.
5. Who did you wish to speak to?
6. The keynote address will be delivered by Seth Goodwin, who is the author of six popular books on marketing, has written two novels, and writes a column for "Fortune" magazine.

7. Often the reputation of an entire company depend on one employee that officially represents that company to the public.

8. The executive director, along with his staff, are working quickly to determine who should receive the Award.

9. Him and his co-workers, the top bowling team in the tournament, will represent our Company in the league finals on saturday.

10. Listening on the extension, details of the embezzlement plot were overheard by the Security Chief.

11. The acceptance of visa cards are in response to our customer's demand for a more efficient and convenient way of paying for parking here at San Diego International airport.

12. The human resources dept. interviewed dozens of people, they are seeking the better candidate for the opening.

13. Libraries' can be a challenging; yet lucrative market if you learn how to work the "system" to gain maximum visibility for you're products and services.

14. Either a supermarket or a discount art gallery are scheduled to open in the Mall.

15. I have told my supervisor that whomever shares my office with me cannot wear perfume, use spray deodorant, or other scented products.

Level 3: Document Critique

The following document may contain errors in grammar, capitalization, punctuation, abbreviation, number style, vocabulary, and spelling. You will also find errors related to topics in this chapter. Concentrate on using the "you" attitude, emphasizing the positive, being polite, and using bias-free language as you improve this memo. Correct all errors using standard proofreading marks (see Appendix C).

Memo

TO:	Blockbuster mngrs.
FROM:	Tom Dooley, deputy chairmen, Viacom, Inc.
	in care of Blockbuster Entertainment Group
	Corporate headquarters, Renaissance Tower
	1201 Elm street; Dallas TX 75270
DATE:	May 8 2009
SUB:	Recent Cash Flow and consumer response—Survey

Now that our stores have been re-organized with your hard work and cooperation, we hope revenues will rise to new heights; if we reemphasize video rentals as Blockbusters core business and reduce the visibility of our sideline retail products. Just in case though, we want to be certain that these changes are having the postive affect on our cash flow that we all except and look forward to.

To help us make that determination, respond to the following survey questions and fax them back. Answer concisely; but use extra paper if necessary—for details and explanations.

When you finish the survey it will help headquarters improve service to you; but also, help us all improve service to our customers. Return your survey before before May 15 to my attention. Then blockbuster hopefully can thrive in a marketplace, that critics say we cannot conquer. Blockbuster must choose wisely and serve it's customers well in a difficult video-rental business environment.

Times are very tough but if we work hard at it its possible we might make Blockbuster 'the man on the streets' favorite 'place to go to rent videos!'

" Writing Business Messages

LEARNING OBJECTIVES

After studying this chapter, you will be able to

1. Explain the importance of adapting your messages to the needs and expectations of your audience

2. Define *"you" attitude* and describe the role of this attitude in successful communication

3. Discuss four ways of achieving a tone that is conversational but still businesslike

4. Explain the meaning of plain English and its value in business communication

5. Briefly describe how to select words that are not only correct but also effective

6. Explain how sentence style affects emphasis within a message

7. List five ways to develop coherent paragraphs

8. Identify the most common software features that help you craft messages more efficiently

[from the real world]

"Has your career blue screened?"[1]

—Headline from an online ad promoting Dice.com, a job-posting website that specializes in technical careers
www.dice.com

The Dice.com headline at left makes perfect sense to some readers—and perfect nonsense to many others. The company's primary audience, computer programmers and other technology specialists, knows that "blue screened" is slang for "crashed" (the term comes from the blue screen that appears on many PCs when they stop running). By using this slang term, Dice.com sends a strong signal that it understands and knows how to communicate with its target audience. In other words, the company has *adapted* its message to its target audience, an essential step in composing successful messages. At the same time, using "blue screened" would be a huge mistake for generalized job-posting websites such as Monster.com that try to attract people from every career field, because many readers in this broader audience have no idea what the term means.

No matter who your audience is, with a solid plan in place (see Chapter 3), you're ready to choose the words and craft the sentences and paragraphs that will carry your ideas to their intended audiences. Figure 4.1 lists the tasks involved in adapting to your audience and composing your message.

ADAPTING TO YOUR AUDIENCE

Audiences are more likely to respond positively when they believe messages address their concerns.

In any communication situation, audiences are most likely to notice, pay attention to, and respond to messages that promise to address their concerns. Dice.com could've written "Has your career crashed?" or "Has your career stalled?" However, when computer specialists read "blue screened," they're more likely to conclude that Dice.com understands the special nature of technology careers and the unique needs of software designers and other "techies."

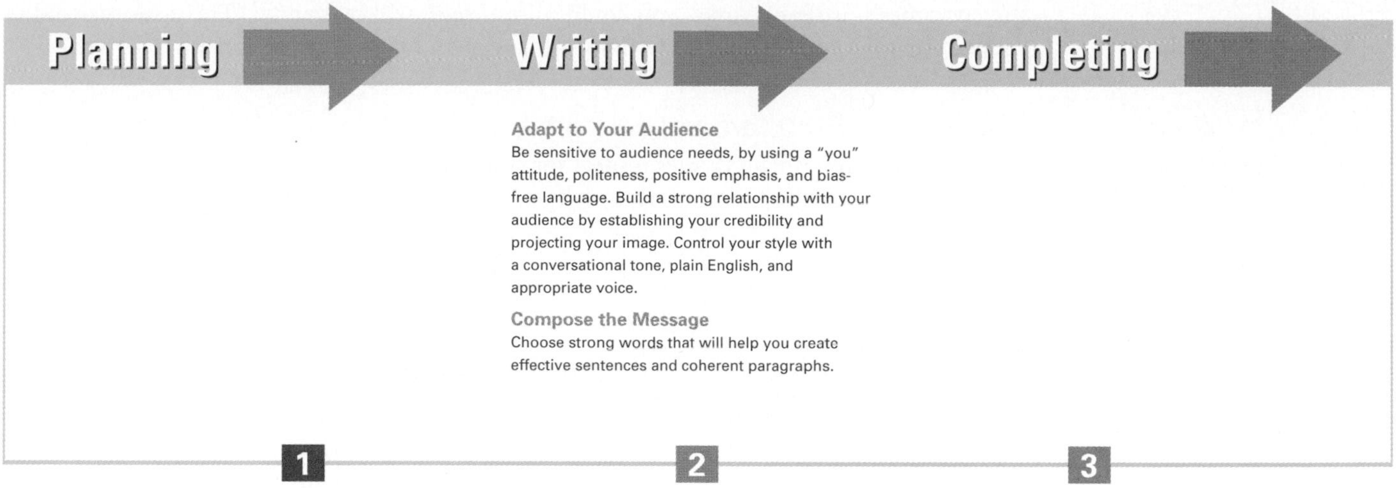

| Planning | ➡ | Writing | ➡ | Completing | ➡ |

Adapt to Your Audience
Be sensitive to audience needs, by using a "you" attitude, politeness, positive emphasis, and bias-free language. Build a strong relationship with your audience by establishing your credibility and projecting your image. Control your style with a conversational tone, plain English, and appropriate voice.

Compose the Message
Choose strong words that will help you create effective sentences and coherent paragraphs.

1   **2**   **3**

Figure 4.1   Step Two in the Three-Step Writing Process: Writing Your Message
The second step in the three-step writing process includes two vital tasks: adapting to your audience and composing your message.

Being Sensitive to Your Audience's Needs

In any business message, you can use all the right words and still not be sensitive to your audience members and their needs. To demonstrate true audience sensitivity, adopt the "you" attitude, maintain good standards of etiquette, emphasize the positive, and use bias-free language.

Using the "You" Attitude

You are already becoming familiar with the audience-centered approach, trying to see a subject through your audience's eyes. Now you want to project this approach in your messages by adopting a **"you" attitude**—that is, by speaking and writing in terms of your audience's wishes, interests, hopes, and preferences.

On a simple level, you can adopt the "you" attitude by replacing terms that refer to yourself and your company with terms that refer to your audience. In other words, use *you* and *your* instead of *I, me, mine, we, us,* and *ours:*

> You can best implement the "you" attitude by expressing your message in terms of the audience's interests and needs.

Instead of This	Write This
To help us process this order, we must ask for another copy of the requisition.	So that your order can be filled promptly, please send another copy of the requisition.
We are pleased to announce our new flight schedule from Atlanta to New York, which is every hour on the hour.	Now you can take a Delta flight from Atlanta to New York every hour on the hour.

Even so, using *you* and *your* requires finesse. If you overdo it, you're likely to create some rather awkward sentences, and you run the risk of sounding overly enthusiastic and artificial.[2] Also, keep in mind that the "you" attitude is not intended to be manipulative or insincere. Nor is the "you" attitude simply a matter of using one pronoun rather than another; it's a matter of genuine empathy. You can use *you* 25 times in a single page and still ignore your audience's true concerns. In other words, it's the thought and sincerity that count, not the pronoun *you*. If you're talking to a retailer, try to think like a retailer; if you're dealing with a production supervisor, put yourself in that position; if you're writing to a dissatisfied customer, imagine how you would feel at his or her end of the transaction.

Be aware that on some occasions, it's better to avoid using *you*, particularly if doing so will sound overly authoritative or accusing. For instance, instead of saying, "You failed to deliver

> Avoid using *you* and *your* when doing so
> ■ Makes you sound dictatorial
> ■ Makes someone else feel guilty
> ■ Goes against your organization's style

69

the customer's order on time," you could minimize ill will by saying, "The customer didn't receive the order on time," or "Let's figure out a system that will ensure on-time deliveries."

Maintaining Standards of Etiquette

Although you may be tempted now and then to be brutally frank, try to express the facts in a kind and thoughtful manner.

Good etiquette not only indicates respect for your audience but also helps foster a more successful environment for communication by minimizing negative emotional reaction:

Instead of This	Write This
Once again, you've managed to bring down the website through your incompetent programming.	Let's review the last website update so that we can identify potential problems before the next update.
You've been sitting on our order for two weeks, and we need it now!	Our production schedules depend on timely delivery of parts and supplies, but we have not yet received the order you promised to deliver two weeks ago. Please respond today with a firm delivery commitment.

Use extra tact when communicating with people higher up the organization chart than you or outside the company.

Of course, some situations require more diplomacy than others. If you know your audience well, a less formal approach might be more appropriate. However, when you are communicating with people who outrank you or with people outside your organization, an added measure of courtesy is usually needed.

Written communication and most forms of electronic media generally require more tact than oral communication (see Figure 4.2). When you're speaking, your words are softened by your tone of voice and facial expression. Plus, you can adjust your approach according to the feedback you get. If you inadvertently offend someone in writing or in a podcast, for example, you usually don't get the immediate feedback you would need to resolve the situation. In fact, you may never know that you offended your audience.

Emphasizing the Positive

You can communicate negative news without being negative.

Sensitive communicators understand the difference between delivering negative news and being negative. For example, when Alaska Airlines instituted surcharges for heavy luggage in an attempt to reduce injuries to baggage handlers, the company presented the change to passengers in a positive light with the message "Pack Light & Save."[3] Never try to hide the negative news but look for positive points that will foster a good relationship with your audience:[4]

Instead of This	Write This
It is impossible to repair your laptop today.	Your computer can be ready by Tuesday. Would you like a loaner until then?
We wasted $300,000 advertising in that magazine.	Our $300,000 advertising investment did not pay off; let's analyze the experience and apply the insights to future campaigns.

Show audience members how they will benefit by responding to your message.

If you're trying to persuade audience members to perform a particular action, point out how doing so will benefit them:

Instead of This	Write This
We will notify all three credit reporting agencies if you do not pay your overdue bill within 10 days.	Paying your overdue bill within 10 days will prevent a negative entry on your credit record.
I am tired of seeing so many errors in the customer service blog.	Proofreading your blog postings will help you avoid embarrassing mistakes that generate more customer service complaints.

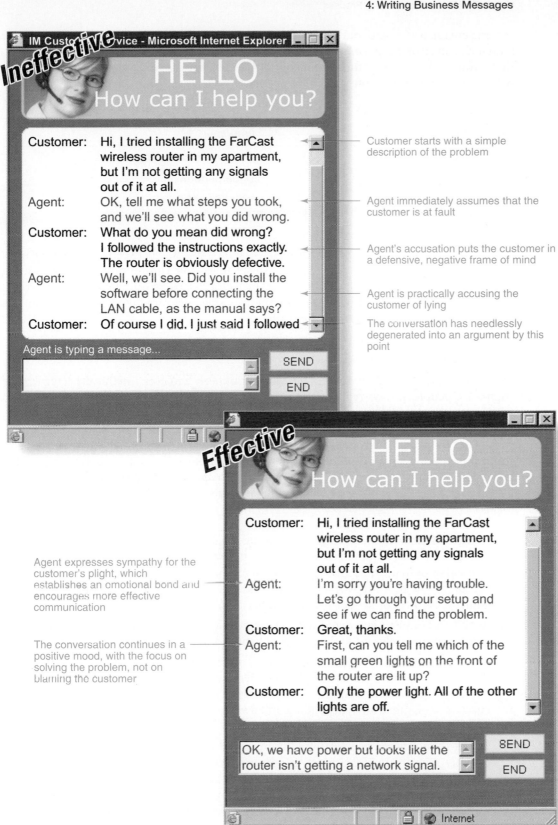

Customer starts with a simple description of the problem

Agent immediately assumes that the customer is at fault

Agent's accusation puts the customer in a defensive, negative frame of mind

Agent is practically accusing the customer of lying

The conversation has needlessly degenerated into an argument by this point

Agent expresses sympathy for the customer's plight, which establishes an emotional bond and encourages more effective communication

The conversation continues in a positive mood, with the focus on solving the problem, not on blaming the customer

Figure 4.2 Fostering a Positive Relationship with an Audience
In the "ineffective" example, notice how the customer service agent's unfortunate word choices immediately derail this instant messaging exchange. In the "effective" example, a more sensitive approach allows both people to focus on solving the problem.

Try to avoid words with negative connotations; use meaningful euphemisms instead.

In general, try to state your message without using words that might hurt or offend your audience. Substitute *euphemisms* (milder synonyms) for terms with unpleasant connotations. You can be honest without being harsh. Gentle language won't change the facts, but it will make them more acceptable:

Instead of This	Write This
Cheap merchandise	Economy merchandise
Failing	Underperforming
Fake	Imitation or faux

Be aware that when using euphemisms, you walk a fine line between softening the blow and hiding the facts. It would be unethical to speak to your community about "relocating refuse" when you're really talking about your plans for disposing of toxic waste. Even if it is unpleasant, people respond better to an honest message delivered with integrity than to a sugarcoated message that obscures the truth.

Using Bias-Free Language

Avoid biased language that might offend your audience.

Bias-free language avoids words and phrases that unfairly and even unethically categorize or stigmatize people in ways related to gender, race, ethnicity, age, or disability. Contrary to what some might think, biased language is not simply about "labels." To a significant degree, language reflects the way people think and what they believe, and biased language may well perpetuate the underlying stereotypes and prejudices that it represents.[5] Moreover, because communication is all about perception, being fair and objective isn't enough; to establish a good relationship with your audience, you must also *appear* to be fair.[6] Good communicators make every effort to change biased language (see Table 4.1). Bias can take a variety of forms:

- **Gender bias.** Avoid sexist language by using the same labels for everyone, regardless of gender. Don't call a woman *chairperson* and then call a man *chairman*. Reword sentences to use *they* or to use no pronoun at all rather than refer to all individuals as *he*. Note that the preferred title for women in business is *Ms.*, unless the individual asks to be addressed as *Miss* or *Mrs.* or has some other title, such as *Dr.*

- **Racial and ethnic bias.** Avoid identifying people by race or ethnic origin unless such identification is relevant to the matter at hand—and it rarely is.

- **Age bias.** Mention the age of a person only when it is relevant. Moreover, be careful of the context in which you use words that refer to age; such words carry a variety of positive and negative connotations. For example, *young* can imply youthfulness, inexperience, or even immaturity, depending on how it's used.

- **Disability bias.** As with other labels, physical, mental, sensory, or emotional impairments should never be mentioned in business messages unless those conditions are directly relevant to the subject. If you must refer to someone's disability, put the person first and the disability second.[7] For example, by saying "employees with physical disabilities," not "handicapped employees," you focus on the whole person, not the disability. Finally, never use outdated terminology such as *crippled* or *retarded.*

Building Strong Relationships with Your Audience

Focusing on your audience's needs is vital to effective communication, but you must also attend to your own priorities as a communicator. You can address your own needs while building a positive relationship by establishing your credibility and projecting your company's image.

TABLE 4.1 Overcoming Bias in Language

Examples	Unacceptable	Preferable
Gender Bias		
Using words containing *man*	Man-made	Artificial, synthetic, manufactured, constructed, human-made
	Mankind	Humanity, human beings, human race, people
	Manpower	Workers, workforce
	Businessman	Executive, manager, businessperson
	Salesman	Sales representative, salesperson, clerk
	Foreman	Supervisor
Using female-gender words	Actress, stewardess	Actor, flight attendant
Using special designations	Woman doctor, male nurse	Doctor, nurse
Using *he* to refer to "everyone"	The average worker . . . he	The average worker . . . he or she *OR* Average workers . . . they
Identifying roles with gender	The typical executive spends four hours of his day in meetings.	Most executives spend four hours a day in meetings.
	the consumer . . . she	consumers . . . they
	the nurse/teacher . . . she	nurses/teachers . . . they
Identifying women by marital status	Mrs. Norm Lindstrom	Maria Lindstrom *OR* Ms. Maria Lindstrom
	Norm Lindstrom and Ms. Drake	Norm Lindstrom and Maria Drake *OR* Mr. Lindstrom and Ms. Drake
Racial and Ethnic Bias		
Assigning stereotypes	My African American assistant speaks more articulately than I do.	My assistant speaks more articulately than I do.
	Jim Wong is an unusually tall Asian.	Jim Wong is tall.
Identifying people by race or ethnicity	Mario M. Cuomo, Italian American politician and ex-governor of New York	Mario M. Cuomo, politician and ex-governor of New York
Age Bias		
Including age when irrelevant	Mary Kirazy, 58, has just joined our trust department.	Mary Kirazy has just joined our trust department.
Disability Bias		
Putting the disability before the person	Crippled workers face many barriers on the job.	Workers with physical disabilities face many barriers on the job.
	An epileptic, Tracy has no trouble doing her job.	Tracy's epilepsy has no effect on her job performance.

Establishing Your Credibility

The response to every message you send depends heavily on audience perceptions of your **credibility**, a measure of your believability based on how reliable you are and how much trust you evoke in others. Whether you're working to build credibility with a new audience, to maintain credibility with an existing audience, or to restore credibility after a mistake, emphasize the following:

- **Honesty.** Demonstrating honesty and integrity will earn you the respect of your audiences, even if they don't always agree with or welcome your messages.

People are more likely to react positively to your message when they have confidence in you.

To enhance your credibility, emphasize factors such as honesty, objectivity, and awareness of audience needs.

- **Objectivity.** Show that you can distance yourself from emotional situations and look at all sides of an issue.
- **Awareness of audience needs.** Let your audience members know that you understand what's important to them.
- **Credentials, knowledge, and expertise.** Audiences need to know that you have whatever it takes to back up your message, whether it's education, professional certification, special training, past successes, or simply the fact that you've done your research.
- **Endorsements.** If your audience members don't know anything about you, try to get assistance from someone they do know and trust.
- **Performance.** Demonstrating impressive communication skills is not enough; people need to know they can count on you to get the job done.
- **Confidence.** Audiences need to know that you believe in yourself and your message. If you are convinced that your message is sound, you can state your case confidently, without sounding boastful or arrogant.
- **Sincerity.** Support your points with evidence, not empty terms such as *amazing*, *incredible*, or *extraordinary*. To praise an employee, for instance, don't say "you are the most fantastic employee I could ever imagine." Instead, point out specific qualities that warrant praise.

Finally, keep in mind that credibility can take days, months, even years to establish—and it can be wiped out in an instant. An occasional mistake or letdown is usually forgiven, but major lapses in honesty or integrity can destroy your reputation. On the other hand, when you do establish credibility, communication becomes much easier because you no longer have to spend time and energy convincing people that you are a trustworthy source of information and ideas.

Projecting the Company's Image

Your company's interests and reputation take precedence over your personal communication style.

When you communicate with outsiders, on even the most routine matter, you serve as a spokesperson for your organization. The impression you make can enhance or damage the reputation of the entire company. Thus, your own views and personality must be subordinated, at least to some extent, to the interests and style of your company.

Many organizations have specific communication guidelines that show everything from the correct use of the company name to preferred abbreviations and other grammatical details. Specifying a desired style of communication is more difficult, however. Observe more experienced colleagues to see how they communicate and never hesitate to ask for editorial help to make sure you're conveying the appropriate tone. For instance, with clients entrusting thousands or millions of dollars to it, an investment firm communicates in a style quite different from that of a clothing retailer. And a clothing retailer specializing in high-quality business attire communicates in a style different from that of a store catering to the latest trends in casual wear.

Controlling Your Style and Tone

Style is the way you use words to achieve a certain **tone**, or the overall feel of your writing. You can vary your style—your sentence structure and vocabulary—to sound forceful or objective, personal or formal, colorful or dry. The right choice depends on the nature of your message and your relationship with the reader.

Creating a Conversational Tone

Most business messages aim for a conversational style that is warm but businesslike.

The tone of your business messages can range from informal to conversational to formal. If you're in a large organization and you're communicating with your superiors or with customers, your tone may tend to be more formal and respectful.[8] However, that formal tone might sound distant and cold if used with close colleagues.

Compare the three versions of the message in Table 4.2. The first is too formal and stuffy for today's audiences, whereas the third is too casual for any audience other than close associates or friends. The second message demonstrates the conversational tone used in most business communication—plain language that sounds businesslike without being stuffy or full of jargon. You can achieve a tone that is conversational but still businesslike following these guidelines:

- **Avoid obsolete and pompous language.** Most companies now shy away from such dated phrases as "attached please find" and "please be advised that." Similarly, avoid using obscure words, stale or clichéd expressions, and overly complicated sentences to impress others.

- **Avoid preaching and bragging.** Few things are more irritating than know-it-alls who like to preach or brag. However, if you need to remind your audience of something that should be obvious, try to work in the information casually, perhaps in the middle of a paragraph, where it will sound like a secondary comment rather than a major revelation. Also, avoid bragging about your accomplishments or those of your organization (unless your audience is a part of your organization).

TABLE 4.2 Formal, Conversational, and Informal Tones

Tone	When It's Used	Example
Formal	Reserved for the most formal occasions	Dear Ms. Navarro: Enclosed please find the information that was requested during our telephone communication of May 14. As was mentioned at that time, Midville Hospital has significantly more doctors of exceptional quality than any other health facility in the state. As you were also informed, our organization has quite an impressive network of doctors and other health-care professionals with offices located throughout the state. In the event that you should need a specialist, our professionals will be able to make an appropriate recommendation. In the event that you have questions or would like additional information, you may certainly contact me during regular business hours. Most sincerely yours, Samuel G. Berenz
Conversational	Preferred for most business communication	Dear Ms. Navarro: Here's the information you requested during our phone conversation on Friday. As I mentioned, Midville Hospital has the best doctors and more of them than any other hospital in the state. In addition, we have a vast network of doctors and other health professionals with offices throughout the state. If you need a specialist, they can refer you to the right one. If you would like more information, please call any time between 9:00 and 5:00, Monday through Friday. Sincerely, Samuel G. Berenz
Informal	Reserved for communication with friends and close associates	Hi Gabriella: Hope all is well. Just sending along the information you asked for. As I said on Friday, Midville Hospital has more and better doctors than any other hospital in the state. We also have a large group of doctors and other health professionals with offices close to you at work or at home. Need a specialist? They'll refer you to the right one. Just give me a ring if you want to know more. Any time from 9:00 to 5:00 should be fine. Take care, Sam

- **Be careful with intimacy.** Business messages should generally avoid intimacy, such as sharing personal details or adopting a casual, unprofessional tone. However, when you have a close relationship with audience members, such as among the members of a close-knit team, a more intimate tone is sometimes appropriate and even expected.
- **Be careful with humor.** Never use humor in formal messages or when you're communicating across cultural boundaries. Humor can easily backfire and divert attention from your message. If you don't know your audience well or you're not skilled at using humor in a business setting, don't use it at all.

Using Plain English

What do you think this sentence is trying to say?

> We continually exist to synergistically supply value-added deliverables such that we may continue to proactively maintain enterprise-wide data to stay competitive in tomorrow's world.[9]

If you don't have any idea what it means, you're not alone. However, this is a real sentence from a real company. This sort of incomprehensible, buzzword-filled writing is driving a widespread call to use *plain English* or *plain language*.[10]

> Audiences can understand and act on plain English without reading it over and over.

Plain English is a way of presenting information in a simple, unadorned style so that your audience can easily grasp your meaning—language that intended recipients "can read, understand and act upon the first time they read it."[11] You can see how this definition supports using the "you" attitude and shows respect for your audience. Murky, pompous, or unnecessarily complex writing is the very antithesis of the "you" attitude. Bear in mind that plain English doesn't have to be simplistic, dull, or imprecise. The point is to be clear, not lifeless.

For all its advantages, plain English does have some limitations. For instance, it sometimes lacks the precision or subtlety necessary for scientific research, legal documents, engineering plans, intense feeling, and personal insight.

Selecting Active or Passive Voice

Your choice of active or passive voice affects the tone of your message. You are using **active voice** when the subject performs the action and the object receives the action: "Jodi sent the e-mail message." You're using **passive voice** when the subject receives the action: "The e-mail message was sent by Jodi." As you can see, the passive voice combines the helping verb *to be* with a form of the verb that is usually the past tense.

> Active sentences are usually stronger than passive ones.

Using the active voice helps make your writing more direct, livelier, and easier to read (see Table 4.3). Passive voice is not wrong grammatically, but it can be cumbersome, lengthy, and vague. In most cases, the active voice is the best choice.[12] Nevertheless, using the passive voice can help you demonstrate the "you" attitude in some situations:

> Use passive sentences to soften bad news, to put yourself in the background, or to create an impersonal tone when needed.

- When you want to be diplomatic about pointing out a problem or an error of some kind
- When you want to point out what's being done without taking or attributing either the credit or the blame
- When you want to avoid personal pronouns (*I* and *we*) in order to create an objective tone

The second half of Table 4.3 illustrates several situations in which the passive voice helps you focus your message on your audience.

COMPOSING YOUR MESSAGE

Now that you have some insights into how to adapt to your audience, you're ready to begin composing your message. As you compose your first draft, try to let your creativity flow. Don't try to draft and edit at the same time or worry about getting everything perfect. Make up words if you can't think of the right word, draw pictures, talk out loud—do whatever it

TABLE 4.4	Finding Words That Communicate with Power

Weak Phrases	Stronger Alternatives
Wealthy businessperson	Tycoon
Growth cycle	Economic boom
Hard times	Slump

Unfamiliar Words	Familiar Words
Ascertain	Find out, learn
Consummate	Close, bring about
Peruse	Read, study
Circumvent	Avoid
Increment	Growth, increase
Unequivocal	Certain

Clichés and Buzzwords	Plain Language
An uphill battle	A challenge
Writing on the wall	Prediction
Call the shots	Be in charge
Take by storm	Attack
Cost an arm and a leg	Expensive
A new ballgame	Fresh start
Fall through the cracks	Be overlooked
Think outside the box	Be creative
Run it up the flagpole	Find out what people think about it
Eat our own dog food	Use our own products
Mission critical	Vital
Disintermediate	Get rid of

- **Avoid clichés and use buzzwords carefully.** Although familiar words are generally the best choice, beware of *clichés*, terms and phrases so common that they have lost some of their power to communicate. When you are searching for a way to say something, terms and phrases that automatically pop to mind are likely to be clichés (such as *outside the box* for *fresh* or *creative*). Avoid clichés. *Buzzwords*, newly coined terms often associated with recent technology, business, or cultural changes, are slightly more difficult to handle than clichés because in small doses and in the right situation, they can actually be useful. The careful use of a buzzword can signal that you're an insider, someone in the know.[14] However, buzzwords quickly become clichés, and using them too late in their "life cycle" can mark you as an outsider desperately trying to look like an insider. When people use clichés and overuse buzzwords, they often sound as though they don't know how to express themselves otherwise and don't invest the energy required for original writing.[15]

> Avoid clichés, be extremely careful with trendy buzzwords, and use jargon only when your audience is completely familiar with it.

- **Use jargon carefully.** Handle technical or professional terms with care. Using them with the wrong audience can confuse and frustrate readers, but *not* using them with audiences that routinely communicate using such terms can label you as inexperienced or unaware.

If you need help finding the right words, try some of the visual dictionaries and thesauruses available online. For example, Visuwords (www.visuwords.com) shows words that are similar to or different from a given word and helps you see subtle differences to find the perfect word.[16]

Creating Effective Sentences

Making every sentence count is a key step in creating effective messages. Start by selecting the optimum type of sentence and then arrange words to emphasize the most important point in each sentence.

Choosing from the Four Types of Sentences

Sentences come in four basic varieties: simple, compound, complex, and compound-complex. A **simple sentence** has one main clause (a single subject and a single predicate), although it may be expanded by nouns and pronouns serving as objects of the action and by modifying phrases. Consider this example (with the subject underlined once and the predicate verb underlined twice):

Profits increased in the past year.

A **compound sentence** has two main clauses that express two or more independent but related thoughts of equal importance, usually joined by *and*, *but*, or *or*. In effect, a compound sentence is a merger of two or more simple sentences (independent clauses) that are related. For example:

Wages have declined by 5 percent, and employee turnover has been high.

The independent clauses in a compound sentence are always separated by a comma or by a semicolon (in which case the conjunction—*and*, *but*, or *or*—is dropped).

A **complex sentence** expresses one main thought (the independent clause) and one or more subordinate thoughts (dependent clauses) related to it, often separated by a comma. The subordinate thought, which comes first in the following sentence, could not stand alone:

Although you may question Gerald's conclusions, you must admit that his research is thorough.

A **compound-complex sentence** has two main clauses, at least one of which contains a subordinate clause:

Profits have increased in the past year, and although you may question Gerald's conclusions, you must admit that his research is thorough.

To make your writing as effective as possible, strive for variety and balance using all four sentence types. If you use too many simple sentences, you won't be able to properly express the relationships among your ideas, and your writing will sound choppy and abrupt. If you use too many long, compound sentences, your writing will sound monotonous.

Using Sentence Style to Emphasize Key Thoughts

In every message, some ideas are more important than others. You can emphasize key ideas through your sentence style. One obvious technique is to give important points the most space. When you want to call attention to a thought, use extra words to describe it. Consider this sentence:

The chairperson called for a vote of the shareholders.

To emphasize the importance of the chairperson, you might describe her more fully:

Having considerable experience in corporate takeover battles, the chairperson called for a vote of the shareholders.

You can increase the emphasis even more by adding a separate, short sentence to augment the first:

The chairperson called for a vote of the shareholders. She has considerable experience in corporate takeover battles.

You can also call attention to a thought by making it the subject of the sentence. In the following example, the emphasis is on the person:

I can write letters much more quickly using a computer.

Margin notes:
A simple sentence has one main clause.

A compound sentence has two main clauses.

A complex sentence has one main clause and one subordinate clause.

A compound-complex sentence has two main clauses and at least one dependent clause.

Writing is usually most effective if it balances all four sentence types.

Emphasize specific parts of sentences by
- Devoting more words to them
- Putting them at the beginning or at the end of the sentence
- Making them the subject of the sentence

However, when you change the subject, the computer takes center stage:

The *computer* enables me to write letters much more quickly.

Another way to emphasize an idea is to place it either at the beginning or at the end of a sentence:

Less emphatic: We are cutting the *price* to stimulate demand.

More emphatic: To stimulate demand, we are cutting the *price*.

In complex sentences, the ideal placement of the dependent clause depends on the relationship between the ideas expressed. If you want to emphasize the idea expressed in the dependent clause, put that clause at the end of the sentence (the most emphatic position) or at the beginning (the second most emphatic position). If you want to downplay the idea, position the dependent clause within the sentence.

Dependent clauses can determine emphasis.

Most emphatic: The electronic parts are manufactured in Mexico, *which has lower wage rates than the United States.*

Emphatic: *Because wage rates are lower in Mexico than in the United States,* the electronic parts are manufactured there.

Least emphatic: Mexico, *which has lower wage rates than the United States,* was selected as the production site for the electronic parts.

In every writing project, having a clear plan and strong knowledge of your audience will help you make the most effective sentence choices.

Crafting Coherent Paragraphs

Paragraphs organize sentences related to the same general topic. Readers expect each paragraph to be *coherent*—to present an idea in a logically connected way. They also expect paragraphs to follow one another in a logical sequence of thoughts that make up a complete message. As with sentences, controlling the elements of each paragraph helps your readers grasp the main idea of your document and understand how the specific pieces of support material back up that idea.

Understanding the Elements of a Paragraph

Paragraphs vary widely in length and form, but most contain three basic elements: a topic sentence, support sentences that develop the topic, and transitional words and phrases.

Most paragraphs consist of
- A topic sentence that reveals the subject of the paragraph
- Related sentences that support and expand the topic
- Transitional elements that help readers move between sentences and paragraphs

Topic Sentence   Every properly constructed paragraph is *unified*; it deals with a single topic. The sentence that introduces that topic is called the **topic sentence**. The topic sentence gives readers a summary of the general idea that will be covered in the rest of the paragraph. In business writing, the topic sentence is usually explicit and is often the first sentence in the paragraph. The following examples show how a topic sentence can introduce the subject and suggest the way that subject will be developed:

The medical products division has been troubled for many years by public relations problems. [In the rest of the paragraph, readers will learn the details of the problems.]

Relocating the plant in New York has two main disadvantages. [The disadvantages will be explained in subsequent sentences.]

Support Sentences   In most paragraphs, the topic sentence needs to be explained, justified, or extended with one or more support sentences. These related sentences must all have a bearing on the general subject and must provide enough specific details to make the topic clear:

The medical products division has been troubled for many years by public relations problems. Since 2006 the local newspaper has published 15 articles that portray the division in a negative light. We have been accused of everything from mistreating laboratory animals to polluting the local groundwater. Our facility has been described as a health hazard. Our scientists are referred to as "Frankensteins," and our profits are considered "obscene."

The support sentences are all more specific than the topic sentence. Each one provides another piece of evidence to demonstrate the general truth of the main thought. Also, each sentence is clearly related to the general idea being developed, which gives the paragraph its unity. A paragraph is well developed when (1) it contains enough information to make the topic sentence convincing and interesting and (2) it contains no extraneous, unrelated sentences.

Transitions   **Transitions** are words or phrases that connect ideas by showing how one thought is related to another. They also help alert the reader to what lies ahead so that shifts and changes don't cause confusion. In addition to helping readers understand the connections you're trying to make, transitions give your writing a smooth, even flow.

Ideally, you begin planning transitions while you're outlining, as you decide how the various ideas and blocks of information will be arranged and connected.[17] You can establish transitions in a variety of ways:

Transitional elements include
- Connecting words (conjunctions)
- Repeated words or phrases
- Pronouns
- Words that are frequently paired

- **Use connecting words.** Use words such as *and*, *but*, *or*, *nevertheless*, *however*, *in addition*, and so on.
- **Echo a word or phrase from a previous paragraph or sentence.** "A system should be established for monitoring inventory levels. *This system* will provide . . ."
- **Use a pronoun that refers to a noun used previously.** "Ms. Arthur is the leading candidate for the president's position. *She* has excellent qualifications."
- **Use words that are frequently paired.** "The machine has a *minimum* output of . . . Its *maximum* output is . . .

Some transitions serve as mood changers; that is, they alert the reader to a change in mood from the previous paragraph. Some announce a total contrast with what's gone on before, some announce a cause-and-effect relationship, and some signal a change in time. Here is a list of common transitions:

Additional detail: moreover, furthermore, in addition, besides, first, second, third, finally

Causal relationship: therefore, because, accordingly, thus, consequently, hence, as a result, so

Comparison: similarly, here again, likewise, in comparison, still

Contrast: yet, conversely, whereas, nevertheless, on the other hand, however, but, nonetheless

Condition: although, if

Illustration: for example, in particular, in this case, for instance

Time sequence: formerly, after, when, meanwhile, sometimes

Intensification: indeed, in fact, in any event

Summary: in brief, in short, to sum up

Repetition: that is, in other words, as I mentioned earlier

Consider using a transition whenever it could help the reader understand your ideas and follow you from point to point. You can use transitions inside paragraphs to tie together related points and between paragraphs to ease the shift from one distinct thought to another. In longer reports, a transition that links major sections or chapters is often a complete paragraph that serves as a mini-introduction to the next section or as a summary of the ideas presented in the section just ending.

Developing Paragraphs

The best way to achieve coherence and unity is to use paragraph structures that are familiar to your readers, appropriate to the ideas you're trying to portray, and suited to your purpose. Five of the most common development techniques are illustration, comparison or contrast, cause and effect, classification, and problem and solution (see Table 4.5).

TABLE 4.5 Five Techniques for Developing Paragraphs

Technique	Description	Example
Illustration	Giving examples that demonstrate the general idea	Some of our most popular products are available through local distributors. For example, Everett & Lemmings carries our frozen soups and entrees. The J. B. Green Company carries our complete line of seasonings, as well as the frozen soups. Wilmont Foods, also a major distributor, now carries our new line of frozen desserts.
Comparison or contrast	Using similarities or differences to develop the topic	When the company was small, the recruiting function could be handled informally. The need for new employees was limited, and each manager could comfortably screen and hire her or his own staff. However, our successful bid on the Owens contract means that we will be doubling our labor force over the next six months. To hire that many people without disrupting our ongoing activities, we will create a separate recruiting group within the human resources department.
Cause and effect	Focusing on the reasons for something	The heavy-duty fabric of your Wanderer tent probably broke down for one of two reasons: (1) a sharp object punctured the fabric, and without reinforcement, the hole was enlarged by the stress of pitching the tent daily for a week or (2) the fibers gradually rotted because the tent was folded and stored while still wet.
Classification	Showing how a general idea is broken into specific categories	Successful candidates for our supervisor trainee program generally come from one of several groups. The largest group, by far, consists of recent graduates of accredited business management programs. The next largest group comes from within our own company, as we try to promote promising staff workers to positions of greater responsibility. Finally, we do occasionally accept candidates with outstanding supervisory experience in related industries.
Problem and solution	Presenting a problem and then discussing the solution	Selling handmade toys online is a challenge because consumers are accustomed to buying heavily advertised toys from major chain stores or well-known websites such as Amazon.com. However, if we develop an appealing website, we can compete on the basis of product novelty and quality. In addition, we can provide unusual crafts at a competitive price: a rocking horse of birch, with a hand-knit tail and mane; a music box with the child's name painted on the top; a real teepee, made by Native American artisans.

USING TECHNOLOGY TO COMPOSE AND SHAPE YOUR MESSAGES

Take full advantage of your word processor's formatting capabilities to help produce effective, professional documents in a short time.

Take advantage of the tools in your word processor or online publishing systems (for websites, blogs, and other documents) to write more efficiently and effectively:

- **Style sheets and templates.** Most word processors offer some form of *style sheets*, which are master lists of predefined styles (typeface, type size, and so on) for headlines, paragraph text, and other elements. (Here, the word *style* should not be confused with *writing style*, discussed earlier in the chapter.) Many organizations provide employees with approved style sheets to ensure a consistent look for all company documents. Moreover, style sheets can eliminate hours of design time by making many of your choices for you. *Templates* can go beyond style sheets by defining such factors as page design, available fonts, and other features. Templates can include *boilerplate*, or sections of text that are reused from document to document. Like style sheets, templates save time by making choices for you in advance. (Depending on the version of Microsoft Word you're using, style sheets may have been replaced by templates.)

- **Autocompletion.** A software feature called *autocompletion* (or something similar) inserts a ready-made block of text when you type the first few characters. For example, instead of typing your company's name, address, phone number, fax number, e-mail address, and website URL, you can set the software to enter all this information as soon as you type the first three letters of the company name.

- **Autocorrection.** An automatic feature in some programs instantly corrects spelling and typing errors and converts text to symbols, such as converting (c) to the © copyright symbol.

- **File merge and mail merge.** Today's software makes it easy to combine files, which is an especially handy feature when several members of a team write different sections of a report. For particularly complex reports, you can set up a master document that merges a number of subdocuments automatically when it's time to print. *Mail merge* lets you personalize form letters by inserting names and addresses from a database.

- **Endnotes, footnotes, indexes, and tables of contents.** Your computer can help you track footnotes and endnotes, renumbering them every time you add or delete references. For a report's indexes and table of contents, you can simply flag the items you want to include, and the software assembles the lists for you.

- **Wizards.** Programs such as Microsoft Word offer *wizards* that guide you through the process of creating letters, résumés, and other common documents. Of course, you need to make all the final decisions about the content of your messages; a wizard can only make suggestions.

For the latest information on using technology to compose messages, visit http://real-timeupdates.com/bce and click on Chapter 4. ■

DOCUMENT MAKEOVER

Improve This Letter

To practice correcting drafts of actual documents, visit the "Document Makeovers" section in either MyBCommLab.com or the Companion Website for this text.

If MyBCommLab.com is being used in your class, see your User Guide for specific instructions on how to access the content for this chapter.

If you are accessing this feature through the Companion Website, click on "Document Makeovers" and then select Chapter 4. You will find a letter that contains problems and errors related to what you've learned in this chapter about writing business messages. Use the Final Draft decision tool to create an improved version of this letter. Check the message for appropriate choice of approach, a conversational tone, correct use of active voice, and logical paragraphs. ●

CHAPTER REVIEW AND ACTIVITIES

Chapter Summary

This chapter discusses the second step in the three-step writing process: writing business messages, including the two key tasks of adapting to your audience and composing your message. Adapting to your audience is critical because it enables you to meet the needs and expectations of audience members, and by doing so, you'll increase the chances of reaching them with your intended message.

The "you" attitude (as opposed to the "me" attitude) refers to speaking and writing in terms of your audience's wishes, interests, hopes, and preferences rather than your own. Put another way, it means replacing *I* and *we* with *you*. Writing with this attitude is essential to effective communication because it shows your audience that you have their needs in mind, not just your own.

To achieve a tone that is conversational but still businesslike, avoid obsolete and pompous language, avoid preaching and bragging, be careful with intimacy (sharing personal details or adopting an overly casual tone), and be careful with humor.

Plain English is a way of presenting information in a simple, unadorned style so that your audience can easily grasp your meaning. By writing and speaking in plain terms, you demonstrate the "you" attitude and show respect for your audience.

Selecting words that are not only correct but also effective involves balancing abstract and concrete words, choosing powerful and familiar words, avoiding clichés, using buzzwords carefully, and using jargon carefully.

Sentence style affects emphasis by playing up or playing down specific parts of a sentence. To emphasize a certain point, you can place it at the end of the sentence or make it the subject of the sentence. To deemphasize a point, put it in the middle of the sentence.

Five ways to develop coherent paragraphs are illustration, comparison or contrast, cause and effect, classification, and problem and solution.

Common software features that help you craft messages more efficiently include style sheets and templates; autocompletion; autocorrection; file merge and mail merge; endnotes, footnotes, indexes, and tables of contents; and wizards.

Test Your Knowledge

1. Which writing characteristics should you avoid if you want to achieve a conversational tone?

2. How does an abstract word differ from a concrete word?

3. In what three situations should you use passive voice?

4. How can you use sentence style to emphasize key thoughts?

5. What functions do transitions serve?

Apply Your Knowledge

1. How can you apply the "you" attitude approach if you don't know your audience personally?

2. When composing business messages, how can you be yourself and project your company's image at the same time?

3. What steps can you take to make abstract concepts such as *opportunity* feel more concrete in your messages?

4. Should you bother using transitional elements if the logical sequence of your message is already obvious? Why or why not?

5. **Ethical Choices** Seven million people in the United States are allergic to one or more food ingredients. Every year 30,000 of these people end up in the emergency room after suffering allergic reactions, and 200 of them die. Many of these tragic events are tied to poorly written food labels that either fail to identify dangerous allergens or use scientific terms that most consumers don't recognize.[18] Do food manufacturers have a responsibility to ensure that consumers read, understand, and follow warnings on food products? Explain your answer.

Practice Your Knowledge

Exercises for Perfecting Your Writing

The "You" Attitude Rewrite the following sentences to reflect your audience's viewpoint.

1. We request that you use the order form supplied in the back of our catalog.

2. We insist that you always bring your credit card to the store.

3. We want to get rid of all our 15-inch monitors to make room in our warehouse for the 19-inch screens. Thus we are offering a 25 percent discount on all sales this week.

4. I am applying for the position of bookkeeper in your office. I feel that my grades prove that I am bright and capable, and I think I can do a good job for you.

5. As requested, we are sending the refund for $25.

Emphasizing the Positive Revise these sentences to be positive rather than negative.

6. To avoid the loss of your credit rating, please remit payment within 10 days.

7. We don't make refunds on returned merchandise that is soiled.

8. Because we are temporarily out of Baby Cry dolls, we won't be able to ship your order for 10 days.

9. You failed to specify the color of the blouse that you ordered.

10. You should have realized that waterbeds will freeze in unheated houses during winter. Therefore, our guarantee does not cover the valve damage and you must pay the $9.50 valve-replacement fee (plus postage).

Emphasizing the Positive Revise the following sentences to replace unflattering terms (in italics) with euphemisms.

11. The new boss is _____ (*stubborn*) when it comes to doing things by the book.

12. When you say we've doubled our profit level, you are _____ (*wrong*).

13. Just be careful not to make any _____ (*stupid*) choices this week.

14. Jim Riley is _____ (*incompetent*) for that kind of promotion.

15. Glen monopolizes every meeting by being _____ (*a loudmouth*).

Courteous Communication Revise the following sentences to make them more courteous.

16. You claim that you mailed your check last Thursday, but we have not received it.

17. It is not our policy to exchange sale items, especially after they have been worn.

18. You neglected to sign the enclosed contract.

19. I received your letter, in which you assert that our shipment was three days late.

20. You failed to enclose your instructions for your new will.

Bias-Free Language   Rewrite each of the following sentences to eliminate bias.

21. For an Indian, Maggie certainly is outgoing.

22. He needs a wheelchair, but he doesn't let his handicap affect his job performance.

23. A pilot must have the ability to stay calm under pressure, and then he must be trained to cope with any problem that arises.

24. Candidate Renata Parsons, married and the mother of a teenager, will attend the debate.

25. Senior citizen Sam Nugent is still an active salesman.

Message Composition: Selecting Words   In the following sentences, replace vague phrases (underlined) with concrete phrases. Make up any details you might need.

26. We will be opening our new facility <u>sometime this spring</u>.

27. You can now purchase our new Leaf-Away yard and lawn blower <u>at a substantial savings</u>.

28. After the reception, we were surprised that <u>such a large number attended</u>.

29. The new production line has been operating <u>with increased efficiency</u> on every run.

30. Over the holiday, we hired a crew to <u>expand the work area</u>.

Message Composition: Selecting Words   In the following sentences, replace weak terms (in italics) with words that are stronger:

31. The two reporters_____ (*ran after*) every lead enthusiastically.

32. Even large fashion houses have to match staff size to the normal_____ (*seasonal ups and downs*).

33. The_____ (*bright*) colors in that ad are keeping customers from seeing what we have to sell.

34. Health costs_____ (*suddenly rise*) when management forgets to emphasize safety issues.

35. Once we solved the zoning issue, new business construction _____ (*moved forward*), and the district has been flourishing ever since.

Message Composition: Selecting Words   Rewrite these sentences to replace the clichés with fresh, personal expressions.

36. Being a jack-of-all-trades, Dave worked well in his new selling job.

37. Moving Leslie into the accounting department, where she was literally a fish out of water, was like putting a square peg into a round hole, if you get my drift.

38. I knew she was at death's door, but I thought the doctor would pull her through.

39. Movies aren't really my cup of tea; as far as I am concerned, they can't hold a candle to a good book.

40. It's a dog-eat-dog world out there in the rat race of the asphalt jungle.

Message Composition: Selecting Words   In the following sentences, replace long, complicated words with short, simple ones.

41. Management _____ (*inaugurated*) the recycling policy six months ago.

42. You can convey the same meaning without _____ (*utilizing*) the same words.

43. You'll never be promoted unless you _____ (*endeavor*) to be more patient.

44. I have to wait until payday to _____ (*ascertain*) whether I got the raise.

45. John will send you a copy once he's inserted all the _____ (*alterations*) you've requested.

46. Grand Tree _____ (*fabricates*) office furniture that is both durable and attractive.

47. I understand from your letter that you expect a full refund; _____ (*nevertheless*), your warranty expired more than a year ago.

Message Composition: Selecting Words   Rewrite the following sentences, replacing obsolete phrases with up-to-date versions. Write *none* if you think there is no appropriate substitute.

48. I have completed the form and returned it to my insurance company, as per your instructions.

49. Attached herewith is a copy of our new contract for your records.

50. Even though it will increase the price of the fence, we have decided to use the redwood in lieu of the cedar.

51. Saunders & Saunders has received your request for the Greenwood file, and in reply I wish to state that we will send you copies of Mr. Greenwood's documents only after Judge Taylor makes her ruling and orders us to do so.

52. Please be advised that your account with National Bank has been compromised, and we advise you to close it as soon as possible.

Message Composition: Creating Sentences   Rewrite the following sentences so that they are active rather than passive.

53. The raw data are submitted to the data processing division by the sales representative each Friday.

54. High profits are publicized by management.

55. The policies announced in the directive were implemented by the staff.

56. Our computers are serviced by the Santee Company.

57. The employees were represented by Janet Hogan.

Message Organization: Transitional Elements   Add transitional elements to the following sentences to improve the flow of ideas. (*Note*: You may need to eliminate or add some words to smooth out the sentences.)

58. Steve Case saw infinite possibilities for the Internet. Steve Case was determined to turn his vision into reality. The techies scoffed at his strategy of building a simple Internet service for ordinary people. Case doggedly pursued his dream. He analyzed other online services. He assessed the needs of his customers. He responded to their desires for an easier way to access information over the Internet. In 1992, Steve Case named his company America Online (AOL). Critics predicted the company's demise. By the end of the century, AOL was a profitable powerhouse. AOL grew so big that it was able to merge with the giant traditional media company Time Warner. The merger was widely criticized. The merger did not live up to Case's expectations. He eventually left the company.

59. Facing some of the toughest competitors in the world, Harley-Davidson had to make some changes. The company introduced new products. Harley's management team set out to rebuild the company's production process. New products were coming to market and the company was turning a profit. Harley's quality standards were not on par with those of its foreign competitors. Harley's costs were still among the highest in the industry. Harley made a U-turn and restructured the company's organizational structure. Harley's efforts have paid off.

60. Whether you're indulging in a doughnut in New York or California, Krispy Kreme wants you to enjoy the same delicious taste with every bite. The company maintains consistent product quality by carefully controlling every step of the production process. Krispy Kreme tests all raw ingredients against established quality standards. Every delivery of wheat flour is sampled and measured for its moisture content and protein levels. Krispy Kreme blends the ingredients. Krispy Kreme tests the doughnut mix for quality. Krispy Kreme delivers the mix to its stores. Krispy Kreme knows that it takes more than a quality mix to produce perfect doughnuts all the time. The company supplies its stores with everything they need to produce premium doughnuts—mix, icings, fillings, equipment—you name it.

Activities

Active links for all websites in this chapter can be found online. If MyBCommLab.com is being used in your class, see your User Guide for instructions on accessing the content for this chapter. Otherwise, visit www.pearsonhighered.com/bovee, locate *Business Communication Essentials*, Fourth Edition, click the Companion Website link, select Chapter 4, and then click on "Featured Websites." Please note that links to sites that become inactive after publication of the book will be removed from the Featured Websites section.

1. **Analyze This Message**   Read the following document and then (1) analyze the strengths and weaknesses of each sentence and (2) revise the document so that it follows this chapter's guidelines. The message was written by the marketing manager of an online retailer of baby-related products in the hope of becoming a retail outlet for Inglesina strollers and high chairs. As a manufacturer of stylish, top-quality products, Inglesina (based in Italy) is extremely selective about the retail outlets through which it allows its products to be sold.[19]

Our e-tailing company, Best Baby Gear, specializes in only the very best products for parents of newborns, infants, and toddlers. We constantly scour the world looking for products that are good enough and well-built enough and classy enough—good enough that is to take their place alongside the hundreds of other carefully selected products that adorn the pages of our award-winning website, www.bestbabygear.com. We aim for the fences every time we select a product to join this portfolio; we don't want to waste our time with onesey-twosey products that might sell a half dozen units per annum—no, we want every product to be a top-drawer success, selling at least one hundred units per specific model per year in order to justify our expense and hassle factor in adding it to the abovementioned portfolio. After careful consideration, we thusly concluded that your Inglesina lines meet our needs and would therefore like to add it.

2. **Teamwork**   For this exercise, work with four other students. Each of you should choose one of the following five topics and write one paragraph on it. Be sure one student writes a paragraph using the illustration technique, one using the comparison-or-contrast technique, one using a discussion of cause and effect, one using the classification technique, and one using a discussion of problem and solution. Then exchange paragraphs within the team and pick out the main idea and general purpose of the paragraph one of your teammates wrote. Was everyone able to correctly identify the main idea and purpose? If not, suggest how the paragraph might be rewritten for clarity.

   a. Types of cameras (or dogs or automobiles) available for sale

   b. Advantages and disadvantages of eating at fast-food restaurants

   c. Finding that first full-time job

   d. Good qualities of my car (or house, or apartment, or neighborhood)

   e. How to make a favorite dessert (or barbecue a steak or make coffee)

Expand Your Knowledge

Exploring the Best of the Web

Compose a Better Business Message   At Purdue University's Online Writing Lab (OWL), http://owl.english.purdue.edu, you'll find tools to help you improve your business messages. For advice on composing written messages, for help with grammar, and for referrals to other information sources, you'd be wise to visit this site. Purdue's OWL offers online services and an introduction to Internet search tools. You can also download a variety of handouts on writing skills. Check out the resources at the OWL homepage and then answer the following questions. (Note that some of the advice you read on OWL may differ from the advice in your textbook in some respects.)

Exercises

1. Explain why positive wording in a message is more effective than negative wording. Why should you be concerned about the position of good news or bad news in your written message?

2. What six factors of tone should you consider when conveying your message to your audience?

3. What points should you include in the close of your business message? Why?

Surfing Your Way to Career Success

Bovée and Thill's Business Communication Headline News offers links to hundreds of online resources that can help you with this course, your other college courses, and your career. Visit http://businesscommunicationblog.com and click on "Web Directory." The Working with Words section connects you to a variety of websites and articles on abstract versus concrete words, abusive words, bias-free writing, euphemisms, obsolete language, plain English, and profane words. Identify three websites from this section that could be useful in your business career. For each site, write a two-sentence summary of what the site offers and how it could help you launch and build your career.

MyBCommLab.com

Use MyBCommLab.com to test your understanding of the concepts presented in this chapter and explore additional materials that will bring the ideas to life in video, activities, and an online multimedia e-book. Additionally, you can improve your skill with adjectives and adverbs by using the "Peak Performance Grammar and Mechanics" module within the lab. Take the Pretest to determine whether you have any weak areas. Then review those areas in the Refresher Course. Take the Follow-Up Test to check your grasp of adjectives and adverbs. For an extra challenge, take the Advanced Test. Finally, for even more reinforcement, go to the "Improve Your Grammar, Mechanics, and Usage" section that follows, and complete the "Level 1: Self-Assessment" exercises.

Improve Your Grammar, Mechanics, and Usage

Level 1: Self-Assessment—Adjectives

Review Section 1.4 in the Handbook of Grammar, Mechanics, and Usage and then complete the following 15 items.

In items 1–5, fill in the appropriate form of the adjective that appears in parentheses.

1. Of the two products, this one has the _____ (*great*) potential.

2. The _____ (*perfect*) solution is *d*.

3. Here is the _____ (*interesting*) of all the ideas I have heard so far.

4. Our service is _____ (*good*) than theirs.

5. The _____ (*hard*) part of my job is firing people.

In items 6–10, insert hyphens where required.

6. A highly placed source revealed Dotson's last ditch efforts to cover up the mistake.

7. Please send an extra large dust cover for my photocopier.

8. A top secret document was taken from the president's office last night.

9. A 30 year old person should know better.

10. If I write a large scale report, I want to know that it will be read by upper level management.

In items 11–15, insert required commas, where needed, between adjectives.

11. The two companies are engaged in an all-out no-holds-barred struggle for dominance.

12. A tiny metal shaving is responsible for the problem.

13. She came to the office with a bruised swollen knee.

14. A chipped cracked sheet of glass is useless to us.

15. You'll receive our usual cheerful prompt service.

Level 2: Workplace Applications

The following items contain numerous errors in grammar, capitalization, punctuation, abbreviation, number style, word division, and vocabulary. Rewrite each sentence, correcting all errors. Write *C* for any sentence that is already correct.

1. Its time that you learned the skills one needs to work with suppliers and vendors to get what you want and need.

2. Easy flexible wireless calling plans start for as little as $19 dollars a month.

3. There's several criteria used to select customer's to receive this offer.

4. PetFood Warehouse officially became PETsMART, Jim left the co. due to health reasons.

5. First quarter sales gains are evident in both the grocery store sector (up 1.03%) and the restaurant sector (up 3.17 per cent) according to Food Institute estimates.

6. Whatever your challenge, learning stronger "negotiating" tactics and strategies will improve the way people work and the results that comes from their efforts.

7. To meet the increasing demand for Penta bottled-drinking-water, production capacity is being expanded by Bio-Hydration Research Lab by 80 percent.

8. Seminars begin at 9 A.M. and wrap up at 4:00 P.M.

9. Temple, Texas-based McLane Co. a subsidiary of Wal-Mart has bought a facility in Northfield, Minn that it will use to distribute products to customers such as convenience stores, stores that sell items at a discount, and mass merchants.

10. The British Retail Consortium are releasing the 3rd edition of its Technical Standards on Apr. 22, reported The New York Times.

11. The reason SkillPath is the fastest growing training company in the world is because of our commitment to providing clients with the highest-quality learning experiences possible.

12. According to professor Charles Noussair of the economics department of Purdue University, opinion surveys "Capture the respondent in the role of a voter, not in the role of a consumer".

13. The Study found that people, exposed to Purina banner ads, were almost 50 percent more likely to volunteer Purina as the first Dog Food brand that came to mind.

14. In a consent decree with the food and drug administration, E'Ola International a dietary supplement maker agreed not to sell any more products containing the drug, ephedrine.

15. Dennis Dickson is looking for a company both to make and distribute plaidberries under an exclusive license, plaidberries is blackberries that are mixed with extracts and they are used as a filling.

Level 3: Document Critique

The following document may contain errors in grammar, capitalization, punctuation, abbreviation, number style, vocabulary, and spelling. You will also find errors related to topics in this chapter. Concentrate on using the "you" attitude, emphasizing the positive, being polite, and using bias-free language as you improve this memo. Correct all errors using standard proofreading marks (see Appendix C).[20]

Welcome! Here is your new card for your health Savings Account (HSA)

Using your prepaid card makes HSAs: Fast + Easy + Automatic!!

Step 1: Activate and sign your Card(s)

✓ You **CANNOT** use your card until you perfom these following steps: to activate, go to the websight listed on the back of your Card(s). You can also just following the instructons written on the sticker which should be attached to the front of your card.

✓ Your member ID No. could be one of two things: your Social Security Number or the ID number assigned by your Health Plan

✓ Sign the back of your card and have the other person on the account, if any, sign the other card (you should've received two cards with this letter, by the way)

Step 2: Use Your Card as You need

However, **DO NOT ATTEMPT** to use yoru card for anything expenses other than current year medical expenses—qualified only!—for you or your dependents if you have any

The things your Card can be used for include but are not limited to such as:

✓ Prescriptions, but only those covered by your health plan—obviously

✓ Dental

✓ Vision and eyewear

✓ OTC items if covered

Step 3: Save all receipts!! so you can use them when you do your taxes

Completing Business Messages

LEARNING OBJECTIVES

After studying this chapter, you will be able to

1. Discuss the value of careful revision and list the main tasks involved in completing a business message

2. List four writing techniques you can use to improve the readability of your messages

3. Describe the steps you can take to improve the clarity of your writing

4. Discuss why it's important to make your messages more concise and give four tips on how to do so

5. Explain how design elements help determine the effectiveness of your documents

6. Highlight the types of errors to look for when proofreading

7. Discuss the most important issues to consider when distributing your messages

"Almost all professional people know that success in business partly depends on good communication skills, on writing and speaking clearly and persuasively. Businesspeople who cannot express themselves well are often at a disadvantage in the corporate world."[1]

—*Robert Hartwell Fiske,* Author of *The Dictionary of Concise Writing* www.vocabula.com

Robert Hartwell Fiske knows the value of effective communication, particularly communication that is clear, concise, and efficient. Conversely, poorly written messages can damage company reputations, hinder sales efforts, and damage careers.[2] Careful revision often means the difference between a rambling, unfocused message and a lively, direct message that gets attention and spurs action.

REVISING YOUR MESSAGE

If you have time, put your draft aside for a day or two before you begin the revision process.

After you complete the first draft of your message, you may be tempted to breathe a sigh of relief, send the message on its way, and move on to the next project. Resist that temptation. Successful communicators recognize that the first draft is rarely as tight, clear, and compelling as it needs to be. Careful revision improves the effectiveness of your messages and sends a strong signal to your readers that you respect their time and care about their opinions.[3]

Whenever possible—particularly with important messages—put your first draft aside for a day or two before you begin the revision process so that you can approach the material with a fresh eye. Then start with the "big picture," making sure that the document accomplishes your overall goals, before moving to finer points such as readability, clarity, and conciseness. Figure 5.1 lists the tasks in the third step of the three-step writing process: revising your message to achieve optimum quality and then producing, proofreading, and distributing it.

Evaluating Your Content, Organization, Style, and Tone

When you begin the revision process, focus on content, organization, style, and tone. Today's time-pressed readers want messages that convey important content clearly and quickly.[4] To evaluate the content of your message, make sure it is accurate, relevant to audience's needs, and complete.

Figure 5.1 Step Three in the Three-Step Writing Process: Completing Your Messages
Resist the temptation to cut corners when performing the tasks in the third step of the three-step writing process. You've spent a lot of time and energy planning and writing a strong message, so make sure it is produced and delivered with professional quality.

When you are satisfied with the basic content of your message, review its organization by asking yourself these questions:

- Are all your points covered in the most logical and convincing order?
- Do the most important ideas receive the most space and greatest emphasis?
- Are any points repeated unnecessarily?
- Are details grouped together logically rather than being randomly scattered throughout the document?

With the content in place and effectively organized, next consider whether you have achieved the right tone for your audience. Is your writing formal enough to meet the audience's expectations without being too formal or academic? Is it too casual for a serious subject?

Spend a few extra moments on the beginning and ending of your message; these sections have the greatest impact on the audience. Be sure that the opening of your document is relevant, interesting, and geared to the reader's probable reaction. The opening should also convey the subject and purpose of the message. For longer documents, the opening should help readers understand how the material is organized. Review the conclusion to be sure that it summarizes the main idea and leaves the audience with a positive impression.

The beginning and end of a message have the greatest impact on your readers.

Reviewing for Readability

When you're satisfied with content, organization, and tone, make a second pass to improve readability. You can adopt a number of techniques to make your message easier to read: varying sentence length, using shorter paragraphs, using lists and bullets instead of narrative, and adding effective headings and subheadings. Note that these techniques also make your documents easier to skim, which many businesspeople do before deciding whether to read documents in depth.

Varying Your Sentence Length

Effective documents usually combine a mixture of sentences that are short (up to 15 words or so), medium (15–25 words), and long (more than 25 words). Each sentence length has advantages. Short sentences can be processed quickly and are easier for nonnative speakers and translators to interpret. Medium-length sentences are useful for showing the relationships among ideas. Long sentences are often the best way to convey complex ideas, list multiple related points, or summarize or preview information.

To keep readers' interest, use a variety of short, medium, and long sentences.

Of course, each sentence length also has disadvantages. Too many short sentences in a row can make your writing choppy and disconnected. Medium sentences lack the punch of short sentences and the informative power of longer sentences. Long sentences are usually harder to understand than short sentences because they are packed with information. They are also harder to skim because readers can absorb only a few words per glance.

Keeping Your Paragraphs Short

Short paragraphs are easier to read than long ones.

Unlike the variety needed with sentences, the optimum paragraph length is short to medium in most cases. Large blocks of text can be intimidating, even to the most dedicated reader. Short paragraphs (of 100 words or fewer; this paragraph has 77 words) are easier to read than long ones, and they make your writing look inviting. They also help audiences read more carefully. You can also emphasize an idea by isolating it in a short, forceful paragraph.

However, don't go overboard with short paragraphs. If you break a complex discussion into more paragraphs in order to keep the paragraphs short, you'll need to add enough transitions to ensure a smooth flow and clear connection between ideas. Also, use one-sentence paragraphs only occasionally and only for emphasis.

Using Lists and Bullets to Clarify and Emphasize

Lists are effective tools for highlighting and simplifying material.

An effective alternative to using conventional sentences is to set off important ideas in a list—a series of words, names, or other items. Lists can show the sequence of your ideas, heighten their impact visually, and increase the likelihood that readers will find your key points. In addition, lists simplify complex subjects, highlight the main point, enable skimming, and give readers a breather. Consider the difference between the following two approaches to the same information:

Instead of This	**Write This**
Owning your own business has many advantages. One is the opportunity to build a major financial asset. Another advantage is the satisfaction of working for yourself. As a sole proprietor, you also have the advantage of privacy because you do not have to reveal your financial information or plans to anyone.	Owning your own business has three advantages: • The opportunity to build a major financial asset • The satisfaction of working for yourself • The freedom to keep most of your financial information private

When creating a list, you can separate items with numbers, letters, or *bullets* (a general term for any kind of graphical element that precedes each item). Bullets are generally preferred over numbers, unless the list is in some logical sequence or ranking, or specific list items will be referred to later on. Make your lists easy to read by making all the items parallel (see "Imposing Parallelism" on page 95) and keeping individual items as short as possible.[5] Also, be sure to introduce your lists clearly so that people know what they're about to read.

Adding Headings and Subheadings

Use headings to grab the reader's attention and organize material into short sections.

A **heading** is a brief title that tells readers about the content of the section that follows. **Subheadings** indicate subsections within a major section; complex documents may have several levels of subheadings. Headings and subheadings help in three important ways: They show readers at a glance how the material is organized, they call attention to important points, and they highlight connections and transitions between ideas.

Informative headings are generally more helpful than descriptive ones.

Headings fall into two categories. **Descriptive headings**, such as "Production Costs," identify a topic but do little more. **Informative headings**, such as "A New Way to Cut Costs," put your reader right into the context of your message. They are also helpful in guiding your work as a writer because they specify the information you need to convey in each section. Well-written informative headings are self-contained, which means that readers can skim just the headings and subheadings and understand them without reading the rest of the document. Whatever types of headings you choose, keep them brief and grammatically parallel.

Editing for Clarity

After you've reviewed and revised your message for readability, make sure your message is as clear as possible.

Clarity is essential to getting your message across accurately and efficiently.

Breaking Up Overly Long Sentences

If you find overly long sentences in your writing, you may be trying to make a sentence do more than it can reasonably do, such as expressing two dissimilar thoughts or peppering the reader with too many pieces of supporting evidence at once. (Did you notice how difficult this long sentence was to read?)

Rewriting Hedging Sentences

Sometimes you have to *hedge* or *qualify* a statement when you aren't entirely sure of something, when you can't predict an outcome, or when you don't want to sound arrogant. However, avoid hedging to the point that you lose all authority:

Don't be afraid to present your opinions without qualification; excessive hedging undermines your authority.

Instead of This	Write This
I believe that Mr. Johnson's employment record seems to show that he may be capable of handling the position.	Mr. Johnson's employment record shows that he is capable of handling the position.

Imposing Parallelism

Making your writing *parallel* means expressing two or more similar ideas using the same grammatical structure. Doing so helps your audience understand that the ideas are related, are of similar importance, and are on the same level of generality. Parallel patterns are also easier to read. Parallelism can be achieved by repeating a pattern in words, phrases, clauses, or entire sentences:

When you use parallel grammatical patterns to express two or more ideas, you show that they are comparable thoughts.

Instead of This	Write This
To waste time and missing deadlines are bad habits.	Wasting time and missing deadlines are bad habits.
Interviews are a matter of acting confident and to stay relaxed.	Interviews are a matter of acting confident and staying relaxed.

Correcting Dangling Modifiers

Be careful not to leave modifying phrases "dangling," with no connection to the subject of the sentence. In the first example below, for instance, the poor version seems to say that the *budget* was working as quickly as possible:

Instead of This	Write This
Working as quickly as possible, the budget was soon ready.	Working as quickly as possible, the committee soon had the budget ready.
After a three-week slump, we increased sales.	After a three-week slump, sales increased.

Rewording Long Noun Sequences

Stringing too many nouns together as modifiers can make a sentence difficult to read. You can often clarify such a sentence by putting some of the nouns in a modifying phrase:

Instead of This	Write This
The aluminum window sash installation company will give us an estimate on Friday.	The company that installs aluminum window sashes will give us an estimate on Friday.

Replacing Camouflaged Verbs

Watch for word endings such as *ion*, *tion*, *ing*, *ment*, *ant*, *ent*, *ence*, *ance*, and *ency*. Most of them "camouflage" a verb by changing it into a noun or an adjective—which requires you to add another verb in order to complete your sentence:

Instead of This	Write This
The manager undertook implementation of the rules.	The manager implemented the rules.
Verification of the shipments occurs weekly.	Shipments are verified weekly.

Clarifying Sentence Structure

Subject and predicate should be placed as close together as possible, as should modifiers and the words they modify.

Keep the subject and predicate of a sentence as close together as possible so that readers don't have to read the sentence twice to figure out who did what:

Instead of This	Write This
A 10 percent decline in market share caused by quality problems and an aggressive sales campaign by Armitage, the market leader in the Northeast, was the major problem in 2008.	The major problem in 2008 was a 10 percent loss of market share caused by quality problems and an aggressive sales campaign by Armitage, the market leader in the Northeast.

Similarly, adjectives, adverbs, and prepositional phrases usually make the most sense when they're placed as close as possible to the words they modify:

Instead of This	Write This
These ergonomic chairs are ideal for professionals who must spend many hours working at their computers with their adjustable sitting, kneeling, and standing positions.	With their adjustable sitting, kneeling, and standing positions, these ergonomic chairs are ideal for professionals who must spend many hours working at their computers.

Clarifying Awkward References

Be careful with directional phrases such as *the above-mentioned*, *as mentioned above*, *the afore-mentioned*, *the former*, *the latter*, and *respectively*. They often force readers to jump from point to point to figure out what you're saying. You're usually better off using specific references:

Instead of This	Write This
The Law Office and the Accounting Office distribute computer supplies for legal secretaries and beginning accountants, respectively.	The Law Office distributes computer supplies for legal secretaries; the Accounting Office distributes those for beginning accountants.

Moderating Your Enthusiasm

An occasional adjective or adverb intensifies and emphasizes your meaning, but too many can ruin your writing by making you sound insincere:

Instead of This	Write This
We are beyond delighted to offer you a position on our staff of exceptionally skilled and highly educated employees. The work offers extraordinary challenges and a very large salary.	We are pleased to offer you a position on our staff of skilled and well-educated employees. The work offers challenges and an attractive salary.

Editing for Conciseness

In addition to clarity, readers appreciate conciseness—particularly in new media formats such as blogs and instant messages. The good news is that most first drafts can be cut by as much as 50 percent.[6]

Make your documents tighter by removing unnecessary words.

Deleting Unnecessary Words and Phrases

To test whether a word or phrase is essential, try the sentence without it. If the meaning doesn't change, leave it out. For instance, *very* is often nothing but clutter. There's no need to call someone "very methodical." The person is either methodical or not. Also, some combinations of words have one-word equivalents that are more efficient:

Instead of This	Write This
for the sum of	for
in the event that	if
on the occasion of	on
prior to the start of	before
in the near future	soon
at this point in time	now
due to the fact that	because
in view of the fact that	because
until such time as	when
with reference to	about

In addition, avoid the clutter of unnecessary or poorly placed relative pronouns (*who*, *that*, *which*):

Instead of This	Write This
Cars that are sold after January will not have a six-month warranty.	Cars sold after January will not have a six-month warranty.
Employees who are driving to work should park in the spaces that are marked "Staff."	Employees driving to work should park in the spaces marked "Staff."

However, well-placed relative pronouns and articles prevent confusion. Notice how the meaning changes depending on where *that* is placed in these sentences:

Instead of This	Write This
The project manager told the engineers last week the specifications were changed.	The project manager told the engineers last week *that* the specifications were changed.
	The project manager told the engineers *that* last week the specifications were changed.

Shortening Long Words and Phrases

Short words are generally more vivid and easier to read than long ones. The idea is to use short, simple words, *not* simple concepts:[7]

Instead of This	Write This
During the preceding year, the company accelerated productive operations, an action predicated on the assumption that the company was operating at a financial deficit.	Last year the company sped up operations. The action was based on the belief that the company was losing money.

Also, by using infinitives in place of some phrases, you can shorten your sentences and make them clearer:

Instead of This	Write This
If you want success as a writer, you must work hard.	To be a successful writer, you must work hard.
He went to the library for the purpose of studying.	He went to the library to study.
The employer increased salaries so that she could improve morale.	The employer increased salaries to improve morale.

Eliminating Redundancies

In some word combinations, the words tend to say the same thing. For instance, "visible to the eye" is redundant because *visible* is enough. Eliminate the redundant word(s):

Instead of This	Write This
absolutely complete	complete
basic fundamentals	fundamentals
follows after	follows
reduce down	reduce
refer back	refer
repeat again	repeat
collect together	collect
future plans	plans
return back	return
end result	result
actual truth	truth
final outcome	outcome
surrounded on all sides	surrounded

In addition, avoid using double modifiers that have the same meaning.

Instead of This	Write This
Modern, up-to-date equipment	Modern equipment

Recasting "It Is/There Are" Starters

Whenever a sentence starts with *It is* or *There are*, see whether you can rewrite it to remove this phrase and thereby shorten the sentence:

Instead of This	Write This
It would be appreciated if you would sign the lease today.	Please sign the lease today.
There are five employees in this division who were late to work today.	Five employees in this division were late to work today.

As you make all these improvements, concentrate on how each word contributes to an effective sentence and on how that sentence helps to develop a coherent paragraph. Look for opportunities to make the material more interesting through the use of strong, lively words and phrases (as discussed in Chapter 4). Sometimes you'll find that the most difficult problem in a sentence can be solved by simply removing the problem itself. When you come upon a troublesome element, ask yourself, "Do I need it at all?" Possibly not. In fact, you may find that it was giving you so much grief precisely because it was trying to do an unnecessary job.[8]

Figure 5.2 provides an example of revising for clarity and conciseness. Notice how the changes remove unnecessary words, clarify the message, and demonstrate the "you" attitude. Figure 5.3 shows the revised document.

Evaluating, Editing, and Revising the Work of Others

At many points in your career, you will be asked to evaluate, edit, or revise the work of others. Whether you're suggesting improvements or actually making the improvements yourself (as you might on a wiki site, for example), you can make a contribution using all the skills you've learned in this chapter as well as in Chapters 3 and 4.

Before you dive into someone else's work, recognize the dual responsibility that doing so entails. First, unless you've specifically been asked to rewrite something in your own style, remember that your job is to help the other writer succeed at his or her task, not to impose your writing style or pursue your own agenda. In other words, make sure your input focuses on making the piece more effective, not on making it more like something you would've written. Second, make sure you understand the writer's intent before you begin suggesting or making changes. If you try to edit or revise without knowing what the writer hoped to accomplish, you run the risk of making the piece less effective, not more. With those thoughts in mind, ask yourself the following questions as you evaluate someone else's writing:

When you evaluate, edit, or revise someone else's work, your job is to help that person succeed—not to impose your own style or agenda.

- What is the purpose of this document or message?
- Who is the target audience?
- What information does the audience need?
- Does the document provide this information in a well-organized way?
- Does the writing demonstrate the "you" attitude toward the audience?
- Is the tone of the writing appropriate for the audience?
- Can the readability be improved?
- Is the writing clear? If not, how can it be improved?
- Is the writing as concise as it could be?
- Does the design support the intended message?

You can read more about using these skills in the context of wiki writing in Chapter 6.

Using Technology to Revise Your Message

When it's time to revise and polish your message, take full advantage of your tools. Avoid drudgery and minimize errors by using word-processing functions such as *cut and paste* (taking a block of text out of one section of a document and pasting it in somewhere else) and *search and replace* (tracking down words or phrases and changing them if you need to). Pay close attention to what the tool is doing for you, of course. For example, replacing all occurrences of *power* with *strength* will also change the word *powerful* to *strengthful*.

Spell checkers, computerized thesauruses, grammar checkers, and style checkers can all help with the revision process, but they can't take the place of good writing and editing skills.

Delauny Music
56 Commerce Circle • Davenport, IA 52806
(563) 555-4001 • delaunymusic.net

June 21, 2009

← *Need 7 blank lines here*

Ms. Claudia Banks
122 River Heights Drive
Bettendorf, IA 52722

Dear Ms. Banks:

On behalf of everyone at Delauny Music, it is my pleasure to thank you for your recent purchase of a Yamaha CG1 grand piano. The Cg1 carries more than a century of Yamaha's heritage in design and production of world-class musical instruments and ~~you can bet it~~ will give you many years of playing and listening pleasure. Our commitment to your satisfaction doesn't stop with your purchase, however. ~~Much to the contrary, it continues for as long as you own your piano, which we hope, of course, is for as long as you live.~~ As a vital first step, please remember to call us, ~~your local Yamaha dealer,~~ sometime within three to eight months after your piano was delivered to take advantage of the ~~free~~ Yamaha Servicebond℠ Assurance Program. This free service program includes a thorough evaluation and ~~adjusting~~ *adjustment* of the instrument after you've had some time to play your piano and your piano has had time to adapt to its environment.

In addition to this ~~vital~~ *important* service appointment, a regular program of tuning is ~~absolutely~~ essential to ensure ~~its~~ *your piano's* impeccable performance. Our piano specialists recommend four tunings during the first year and two tunings every year thereafter ~~that~~. As your local Yamaha *dealer*, we are ideally positioned to provide you with optimum service for both regular tuning and any maintenance or repair needs you may have ~~over the years.~~

All of us at Delauny Music thank you for your recent purchase ~~and~~ wish you *We* ~~many~~ many years of satisfaction with your new Yamaha CG1 grand piano.

Sincerely,
~~Respectfully yours in beautiful music,~~

Madeline Delauny
Owner

tjr

Annotations (left side):

Replaces the first sentence with the sentence from below (the two sentences said essentially the same thing)

Changes adjusting to adjustment to make it parallel with evaluation

Replaces its with your piano's to avoid confusion

Simplifies an over-the-top complimentary close

Annotations (right side):

Removes a phrase (you can bet) that is too informal for this fairly formal message

Removes an awkward and unnecessary sentence

Inserts a missing word (dealer)

Removes unnecessary words in several places

Common Proofreading Symbols (see page A-28 for more)	
~~strikethrough~~	Delete text
ℓ	Delete individual character or a circled block of text
∧	Insert text (text to insert is written above)
⊙	Insert period
⋏	Insert comma
⌐	Start new line
⌲	Start new paragraph
≡	Capitalize

Figure 5.2 Improving a Customer Letter Through Careful Revision
Careful revision makes this draft shorter, clearer, and more focused. The proofreading symbols you see here are still widely used whenever printed documents are edited and revised; you can find a complete list of symbols in Appendix C. Note that many business documents are now "marked up" using such technological tools as *revision marks* in Microsoft Word and *comments* in Adobe Acrobat. No matter what the medium, however, careful revision is key to more effective messages.

Delauny Music
56 Commerce Circle • Davenport, IA 52806
(563) 555-4001 • delaunymusic.net

June 21, 2009

Ms. Claudia Banks
122 River Heights Drive
Bettendorf, IA 52722

Dear Ms. Banks:

Thank you for your recent purchase. We wish you many years of satisfaction with your new Yamaha CG1 grand piano. The CG1 carries more than a century of Yamaha's heritage in design and production of world-class musical instruments and will give you many years of playing and listening pleasure.

Our commitment to your satisfaction doesn't stop with your purchase, however. As a vital first step, please remember to call us sometime within three to eight months after your piano was delivered to take advantage of the Yamaha Servicebond℠ Assurance Program. This free service program includes a thorough evaluation and adjustment of the instrument after you've had some time to play your piano and your piano has had time to adapt to its environment.

In addition to this important service appointment, a regular program of tuning is essential to ensure your piano's impeccable performance. Our piano specialists recommend four tunings during the first year and two tunings every year thereafter. As your local Yamaha dealer, we are ideally positioned to provide you with optimum service for both regular tuning and any maintenance or repair needs you may have.

Sincerely,

Madeline Delauny
Owner

tjr

Figure 5.3   A Professional Business Letter
Here is the revised and finished version of the edited letter from Figure 5.2. Note that the *block format* used here is just one of several layout options; Appendix A also describes the *modified block format* and the *simplified format*.

Software tools such as *revision marks* and *commenting* keep track of proposed editing changes electronically and provide a history of a document's revisions. For instance, in Microsoft Word, the revisions appear in a different font color than the original text, giving you a chance to review changes before accepting or rejecting them. Adobe Acrobat lets you attach notes to and mark text changes in PDF files. In addition, Word, Acrobat, and other software tools, including groupware systems, now provide a host of features to keep track of editing changes made by multiple members of a team.

In addition to the many revision tools, four software functions can help bring out the best in your documents. First, a *spell checker* compares your document with an electronic dictionary, highlights unrecognized words, and suggests correct spellings. Using a spell checker is a wonderful way to weed major typos out of your documents, but it is no substitute for good spelling skills. For example, if you use *the* when you mean to use *then*, your spell checker won't notice, because *the* is spelled correctly. Plus, a spell checker can flag words it doesn't recognize as misspelled when they are actually correct. It's up to you to decide whether each flagged word should be corrected or left alone, and it's up to you to find errors that your spell checker has overlooked.

Second, a computer *thesaurus* gives you alternative words, just as a printed thesaurus does. A computer thesaurus is much faster and lets you try multiple alternatives in just a few seconds to see which works best. The best uses of any thesaurus, printed or computerized, are to find fresh, interesting words when you've been using the same word too many times and to find the word that most accurately conveys your intended meaning. Don't use a thesaurus simply to add impressive-sounding words.

Third, a *grammar checker* can perform some helpful review tasks (such as pointing out noun–verb agreement problems) and highlight items you should consider changing, such as passive voice, long sentences, and commonly misused words.

Fourth, a *style checker* can also monitor your word and sentence choices and suggest alternatives that might produce more effective writing. For instance, the style checking options in Microsoft Word range from such basic issues as whether to spell out numbers or use contractions to more subjective matters, such as problems with sentence structure and the use of technical terminology.

By all means, use any software that you find helpful when revising your documents. Just remember that it's unwise to rely on them to do all your revision work and that you're responsible for the final product.

PRODUCING YOUR MESSAGE

The quality of your document design, both on paper and on-screen, affects readability and audience perceptions.

Now it's time to put your hard work on display. The *production quality* of your message—the total effect of page design, graphical elements, typography, screen presence, and so on—plays an important role in its effectiveness. A polished, inviting design not only makes your document easier to read but also conveys a sense of professionalism and importance.[9]

Adding Graphics, Sound, Video, and Hypertext

Take advantage of your software's ability to incorporate other communication elements.

Today's word processors and other software tools make it easy to produce impressive documents that enliven your text with not only full-color graphics but also sound, video, and hypertext links. The software for creating business visuals falls into two basic groups: *presentation software*, which helps you create overhead transparencies and computerized slide shows (electronic presentations are discussed in Chapter 12), and *graphics software*, which ranges from basic tools that help you create simple business diagrams to the comprehensive tools preferred by artists and graphic designers. You can create graphics yourself, use *clip art* (collections of uncopyrighted images), or import or scan in drawings or photographs.

Adding sound bites or video clips to electronic documents can be an effective way to help get your message across. Several systems let you record brief messages and attach them to particular places in a document. The reader then clicks on a speaker icon to play each comment.

You can use Hypertext Markup Language (HTML) to insert *hyperlinks* into your documents. Readers can easily jump from one document to another by clicking on such a link. They can go directly to a website, jump to another section of your document, or go to a different document or program altogether. Using hyperlinks, you can customize your documents to meet the individual information needs of your readers—just as you can on a webpage.

Designing for Readability

Good design enhances the readability of your material.

The design of your document affects readability in two important ways. First, good design improves the effectiveness of your message. Conversely, poor design can act as a barrier to communication. Second, visual design itself sends a nonverbal message to audience members, influencing their perceptions of the communication before they read a single word (see Figure 5.4).

Poor

Subject: Using sports to promote our new Victorinox apparel collection (HTML)

File Edit View Insert Format Tools Actions Help

Send · Attach as Adobe PDF · Options...

To... alden.maxwell@sabrands.com

Cc...

Subject: Using sports to promote our new Victorinox apparel collection

After researching sports marketing results over the past five years, I'm more convinced than ever that sponsoring a sporting event would be an excellent way to build awareness of our new Victorinox line.

- The experiences of other companies show that sports sponsorship is an extremely cost-effective approach to promotion. For example, Volvo found that it can reach as many people by spending $3 million on tennis tournaments as it can by spending $25 million on media advertising.
- If we decide to go forward with a sponsorship, our first priority should be to identify a sport that is popular with our target customers. Auto racing is currently the number-one sport among corporate sponsors: 1. auto racing, 2. golf, 3. Olympics, 4. tennis, 5. running.
- Although the "mainstream" sports currently receive the bulk of corporate spending, we might achieve more impact with a lesser-known event. For instance, Timberline Company recently enjoyed tremendous success with its sponsorship of the Iditarod Dog-Sled Race across Alaska, a contest that appeals to buyers of rugged footwear.

Over the next few days, I plan to do some more research to identify sporting events that would give us the most exposure among urban professionals with an active mindset, who represent ou... possibilities and prepare some p... Tuesday staff meeting.

Disrupts the flow with horizontal lines that add no information value

Uses font styles inconsistently and unnecessarily

Obscures ranked list within the paragraph, making it difficult to distinguish from the rest of the text

Complicates reading with an unnecessary background color

Improved

Subject: Using sports to promote our new Victorinox apparel collection (HTML)

View Insert Format Tools Actions Help

Send · Attach as Adobe PDF · Options...

To... alden.maxwell@sabrands.com

Cc...

Subject: Using sports to promote our new Victorinox apparel collection

Hello Alden,

After researching sports marketing results over the past five years, I'm more convinced than ever that sponsoring a sporting event would be an excellent way to build awareness of our new Victorinox line.

Benefits of Sports Sponsorship
The experiences of other companies show that sports sponsorship is an extremely cost-effective approach to promotion. For example, Volvo found that it can reach as many people by spending $3 million on tennis tournaments as it can by spending $25 million on media advertising.

How to Identify the Best Sport
If we decide to go forward with a sponsorship, our first priority should be to identify a sport that is popular with our target customers. Auto racing is currently the number-one sport among corporate sponsors:

Corporate Spending ($ millions)

Auto racing
Golf
Olympics
Tennis
Running
0   20   40   60   80   100   120

Although the "mainstream" sports currently receive the bulk of corporate spending, we might achieve more impact with a lesser-known event. For instance, Timberline Company recently enjoyed tremendous success with its sponsorship of the Iditarod Dog-Sled Race across Alaska, a contest that appeals to buyers of rugged footwear.

Over the next few days, I plan to do some more research to identify sporting events that would give us the most exposure among urban professionals with an active mindset, who represent our primary market. I plan to pinpoint three or four possibilities and prepare some preliminary cost estimates for discussion at the Tuesday staff meeting.

Uses fonts and colors consistently throughout

Uses white space and paragraph headings effectively to make the document easy to skim

Draws attention to important points with an easy-to-understand graphic

Balances graphics, text, and color to create a polished appearance and to lend credibility

Figure 5.4 Poor and Improved Document Design
Compare these two e-mail screens. They contain virtually the same information but send dramatically different messages to the reader. The unprofessional appearance of the "poor" version makes it uninviting and difficult to read. The amateurish use of color is distracting. In contrast, the "improved" version is clear, inviting, and easy to either read entirely or scan quickly.

For effective design, pay attention to
- Consistency
- Balance
- Restraint
- Detail

To achieve an effective design, pay careful attention to the following design elements:

- **Consistency.** Throughout each message, be consistent in your use of margins, typeface, type size, spacing, color, and position.
- **Balance.** Try to balance the space devoted to text, visuals, and *white space*. For instance, many pages or screens in a row with nothing but text can be intimidating to readers. Conversely, a design can have too many visuals, which breaks the text into disjointed chunks that are more difficult to read.
- **Restraint.** Strive for simplicity. Don't clutter your message with too many design elements, too many colors, or too many decorative touches.
- **Detail.** Pay attention to the details. For instance, headings and subheadings that appear at the bottom of a column or page can annoy readers when the promised information doesn't appear until the next column or page.

Even without special training in graphic design, you can make your printed and electronic messages more effective by understanding the use of white space, margins and line justification, typefaces, and type styles.

White Space

White space separates elements in a document and helps guide the reader's eye.

Any space free of text or artwork is considered **white space** (note that white space isn't necessarily white). White space includes the outside margins, open area surrounding headings, vertical space between columns, and paragraph indents or extra space between paragraphs. To increase the chance that readers will read your documents, be generous with white space; it makes pages less intimidating and easier to read.[10]

Margins and Justification

Most business documents use a flush left margin and a ragged right margin.

Margins define the space around text and between text columns. They're influenced by the way you place lines of type, which can be set (1) justified (flush on the left and flush on the right), (2) flush on the left and "ragged" on the right, (3) flush on the right and ragged on the left, or (4) centered. Justified type is frequently used in magazines, newspapers, and books because it can accommodate more text in a given space. However, without special attention from experienced designers, justified paragraphs often have awkward gaps and variable spacing between words and letters. The effect is both disrupting to look at and difficult to read.[11] Writers without the time or skill needed to "tweak" justified text are better off not using it.

Flush-left, ragged-right type is the best choice for most business messages because it creates an informal, open, and contemporary feel. Spacing between words is consistent, and only long words that fall at the ends of lines are hyphenated.

Centered type is rarely used for text paragraphs but is commonly used for headings and subheadings. Flush-right, ragged-left type is rarely used in business documents.

Typefaces

Serif typefaces are commonly used for text; sans serif typefaces are commonly used for headings.

Typeface, or *font*, refers to the physical design of letters, numbers, and other text characters. Typeface influences the tone of your message, making it look authoritative or friendly, businesslike or casual, classic or modern, and so on (see Table 5.1). Be sure to choose fonts that are appropriate for your message; many of the fonts on your computer are not appropriate for business use.

Serif typefaces have small crosslines (called serifs) at the ends of each letter stroke. Serif faces such as Times Roman are commonly used for body text. They can look busy and cluttered when set in large sizes for headings or other display treatments. **Sans serif typefaces** have no serifs. Sans serif faces such as Helvetica and Arial are ideal for display treatments that use larger type, but they can be difficult to read in long blocks of text.

For most documents, you shouldn't need more than two typefaces, although if you want to make captions or other text elements stand out, you can use another font.[12] You can't go too wrong with a sans serif typeface (such as Arial) for heads and subheads and a serif typeface (such as Times New Roman) for text and captions. Using more typefaces can clutter a document and produce an amateurish look.

Serif Typefaces (Best for text)	Sans Serif Typefaces (Best for headlines; some work well for text)	Specialty Typefaces (For decorative purposes only)
Bookman Old Style	Arial	AMMA
Century Schoolbook	**Eras Bold**	Bauhaus
Courier	Franklin Gothic Book	*EDWARDIAN*
Garamond	Frutiger	*Lucida Handwriting*
Rockwell	Gill Sans	Euclid Ftaltur
Times Roman	Verdana	**STENCIL**

TABLE 5.1 Typeface Personalities: Serious to Casual to Playful

Type Styles

Type style refers to any modification that lends contrast or emphasis to type, including **boldface**, *italic*, and underlining. In general, boldface is the most emphatic, followed by italics and then underlining. Use any type style in moderation. For instance, underlining or using all-uppercase letters can interfere with the reader's ability to recognize the shapes of words, improperly placed boldface or italicized type can slow down your reader, and shadowed or outlined type can seriously hinder legibility.

For most business messages, use a type size of 10 to 12 points for regular text and 12 to 18 points for headings and subheadings. (A point is approximately 1/72 inch.) Resist the temptation to reduce the type size to squeeze in text or to enlarge it to fill up space. Type that is too small is hard to read, whereas extra-large type looks unprofessional.

Avoid using any type style that inhibits your audience's ability to read your messages.

Using Technology to Produce Your Message

Your production tools will vary widely, depending on the software and systems you're using. Some instant messaging and e-mail systems offer limited formatting and production capabilities, whereas most word processors now offer some capabilities that rival those of professional publishing software for many day-to-day business needs. *Desktop publishing* software programs such as QuarkXPress and Adobe InDesign go beyond word processing, offering more advanced layout capabilities and the ability to prepare documents for printing presses. (These programs are used mainly by design professionals.) For online content, web publishing systems make it easy to produce great-looking webpages quickly. Similarly, blogging and wiki systems simplify the production step, making it easy to rapidly post new content. Multimedia production tools such as Microsoft Producer let you combine slides, audio commentary, video clips, and other features into computer-based presentations that used to cost thousands of dollars to create.

No matter what system you're using, become familiar with the basic formatting capabilities. A few hours of exploration on your own or an introductory training course can dramatically improve the production quality of your documents. Depending on the types of messages you're creating, you'll benefit from being proficient with the following features:

Learn to use your communication tools effectively.

- **Templates and style sheets.** As Chapter 4 notes, you can save a tremendous amount of time by using templates and style sheets. Many companies provide these aids to their employees to ensure a consistent look and feel for all print and online documents.

- **Page setup.** Use page setup to control margins, orientation (*portrait* is vertical; *landscape* is horizontal), and the location of *headers* (text and graphics that repeat at the top of every page) and *footers* (similar to headers but at the bottom of the page).

- **Column formatting.** Most business documents use a single column of text per page, but multiple columns can be an attractive format for documents such as newsletters. Using columns is also a handy way to format long lists.

- **Paragraph formatting.** Take advantage of the various paragraph formatting controls to enhance the look of your documents. You can set off quotations by increasing margin width around a single paragraph, subtly compress line spacing to fit a document onto a single page, or use hanging indents to offset the first line of a paragraph.

Paragraph formatting gives you greater control over the look of your documents.

- **Numbered and bulleted lists.** Let your word processor or online publishing system do the busywork of formatting numbered and bulleted lists, too. The software can also automatically renumber lists when you add or remove items, saving you the embarrassment of misnumbered lists.

- **Tables.** Using tables is a great way to display any information that lends itself to rows and columns, including calendars, numeric data, and comparisons. Use paragraph and font formatting thoughtfully within tables for the best look.

- **Photos, illustrations, text boxes, and objects.** Most software tools used for document production, from word processors to blogging systems, let you insert photos and illustrations. *Text boxes* are small blocks of text that stand apart from the main text; they are great for captions, callouts, margin notes, and so on. *Objects* can be anything from a spreadsheet to a sound clip to an engineering drawing.

By improving the appearance of your documents with these tools, you'll improve your readers' impressions of you and your messages, too.

PROOFREADING YOUR MESSAGE

Your credibility is affected by your attention to the details of mechanics and form.

Proofreading is an essential step in completing your messages because it is your last chance to ensure the quality of your documents—and to protect or enhance your reputation as a thinker and a writer.

Look for two types of problems: (1) undetected mistakes from the writing, design, and layout stages and (2) mistakes that crept in during production. For the first category, you can review format and layout guidelines in Appendix A (including standard formats for both letters and memos) and brush up on writing basics with the Handbook of Grammar, Mechanics, and Usage that follows the appendixes. The second category can include anything from computer glitches such as incorrect fonts or misaligned page elements to problems with the ink used in printing. Be particularly vigilant with complex documents and complex production processes that involve teams of people and multiple computers. Strange things can happen as files move from computer to computer, especially when lots of graphics and different fonts are involved.

The types of details to look for when proofreading include language errors, missing material, design errors, and typographical errors.

Far from being a casual scan up and down the page or screen, proofreading should be a methodical procedure in which you look for specific problems. Here is some advice from the pros:

- **Make multiple passes.** Go through the document several times, focusing on a different aspect each time. For instance, look for content errors the first time and layout errors the second time.

- **Use perceptual tricks.** To keep from missing errors that are "in plain sight," try reading pages backward, placing your finger under each word and reading it silently, covering everything but the line you're currently reading, or reading the document aloud.

- **Focus on high-priority items.** Double-check the spelling of names and the accuracy of dates, addresses, and any number that could cause grief if incorrect.

- **Get some distance.** If possible, don't proofread immediately after finishing the document; let your brain wander off to new topics and come back fresh later on.

- **Stay focused and vigilant.** Block out distractions and focus as completely as possible on your proofreading. Avoid reading large amounts of material in one sitting and try not to proofread when you're tired.

- **Take your time.** Quick proofreading is not careful proofreading.

Table 5.2 offers some handy tips to improve your proofreading efforts.

DISTRIBUTING YOUR MESSAGE

With the production finished, you're ready to distribute your message. As with every other aspect of business communication, your options for distribution multiply with every advance in technology. When planning your distribution, consider the following factors:

TABLE 5.2   Proofreading Tips

Look for writing and typing errors

☑ Typographical mistakes

☑ Misspelled words

☑ Grammatical errors

☑ Punctuation mistakes

Look for design and layout errors

☑ Violation of company standards

☑ Page or screen layout errors (such as incorrect margins and column formatting)

☑ Clumsy page breaks

☑ Inconsistent font usage (such as with headings and subheadings)

☑ Alignment problems (such as with columns, headers, footers, and graphics)

☑ Missing or incorrect page and section numbers

☑ Missing or incorrect page headers or footers

☑ Missing or incorrect URLs, e-mail addresses, or other contact information

☑ Missing or incorrect photos and other graphical elements

☑ Missing or incorrect source notes, copyright notices, or other reference items

Look for production errors

☑ Printing problems

☑ Browser compatibility problems

☑ Incorrect or missing tags on blog posts

- **Cost.** Cost isn't a concern for most messages, but for multiple copies of lengthy reports or multimedia productions, it might well be. Weigh the cost and the benefits before you decide.

- **Convenience.** Make sure your audience can conveniently access the material you send. For instance, sending huge files may be fine on a fast local office network, but it can be a major headache for colleagues trying to download them over slower wireless networks.

- **Time.** How soon does the message need to reach the audience? Don't waste money on overnight delivery if the recipient won't read the report for a week.

- **Security and privacy.** The convenience offered by electronic communication needs to be weighed against security and privacy concerns. For the most sensitive messages, your company will probably restrict both the people who can receive the messages and the means you can use to distribute them. In addition, most computer users are wary of opening attachments. Instead of sending Word files (which can be vulnerable to macro viruses and other risks), consider converting your documents to PDF files that can be read in Adobe Reader.

> Consider cost, convenience, time, security, and privacy when choosing a distribution method.

For news on the latest advances in message distribution technologies, visit http://real-timeupdates.com/bce and click on Chapter 5. ∎

DOCUMENT MAKEOVER

Improve This Letter

To practice correcting drafts of actual documents, visit the "Documents Makeovers" section in either MyBCommLab.com or the Companion Website for this text.

If MyBCommLab.com is being used in your class, see your User Guide for specific instructions on how to access the content for this chapter.

If you are accessing this feature through the Companion Website, Click on "Document Makeovers" and then select Chapter 5. You will find a letter that contains problems and errors related to what you've learned in this chapter about revising messages. Use the Final Draft decision tool to create an improved version of this letter. Check the message for organization, readability, clarity, and conciseness. ●

" CHAPTER REVIEW AND ACTIVITIES

Chapter Summary

Revision can make your first draft tighter, clearer, and more compelling. Revision consists of three main tasks: (1) evaluating content, organization, style, and tone; (2) reviewing for readability; and (3) editing for clarity and conciseness. After you revise your message, complete it by using design elements, proofreading to ensure quality, and distributing it to your audience.

Four techniques that improve readability are varying sentence length, keeping paragraphs short, using lists and bullets, and adding headings and subheadings. Varying sentence length helps make your writing more dynamic while emphasizing the most important points. Paragraphs are usually best kept short to make it easier for readers to consume information in manageable chunks. Lists and bullets are effective devices for delineating sets of items, steps, or other collections of related information. Headings and subheadings organize your message, call attention to important information, and help readers make connections between related pieces of information.

As you work to clarify your message, (1) break up overly long sentences, (2) rewrite hedging sentences, (3) impose parallelism, (4) correct dangling modifiers, (5) reword long noun sequences, (6) replace camouflaged verbs, (7) clarify sentence structure, (8) clarify awkward references, and (9) moderate your enthusiasm.

To make messages more concise, include only necessary material and write uncluttered sentences by (1) deleting unnecessary words and phrases, (2) shortening overly long words and phrases, (3) eliminating redundancies, and (4) recasting sentences that begin with "It is" and "There are."

Design elements help determine the effectiveness of your documents. White space provides contrast and balance. Margins define the space around the text and contribute to the amount of white space. Typefaces influence the tone of the message. Type styles—boldface, italics, and underlining—provide contrast or emphasis. When selecting and applying design elements, be consistent throughout your document; balance text, art, and white space; show restraint in the number of elements you use; and pay attention to every detail.

When proofreading the final version of your document, always keep an eye out for errors in grammar, usage, and punctuation. In addition, watch for spelling errors and typos. Make sure that nothing is missing and no extraneous elements are included.

Consider cost, convenience, time, security, and privacy when choosing the method to distribute your messages. Always consider security and privacy issues before distributing messages that contain sensitive or confidential information.

Test Your Knowledge

1. What are the four main tasks involved in completing a business message?

2. What are your responsibilities when you review and edit the work of others?

3. What is parallel construction, and why is it important?

4. How do readers benefit from white space?

5. Why is proofreading an important part of the writing process?

Apply Your Knowledge

1. Why should you let your draft "age" for1 a while before you begin the revision process?

2. Why is it important that your business messages be clear?

3. Why is it important that your business messages be concise?

4. Why is it essential to understand the writer's intent before suggesting or making changes to another person's document?

5. Ethical Choices   What are the ethical implications of murky, complex writing in a document whose goal is to explain how customers can appeal the result of a decision made in the company's favor during a dispute?

Practice Your Knowledge

Exercises for Perfecting Your Writing

Revising Messages: Clarity   Break the following sentences into shorter ones by adding more periods and revising as necessary.

1. The next time you write something, check your average sentence length in a 100-word passage, and if your sentences average more than 16 to 20 words, see whether you can break up some of the sentences.

2. Don't do what the village blacksmith did when he instructed his apprentice as follows: "When I take the shoe out of the fire, I'll lay it on the anvil, and when I nod my head, you hit it with the hammer." The apprentice did just as he was told, and now he's the village blacksmith.

3. Unfortunately, no gadget will produce excellent writing, but using spell checkers and grammar checkers can help by catching common spelling errors and raising grammatical points that writers might want to reconsider, such as suspect sentence structure and problems with noun–verb agreement.

4. Know the flexibility of the written word and its power to convey an idea, and know how to make your words behave so that your readers will understand.

Revising Messages: Conciseness   Cross out unnecessary words in the following sentences.

5. The board cannot act without a consensus of opinion.

6. To surpass our competitors, we need new innovations both in products and in company operations.

7. George McClannahan has wanted to be head of engineering a long period of time, and now he has finally gotten the promotion.

8. Don't pay more than you have to; you can get our new fragrance for a price of just $50.

Revising Messages: Conciseness   Revise the following sentences, using shorter, simpler words.

9. The antiquated calculator is ineffectual for solving sophisticated problems.

10. It is imperative that the pay increments be terminated before an inordinate deficit is accumulated.

11. There was unanimity among the executives that Ms. Jackson's idiosyncrasies were cause for a mandatory meeting with the company's personnel director.

12. The impending liquidation of the company's assets was cause for jubilation among the company's competitors.

Revising Messages: Conciseness   Use infinitives as substitutes for the overly long phrases in the following sentences.

13. For living, I require money.

14. They did not find sufficient evidence for believing in the future.

15. Bringing about the destruction of a dream is tragic.

Revising Messages: Conciseness   Condense the following sentences to as few words as possible; revise as needed to maintain clarity and sense.

16. We are of the conviction that writing is important.

17. In all probability, we're likely to have a price increase.

18. Our goals include making a determination about that in the near future.

19. When all is said and done at the conclusion of this experiment, I'd like to summarize the final windup.

Revising Messages: Modifiers   Remove all the unnecessary modifiers from the following sentences.

20. Tremendously high pay increases were given to the extraordinarily skilled and extremely conscientious employees.

21. The union's proposals were highly inflationary, extremely demanding, and exceptionally bold.

Revising Messages: Hedging   Rewrite the following sentences so that they no longer contain any hedging.

22. It would appear that someone apparently entered illegally.

23. It may be possible that sometime in the near future the situation is likely to improve.

24. Your report seems to suggest that we might be losing money.

25. I believe Nancy apparently has somewhat greater influence over employees in the word-processing department.

Revising Messages: Indefinite Starters   Rewrite the following sentences to eliminate the indefinite starters.

26. There are several examples here to show that Elaine can't hold a position very long.

27. It would be greatly appreciated if every employee would make a generous contribution to Mildred Cook's retirement party.

28. It has been learned in Washington today from generally reliable sources that an important announcement will be made shortly by the White House.

29. There is a rule that states that we cannot work overtime without permission.

Revising Messages: Parallelism   Revise the following sentences to fix the parallelism problems.

30. Mr. Hill is expected to lecture three days a week, to counsel two days a week, and must write for publication in his spare time.

31. She knows not only accounting, but she also reads Latin.

32. Both applicants had families, college degrees, and were in their thirties, with considerable accounting experience but few social connections.

33. This book was exciting, well written, and held my interest.

Revising Messages: Awkward Pointers   Revise the following sentences to delete the awkward pointers.

34. The vice president in charge of sales and the production manager are responsible for the keys to 34A and 35A, respectively.

35. The keys to 34A and 35A are in executive hands, with the former belonging to the vice president in charge of sales and the latter belonging to the production manager.

36. The keys to 34A and 35A have been given to the production manager, with the aforementioned keys being gold embossed.

37. A laser printer and an inkjet printer were delivered to John and Megan, respectively.

Revising Messages: Dangling Modifiers   Rewrite the following sentences to clarify the dangling modifiers.

38. Running down the railroad tracks in a cloud of smoke, we watched the countryside glide by.

39. Lying on the shelf, Ruby saw the seashell.

40. Based on the information, I think we should buy the property.

41. Being cluttered and filthy, Sandy took the whole afternoon to clean up her desk.

Revising Messages: Noun Sequences   Rewrite the following sentences to eliminate the long strings of nouns.

42. The focus of the meeting was a discussion of the bank interest rate deregulation issue.

43. Following the government task force report recommendations, we are revising our job applicant evaluation procedures.

44. The production department quality assurance program components include employee training, supplier cooperation, and computerized detection equipment.

45. The supermarket warehouse inventory reduction plan will be implemented next month.

Revising Messages: Sentence Structure   Rearrange each of the following sentences to bring the subjects closer to their verbs.

46. Trudy, when she first saw the bull pawing the ground, ran.

47. It was Terri who, according to Ted, who is probably the worst gossip in the office (Tom excepted), mailed the wrong order.

48. William Oberstreet, in his book *Investment Capital Reconsidered*, writes of the mistakes that bankers through the decades have made.

49. Judy Schimmel, after passing up several sensible investment opportunities, despite the warnings of her friends and family, invested her inheritance in a jojoba plantation.

Revising Messages: Camouflaged Verbs   Rewrite each of the following sentences so that the verbs are no longer camouflaged.

50. Adaptation to the new rules was performed easily by the employees.

51. The assessor will make a determination of the tax due.

52. Verification of the identity of the employees must be made daily.

53. The board of directors made a recommendation that Mr. Ronson be assigned to a new division.

Activities

Active links for all websites in this chapter can be found online. If MyBCommLab.com is being used in your class, see your User Guide for instructions on accessing the content for this chapter. Otherwise, visit www.pearsonhighered.com/bovee, locate *Business Communication Essentials*, Fourth Edition, click the Companion Website link, select Chapter 5, and then click on "Featured Websites." Please note that links to sites that become inactive after publication of the book will be removed from the Featured Websites section.

1. **Analyze This Message**   Read the following document and (1) analyze the strengths and weaknesses of each sentence and (2) revise it so that it follows the guidelines in Chapters 3 through 5.

   I have so many questions I would like to ask you: Did you encounter any unforeseen costs when you were first starting up your franchise? Did you have trouble fitting into the franchise mold? How much say did you have in the location of your store? In its size? How long did it take you to start making a profit? How many hours a week do you work? Do you have any costs that are not covered by the franchise fee? How do you calculate royalty and advertising fees? How much say do you have in choosing suppliers? Do Subway's advertising programs satisfy your needs? How much did Subway help you in the beginning?

   As a potential franchisee, I am investigating Subway operations. Can you help me answer some of these questions? With your experience, you can provide the kind of information I need. Can you help me? I would be so grateful. You can reach me at (918) 555-9983, day or evening. My mobile phone is (918) 555-8838.

   Please let me hear from you soon; I hope to make my franchise decision fairly quickly.

2. **Internet**   Visit the stock market page of Bloomberg's website, at www.bloomberg.com, and evaluate the use of design in presenting the latest news. What design improvements can you suggest to enhance readability of the information posted on this page?

3. **Proofreading Messages: E-Mail**   Proofread the following e-mail message and revise it to correct any problems you find.

Our final company orrientation of the year will be held on Dec. 20. In preparation for this sesssion, please order 20 copies of the Policy handbook, the confindentiality agreenemt, the employee benefits Manual, please let me know if you anticipate any delays in obtaining these materials.

Expand Your Knowledge

Exploring the Best of the Web

Write It Right: Tips to Help You Rethink and Revise   Are you sure that readers perceive your written message as you intended? If you want help revising a message that you're completing, use the Paradigm Online Writing Assistant (POWA), at www.powa.org. With this interactive writer's guide, you can select topics to get tips on how to edit your work, reshape your thoughts, and rewrite for clarity. Read discussions about perfecting your writing skills, and for practice, complete one of the many online activities provided to reinforce what you've learned. Or select the Forum to talk about writing. Explore POWA's advice and then answer the following questions.

Exercises

1. Why is it best to write out ideas in a rough format and later reread your message to revise its content? When revising your message, what questions can you ask about your writing?

2. Name the four elements of the "writing context." Imagine that you're the reader of your message. What questions might you ask?

3. When you revise a written message, what is the purpose of "tightening"? What is one way to tighten your writing as you complete a message?

Surfing Your Way to Career Success

Bovée and Thill's Business Communication Headline News offers links to hundreds of online resources that can help you with this course, your other college courses, and your career. Visit http://businesscommunicationblog.com and click on "Web Directory." The Interpersonal section connects you to a variety of websites and articles on effective questions, interpersonal dialogs, listening, and feedback. Identify three websites from this section that could be useful in your business career. For each site, write a two-sentence summary of what the site offers and how it could help you launch and build your career.

MyBCommLab.com

Use MyBCommLab.com to test your understanding of the concepts presented in this chapter and explore additional materials that will bring the ideas to life in video, activities, and an online multimedia e-book. Additionally, you can continue to improve your skill with adjectives and adverbs by using the "Peak Performance Grammar and Mechanics" module within the lab. Take the Pretest to determine whether you have any weak areas. Then review those areas in the Refresher Course. Take the Follow-Up Test to check your grasp of adjectives and adverbs. For an extra challenge, take the Advanced Test. Finally, for even more reinforcement, go to the "Improve Your Grammar, Mechanics, and Usage" section that follows, and complete the "Level 1: Self-Assessment" exercises.

Improve Your Grammar, Mechanics, and Usage

Level 1: Self-Assessment—Adverbs

Review Section 1.5 in the Handbook of Grammar, Mechanics, and Usage and then complete the following 15 items.

In items 1–5, circle the correct adjective or adverb provided in parentheses.

1. Their performance has been (*good, well*).

2. I (*sure, surely*) do not know how to help you.

3. He feels (*sick, sickly*) again today.

4. Customs dogs are chosen because they smell (*good, well*).

5. The redecorated offices look (*good, well*).

In items 6–10, provide the correct form of the adverb in parentheses:

6. Which of the two programs computes _____ (*fast*)?

7. Kate has held five jobs over 13 years, and she was _____ (*recently*) employed by Graphicon.

8. Could they be _____ (*happily*) employed than they are now?

9. Of the two we have in stock, this model is the _____ (*well*) designed.

10. Of all the arguments I've ever heard, yours is the _____ (*logically*) reasoned.

In items 10–15, rewrite the sentences to correct double negatives.

11. He doesn't seem to have none.

12. That machine is scarcely never used.

13. They can't get no replacement parts until Thursday.

14. It wasn't no different from the first event we promoted.

15. We've looked for it, and it doesn't seem to be nowhere.

Level 2: Workplace Applications

The following items contain numerous errors in grammar, capitalization, punctuation, abbreviation, number style, word division, and vocabulary. Rewrite each sentence, correcting all errors. Write *C* for any sentence that is already correct.

1. All too often, whomever leaves the most out of his cost estimate is the one who wins the bid—if you can call it winning.

2. Carol Bartz CEO for fourteen years guided Autodesk; from a small company, to it's pre-eminent position in the computer aided design (cad) software market.

3. Shoppers were disinterested in the world-wide Web initially because many hyped services, offered no real cost or convenience advantages over offline stores.

4. Different jobs and different customers call for different pricing, estimating, and negotiating strategies.

5. Get to know the customer and their expectations, get the customer to talk about their primary use for you're product.

6. To homeowners, who feel they have found a competent contractor who has they're best interest's at heart, price will not matter nearly as much.

7. If I was you, I would of avoided investing in large conglomerates in light of the collapse of energy trader, Enron Corp., over accounting irregularities.

8. Outdoor goods retailer REI has had significant, success with in-store kiosks that let customers choose between several types of merchandise.

9. To people in some areas of cyberspace "Advertising" is a four letter word but "Marketing" is perfectly acceptable.

10. In any business effort, making money requires planning. Strategic marketing, a good product, good customer service, considerable shrewdness—and much hard work.

11. Investors must decide weather to put their capitol into bonds or CDs.

12. Running at full capacity, millions of Nike shoes are being produced by manufacturing plants every day.

13. Metropolis' stationary has a picture of the Empire state building on it.

14. Starbucks are planning to add fruit drinks to their menu in states throughout the south.

15. Credit ratings ain't what they used to be.

Level 3: Document Critique

The following document contains errors in grammar, punctuation, capitalization, abbreviation, number style, vocabulary, and spelling. You will also find errors related to topics in this chapter. For example, look for ways to improve long words and phrases, redundancies, dangling modifiers, camouflaged verbs, and problems with parallelism as you improve this memo. Correct all errors using standard proofreading marks (see Appendix C).

Memorandum

TO: Metro power Employees
FROM: Susannah Beech, Hr Administrator
SUBJECT: Ways to improve your response to technology failures
Date: 22 September 2009

Dear Metro Employees:

There is always a chance of racing toward a deadline and suddenly having equipment fall. The following includes a few proposed suggestions to help you stave off, and cope with, technical equipment and system failures:

- Stay cool. There are many technical failures so they are commonplace in business; and it is likely that your bosses and co-workers will understand that you're having a prolbem and why.

- Practice preventive maintenance: Use cleaning cloths and sprays regularly, liquids and foods should be kept away from keyboards and printers; and you should make sure systems are shut down when you leave at night.

- It is important for faster repair asistance to promptly report computer failures to Bart Stone assistant director of information services ext. 2238, who will get to your poblem as soon as it is humanly possible for him to do so but you must keep in mind that there are many people demanding his focused attention at any given time;

- If you suspect that a problem may be developing, don't wait until the crucial last moment to call for assistance.

- When a last-minute technical failure of equipment threatens to disrupt your composure you might want to consider taking a walk to calm down.

The last suggestion is perhaps the most important to keep your career on track. Lost tempers; taking out your feelings in violent outbursts, and rude language are threatening to co-workers and could result in a reprimand or other disciplinary action. By calling technical support lines for help, your equipment can stay in good working order and your temper will stay calm.

The timely implemention of repairs is important, so ask your supervisor for a list of support numbers to keep handy. Then, the next time you experience a technology giltch in your equipment or systems, there are going to be quite a few numbers handy for you to call to help you handle it as just another aspect of your business regeem.

Sincerely,

Susannah Beech

Human Resources administrator

Brief Business Messages

CHAPTER 6: Crafting Messages for Electronic Media

CHAPTER 7: Writing Routine and Positive Messages

CHAPTER 8: Writing Negative Messages

CHAPTER 9: Writing Persuasive Messages

Crafting Messages for Electronic Media

LEARNING OBJECTIVES

After studying this chapter, you will be able to

1. Compare the strengths and weaknesses of the print and electronic media available for short messages

2. Explain how business e-mail differs from personal e-mail and explain the importance of e-mail subject lines

3. Identify guidelines for effective instant messaging (IM) in the workplace

4. Explain the role of blogging in business communication

5. Explain how to adapt the three-step writing process for podcasts

6. Offer guidelines for becoming a valuable wiki contributor

[from the real world]

"I blogged. You flamed. We changed."
—Bill Owens,
Southwest Airlines employee and member of the Nuts About Southwest blogging team
www.blogsouthwest.com

When Bill Owens posted what he thought was a routine message about Southwest's reservation policies, the response from readers of the company's Nuts About Southwest blog was anything but routine. Hundreds of passengers left comments on the blog, many of them disappointed, frustrated, and even angry. As he wrote in a follow-up post, "Talk about sticking your head in a hornet's nest!" Management decisions that customers don't agree with are nothing new, of course. However, this online conversation between Southwest Airlines and its customers represents a revolutionary development in the history of business communication: the ability for customers and other audiences to quickly, easily, and publicly talk back to companies. Interactive communication can even pressure managers to make changes, as blog readers did in this instance.[1] As you'll read in this chapter, blogs are among several recent innovations that are changing the nature of business communication.

CHOOSING ELECTRONIC MEDIA FOR BRIEF MESSAGES

Today you have multiple options for sending short messages:
- E-mail messages
- Instant messages
- Text messages
- Blog postings
- Podcasts
- Wikis

Today's business communicators have a broad range of options for sending short messages (note that many of these media options are used for longer messages as well):

- **E-mail.** Thanks to its high speed and low cost, e-mail is now a primary medium for most companies. However, as technologies continue to evolve and users tire of fighting the flood of spam, viruses, and other problems related to e-mail, this medium is in turn being replaced in many instances by instant messaging, blogging, wikis, and other tools that provide better support for instant communication and real-time collaboration.

- **Instant messaging (IM).** IM usage now rivals e-mail in many companies. It offers even greater speed than e-mail as well as simple operation and—so far at least—fewer problems with unwanted messages.

- **Text messaging.** Phone-based text messaging is just beginning to make inroads into business communication, with marketing messages being one of the first applications.[2]

- **Blogs.** The ability to update content quickly and easily makes blogs a natural for communicators who need to get messages out in a hurry. Bloggers can publish information to vast audiences with relatively little effort.

- **Podcasts.** Podcasts, the online equivalent of recorded audio or video broadcasts, are starting to replace or supplement many conference calls, training courses, and other communication activities.
- **Wikis.** Wikis present the opportunity for rapid collaboration among geographically dispersed groups, making them ideal for today's flexible organization structures.

The wide reach and interactivity of electronic media are changing the very nature of businesses communication. As Chapter 1 notes, customers are no longer content to be passive listeners in a one-way process controlled by business. They now expect to be active participants in a real conversation—and not only with companies but with other customers. Blogs, "microblog" tools such as Twitter, podcasts, bookmarking and tagging sites (such as del.icio.us and Digg), photo- and video-sharing sites (such as Flickr and YouTube), wikis, and other electronic tools are considered **social media**, in which all participants can contribute to the conversation.[3] Social media are the centerpiece of **Web 2.0**, a label applied to technologies that promote interaction, audience involvement, and *user-generated content*—in contrast to the unidirectional publishing model of the first generation of websites.

With social media, audiences expect to participate in conversations, rather than being passive recipients of messages.

Although social media have reduced the amount of control that businesses have over the content and the process of communication,[4] today's smart companies are learning how to adapt their communication efforts to this new media landscape and to welcome customers' participation. Social media are also revolutionizing internal communication, breaking down traditional barriers in the organizational hierarchy, promoting the flow of information and ideas, and enabling "value networks" of companies to collaborate on a global scale.[5]

However, while most of your business communication is likely to be via electronic means, don't automatically dismiss the benefits of printed messages. Here are several situations in which you should use a printed message over electronic alternatives:

- When you want to make a formal impression
- When you are legally required to provide information in printed form
- When you want to stand out from the flood of electronic messages

Obviously, if you can't reach a particular audience electronically, you'll also need to use a printed message.

CREATING EFFECTIVE E-MAIL MESSAGES

Business e-mail is a more formal medium than you are probably accustomed to with e-mail for personal communication (see Figure 6.1). Consequently, it's important to approach e-mail as a professional communication medium and an important company resource.

Adapting the Three-Step Process for Successful E-Mail

The expectations of writing quality for business e-mail are higher than for personal e-mail, and the consequences of bad writing or poor judgment can be much more serious. For example, e-mail messages and other electronic documents have the same legal weight as printed documents, and they are often used as evidence in lawsuits and criminal investigations.[6] Other concerns include the possibility of disclosing confidential information and exposing company networks to security problems.

Business e-mail messages are more formal than the e-mail messages you send to family and friends.

Many companies now have formal e-mail policies that specify how employees can use e-mail, including restrictions against using company e-mail service for personal messages and sending material that might be deemed objectionable. In addition, many employers now monitor e-mail, either automatically with software programmed to look for sensitive content or manually via security staff actually reading selected e-mail messages. Roughly one-quarter of U.S. companies have fired employees for misuse of e-mail or the Internet.[7]

E-mail presents considerable legal hazards, and many companies have formal e-mail policies.

Regardless of formal policies, every e-mail user has a responsibility to avoid actions that could cause trouble, from downloading virus-infected software to sending objectionable

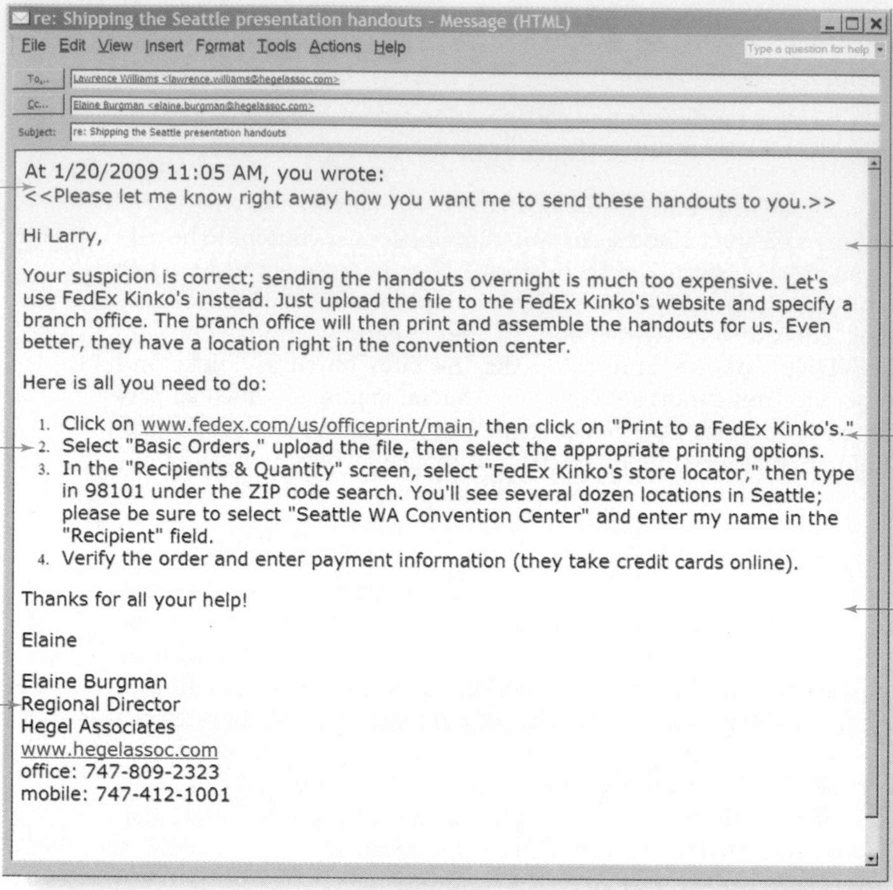

Includes enough of the original message to remind Williams why she is writing— but doesn't clutter the screen with the entire original message

Uses the numbered list feature to itemize the steps she wants Williams to follow

Uses the e-mail signature feature to include her contact information

Opens with an informal salutation appropriate for communication between colleagues

Includes the URL of the website she wants Williams to visit, so all he needs to do is click on the link

Ends with a warm complimentary close

re: Shipping the Seattle presentation handouts - Message (HTML)

File Edit View Insert Format Tools Actions Help

Type a question for help

To... | Lawrence Williams <lawrence.williams@hegelassoc.com>
Cc... | Elaine Burgman <elaine.burgman@hegelassoc.com>
Subject: | re: Shipping the Seattle presentation handouts

At 1/20/2009 11:05 AM, you wrote:
<<Please let me know right away how you want me to send these handouts to you.>>

Hi Larry,

Your suspicion is correct; sending the handouts overnight is much too expensive. Let's use FedEx Kinko's instead. Just upload the file to the FedEx Kinko's website and specify a branch office. The branch office will then print and assemble the handouts for us. Even better, they have a location right in the convention center.

Here is all you need to do:

1. Click on www.fedex.com/us/officeprint/main, then click on "Print to a FedEx Kinko's."
2. Select "Basic Orders," upload the file, then select the appropriate printing options.
3. In the "Recipients & Quantity" screen, select "FedEx Kinko's store locator," then type in 98101 under the ZIP code search. You'll see several dozen locations in Seattle; please be sure to select "Seattle WA Convention Center" and enter my name in the "Recipient" field.
4. Verify the order and enter payment information (they take credit cards online).

Thanks for all your help!

Elaine

Elaine Burgman
Regional Director
Hegel Associates
www.hegelassoc.com
office: 747-809-2323
mobile: 747-412-1001

Figure 6.1 E-Mail for Business Communication
In this response to an e-mail query from a colleague, Elaine Burgman takes advantage of her e-mail system's features to create an efficient and effective message.

photographs. *E-mail hygiene* refers to all the efforts that companies are making to keep e-mail clean and safe—from spam blocking and virus protection to content filtering.[8]

Planning E-Mail Messages

Attention to etiquette is vital with e-mail communication.

Because sending e-mail is so easy, it is often overused and misused. Many busy professionals now struggle to keep up with the flow of e-mail messages; some report receiving as many as 50 messages per hour from colleagues and clients.[9] The flood of messages from an expanding array of electronic sources can significantly affect employees' ability to focus on their work. In one recent study, in fact, workers exposed to a constant barrage of e-mail, IM, and phone calls experienced an average 10-point drop in their functioning IQ.[10] You can help keep electronic messages from causing problems in your organization by following the tips in Table 6.1.

Do your part to stem the flood of e-mail by making sure you don't send unnecessary messages or cc people who don't really need to see particular messages.

When analyzing the audience for your e-mail messages, think twice before sending copies to multiple recipients with the *cc* (courtesy copy) function. Let's say you send a message to your boss and cc five colleagues simply because you want them to see that you're giving the boss some good information. Those five people now not only have to read your message but might also feel compelled to reply so that the boss doesn't think they're being negligent. Then everyone will start replying to *those* replies, and on and on. What should have been a single message exchange between you and your boss quickly turns into a flurry of messages that wastes everybody's time.

Finally, be sure to respect the chain of command. In many companies, any employee can e-mail anyone else, including the president and CEO. However, take care that you don't abuse this freedom. For instance, don't send an e-mail complaint straight to the top just because it's easy to do so. Your e-mail will usually be more effective if you follow the organizational hierarchy and give each person a chance to address the situation in turn.

TABLE 6.1   Tips for Effective E-Mail Messages

Tip	Why It's Important
When you request information or action, make it clear what you're asking for, why it's important, and how soon you need it; don't make your reader write back for details.	People will be tempted to ignore your messages if they're not clear about what you want or how soon you want it.
When responding to a request, either paraphrase the request or include enough of the original message to remind the reader what you're replying to.	Some businesspeople get hundreds of e-mail messages per day and may need to be reminded what your specific response is about.
If possible, avoid sending long, complex messages via e-mail.	Long messages are easier to read as attached reports or web content.
Adjust the level of formality to the message and the audience.	Overly formal messages to colleagues can be perceived as stuffy and distant; overly informal messages to customers or top executives can be perceived as disrespectful.
Activate a signature file, which automatically pastes your contact information into every message you create.	A signature file saves you the trouble of retyping vital information and ensures that recipients know how to reach you through other means.
Don't let unread messages pile up in your in-basket.	You'll miss important information and create the impression that you're ignoring other people.
Never type in all caps.	ALL CAPS ARE INTERPRETED AS SCREAMING.
Don't overformat your messages with background colors, multicolored type, unusual fonts, and so on.	Such messages can be difficult and annoying to read on-screen.
Remember that messages can be forwarded anywhere and saved forever.	A moment of anger or poor judgment could haunt you for the rest of your career.
Use the "return receipt requested" feature only for the most critical messages.	This feature triggers a message back to you whenever someone receives or opens your message; many consider this an invasion of privacy.
Make sure your computer has up-to-date virus protection.	One of the worst breaches of "netiquette" is infecting other computers because you haven't bothered to protect your own system.
Pay attention to grammar, spelling, and capitalization.	Some people don't think e-mail needs formal rules, but careless messages make you look unprofessional and can annoy readers.
Use acronyms sparingly.	Shorthand such as *IMHO* ("in my humble opinion") and *LOL* ("laughing out loud") can be useful in informal correspondence with colleagues, but don't use them in other messages.

Writing E-Mail Messages

The casual style you're no doubt accustomed to for personal e-mail is inappropriate for most business communication. The time you might save with a careless approach won't make up for the damage it can do to your career.[11] First, haphazard planning and sloppy writing may require less time for writers, but they usually demand *more* time from readers. Second, people who care about effective communication—a group that includes the managers and executives who decide whether you'll get promoted and how much you'll get paid—often judge the quality of your *work* by the quality of your *writing*.

Writing Effective Subject Lines   The subject line is one of the most important parts of every e-mail message because it helps recipients decide which messages to read and when to read them. To capture your audience's attention, make sure your subject line is informative

A poorly written subject line could lead to a message being deleted or ignored.

and compelling. Go beyond simply describing or classifying your message; use the opportunity to build interest with keywords, quotations, directions, or questions:[12]

Instead of This	Write This
July sales results	July sales results: good news and bad news
Tomorrow's meeting	Be ready for some tough questions at Friday's meeting
Marketing reports	Marketing reports are due Monday morning
Status report	Website redesign is falling behind schedule

For example, "July sales results" accurately describes the content of the message, but "July sales results: good news and bad news" is more intriguing. Readers will want to know why some news is good and some is bad.

Also, if you and someone else are replying back and forth based on the same original message, it's a good idea to periodically modify the subject line of your message to reflect the revised message content. When numerous messages have identical subject lines, trying to find a particular one can be confusing and frustrating.

Keeping Your Emotions Under Control   Given the spontaneous nature of e-mail (and other electronic media), you will sometimes need to work hard to keep your emotions from getting the best of you when you're writing. A message that contains insensitive, insulting, or critical comments is called a *flame*. If you're angry, walk away from your computer and calm down before firing off an e-mail message. Ask yourself two questions: First, "Would I say this to my audience face to face?" And second, "Am I comfortable with this message becoming a permanent part of the company's communication history?"

Because e-mail messages (and other lean media) lack the ability to convey nuances, they raise the risk of miscommunication and unnecessary conflict.[13] Whenever you feel angry or just confused by something you've read in an e-mail message, consider picking up the phone to clarify the situation. A brief conversation can often prevent or repair frayed nerves.

> Keep your emotions in check when you compose e-mail messages; *flaming* can damage relationships—and your reputation.

Completing E-Mail Messages

Particularly for important messages, taking a few moments to revise and proofread might save you hours of headaches and damage control. Also, lean in favor of simplicity when it comes to producing your e-mail messages. A clean, easily readable font, in black on a white background, is sufficient for nearly all e-mail messages. Take advantage of your e-mail system's ability to include an **e-mail signature**, a small file that automatically includes such items as your full name, title, company, and contact information at the end of your messages.

When you're ready to distribute your message, pause to verify what you're doing before you click Send. Make sure you've included everyone necessary—and no one else. Did you click Reply All when you meant to click only Reply? The difference could be embarrassing or even career threatening. Don't include people in the cc (courtesy copy) or bcc (blind courtesy copy) fields unless you know how these features work. (Everyone who receives the message can see who is on the cc line but not who is on the bcc line.) Also, don't set the message priority to "high" or "urgent" unless your message is truly urgent.

For the latest information on using e-mail in business, visit http://real-timeupdates .com/bce and click on Chapter 6.

CREATING EFFECTIVE INSTANT MESSAGES AND TEXT MESSAGES

> IM is taking the place of e-mail for routine communication in many companies.

While e-mail is here to stay as a business medium, its disadvantages—including viruses, spam, and rampant overuse—are driving many people to explore alternatives.[14] One of the most important of those alternatives is **instant messaging (IM)**. For both routine communication and exchanges during online meetings, IM is now widely used throughout the business world and is beginning to overtake and even replace e-mail for internal communication in many companies.[15] Business-grade IM systems offer a range of capabilities, including basic chat, *presence awareness* (the ability to quickly see which people are at their desks and available to IM), remote display of documents, video capabilities, remote control of other computers, automated newsfeeds from blogs and websites, and automated bot capabilities.[16]

Text messaging is beginning to find applications in business as well. Although both IM and text messaging perform the similar function of nearly instantaneous communication between devices, IM is primarily a computer-based technology, whereas text messaging is primarily a phone-based technology. (Of course, as often happens, continuing innovation blurs the lines between technologies, and now you can send a text message to a phone from your computer and so on.) Text messaging has long been popular in other parts of the world, where it is often referred to as *short messaging service (SMS)*, and phones have had texting capability for years. With text messaging now well entrenched among young consumers in North America, expanded business applications are likely to follow. In addition to person-to-person communication between colleagues, text messaging is taking off in such areas as marketing (responding to product information requests, for example) and entertainment (for example, letting viewers predict the outcome of sporting events or place votes on reality television programs).[17]

Because IM is currently more versatile and more widely used in business than text messaging, the following sections focus on IM. However, as text messaging evolves along with wireless devices and networking, you can expect that many of the benefits, risks, and guidelines that pertain to IM will eventually pertain to text messaging as well.

> Phone-based text messaging is fast and portable but not as versatile as computer-based IM.

Understanding the Benefits and Risks of IM

The benefits of IM include its capability for rapid response to urgent messages, lower cost than phone calls and e-mail, ability to mimic conversation more closely than e-mail, and availability on a wide range of devices, from PCs to mobile phones to PDAs.[18] In addition, unlike email, IM can't get misused as a broadcast method ("blasting" messages to dozens, hundreds, or thousands of recipients at once).[19]

Of course, wherever technology goes, trouble seems to follow. The potential drawbacks of IM include security problems (the risks of computer viruses and the worry that sensitive messages might be intercepted by outsiders), the need for *user authentication* (making sure that online correspondents are really who they appear to be), the challenge of logging messages for later review and archiving, and incompatibility between competing IM systems. Fortunately, with the growth of *enterprise instant messaging (EIM)*, IM systems designed for large-scale corporate use, many of these problems are being overcome. Security remains an ongoing concern, however, with attacks on IM systems, both public and corporate, continuing to rise.[20] A new breed of virus spread by bots is a particular concern. IM users who fall prey to these bots believe they are chatting with a trusted correspondent when in fact they are exchanging information with an automated bot that imitates human IM chat. The bot encourages the user to download a file or otherwise expose his or her computer to malicious software and then spreads the virus through the user's IM address book.[21]

> IM offers many benefits:
> - Rapid response
> - Low cost
> - Ability to mimic conversation
> - Wide availability

Adapting the Three-Step Process for Successful IM

Although instant messages are often conceived, written, and sent within a matter of seconds, the principles of the three-step process still apply:

- **Planning instant messages.** Except for simple exchanges, take a moment to plan IM "conversations" in much the same way you would plan an important conversation. A few seconds of planning can help you deliver information in a coherent, complete way that minimizes the number of individual messages required.

- **Writing instant messages.** As with e-mail, the appropriate writing style for business IM is more formal than the style you may be accustomed to with personal IM or text

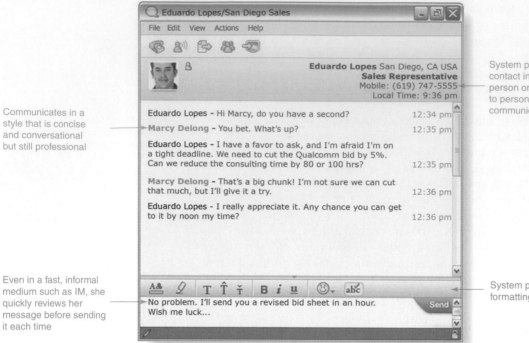

Communicates in a style that is concise and conversational but still professional

System provides position and contact information and a photo of the person on the other end, which helps to personalize this purely electronic communication

Even in a fast, informal medium such as IM, she quickly reviews her message before sending it each time

System provides simple formatting tools and a spell checker

Figure 6.2 Instant Messaging for Business Communication
Instant messaging is widely used in business, but you should not use the same informal style of communication you probably use for IM with your friends and family.

messaging (see Figure 6.2). Find out if your company discourages the use of IM acronyms (such as *FWIW* for "for what it's worth" or *HTH* for "hope that helps").

- **Completing instant messages.** The only task in the completing stage is to send your message. Just quickly scan it before sending, to make sure you don't have any missing or misspelled words and verify that your message is clear and complete.

When using IM, be aware of the potential for constant interruptions and wasted time.

To use IM effectively, keep in mind some important behavioral issues: the potential for constant interruptions, the ease of accidentally mixing personal and business messages, the risk of being out of the loop (if a hot discussion or an impromptu meeting flares up when you're away from your PC or other IM device), and the "vast potential for wasted time" (in the words of MIT labor economist David Autor). On top of all that, users are at the mercy of other people's typing abilities, which can make IM agonizingly slow.[22]

Understand the guidelines for successful business IM before you begin to use it.

Regardless of the system you're using, you can make IM more efficient and effective by heeding these tips:[23]

- Avoid the temptation to use IM just because you're bored; make sure you have a purpose before you IM anyone.

- Unless a meeting is scheduled, make yourself unavailable for IM when you need to focus on other work.

- If you're not on a secure system, don't send confidential information.

- Be extremely careful about sending personal messages—and don't send them at all if your company's policy forbids them.

- Unless your system is set up for it, don't use IM for lengthy, complex messages; e-mail is better for those.

- Whenever possible, avoid carrying on multiple IM conversations at once.

- If your IM system has filters for *spim*, the IM version of e-mail spam, make sure they're active and up to date.[24]

For the latest information on using IM in business, visit http://real-timeupdates.com/bce and click on Chapter 6.

CREATING EFFECTIVE BUSINESS BLOGS

A **blog** (short for *web log*) is an online journal that is much easier to personalize and update than a conventional website. In a sense, a blog combines the global reach and reference value of a conventional website with the conversational exchanges of e-mail or IM. Good business blogs pay close attention to several important elements:

Blogs have a unique ability to encourage interaction with a large, geographically dispersed audience.

- **Communicating with personal style and an authentic voice.** Most business messages designed for large audiences are carefully scripted and written in a "corporate voice" that is impersonal and objective. In contrast, successful business blogs are written by individuals and exhibit their personal style. Audiences relate to this fresh approach and often build closer emotional bonds with the blogger's organization as a result. For instance, Microsoft's Channel 9 video blog, or *vlog* (http://channel9.msdn.com), features informal, personable video clips in which several of the company's technical experts answer questions and criticisms from software developers.[25]

- **Delivering new information quickly.** Today's blogging tools let you post new material within minutes of writing it or filming it. Not only does this feature allow you to respond quickly when needed—such as during a corporate crisis—it also lets your audiences know that an active conversation is taking place. Blogs that don't offer a continuous stream of new and interesting content are quickly ignored in today's online environment.

- **Choosing topics of peak interest to audiences.** Successful blogs cover topics that readers care about. For instance, General Motors's popular FastLane blog (http://fastlane.gmblogs.com) features top executives writing about GM cars and responding to questions and criticisms from car enthusiasts. The people who read the blog and write comments obviously care about cars and want the latest information from GM.[26]

- **Encouraging audiences to join the conversation.** Not all blogs invite comments, although most do, and many bloggers consider comments to be an essential feature. Blog comments can be a valuable source of news, information, and insights. In addition, the relatively informal nature of blogging seems to make it easier for companies to let their guard down and converse with their audiences. To guard against comments that are not helpful or appropriate, many bloggers review all comments and post only the most helpful or interesting ones.

Most business blogs invite readers to leave comments.

Understanding the Business Applications of Blogging

Blogs are a potential solution whenever you have a continuing stream of information to share with an online audience—and particularly when you want the audience to have the opportunity to respond. Here are some of the many ways businesses are using blogs:[27]

The business applications of blogs include a wide range of internal and external communication tasks.

- **Project management and team communication.** Using blogs is a good way to keep project teams up to date, particularly when team members are geographically dispersed. For instance, the trip reports that employees file after visiting customers or other external parties can be enhanced vividly with *mobile blogs*, or *moblogs*.

- **Company news.** Companies can use blogs to keep employees informed about general business matters, from facility news to benefit updates. Blogs also serve as online community forums, giving everyone in the company a chance to raise questions and voice concerns.

- **Customer support.** Building on the tradition of online customer support forums that have been around since the earliest days of the Internet, customer support blogs answer questions, offers tips and advice, and inform customers about new products.

- **Public relations and media relations.** Many company employees and executives now share company news with both the general public and journalists via their blogs. Wal-Mart encourages employees to share candid opinions with the public, even when those opinions are negative comments on products the company sells.[28]

- **Recruiting.** Using a blog is a great way to let potential employees know more about your company, the people who work there, and the nature of the company culture.

- **Policy and issue discussions.** Executive blogs in particular provide a public forum for discussing legislation, regulations, and other broad issues of interest to an organization.

- **Crisis communication.** Using blogs is a convenient way to provide up-to-the-minute information during emergencies, correct misinformation, or respond to rumors.

- **Market research.** In addition to using their own blogs to solicit feedback, today's companies should monitor blogs that are likely to discuss them, their executives, and their products. *Reputation analysts* such as Evolve24 (www.evolve24.com) have developed ways to automatically monitor blogs and other online sources to see what people are saying about their corporate clients.[29]

- **Brainstorming.** Online brainstorming via blogs offers a way for people to toss around ideas and build on each others' contributions.

- **Employee engagement.** Blogs can enhance communication across all levels of a company. For example, as part of a program to align its corporate culture with changes in the global beverage market, Coca-Cola solicited feedback via blog comments from more than 20,000 employees.[30]

- **Viral marketing.** Bloggers often make a point of providing links to other blogs and websites that interest them, giving marketers a great opportunity to have their messages spread. *Viral marketing* refers to the transmission of messages in much the same way that biological viruses are transmitted from person to person.

> Blogs are an ideal medium for viral marketing, the organic spread of product-related messages from one audience member to another.

- **E-mail replacement.** Many companies have switched from e-mail to blogs as a more convenient way to distribute information to customers and other audiences. Using *newsfeeds* from a company's blog, audiences can subscribe to categories of information that interest them. These messages are then delivered via an *aggregator*, bypassing the increasingly clogged e-mail channel.

The uses of blogs are limited only by your creativity, so be on the lookout for new ways you can use them to foster positive relationships with colleagues, customers, and other important audiences (see Figure 6.3).

Adapting the Three-Step Process for Successful Blogging

The three-step writing process is easy to adapt to blogging tasks. The planning step is particularly important if you're considering starting a blog because you're planning an entire communication channel, not just a single message. Pay close attention to your audience, your purpose, and your scope:

> Before you launch a blog, make sure you have a clear understanding of your target audience, the purpose of your blog, and the scope of subjects you plan to cover.

- **Audience.** Except with team blogs and other efforts that have an obvious and well-defined audience, defining your target audience can be challenging. You want an audience large enough to justify the time you'll be investing but narrow enough that you can provide a clear focus for the blog. For instance, if you work for a firm that develops computer games, would you focus your blog on "hardcore" players, the type who spend thousands of dollars on super-fast PCs optimized for video games, or would you broaden the reach to include all video gamers? The decision often comes down to business strategy.

- **Purpose.** A business blog needs to have a business-related purpose that is important to your company and to your chosen audience. Moreover, the purpose has to "have legs"—that is, it needs to be something that can drive the blog's content for months or years—rather than focus on a single event or an issue of only temporary

The headline and tagline combine to clearly indicate the source and the nature of this blog

Postings can be either complete articles or introductions that have links to the complete pieces

Postings are accompanied by a line that indicates who posted the material and when; most blogs also allow visitors to comment on posts

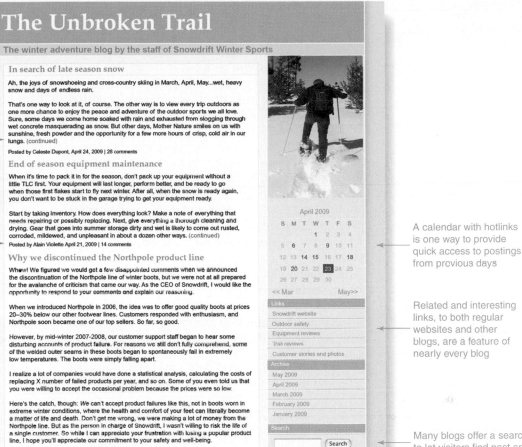

The Unbroken Trail

The winter adventure blog by the staff of Snowdrift Winter Sports

In search of late season snow

Ah, the joys of snowshoeing and cross-country skiing in March, April, May...wet, heavy snow and days of endless rain.

That's one way to look at it, of course. The other way is to view every trip outdoors as one more chance to enjoy the peace and adventure of the outdoor sports we all love. Sure, some days we come home soaked with rain and exhausted from slogging through wet concrete masquerading as snow. But other days, Mother Nature smiles on us with sunshine, fresh powder and the opportunity for a few more hours of crisp, cold air in our lungs. (continued)

Posted by Celeste Dupont, April 24, 2009 | 28 comments

End of season equipment maintenance

When it's time to pack it in for the season, don't pack up your equipment without a little TLC first. Your equipment will last longer, perform better, and be ready to go when those first flakes start to fly next winter. After all, when the snow is ready again, you don't want to be stuck in the garage trying to get your equipment ready.

Start by taking inventory. How does everything look? Make a note of everything that needs repairing or possibly replacing. Next, give everything a thorough cleaning and drying. Gear that goes into summer storage dirty and wet is likely to come out rusted, corroded, mildewed, and unpleasant in about a dozen other ways. (continued)

Posted by Alain Violette April 21, 2009 | 14 comments

Why we discontinued the Northpole product line

Whew! We figured we would get a few disappointed comments when we announced the discontinuation of the Northpole line of winter boots, but we were not at all prepared for the avalanche of criticism that came our way. As the CEO of Snowdrift, I would like the opportunity to respond to your comments and explain our reasoning.

When we introduced Northpole in 2006, the idea was to offer good quality boots at prices 20–30% below our other footwear lines. Customers responded with enthusiasm, and Northpole soon became one of our top sellers. So far, so good.

However, by mid-winter 2007-2008, our customer support staff began to hear some disturbing accounts of product failure. For reasons we still don't fully comprehend, some of the welded outer seams in these boots began to spontaneously fail in extremely low temperatures. The boots were simply falling apart.

I realize a lot of companies would have done a statistical analysis, calculating the costs of replacing X number of failed products per year, and so on. Some of you even told us that you were willing to accept the occasional problem because the prices were so low.

Here's the catch, though: *We* can't accept product failures like this, not in boots worn in extreme winter conditions, where the health and comfort of your feet can literally become a matter of life and death. Don't get me wrong, we were making a lot of money from the Northpole line. But as the person in charge of Snowdrift, I wasn't willing to risk the life of a single customer. So while I can appreciate your frustration with losing a popular product line, I hope you'll appreciate our commitment to your safety and well-being.

Posted by Joel Canyard, April 18, 2009 | 156 comments

April 2009

S	M	T	W	T	F	S
			1	2	3	4
5	6	7	8	9	10	11
12	13	14	15	16	17	18
19	20	21	22	23	24	25
26	27	28	29	30		

<< Mar   May>>

Links
Snowdrift website
Outdoor safety
Equipment reviews
Trail reviews
Customer stories and photos

Archive
May 2009
April 2009
March 2009
February 2009
January 2009

Search
[   ] [Search]

Subscribe
[XML]

A calendar with hotlinks is one way to provide quick access to postings from previous days

Related and interesting links, to both regular websites and other blogs, are a feature of nearly every blog

Many blogs offer a search box to let visitors find past articles

Most blogs provide one or more ways for readers to subscribe via a newsfeed

Figure 6.3 Elements of an Effective Business Blog
Blogs exist in many forms and formats, but visitors expect a few basic elements, such as access to archives, links to related information, and a convenient way to subscribe to an automatic newsfeed. Note the style and tone of the writing in this blog; it is far more engaging and conversational than the traditional "corporate voice." Moreover, it is about the *customers*, not the *company*.

interest. For instance, if you're a technical expert, you might create a blog to give the audience tips and techniques for using your company's products more effectively—a never-ending subject that's important to both you and your audience. This would be the general purpose of your blog; each posting would have a specific purpose within the context of that general purpose. Finally, if you are not writing an official company blog but rather blogging as an individual employee, make sure you understand your employer's blogging guidelines. As with e-mail and IM, more and more companies are putting policies in place to prevent employee mistakes with blogging.[31]

- **Scope.** Defining the scope of your blog can be a bit tricky. You want to cover a subject area that is broad enough to offer discussion possibilities for months or years but narrow enough to have an identifiable focus. For instance, GM's FastLane blog is about GM cars only—not GM's stock price, labor negotiations, and so on.

After you begin writing your blog, the careful planning needs to continue with each message. Unless you're posting to a restricted-access blog, such as an internal blog on a company intranet, you can never be sure who might see your posts. Other bloggers might link to them months or years later.

Write blog postings in a comfortable—but not careless—style.

Write in a comfortable, personal style. Blog audiences don't want to hear from your company; they want to hear from *you*. Bear in mind, though, that *comfortable* does not mean *careless*. Sloppy writing damages your credibility. Successful blog content also needs to be interesting, valuable to readers, and as brief as possible.[32] In addition, while audiences expect you to be knowledgeable in the subject area your blog covers, you don't need to know everything about a topic. If you don't have all the information yourself, provide links to other blogs and websites that supply relevant information. In fact, many blog audiences consider carefully screened links to be an essential part of blogging.

Completing messages for your blog is usually quite easy. Evaluate the content and readability of your message, proofread to correct any errors, and post using your blogging system's tools for doing so. Be sure to include one or more *newsfeed* options (often called *RSS newsfeeds*) so that your audience can automatically receive headlines and summaries of new blog posts. Whatever blogging system you are using can provide guidance on setting up newsfeeds. Finally, make your material easier to find by **tagging** it with descriptive words. Visitors to your blog who want to read everything you've written about recruiting just click on that word to see all your posts on that subject. Tagging can also help audiences locate your posts on blog trackers such as Technorati (http://technorati.com) or on **social bookmarking** or *social news* sites such as Delicious (http://delicious.com) and Digg (www.digg.com).

Table 6.2 summarizes a number of suggestions for successful blogging. For the latest information on using blogs in business, visit http://real-timeupdates.com/bce and click on Chapter 6.

CREATING EFFECTIVE PODCASTS

Podcasting can be used to deliver a wide range of audio and video messages.

Podcasting offers a number of interesting possibilities for business communication. Its most obvious use is to replace existing audio and video messages, such as one-way teleconferences in which a speaker provides information without expecting to engage in conversation with the listeners. Training is another good use of podcasting. One of the first podcasts recorded by technical experts at IBM gave other employees advice on setting up blogs, for example.[33] Sales representatives who travel to meet with potential customers can listen to audio podcasts or view video podcasts to get the latest information on their companies' products. Podcasts are also an increasingly common feature on blogs, letting audiences listen to or watch recordings of their favorite bloggers. New services can even transcribe blogs into podcasts and vice versa.[34]

As more businesspeople become comfortable with podcasting, it should find applications in a variety of new areas, wherever audio or video content can convey business messages effectively. For instance, real estate agents can record audio podcasts that potential homebuyers can listen to while walking through houses. Marketing departments can replace expensive printed brochures with video podcasts that demonstrate new products in action. Human resources departments can offer video tours of their companies to entice new recruits.

Adapting the Three-Step Process for Successful Podcasting

Steering devices such as transitions, previews, and reviews are vital in podcasts.

Although it might not seem obvious at first, the three-step writing process adapts quite nicely to podcasting. First, focus the planning step on analyzing the situation, gathering the information you'll need, and organizing your material. One vital planning step depends on whether you intend to create podcasts for limited use and distribution (such as a weekly audio update to your virtual team) or to create a *podcasting channel* with regular recordings on a consistent theme, designed for a wider public audience. As with planning a blog, if you intend to create a podcasting channel, be sure to think

TABLE 6.2 Tips for Effective Business Blogging

Tip	Why It's Important
Don't blog without a clear plan.	Without a clear plan, your blog is likely to wander from topic to topic and fail to build a sense of community with your audience.
Post frequently; the whole point of a blog is fresh material.	If you won't have a constant supply of new information or new links, create a traditional website instead.
Make it about your audience and the issues that are important to them.	Readers want to know how your blog will help them, entertain them, or give them a chance to communicate with others who have similar interests.
Write in an authentic voice; never create an artificial character who supposedly writes a blog.	*Flogs*, or fake blogs, violate the spirit of blogging, show disrespect for your audience, and will turn audiences against you as soon as they uncover the truth.
Link generously—but carefully.	Providing interesting links to other blogs and websites is a fundamental aspect of blogging, but make sure the links will be of value to your readers and don't point to inappropriate material.
Keep it brief.	Most online readers don't have the patience to read lengthy reports.
Don't post anything you wouldn't want the entire world to see.	Future employers, government regulators, competitors, journalists, and community critics are just a few of the people who might eventually see what you've written.
Don't engage in blatant product promotion.	Readers who think they're being advertised to will stop reading.
Take time to write compelling, specific headlines for your postings.	Readers usually decide within a couple seconds whether to read your postings; boring or vague headlines will turn them away instantly.
Pay attention to spelling, grammar, and mechanics.	No matter how smart or experienced you are, poor-quality writing undermines your credibility with intelligent audiences.
Respond to criticism openly and honestly.	Hiding sends the message that you don't have a valid response to the criticism. If your critics are wrong, patiently explain why you think they're wrong. If they are right, explain how you'll fix the situation.
Listen and learn.	If you don't take the time to analyze the comments people leave on your blog or the comments other bloggers make about you, you're missing out on one of the most valuable aspects of blogging.
Respect intellectual property.	You not only have an ethical obligation to not use material you don't own, doing so can also violate copyright laws.
Be scrupulously honest and careful with facts.	Honesty is an absolute requirement for every ethical business communicator, of course, but you need to be extra careful online because inaccuracies (both intentional and unintentional) are likely to be discovered quickly and shared widely.

through the range of topics you want to address over time to verify that you have a sustainable purpose. If you bounce from one theme to another, you risk losing your audience.[35]

As you organize and begin to think about the words or images you'll use as content, pay close attention to previews, transitions, and reviews. These steering devices are especially vital in audio and video recordings because these formats lack the "street signs" (such as headings) that audiences rely on in print media. Moreover, scanning back and forth to find specific parts of an audio or video message is much more difficult than with textual messages, so you need to do everything possible to make sure your audience successfully receives and interprets your message on the first try.

One of the attractions of podcasting is the conversational, person-to-person feel of the recordings, so unless you need to capture exact wording, speaking from an outline and notes rather than a prepared script is often the best choice. However, no one wants to listen

Generous use of previews, transitions, and reviews helps podcast audiences follow the thread of your recording.

Figure 6.4 The Podcasting Process
Creating a podcast requires a few easy steps, and basic podcasts can be created using free or low-cost hardware and software.

to rambling podcasts that struggle to make a point, so don't try to make up your content on the fly. Effective podcasts, like effective stories, have a clear beginning, middle, and end.

Plan your podcast content carefully; editing is more difficult with podcasts than with textual messages.

In the completing step, keep in mind that editing podcasts is more difficult and more time consuming than editing textual media. Take extra care to revise your script or think through your speaking notes before you begin to record. The closer you can get to recording your podcasts in one take, the more productive you'll be. When each recording is ready, use your system's tools to prepare the audio file and publish it via a newsfeed.

Finally, consider integrating your podcasting efforts with a related blog. Not only can you provide additional information, you can also use the commenting feature of the blog to encourage feedback from your audience.[36]

Assembling a Podcasting System

For basic podcasts, your computer probably has most of the hardware you already need, and you can download recording software.

The equipment needed to record podcasts depends on the degree of production quality you want to achieve. For basic podcasts, such as those you might record for internal audiences, most contemporary personal computers probably have the equipment you need: a low-cost microphone (most laptop computers now have built-in microphones), a sound card to convert the microphone signal to digital format (most computers have them now), and some recording software (free versions are available online). Many handheld digital recorders can also record audio files that you can upload to a PC for editing and distribution.

However, a basic system might not deliver the audio quality or production flexibility you need for a public podcast. For instance, the microphone built into your laptop can't reproduce sound nearly as well as a professional-quality microphone can; and because it's physically located on the computer, the built-in microphone will pick up the noise from the computer's fan. Similarly, the low-cost sound cards built into many computers can add a significant amount of noise to your signal.[37]

For higher-quality podcasts, you'll probably need additional hardware and software.

If you need higher production quality or greater flexibility, you'll need additional pieces of hardware and software, such as an audio processor (to filter out extraneous noise and otherwise improve the audio signal), a mixer (to combine multiple audio or video signals), a better microphone, and more sophisticated recording and editing software (see Figure 6.4). You may also need to improve the acoustics of the room in which you are recording, to minimize echoes, noise, and other problems. To learn more about the technical requirements of podcasting, pick up one of the many new books on the subject. Some of them even come with free recording software.[38]

For the latest information on using podcasts in business, visit http://real-timeupdates.com/bce and click on Chapter 6.

COLLABORATING ON WIKIS

Wikis enable collaboration on writing projects ranging from brief articles to long reports and reference works.

As Chapter 2 points out, using wikis is a great way for teams and other groups to collaborate on writing projects, from brief articles to long reports and reference works. Unlike typical websites, wikis don't require contributors to have much technical expertise in order to create or edit content. Wikis also provide the opportunity to post new or revised material without prior approval. This approach is quite different from a *web content management system*, in which both the organization of the website and the *workflow* (the rules for creating, editing, reviewing, and approving content) are tightly controlled.[39]

Understanding the Wiki Philosophy

The benefits of wikis are compelling, but they do require a unique approach to writing. To be a valuable wiki contributor, keep these points in mind:[40]

- Writers need to let go of traditional expectations of authorship, including individual recognition and control. The value of a wiki stems from the collective insight of all its contributors.
- Team members sometimes need to be encouraged to edit and improve each other's work.
- Using page templates and other formatting options can help you ensure that your content fits the same style as the rest of the wiki.
- Many wikis provide both editing and commenting capabilities, and participants should use the appropriate tool for each. In other words, don't insert comments or questions into the main content; use the "talk page" or other commenting feature if you want to discuss the content.
- New users should take advantage of the *sandbox*, if available; this is a "safe," nonpublished section of the wiki where team members can practice editing and writing.

Wikis usually have guidelines to help new contributors integrate their work into the group's ongoing effort. Be sure to read and understand these guidelines, and don't be afraid to ask for help.

Understand the unique philosophy of wiki collaboration before you add or modify content on a wiki.

Adapting the Three-Step Process for Successful Wiki Writing

You can easily adapt the three-step writing process for wikis, depending on whether you are creating a new wiki, adding new material to an existing wiki, or revising existing material on a wiki.

If you are creating a new wiki, think through your long-term purpose carefully, just as you would with a new blog or podcast channel. Will the wiki be a one-time event (creating a report, for example) or an ongoing effort (such as maintaining "help" files for a software program)? Who will be allowed to add or modify content? Will you or someone else serve as editor, reviewing all additions and changes? What rules and guidelines will you establish to guide the growth of the wiki? What security measures might be required? For instance, the PlayStation development team at Sony uses a wiki to keep top managers up to date on new products, and because this information is highly confidential, access to the wiki is tightly controlled.[41]

If you are adding a page or an article to an existing wiki, figure out how this new material fits in with the existing structure of the wiki. Find out if any similar material already exists; it might be better to expand an existing article or add a subpage than to create a new item. Also, learn the wiki's preferred style for handling incomplete articles. For example, on the wiki that contains the user documentation for the popular WordPress blogging software, contributors are discouraged from adding new pages until the content is "fairly complete and accurate." Writers are instead encouraged to insert incomplete pages (usually called "stubs" in wiki parlance) and rough drafts under their personal pages until they are ready to be added to the main wiki content.[42]

If you are revising or updating an existing wiki article, use the checklist on page 99 in Chapter 5 to evaluate the content before you make changes. If you don't agree with published content and plan to revise it, you can use the wiki's discussion facility to share your concerns with other contributors. A well-run wiki encourages discussions and even robust disagreements, as long as everyone remains civil and respectful. If two or more contributors get into an "edit war," an editor may need to step in to resolve the conflict.[43]

For the latest information on using wikis in business, visit http://real-timeupdates.com/bce and click on Chapter 6.

The three-step writing process works well with wikis, whether you're creating a wiki, adding content, or revising existing content.

DOCUMENT MAKEOVER

Improve This Blog

To practice correcting drafts of actual documents, visit the "Document Makeovers" section in either MyBCommLab.com or the Companion Website for this text.

If MyBCommLab.com is being used in your class, see your User Guide for specific instructions on how to access the content for this chapter.

If you are accessing this feature through the Companion Website, click on "Document Makeovers" and then select Chapter 6. You will find a blog posting that contains problems and errors related to what you've learned in this chapter about writing for electronic media. Use the Final Draft decision tool to create an improved version of this posting. ●

" CHAPTER REVIEW AND ACTIVITIES

Chapter Summary

The media options for sending short messages each have advantages and disadvantages. Printed memos and letters offer a degree of formality that is sometimes difficult to achieve with electronic media, but they lack the speed, richness, and convenience of electronic media. E-mail offers high speed, low cost, and widespread availability, but it suffers from overuse and a variety of spam, security, and privacy problems. Computer-based instant messaging is even faster than e-mail, is simple to use, and hasn't yet accumulated problems with spam, security, and privacy to the same degree that e-mail has. Phone-based text messaging offers high speed and portability, but it can't yet perform the wide array of functions now available in business-grade IM. Blogging offers a fast, simple way to publish information online and to reach wide audiences. Blogging's biggest downside is competition from the millions of other blogs on the Internet. Podcasts offer a simple way for anyone to broadcast audio or video messages. However, they require more work to create than blogs, and high-quality podcasts require some additional recording equipment. Wikis make it easy for teams and other groups to collaborate across time and distance. Their primary disadvantage is a lack of editorial control, but wiki administrators can limit access to help ensure quality content.

Business e-mail differs from personal e-mail in two important respects: First, the expectations of writing quality and formality are higher, and second, from a legal perspective, business e-mail messages need to be given the same respect as printed business documents. The wording of an e-mail message's subject line often determines when—and whether—recipients open and read the message. Effective subject lines are both informative (concisely identifying what the message is about) and compelling (giving readers a reason to read the message).

As with e-mail, business IM needs to be treated as a professional medium to ensure safe and effective communication. Make yourself unavailable when you need to focus on other work, refrain from sending confidential information if you're not on a secure system, refrain from sending personal messages at work, avoid using IM for lengthy and complex messages, avoid carrying on multiple IM conversations at once, avoid IM slang with anyone other than close colleagues, and keep spim filters and other security and privacy measures current.

Blogs are used in numerous ways in business today, such as for project management and team communication, company news, customer support, public relations and media relations, employee recruiting, policy and issue discussions, crisis communication, market research, brainstorming, and viral marketing.

Although you record audio or video when creating podcasts rather than write messages, using the three-step process is an effective way to develop podcasts as well. Focus the planning step on analyzing the situation, gathering the information you'll need, and organizing your material. If you plan to create a series of podcasts on a given theme (the equivalent of starting a radio or television show), make sure you've identified a range of topics extensive enough to keep you going over time. As you organize and begin to think about the words or images you'll use as content, pay close attention to previews, transitions, and reviews so that audiences don't get lost while listening or watching. Finally, consider the necessary level of production quality; good-quality podcasts usually require some specialized hardware and software.

To become a valuable wiki contributor, let go of traditional expectations of authorship, including individual recognition and control; don't be afraid to edit and improve existing content; use page templates and other formatting options to make sure your content is formatted in the same style as the rest of the wiki; keep edits and comments separate by using the "talk page" to discuss content, rather than inserting comments directly into the text; take advantage of the sandbox to learn how use the wiki's writing and editing tools; and understand and follow the wiki's contributor guidelines.

Test Your Knowledge

1. What four electronic media choices are replacing traditional memos and letters in many instances?

2. Why are subject lines in e-mail messages important?

3. Should you use common IM slang terms and abbreviations such as *IMHO* ("in my humble opinion") or *TY* ("thank you") in business IM? Why or why not?

4. Why does a personal style of writing help blogs build stronger relationships with audiences?

5. Would it be a good idea to replace a printed employee handbook (which covers such topics as employment policies, dress code, safety rules, compensation policies, and benefit plans) with a wiki that is open to contributions from all employees in the company? Why or why not?

Apply Your Knowledge

1. Are instant messaging and blogging replacing many instances of e-mail for the same reasons that e-mail replaced many instances of printed memos and letters? Explain your answer.

2. If one of the benefits of blogging is the personal, intimate style of writing, is it a good idea to limit your creativity by adhering to conventional rules of grammar, spelling, and mechanics? Why or why not?

3. In your work as a video game designer, you know that eager players search the web for any scrap of information they can find about upcoming releases. In fact, to build interest, your company's public relations department carefully doles out small bits of information in the months before a new title hits the market. However, you and others in the company are also concerned about competitors getting their hands on all this "prerelease" information. If they learn too much too soon, they can use the

information to improve their own products more quickly. You and several other designers and programmers maintain blogs that give players insights into game design techniques and that occasionally share tips and tricks. You have thousands of readers, and you know your blog helps build customer loyalty. The company president wants to ban blogging entirely so that bloggers don't accidentally share too much prerelease information about upcoming games. Would this be a wise move? Why or why not?

4. What factors should you consider before replacing your company's employee newsletter, which is currently sent by e-mail, with a podcast?

5. **Ethical Choices**   Your company markets products that incorporate a particular technology, and several competitors use a different technology. When customers choose products in this industry, the decision is as much about the underlying technology as it is about specific product designs. Consequently, much of your company's promotional activities focus on the technology the firm uses. Your boss now wants you to write an article about this technology for Wikipedia, and she gave you a not-so-subtle hint to highlight the technology's strengths and ignore its weaknesses.

   To whom does your loyalty primarily lie—your employer, who wants to promote a specific technology, or Wikipedia readers, who want balanced coverage? How should you respond to your boss's request?

Practice Your Knowledge

Exercises for Perfecting Your Writing

Form and Audience   You are in charge of public relations for a cruise line that operates out of Miami. You are shocked to read a letter in a local newspaper from a disgruntled passenger, complaining about the service and entertainment on a recent cruise. You will have to respond to these publicized criticisms in some way.

1. What audiences will you need to consider in your response?

2. For each of these audiences, which medium (or media) should you use to send your message?

Better Blogging   The members of the project team of which you are the leader have enthusiastically embraced blogging as a communication medium. Unfortunately, as emotions heat up during the project, some of the blog postings are getting too casual, too personal, and even sloppy. Because your boss and other managers around the company also read this project blog, you don't want the team to look unprofessional in anyone's eyes. Revise the following blog posting so that it communicates in a more businesslike manner while retaining the informal, conversational tone of a blog (be sure to correct any spelling and punctuation mistakes you find as well).

3. Well, to the profound surprise of absolutely nobody, we are not going to be able meet the June 1 commitment to ship 100 operating tables to Southeast Surgical Supply. (For those of you who have been living in a cave the past six month, we have been fighting to get our hands on enough high-grade chromium steel to meet our production schedule.) Sure enough, we got news, this morning that we will only get enough for 30 tables. Yes, we look lik fools for not being able to follow through on promises we made to the customer, but no, this didn't have to happpen. Six month's ago, purchasing warned us about shrinking supplies and suggested we advance-buy as much

as we would need for the next 12 months, or so. We naturally tried to followed their advice, but just as naturally were shot down by the bean counters at corporate who trotted out the policy about never buying more than three months worth of materials in advance. Of course, it'll be us—not the bean counters who'll take the flak when everybody starts asking why revenues are down next quarter and why Southeast is talking to our friends at Crighton Manuf!!! Maybe, some day this company will get its head out of the sand and realize that we need to have some financial flexibility in order to compete.

Teamwork   Working with at least two other students, identify the best medium to use for each of the following messages. For each of these message needs, choose a medium that you think would work effectively and explain your choice. (More than one medium could work in some cases; just be able to support your particular choice.)

4. A technical support service for people trying to use their digital music players

5. A message of condolence to the family of an employee who passed away recently

6. A message from the CEO of a small company, explaining that she is leaving the company to join a competitor

7. A series of observations on the state of the industry

8. A series of messages, questions, and answers surrounding the work of a project team

E-Mail Subject Lines   Using your imagination to make up whatever details you need, revise the following e-mail subject lines to make them more informative:

9. New budget figures

10. Marketing brochure—your opinion

11. Production schedule

Activities

Active links for all websites in this chapter can be found online. If MyBCommLab.com is being used in your class, see your User Guide for instructions on accessing the content for this chapter. Otherwise, visit www.pearsonhighered.com/bovee, locate *Business Communication Essentials*, Fourth Edition, click the Companion Website link, select Chapter 6, and then click on "Featured Websites." Please note that links to sites that become inactive after publication of the book will be removed from the Featured Websites section.

1. **Analyze This Message**   Read the following blog post and (1) analyze the strengths and weaknesses of each sentence and (2) revise it so that it follows the guidelines in this chapter.

[headline]

We're DOOMED!!!!!

[post]

I was at the Sikorsky plant in Stratford yesterday, just checking to see how things were going with the assembly line retrofit we did for them last year. I think I saw the future, and it ain't pretty. They were demo'ing a prototype robot from Motoman that absolutely blows our stuff out of the water. They wouldn't let me really see it, but based on the 10-second glimpse I got, it's smaller, faster, and more maneuverable than any of our units. And when I asked about the price, the guy just grinned. And it wasn't the sort of grin designed to make me feel good.

I've been saying for years that we need to pay more attention to size, speed, and maneuverability instead of just relying on our historical strengths of accuracy and payload capacity, and you'd have to be blind not to agree that this experience proves me right. If we can't at least show a design for a better unit within two or three months, Motoman is going to lock up the market and leave us utterly in the dust.

Believe me, being able to say "I told you so" right now is not nearly as satisfying as you might think!!

2. **Improving an Agent's IM Skills**   Review the following IM exchange and explain how the customer service agent could have handled the situation more effectively.

AGENT:	Thanks for contacting Home Exercise Equipment. What's up?
CUSTOMER:	I'm having trouble assembling my home gym.
AGENT:	I hear that a lot! LOL
CUSTOMER:	So is it me or the gym?
AGENT:	Well, let's see <g>. Where are you stuck?
CUSTOMER:	The crossbar that connects the vertical pillars doesn't fit.
AGENT:	What do you mean doesn't fit?
CUSTOMER:	It doesn't fit. It's not long enough to reach across the pillars.
AGENT:	Maybe you assembled the pillars in the wrong place. Or maybe we sent the wrong crossbar.
CUSTOMER:	How do I tell?
AGENT:	The parts aren't labeled so could be tough. Do you have a measuring tape? Tell me how long your crossbar is.

3. **Revising an E-Mail Message: Break-Time Blues—Message Requesting a New Employee Procedure**   The following e-mail message contains numerous errors related to what you've learned about planning and writing business messages. First, list the flaws you find in this version. Then use the following steps to plan and write a better memo.

TO:	Felicia August <fb_august@evertrust.com>
CC:	
SUBJECT:	Compliance with new break procedure

Some of you may not like the rules about break times; however, we determined that keeping track of employees while they took breaks at times they determined rather than regular breaks at prescribed times was not working as well as we would have liked it to work. The new rules are not going to be an option. If you do not follow the new rules, you could be docked from your pay for hours when you turned up missing, since your direct supervisor will not be able to tell whether you were on a "break" or not and will assume that you have walked away from your job. We cannot be responsible for any errors that result from your inattentiveness to the new rules. I have already heard complaints from some of you and I hope this memo will end this issue once and for all. The decision has already been made.

Starting Monday, January 1, you will all be required to take a regular 15-minute break in the morning and again in the afternoon, and a regular thirty-minute lunch at the times specified by your supervisor, NOT when you think you need a break or when you "get around to it."

There will be no exceptions to this new rule!

Felicia August

Manager

Billing and accounting

a. Describe the flaws you discovered in this e-mail message.

b. Develop a plan for rewriting the message. Use the following steps to organize your efforts before you begin writing:

1. Determine the purpose.
2. Identify and analyze your audience.
3. Define the main idea.
4. Outline the major supporting points.
5. Choose between a direct and an indirect approach.

c. Now rewrite the e-mail message. Don't forget to leave ample time for revision of your own work before you turn it in.

4. **Revising a Memo: Moving Day—Blog Posting Informing Employees About an Office Relocation**   From what you've learned about planning and writing business messages, you should be able to identify numerous errors made by the writer of the following blog

posting. List them below and then plan and write a better post, following the guidelines given.

[headline]

Get Ready!

[post]

We are hoping to be back at work soon, with everything running smoothly, same production schedule and no late projects or missed deadlines. So you need to clean out your desk, put your stuff in boxes, and clean off the walls. You can put the items you had up on your walls in boxes, also.

We have provided boxes. The move will happen this weekend. We'll be in our new offices when you arrive on Monday.

We will not be responsible for personal belongings during the move.

Posted by David Burke at 10:42 AM 09-27-09.

   a. Describe the flaws you discovered in this blog post.

   b. Develop a plan for rewriting the post. Use the following steps to organize your efforts before you begin writing:

      1. Determine the purpose.

      2. Identify and analyze your audience.

      3. Define the main idea.

      4. Outline the major supporting points.

      5. Choose between direct and indirect approaches.

   c. Now rewrite the post. Don't forget to leave ample time for revision of your own work before you turn it in.

5. Podcasting: Where Are We Going with This, Boss? You've recently begun recording a weekly podcast to share information with your large and far-flung staff. After a month, you ask for feedback from several of your subordinates, and you're disappointed to learn that some people stopped listening to the podcast after the first couple weeks. Someone eventually admits that many staffers feel the recordings are too long and rambling, and the information they contain isn't valuable enough to justify the time it takes to listen. You aren't pleased, but you want to improve. An assistant transcribes the introduction to last week's podcast so you can review it. You immediately see two problems. Revise the introduction based on what you've learned in this chapter.

So there I am, having lunch with Selma Gill, who just joined and took over the Northeast sales region from Jackson Stroud. In walks our beloved CEO with Selma's old boss at Uni-Plex; turns out they were finalizing a deal to co-brand our products and theirs and to set up a joint distribution program in all four domestic regions. Pretty funny, huh? Selma left Uni-Plex because she wanted sell our products instead, and now she's back selling her old stuff, too. Anyway, try to chat with her when you can; she knows the biz inside and out and probably can offer insight into just about any sales challenge you might be running up against. We'll post more info on the co-brand deal next week; should be a boost for all of us. Other than those two news items, the other big news this week is the change in commission reporting. I'll go into the details in minute, but when you log onto the intranet, you'll now see your sales results split out by product line and industry sector. Hope this helps you see where you're doing well and where you might beef things up a bit. Oh yeah, I almost forgot the most important bit. Speaking of our beloved CEO, Thomas is going to be our guest of honor, so to speak, at the quarterly sales meeting next week and wants an update on how petroleum prices are affecting customer behavior. Each district manager should be ready with a brief report. After I go through the commission reporting scheme, I'll outline what you need to prepare.

6. Podcasting: Advice for a Beginning Podcaster To access this podcast exercise, visit http://real-timeupdates.com/bce, click on "Student Assignments," and select Chapter 6, page 135, Activity 6. Download and listen to this podcast. Identify at least three ways in which the podcast could be improved and draft a brief e-mail message that you could send to the podcaster with your suggestions for improvement.

7. Wikis: Revising Web Content with a "You" Attitude To access this wiki exercise, visit http://real-timeupdates.com/bce, click on "Student Assignments," and select Chapter 6, page 135, Activity 7. Follow the instructions for evaluating the existing content and revising it to make it more reader oriented.

Expand Your Knowledge

Exploring the Best of the Web

Ready to Start Blogging?   Blogging is easy to do if you have the right information. Start with the helpful tutorials at www.website101.com/RSS-Blogs-Blogging. More than 30 brief articles cover everything from creating a blog to attracting more readers to setting up RSS newsfeeds. Learn the techniques for adding audio and photo files to your blog. Review how search engines treat blogs and how you can use search engines to help more people find your blog. Then answer the following questions.

Exercises

1. What are five ways to attract more readers to your blog?

2. Why are blogs good for marketing?

3. What is a newsfeed, and why is it a vital part of blogging?

Surfing Your Way to Career Success

Bovée and Thill's Business Communication Headline News offers links to hundreds of online resources that can help you with this course, your other college courses, and your career. Visit http://businesscommunicationblog.com and click on "Web Directory." The Letters, Memos, E-Mail, Instant Messages, Blogs, and Web Content section connects you to a variety of websites and articles on routine, positive, and negative messages; persuasive messages; letters and memos; e-mail; IM; blogging; and web writing. Identify three websites from this section that could be useful in your business career. For each site, write a two-sentence summary of what the site offers and how it could help you launch and build your career.

MyBCommLab.com

Use MyBCommLab.com to test your understanding of the concepts presented in this chapter and explore additional materials that will bring the ideas to life in video, activities, and an online multimedia e-book. Additionally, you can improve your skill with prepositions, conjunctions, and articles by using the "Peak Performance Grammar and Mechanics" module within the lab. Take the Pretest to determine whether you have any weak areas. Then review those areas in the Refresher Course. Take the Follow-Up Test to check your grasp of prepositions, conjunctions, and articles. For an extra challenge, take the Advanced Test. Finally, for even more reinforcement, go to the "Improve Your Grammar, Mechanics, and Usage" section that follows the cases, and complete the "Level 1: Self-Assessment" exercises.

CASES

▼ *Apply the three-step writing process to the following cases, as assigned by your instructor.*

BLOGGING SKILLS

1. Come on to Comic-Con: Explaining the Benefits of Attending

Comic-Con International is an annual convention that highlights a wide variety of pop culture and entertainment media, from comic books and collectibles to video games and movies. From its early start as a comic book convention that attracted several hundred fans and publishing industry insiders, Comic-Con has become a major international event, with more than 120,000 attendees.

Your task Several readers of your pop culture blog have been asking for your recommendation about visiting Comic-Con in San Diego next summer. Write a two- or three-paragraph posting for your blog that explains what Comic-Con is and what visitors can expect to experience at the convention. Be sure to address your posting to fans, not industry insiders. You can learn more at www.comic-con.org.[44]

2. Keeping the Fans Happy: Analyzing Advertising on ESPN.com

ESPN leads the pack both online and off. Its well-known cable television sports channels are staple fare for sports enthusiasts, and ESPN.com (http://espn.go.com) is the leader in sports websites. Advertisers flock to ESPN.com because it delivers millions of visitors in the prime 18- to 34-year-old demographic group. With a continually refreshed offering of sporting news, columnists, video replays, and fantasy leagues (online competitions in which participants choose players for their teams, and the outcome is based on how well the real players do in actual live competition), ESPN.com has become one of the major advertising venues on the web.

As an up-and-coming web producer for ESPN.com, you're concerned about the rumblings of discontent you've heard from friends and read in various blogs and other sources. ESPN.com remains popular with millions of sports fans, but some say they are getting tired of all the ads—both ads on the site itself and pop-up ads. A few say they are switching to other websites with fewer advertising intrusions. Your site traffic numbers are holding fairly steady for now, but you're worried that the few visitors leaving ESPN.com might be the start of a significant exodus in the future.

Your task Write an e-mail message to your manager, expressing your concern about the amount of advertising content on ESPN.com. Acknowledge that advertising is a vital source of revenue but share what you're learned about site visitors who claim to be migrating to other sites. Offer to lead a comprehensive review effort that will compare the advertising presence on ESPN.com with that of other sports websites and explore ways to maintain strong advertising sales without alienating readers.[45]

3. Must Be an Opportunity in Here Somewhere: The Growing Market of Women Living Without Husbands
For the first time in history (aside from special situations such as major wars), more than half—51 percent—of all U.S. adult women now live without a spouse. (In other words, they live alone, with roommates, or as part of an unmarried couple.) Twenty-five percent have never married, and 26 percent are divorced, widowed, or married but living apart from their spouses. In the 1950s and into the 1960s, only 40 percent of women lived without a spouse, but every decade since, the percentage has increased. In your work as a consumer trend specialist for Seymour Powell (www.seymourpowell.com), a product design firm based in London that specializes in the home, personal, leisure, and transportation sectors, it's your business to recognize and respond to demographic shifts such as this.

Your task With a small team of classmates, brainstorm possible product opportunities that respond to this trend. In an e-mail message to be sent to the management team at Seymour Powell, list your ideas for new or modified products that might sell well in a society in which more than half of all adult women live without a spouse. For each idea, provide a one-sentence explanation of why you think the product has potential.[46]

4. Help Is on the Way: Encouraging Ford Dealers
The "Big Three" U.S. automakers—General Motors, Chrysler, and Ford—haven't had much good news to share lately. Ford, in particular, has been going through a rough time, losing billions of dollars and being overtaken in sales volume by Toyota.

Your task Write an e-mail message to be sent to all Ford dealers in North America, describing an exciting new model about to be introduced to the public. For this exercise, you can use either an upcoming Ford model you have researched in the automotive media or a fictitious car of your own imagination (make sure it's something that could conceivably be introduced by Ford).[47]

5. Legitimate and Legal: Defending Technology Sales to Chinese Police Agencies
Cisco, a leading manufacturer of computer networking equipment, is one of several technology companies that have been criticized recently for selling high-tech equipment to police agencies in China. After the Chinese government killed hundreds of protestors in Tiananmen Square in 1989, U.S. officials began restricting the export of products that could be used by Chinese security forces. The restrictions cover a range of low-tech devices, from helmets and handcuffs to fingerprint powder and teargas, but not certain high-tech products, such as the networking equipment that Cisco sells, which can conceivably be used by security forces in ways that violate human rights. Critics contend that by not restricting products such as Cisco's, the U.S. government is not enforcing the full intent of the restrictions. Moreover, they suggest that Cisco could be enabling abuse. For example, its Chinese marketing brochure promotes the equipment's ability to "strengthen police control."

Your task Write a brief post for the Cisco executive blog that explains the following points: The company rigorously follows all U.S. export regulations; the company's marketing efforts in China are consistent with the way it markets products to other police organizations throughout the world; the products are simply tools, and like all other tools, they can be applied in good or bad ways, and responsible application is the customer's responsibility, not Cisco's; and if Cisco didn't sell this equipment to the Chinese government, another company from another country would.[48]

6. The Very Definition of Confusion: Helping Consumers Sort Out High-Definition Television
High-definition television can be a joy to watch—but, oh, what a pain to buy. The field is littered with competing technologies and arcane terminology that is meaningless to most consumers. Moreover, it's nearly impossible to define one technical term without invoking two or three others, leaving consumers swimming in an alphanumeric soup of confusion. The manufacturers themselves can't even agree on which of the *18* different digital TV formats truly qualify as "high definition." As a sales support manager for Crutchfield (www.crutchfield.com), a leading online retailer of audio and video systems, you understand the frustration buyers feel; your staff is deluged daily by their questions.

Your task To help your staff respond quickly to consumers who ask questions via Crutchfield's online IM chat service, you are developing a set of "canned" responses to common questions. When a consumer asks one of these questions, a sales advisor can simply click on the ready-made answer. Start by writing concise, consumer-friendly definitions of the following terms: *resolution*, *HDTV*, *1080p*, and *HDMI*. (On the Crutchfield website, click on "Learn," "TVs, Blu-ray & Gaming," and then "Televisions" to learn more about these terms. Answers.com and CNET.com are two other handy sources.)[49]

[PODCASTING SKILLS] [PORTFOLIO BUILDER]

7. Based on My Experience: Recommending Your College or University With any purchase decision, from a restaurant meal to a college education, recommendations from satisfied customers are often the strongest promotional messages.

Your task Write a script for a one- to two-minute podcast (roughly 150 to 250 words) explaining why your college or university is a good place to get an education. Your audience is high school juniors and seniors. You can choose to craft a general message, something that would be useful to all prospective students, or you can focus on a specific academic discipline, the athletic program, or some other important aspect of your college experience. Either way, make sure your introductory comments make it clear whether you are offering a general recommendation or a specific recommendation. If your instructor asks you to do so, record the podcast and submit the file electronically.

[BLOGGING SKILLS]

8. Look Sharp: Travel Safety Tips for New Employees As the travel director for a global management consulting firm, your responsibilities range from finding the best travel deals to helping new employees learn the ins and outs of low-risk, low-stress travel. One of the ways in which you dispense helpful advice is through an internal blog.

Your task Research advice for safe travel and identify at least six tips that every employee in your company should know. Write a brief blog posting that introduces and identifies the six tips.

[E-MAIL SKILLS]

9. Your Work Does Matter: Encouraging an Unhappy Colleague You certainly appreciate your company's "virtual team" policy of letting employees live wherever they want while using technology to communicate and collaborate. The company is headquartered in a large urban area, but you get to live in the mountains, only a step or two away from some of the best fly fishing in the world. Most of the time, this approach to work couldn't get any better.

However, the lack of face-to-face contact with your colleagues definitely has disadvantages. For example, when a teammate seems to be upset about something, you wish you could go for a walk with the person and talk it out rather than rely on phone calls, e-mail, or IM. In the past couple weeks, Chris Grogan, the graphic designer working with you on a new e-commerce website project, seems to be complaining about everything. His negative attitude is starting to wear down the team's enthusiasm at a critical point in the project. In particular, he has complained several times that no one on the team seems to care about his design work. It is rarely mentioned in team teleconferences, and no one asks him about it. That part is true, actually, but the reason is that there is nothing wrong with his

work; some critical technical issues unrelated to the graphic design are consuming everyone's attention.

Your task After a couple unsuccessful attempts at encouraging Grogan over the phone, you decide to write a brief e-mail message to assure him of the importance of his work on this project and the quality of his efforts. Let him know that graphic design is a critical part of the project's success and that as soon as those technical issues are resolved and the project is completed, everyone will have a chance to appreciate his contribution to the project. Make up whatever details you need to craft your message.

[E-MAIL SKILLS] [PORTFOLIO BUILDER]

10. She's One of Us: Promoting a New Lifestyle Magazine Consumers looking for beauty, health, and lifestyle magazines have an almost endless array of choices, but even in this crowded field, Logan Olson found her own niche. Olson, who was born with congenital heart disease, suffered a heart attack at age 16 that left her in a coma and caused serious brain damage. The active and outgoing teen had to relearn everything from sitting up to feeding herself. As she recovered, she looked for help and advice in conquering such daily challenges as finding fashionable clothes that were easier to put on and makeup that was easier to apply. Mainstream beauty magazines didn't seem to offer any information for young women with disabilities, so she started her own magazine. Oprah Winfrey has *Oprah*, and now Logan Olson has *Logan*. The magazine not only gives young women tips on buying and using a variety of products but lets women with disabilities know there are others out there like them, facing and meeting the same challenges.

Your task Write a promotional e-mail message to be sent to young women with disabilities as well as families and friends who might like to give gift subscriptions, promoting the benefits of subscribing to *Logan*. You can learn more about *Logan* at www.loganmagazine.com.[50]

[E-MAIL SKILLS] [PORTFOLIO BUILDER]

11. We're the One: Explaining Why a Company Should Hire Your Firm You work for Brainbench (www.brainbench.com), one of many companies that offer employee screening services. Brainbench's offerings include a variety of online products and consulting services, all designed to help employers find and develop the best possible employees. For example, Brainbench's Pre-Hire Testing products help employers test for job skills, communication skills, personality, and employment history red flags (such as chronic absenteeism or performance problems). Employers use these test results to either screen out candidates entirely or ask focused interview questions about areas of concern.

Sonja Williamson, the human resources director of a large retail company, has just e-mailed your sales team. She would like an overview of the Pre-Hire Testing products and some background on your company.

Your task Write an e-mail response to Williamson's query. Be sure to thank her for her interest, briefly describe the Pre-Hire Testing products, and summarize Brainbench's qualifications. Include at least one hyperlink to the Brainbench website and consider attaching one or more PDF files from the website as well.

[PODCASTING SKILLS]

12. Podcasting Pitch: Training People to Sell Your Favorite Product

What product do you own (or use regularly) that you can't live without? It could be something as seemingly minor as a favorite pen or something as significant as a medical device that you literally can't live without. Now imagine that you're a salesperson for this product; think about how you would sell it to potential buyers. How would you describe it, and how would you explain the benefits of owning it? After you've thought about how you would present the product to others, imagine that you've been promoted to a sales manager position, and it is your job to train other people to sell the product.

Your task Write the script for a brief podcast (200 to 300 words) that summarizes for your sales staff the most important points to convey about the product. Imagine that they'll listen to your podcast while driving to a customer's location or preparing for the day's activity in a retail store (depending on the nature of the product). Be sure to give your staffers a concise overview message about the product and several key support points.

[E-MAIL SKILLS]

13. Time to Think: E-Mail Requesting a Change in Your Workload

The description of your job as a global marketing manager for New Balance is full of responsibilities that require creative thinking, from predicting consumer and retailing trends to establishing seasonal priorities for the global merchandising effort. You love these challenges—in fact, they're the main reason you took the job at this respected maker of athletic shoes and apparel. Unfortunately, between department meetings, status reports, budgets, and an endless array of other required chores, you hardly have time to think at all, much less engage in the sort of unstructured, "blue sky" thinking that is crucial to creative strategizing. You have virtually no time at work for such thinking, and after 50 or 60 hours a week at the office or on the road, you're too exhausted to brainstorm on your own time.

Your task Write an e-mail message to your boss, Paul Heffernan, the executive vice president of global marketing, persuading him that you need to reshuffle your assignments to free up more time to think. This is a tricky request because you know that Heffernan faces the same challenge. However, you're convinced that by spending less time on tasks that could be done by someone else (or perhaps shouldn't be done at all), you'll be able to do a better job of creating marketing strategies—and maybe even set a good example for other New Balance executives. You have a preliminary list of changes you'd like to make, but you know you need to discuss the entire scope of your

job with Heffernan before finalizing the list. Your purpose: Invite him to lunch to begin a discussion of reshaping your responsibilities.[51]

[PODCASTING SKILLS]

14. Why Me? Introducing Yourself to a Potential Employer

While writing the many letters and e-mail messages that are part of the job search process, you find yourself wishing that you could just talk to some of these companies so your personality could shine through. Well, you've just gotten that opportunity. One of the companies that you've applied to has e-mailed you back, asking you to submit a two-minute podcast introducing yourself and explaining why you would be a good person to hire.

Your task Identify a company that you'd like to work for after graduation and select a job that would be a good match for your skills and interests. Write a script for a two-minute podcast (two minutes represents roughly 250 words for most speakers). Introduce yourself and the position you're applying for, describe your background, and explain why you think you're a good candidate for the job. Make up any details you need. If your instructor asks you to do so, record the podcast and submit the file.

[SOCIAL NETWORKING SKILLS]

15. "Hi, My Name Is . . .": Introducing Yourself on a Business Network

Business networking websites such as www.linkedin.com, www.ryze.com, and www.spoke.com have become popular places for professionals to make connections that would be difficult or impossible to make without the Internet. (You might be familiar with MySpace, Facebook, or Friendster, sites that help individuals meet through networks of people they already know and trust.) These business-oriented sites follow the same principle, but instead of using them to find new friends or dates, you use them to find new customers, new suppliers, or other important business connections. For instance, you might find that the ideal contact person in a company you'd like to do business with is the aunt of your boss's tennis partner.

An important aspect of business networking is being able to provide a clear description of your professional background and interests. For example, a manufacturing consultant can list the industries in which she has experience, the types of projects she has worked on, and the nature of work she'd like to pursue in the future (such as a full-time position for a company or additional independent projects).

Your task Write a brief statement to introduce yourself, including your educational background, your job history, and the types of connections you'd like to make. Feel free to "fast forward" to your graduation and list your degree, the business specialty you plan to pursue, and any relevant experience. If you have business experience already, feel free to use that information instead. Make sure your statement is clear, concise (no more than two sentences), and compelling so that anyone looking for someone like you would want to get in touch with you after reading your introduction.

Improve Your Grammar, Mechanics, and Usage

Level 1: Self-Assessment—Prepositions and Conjunctions

Review Sections 1.6.1 and 1.6.2 in the Handbook of Grammar, Mechanics, and Usage and then complete the following items.

Rewrite items 1–5, deleting unnecessary words and prepositions and adding required prepositions:

1. Where was your argument leading to?

2. I wish he would get off of the phone.

3. This is a project into which you can sink your teeth.

4. U.S. Mercantile must become aware and sensitive to its customers' concerns.

5. We are responsible for aircraft safety in the air, the hangars, and the runways.

In items 6–10, write the correct preposition in the blank:

6. Dr. Namaguchi will be talking _____ the marketing class, but she has no time for questions.

7. Matters like this are decided after thorough discussion _____ all seven department managers.

8. We can't wait _____ their decision much longer.

9. Their computer is similar _____ ours.

10. This model is different _____ the one we ordered.

In items 11–15, rewrite the sentences in the space provided to make phrases parallel.

11. She is active in not only a civic group but also in an athletic organization.

12. That is either a mistake or was an intentional omission.

13. The question is whether to set up a booth at the convention or be hosting a hospitality suite.

14. We are doing better in both overall sales and in profits.

15. She had neither the preferred educational background, nor did she have suitable experience.

Level 2: Workplace Applications

The following items contain numerous errors in grammar, capitalization, punctuation, abbreviation, number style, word division, and vocabulary. Rewrite each sentence, correcting all errors. Write *C* for any sentence that is already correct.

1. Peabody Energys commitment to environmental excellence is driven by the companies' mission statement which states that when mining is complete, the company will leave the land in a condition equal or better than it was before mining.

2. In 1998, Blockbuster opened a state of the art distribution center in McKinney, Texas, just North of the company's Dallas Headquarters.

3. Miss Tucci was responsible for developing Terraspring's business plan, establishing the brand, and for launching the company.

4. The principle goals of the new venture will be to offer tailored financial products and meeting the needs of the community.

5. Nestle Waters North America are the number one bottled water company in the US. and Canada.

6. The reason egg prices dropped sharply is because of a Post Easter reduction in demand.

7. Joining bank officials during the announcement of the program were U.S. congressman Luis V. Guitierrez, Carlos Manuel Sada Solana, General Consul of Mexico in the Midwest, and "Don Francisco", the leading hispanic entertainment figure in the United States and Latin America.

8. The summer advertising campaign is the most unique in 7-Eleven's history.

9. Upon introducing it's new Quadruple Fudge flavor, consumers are expected to flock to Baskin-Robbins ice cream parlors.

10. The signing of a Trade Pact between the european union and Chile, is being delayed by european negotiators who insist the deal includes an agreement requiring Chile to stop using the names Cognac, Champagne, and Burgundy.

11. Federal Trade commissioner, Mrs. Sheila F. Anthony called on the dietary supplement industry to institute better self regulation, and called on the media to refuse ads containing claims that are obviously false.

12. Founded in 1971, GSD&M has grown to become a nationally-acclaimed advertising agency with more than 500 employees and having billings of over $1 billion dollars.

13. Although marketing may seem to be the easier place to cut costs during a downturn its actually the last place you should look to make strategic cuts.

14. After closing their plant in Mecosta county, Green Mountain will have less than 200 employees.

15. The purchasing needs of professional's differ from blue collar workers.

Level 3: Document Critique

The following document may contain errors in grammar, capitalization, punctuation, abbreviation, number style, vocabulary, and spelling. You may also find errors related to topics in this chapter, such as the subject line. Correct all errors using standard proofreading marks (see Appendix C).

TO: George Kimball <g.kimball@sprenco.com>
CC:
SUBJECT: My trip back East

Dear George:

I went back to New York for apresentation the 15th of this month and I found it very informative. The sponsor of my visat was Vern Grouper. Vern is the Manager of IS at headquarters; that is, their centralized information systems operation. They've got quite a bit of power out there. And they do encourage us to utilize their capibilities, there services, and experiences to whatever extent will be beneficial to us. However, you could say it would be my observation that although they have a tremendous amount of computing capability that capability is directed toward a business dimension very different than ours and unlike anything we have. However, their are certain services that might be performed in our behalf by headquarters. For example, we could utilize people such as Vern to come and address our IS advisory group since I am planning on convening that group on a monthly basis.

By the way, I need to talk to you about the IS advicory group when you get a chance. I have 1 or 2 thoughts about some new approaches we can take with it I'd like to run by you if you don't mind. Its not too complicated just some simple ideas.

Let me know what you think of this idea about Vern coming here. If you like it than I will go ahead and set things in motion with Vern.

Sincerely,

John

Writing Routine and Positive Messages

LEARNING OBJECTIVES

After studying this chapter, you will be able to

1. Apply the three-step writing process to routine and positive messages
2. Outline an effective strategy for writing routine requests
3. Explain how to ask for specific action in a courteous manner
4. Describe a strategy for writing routine replies and positive messages
5. Discuss the importance of knowing who is responsible when granting claims and requests for adjustment
6. Explain how creating informative messages differs from responding to information requests
7. Describe the importance of goodwill messages and explain how to make them effective

[from the real world]

"To succeed, I don't need to be Shakespeare; I must, though, have a sincere desire to inform."
—Warren Buffett, Legendary investor and chairman of Berkshire Hathaway
www.berkshirehathaway. com

Warren Buffett's financial acumen has made him and many of his shareholders wealthy, but he is recognized almost as widely for his communication skills. His letters, essays, and annual reports communicate complex financial topics in simple language that his readers can easily understand. His approach is simple: Even for a document that will be read by thousands of people, he visualizes a single person (often one of his sisters) as his audience. He treats this audience member as an intelligent human being who just doesn't have the same level of experience with the subject matter that he has. From there, he proceeds to organize and write his messages in a way that clarifies all the essential information and doesn't try to impress or obscure with complicated language. Whether you're writing an e-mail message to your boss or a report for an audience of thousands, Buffett's approach is a great example to follow.[1]

USING THE THREE-STEP WRITING PROCESS FOR ROUTINE AND POSITIVE MESSAGES

Most business communication is about routine matters: orders, company policies, claims, credit, employees, products, operations, and so on. Such messages are rarely long or complex, but the three-step writing process still gives you a great way to produce effective messages efficiently:

- **Step 1: Plan your message.** Analyze the situation and make sure that your purpose is clear, gather the information your audience needs to know, select the most appropriate medium, and organize your information effectively.

- **Step 2: Write your message.** Adapt to your audience as the situation requires, maintaining a "you" attitude, being polite, emphasizing the positive, and using bias-free language (see Figure 7.1). Use plain English and write in the active voice.

- **Step 3: Complete your message.** Spend a few moments to revise your messages to make sure they are clear and concise. Use templates and style sheets to speed up the production

Even simple messages can benefit from thoughtful planning.

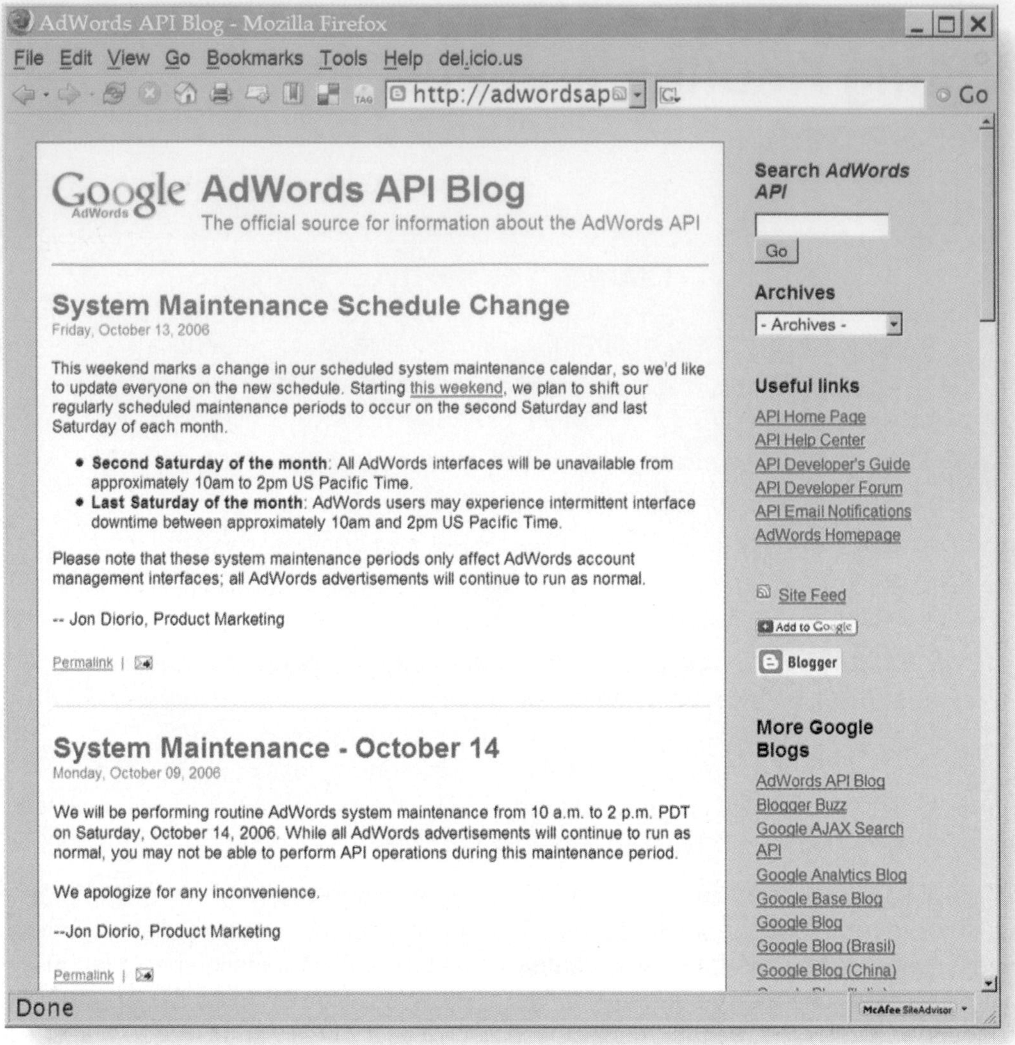

Figure 7.1   Routine Messages
Routine and positive messages are best conveyed using a direct approach. Google uses this blog to keep users of its AdWords search engine advertising system up to date on maintenance interruptions and other important news.

of routine messages. Finally, make sure you know how to take full advantage of whatever medium you're using to distribute your messages, whether it's e-mail, instant messaging, blogging, or any other system.

MAKING ROUTINE REQUESTS

Making requests—for information, action, products, adjustments, or other matters—is a routine part of business. In most cases, your audience will be prepared to comply, as long as you're not being unreasonable or asking people to do work they would expect you to do yourself. By applying a clear strategy and tailoring your approach to each situation, you'll be able to generate effective requests quickly.

Strategy for Routine Requests

For routine requests and positive messages

- State the request or main idea
- Give necessary details
- Close with a cordial request for specific action

Like all other business messages, routine requests have three parts: an opening, a body, and a close. Using the direct approach, open with your main idea, which is a clear statement of your request. Use the body to give details and justify your request and then close by requesting specific action.

Stating Your Request Up Front

Begin routine requests by placing your request first. Of course, getting right to the point is not license to be abrupt or tactless:

- **Pay attention to tone.** Instead of demanding action ("Send me the latest version of the budget spreadsheet"), soften your request with words such as *please* and *I would appreciate*.
- **Assume that your audience will comply.** You can generally make the assumption that your audience members will comply when they clearly understand the reason for your request.
- **Be specific.** State precisely what you want. For example, if you request the latest market data from your research department, be sure to say whether you want a 1-page summary or 100 pages of raw data.

Take care that your direct approach doesn't come across as abrupt or tactless.

Explaining and Justifying Your Request

Use the body of your message to explain your request. Make the explanation a smooth and logical outgrowth of your opening remarks. If complying with the request could benefit the reader, be sure to mention this. You can also use the body to ask questions that will help you organize the message and help your audience identify the information you need. When asking such questions, consider these tips:

- **Ask the most important questions first.** If cost is your main concern, you might begin with a question such as "How much will it cost to have our new website created by an outside firm?" Then you may want to ask more specific but related questions, such as whether discounts are available for paying early.
- **Ask only relevant questions.** To help expedite the response to your request, ask only questions that are central to your main request.
- **Deal with only one topic per question.** If you have an unusual or complex request, break it down into specific, individual questions so that the reader can address each one separately. This consideration not only shows respect for your audience's time but also gets you a more accurate answer in less time.

If you have multiple requests or questions, start with the most important one.

Requesting Specific Action in a Courteous Close

Close your message with three important elements: (1) a specific request that includes any relevant deadlines, (2) information about how you can be reached (if it isn't obvious), and (3) an expression of appreciation or goodwill. For example: "Please send the figures by April 5 so that I can return first-quarter results to you before the April 15 board meeting. I appreciate your help." Concluding your note with "Thank you" or "Thanks for your help" is fine, although "Thank you in advance" is considered a bit stuffy and presumptuous.

Close request messages with
- *A request for some specific action*
- *Information about how you can be reached*
- *An expression of appreciation*

Common Examples of Routine Requests

The most common types of routine messages are asking for information and action, asking for recommendations, and making claims and requesting adjustments.

Asking for Information and Action

When you need to know about something, to elicit an opinion from someone, or to request a simple action, you usually need only ask. In essence, simple requests say

- What you want to know or what you want readers to do
- Why you're making the request
- Why it may be in your readers' interest to help you (if applicable)

For simple requests, a straightforward request gets the job done with a minimum of fuss. In more complex situations, you may need to provide more extensive reasons and justification for your request. Naturally, be sure to adapt your request to your audience and the situation (see Figure 7.2).

Planning ➤ **Writing** ➤ **Completing** ➤

Analyze the Situation
Verify that the purpose is to request information from company managers.

Gather Information
Gather accurate, complete information about local competitive threats.

Select the Right Medium
Choose e-mail for this internal message, which also allows the attachment of a Word document to collect the information.

Organize the Information
Clarify that the main idea is collecting information that will lead to a better competitive strategy, which will in turn help the various district managers.

Adapt to Your Audience
Show sensitivity to audience needs with a "you" attitude, politeness, positive emphasis, and bias-free language. The writer already has credibility as manager of the department.

Compose the Message
Maintain a style that is conversational but still businesslike, using plain English and appropriate voice.

Revise the Message
Evaluate content and review readability; avoid unnecessary details.

Produce the Message
Simple e-mail format is all the design this message needs.

Proofread the Message
Review for errors in layout, spelling, and mechanics.

Distribute the Message
Deliver the message via the company's e-mail system.

| **1** | **2** | **3** |

Identifies the subject of the e-mail

Acknowledges that responding to the request will require some work, but the result will benefit everyone

Eudora – [All District Mgrs, Competitive Threat Analysis]
File Edit Mailbox Message Transfer Special Tools Window Help

To: <All District Mgrs>
From: hh_clausen@early-ed.com
Subject: Competitive Threat Analysis
Cc:
Bcc:
Attached: C:\Strategic planning\Competitive Analysis template.doc;

Hello everyone,

At last week's off-site meeting, Charles asked me to coordinate our companywide competitive threat analysis project. In order to devise a comprehensive strategic response that is sensitive to local market variations, we need your individual insights and advice.

To minimize the effort for you and to ensure consistent data collection across all regions, I've attached a template that identifies all the key questions we'd like to have answered. I realize this will require several hours of work on your part, but the result will be a truly nationwide look at our competitive situation. From this information, we can create a plan for next fiscal year that makes the best use of finite resources while adapting to your local district needs.

To allow sufficient time to compile your inputs before the November 13 board meeting, please e-mail your responses to me by November 8. Thanks for your help and timely attention to this important project.

Helene

Helene H. Clausen
Director, Strategic Initiatives
Early Education Solutions, Inc.
14445 Lawson Blvd, Suite 455
Denver, CO 80201
tel: 303-555-1200
fax: 303-555-1210
www.early-ed.com

Gets right to the point of the message

Explains the benefit of responding to the request

Provides a clear and meaningful deadline, then closes in a courteous manner

Pointers for Making a Routine Request
• Your readers will respond favorably, so be direct.
• Use a polite, personal tone and don't demand a response.
• Justify the request or explain its importance.
• Explain the benefits of responding.
• Close courteously, with a request for specific action.

Figure 7.2 Effective Message Requesting Action
In this e-mail request to district managers across the country, Helene Clausen asks them to fill out an attached information collection form. Although the request is not unusual and responding to it is part of the managers' responsibility, Clausen asks for their help in a courteous manner and points out the benefits of responding.

Asking for Recommendations

The need to inquire about people arises often in business. For example, before awarding credit, contracts, jobs, promotions, scholarships, or other benefits, some companies ask applicants to supply contact information for references who can vouch for their ability, skills, integrity, character, and other qualities. Before you volunteer someone's name as a reference, make sure you have permission to do so. Some people are not comfortable writing recommendation letters, and some organizations have policies that prohibit employees from endorsing former colleagues or suppliers.

Always ask for permission before using someone as a reference.

If you're applying for a job and your potential employer asks for references, you might want to ask a former instructor or professional associate to write a letter of recommendation. Because requests for recommendations and references are routine, you can organize your inquiry using the direct approach (see Figure 7.3). Open your message by clearly stating

Planning

Analyze the Situation
Verify that the purpose is to request a recommendation letter from a college professor.

Gather Information
Gather information on classes and dates to help the reader recall you and to clarify the position you seek.

Select the Right Medium
The letter format gives this message an appropriate level of formality, although many professors prefer to be contacted by e-mail.

Organize the Information
Messages like this are common and expected, so a direct approach is fine.

Writing

Adapt to Your Audience
Show sensitivity to audience needs with a "you" attitude, politeness, positive emphasis, and bias-free language.

Compose the Message
The style is respectful and businesslike, while still using plain English and appropriate voice.

Completing

Revise the Message
Evaluate content and review readability; avoid unnecessary details.

Produce the Message
Simple memo format is all the design this message needs.

Proofread the Message
Review for errors in layout, spelling, and mechanics.

Distribute the Message
Deliver the message via postal mail or e-mail if you have the professor's e-mail address.

1   **2**   **3**

1181 Ashport Drive
Tate Springs, TN 38101
March 14, 2009

Professor Lyndon Kenton
School of Business
University of Tennessee, Knoxville
Knoxville, TN 37916

Dear Professor Kenton:

I recently interviewed with Strategic Investments and have been called for a second interview for their Analyst Training Program (ATP). They have requested at least one recommendation from a professor, and I immediately thought of you. May I have a letter of recommendation from you?

Opens by stating the purpose of the letter and making the request, assuming the reader will want to comply with the request

Includes information near the opening to refresh the reader's memory about this former student

As you may recall, I took BUS 485, Financial Analysis, from you in the fall of 2007. I enjoyed the class and finished the term with an "A." Professor Kenton, your comments on assertiveness and cold-calling impressed me beyond the scope of the actual course material. In fact, taking your course helped me decide on a future as a financial analyst.

My enclosed résumé includes all my relevant work experience and volunteer activities. I would also like to add that I've handled the financial planning for our family since my father passed away several years ago. Although I initially learned by trial and error, I have increasingly applied my business training in deciding what stocks or bonds to trade. This, I believe, has given me a practical edge over others who may be applying for the same job.

Refers to résumé in the body and mentions experience that could set applicant apart from other candidates

Gives a deadline for response and includes information about the person expecting the recommendation

If possible, Ms. Blackmon in Human Resources needs to receive your letter by March 30. For your convenience, I've enclosed a preaddressed, stamped envelope.

Mentions the pre-addressed, stamped envelope to encourage a timely response

I appreciate your time and effort in writing this letter of recommendation for me. It will be great to put my education to work, and I'll keep you informed of my progress. Thank you for your consideration in this matter.

Sincerely,

Joanne Tucker

Joanne Tucker

Enclosure

Figure 7.3   Effective Request for a Recommendation
This writer uses a direct approach when asking for a recommendation from a former professor. Note how she takes care to refresh the professor's memory, since the class was taken a year and a half ago. She also indicates the date by which the letter is needed and points to the enclosure of a stamped, preaddressed envelope.

that you're applying for a position and that you would like your reader to write a letter of recommendation. If you haven't had contact with the person for some time, use the opening to recall the nature of the relationship you had, the dates of association, and any special events that might bring a clear, favorable picture of you to mind. Consider including an updated résumé if you've had significant career advancement since your last contact.

Close your letter with an expression of appreciation and the full name and address of the person to whom the letter should be sent. When asking for an immediate

Refresh the memory of any potential reference you haven't been in touch with for a while.

recommendation, you should also mention the deadline. You'll make a response more likely if you enclose a stamped, preaddressed envelope, which is a considerate step in any event.

Making Claims and Requesting Adjustments

If you're dissatisfied with a company's product or service, you can opt to make a **claim** (a formal complaint) or request an **adjustment** (the settlement of a claim). In either case, maintaining a professional tone in all your communication will help you get the situation resolved sooner. In addition, be sure to document your initial complaint and all correspondence after that.

In most cases, and especially in your initial contact, you can assume that a fair adjustment will be made. A direct approach is therefore appropriate. Open with a straightforward statement of the problem and then give a complete, specific explanation in the body. Provide any information a reader would need to verify your complaint. In your close, politely request specific action or convey a sincere desire to find a solution. And if appropriate, suggest that the business relationship will continue if the problem is solved satisfactorily.

Companies often accept the customer's explanation of what's wrong, so maintain good ethics by being entirely honest when filing claims. Also, be prepared to back up your claim with invoices, sales receipts, credit card statements, dated correspondence, and any other relevant documents. Send copies and keep the originals for your files.

If the remedy is obvious, tell your reader exactly what you expect from the company, such as issuing a refund or performing a service again. In some cases, you might ask the reader to resolve a problem. However, if you're uncertain about the precise nature of the trouble, you could ask the company to make an assessment and advise you on how the situation could be fixed. Supply your contact information so that the company can discuss the situation with you if necessary. Compare the poor and improved versions in Figure 7.4 for an example of making an effective claim.

SENDING ROUTINE REPLIES AND POSITIVE MESSAGES

Just as you'll make numerous requests for information and action throughout your career, you'll also respond to similar requests from other people. When you are responding positively to a request, sending routine announcements, or sending a positive or goodwill message, you have several goals: to communicate the information or the good news, answer all questions, provide all required details, and leave your reader with a good impression of you and your firm.

Strategy for Routine Replies and Positive Messages

Because readers receiving routine replies and positive messages will generally be interested in what you have to say, you'll usually use the direct approach. Place your main idea (the positive reply or the good news) in the opening. Use the body to explain all the relevant details, and close cordially, perhaps highlighting a benefit to your reader.

Starting with the Main Idea

By opening with the main idea or good news, you prepare your audience for the details that follow. Make your opening clear and concise. Although the following introductory statements make the same point, one is cluttered with unnecessary information that buries the purpose, whereas the other is brief and to the point:

Instead of This	Write This
I am pleased to inform you that after deliberating the matter carefully, our human resources committee has recommended you for appointment as a financial analyst.	We would like to offer you the position of financial analyst in our Cleveland headquarters.

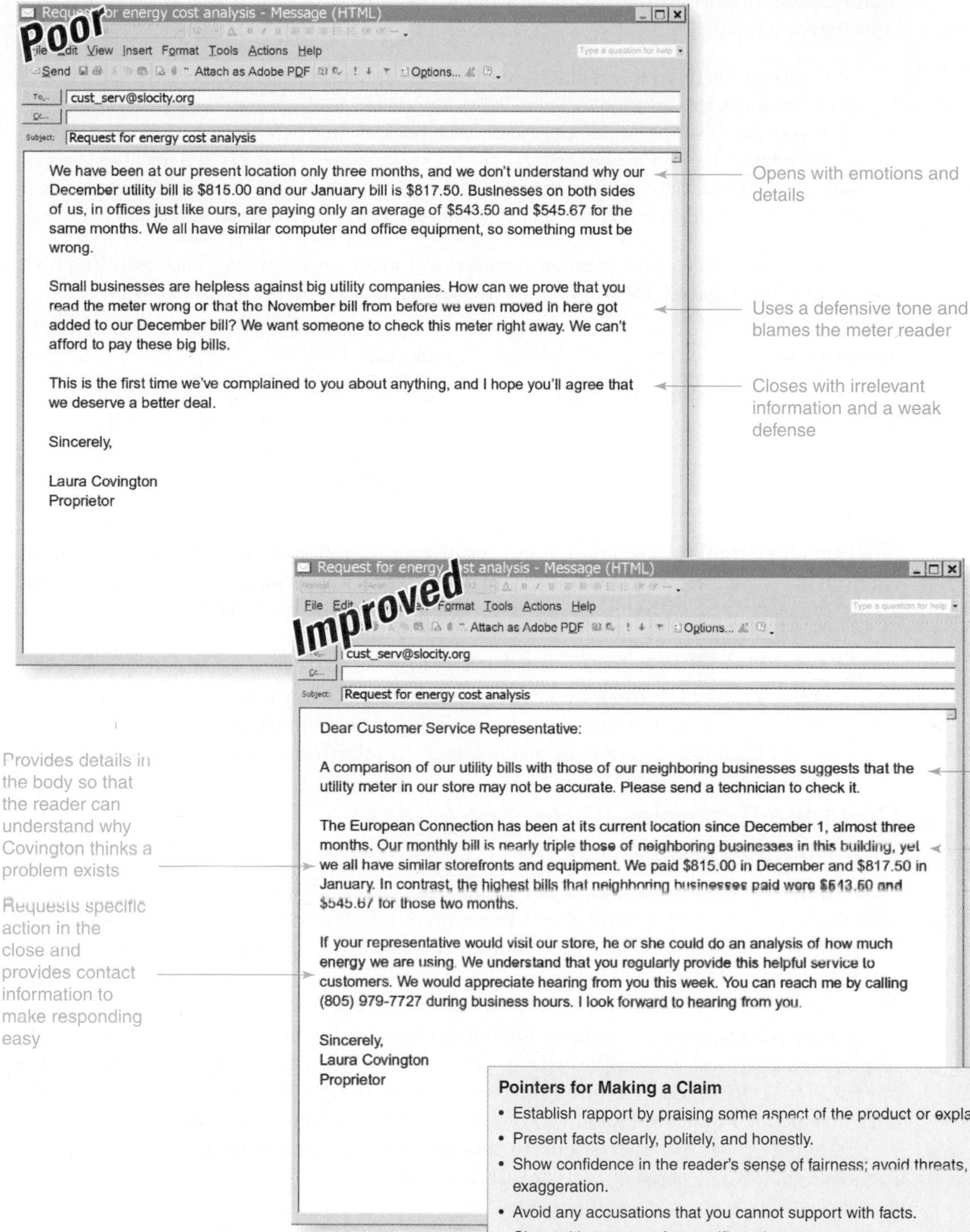

Poor

[Email window: Request for energy cost analysis - Message (HTML)]

To: cust_serv@slocity.org
Cc:
Subject: Request for energy cost analysis

We have been at our present location only three months, and we don't understand why our December utility bill is $815.00 and our January bill is $817.50. Businesses on both sides of us, in offices just like ours, are paying only an average of $543.50 and $545.67 for the same months. We all have similar computer and office equipment, so something must be wrong.

Small businesses are helpless against big utility companies. How can we prove that you read the meter wrong or that the November bill from before we even moved in here got added to our December bill? We want someone to check this meter right away. We can't afford to pay these big bills.

This is the first time we've complained to you about anything, and I hope you'll agree that we deserve a better deal.

Sincerely,

Laura Covington
Proprietor

— Opens with emotions and details

— Uses a defensive tone and blames the meter reader

— Closes with irrelevant information and a weak defense

Improved

[Email window: Request for energy cost analysis - Message (HTML)]

To: cust_serv@slocity.org
Cc:
Subject: Request for energy cost analysis

Dear Customer Service Representative:

A comparison of our utility bills with those of our neighboring businesses suggests that the utility meter in our store may not be accurate. Please send a technician to check it.

The European Connection has been at its current location since December 1, almost three months. Our monthly bill is nearly triple those of neighboring businesses in this building, yet we all have similar storefronts and equipment. We paid $815.00 in December and $817.50 in January. In contrast, the highest bills that neighboring businesses paid were $543.50 and $545.67 for those two months.

If your representative would visit our store, he or she could do an analysis of how much energy we are using. We understand that you regularly provide this helpful service to customers. We would appreciate hearing from you this week. You can reach me by calling (805) 979-7727 during business hours. I look forward to hearing from you.

Sincerely,
Laura Covington
Proprietor

Provides details in the body so that the reader can understand why Covington thinks a problem exists

Requests specific action in the close and provides contact information to make responding easy

— Opens by clearly and calmly stating the problem

— Presents details clearly, concisely, and completely

Pointers for Making a Claim

- Establish rapport by praising some aspect of the product or explaining why you purchased it.
- Present facts clearly, politely, and honestly.
- Show confidence in the reader's sense of fairness; avoid threats, sarcasm, hostility, or exaggeration.
- Avoid any accusations that you cannot support with facts.
- Close with a request for specific action.

Figure 7.4   Poor and Improved Versions of a Claim
Note the difference in both tone and information content in these two versions. The poor version is emotional and unprofessional, whereas the improved version communicates calmly and clearly.

The best way to write a clear opening is to have a clear idea of what you want to say. Before you begin to write, ask yourself, "What is the single most important message I have for the audience?"

Providing Necessary Details and Explanation

Use the body of your message to explain your point completely so that your audience will experience no confusion or lingering doubt. In addition to providing details in the body, maintain the supportive tone established in the opening. This tone is easy to continue when your message is entirely positive, as in this example:

> Your educational background and internship have impressed us, and we believe you would be a valuable addition to Green Valley Properties. As discussed during your interview, your salary will be $4,300 per month, plus benefits. In that regard, you will meet with our benefits manager, Paula Sanchez, at 8 a.m. on Monday, March 21. She will assist you with all the paperwork necessary to tailor our benefit package to your family situation. She will also arrange various orientation activities to help you acclimate to our company.

Try to embed any negative information in a positive context.

However, if your routine message is mixed and must convey mildly disappointing information, put the negative portion of your message into as favorable a context as possible:

Instead of This	Write This
No, we no longer carry the Sportsgirl line of sweaters.	The new Olympic line has replaced the Sportsgirl sweaters that you asked about. Olympic features a wider range of colors and sizes and more contemporary styling.

The more complete description is less negative and emphasizes how the audience can benefit from the change. However, if the negative news is likely to be a shock or particularly unpleasant for the reader, you'll want to use the indirect approach (discussed in Chapter 8).

Ending with a Courteous Close

Make sure audience members understand what to do next and how that action will benefit them.

Your message is more likely to succeed if your readers are left feeling that you have their best interests in mind. You can accomplish this by highlighting a benefit to the audience or by expressing appreciation or goodwill. If follow-up action is required, clearly state who will do what next.

Common Examples of Routine Replies and Positive Messages

Most routine and positive messages fall into six main categories: answers to requests for information and action, grants of claims and requests for adjustment, recommendations, informative messages, good-news announcements, and goodwill messages.

Answering Requests for Information and Action

Every professional answers requests for information and action from time to time. If the response to a request is a simple "yes" or some other straightforward information, a direct approach is appropriate. A prompt, gracious, and thorough response will positively influence how people think about you and the organization you represent (see Figure 7.5).

To handle repetitive queries quickly and consistently, companies usually develop form responses that can be personalized for each recipient. For instance, the mail merge capability in your word processor lets you personalize specific fields within the document, such as the recipient's name. If you have time and the message is important, go beyond this and revise the content of each message with information that's unique to each recipient (see Figure 7.6).

Granting Claims and Requests for Adjustment

Even the best-run companies make mistakes, from billing customers incorrectly to delivering products that fail to perform properly. In other cases, the customer or a third party might be responsible for the mistake, such as misusing a product or damaging it in shipment. Each of these events represents a turning point in your relationship with your customer. If you handle the situation well, your customer will likely be even more loyal than before because you've proven that you're serious about customer satisfaction. However, if a customer believes that you mishandled a complaint, you'll make the situation even worse. Dissatisfied customers often take their business elsewhere and are likely to tell numerous friends and colleagues about the negative experience. A transaction that might be worth only a few dollars by itself could cost you many times that amount in lost business.

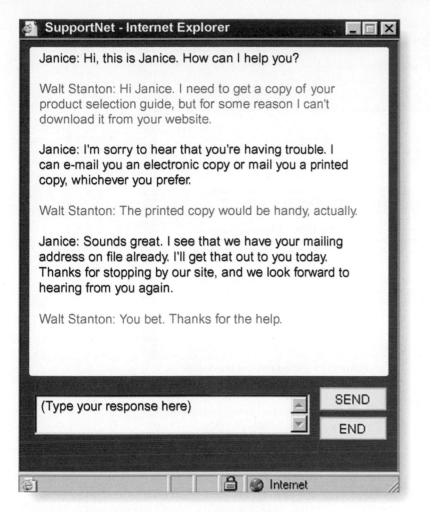

Figure 7.5   Effective IM Response to Information Request
This quick and courteous exchange is typical of IM communication in such areas as customer service and technical support. The agent (Janice) solves the problem quickly and leaves the customer with a positive impression of the company.

Consequently, view every mistake as an opportunity to improve a relationship. Unless you have strong reason to believe otherwise, start from the assumption that the information the customer provided is correct. From there, your response to the complaint depends on both your company's policies for resolving such issues and your assessment of whether the company, the customer, or some third party is at fault.

Responding to a Claim When Your Company Is at Fault   Before you respond when your firm is at fault, make sure you know your company's policies in such cases, which might even dictate specific legal and financial steps to be taken. Most routine responses should take your company's specific policies into account and address the following points:

- Acknowledge receipt of the customer's claim or complaint.
- Sympathize with the customer's inconvenience or frustration.
- Take (or assign) personal responsibility for setting matters straight.
- Explain precisely how you have resolved, or plan to resolve, the situation.
- Take steps to repair the relationship.
- Follow up to verify that your response was correct.

In addition to these positive steps, maintain professional demeanor by avoiding some key negative steps as well: Don't blame anyone in your organization by name, don't make

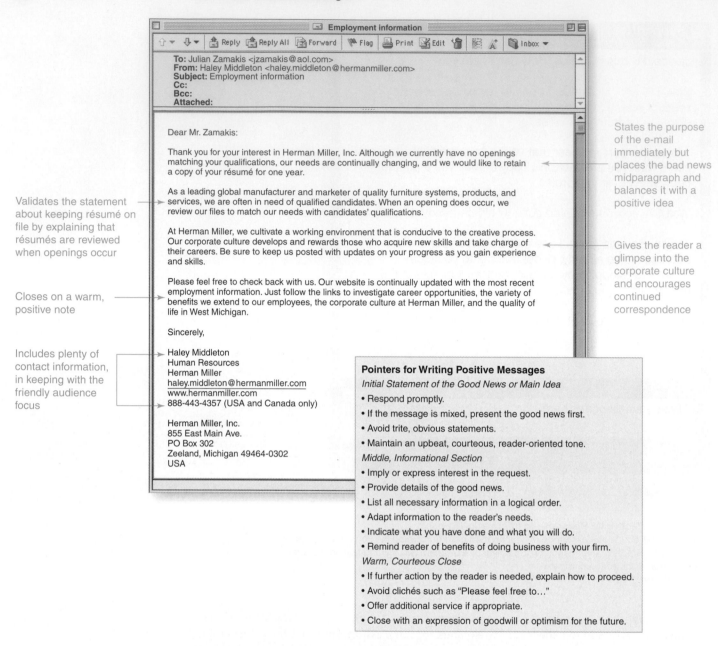

Figure 7.6   Personalized Reply to a Request for Information
This e-mail message personalizes a standardized response by including the recipient's name in the greeting.

exaggerated apologies that sound insincere, don't imply that the customer is at fault, and don't promise more than you can deliver.

Responding to a Claim When the Customer Is at Fault

Communication about a claim is a delicate matter when the customer is clearly at fault. You can refuse the claim and attempt to justify your refusal or simply do what the customer asks. If you refuse the claim, you may lose your customer—as well as many of the customer's friends and colleagues, who will hear only one side of the dispute. You must weigh the cost of making the adjustment against the cost of losing future business from one or more customers.

To grant a claim when the customer is at fault, try to discourage repeated mistakes without insulting the customer.

If you choose to grant the claim, simply open with that good news. However, the body needs special attention because you need to discourage repeated mistakes without insulting the customer (see Figure 7.7). Close in a courteous manner that expresses your appreciation for the customer's business.

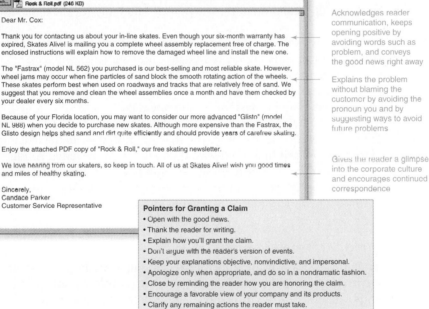

Planning

Analyze the Situation
Verify that the purpose is to grant the customer's claim, tactfully educate him, and encourage further business

Gather Information
Gather information on product care, warranties, and resale information.

Select the Right Medium
An e-mail message is appropriate in this case because the customer contacted the company via e-mail.

Organize the Information
You're responding with a positive answer, so a direct approach is fine.

Writing

Adapt to Your Audience
Show sensitivity to audience needs with a "you" attitude, politeness, positive emphasis, and bias-free language.

Compose the Message
Style is respectful while still managing to educate the customer on product usage and maintenance.

Completing

Revise the Message
Evaluate content and review readability; avoid unnecessary details.

Produce the Message
Emphasize a clean, professional appearance.

Proofread the Message
Review for errors in layout, spelling, and mechanics.

Distribute the Message
E-mail the reply.

1   **2**   **3**

Subtly promotes a more appropriate product for the customer

Closes on a positive note that conveys an attitude of excellent customer service

Acknowledges reader communication, keeps opening positive by avoiding words such as problem, and conveys the good news right away

Explains the problem without blaming the customer by avoiding the pronoun you and by suggesting ways to avoid future problems

Gives the reader a glimpse into the corporate culture and encourages continued correspondence

re: Warranty repair? (HTML)

To: SteveC955@verizon.net
Cc:
Subject: re: Warranty repair?
Attach: Rock & Roll.pdf (246 KB)

Dear Mr. Cox:

Thank you for contacting us about your in-line skates. Even though your six-month warranty has expired, Skates Alive! is mailing you a complete wheel assembly replacement free of charge. The enclosed instructions will explain how to remove the damaged wheel line and install the new one.

The "Fastrax" (model NL 562) you purchased is our best-selling and most reliable skate. However, wheel jams may occur when fine particles of sand block the smooth rotating action of the wheels. These skates perform best when used on roadways and tracks that are relatively free of sand. We suggest that you remove and clean the wheel assemblies once a month and have them checked by your dealer every six months.

Because of your Florida location, you may want to consider our more advanced "Glisto" (model NL 988) when you decide to purchase new skates. Although more expensive than the Fastrax, the Glisto design helps shed sand and dirt quite efficiently and should provide years of carefree skating.

Enjoy the attached PDF copy of "Rock & Roll," our free skating newsletter.

We love hearing from our skaters, so keep in touch. All of us at Skates Alive! wish you good times and miles of healthy skating.

Sincerely,
Candace Parker
Customer Service Representative

Pointers for Granting a Claim
- Open with the good news.
- Thank the reader for writing.
- Explain how you'll grant the claim.
- Don't argue with the reader's version of events.
- Keep your explanations objective, nonvindictive, and impersonal.
- Apologize only when appropriate, and do so in a nondramatic fashion.
- Close by reminding the reader how you are honoring the claim.
- Encourage a favorable view of your company and its products.
- Clarify any remaining actions the reader must take.

Figure 7.7   Responding to a Claim When the Customer Is at Fault
In the interest of positive customer relationships, this company agreed to provide replacement parts for a customer's in-line skates, even though the product is outside its warranty period. (For the sake of clarity, the content of the customer's original e-mail message is not reproduced here.)

Responding to a Claim When a Third Party Is at Fault   Sometimes neither your company nor your customer is at fault. For example, ordering a book from Amazon involves not only Amazon but also a delivery service such as FedEx or the U.S. Postal Service, the publisher and possibly a distributor of the book, a credit card issuer, and a company that processes credit card transactions. If something goes wrong, any one of these other partners might be at fault, but the customer is likely to blame Amazon because that is the entity that receives the customer's payment.

No general advice applies to every case involving a third party, so evaluate the situation carefully and know your company's policies before responding. For instance, an online

When a third party is at fault, your response depends on your company's agreements with that organization.

retailer and the companies that manufacture its merchandise might have an agreement specifying that the manufacturers automatically handle all complaints about product quality. However, regardless of who eventually resolves the problem, if customers contact you, you need to respond with messages that explain how the problem will be solved. Pointing fingers is both unproductive and unprofessional; resolving the situation is the only issue customers care about.

Providing Recommendations

When writing a letter of recommendation, your goal is to convince readers that the person being recommended has the characteristics necessary for the job, project assignment, or other objective the person is seeking. A successful recommendation letter contains a number of relevant details:

- The candidate's full name
- The position or other objective the candidate is seeking
- The nature of your relationship with the candidate
- An indication of whether you're answering a request from the person or taking the initiative to write
- Facts and evidence relevant to the candidate and the opportunity
- Your overall evaluation of the candidate's suitability for the opportunity

As surprising as this might sound, the most difficult recommendation letters to write are often those for truly outstanding candidates. Your audience will have trouble believing uninterrupted praise for someone's talents and accomplishments. To enhance your credibility—and the candidate's—illustrate your general points with specific examples that highlight the candidate's abilities and fitness for the job opening.

A serious shortcoming cannot be ignored in a recommendation, but beware of being libelous:

- Include only relevant, factual information
- Avoid value judgments
- Balance criticisms with favorable points

If the candidate has shortcomings that are relevant to the opportunity, you'll need to decide how to handle the situation. You may opt not to write the letter, in which case you're not necessarily obliged to explain why. If you do write the letter, you have an ethical obligation not to hide negative information. You don't have to present the shortcomings as simple criticisms, however. A good option is to list them as areas for improvement, particularly if the person is already committed to making improvements (see Figure 7.8).

Creating Informative Messages

When writing informative messages

- State the purpose at the beginning and briefly mention the nature of the information you are providing
- Provide the necessary details
- End with a courteous close

All companies send routine informative messages, such as reminder notices and policy statements. Use the opening to state the purpose (to inform) and briefly mention the nature of the information you are providing. Unlike the replies discussed earlier, informative messages are not solicited by your reader, so make it clear up front why the reader is receiving this particular message. In the body, provide the necessary details. End your message with a courteous close.

Most informative communications are neutral and straightforward, but some may require additional care. For instance, policy statements or procedural changes may be good news for a company, such as by saving money. However, it may not be obvious to employees that such savings may make available additional employee resources or even pay raises. In instances in which the reader may not initially view the information positively, use the body of the message to highlight the potential benefits from the reader's perspective.

Fostering Goodwill

Goodwill is the positive feeling that encourages people to maintain a business relationship.

All business messages should be written with an eye toward fostering positive relationships with audiences, but some messages are written specifically to build goodwill. You can use these messages to enhance your relationships with customers, colleagues, and other businesspeople by sending friendly, even unexpected, notes with no direct business purpose.

Point1 Promotions

105 E. Madison
Ann Arbor, MI 48103
tel: 800-747-9786
e-mail: info@point1promo.net
www.point1promo.net

November 14, 2009

Ms. Clarice Gailey
Director of Operations
McNally and Associates, Inc.
8688 Southgate Ave.
Augusta, GA 30906

Dear Ms. Gailey:

I am pleased to recommend Talvin Biswas for the marketing position at McNally and Associates. Mr. Biswas has worked with Point1 Promotions as an intern for the past two summers while working toward his degree in marketing and advertising. His duties included customer correspondence, web content updates, and direct-mail campaign planning.

As his supervisor, in addition to knowing his work here, I also know that Mr. Biswas has served as secretary for the International Business Association at the University of Michigan. He tutored other international students in the university's writing center. His fluency in three languages (English, French, and Hindi) and thorough knowledge of other cultures will make him an immediate contributor to your international operations.

Mr. Biswas is a thoughtful and careful professional who will not hesitate to contribute ideas when invited to do so. In addition, because Mr. Biswas learns quickly, he will learn your company's routine with ease.

Mr. Biswas will make an excellent addition to your staff at McNally and Associates. If I can provide any additional information, please call or fax me at the numbers above. If you prefer to communicate by e-mail, my address is angela_leclerc@point1promo.net.

Sincerely,

Angela LeClerc

Angela LeClerc
Vice President, Marketing

Margin annotations:

Specifies duration and nature of relationship in the body to give weight to the evaluation

Closes by inviting reader to discuss the candidate further

Clearly states candidate's full name and the main point of the letter in the opening

Begins the close by summarizing the supportive evaluation

Pointers for Writing Recommendation Letters

- Take great care to avoid a lawsuit (either for including too much negative information or for omitting negative information).
- Follow your company's policies in all details; verify only the dates of employment and job titles if that is all the information your company allows to be released.
- Release information only to people who have written authorization from the former employee.
- Consider collaborating with the former employee so that the contents of the letter meet both of your needs.
- If you are unable or unwilling to represent your company in a professional capacity, offer to be a personal reference instead.
- Comment only on your direct experience working with the former employee.
- Limit your remarks to provable facts; avoid hyperbole.
- Ask your human resource department to review the letter before you send it.

Figure 7.8   Effective Recommendation Letter
This letter clearly states the nature of the writer's relationship to the candidate and provides specific examples to support the writer's endorsements.

Effective goodwill messages must be sincere and honest. Otherwise, you'll appear to be interested in personal gain rather than in benefiting customers, fellow workers, or your organization. To come across as sincere, avoid exaggerating and support compliments with specific evidence. In addition, readers often regard more restrained praise as being more sincere:

Make sure your compliments are both sincere and honest.

Instead of This	Write This
Words cannot express my appreciation for the great job you did. Thanks. No one could have done it better. You're terrific! You've made the whole firm sit up and take notice, and we are ecstatic to have you working here.	Thanks again for taking charge of the meeting in my absence and doing such an excellent job. With just an hour's notice, you pulled the legal and public relations departments together to present a united front in the negotiations. Your dedication and communication abilities have been noted and are truly appreciated.

Sending Congratulations

One prime opportunity for sending goodwill messages is to congratulate individuals or companies for significant business achievements—perhaps for being promoted or for attaining product sales milestones. Other reasons for sending congratulations include the highlights in people's personal lives, such as weddings, births, graduations, and success in nonbusiness competitions. You may congratulate business acquaintances on their own achievements or on the accomplishments of a spouse or child. You may also take note of personal events, even if you don't know the reader well. If you're already friendly with the reader, a more personal tone is appropriate.

Sending Messages of Appreciation

An important business quality is the ability to recognize the contributions of employees, colleagues, suppliers, and other associates. Your praise does more than just make the person feel good; it encourages further excellence. A message of appreciation may also become an important part of someone's personnel file. So when you write a message of appreciation, try to specifically mention the person or people you want to praise, as in this example:

> Thank you and everyone on your team for the heroic efforts you took to bring our servers back up after last Friday's flood. We were able to restore business right on schedule first thing Monday morning. You went far beyond the level of contractual service in restoring our data center within 16 hours. I would especially like to highlight the contribution of networking specialist Julienne Marks, who worked for 12 straight hours to reconnect our Internet service. If I can serve as a reference in your future sales activities, please do not hesitate to ask.

Hearing a sincere thank you can do wonders for morale.[2] Moreover, in today's electronic media environment, a handwritten thank-you note can be a particularly welcome acknowledgment.[3]

Offering Condolences

In times of serious trouble and deep sadness, well-written condolences and expressions of sympathy can mean a great deal to people who've experienced loss. This type of message is difficult to write, but don't let the difficulty of the task keep you from responding promptly.

Open a condolence message with a brief statement of sympathy, such as "I was deeply sorry to hear of your loss" in the event of a death, for example. In the body, mention the good qualities or the positive contributions made by the deceased. State what the person meant to you or your colleagues. In closing, you can offer your condolences and your best wishes. Here are a few general suggestions for writing condolence messages:

- **Keep reminiscences brief.** Recount a memory or an anecdote (even a humorous one) but don't dwell on the details of the loss, lest you add to the reader's anguish.
- **Write in your own words.** Write as if you were speaking privately to the person. Don't quote "poetic" passages or use stilted or formal phrases. If the loss is a death, refer to it as such rather than as "passing away" or "departing."
- **Be tactful.** Mention your shock and dismay but remember that bereaved and distressed loved ones take little comfort in lines such as "Richard was too young to die."
- **Take special care.** Be sure to spell names correctly and to be accurate in your review of facts. Try to be prompt.
- **Write about special qualities of the deceased.** You may have to rely on reputation to do this, but let the grieving person know you valued his or her loved one.
- **Write about special qualities of the bereaved person.** A pat on the back helps a bereaved family member feel more confident about handling things during such a traumatic time.[4]

Supervisor George Bigalow sent the following condolence letter to his administrative assistant, Janice Case, after learning of the death of Janice's husband:

> My sympathy to you and your children. All your friends at Carter Electric were so very sorry to learn of John's death. Although I never had the opportunity to meet him, I do

know how very special he was to you. Your tales of your family's camping trips and his rafting expeditions were always memorable.

For the latest information on writing routine and positive messages, visit http://real-timeupdates.com/bce and click on Chapter 7. ■

DOCUMENT MAKEOVER

Improve This E-Mail Message

To practice correcting drafts of actual documents, visit the "Document Makeovers" section in either MyBCommLab.com or the Companion Website for this text.

If MyBCommLab.com is being used in your class, see your User Guide for specific instructions on how to access the content for this chapter.

If you are accessing this feature through the Companion Website, click on "Document Makeovers" and then select Chapter 7. You will find an e-mail message that contains problems and errors related to what you've learned in this chapter about writing routine and positive messages. Use the Final Draft decision tool to create an improved version of this e-mail message. ●

CHAPTER REVIEW AND ACTIVITIES

Chapter Summary

To plan routine messages, take a few moments to analyze your purpose and audience, investigate your readers' needs and make sure that you have all the facts to satisfy them, and adapt your message to your audience. When writing these messages, use the direct approach, as long as your readers' reaction will be positive (or at least neutral). Completing routine messages means making them as professional as possible by revising for clarity and conciseness, selecting appropriate design elements and delivery methods, and proofreading with care.

When writing a routine request, open by stating your specific request. Use the body to justify your request and explain its importance. Close routine requests by asking for specific action (including a deadline, if appropriate) and expressing goodwill.

A courteous close contains three important elements: (1) a specific request, (2) information about how you can be reached (if it isn't obvious), and (3) an expression of appreciation or goodwill.

Your response to a claim or a request for an adjustment can vary significantly, depending on which party you determine to be at fault. If your company is at fault, your message should acknowledge the complaint, take responsibility, sympathize, explain how you will resolve the situation, and take steps to repair the relationship. If the customer is at fault, you have to decide whether to grant the claim in the interest of keeping the customer's business. If a third party is at fault, your response will be determined by whatever arrangements are in place between your company and the third party.

The key difference between creating informative messages and responding to information requests is a matter of who initiates the communication. When you create an informative message, your audience members may or may not be expecting it and may or may not be motivated to read it, so you need to gauge their potential reaction and plan your message accordingly. In contrast, when someone else initiates the request, that person will obviously be anticipating your response.

Goodwill messages are important for building relationships with customers, colleagues, and other businesspeople. These include messages of congratulations, appreciation, and condolence. To make goodwill messages effective, make them honest, sincere, and factual.

Test Your Knowledge

1. What are three guidelines for asking a series of questions in a routine request?

2. Should you use the direct or indirect approach for most routine messages? Why?

3. What six pieces of information must be included in a letter of recommendation?

4. How can you avoid sounding insincere when writing a goodwill message?

5. What are six guidelines for writing condolence messages?

Apply Your Knowledge

1. Why is it good practice to explain that replying to a request could benefit the reader?

2. Your company's error cost an important business customer a new client; you know it, and your customer knows it. Do you apologize, or do you refer to the incident in a positive light without admitting any responsibility? Briefly explain.

3. You've been asked to write a letter of recommendation for an employee who worked for you some years ago. You recall that the employee did an admirable job, but you can't remember any specific information at this point. Should you write the letter anyway? Explain.

4. Every time you send a direct-request memo to Ted Jackson, he delays or refuses to comply. You're beginning to get impatient. Should you send Jackson an e-mail message to ask what's wrong? Complain to your supervisor about Jackson's uncooperative attitude? Arrange a face-to-face meeting with Jackson? Bring up the problem at the next staff meeting? Explain.

5. **Ethical Choices**   You have a complaint against one of your suppliers, but you have no documentation to back it up. Should you request an adjustment anyway? Why or why not?

Practice Your Knowledge

Exercises for Perfecting Your Writing

Revising Messages: Direct Approach   Revise the following short e-mail messages so that they are more direct and concise; develop a subject line for each revised message.

1. I'm contacting you about your recent order for a High Country backpack. You didn't tell us which backpack you wanted, and you know we make a lot of different ones. We have the canvas models with the plastic frames and vinyl trim, and we have

the canvas models with leather trim, and we have the ones that have more pockets than the other ones. Plus they come in lots of different colors. Also they make the ones that are large for a big-boned person and the smaller versions for little women or kids.

Subject line: _____

2. Thank you for contacting us about the difficulty you had collecting your luggage at the Denver airport. We are very sorry for the inconvenience this has caused you. As you know, traveling can create problems of this sort regardless of how careful the airline personnel might be. To receive compensation, please send us a detailed list of the items that you lost and complete the following questionnaire. You can e-mail it back to us.

Subject line: _____

3. Sorry it took us so long to get back to you. We were flooded with résumés. Anyway, your résumé made the final ten, and after meeting three hours yesterday, we've decided we'd like to meet with you. What is your schedule like for next week? Can you come in for an interview on June 15 at 3:00 p.m.? Please get back to us by the end of this work week and let us know if you will be able to attend. As you can imagine, this is our busy season.

Subject line: _____

Revising Messages: Direct Approach   Rewrite the following sentences so that they are direct and concise.

4. We wanted to invite you to our special 40 percent off by-invitation-only sale. The sale is taking place on November 9.

5. We wanted to let you know that we are giving an MP3 player with every $100 donation you make to our radio station.

6. The director planned to go to the meeting that will be held on Monday at a little before 11:00 A.M.

7. In today's meeting, we were happy to have the opportunity to welcome Paul Eccelson. He reviewed some of the newest types of order forms. If you have any questions about these new forms, feel free to call him at his office.

Teamwork   With another student, conduct an audience analysis of the following message topic: A notice to all employees about the placement of recycling bins by the elevator doors.

8. What is the purpose of this message?

9. What is the most appropriate format for communicating this written message?

10. How is the audience likely to respond to this message?

11. Based on this audience analysis, would you use the direct or the indirect approach for this message? Explain your reasoning.

Revising Messages: Closing Paragraphs   Rewrite each of the following closing paragraphs to be concise, courteous, and specific.

12. I need your response sometime soon so I can order the parts in time for your service appointment. Otherwise your air-conditioning system may not be in tip-top condition for the start of the summer season.

13. Thank you in advance for sending me as much information as you can about your products. I look forward to receiving your package in the very near future.

14. To schedule an appointment with one of our knowledgeable mortgage specialists in your area, you can always call our hotline at 1-800-555-8765. This is also the number to call if you have more questions about mortgage rates, closing procedures, or any other aspect of the mortgage process. Remember, we're here to make the home-buying experience as painless as possible.

Activities

Active links for all websites in this chapter can be found online. If MyBCommLab.com is being used in your class, see your User Guide for instructions on accessing the content for this chapter. Otherwise, visit www.pearsonhighered.com/bovee, locate *Business Communication Essentials*, Fourth Edition, click the Companion Website link, select Chapter 7, and then click on "Featured Websites." Please note that links to sites that become inactive after publication of the book will be removed from the Featured Websites section.

1. **Analyze This Message**   Read the following document and (1) analyze the strengths and weaknesses of each sentence and (2) revise the document so that it follows this chapter's guidelines.

   Our college is closing its dining hall for financial reasons, so we want to do something to help the students prepare their own food in their dorm rooms if they so choose. Your colorful ad in *Collegiate Magazine* caught our eye. We need the following information before we make our decision.

   1. Would you be able to ship the microwaves by August 15th? I realize this is short notice, but our board of trustees just made the decision to close the dining hall last week and we're scrambling around trying to figure out what to do.
   2. Do they have any kind of a warranty? College students can be pretty hard on things, as you know, so we will need a good warranty.
   3. How much does it cost? Do you give a discount for a big order?
   4. Do we have to provide a special outlet?
   5. Will students know how to use them, or will we need to provide instructions?

   As I said before, we're on a tight time frame and need good information from you as soon as possible to help us make our decision about ordering. You never know what the board might come up with next. I'm looking at several other companies, also, so please let us know ASAP.

2. **Analyze This Message**   Read the following document and (1) analyze the strengths and weaknesses of each sentence and (2) revise the document so that it follows this chapter's guidelines.

   At a local business-supply store, I recently purchased your "Negotiator Pro" for my computer. I bought the CD because I saw your ad for it in *Macworld* magazine, and it looked as if it might be an effective tool for use in my corporate seminar on negotiation.

   Unfortunately, when I inserted it in my office computer, it wouldn't work. I returned it to the store, but since I had already opened it, they refused to exchange it for a CD that would work or give me a refund. They told me to contact you and that you might be able to send me a version that would work with my computer.

   You can send the information to me at the letterhead address. If you cannot send me the correct disk, please refund my $79.95. Thanks in advance for any help you can give me in this matter.

3. **Analyze This Message**   Read the following document and (1) analyze the strengths and weaknesses of each sentence and (2) revise the document so that it follows this chapter's guidelines.

   I'm contacting you about your recent e-mail request for technical support on your cable Internet service. Part of the problem we have in tech support is trying to figure out exactly what each customer's specific problem is so that we can troubleshoot quickly and get you back in business as quickly as possible. You may have noticed that in the online support request form, there are a number of fields to enter your type of computer, operating system, memory, and so on. While you did tell us you were experiencing slow download speeds during certain times of the day, you didn't tell us which times specifically, nor did you complete all the fields telling us about your computer. Please return to our support website and resubmit your request, being sure to provide all the necessary information; then we'll be able to help you.

4. **Analyze This Message**   Read the following document and (1) analyze the strengths and weaknesses of each sentence and (2) revise the document so that it follows this chapter's guidelines.

Your letter to Kunitake Ando, President of Sony, was forwarded to me because I am the human resources director. In my job as head of HR, I have access to performance reviews for all of the Sony employees in the United States. This means, of course, that I would be the person best qualified to answer your request for information on Nick Oshinski.

In your letter of the 15th, you asked about Nick Oshinski's employment record with us because he has applied to work for your company. Mr. Oshinski was employed with us from January 5, 1998, until March 1, 2008. During that time, Mr. Oshinski received ratings ranging from 2.5 up to 9.6, with 10 being the top score. As you can see, he must have done better reporting to some managers than to others. In addition, he took all vacation days, which is a bit unusual. Although I did not know Mr. Oshinski personally, I know that our best workers seldom use all the vacation time they earn. I do not know if that applies in this case.

In summary, Nick Oshinski performed his tasks well depending on who managed him.

5. **Internet**   Visit the Workplace eCards section of the Blue Mountain site, at www.bluemountain.com, and analyze one of the electronic greeting cards bearing a goodwill message of appreciation for good performance. Under what circumstances would you send this electronic message? How could you personalize it for the recipient and the occasion? What would be an appropriate close for this message?

6. **Ethical Choices**   Your company markets a line of automotive accessories for people who like to "tune" their cars for maximum performance. A customer has just written a furious e-mail, claiming that a supercharger he purchased from your website didn't deliver the extra engine power he expected. Your company has a standard refund process to handle situations such as this, and you have the information you need to inform the customer about that. You also have information that could help the customer find a more compatible supercharger from one of your competitors, but the customer's e-mail message is so abusive that you don't feel obligated to help. Is this an appropriate response? Why or why not?

7. **Planning a Letter: Air Rage Fiasco**   You've been administrative assistant to Samantha Alberts, vice president of sales for Richter Office Solutions, for two years. You handle all her travel arrangements, and you've never seen her so upset. The "air rage" incident happened on Friday, and now it's Monday, but she's still pale and shaky.

"There we were, cruising over the Atlantic, and the guy just erupted! I couldn't believe it!" she says for the third time.

She was flying back from a conference in London to make a presentation at your New York branch. Then she was to catch a plane home to San Francisco on Saturday. With airline security so tight these days, she expected a calm flight and lots of time to prepare her presentation notes as she crossed the ocean. As it turned out, she spent most of that time fearing for her life.

"What made the guy angry?" you ask.

"Apparently some passengers complained about 'offensive images' he was viewing on his laptop. When the flight attendant politely asked him to stop, the guy went nuts and started hitting people, swearing all the while. At first I thought he was a hijacker and I was going to die on that plane! Thank goodness several crew members and passengers were able to subdue him and handcuff him into a back row seat. But we still had hours over the Atlantic before the pilot could land, so we had to listen to him screaming profanity. Finally, a passenger who was a pediatrician injected him with a sedative."

"Did they arrest him?" you want to know.

"As soon as we got on the ground. Police cars were everywhere. He just kept muttering, 'I thought they were going to kill me.'" She shudders. "But the flight attendants and airline officials were wonderful. They told us to write to the airline, explain the details, and ask for a refund."

"Of course, I was late and unprepared for my presentation. When they heard what happened, the folks in our New York office just handed me a cup of herb tea, sat me on a couch with a blanket, and told me to forget about making any presentations that day."

Samantha leaves you her ticket stubs and other documents. She's expecting you to write the refund request to British Airways Ticket Refunds USA, 75-20 Astoria Blvd., Jackson Heights, NY 11370. Before you begin, consider these questions:[5]

    a. For the purpose of this exercise, what details will you need to make up to write the request?

    b. Will you use a direct or indirect approach? Why?

    c. What tone should you adopt? What should you avoid?

    d. How will you support the claim?

    e. What would be an effective closing for this request?

8. Planning a Letter: Intercultural Condolences   You've been working two years as administrative assistant to Ron Glover, vice president of global workforce diversity at IBM's Learning Center in Armonk, New York. After listening to many of his speeches on maintaining multicultural sensitivity in the workplace, you know you're facing a sensitive situation right now. You need to stop and think before you act.

The husband of your co-worker Chana Panichpapiboon was killed in a bus accident yesterday, along with 19 others. The bus skidded on icy pavement into a deep ravine, tipping over and crushing the occupants before rescue workers could get to them.

You met her husband, Surin, last year at a company banquet. You can still picture his warm smile and the easy way he joked with you and others over chicken Florentine, even though you were complete strangers to him. He was only 32 years old, and he left Chana with two children, a 12-year-old boy, Arsa, and a 10-year-old girl, Veera. His death is a terrible tragedy.

Normally, you'd write a condolence letter immediately. But Chana Panichpapiboon is a native of Thailand, and so was Surin. You know you'd better do a little research first. Is Chana Buddhist or Catholic? Is there anything about the typical Western practice of expressing sympathy that might be inappropriate? Offensive?

After making some discreet inquiries among Chana's closest friends at work, you learn that she is Theravada Buddhist, as are most people in Thailand. In a reference book your boss lends you about doing business around the world, you read that in Thailand, "the person takes precedence over rule or law" and "people gain their social position as a result of karma, not personal achievement," which means Chana may believe in reincarnation. But the book also says that Theravada Buddhists are free to choose which precepts of their religion, if any, they will follow. So Chana's beliefs are still a mystery.

You do know that her husband was very important to her and much loved by all their family. That, at least, is universal. And you're considering using a poetic line you remember, "The hand of time lightly lays, softly soothing sorrow's wound." Is it appropriate?

You've decided to handwrite the condolence note on a blank greeting card you've found that bears a peaceful, "Eastern-flavor" image. You know you're risking a cultural gaffe, but you don't want to commit the offense of not writing at all. Use the following questions to help you think through your choices before you begin writing:[6]

    a. If you had to choose among these sentences, which one would make the best opening?

        1. I was so sorry to hear the news about your husband.

        2. What a terrible tragedy you have suffered.

        3. If there's anything I can do for you, Chana, please let me know.

        4. You and your children must be so upset, and who could blame you?

b. In the body of the letter, you want to express something meaningful, but you're concerned about Chana's beliefs and you're not sure what's safe. Choose the best idea from the following:

1. You could quote the poem about "the hand of time" mentioned in the case.
2. You could express your sorrow for Chana's children.
3. You could mention something nice about Surin you learned during your brief meeting.

c. For your closing paragraph, which of these ideas is best?

1. Take a moment to express your thoughts about death and the hereafter.
2. Say something positive and encouraging about Chana.
3. Explain that you don't understand her religious beliefs and aren't sure what's appropriate to say at this time.
4. All of the above.

d. In the following list, circle all the words you should avoid as you write:

1. Death
2. Departure
3. Karma
4. Unbearable

Now write the condolence letter in your own words. Remember that sincerity is the most important tool in overcoming differences of custom or tradition.

9. Revising a Letter: Vacation Planning   The following letter requesting information about resorts in Florida contains numerous errors, based on what you've learned in this chapter. Read the letter carefully and analyze its flaws. Then use the steps that follow to outline and write a better version of the request.

5493 Beechwood Drive
Trenton, N.J. 08608
April 12, 2009

Florida Resort Bureau
1555 Palm Beach Lakes Boulevard
West Palm Beach, FL 33401

Dear Sir:

My wife and I are planning a late September vacation with our two teenage children. We need this information in the next two weeks so I can schedule my time off from work in the fall. I enjoy the beach and the golf course, but we also want to be near night entertainment suitable for the whole family. I am particularly interested in resort areas that have public transportation available; some family members may want to participate in activities away from the resort.

In addition to the brochures your advertisement promises, will you please also tell me which resorts are near large cities, which are reached by public transportation and have attractions for teenagers and do the off-season rates include all the amenities? Can you tell me additionally about the weather during September in Florida, and who we should call for concert schedules during our vacation?

Your advertisement about Florida resorts in the April 2009 issue of *Smithsonian* magazine caught my eye.

Frank C. Atlas

a. Describe the flaws you discovered in this letter requesting information.
b. Develop a plan for rewriting the letter. Use the following steps to organize your efforts before you begin writing:

1. Create a clear statement of your request.
2. Decide what explanation is needed to justify your request.
3. Determine whether you can use lists effectively in your letter.

4. Ask for specific action.

5. Mention a deadline and reason to respond, if appropriate.

c. Now rewrite the letter. Don't forget to leave ample time for revision of your own work before you turn it in.

Exploring the Best of the Web

Get Some Great Recommendations for Recommendation Letters Whether you're continuing to graduate school or entering the workforce with your undergraduate degree, recommendation letters could play an important role in the next few steps of your career. From selecting the people to ask for recommendation letters to knowing what makes an effective letter, About.com extends the advice offered in this chapter with real-life examples and suggestions. Visit About.com's Business School website, at http://businessmajors. about.com, and click on "Recommendation Letters." Read the advice you find and then answer the following questions.

Exercises

1. What is a good process for identifying the best people to ask for recommendation letters?

2. What information should you provide to letter writers to help them produce a credible and compelling letter on your behalf?

3. What are the most common mistakes you need to avoid with recommendation letters?

Surfing Your Way to Career Success

Bovée and Thill's Business Communication Headline News offers links to hundreds of online resources that can help you with this course, your other college courses, and your career. Visit http://businesscommunicationblog.com and click on "Web Directory." The Communication on the Job section connects you to a variety of websites and articles on committees and teams, group communication, team conflict, negotiation, office politics, and the grapevine. Identify three websites from this section that could be useful in your business career. For each site, write a two-sentence summary of what the site offers and how it could help you launch and build your career.

MyBCommLab.com

Use MyBCommLab.com to test your understanding of the concepts presented in this chapter and explore additional materials that will bring the ideas to life in video, activities, and an online multimedia e-book. Additionally, you can improve your skill with sentences by using the "Peak Performance Grammar and Mechanics" module within the lab. Take the Pretest to determine whether you have any weak areas. Then review those areas in the Refresher Course. Take the Follow-Up Test to check your grasp of sentences. For an extra challenge, take the Advanced Test. Finally, for even more reinforcement, go to the "Improve Your Grammar, Mechanics, and Usage" section that follows the cases, and complete the "Level 1: Self-Assessment" exercises.

CASES

▼ *Apply the three-step writing process to the following cases, as assigned by your instructor.*

[E-MAIL SKILLS]

1. Breathing Life Back into Your Biotech Career: E-Mail Requesting a Recommendation After five years of work in the human resources department at Cell Genesys (a company that is developing cancer treatment drugs), you were laid off in a round of cost-cutting moves that rippled through the biotech industry in recent years. The good news is that you found stable employment in the grocery distribution industry. The bad news is that in the three years since you left Cell Genesys, you truly miss working in the exciting biotechnology field and having the opportunity to be a part of something as important as helping people recover from life-threatening diseases. You

know that careers in biotech are uncertain, but you have a few dollars in the bank now, so you're more willing to accept the risk of being laid off at some point in the future.

Your task Draft an e-mail to Calvin Morris, your old boss at Cell Genesys, reminding him of the time you worked together and asking him to write a letter of recommendation for you.[7]

[IM SKILLS]

2. Trans-Global Exchange: Instant Message Request for Information from Chinese Manufacturer Thank goodness your company, Diagonal Imports, chose the instant messaging software produced by IBM Lotus, called Sametime. Other products might allow you to carry on real-time exchanges with colleagues on the other side of the planet, but Sametime supports bidirectional machine translation, and you're going to need it.

It seems that production on a popular line of decorative lighting appliances produced at your Chinese manufacturing plant inexplicably came to a halt last month. As the product manager in the United States, you have many resources you could call on to help, such as new sources for faulty parts. But you can't do anything if you don't know the details. You've tried telephoning top managers in China, but they're evasive, telling you only what they think you want to hear.

Finally, your friend Kuei-chen Tsao has returned from a business trip. You met her during your trip to China last year. She doesn't speak English, but she's the line engineer responsible for this particular product: a fiber-optic lighting display, featuring a plastic base with a rotating color wheel. As the wheel turns, light emitted from the spray of fiber-optic threads changes color in soothing patterns. Product #3347XM is one of Diagonal's most popular items, and you've got orders from novelty stores around the United States waiting to be filled. Kuei-chen should be able to explain the problem, determine whether you can help, and tell you how long before regular shipping resumes.

Your task Write the first of what you hope will be a productive instant messaging exchange with Kuei-Chen. Remember that your words will be machine translated.[8]

[TEXT MESSAGING SKILLS]

3. Tracking the New Product Buzz: Text Message to Colleagues at a Trade Show The vast Consumer Electronics Show (CES) is the premier promotional event in the electronics industry. More than 130,000 industry insiders from all over the world come to see the exciting new products on display from nearly 1,500 companies—everything from video game gadgets to Internet-enabled refrigerators with built-in computer screens. You've just stumbled on a video game controller that has a built-in webcam to allow networked gamers to see and hear each other while they play. Your company also makes game controllers, and you're worried that your customers will flock to this new controller-cam. You need to know how much "buzz" is circulating around the show: Have people seen it? What are they saying about it? Are they excited about it?

Your task Compose a text message to your colleagues at the show, alerting them to the new controller-cam and asking them to listen for any buzz that it might be generating among the attendees at the Las Vegas Convention Center and the several surrounding hotels where the show takes place. Here's the catch: Your text messaging service limits messages to 160 characters, including spaces and punctuation, so your message can't be any longer than this.[9]

[E-MAIL SKILLS] [PORTFOLIO BUILDER]

4. That's Not the Way Things Really Are: Correcting Economic Misinformation As the CEO of a small manufacturing company, your interests and responsibilities range far beyond the four walls of the factory. You have to be in tune with the global economy, politics, taxation policies, and other external forces that affect your company and your employees. Along with your peers in other companies, you've learned to speak out on issues—particularly when you believe that misguided government policies or misinformed public opinions threaten the viability of your company, your industry, and the economy as a whole.

An item in this morning's newspaper certainly got your attention. A prominent national political leader claimed that job-growth figures in recent years prove that the government's economic policies are working. The economy is in reasonably good shape, considering the battering it has taken in recent years, but you believe the situation would improve considerably if the government would address a variety of issues, from health-care costs to economic incentives for investing in manufacturing upgrades. Moreover, you know that the politician's claim about job growth is only partly true. Yes, the U.S. economy added nearly 2 million new jobs in the past five years, but a recent *BusinessWeek* article pointed out that virtually all those jobs were in health care. Not only did all other industries not add jobs as a whole, but the dramatic rise in health-care employment suggests no end to the rise in health-care costs.

Your task Write a brief e-mail message (no more than 300 words) to the editor of the newspaper. Correct the impression that job growth is occurring throughout the economy and encourage political leaders to address problems that you believe continue to limit growth in other industries, including health-care costs, taxation policies in the manufacturing sector, and unfair competitive practices from companies in certain other countries. Make up whatever information you need to back up your claims.[10]

[PODCASTING SKILLS] [PORTFOLIO BUILDER]

5. Listening to Business: Using the iPod to Train Employees As a training specialist in the human resources department at Winnebago Industries, you're always on the lookout for new ways to help employees learn vital job skills. While watching a production worker page through a training manual while learning how to assemble a new recreational vehicle, you get what seems to be a great idea: Record the assembly instructions as audio files that workers can listen to while performing the necessary steps. With audio instructions, they wouldn't need to keep shifting their eyes between the product and the manual—and constantly losing their place. They could focus on the product and listen for each instruction. Plus, the new system wouldn't cost much at all; any computer can record the audio files, and you'd simply make them available on an intranet site for download into iPods or other digital music players.

Your task You immediately run your new idea past your boss, who has heard about podcasting but doesn't think it has any place in business. He asks you to prove the viability of the idea by recording a demonstration. Choose a process that you engage in yourself—anything from replacing the strings on a guitar to sewing a quilt to changing the oil in a car—and write a brief (one page or less) description of the process that could be recorded as an audio file. Think carefully about the limitations of the audio format as a replacement for printed text (for instance, do you need to tell people to pause the audio while they perform a time-consuming task?).

E-MAIL SKILLS

6. Auto-Talk: E-Mail Messages for Highway Bytes Computers to Be Sent Automatically

You are director of customer services at Highway Bytes, which markets a series of small, handlebar-mounted computers for bicyclists. These Cycle Computers do everything, from computing speed and distance traveled to displaying street maps. Serious cyclists love them, but your company is growing so fast that you can't keep up with all the customer service requests you receive every day. Your boss wants not only to speed up response time but also to reduce staffing costs and allow your technical experts the time they need to focus on the most difficult and important questions.

You've just been reading about automated response systems, and you quickly review a few articles before discussing the options with your boss. Artificial intelligence researchers have been working for decades to design systems that can actually converse with customers, ask questions, and respond to requests. Some of today's systems have vocabularies of thousands of words and the ability to understand simple sentences. For example, *chatterbots* are automated bots that can actually mimic human conversation. (You can see what it's like to carry on a conversation with some of these bots by visiting www.botspot.com, clicking on "Artificial Life Bots," and then selecting "Chatterbots.")

Unfortunately, even though chatterbots hold a lot of promise, human communication is so complex that a truly automated customer service agent could take years to perfect (and may even prove to be impossible). However, the simplest automated systems, called *autoresponders* or *e-mail-on-demand*, are fast and extremely inexpensive. They have no built-in intelligence, so they do nothing more than send back the same reply to every message they receive.

You explain to your boss that although some of the messages you receive require the attention of your product specialists, many are simply requests for straightforward information. In fact, the customer service staff already answers some 70 percent of e-mail queries with three ready-made attachments:

- **Installing Your Cycle Computer.** Gives customers advice on installing the cycle computer the first time or reinstalling it on a new bike. In most cases, the computer and wheel sensor bolt directly to the bike without modification, but certain bikes require extra work.
- **Troubleshooting Your Cycle Computer.** Provides a step-by-step guide to figuring out what might be wrong with a malfunctioning cycle computer. Most problems are simple, such as dead batteries or loose wires, but others are beyond the capabilities of your typical customer.
- **Upgrading the Software in Your Cycle Computer.** Tells customers how to attach the cycle computer to their home or office PC and download new software from Highway Bytes.

Your boss is enthusiastic when you explain that you can program your current e-mail system to look for specific words in incoming messages and then respond, based on what it finds. For example, if a customer message contains the word "installation," you can program the system to reply with the "Installing Your Cycle Computer" attachment. This reconfigured system should be able to handle a sizeable portion of the hundreds of e-mails your customer service group gets every week.

Your task First, draft a list of key words that you'll want your e-mail system to look for. You'll need to be creative and spend some time with a thesaurus. Identify all the words and word combinations that could identify a message as pertaining to one of the three subject areas. For instance, the word *attach* would probably indicate a need for the installation material, whereas *new software* would most likely suggest a need for the upgrade attachment.

Second, draft three short e-mail messages to accompany each ready-made attachment, explaining that the attached document answers the most common questions on a particular subject (installation, troubleshooting, or upgrading). Your messages should invite recipients to write back if the attached document doesn't solve the problem, and don't forget to provide the e-mail address: support2@highwaybytes.com.

Third, draft a fourth message to be sent out whenever your new system is unable to figure out what the customer is asking for. Simply thank the customer for writing and explain that the query will be passed on to a customer service specialist who will respond shortly.

7. The Special Courier: Letter of Recommendation for an Old Friend

In today's mail you get a letter from Non-Stop Messenger Service, 899 Sparks St., Ottawa, Ontario K1A 0G9, Canada. It concerns a friend of yours who has applied for a job. Here is the letter:

> Kathryn Norquist has applied for the position of special courier with our firm, and she has given us your name as a reference. Our special couriers convey materials of considerable value or confidentiality to their recipients. It is not an easy job. Special couriers must sometimes remain alert for periods of up to 20 hours, and they cannot expect to follow the usual "three square meals and eight hours' sleep" routine because they often travel long distances on short notice. On occasion, a special courier must react quickly and decisively to threatening situations.
>
> For this type of work, we hire only people of unquestioned integrity, as demonstrated both by their public records and by references from people, like you, who have known them personally or professionally.
>
> We would appreciate a letter from you, supplying detailed answers to the following questions: (1) How long and in what circumstances have you known the applicant? (2) What qualities does she possess that would qualify her for the position of special courier? (3) What qualities might be improved before she is put on permanent assignment in this job?

As vice president of human resources at DHL, you know how much weight a strong personal reference can carry, and you don't really mind that Kathryn never contacted you for permission to list your name—that's Kathryn. You met her during your sophomore year at San Diego State University—that would have been 1994—and you two were roommates for several years after. Her undergraduate degree was in journalism, and her investigative reporting was relentless. You have never known anyone who could match Kathryn's stamina when she was on a story. Of course, when she was between stories, she could sleep longer and do less than anyone else you have ever known.

After a few years of reporting, Kathryn went back to school and earned her MBA from the University of San Diego, and after that you lost track of her for awhile. Somebody said that she had joined the FBI—or was it the CIA?—you never really knew. You received a couple of postcards from Paris and one from Madrid.

Two years ago, you met Kathryn for dinner. Only in town for the evening, she was on her way to Borneo to "do the text" for a photographer friend of hers who worked for *National Geographic*. Last year, you read the article on the shrinking habitat for orangutans. It was powerful.

Although you're in no position to say much about Kathryn's career accomplishments, you can certainly recommend her energy and enthusiasm, her ability to focus on a task or assignment, her devotion to ethics, and her style. She always seems unshakable—organized, thorough, and honorable, whether digging into political corruption or trudging the jungles of Borneo. You're not sure that her free spirit would flourish in a courier's position, and you wonder if she wouldn't be a bit overqualified for the job. But knowing Kathryn, you're confident she wouldn't apply for a position unless she truly wanted it.

Your task Supplying any details you can think of, write as supportive a letter as possible about your friend Kathryn to Roscoe de la Penda, Human Resources Specialist, Non-Stop Messenger.

[E-MAIL SKILLS]

8. Lighten Up: E-Mail Reply to a Website Designer at Organizers Unlimited

When Kendra Williams, owner of Organizers Unlimited, wanted to create a website to sell her Superclean Organizer, she asked you, her assistant, to find a designer. After some research, you found three promising individuals. Williams chose Pete Womack, whose résumé impressed both of you. Now he's e-mailed his first design proposal, and Williams is not happy.

"I detest cluttered websites!" she explodes. "This homepage has too many graphics and animations, too much 'dancing baloney.' He must have included at least a megabyte of bouncing cotton balls and jogging soap bars! Clever, maybe, but we don't want it! If the homepage takes too long to load, our customers won't wait for it, and we'll lose sales."

Williams's dislike of clutter is what inspired her to invent the Superclean Organizer in the first place, a neat device for organizing bathroom items.

Your task "You found him," says Williams, "now you can answer and tell him what's wrong with this design." Before you write the e-mail reply to Womack, explaining the need for a simpler homepage, read some of the articles offering tips at www.sitepoint.com. On the homepage, under "Before You Code," select "Site Planning" and under "Design and Layout" select "Design Principles." Use these ideas to support your message.[11]

[BLOGGING SKILLS]

9. Leveraging the Good News: Blog Announcement of a Prestigious Professional Award

You and your staff in the public relations (PR) department at Epson of America were delighted when the communication campaign you created for the new PictureMate Personal Photo Lab (www.epson.com/picturemate) was awarded the prestigious Silver Anvil award by the Public Relations Society of America. Now you'd like to give your team a pat on the back by sharing the news with the rest of the company.

Your task Write a one-paragraph message for the PR department blog (which is read by people throughout the company but is not accessible outside the company), announcing the award. Take care not to "toot your own horn" as the manager of the PR department and use the opportunity to compliment the rest of the company for designing and producing such an innovative product.[12]

10. Our Sympathy: Condolence Letter to an Aetna Underwriter

As chief administrator for the underwriting department of Aetna Health Plans in Walnut Creek, California, you're facing a difficult task. One of your best underwriters, Hector Almeida, recently lost his wife in an automobile accident (he and his teenaged daughter weren't with her at the time). Because you're the boss, everyone in the close-knit department is looking to you to communicate the group's sympathy and concern.

Someone suggested a simple greeting card that everyone could sign, but that seems so impersonal for someone you've worked with every day for nearly five years. So you decided to write a personal note on behalf of the whole department. You met Hector's wife, Rosalia, at a few company functions, although you knew her mostly through Hector's frequent references to her. Although you didn't know her well, you do know important things about her life, which you can celebrate in the letter.

Right now he's devastated by the loss. But if anyone can overcome this tragedy, Hector can. He's always determined to get a job done no matter what obstacles present themselves, and he does it with an upbeat attitude. That's why everyone in the office likes him so much.

You also plan to suggest that when he returns to work, he might like to move his schedule up an hour so that he'll have more time to spend with his daughter, Lisa, after school. It's your way of helping make things a little easier for them during this period of adjustment.

Your task Write the letter to Hector Almeida, who lives at 47 West Ave., #10, Walnut Creek, CA 94596. Feel free to make up any details you need.[13]

11. Unhappy Customer: Claim Letter from You Requesting an Adjustment As a consumer, you've probably bought something that didn't work right or paid for a service that didn't turn out the way you expected. Maybe it was a pair of jeans with a rip in a seam that you didn't find until you got home or a watch that broke a week after you bought it. Or maybe your family hired a lawn service to do some yard work, and no one from the company showed up on the day promised. When a man finally appeared, he did not do what he'd been hired for but did other things that wound up damaging valuable plants.

You'd be wise to write a claim letter asking for a refund, repair, replacement, or other adjustment. You'll need to include all the details of the transaction, plus your contact address and phone number.

Your task To practice writing claim letters, choose an experience like this from your own background or make up details for these imaginary situations. If your experience is real, you might want to mail the letter. The reply you receive will provide a good test of your claim-writing skills.

[BLOGGING SKILLS]

12. Here's How It Will Work: Explaining the Brainstorming Process Austin, Texas, advertising agency GSD&M Advertising brainstorms new advertising ideas using a process it calls *dynamic collaboration*. A hand-picked team of insiders and outsiders are briefed on the project and given a key question or two to answer. The team members then sit down at computers and anonymously submit as many responses as they can within five minutes. The project moderators then pore over these responses, looking for any sparks that can ignite new ways of understanding and reaching out to consumers.

Your task For these brainstorming sessions, GSD&M recruits an eclectic mix of participants from inside and outside the agency—figures as diverse as economists and professional video gamers. To make sure everyone understands the brainstorming guidelines, prepare a message to be posted on the project blog. In your own words, convey the following four points as clearly and succinctly as you can:

- **Be yourself.** We want input from as many perspectives as possible, which is why we recruit such a diverse array of participants. Don't try to get into what you believe is the mindset of an advertising specialist; we want you to approach the given challenge using whatever analytical and creative skills you normally employ in your daily work.
- **Create, don't edit.** Don't edit, refine, or self-censor while you're typing during the initial five-minute session. We don't care if your ideas are formatted beautifully, phrased poetically, or even spelled correctly. Just crank 'em out as quickly as you can.
- **It's about the ideas, not the participants.** Just so you know up front, all ideas are collected anonymously. We can't tell who submitted the brilliant ideas, the boring ideas, or the already-tried-that ideas. So while you won't get personal credit, you can also be crazy and fearless. Go for it!

- **The winning ideas will be subjected to the toughest of tests.** Just in case you're worried about submitting ideas that could be risky, expensive, or difficult to implement—don't fret. As we narrow down the possibilities, the few that remain will be judged, poked, prodded, and assessed from every angle. In other words, let us worry about containing the fire; you come up with the sparks.[14]

[E-MAIL SKILLS]   [PORTFOLIO BUILDER]

13. Window Shopping at Wal-Mart: Offering Advice to the Webmaster Wal-Mart has grown to international success because it rarely fails to capitalize on a marketing scheme, and its website is no exception. To make sure the website remains effective and relevant, the webmaster asks various people to check out the site and give their feedback. As administrative assistant to Wal-Mart's director of marketing, you have just received a request from the webmaster to visit Wal-Mart's website and give your feedback.

Your task Visit www.walmart.com and do some online "window shopping." As you browse through the site, consider the language, layout, graphics, and overall ease of use. In particular, look for aspects of the site that might be confusing or frustrating—annoyances that could prompt shoppers to abandon their quests and head to a competitor such as Target. Summarize your findings and recommendations in an e-mail message to the webmaster.

[BLOGGING SKILLS]   [PORTFOLIO BUILDER]

14. Green Is the New Green: Blog Update on Energy Savings Adobe Systems is well known as the maker of Reader, Acrobat, Photoshop, Flash, and other programs that are fundamental tools in the Internet Age. It is also becoming well known as one of the "greenest" companies in the country, adopting a variety of techniques and technologies that have not only reduced its energy usage considerably but also cut nearly $1 million per year from its utility bills. In 2006, Adobe became the first company ever to receive Platinum Certification from the U.S. Green Building Council.

Your task Write a one- or two-paragraph post for an internal blog at Adobe, letting employees know how well the company is doing in its efforts to reduce energy usage and thanking employees for the energy-saving ideas they've submitted and the individual efforts they've made to reduce, reuse, and recycle. Learn more about the company's accomplishments by searching for the news release "Adobe Headquarters Awarded Highest Honors from U.S. Green Building Council," available on the Adobe website, at www.adobe.com/aboutadobe/pressroom. Select a few key details from this news release to include in your message.[15]

15. Congrats on That: Complimenting a Former Business Acquaintance for National Recognition You pull the new issue of *Fortune* magazine out of the stack of mail and are quite pleased to see Indra Nooyi on the cover. Not only was Nooyi recently appointed CEO of PepsiCo, but *Fortune* has just named her the most powerful woman in American business. You got to know her briefly when PepsiCo acquired your previous employer, Quaker Oats, in 2001. You haven't spoken to her since then, but you have followed her accomplishments in the business media.

Your task Write a brief letter (no more than one page), congratulating Nooyi on her promotion to CEO and on being recognized by *Fortune*. Make up any details you need to create a credible message. You can learn more about Nooyi's career and accomplishments in the news release "PepsiCo's Board of Directors Appoints Indra K. Nooyi as Chief Executive Officer Effective October 1, 2006," on the PepsiCo website, www.pepsico.com (look under "News," "PepsiCo Releases," "2006"). Address the letter to Indra Nooyi, CEO, PepsiCo, Inc., 700 Anderson Hill Road, Purchase, NY 10577.

Improve Your Grammar, Mechanics, and Usage

Level 1: Self-Assessment—Periods, Question Marks, and Exclamation Points

Review Sections 2.1, 2.2, and 2.3 in the Handbook of Grammar, Mechanics, and Usage, and then complete the following 15 items.

In items 1–15, add periods, question marks, and exclamation points wherever they are appropriate.

1. Dr Eleanor H Hutton has requested information on TaskMasters, Inc

2. That qualifies us as a rapidly growing new company, don't you think

3. Our president, Daniel Gruber, is a CPA On your behalf, I asked him why he started the company

4. In the past three years, we have experienced phenomenal growth of 800 percent

5. Contact me at 1358 N Parsons Avenue, Tulsa, OK 74204

6. Jack asked, "Why does he want to know Maybe he plans to become a competitor"

7. The debt load fluctuates with the movement of the US prime rate

8. I can't believe we could have missed such a promising opportunity

9. Is consumer loyalty extinct Yes and No.

10. Johnson and Kane, Inc, has gone out of business What a surprise

11. Will you please send us a check today so that we can settle your account

12. Mr James R Capp will be our new CEO, beginning January 20, 2009

13. The rag doll originally sold for $1098, but we have lowered the price to a mere $599

14. Will you be able to make the presentation at the conference, or should we find someone else

15. So I ask you, "When will we admit defeat" Never

Level 2: Workplace Applications

The following items contain numerous errors in grammar, capitalization, punctuation, abbreviation, number style, word division, and vocabulary. Rewrite each sentence, correcting all errors. Write *C* for any sentence that is already correct.

1. Attached to both the Train Station and the Marriott hotel, one doesnt even need to step outside the convention center to go from train to meeting room.
2. According to Federal statistics, 61 percent of the nations employers have less than 5 workers.
3. "The problem", said Business Owner Mike Millorn, "Was getting vendor's of raw materials to take my endeavor serious."
4. After pouring over trade journals, quizzing industry experts, and talks with other snack makers, the Harpers' decided to go in the pita chip business.
5. Some argue that a Mac with half as much RAM and a slower processor is as fast or faster than a PC.
6. The couple has done relatively little advertising, instead they give away samples in person at trade shows, cooking demonstrations, and in grocery stores.
7. CME Information Services started by videotaping doctor's conventions, and selling the recorded presentations to nonattending physicians that wanted to keep track of the latest developments.
8. For many companies, the two biggest challenges to using intranets are: getting people to use it and content freshness.
9. Company meetings including 'lunch and learn' sessions are held online often.
10. Most Children's Orchard franchisees, are men and women between the ages of 30–50; first time business owners with a wide range of computer skills.
11. Joining the company in 1993, she had watched it expand and grow from a single small office to a entire floor of a skyscraper.
12. One issue that effected practically everyone was that they needed to train interns.
13. The website includes information on subjects as mundane as the filling out of a federal express form, and as complex as researching a policy issue.
14. "Some management theories are good, but how many people actually implement them the right way?", says Jack Hartnett President of D. L. Rogers Corp.
15. Taking orders through car windows, customers are served by roller-skating carhops at Sonic restaurants.

Level 3: Document Critique

The following document may contain errors in grammar, punctuation, capitalization, abbreviation, number style, vocabulary, and spelling. You will also find errors related to topics in this chapter. For example, consider the organization and relevance of material as you improve this routine request for information. Correct all errors using standard proofreading marks (see Appendix C).

Risa Zenaili

883 Middleton Aven.

Bartlesville OK 74005

918-555-9983

rzenaili@ppri.com

March 13 2009

Tharita Jones Owner

Subway Restaurant

120 W Greenfield Str.

Tulsa, Oklahoma, 74133

Dear Ms. Jones,

I am investigatting careers in vareous fast-food enviroments, since I expect to complete my degreee in business administration within the next 3 years and that should leave me enough time to grow into a management position. Subway gave me your name when I asked for a franchise owner who might be willing to answer some questions about managment careers with the company. You may be able to provide the kind of informaton I'll never get from coporate brochures.

For example I'd like to know how long I can expect to work at an entry level before promotions are considered. How many levels must I rise before reaching assistant manager. And how many before I would be considered as manager, assuming I've performed well. Sometimes a person is promoted because they are qualified and sometimes it just because they willing to work long hours, so I want to know this before I commit myself!

I'm looking for a company that will offer me the best future in the most promising environment and since there are so many to choose from I am trying to be very careful in making this choice. I'd be really gratefull if you could take a moment to share any advice or encouragment you might have for me because as you know this kind of decision is one we all must make one day and it will effect us for a long, long time to come

I also like to know: How many hour a week can I expect to work to be on management career track? Once I reach management level: will those hours increase?
What qualifications do you look for in your managers and assitant managers? Plus: Benefits the company offers, special training—availibility and qualifications; how to improve my chances for promation if I choose Subway?

Please let me hear from you before the end of the month.

If you prefer to call than write; you reach me at 918 555-9983 day or evening. My cell phone number is (918) 555-8838. Or you can send a reply to me at the address above or to my e-mail address rzeinali@earthlink.net.

Sincerely:

Risa Zeinali

Writing Negative Messages

LEARNING OBJECTIVES

After studying this chapter, you will be able to

1. Apply the three-step writing process to negative messages
2. Explain the differences between the direct and the indirect approaches to negative messages, including when it's appropriate to use each one
3. Identify the ethical risks of using the indirect approach
4. Define *defamation* and explain how to avoid it in negative messages
5. Discuss the challenge presented by online rumors and attacks
6. List three guidelines for delivering negative news to job applicants and give a brief explanation of each one

[from the real world]

"... from a Homer Simpson design to a Superman design . . ."
—*Derrick Kuzak,*
Group vice president,
Global Product
Development Ford
Motor Company
www.ford.com

Salespeople and executives often try to build interest in their new products by explaining how the new offerings improve on existing products. But comparing your current product to a bulbous, blundering, donut-gobbling cartoon character who makes a mess of everything he touches? That's exactly what Ford's Derrick Kuzak did when he tried to explain how an upcoming Taurus model was significantly more attractive than the current one. CEO Alan Mulally also called the upcoming car the "the one we should have made originally." The Taurus model Kuzak and Mulally were referring to was indeed a disappointment in the marketplace, and some observers admired the company's honesty in admitting to failure. However, one has to wonder if it was a good idea to be so openly negative. After all, that Homeresque product was designed, built, and marketed by Ford employees, and they might not be so happy to have their work criticized in public by their own managers.[1]

USING THE THREE-STEP WRITING PROCESS FOR NEGATIVE MESSAGES

Five goals of negative messages:
- Give the bad news
- Ensure its acceptance
- Maintain reader's goodwill
- Maintain organization's good image
- Reduce future correspondence on the matter

Delivering negative information is rarely easy and never enjoyable, but with some helpful guidelines, you can craft messages that minimize negative reactions. When you need to deliver bad news, you have five goals: (1) to convey the bad news, (2) to gain acceptance for it, (3) to maintain as much goodwill as possible with your audience, (4) to maintain a good image for your organization, and (5) if appropriate, to reduce or eliminate the need for future correspondence on the matter. Accomplishing all five goals requires careful attention to planning, writing, and completing your message.

Step 1: Planning Negative Messages

Careful planning is necessary to avoid alienating your readers.

When planning negative messages, you can't avoid the fact that your audience does not want to hear what you have to say. To minimize the damage to business relationships and to encourage the acceptance of your message, plan carefully. With a clear purpose and your audience's needs in mind, gather the information your audience will need in order to understand and accept your message.

TABLE 8.1 Choosing Positive Words

Negative Phrasings	Positive Alternatives
Your request doesn't make any sense.	Please clarify your request.
The damage won't be fixed for a week.	The item will be repaired next week.
Although it wasn't our fault, there will be an unavoidable delay in your order.	We will process your order as soon as we receive an aluminum shipment from our supplier, which we expect to happen within 10 days.
You are clearly dissatisfied.	We are doing what we can to make things right.
I regret the misunderstanding.	I'll try my best to be more clear from now on.
I was shocked to learn that you're unhappy.	Thank you for sharing your concerns about the service you received while shopping with us.
Unfortunately, we haven't received it.	It hasn't arrived yet.
The enclosed statement is wrong.	Please recheck the enclosed statement.

Selecting the right medium is critical. For instance, experts advise that bad news for employees always be delivered in person whenever possible, both to show respect for the employees and to give them an opportunity to ask questions. However, delivering bad news is never easy, and an increasing number of managers appear to be using e-mail and other electronic media to convey negative messages to employees.[2]

Choose the medium with care when preparing negative messages.

Finally, when you are delivering bad news, the organization of your message requires particular care. This chapter presents in-depth advice on using both direct and indirect approaches to organization.

Use the appropriate organization to help readers accept your negative news.

Step 2: Writing Negative Messages

By writing clearly and sensitively, you can take some of the sting out of bad news and help your reader accept the decision and move on. If your credibility hasn't already been established with an audience, clarify your qualifications so message recipients won't question your authority or ability.

When you use language that conveys respect and avoids an accusing tone, you protect your audience's pride. This kind of communication etiquette is always important, but it demands special care with negative messages. Moreover, you can ease the sense of disappointment by using positive words rather than negative, counterproductive ones (see Table 8.1).

Step 3: Completing Negative Messages

The need for careful attention to detail continues as you complete your message. Revise your content to make sure everything is clear, complete, and concise—even small flaws can be magnified in readers' minds as they react to your negative news. Produce clean, professional documents and proofread carefully to eliminate mistakes. Finally, be sure to deliver messages promptly; withholding bad news can be unethical and even illegal.

DEVELOPING NEGATIVE MESSAGES

One of the most critical decisions in planning negative messages is choosing whether to use the direct or indirect approach. To help decide in any situation you encounter, ask yourself the following questions:

- **Will the bad news come as a shock?** In some instances, negative news is expected from time to time, so the direct approach is usually acceptable. However, if the bad news might come as a shock, use the indirect approach to help your reader prepare.

- **Does the reader prefer short messages that get right to the point?** For example, if you know that your boss always wants messages that get right to the point, even when they deliver bad news, use the direct approach.

- **How important is this news to the reader?** For minor or routine scenarios, the direct approach is nearly always best. However, if the reader has an emotional investment in the situation or the consequences to the reader are considerable, the indirect approach is often better.

- **Do you need to maintain a close working relationship with the reader?** The indirect approach lets you soften the blow of bad news and preserve a close relationship.

- **Do you need to get the reader's attention?** If someone has ignored repeated messages, the direct approach can help you get his or her attention.

- **What is your organization's preferred style?** Some companies have a distinct communication style, ranging from blunt and direct to gentle and indirect.

Using the Direct Approach Effectively

Use the direct approach when your negative answer or information will have minimal personal impact.

A negative message using the direct approach opens with the bad news, proceeds to the reasons for the situation or the decision, and ends with a positive statement aimed at maintaining a good relationship with the audience (see Figure 8.1). The message may also offer alternatives or a plan of action to fix the situation under discussion. Stating the bad news at the beginning can have two advantages: (1) It makes a shorter message possible, and (2) it requires less time for the audience to reach the main idea of the message.

Opening with a Clear Statement of the Bad News

If you've chosen the direct approach to convey bad news, come right out and say it. Maintain a calm, professional tone that keeps the focus on the news and not on individual failures. Also, if necessary, remind the reader why you're writing. The following are examples of the direct approach:

Reminds the reader that he or she applied for life insurance with your firm and announces your decision

Transnation Life is unable to grant your application for SafetyNet term life insurance.

Eases into the bad news with a personal acknowledgment to the staff, even though it delivers the news directly and immediately

Despite everyone's best efforts to close more sales this past quarter, revenue fell 14 percent compared to the third quarter last year.

Notice that the second example manages to ease into the bad news, even though it delivers the bad news directly and quickly. In both instances, the recipient gets the news immediately.

Figure 8.1 Choosing the Indirect or Direct Approach for Negative Messages
Analyze the situation carefully before choosing your approach to organizing negative messages.

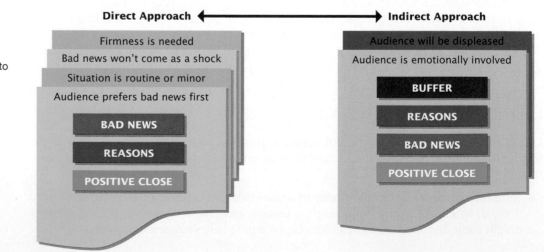

Providing Reasons and Additional Information

In most cases, you'll follow the direct opening with an explanation of why the news is negative:

> Transnation Life is unable to grant your application for SafetyNet term life insurance. The SafetyNet program has specific health history requirements that your application does not meet.

Offers a general explanation as the reason the application was denied and discourages further communication on the matter

> Despite everyone's best efforts to close more sales this past quarter, revenue fell 14 percent compared to the third quarter last year. Reports from the field offices indicate that the economic downturn in Asia has reduced demand for our products.

Lets readers know why the news is negative and reassures them that job performance is not the reason

The extent of your explanation depends on the nature of your news and your relationship with the reader. In the first example, the insurance company provides a general reason for the denial because listing a specific health issue might encourage additional communication from the reader to negotiate or to explain the situation. The company's decision is final, and any further communication on the issue would be counterproductive for both parties. In other situations, it's a good idea to follow the explanation with a statement of how you plan to correct or respond to the negative news. In the case of the sales decline, you might follow by telling the staff you plan to increase advertising to help stimulate sales.

The amount of detail you provide depends on your relationship with the audience.

You will encounter situations in which explaining negative news is neither appropriate nor helpful, such as when the reasons are confidential, excessively complicated, or irrelevant to the reader. To maintain a cordial working relationship with the reader, you might want to explain why you can't provide the information.

Sometimes you should not provide detailed reasons.

When a company has made a serious mistake, those who communicate the negative news need to address the question of apologies. This question does not have a simple answer. To some people, an apology simply means an expression of sympathy that something negative has happened to another person. Others think it means admitting fault and taking responsibility for specific compensations or corrections to atone for the mistake.

Whether apologizing is appropriate depends on a number of factors.

Some experts have advised that companies never apologize, as apologies might be taken as confessions of guilt that could be used against them in lawsuits. However, several states have laws that specifically prevent expressions of sympathy from being used as evidence of legal liability. In fact, judges, juries, and plaintiffs tend to be more forgiving of companies that express sympathy for wronged parties.[3]

The best general advice in the event of a serious mistake or accident is to immediately and sincerely express sympathy and offer help, if appropriate, without admitting guilt; then seek the advice of your company's lawyers before elaborating. A straightforward, sincere apology can go a long way toward healing wounds and rebuilding relationships. As one recent survey concluded, "The risks of making an apology are low, and the potential reward is high."[4]

Closing on a Positive Note

After you've explained your negative news, close the message in a positive and respectful manner, as in the following examples:

Close your message in a positive but respectful tone.

> Transnation Life is unable to grant your application for SafetyNet term life insurance. The SafetyNet program has specific health history requirements that your application does not meet. We wish you success in finding coverage through another provider.

Ends on a respecful note, knowing that life insurance is an important subject for the reader, but also makes it clear that the company's decision is final

> Despite everyone's best efforts to close more sales this past quarter, revenue fell 14 percent compared to the third quarter last year. Reports from the field offices indicate that the economic downturn in Asia has reduced demand for our products. However, I continue to believe that we have the best product for these customers, and we'll continue to explore ways to boost sales in these key markets.

Helps readers respond to the news by letting them know that the company plans to fix the situation, even if the plan for doing so isn't clear yet

Notice how both examples deliver bad news quickly and efficiently and then move on. Consider offering your readers an alternative solution, if you can. For instance, if you know that another insurance company has a program for higher-risk policies, you can alert your reader to that opportunity. In many instances, you won't be able to justify spending much time researching and communicating alternatives. However, to preserve an important business relationship, it often makes sense to devote some time to this task.

Using the Indirect Approach Effectively

The indirect approach helps readers prepare for the bad news by outlining the reasons for the situation before presenting the bad news itself. However, the indirect approach is not meant to obscure bad news, delay it, or limit your responsibility. The purpose of this approach is to ease the blow and help readers accept the news. When done poorly, the indirect approach can be disrespectful and even unethical. But when done well, it is a good example of "you"-oriented communication crafted with attention to both ethics and etiquette.

Opening with a Buffer

The first step in using the indirect approach is to write a **buffer**, a neutral, noncontroversial statement that is closely related to the point of the message. A buffer establishes common ground with your reader, and if you're responding to a request, a buffer validates that request. Some critics believe that using a buffer is manipulative and unethical—or even dishonest. However, buffers are unethical only if they're insincere or deceptive. Showing consideration for the feelings of others is never dishonest.

A poorly written buffer might trivialize the reader's concerns, divert attention from the problem with insincere flattery or irrelevant material, or mislead the reader into thinking your message actually contains good news. A good buffer, on the other hand, can express your appreciation for being considered (if you're responding to a request), assure your reader of your attention to the request, or indicate your understanding of the reader's needs.

Say that a manager of an order fulfillment department has requested some temporary staffing help from your department, and you won't be able to fulfill that request. The following examples are possible responses:

- Our department shares your goal of processing orders quickly and efficiently.
- As a result of the last downsizing, every department in the company is running shorthanded.
- You folks are doing a great job over there, and I'd love to be able to help out.
- Those new state labor regulations are driving me crazy over here; how about in your department?

Only the first of these buffers can be considered effective; the other three are likely to damage your relationship with the other manager. Whichever approach you choose, make sure your buffer is respectful, relevant, and neutral (see Table 8.2).

Providing Reasons and Additional Information

An effective buffer serves as a transition to the next part of your message, in which you build up the explanations and information that will culminate in your negative news. An ideal explanation section leads readers to your conclusion before you come right out and say it. The reader has followed your line of reasoning and is ready for the answer. By giving your reasons effectively, you help maintain focus on the issues at hand and defuse the emotions that always accompany significantly bad news.

As you lay out your reasons, guide your readers' responses by starting with the most positive points first and moving forward to increasingly negative ones. Provide enough detail for the audience to understand your reasons but be concise. Your reasons need to convince your audience that your decision is justified, fair, and logical.

Whenever possible, avoid hiding behind company policy to cushion your bad news. Skilled and sympathetic communicators explain company policy (without referring to it as "policy") so that the audience can try to meet the requirements at a later time. Consider this response to a job applicant:

- Because these management positions are quite challenging, the human relations department has researched the qualifications needed to succeed in them. The findings show that the two most important qualifications are a bachelor's degree in business administration and two years' supervisory experience.

Margin notes

Use the indirect approach when some preparation will help your audience accept your bad news.

A buffer establishes common ground with the reader.

Poorly written buffers mislead or insult the reader.

Establishes common ground with the reader and validates the concerns that prompted the original request—without promising a positive answer

Establishes common ground but in a negative way that downplays the recipient's concerns

Potentially misleads the reader into concluding that you will comply with the request

Trivializes the reader's concerns by opening with an irrelevant issue

Phrase your reasons to signal the negative news ahead.

Don't hide behind company policy when you deliver bad news.

Shows that the decision is based on a methodical analysis and not on some arbitrary guideline

Establishes the criteria behind the decision and lets the reader know what to expect

TABLE 8.2 Types of Buffers

Buffer Type	Strategy	Example
Agreement	Find a point on which you and the reader share similar views.	We both know how hard it is to make a profit in this industry.
Appreciation	Express sincere thanks for receiving something.	Your check for $127.17 arrived yesterday. Thank you.
Cooperation	Convey your willingness to help in any way you realistically can.	Employee Services is here to smooth the way for all of you who work to achieve company goals.
Fairness	Assure the reader that you've closely examined and carefully considered the problem, or mention an appropriate action that has already been taken.	For the past week, we have carefully monitored those using the photocopying machine to see whether we can detect any pattern of use that might explain its frequent breakdowns.
Good news	Start with the part of your message that is favorable.	A replacement knob for your range is on its way, shipped February 10 via UPS.
Praise	Find an attribute or an achievement to compliment.	The Stratford Group clearly has an impressive record of accomplishment in helping clients resolve financial reporting problems.
Resale	Favorably discuss the product or company related to the subject of the letter.	With their heavy-duty, full-suspension hardware and fine veneers, the desks and file cabinets in our Montclair line have become a hit with value-conscious professionals.
Understanding	Demonstrate that you understand the reader's goals and needs.	So that you can more easily find a printer that has the features you need, we are enclosing a brochure that describes all the Panasonic printers currently available.

The paragraph does a good job of stating reasons for the refusal:

- It provides enough detail to logically support the refusal.
- It implies that the applicant is better off avoiding a position in which he or she might fail.
- It doesn't apologize for the decision because no one is at fault.
- It avoids negative personal statements (such as "You do not meet our requirements").

Well-written reasons are
- Detailed
- Tactful
- Individualized
- Unapologetic
- Positive

Even valid, well-thought-out reasons won't convince every reader in every situation, but if you've done a good job of laying out your reasoning, then you've done everything you can to prepare the reader for the main idea, which is the negative news itself.

Continuing with a Clear Statement of the Bad News

After you've thoughtfully and logically established your reasons and readers are prepared to receive the bad news, you can use three techniques to convey the negative information as clearly and as kindly as possible. First, deemphasize the bad news:

- Minimize the space or time devoted to the bad news—without trivializing it or withholding any important information. In other words, don't repeat it or belabor it.
- Subordinate bad news within a complex or compound sentence ("My department is already shorthanded, <u>so I'll need all my staff for at least the next two months</u>").
- Embed bad news in the middle of a paragraph or use parenthetical expressions ("Our profits, <u>which are down</u>, are only part of the picture").

To handle bad news
- Deemphasize the bad news visually and grammatically
- Use a conditional statement, if appropriate
- Tell what you did do, not what you didn't do

However, keep in mind that it's possible to abuse this notion of deemphasizing bad news. For instance, if the primary point of your message is that profits are down, it would be inappropriate to marginalize that news by burying it in the middle of a sentence. State the negative news clearly and then make a smooth transition to any positive news that might balance the story.

Second, use a conditional (*if* or *when*) statement to imply that the audience could have received, or might someday receive, a favorable answer ("<u>When you have more managerial experience</u>, you are welcome to reapply"). Such a statement could motivate the audience.

Don't disguise bad news when you emphasize the positive.

Third, emphasize what you can do or have done rather than what you cannot do. Also, by implying the bad news, you may not need to actually state it, thereby making the bad news less personal ("The five positions currently open <u>have been filled</u> with people whose qualifications match those uncovered in our research"). However, make sure your audience understands the entire message—including the bad news. If an implied message might lead to uncertainty, state your decision in direct terms. Just be sure to avoid overly blunt statements that are likely to cause pain and anger:

Instead of This	Write This
I *must refuse* your request.	I will be out of town on the day you need me.
We *must deny* your application.	The position has been filled.
I *am unable* to grant your request.	Contact us again when you have established . . . .
We *cannot afford* to continue the program.	The program will conclude on May 1.
Much as I would like to attend	Our budget meeting ends too late for me to attend.
We *must reject* your proposal.	We've accepted the proposal from AAA Builders.
We *must turn down* your extension request.	Please send in your payment by June 14.

Closing on a Positive Note

The conclusion is your opportunity to emphasize your respect for your audience, even though you've just delivered unpleasant news. If you can find a positive angle that's meaningful to your audience, by all means consider adding it to your conclusion. However, don't try to pretend that the negative news didn't happen or that it won't affect the reader. Suggest alternative solutions if such information is available. In a message to a customer or potential customer, the ending can include **resale information** (favorable comments about a product or service that the customer has already purchased) or **sales promotion** (favorable comments that encourage interest in goods or services the reader has not yet committed to purchase). If you've asked readers to decide between alternatives or to take some action, make sure that they know what to do, when to do it, and how to do it. Whatever type of conclusion you use, follow these guidelines:

A positive close
- Builds goodwill
- Offers a suggestion for action
- Provides a look toward the future

- Don't refer to, repeat, or apologize for the bad news and refrain from expressing any doubt that your reasons will be accepted.
- Encourage additional communication *only* if you're willing to discuss your decision further.
- Don't anticipate problems. (Avoid statements such as "Should you have further problems, please let us know.")
- Avoid clichés that are insincere in view of the bad news. (If you can't help, don't say, "If we can be of any help, please contact us.")

Finally, keep in mind that the closing is the last thing the audience has to remember you by. Try to make the memory a positive one.

EXPLORING COMMON EXAMPLES OF NEGATIVE MESSAGES

The following sections offer examples of the most common negative messages, dealing with topics such as routine business matters, employment, and organizational news.

Sending Negative Messages on Routine Business Matters

Most companies receive numerous requests for information and donations or invitations to join various organizations. As you progress in your career and become more visible in your industry and community, you will probably receive a wide variety of invitations to speak or to volunteer your time. In addition, routine business matters such as credit applications and requests for adjustment will often require negative responses. Neither you nor your company will be able to say yes to every request. Crafting negative responses quickly and graciously is an important skill for many professionals.

Refusing Routine Requests

When you are unable to meet a routine request, your primary communication challenge is to give a clear negative response without generating negative feelings or damaging either your personal reputation or the company's. As simple as these messages may appear to be, they can test your skills as a communicator because you often need to deliver negative information while maintaining a positive relationship with the other party.

Saying no is a routine part of business and shouldn't reflect negatively on you. If you said yes to every request that crossed your desk, you'd never get any work done. The direct approach will work best for most routine negative responses. It helps your audience get your answer quickly and move on to other possibilities, and it also helps you save time because the direct approach is often easier to write. The indirect approach works best when the stakes are high for you or for the receiver, when you or your company has an established relationship with the person making the request, or when you're forced to decline a request that you might have said yes to in the past (see Figure 8.2).

When turning down an invitation or a request for a favor, consider your relationship with the reader.

Consider the following points as you develop routine negative messages:

- **Manage your time carefully.** Focus your limited time on the most important relationships and requests; craft quick, standard responses for less important situations.

- **If the matter is closed, don't imply that it's still open.** If your answer is truly no, don't use phrases such as "Let me think about it and get back to you" as a way to delay saying no.

- **Offer alternative ideas if you can.** However, remember to use your time wisely in such matters. Unless the relationship is vital to your company, you probably shouldn't spend time researching alternatives for the other person.

- **Don't imply that other assistance or information might be available if it isn't.** A disingenuous attempt to soothe hostile feelings could simply lead to another request you'll have to refuse.

If you aren't in a position to offer additional information or assistance, don't imply that you are.

Handling Bad News About Transactions

Bad-news messages about transactions are always unwelcome and usually unexpected. You have three goals in writing these messages: to modify the customer's expectations regarding the transaction, to explain how you plan to resolve the situation, and to repair whatever damage might have been done to the business relationship.

The specific content and tone of each message can vary widely, depending on the nature of the transaction and your relationship with the customer. Telling an individual consumer that his new sweater will be arriving a week later than you promised is a much simpler task than telling General Motors that 30,000 transmission parts will be a week late (especially when you know the company will be forced to idle a multimillion-dollar production facility as a result).

Some negative messages regarding transactions carry significant business ramifications.

Negative messages about transactions come in two basic flavors. If you haven't done anything specific to set the customer's expectations—such as promising delivery within 24 hours—the message simply needs to inform the customer, with little or no emphasis on apologies (see Figure 8.3).

Your approach to bad news about business transactions depends on the customer's expectations.

If you did set the customer's expectations and now find you can't meet them, your task is more complicated. In addition to resetting the expectations and explaining how you'll resolve the problem, you may need to include an element of apology. The scope of the apology depends on the magnitude of the mistake. For a customer who ordered a sweater, a simple apology, followed by a clear statement of when the sweater will arrive, would probably be sufficient. For larger business-to-business transactions, the customer may want an explanation of what went wrong in order to judge whether you'll be able to perform as you promise in the future.

If you've failed to meet expectations that you set for the customer, consider an element of apology.

To help repair the damage to the relationship and encourage repeat business, many companies offer discounts on future purchases, free merchandise, or other considerations. Even modest efforts can go a long way toward rebuilding the customer's confidence in

Planning

Analyze the Situation
Verify that the purpose is to decline a request and offer alternatives; audience is likely to be surprised by the refusal.

Gather Information
Determine audience needs and obtain the necessary information.

Select the Right Medium
For formal messages, printed letters on company letterhead are best.

Organize the Information
The main idea is to refuse the request so limit your scope to that; select the indirect approach based on the audience and the situation.

Writing

Adapt to Your Audience
Adjust the level of formality based on your degree of familiarity with the audience; maintain a positive relationship by using the "you" attitude, politeness, positive emphasis, and bias-free language.

Compose the Message
Use a conversational but professional style and keep the message brief, clear, and as helpful as possible.

Completing

Revise the Message
Evaluate content and review readability to make sure the negative information won't be misinterpreted; make sure your tone stays positive without being artificial.

Produce the Message
Maintain a clean, professional appearance on company letterhead.

Proofread the Message
Review for errors in layout, spelling, and mechanics.

Distribute the Message
Deliver your message using the chosen medium.

1   **2**   **3**

InfoTech

927 Dawson Valley Road, Tulsa, Oklahoma 74151
Voice: (918) 669-4428   Fax: (918) 669-4429
www.infotech.com

March 6, 2009

Dr. Sandra Wofford, President
Whittier Community College
333 Whittier Avenue
Tulsa, OK 74150

Dear Dr. Wofford:

[Buffers negative response by demonstrating respect and recapping the request] Infotech has been happy to support Whittier Community College in many ways over the years, and we appreciate the opportunities you and your organization provide to so many deserving students. Thank you for considering our grounds for your graduation ceremony on June 3.

[States a meaningful reason for the negative response, without apologizing (because the company is not at fault)] We would certainly like to accommodate Whittier as we have in years past, but our companywide sales meetings will be held this year during the weeks of May 29 and June 5. With more than 200 sales representatives and their families from around the world joining us activities will be taking place throughout our facility.

[Suggests an alternative, showing that Kwan cares about the college and has given the matter some thought] My assistant, Robert Seagers, suggests you contact the Municipal Botanical Gardens as a possible graduation site. He recommends calling Jerry Kane, director of public relations.

[Closes by emphasizing the importance of the relationship and the company's continuing commitment] We remain firm in our commitment to you, President Wofford, and to the fine students you represent. Through our internship program, academic research grants, and other initiatives, we will continue to be a strong corporate partner to Whittier College and will support your efforts as you move forward.

Sincerely,

May Yee Kwan

May Yee Kwan
Public Relations Director

lc

Pointers for Writing Negative Messages
- Carefully choose a direct or indirect approach.
- If using an indirect approach, establish rapport without implying that a positive response is coming.
- Smoothly transition from the buffer to the reasons for the negative response or news; help the reader anticipate the bad news before reaching it.
- Explain how the decision or news might benefit your audience—but only if it really does benefit them.
- Apologize only if appropriate and only if allowed by company policy.
- State the negative news as positively as possible, but without misleading your audience.
- Maintain a calm, objective tone throughout.
- Carefully consider the amount of detail to include.
- Don't invite questions or discussion if the decision is final.
- Close with a positive—but honest—outlook on the future.

Figure 8.2 Effective Letter Declining a Favor
In declining a request to use her company's facilities, May Yee Kwan took note of the fact that her company has a long-standing relationship with the college and wants to maintain that positive relationship. Because the news is unexpected based on past experience, she chose an indirect approach to build up to her announcement.

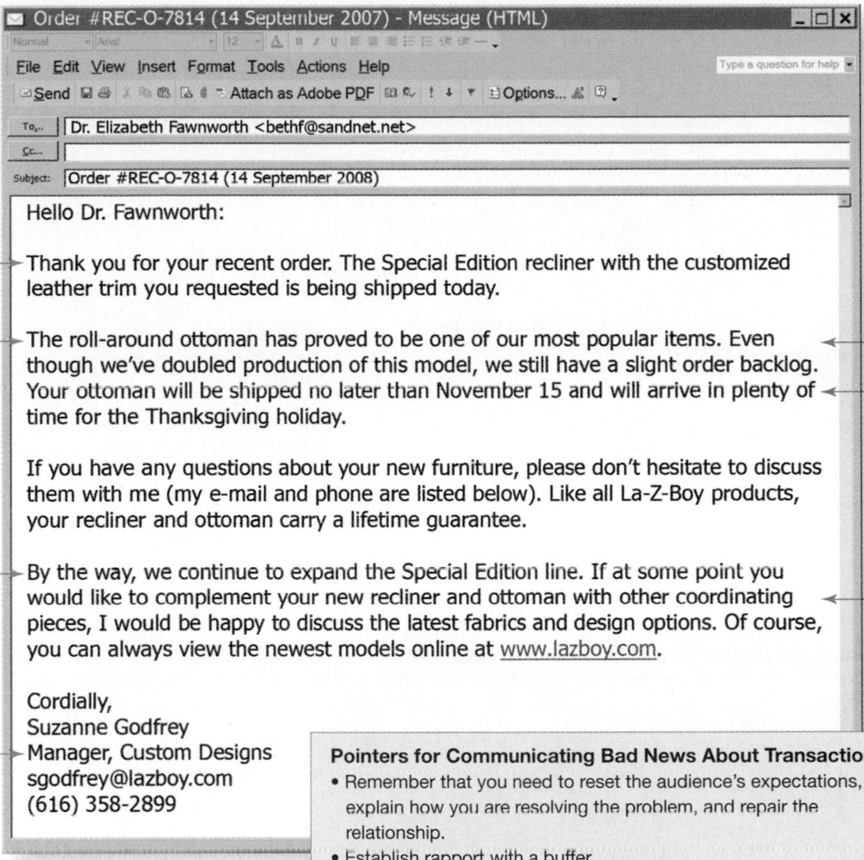

Annotations (left margin):

- Conveys the good news first in the buffer
- Implies the actual bad news by telling the reader what's being done, not what can't be done
- Fosters a positive ongoing relationship by inviting inquiries and reminding the customer of a key benefit
- Includes helpful contact information

E-mail message:

Order #REC-O-7814 (14 September 2007) - Message (HTML)

File Edit View Insert Format Tools Actions Help

Send | Attach as Adobe PDF | Options...

To..: Dr. Elizabeth Fawnworth <bethf@sandnet.net>

Cc..:

Subject: Order #REC-O-7814 (14 September 2008)

Hello Dr. Fawnworth:

Thank you for your recent order. The Special Edition recliner with the customized leather trim you requested is being shipped today.

The roll-around ottoman has proved to be one of our most popular items. Even though we've doubled production of this model, we still have a slight order backlog. Your ottoman will be shipped no later than November 15 and will arrive in plenty of time for the Thanksgiving holiday.

If you have any questions about your new furniture, please don't hesitate to discuss them with me (my e-mail and phone are listed below). Like all La-Z-Boy products, your recliner and ottoman carry a lifetime guarantee.

By the way, we continue to expand the Special Edition line. If at some point you would like to complement your new recliner and ottoman with other coordinating pieces, I would be happy to discuss the latest fabrics and design options. Of course, you can always view the newest models online at www.lazboy.com.

Cordially,
Suzanne Godfrey
Manager, Custom Designs
sgodfrey@lazboy.com
(616) 358-2899

Annotations (right margin):

- Explains the delay
- Cushions bad news with a pledge to ship by a definite time
- Encourages future purchasing, but in a way that addresses the customer's needs, not La-Z-Boy's

Pointers for Communicating Bad News About Transactions
- Remember that you need to reset the audience's expectations, explain how you are resolving the problem, and repair the relationship.
- Establish rapport with a buffer.
- If the news is mixed, use the good news as a buffer.
- Explain the reasons without laying the blame or making excuses.
- Describe exactly what will happen and when; focus on solutions, not problems.
- Reinforce the customer's confidence by emphasizing the advantages of doing business with you.
- Express the negative news succinctly and clearly.
- Suggest alternatives, if appropriate.
- Consider including tactful resale information to encourage future business.
- Close on a positive note that shows continued attention to the customer's needs.

Figure 8.3   Effective E-Mail Advising of a Back Order
This message, which is combination of good and bad news, uses the indirect approach—with the good news serving as a buffer for the bad news. In this case, the customer wasn't promised delivery by a certain date, so the writer simply informs the customer when to expect the rest of the order. The writer also takes steps to repair the relationship and encourage future business with her firm.

your company. Business-to-business purchasing contracts often include performance clauses that legally entitle the customer to discounts or other restitution in the event of late delivery.

Refusing Claims and Requests for Adjustment

Customers who make a claim or request an adjustment tend to be emotionally involved, so the indirect method is usually the best approach for a refusal. Your job as a writer is to avoid accepting responsibility for the unfortunate situation and yet avoid blaming or accusing the customer. To steer clear of these pitfalls, pay special attention to the tone of your letter. Demonstrate that you understand and have considered the complaint carefully and then rationally explain why you are refusing the request. End the letter on a respectful and action oriented note (see Figure 8.4).

Use the indirect approach in most cases of refusing claims.

Planning → **Writing** → **Completing**

Analyze the Situation
Verify that the purpose is to refuse a warranty claim and offer alternatives; the audience's likely reaction is disappointment and surprise.

Gather Information
Verify warranty information and research alternatives to present to the customer.

Select the Right Medium
Choose the best medium to deliver this message; the customer submitted the claim via e-mail, so a response via e-mail is appropriate.

Organize the Information
Focus on the main idea, which is to refuse the claim; select the indirect approach based on the audience and the situation.

Adapt to Your Audience
Adjust the level of formality based on the degree of familiarity with the audience (relatively formal is best in this case); maintain a positive relationship by using the "you" attitude, politeness, positive emphasis, and bias-free language.

Compose the Message
Use a conversational but professional style and keep the message brief, clear, and as helpful as possible.

Revise the Message
Evaluate content and review readability to make sure the negative information won't be misinterpreted; make sure your tone stays positive without being artificial.

Produce the Message
Emphasize a clean, professional appearance.

Proofread the Message
Review for errors in layout, spelling, and mechanics.

Distribute the Message
Deliver your message via e-mail.

1   **2**   **3**

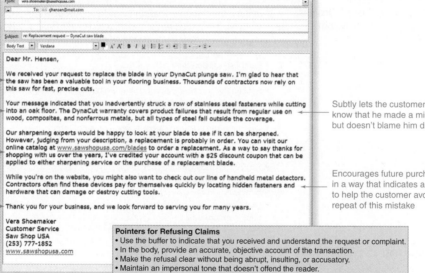

Buffers the bad news by starting with a point on which the writer and reader agree

States the bad news indirectly while emphasizing the appropriate uses of the product

Gives the customer options for the next step, including a helpful link to the company's website

Closes on a positive note by thanking the customer and looking to the future

Subtly lets the customer know that he made a mistake, but doesn't blame him directly

Encourages future purchasing in a way that indicates a desire to help the customer avoid a repeat of this mistake

Dear Mr. Hensen,

We received your request to replace the blade in your DynaCut plunge saw. I'm glad to hear that the saw has been a valuable tool in your flooring business. Thousands of contractors now rely on this saw for fast, precise cuts.

Your message indicated that you inadvertently struck a row of stainless steel fasteners while cutting into an oak floor. The DynaCut warranty covers product failures that result from regular use on wood, composites, and nonferrous metals, but all types of steel fall outside the coverage.

Our sharpening experts would be happy to look at your blade to see if it can be sharpened. However, judging from your description, a replacement is probably in order. You can visit our online catalog at www.sawshopusa.com/blades to order a replacement. As a way to say thanks for shopping with us over the years, I've credited your account with a $25 discount coupon that can be applied to either sharpening service or the purchase of a replacement blade.

While you're on the website, you might also want to check out our line of handheld metal detectors. Contractors often find these devices pay for themselves quickly by locating hidden fasteners and hardware that can damage or destroy cutting tools.

Thank you for your business, and we look forward to serving you for many years.

Vera Shoemaker
Customer Service
Saw Shop USA
(253) 777-1852
www.sawshopusa.com

Pointers for Refusing Claims
• Use the buffer to indicate that you received and understand the request or complaint.
• In the body, provide an accurate, objective account of the transaction.
• Make the refusal clear without being abrupt, insulting, or accusatory.
• Maintain an impersonal tone that doesn't offend the reader.
• Don't apologize for refusing, since your company hasn't done anything wrong.
• If appropriate, offer an alternative solution.
• Emphasize your continued desire for a positive relationship with the customer.
• Close with resale information if appropriate.
• Make any suggested actions easy for the reader to follow.

Figure 8.4 Effectively Refusing a Claim
Vera Shoemaker diplomatically refuses this customer's request for a new saw blade. Without blaming the customer (even though the customer clearly made a mistake), she points out that the saw blade is not intended to cut steel, so the warranty doesn't cover a replacement in this instance.

If you deal with enough customers over a long-enough period, chances are you'll get a request that is particularly outrageous. You may even be convinced that the person is being dishonest. However, you must resist the temptation to call the person dishonest or incompetent. If you don't, you could be sued for **defamation**, a false statement that damages someone's reputation. (Written defamation is called *libel*; spoken defamation is called *slander*.) To successfully sue for defamation, the aggrieved party must prove (1) that the statement is false, (2) that the language injures the person's reputation, and (3) that the statement has been communicated to others.

To avoid being accused of defamation, follow these guidelines:

- Avoid using any kind of abusive language or terms that could be considered defamatory. If you wish to express your own personal opinions about a sensitive matter, use your own stationery (not company letterhead), and don't include your job title or position. Be aware that by doing so, you take responsibility for your own opinions, you are no longer acting within the scope of your duties with the company, and you are personally liable for any resulting legal action.
- Never let anger or malice motivate your messages.
- Consult your company's legal department or an attorney whenever you think a message might have legal consequences.
- Communicate honestly and make sure that what you're saying is what you believe to be true.
- Emphasize a desire for a good relationship in the future.

You can help avoid defamation by not responding emotionally.

Remember that nothing positive can come out of antagonizing a customer, a colleague, or another business contact—even if that person has verbally abused you or others. Calmly reject the claim or request for adjustment and move on to the next challenge.

Sending Negative Employment Messages

All managers must convey bad news to individual employees from time to time. You can use the direct approach when writing to job applicants or when communicating with other companies to send a negative reference to a prospective employer. But it's best to use the indirect approach when giving negative performance reviews to employees; they will most certainly be emotionally involved. In addition, choose the media you use for these messages with care. E-mail and other written forms let you control the message and avoid personal confrontation, but one-on-one conversations are more sensitive and promote the interaction often needed to confront problems and discuss solutions.

Refusing Requests for Recommendation Letters

Many states have passed laws to protect employers who provide open and honest job references for former employees, but legal hazards persist.[5] That's why many employers still refuse to write recommendation letters—especially for former employees whose job performance was unsatisfactory. When sending refusals to prospective employers, be brief and direct:

Our human resources department has authorized me to confirm that Yolanda Johnson worked for Tandy, Inc., for three years, from June 1999 to July 2001. Best of luck as you interview administrative applicants.

Implies that company policy prohibits the release of any more information but does provide what information is available

Ends on a positive note

This message doesn't need to say, "We cannot comply with your request." It simply gets down to the business of giving readers the information that is allowable.

Refusing an applicant's direct request for a recommendation letter is another matter. Any refusal to cooperate may seem like a personal slight and a threat to the applicant's future. Diplomacy and preparation help readers accept your refusal:

In letters informing prospective employers that you will not provide a recommendation, be direct, brief, and factual (to avoid legal pitfalls).

Thank you for letting me know about your job opportunity with Coca-Cola. Your internship there and the MBA you've worked so hard to earn should place you in an excellent position to land the marketing job.

Uses the indirect approach because the other party is probably expecting a positive response

Although we do not send out formal recommendations here at PepsiCo, I can certainly send Coca-Cola a confirmation of your employment dates. And if you haven't considered this already, be sure to ask several of your professors to write evaluations of your marketing skills. Best of luck to you in your career.

Announces that the writer cannot comply with the request, without explicitly blaming it on "policy"

Offers to fulfill as much of the request as possible and then offers an alternative

Ends on a positive note

This letter tactfully avoids hurting the reader's feelings because it makes positive comments about the reader's recent activities, implies the refusal, suggests an alternative, and uses a polite close.

Rejecting Job Applications

Traditionally, businesses made a point of always responding to applications, but the rapid growth of e-mailed résumés and online job sites such as Monster.com have flooded some companies with so many applicants that they say they can no longer reply to them all.[6] However, you should make every effort to respond; failing to do so builds ill will and can harm your company's reputation.

As you write, bear in mind that poorly written rejection letters have negative consequences, ranging from the loss of qualified candidates for future openings to the loss of potential customers (not only the rejected applicants but also their friends and family members).[7] Poorly phrased rejection letters can even invite legal troubles. When delivering bad news to job applicants, follow three guidelines:[8]

Experts disagree on whether the direct or indirect approach is better for rejecting job applications.

- **Choose your approach carefully.** Experts disagree on whether the direct or indirect approach is best for rejection letters. On the one hand, job applicants know they won't get many of the positions they apply for, so negative news during a job search may be disappointing but is rarely shocking. On the other hand, people put their hopes and dreams on the line when they apply for work, so job applicants have a deep emotional investment in the process, which is one of the factors to consider in using the indirect approach. If you opt for the indirect approach, be careful not to mislead the reader with effusive praise or delay the bad news for more than a sentence or two. A simple "Thank you for considering ABC as the place to start your career" is a quick and courteous buffer.

- **Clearly state why the applicant was not selected.** Make your rejection less personal by stating that you hired someone with more experience or whose qualifications match the position requirements more closely.

- **Close by suggesting alternatives.** If you believe the applicant is qualified, mention other openings within your company. You might suggest professional organizations that could help the applicant find employment. Such suggestions may help the applicant be less disappointed and view your company more positively.

A rejection letter need not be long. After all, the applicant wants to know only one thing: Did I land the job? Your brief message should convey the information clearly and with tactful consideration for the applicant's feelings (see Figure 8.5).

Giving Negative Performance Reviews

An important goal of any performance evaluation is giving the employee a plan of action for improving his or her performance.

Few other communication tasks require such a broad range of skills and strategy as those needed for employee performance reviews. The main purpose of these reviews is to improve employee performance by (1) emphasizing and clarifying job requirements, (2) giving employees feedback on their efforts toward fulfilling those requirements, and (3) guiding continued improvements. In addition to improving employee performance, performance reviews help companies set organizational standards and communicate organizational values.[9] Whether the review is generally positive or generally negative, the tone should be objective and unbiased, the language nonjudgmental, and the focus on problem resolution.[10]

Criticizing the performance of an underperforming employee is never pleasant, but it is a vital responsibility for managers. First, without clear feedback, an employee may not understand the need to improve. Second, if you fire an employee for incompetence after he or she receives nothing but positive performance evaluations, the employee can sue your company, maintaining that you had no cause to terminate employment.[11] Also, your company could be sued for negligence if an injury is caused by an employee who received a negative evaluation but received no corrective action (such as retraining).[12]

When you need to give a negative performance review, follow these guidelines:[13]

- **Confront the problem right away.** Avoiding performance problems only makes them worse and opens the company to legal difficulties.[14]

- **Plan your message.** Be clear about your concerns and include examples of the employee's specific actions. Think about any possible biases you may have and get feedback from others. Collect and verify all relevant facts (both strengths and weaknesses).

Address performance problems in private.

- **Deliver the message in private.** Whether in writing or in person, be sure to address the performance problem privately.

Opens with an excessively positive tone that misleads the reader into thinking the answer will be positive

Includes an inappropriate apology; the company did nothing wrong so therefore has no need to apologize; also fails to explain why the candidate was not chosen

Closes with a weak, insincere request

Further sets the stage for the negative news by thoughtfully explaining the context in which the decision was made

Moderates the bad news with honest, specific encouragement

Buffers the upcoming bad news with a sincere thanks for being considered

Presents the bad news as a logical consequence of the decision-making process

Closes in a respectful, positive manner

Figure 8.5 Ineffective and Effective E-Mails Rejecting a Job Application
This e-mail response was drafted by Marvin Fichter to communicate bad news to Carol DeCicco following her interview with Bradley Jackson. After reviewing the first draft, Fichter made several changes to improve the communication. The revised e-mail helps DeCicco understand that (1) she would have been hired if she'd had more tax experience and (2) she shouldn't be discouraged.

- **Focus on the problem not the person.** Discuss the problems caused by the employee's behavior, comparing the employee's performance with what's expected, with company goals, or with job requirements. Identify the consequences of continuing poor performance and show that you're committed to helping solve the problem.

- **Ask for a commitment from the employee.** Help the employee understand that planning for and making improvements are the employee's responsibility. However, finalize decisions jointly so that you can be sure any action to be taken is achievable. Set a schedule for improvement and for following up with evaluations of that improvement.

Even if your employee's performance has been disappointing, look for opportunities to begin the performance review with some positive points. Then clearly and tactfully state how the employee can better meet the responsibilities of the job.[15] Remember that the ultimate goal is not simply to criticize but to help the employee succeed.

Terminating Employment

If an employee's performance cannot be brought up to company standards or if other factors such as declining sales cause a reduction in the workforce, a company often has no choice but to terminate employment. When writing a termination message, you have three goals: (1) Present the reasons for this difficult action, (2) avoid statements that might expose the company to a wrongful termination lawsuit, and (3) leave the relationship between the terminated employee and the firm as favorable as possible. For both legal and personal reasons, present specific justification for asking the employee to leave.[16] If the employee is working under contract, your company's lawyers will be able to tell you whether the employee's performance is legal grounds for termination.

Make sure that all your reasons are accurate and verifiable. Whenever possible, avoid words that are open to interpretation, such as *unsatisfactory* and *difficult*. Make sure the employee leaves with feelings that are as positive as the circumstances allow. You can do so by telling the truth about the termination and by helping as much as you can to make the employee's transition as smooth as possible.[17]

Sending Negative Organizational News

In special cases, you might need to issue negative announcements regarding some aspect of your products, services, or operations. These messages include news of changes that negatively affect one or more groups (such as losing a major contract or canceling a popular product); announcements of workforce reductions; and *crisis communication* regarding environmental incidents, workplace accidents, or other traumatic situations.

When making negative announcements, follow these guidelines:

- **Match your approach to the situation.** For example, in an emergency such as product tampering or a toxic spill, get to the point immediately.
- **Consider the unique needs of each group.** When a facility closes, for instance, employees need time to find new jobs, and community leaders may need to be prepared to help people who have lost their jobs.

- **Minimize the element of surprise whenever possible.** Give affected groups as much time as possible to prepare and respond.
- **If possible, give yourself enough time to plan and manage a response.** Make sure you're ready with answers to expected questions.
- **Look for positive angles but don't exude false optimism.** Laying off 10,000 people does not give them "an opportunity to explore new horizons." It's a traumatic event that can affect employees, their families, and their communities for years. The best you may be able to do is to thank people for their past support and to wish them well in the future.

- **Seek expert advice.** Many significant negative announcements have important technical, financial, or legal elements that require the expertise of lawyers, accountants, or other specialists.

Social media have created a major new challenge regarding negative company information: responding to online rumors and attacks on a company's reputation. Disappointed consumers can now communicate through blogs, social networking sites, advocacy sites such as www.walmartwatch.com, and complaint websites such as www.planetfeedback.com. These channels give customers who feel they've been wronged a chance to speak out and potentially influence corporate behavior. However, such sites can also give rise to false rumors and unfair criticisms that can spread around the world in a matter of minutes. In response, many companies now monitor blogs and other online sources to catch and respond to negative messages. Some have even set up special websites, such as www.walmartfacts.com, to answer

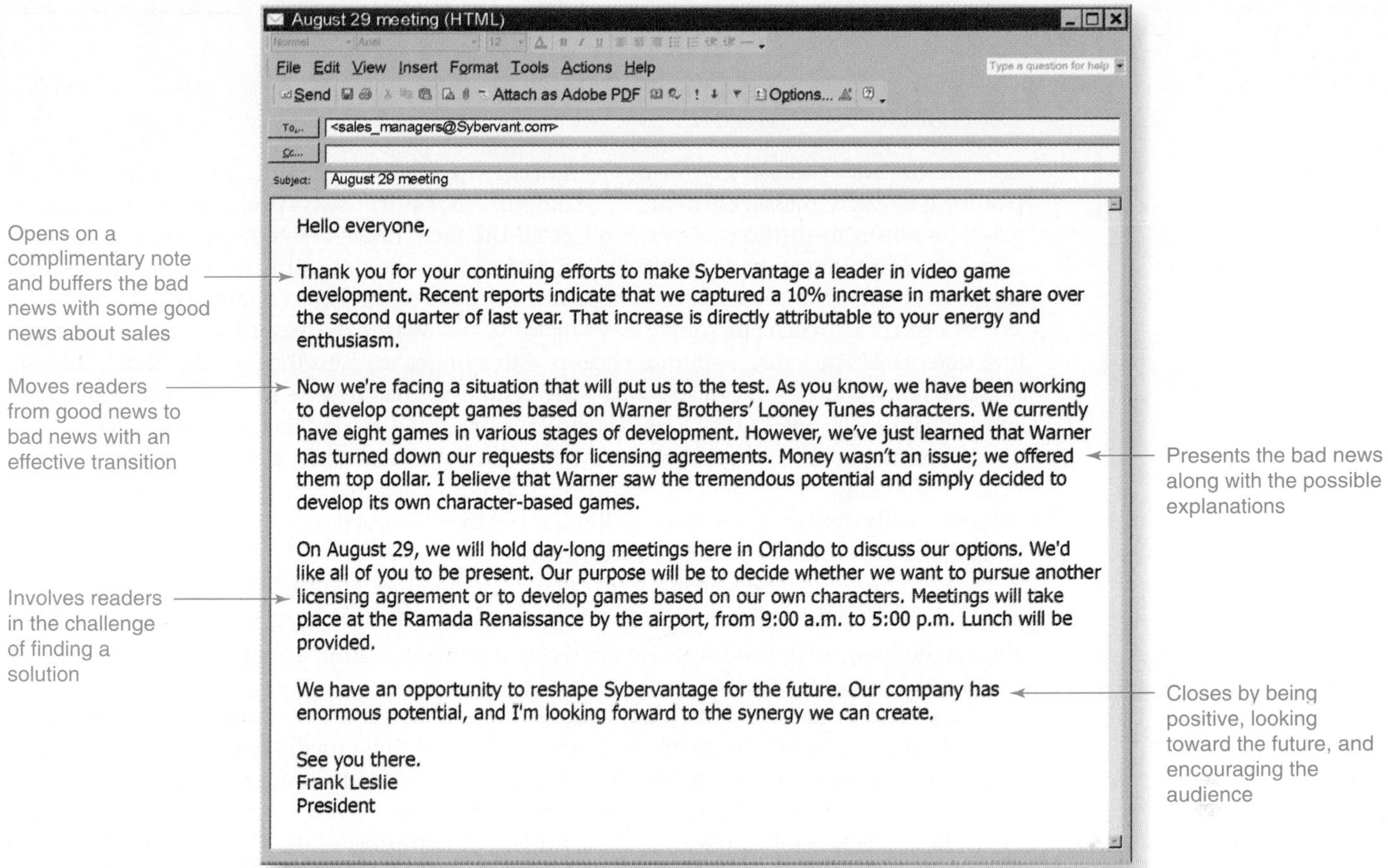
August 29 meeting (HTML)

File Edit View Insert Format Tools Actions Help

Send Attach as Adobe PDF Options...

To... <sales_managers@Sybervant.com>

Cc...

Subject: August 29 meeting

Hello everyone,

Thank you for your continuing efforts to make Sybervantage a leader in video game development. Recent reports indicate that we captured a 10% increase in market share over the second quarter of last year. That increase is directly attributable to your energy and enthusiasm.

Now we're facing a situation that will put us to the test. As you know, we have been working to develop concept games based on Warner Brothers' Looney Tunes characters. We currently have eight games in various stages of development. However, we've just learned that Warner has turned down our requests for licensing agreements. Money wasn't an issue; we offered them top dollar. I believe that Warner saw the tremendous potential and simply decided to develop its own character-based games.

On August 29, we will hold day-long meetings here in Orlando to discuss our options. We'd like all of you to be present. Our purpose will be to decide whether we want to pursue another licensing agreement or to develop games based on our own characters. Meetings will take place at the Ramada Renaissance by the airport, from 9:00 a.m. to 5:00 p.m. Lunch will be provided.

We have an opportunity to reshape Sybervantage for the future. Our company has enormous potential, and I'm looking forward to the synergy we can create.

See you there.
Frank Leslie
President

Figure 8.6 Effective E-Mail Providing Bad News About Company Operations
In this message to employees at Sybervantage, Frank Leslie shares the unpleasant news that a hoped-for licensing agreement with Warner Brothers has been rejected. Rather than dwell on the bad news, he focuses on options for the future. The upbeat close diminishes the effect of the bad news without hiding or downplaying the news itself.

public criticisms. Even if your company hasn't been the focus of complaints, stay tuned to public opinion and be ready to respond immediately.[18]

Negative situations will test your skills both as a communicator and as a leader. Inspirational leaders try to seize such opportunities as an opportunity to reshape or reinvigorate the organization, and they offer encouragement to those around them (see Figure 8.6).

For the latest information on writing negative messages, visit http://real-timeupdates.com/bce and click on Chapter 8. ■

DOCUMENT MAKEOVER

Improve This Memo

To practice correcting drafts of actual documents, visit the "Document Makeovers" section in either MyBCommLab.com or the Companion Website for this text.

If MyBCommLab.com is being used in your class, see your User Guide for specific instructions on how to access the content for this chapter.

If you are accessing this feature through the Companion Website, click on "Document Makeovers" and then select Chapter 8. You will find a memo that contains problems and errors related to what you've learned in this chapter about writing negative business messages. Use the Final Draft decision tool to create an improved version of this memo. Check the message for the use of buffers, apologies, explanations, subordination, embedding, positive action, conditional phrases, and upbeat perspectives. ●

" CHAPTER REVIEW AND ACTIVITIES

Chapter Summary

Because the way you say no can be far more damaging than the fact that you're saying it, planning negative messages is crucial. Make sure your purpose is specific and use an appropriate medium to fit the message. Collect all the facts necessary to support your negative decision, adapt your tone to the situation, and choose the optimum approach. Use positive words to construct diplomatic sentences and pay close attention to quality.

The direct approach puts the bad news up front, follows with the reasons, and closes with a positive statement. The indirect approach begins with a buffer, explains the reasons, clearly states the negative news, and closes with a positive statement. If the bad news is not unexpected, the direct approach is usually fine, but if the news is shocking or painful, the indirect approach is better.

When using the indirect approach, pay careful attention to avoid obscuring the bad news, trivializing the audience's concerns, or even misleading your audience into thinking you're actually delivering good news. Remember that the purpose of the indirect approach is to cushion the blow, not to avoid delivering it.

Defamation is a false statement that damages someone's reputation. Written defamation is called *libel*; spoken defamation is called *slander*. To avoid charges of defamation, avoid abusive language, communicate honestly, keep your emotions under control, and consult with legal advisors if needed.

Blogs and other online media give consumers and others the opportunity to vent their frustrations with faulty products and poor service, but these media also enable the dissemination of false rumors and unfair attacks. Companies need to stay on top of what is being said about them online and be ready to respond quickly.

When rejecting job applicants, (1) consider your approach carefully, (2) state clearly why the applicant was not selected, and (3) consider suggesting alternatives if you know of an opportunity that is a better fit for a particular applicant.

Test Your Knowledge

1. What are the five main goals in delivering bad news?

2. What questions should you ask yourself when choosing between the direct and indirect approaches?

3. What is the sequence of elements in a negative message organized using the indirect approach?

4. What is a buffer, and why do some critics consider it unethical?

5. When using the indirect approach to announce a negative decision, what is the purpose of presenting your reasons before explaining the decision itself?

Apply Your Knowledge

1. Why is it important to end negative messages on a positive note? Explain.

2. What new challenges do social media present to today's companies when it comes to negative information?

3. If the purpose of your letter is to convey bad news, should you take the time to suggest alternatives to your reader? Why or why not?

4. Why should a company always try to respond to all job applicants?

5. **Ethical Choices**   Is intentionally deemphasizing bad news the same as distorting graphs and charts to deemphasize unfavorable data? Why or why not?

Practice Your Knowledge

Exercises for Perfecting Your Writing

Teamwork   Working alone, revise the following statements to deemphasize the bad news without hiding it or distorting it. (*Hint:* Minimize the space devoted to the bad news, subordinate it, embed it, or use the passive voice.) Then team up with a classmate and read each other's revisions. Did you both use the same approach in every case? Which approach seems to be most effective for each of the revised statements?

1. The airline can't refund your money. The "Conditions" section on the back of your ticket states that there are no refunds for missed flights. Sometimes the airline makes exceptions, but only when life and death are involved. Of course, your ticket is still valid and can be used on a flight to the same destination.

2. I'm sorry to tell you, we can't supply the custom decorations you requested. We called every supplier and none of them can do what you want on such short notice. You can, however, get a standard decorative package on the same theme in time. I found a supplier that stocks these. Of course, it won't have quite the flair you originally requested.

3. We can't refund your money for the malfunctioning MP3 player. You shouldn't have immersed the unit in water while swimming; the users manual clearly states the unit is not designed to be used in adverse environments.

Indirect Approach: Buffers   Answer the following pertaining to buffers.

4. You have to tell a local restaurant owner that your plans have changed and you have to cancel the 90-person banquet scheduled for next month. Do you need to use a buffer? Why or why not?

5. Write a buffer for a letter declining an invitation to speak at the association's annual fund-raising event. Show your appreciation for being asked.

6. Write a buffer for a letter rejecting a job applicant who speaks three foreign languages fluently. Include praise for the applicant's accomplishments.

Indirect or Direct Approach   Select which approach you would use (direct or indirect) for the following negative messages.

7. An e-mail message to your boss, informing her that one of your key clients is taking its business to a different accounting firm

8. An e-mail message to a customer, informing her that one of the books she ordered from your website is temporarily out of stock

9. A letter to a customer, explaining that the DVD burner he ordered for his new custom computer is on back order and that, as a consequence, the shipping of the entire order will be delayed

Activities

Active links for all websites in this chapter can be found online. If MyBCommLab.com is being used in your class, see your User Guide for instructions on accessing the content for this chapter. Otherwise, visit www.pearsonhighered.com/bovee, locate *Business Communication Essentials*, Fourth Edition, click the Companion Website link, select Chapter 8, and then click on "Featured Websites." Please note that links to sites that become inactive after publication of the book will be removed from the Featured Websites section.

1. **Analyze This Message**   Read the following document and (1) analyze the strengths and weaknesses of each sentence and (2) revise each document so that it follows this chapter's guidelines.

    Your spring fraternity party sounds like fun. We're glad you've again chosen us as your caterer. Unfortunately, we have changed a few of our policies, and I wanted you to know about these changes in advance so that we won't have any misunderstandings on the day of the party.

    We will arrange the delivery of tables and chairs as usual the evening before the party. However, if you want us to set up, there is now a $100 charge for that service. Of course, you might want to get some of the brothers and pledges to do it, which would save you money. We've also added a small charge for cleanup. This is only $3 per person (you can estimate because I know a lot of people come and go later in the evening).

    Other than that, all the arrangements will be the same. We'll provide the skirt for the band stage, tablecloths, bar setup, and of course, the barbecue. Will you have the tubs of ice with soft drinks again? We can do that for you as well, but there will be a fee.

    Please let me know if you have any problems with these changes and we'll try to work them out. I know it's going to be a great party.

2. **Analyze This Message**   Read the following document and (1) analyze the strengths and weaknesses of each sentence and (2) revise the message so that it follows this chapter's guidelines.

    I am responding to your letter of about six weeks ago asking for an adjustment on your wireless hub, model WM39Z. We test all our products before they leave the factory; therefore, it could not have been our fault that your hub didn't work.

    If you or someone in your office dropped the unit, it might have caused the damage. Or the damage could have been caused by the shipper if he dropped it. If so, you should file a claim with the shipper. At any rate, it wasn't our fault. The parts are already covered by warranty. However, we will provide labor for the repairs for $50, which is less than our cost, since you are a valued customer.

    We will have a booth at the upcoming trade fair there and hope to see you or someone from your office. We have many new models of computing and networking accessories that we're sure you'll want to see. I've enclosed our latest catalog. Hope to see you there.

3. **Analyze This Message**   Read the following document and (1) analyze the strengths and weaknesses of each sentence and (2) revise the message so that it follows this chapter's guidelines.

    I regret to inform you that you were not selected for our summer intern program at Equifax. We had over a thousand résumés and cover letters to go through and simply could not get to them all. We have been asked to notify everyone that we have already selected students for the 25 positions based on those who applied early and were qualified.

We're sure you will be able to find a suitable position for summer work in your field and wish you the best of luck. We deeply regret any inconvenience associated with our reply.

4. **Ethical Choices**   The insurance company where you work is planning to raise all premiums for health-care coverage. Your boss has asked you to read a draft of her letter to customers, announcing the new, higher rates. The first two paragraphs discuss some exciting medical advances and the expanded coverage offered by your company. Only in the final paragraph do customers learn that they will have to pay more for coverage starting next year. What are the ethical implications of this draft? What changes would you suggest?

5. **Revising an E-Mail Message: Budgetary Cutbacks at Black & Decker**   The following e-mail message about travel budget cutbacks contains numerous blunders. Using what you've learned in the chapter, read the message carefully and analyze its faults. Then use the questions that follow to outline and write an improved message.

DATE: Wed, 28 May 2009 4:20:15 -0800
FROM: M. Juhasz, Travel & Meeting Services <mjuhasz@blackanddecker.com>
TO: [mailing list]
SUBJECT: Travel Budget Cuts Effective Immediately

Dear Traveling Executives:

We need you to start using some of the budget suggestions we are going to issue as a separate memorandum. These include using videoconference equipment instead of traveling to meetings, staying in cheaper hotels, arranging flights for cheaper times, and flying from less-convenient but also less-expensive suburban airports.

The company needs to cut travel expenses by fifty percent, just as we've cut costs in all departments of Black & Decker. This means you'll no longer be able to stay in fancy hotels and make last-minute, costly changes to your travel plans.

You'll also be expected to avoid hotel phone surcharges. Compose your e-mail offline when you're in the hotel. And never return a rental car with an empty tank! That causes the rental agency to charge us a premium price for the gas they sell when they fill it up upon your return.

You'll be expected to make these changes in your travel habits immediately.

Sincerely,
M. Juhasz

Travel & Meeting Services

   a. Describe the flaws in this bad-news e-mail about company operations.

   b. Develop a plan for rewriting the e-mail to company insiders, using the direct approach. The following steps will help you organize your efforts before you begin writing:

   1. Create an opening statement of the bad news, using the "you" attitude.

   2. Decide what explanation is needed to justify the news.

   3. Determine whether you can use lists effectively.

   4. Choose some positive suggestions you can include to soften the news.

   5. Develop an upbeat closing.

   c. Now rewrite the e-mail. Don't forget to leave ample time for revision of your work before you turn it in.

6. **Teamwork: Revising a Letter—Refusal from Home Depot to New Faucet Manufacturer**   The following letter rejecting a faucet manufacturer's product presentation contains many errors in judgment. Working with your classmates in a team effort, you should be able to improve its effectiveness as a negative message. First, analyze and discuss the letter's flaws. How can it be improved? Use the following questions to help guide your discussion and development of an improved version.

July 15, 2009

Pamela Wilson, Operations Manager
Sterling Manufacturing
133 Industrial Avenue
Gary, IN 46403

Dear Ms. Wilson:

We regret to inform you that your presentation at Home Depot's recent product review sessions in St. Petersburg did not meet our expert panelists' expectations. We require new products that will satisfy our customers' high standards. Yours did not match this goal.

Our primary concern is to continue our commitment to product excellence, customer knowledge, and price competitiveness, which has helped make Home Depot a Fortune 500 company with more than a thousand stores nationwide. The panel found flaws in your design and materials. Also, your cost per unit was too high.

The product review sessions occur annually. You are allowed to try again; just apply as you did this year. Again, I'm sorry things didn't work out for you this time.

Sincerely,

Hilary Buchman, Assistant to the Vice President, Sales

HB:kl

    a. Describe the problems with this letter rejecting a product presentation.

    b. Develop a plan for rewriting the letter, using the indirect approach. Organize your thinking before you begin writing, using the following tactics:

        1. Select a buffer for the opening, using the "you" attitude.

        2. Choose the reasons you'll use to explain the rejection.

        3. Develop a way to soften or embed the bad news.

        4. Create a conditional (if/then) statement to encourage the recipient to try again.

        5. Find a way to close on a positive, encouraging note.

    c. Now rewrite the letter. Don't forget to leave ample time for revision of your work before you turn it in.

Expand Your Knowledge

Exploring the Best of the Web

Protect Yourself When Sending Negative Employment Messages A visit to the Business Owner's Toolkit website, www.toolkit.com, can help you reduce your legal liability, whether you are laying off an employee, firing an employee, or contemplating a companywide reduction in your workforce. Find out the safest way to fire someone from a legal standpoint before it's too late. Learn why it's important to document disciplinary actions. Discover why some bad news should be given face-to-face and never by letter or over the phone. Read the site's advice under "Firing and Termination" and then answer the following questions.

Exercises

1. What should a manager communicate to an employee during a termination meeting?

2. Why is it important to document employee disciplinary actions?

3. What steps should you take before firing an employee for misconduct or poor performance?

Surfing Your Way to Career Success

Bovée and Thill's Business Communication Headline News offers links to hundreds of online resources that can help you with this course, your other college courses, and your career. Visit http://businesscommunicationblog.com and click on "Web Directory." The Internet and the World Wide Web section connects you to a variety of websites and articles on website design and development, HTML, web graphics, RSS, wikis, and related topics. Identify three websites from this section that could be useful in your business career. For each site, write a two-sentence summary of what the site offers and how it could help you launch and build your career.

MyBCommLab.com

Use MyBCommLab.com to test your understanding of the concepts presented in this chapter and explore additional materials that will bring the ideas to life in video, activities, and an online multimedia e-book. Additionally, you can improve your skill with commas, semicolons, and colons by using the "Peak Performance Grammar and Mechanics" module within the lab. Take the Pretest to determine whether you have any weak areas. Then review those areas in the Refresher Course. Take the Follow-Up Test to check your grasp of commas, semicolons, and colons. For an extra challenge, take the Advanced Test. Finally, for even more reinforcement, go to the "Improve Your Grammar, Mechanics, and Usage" section that follows the cases, and complete the "Level 1: Self-Assessment" exercises.

CASES

▼ *Apply the three-step writing process to the following cases, as assigned by your instructor.*

[BLOGGING SKILLS] [PORTFOLIO BUILDER]

1. Removing the Obstacles on the On-ramp: Blog Posting to Ernst & Young Employees
Like many other companies these days, the accounting firm Ernst & Young is fighting a brain drain as experienced executives and professionals leave in mid-career to pursue charitable interests, devote more time to family matters, and pursue a variety of other dreams or obligations. The problem is particularly acute among women, who, on average, step off the career track more often than men do. As general manager of the largest division of Ernst & Young, you've been tapped to draft a set of guidelines to make it easier for employees who've taken some time off to move back into the company.

However, as soon as word gets out about what you're planning, several of your top performers, people who've never left the company for personal time off—or "taken the off-ramp," in current buzzword-speak—march into your office to complain. They fear that encouraging the "off-rampers" to return isn't fair to the employees who've remained loyal to the firm, as they put it. One goes as far to say that anyone who leaves the company doesn't deserve to be asked back. Two others claim that the additional experience and skills they've gained as they continued to work should guarantee them higher pay and more responsibilities than employees who took time off for themselves.[19]

Your task As unhappy as these several employees are, the program needs to be implemented if Ernst & Young hopes to bring off-rampers back into the company—thereby making sure they don't go work for competitors instead. However, you also can't afford to antagonize the existing workforce, and if the people who've already complained are any indication, you have a sizable morale problem on your hands. You decide that your first step is to clearly explain why the program is necessary, including how it will benefit everyone in the company by making Ernst & Young more competitive. Write a short posting for the company's internal blog, explaining that despite the objections some employees have raised, the firm is going ahead with the program as planned. Balance this news (which some employees will obviously view as negative) with positive reassurances that all current employees will be treated fairly in terms of both compensation and promotion opportunities. Close with a call for continued communication on this issue, inviting people to meet with you in person or to post their thoughts on the blog.

[PORTFOLIO BUILDER]

2. Listen to the Music, Partner: Delivering an Ultimatum to a Business Associate
You're a marketing manager for Stanton, one of the premier suppliers of DJ equipment (turntables, amplifiers, speakers, mixers, and related accessories). Your company's latest creation, the FinalScratch system, has been flying off retailers' shelves. Both professional and amateur DJs love the way that FinalScratch gives them the feel of working with vinyl records by letting them control digital music files from any analog turntable or CD player, while giving them access to the endless possibilities of digital music technology. (For more information about the product, go to www.stantondj.com.) Sales are strong everywhere except in Music99 stores, a retail chain in the Mid-Atlantic region. You suspect the cause: The owners of this chain refused to let their salespeople attend the free product training you offered when FinalScratch was introduced, claiming that their people were smart enough to train themselves.

To explore the situation, you head out from Stanton headquarters in Hollywood, Florida, on an undercover shopping mission. After visiting a few Music99 locations, you're appalled by what you see. The salespeople in these stores clearly don't understand the FinalScratch concept, so they either give potential customers bad information about it or steer them to products from your competitors. No wonder sales are so bad at this chain.[20]

Your task You're tempted to pull your products out of this chain immediately, but based on your experience in this market, you know how difficult and expensive it is to recruit new retailers. However, this situation can't go on; you're losing thousands of dollars of potential business every week. Write a letter to Jackson Fletcher, the CEO of Music99 (14014 Preston Pike, Dover, Delaware, 19901), expressing your disappointment in what you observed and explaining that the Music99 sales staff will need to agree to attend product training or else your company's management team will consider terminating the business relationship. You've met Mr. Fletcher in person once and talked on the phone several times, and you know him well enough to know that he will not be pleased by this ultimatum. Music99 does a good job selling other Stanton products—and he'll probably be furious to learn that you were "spying" on his sales staff.

[E-MAIL SKILLS]

3. Message to the Boss: Refusing a Project on Ethical Grounds
A not-so-secret secret is getting more attention than you'd really like after an article in *BusinessWeek* gave the world an inside look at how much money you and other electronics retailers make from extended warranties (sometimes called service contracts). The article explained that typically half of the warranty price goes to the salesperson as a commission and that only 20 percent of the total amount customers pay for warranties eventually goes to product repair.

You also know why extended warranties are such a profitable business. Many electronics products follow a predictable pattern of failure: a high failure rate early in their lives, then a "midlife" period during which failures go way down, and finally an "old age" period when failure rates ramp back up again (engineers refer to the phenomenon as the *bathtub curve* because it looks like a bathtub from the side—high at both ends and low in the middle). Those early failures are usually covered by manufacturers' warranties, and the extended warranties you sell are designed to cover that middle part of the life span. In other words, many extended warranties cover the period of time during which consumers are *least* likely to need them and offer no coverage when consumers need them *most*. (Consumers can actually benefit from extended warranties in a few product categories, including laptop computers and plasma TVs. Of course, the more sense the warranty makes for the consumer, the less financial sense it makes for your company.)[21]

Your task Worried that consumers will start buying fewer extended warranties, your boss has directed you to put together a sales training program that will help cashiers sell the extended warranties even more aggressively. The more you ponder this challenge, though, the more you're convinced that your company should change its strategy so it doesn't rely so much on profits from these warranties. In addition to offering questionable value to the consumer, they risk creating a consumer backlash that could lead to lower sales of all your products. You would prefer to voice your concerns to your boss in person, but both of you are traveling on hectic schedules for the next week. You'll have to write an e-mail instead. Draft a brief message explaining why you think the sales training specifically and the warranties in general are both bad ideas.

[**PHONE SKILLS**]

4. When a Recall Isn't Really a Recall: Voice Recording Informing Customers That an Unsafe Product Won't Be Replaced
Vail Products of Toledo, Ohio, manufactured a line of beds for use in hospitals and other institutions where there is a need to protect patients who might otherwise fall out of bed and injure themselves (including patients with cognitive impairments or patterns of spasms or seizures). These "enclosed bed systems" use a netted canopy to keep patients in bed rather than the traditional method of using physical restraints such as straps or tranquilizing drugs. The intent is humane, but the design is flawed: At least 30 patients have become trapped in the various parts of the mattress and canopy structure, and 8 of them have suffocated.

Working with the U.S. Food and Drug Administration (FDA), Vail issued a recall on the beds, as manufacturers often do in the case of unsafe products. However, the recall is not really a recall. Vail will not be replacing or modifying the beds, nor will it accept returns. Instead, the company is urging institutions to move patients to other beds if possible. Vail has also sent out revised manuals and warning labels to be placed on the beds. In addition, the company announced that it is ceasing production of enclosed beds.

Your task A flurry of phone calls from concerned patients, family members, and institutional staff is overwhelming the support staff. As a writer in Vail's corporate communications office, you've been asked to draft a short script to be recorded on the company's phone system. When people call the main

number, they'll hear "Press 1 for information regarding the recall of Model 500, Model 1000, and Model 2000 enclosed beds." After they press 1, they'll hear the message you're about to write, explaining that although the action is classified as a recall, Vail will not be accepting returned beds, nor will it replace any of the affected beds. The message should also assure customers that Vail has already sent revised operating manuals and warning labels to every registered owner of the beds in question. The phone system has limited memory, and you've been directed to keep the message to 75 words or less.[22]

[**E-MAIL SKILLS**] [**PORTFOLIO BUILDER**]

5. Sorry, but We Don't Have a Choice: E-Mail About Monitoring Employee Blogs
You can certainly sympathize with employees when they complain about having their e-mail and instant messages monitored, but you're implementing a company policy that all employees agree to abide by when they join the company. Your firm, Webcor Builders of San Mateo, California, is one of the estimated 60 percent of U.S. companies with such monitoring systems in place. More and more companies are using these systems (which typically operate by scanning messages for key words that suggest confidential, illegal, or otherwise inappropriate content) in an attempt to avoid instances of sexual harassment and other problems.

As the chief information officer, the manager in charge of computer systems in the company, you're often the target when employees complain about being monitored. Consequently, you know you're really going to hear it when employees learn that the monitoring program will be expanded to personal blogs as well.[23]

Your task Write an e-mail to be distributed to the entire workforce, explaining that the automated monitoring program is about to be expanded to include employees' personal blogs. Explain that while you sympathize with employee concerns regarding privacy and freedom of speech, the management team's responsibility is to protect the company's intellectual property and the value of the company name. Therefore, employees' personal blogs will be added to the monitoring system to ensure that employees don't intentionally or accidentally expose company secrets or criticize management in a way that could harm the company.

[**PHONE SKILLS**]

6. Reacting to a Lost Contract: Phone Call Rescinding a Job Offer
As the human resources manager at Alion Science and Technology, a military research firm in McLean, Virginia, you were thrilled when one of the nation's top computer visualization specialists accepted your job offer. Claus Gunnstein's skills would make a major contribution to Alion's work in designing flight simulators and other systems. Unfortunately, the day after he accepted the offer, Alion received news that a major Pentagon contract had been canceled. In addition to letting several dozen current employees know that the company will be forced to lay them off, you need to tell Gunnstein that Alion has no choice but to rescind the job offer.[24]

Your task Outline the points you'll need to make in a telephone call to Gunnstein. Pay special attention to your opening and closing statements. (You'll review your plans for the phone call with Alion's legal staff to make sure everything you say follows employment law guidelines; for now, just focus on the way you'll present the negative news to Gunnstein. Feel free to make up any details you need.)

[IM SKILLS]

7. Midair Letdown: Instant Message About Flight Cancellations at United Airlines In the old days, airline passengers usually didn't learn about cancelled connecting flights until after they'd landed. Sometimes a pilot would announce cancellations just before touching down at a major hub, but how were passengers to notify waiting relatives or business associates on the ground?

As a customer service supervisor for United Airlines, you've just received information that all United flights from Chicago's O'Hare International Airport to Boston's Logan International have been cancelled until further notice. A late winter storm has already blanketed Boston with snow, and freezing rain is expected overnight. The way the weather report looks, United will probably be lodging Boston-bound connecting passengers in Chicago-area hotels tonight. Meanwhile, you'll be using some of United's newest communication tools to notify travelers of the bad news.

United Airlines now partners with Verizon Airfone to provide JetConnect information services, giving travelers access to instant messaging and other resources while they're airborne. For a small fee, they can plug their laptop computers into the Airfone jack and activate their own instant messaging software to send and receive messages. If they've signed up for United's EasyUpdate flight status notification service, they'll also receive instant message alerts for flight cancellations, delays, seating upgrades, and so on.

Your task Write the cancellation alert, staying within the 65-word limit of many instant messaging programs. You might want to mention the airline's policy of providing overnight lodging for passengers who planned to use the Boston route as a connecting flight to complete journeys in progress.[25]

[E-MAIL SKILLS]

8. Career Moves: E-Mail Refusing to Write a Recommendation Tom Weiss worked in the office at Opal Pools and Patios for four months, under your supervision (you're office manager). On the basis of what he told you he could do, you started him off as a file clerk. However, his organizational skills proved inadequate for the job, so you transferred him to logging in accounts receivable, where he performed almost adequately. Then he assured you that his "real strength" was customer relations, so you moved him to the complaint department. After he spent three weeks making angry customers even angrier, you were convinced that no place in your office was appropriate for the talents of Mr. Weiss. Five weeks ago, you encouraged him to resign before being formally fired.

Today's e-mail brings a request from Weiss, asking you to write a letter recommending him for a sales position with a florist shop. You can't assess Weiss's sales abilities, but you do know him to be an incompetent file clerk, a careless bookkeeper, and an insensitive customer service representative. Someone else is more likely to deserve the sales job, so you decide that you have done enough favors for Tom Weiss for one lifetime and plan to refuse his request.

Your task Write an e-mail reply to Mr. Weiss (tomweiss@aol.com), indicating that you have chosen not to write a letter of recommendation for him.

[INTERCULTURAL SKILLS]

9. Juggling Diversity and Performance: Memo Giving a Negative Performance Review at AT&T As billing adjustments department manager at AT&T, you've been trained to handle a culturally diverse workforce. One of your best recent hires is 22-year-old Jorge Gutierrez. In record time, he was entering and testing complex price changes, mastering the challenges of your monumental computerized billing software. He was a real find—except for one problem: His close family ties often distract him from work duties.

His parents immigrated from Central America when Jorge and his sisters were young children, and you understand and deeply respect the importance that family plays in the lives of many Hispanic Americans. However, every morning Gutierrez's mother calls to be sure he got to work safely. Then his father calls. And three times this month, his younger sister has called him away from work with three separate emergencies. Friends and extended family members seem to call at all hours of the day.

Gutierrez says he's asked friends and family members not to call his office number. Now they dial his mobile phone instead. He's reluctant to shut off his mobile phone during work hours, in case someone in his family needs him.

At this point, you have given Gutierrez several verbal warnings. You really can't afford to lose him, so you're hoping that a written negative review will give him greater incentive to persuade friends and relatives. You'll deliver the letter in a one-on-one meeting and help him find ways to resolve the issue within a mutually agreed-upon time frame.

Your task Write the memo, using suggestions in this chapter to help you put the bad news in a constructive light. Avoid culturally biased remarks or innuendos.

[IM SKILLS]

10. Quick Answer: Instant Message Turning Down an Employee Request at Hewlett-Packard If she'd asked you a week ago, Lewinda Johnson might have been granted her request to attend a conference on the use of blogging for business, which is being held in New York City next month. Instead, Johnson waited until you were stuck in this meeting, and she needs your response within the hour. She'll have to take no for an answer: With travel budgets under tight restrictions, you would need at least three days to send her request up the chain of command. Furthermore, Johnson hasn't given you sufficient justification for her attendance, since she's already familiar with blogging.

Your task Write a 60- to 75-word instant message to Lewinda Johnson, declining her request. Decide whether the direct or indirect approach is appropriate.[26]

[WEB WRITING SKILLS]

11. Coffee Offer Overflow: Undoing a Marketing Mistake at Starbucks Marketing specialists usually celebrate when target audiences forward their messages to friends and family—essentially acting as unpaid advertising and sales representatives. In fact, the practice of viral marketing (see page 124) is based on this hope. For one Starbucks regional office, however, viral marketing started to make the company just a bit sick. The office sent employees in the Southeast an e-mail coupon for a free iced drink and invited them to share the coupon with family and friends. To the surprise of virtually no one who understands the nature of online life, the e-mail coupon multiplied rapidly, to the point that Starbucks stores all around the country were quickly overwhelmed with requests for free drinks. The company decided to immediately terminate the free offer, a month ahead of the expiration date on the coupon.[27]

Your task Write a one-paragraph message that can be posted on the Starbucks website and in individual stores, apologizing for the mix-up and explaining that the offer is no longer valid.

[BLOGGING SKILLS]

12. We're Going to Catch Some Flak for This: Alerting Employees to the Removal of a Popular Product XtremityPlus is known for its outlandish extreme-sports products, and the Looney Launch is no exception. Fulfilling the dream of every childhood daredevil, the Looney Launch is an aluminum and fiberglass contraption that quickly unfolds to create the ultimate bicycle jump. The product has been selling as fast as you can make it, even though it comes plastered with warning labels proclaiming that its use is inherently dangerous.

As XtremityPlus's CEO, you were nervous about introducing this product, and your fears were just confirmed: You've been notified of the first lawsuit by a parent whose child broke several bones after crash-landing off a Looney Launch.

Your task Write a post for your internal blog, explaining that the Looney Launch is being removed from the market immediately. Tell your employees to expect some negative reactions from enthusiastic customers and retailers but explain that (a) the company can't afford the risk of additional lawsuits and (b) even for XtremityPlus, the Looney Launch pushes the envelope a bit too far. The product is simply too dangerous to sell in good conscience.

[BLOGGING SKILLS] [PORTFOLIO BUILDER]

13. Communicating in a Crisis: Informing the Local Community About a Serious Accident One of your company's worst nightmares has just come true. EQ Industrial Services (EQIS), based in Wayne, Michigan, operates a number of facilities around the country that dispose of, recycle, and transport hazardous chemical wastes. Last night, explosions and fires broke out at the company's Apex, North Carolina, facility, forcing the evacuation of 17,000 local residents.

Your task It's now Friday, the day after the fire. Write a brief post for the company's blog, covering the following points:

- A fire did break out at the Apex facility at approximately 10 P.M. Thursday.
- No one was in the facility at the time.
- Because of the diverse nature of the materials stored at the plant, the cause of the fire is not yet known.
- Rumors that the facility stores extremely dangerous chlorine gas and that the fire was spreading to other nearby businesses are not true.
- Special industrial firefighters hired by EQIS have already brought the fire under control.
- Residents in the immediate area were evacuated as a precaution, and they should be able to return to their homes tomorrow, pending permission by local authorities.
- Several dozen residents were admitted to local hospitals with complaints of breathing problems, but many have been released already; about a dozen emergency responders were treated as well.
- At this point (Friday afternoon), tests conducted by the North Carolina State Department of Environment and Natural Resources "had not detected anything out of the ordinary in the air."

Conclude by thanking the local police and fire departments for their assistance and directing readers to EQIS's toll-free hot line for more information.[28]

[PODCASTING SKILLS]

14. Say Good-bye to the Concierge: Podcast Announcing the End of a Popular Employee Benefit An employee concierge seemed like a great idea when you added it as an employee benefit last year. The concierge handles a wide variety of personal chores for employees, everything from dropping off their dry cleaning to ordering event tickets to sending flowers. Employees love the service, and you know that the time they save can be devoted to work or family activities. Unfortunately, profits are way down, and concierge usage is up—up so far that you'll need to add a second concierge to keep up with the demand. As painful as it will be for everyone, you decide that the company needs to stop offering the service.

Your task Script a brief podcast announcing the decision and explaining why it was necessary. Make up any details you need.

If your instructor asks you to do so, record your podcast and submit the file.

[PORTFOLIO BUILDER]

15. What We Have Here Is a Failure to Communicate: Writing a Negative Performance Review Elaine Bridgewater, the former professional golfer you hired to oversee your golf equipment company's relationship with retailers, knows the business inside and out. As a former touring pro, she has unmatched credibility. She also has seemingly boundless energy, solid technical knowledge, and an engaging personal style. Unfortunately, she hasn't been quite as attentive as she needs to be when it comes to communicating with retailers. You've been getting complaints about voice-mail messages gone unanswered for days, confusing e-mails that require two or three rounds of clarification, and reports that are haphazardly thrown together. As valuable as Bridgewater's other skills are, she's going to cost the company sales if this goes on much longer. The retail channel is vital to your company's survival, and she's the employee most involved in the channel.

Your task Draft a brief (one page maximum) informal performance appraisal and improvement plan for Bridgewater. Be sure to compliment her on the areas in which she excels but don't shy away from highlighting the areas in which she needs to improve, too: punctual response to customer messages; clear writing; and careful revision, production, and proofreading. Use what you've learned in this course so far to supply any additional advice about the importance of these skills.

Improve Your Grammar, Mechanics, and Usage

Level 1: Self-Assessment—Semicolons and Colons

Review Sections 2.4 and 2.5 in the Handbook of Grammar, Mechanics, and Usage, and then complete the following 15 items.

In items 1–15, insert all required semicolons, colons, and commas.

1. This letter looks good that one doesn't.

2. I want to make one thing perfectly clear neither of you will be promoted if sales figures don't improve.

3. The Zurich airport has been snowed in therefore I won't be able to meet with you before January 4.

4. His motivation was obvious to get Meg fired.

5. Only two firms have responded to our survey J. J. Perkins and Tucker & Tucker.

6. Send a copy to Mary Kent Marketing Director Robert Bache Comptroller and Dennis Mann Sales Director.

7. Please be sure to interview these employees next week Henry Gold Doris Hatch and George Iosupovich.

8. We have observed your hard work because of it we are promoting you to manager of your department.

9. You shipped three items on June 7 however we received only one of them.

10. The convention kit includes the following response cards, giveaways, brochures, and a display rack.

11. The workers wanted an immediate wage increase they had not had a raise in nearly two years.

12. This then is our goal for 2009 to increase sales 35 percent.

13. His writing skills are excellent however he still needs to polish his management style.

14. We would like to address three issues efficiency profitability and market penetration.

15. Remember this rule When in doubt leave it out.

Level 2: Workplace Applications

The following items contain numerous errors in grammar, capitalization, punctuation, abbreviation, number style, word division, and vocabulary. Rewrite each sentence, correcting all errors. Write *C* for any sentence that is already correct.

1. Hector's, Julie's, and Tim's report was well-received by the Committee.

2. Everyone who are interested in signing up for the training seminar must do so by 3:00 o'clock PM on friday.

3. David Stern is a management and training expert that has spent a major part of his career coaching, counseling, and giving advise both to managers and workers.

4. Be aware and comply with local "zoning ordnances" and building codes.

5. Garrett didn't seem phased when her supervisor didn't except her excuse for being late, she forgot to set her alarm.

6. Copyright laws on the Internet is not always clearly defined, be sure your research doesn't extend to "borrowing" a competitors' keywords or copy.

7. Sauder Woodworking, in Archibald, Ohio sell a line of ready to assemble computer carts, desks, file cabinets, and furniture that is modular that can be mixed and matched to meet each business owners' personal taste.

8. Spamming is the most certain way to loose you're e-mail account, Web site, and you're reputation.

9. Us programmers have always tried to help others learn the tricks of the trade, especially Roger and myself.

10. The person whom was handling Miss Martinez' account told her that an error had been made by the bank in her favor.

11. "The trouble with focus groups" says Marketing Expert Frances Knight, "Is that consumers rarely act in real life they way they do in a "laboratory" setting."

12. In a industry in which design firms tend to come and go Skyline has licensed seventy products and grown to 8 employees.

13. If youv'e ever wondered why fast food restaurants are on the left and gift shops are on the right as you walk toward the gate into a newly-constructed airport you should read Malcolm Gladwells article, 'The Science of Shopping,' in the *New Yorker*.

14. Anyone whose starting a business should consider using their life story, as a way to generate customer's interest.

15. Having been in business since 1993, over 1000s of sales calls has been made by Mr. Jurzang, on prospects for his minority owned company.

Level 3: Document Critique

The following e-mail message may contain errors in grammar, capitalization, punctuation, abbreviation, number style, vocabulary, and spelling. You may also discover problems with wordiness, usage, and appropriateness of tone for negative messages. Correct all errors using standard proofreading marks (see Appendix C).

TO: <all.employees>
SUBJECT: Health insurance—Changes

Unlike many companies, Bright Manufacturing has always paid a hundred % of medical car insurance for it's employees, absorbing the recent 10–20 percent annual cost increases in order to provide this important benefit. This year; Blue Cross gave us some terrible news: the cost increase for our employee's medical coverage would be a staggering fourty percent per month next year

To mange the increase and continue to offer you and your family highquality medical coverage we have negotiated several changes with Blue Cross; a new cost saving alternative is also being offered by us:
Under the Blue Cross Plus plan, copay amounts for office visits will be ten dollars next year/ $50 for emergency room visits.

80 % of employees' insurance coverage (including 10 percent of the cost increase) will be paid by Bright next year and 100 % of the prescription drug costs (including a 23 percent cost increase). The remaining twenty percent of medical coverage will be deducted by us monthly from your salary, if you choose to remain on a Blue Cross Plus plan. We realize this is alot, but its still less than many companies charge their employees.

A fully paid alternative health plan, Blue Cross HMO, will now be provided by Bright at no cost to employees. But be warned that there is a deadline. If you want to switch to this new plan you must do so during our open enrollment period, Nov. 20 to December 1, and we will not consder applications for the change after that time so don't get your forms in late.

There are forms available in the Human Resources office for changing your coverage. They must be returned between November 20 and December 1. If you wish to remain on a Blue Cross Plus policy, you do not need to notify us; payroll deductions for company employees on the plan will occur automatic beginning January first.

If you have questions, please call our new Medical Benefits Information line at ext. 3392. Our Intranet sight will also provide you easy with information about health care coverage online if you click the "Medical Benefits" icon. Since our founding in 1946, we have provided our company employees with the best medical coverage available. We all hate rising costs and although things are looking bleak for the future but we're doing all we can do to hold on to this helpful benefit for you.

Lucinda Goodman, Benefits Mangr., Human resources

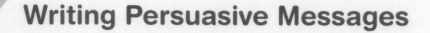

CHAPTER

9

Writing Persuasive Messages

LEARNING OBJECTIVES

After studying this chapter, you will be able to

1. Apply the three-step writing process to persuasive messages
2. Identify seven ways to establish credibility in persuasive messages
3. Describe the AIDA model for persuasive messages
4. Distinguish between emotional and logical appeals and discuss how to balance them
5. Explain why it is important to identify potential objections before you start writing persuasive messages
6. Explain how your writing approach should be modified for conversation marketing
7. Identify steps you can take to avoid ethical lapses in marketing and sales messages

The "you" attitude is important in any business message, but it's absolutely vital in persuasive writing. If your audience members don't believe that you have their best interests at heart, they won't be easily persuaded by anything you write. Follow the advice of successful persuasive writers such as Brian Clark: Audiences don't really care about what you have to say until you've demonstrated—sometimes more than once—that you care about what's important to them.[1]

USING THE THREE-STEP WRITING PROCESS FOR PERSUASIVE MESSAGES

Persuasion is the attempt to change someone's attitudes, beliefs, or actions.

Whether you're convincing your boss to open a new office in Europe or encouraging potential customers to try your products, you'll use many of the same techniques of **persuasion**—the attempt to change an audience's attitudes, beliefs, or actions.[2] Because persuasive messages ask audiences to give something of value (money in exchange for a product, for example) or take substantial action (such as changing a corporate policy), they are more challenging to write than routine messages. Successful professionals understand that persuasion is not about trickery or getting people to act against their own best interests; it's about letting audiences know they have choices and presenting your offering in the best possible light.[3]

Step 1: Planning Persuasive Messages

Having a great idea or a great product is not enough; you need to be able to convince others of its merits.

In today's information-saturated business environment, having a great idea or a great product is no longer enough. Every day, untold numbers of good ideas go unnoticed and good products go unsold simply because the messages meant to promote them aren't compelling enough to be heard above the competitive noise. Creating successful persuasive messages in these challenging situations demands careful attention to all four tasks in the planning step, starting with an insightful analysis of your purpose and your audience.

Analyzing Your Situation

In defining your purpose, make sure you're clear about what you really hope to achieve. Suppose you want to persuade company executives to support a particular research project. But what does "support" mean? Do you want them to pat you on the back and wish you well? Or do you want them to give you a staff of five researchers and a $1 million annual budget?

The best persuasive messages are closely connected to your audience's desires and interests.[4] Consider these important questions: Who is my audience? What are my audience members' needs? What do I want them to do? How might they resist? Are there alternative positions I need to examine? What does the decision maker consider to be the most important issue? How might the organization's culture influence my strategy?

To understand and categorize audience needs, you can refer to specific information, such as **demographics** (the age, gender, occupation, income, education, and other quantifiable characteristics of the people you're trying to persuade) and **psychographics** (personality, attitudes, lifestyle, and other psychological characteristics). When analyzing your audiences, take into account their cultural expectations and practices so that you don't undermine your persuasive message by using an inappropriate appeal or by organizing your message in a way that seems unfamiliar or uncomfortable to your readers.

If you aim to change someone's attitudes, beliefs, or actions, it is vital to understand his or her **motivation**—the combination of forces that drive people to satisfy their needs. Obviously, the more closely a persuasive message aligns with a recipient's existing motivation, the more effective the message is likely to be (see Figure 9.1). For example, if you try to persuade consumers to purchase a product on the basis of its fashion appeal, that message will connect with consumers who are motivated by a desire to be in fashion but probably won't connect with consumers driven more by practical function or financial concerns.

> Clarifying your purpose is an essential step with persuasive messages.

> Demographics include characteristics such as age, gender, occupation, income, and education.

> Psychographics include characteristics such as personality, attitudes, and lifestyle.

Figure 9.1   Appealing to Audience Motivations
The social networking website ClubMom promotes itself to mothers by using both emotional appeals (such as "A few blogs a day keep the insanity away!") and logical appeals (such as "Earn points by shopping with ClubMom partners").

Gathering Information

When your situation analysis is complete, you need to gather the information necessary to close the gap between what your audience knows, believes, or feels right now and what you want them to know, believe, or feel as a result of receiving your message. You'll learn more about the types of information to offer when you read "Developing Persuasive Business Messages" later in the chapter. Chapter 10 presents advice on how to find the information you need.

Selecting the Right Medium

You may need to use multiple media to reach your entire audience.

Media choices are always important, of course, but these decisions are particularly sensitive with persuasive messages because such messages are often unexpected or even unwelcome. For instance, some people don't mind promotional e-mail messages for products they're interested in; others resent every piece of commercial e-mail they receive. The emergence of permission-based marketing (see page 215) helps marketers avoid antagonizing their target audiences.

Social media (see Chapter 6) provide some exciting options for persuasive messages, particularly marketing and sales messages. However, as "Writing Persuasive Messages for Social Media" on page 213 explains, messages in these media require a unique approach.

Another important area of development in media for persuasive messages is combining personal attention with technological reach and efficiency. For example, a customer support agent can carry on multiple instant messaging conversations at once, responding to one customer while other customers are typing messages. Even perceptions of human interaction created by animated *avatars* such as IKEA's "Anna" (www.ikea.com) can create a more sociable experience for shoppers, which can make websites more effective as a persuasive medium.[5]

Organizing Your Information

The most effective main ideas for persuasive messages have one thing in common: They are about the receiver, not the sender. For instance, if you're trying to convince others to join you in a business venture, explain how it will help them, not how it will help you.

Limit your scope to include only the information needed to help your audience take the next step toward making a favorable decision.

Limiting your scope is vital. If you seem to be wrestling with more than one main idea, you haven't zeroed in on the heart of the matter. If you try to craft a persuasive message without focusing on the one central problem or opportunity your audience truly cares about, chances are you won't be able to persuade successfully.[6]

Most persuasive messages use the indirect approach.

Because the nature of persuasion is to convince people to change their attitudes, beliefs, or actions, most persuasive messages use the indirect approach. That means you'll want to explain your reasons and build interest before asking for a decision or for action—or perhaps even before revealing your purpose. In contrast, when you have a close relationship with your audience, and the message is welcome or at least neutral, the direct approach can be effective.

Your choice of approach is influenced by your position (or authority within the organization) relative to your audience's.

The choice between the direct and indirect approaches is also influenced by the extent of your authority, expertise, or power in an organization. For instance, if you are a highly regarded technical expert with years of experience, you might use the direct approach in a message to top executives. In contrast, if you aren't well known and therefore need to rely more on the strength of your message than the power of your reputation, the indirect approach will probably be more successful.

Step 2: Writing Persuasive Messages

Persuasive messages are often unexpected or even unwelcome, so the "you" attitude is crucial.

Encourage a positive response to your persuasive messages by (1) using positive and polite language, (2) understanding and respecting cultural differences, (3) being sensitive to organizational cultures, and (4) taking steps to establish your credibility.

Positive language usually happens naturally with persuasive messages because you're promoting an idea or a product you believe in. However, take care not to inadvertently insult your readers by implying that they've made poor choices in the past.

Be sure to understand cultural expectations as well. For example, a message that seems forthright and direct in a low-context culture might seem brash and intrusive in a high-context culture.

Just as social culture affects the success of a persuasive message, so too does the culture within various organizations. Some organizations handle disagreement and conflict in an indirect, behind-the-scenes way, whereas others accept and even encourage open discussion and sharing of differing viewpoints.

Finally, when trying to persuade a skeptical or hostile audience, you must convince people that you know what you're talking about and that you're not trying to mislead them. Use these techniques:

- Use simple language to avoid suspicions of fantastic claims and emotional manipulation.
- Provide objective evidence for the claims and promises you make.
- Identify your sources, especially if your audience already respects those sources.
- Establish common ground by emphasizing beliefs, attitudes, and background experiences you have in common with the audience.
- Be objective and present fair and logical arguments.
- Display your willingness to keep your audience's best interests at heart.
- Avoid the "hard sell," an aggressive approach that uses strong, emotional language and high-pressure tactics to convince people to make a firm decision in a hurry.

Whenever possible, try to build your credibility *before* you present a major proposal or ask for a major decision. That way, audiences don't have to evaluate both you and your message at the same time.[7]

Cultural differences influence your persuasion attempts.

Audiences often respond unfavorably to over-the-top language, so keep your writing simple and straightforward.

Step 3: Completing Persuasive Messages

Credibility is an essential element of persuasion, so the production quality of your messages is vital. If your message shows signs of carelessness or incompetence, people might think *you* are careless or incompetent as well.

When you evaluate your content, try to judge your argument objectively and try not to overestimate your credibility. When revising for clarity and conciseness, carefully match the purpose and organization to audience needs. If possible, ask an experienced colleague who knows your audience well to review your draft. Your design elements must complement, not detract from, your argument. In addition, meticulous proofreading will identify any mechanical or spelling errors that would weaken your persuasive potential. Finally, make sure your distribution methods fit your audience's expectations as well as your purpose.

Sloppy production undermines your credibility, so revise and proofread with care.

DEVELOPING PERSUASIVE BUSINESS MESSAGES

Your success as a businessperson is closely tied to your ability to convince others to accept new ideas, change old habits, or act on your recommendations. Unless your career takes you into marketing and sales, most of your messages will consist of *persuasive business messages*, which are any persuasive messages designed to elicit a preferred response in a nonsales situation.

Strategies for Persuasive Business Messages

Even if you have the power to compel others to do what you want them to do, persuading them is more effective than forcing them. People who are forced into accepting a decision or plan are less motivated to support it and more likely to react negatively than if they're persuaded.[8] Within the context of the three-step process, effective persuasion involves four essential strategies: framing your arguments, balancing emotional and logical appeals, reinforcing your position, and anticipating objections.

TABLE 9.1   The AIDA Model

Phase	Objective
Attention	Get the reader's attention with the benefit that is of real interest or value.
Interest	Build the reader's interest by further explaining benefits and appealing to his or her logic or emotions.
Desire	Build desire by providing additional supporting details and answering potential questions.
Action	Motivate the reader to take the next step by closing with a compelling call to action and providing a convenient means for the reader to respond.

Framing Your Arguments

The AIDA model is a useful approach for many persuasive messages:
- Attention
- Interest
- Desire
- Action

Many persuasive messages follow some variation of the indirect approach. One of the most commonly used variations is called the **AIDA model**, which organizes your presentation into four phases (see Table 9.1):

- **Attention.** Your first objective is to encourage your audience to want to hear about your problem, idea, or new product—whatever your main idea is. Be sure to find some common ground on which to build your case.

- **Interest.** Provide additional details that prompt audience members to imagine how the solution might benefit them.

- **Desire.** Help audience members embrace your idea by explaining how the change will benefit them and answering potential objections.

- **Action.** Suggest the specific action you want your audience to take. Include a deadline, when applicable.

The AIDA model is ideal for the indirect approach.

The AIDA model is tailor-made for using the indirect approach, allowing you to save your main idea for the action phase (see Figure 9.2). However, it can also work with the direct approach, in which case you use your main idea as an attention-getter, build interest with your argument, create desire with your evidence, and emphasize your main idea in the action phase with the specific action you want your audience to take.

When your AIDA message uses the indirect approach and is delivered by memo or e-mail, keep in mind that your subject line usually catches your reader's eye first. Your challenge is to make it interesting and relevant enough to capture reader attention without revealing your main idea. If you put your request in the subject line, you're likely to get a quick "no" before you've had a chance to present your arguments:

Instead of This	Write This
Proposal to install new phone message system	Reducing the cost of our toll-free number

The AIDA approach has limitations:
- It essentially talks *at* audiences, not *with* them
- It focuses on one-time events not long-term relationships

With either the direct or indirect approach, AIDA and similar models do have limitations. First, AIDA is a unidirectional method that essentially talks *at* audiences, not *with* them. Second, AIDA is built around a single event, such as asking an audience for a decision, rather than on building a mutually beneficial, long-term relationship.[9] AIDA is still a valuable tool for the right purposes, but as you'll read later in the chapter, a conversational approach is more compatible with today's social media.

Balancing Emotional and Logical Appeals

Emotional appeals attempt to connect with the reader's feelings or sympathies.

Few persuasive appeals are purely logical or purely emotional, and a key skill is finding the right balance for each message. An **emotional appeal** calls on feelings or audience sympathies. For instance, you can make use of the emotion inspired by words such as *freedom*,

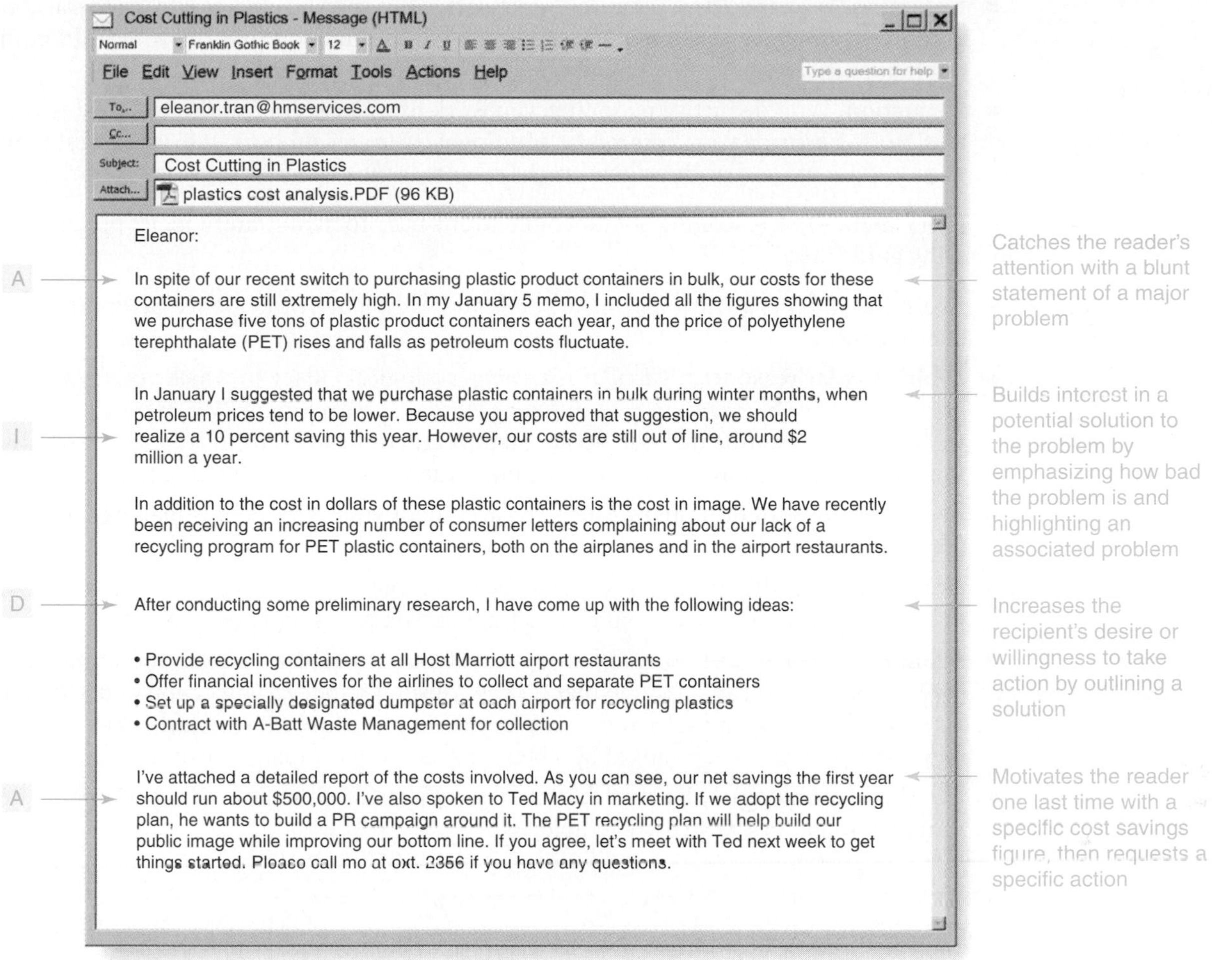

```
┌──────────────────────────────────────────────────────────────────────┐
│ ✉ Cost Cutting in Plastics - Message (HTML)              _ □ ✕        │
├──────────────────────────────────────────────────────────────────────┤
│ Normal    ▾ Franklin Gothic Book ▾ 12 ▾ A ▪ B I U ▦▦▦ ▤▤ ⟨⟨ ⟩⟩ ─ ▪   │
│ File  Edit  View  Insert  Format  Tools  Actions  Help   [Type a question for help ▾]│
├──────────────────────────────────────────────────────────────────────┤
│ To...  │ eleanor.tran@hmservices.com                                   │
│ Cc...  │                                                                │
│ Subject: │ Cost Cutting in Plastics                                    │
│ Attach... │ 🗎 plastics cost analysis.PDF (96 KB)                       │
└──────────────────────────────────────────────────────────────────────┘
```

Eleanor:

(A) In spite of our recent switch to purchasing plastic product containers in bulk, our costs for these containers are still extremely high. In my January 5 memo, I included all the figures showing that we purchase five tons of plastic product containers each year, and the price of polyethylene terephthalate (PET) rises and falls as petroleum costs fluctuate.

> Catches the reader's attention with a blunt statement of a major problem

(I) In January I suggested that we purchase plastic containers in bulk during winter months, when petroleum prices tend to be lower. Because you approved that suggestion, we should realize a 10 percent saving this year. However, our costs are still out of line, around $2 million a year.

In addition to the cost in dollars of these plastic containers is the cost in image. We have recently been receiving an increasing number of consumer letters complaining about our lack of a recycling program for PET plastic containers, both on the airplanes and in the airport restaurants.

> Builds interest in a potential solution to the problem by emphasizing how bad the problem is and highlighting an associated problem

(D) After conducting some preliminary research, I have come up with the following ideas:

- Provide recycling containers at all Host Marriott airport restaurants
- Offer financial incentives for the airlines to collect and separate PET containers
- Set up a specially designated dumpster at each airport for recycling plastics
- Contract with A-Batt Waste Management for collection

> Increases the recipient's desire or willingness to take action by outlining a solution

(A) I've attached a detailed report of the costs involved. As you can see, our net savings the first year should run about $500,000. I've also spoken to Ted Macy in marketing. If we adopt the recycling plan, he wants to build a PR campaign around it. The PET recycling plan will help build our public image while improving our bottom line. If you agree, let's meet with Ted next week to get things started. Please call me at ext. 2366 if you have any questions.

> Motivates the reader one last time with a specific cost savings figure, then requests a specific action

---

Pointers for Developing Persuasive Messages
- Open with a reader benefit, stimulating question, eye-opening fact, or other attention-getter.
- Balance emotional and logical appeals to help the audience accept your message.
- Indicate that you understand the reader's concerns.
- Elaborate on the principal benefits as you continue to stimulate interest and build desire.
- Support your claims with relevant evidence.
- Confidently ask for a decision, stressing the positive results of the action.
- Include pertinent action details such as deadlines.
- Make the desired response simple to understand and easy to accomplish.
- Close with one last reminder of how the audience can benefit.

Figure 9.2 Persuasive Message Using the AIDA Model
Randy Thumwolt uses the AIDA model in a persuasive message about a program that would try to reduce Host Marriott's annual plastics costs and try to curtail consumer complaints about the company's recycling record. Note how Thumwolt "sells the problem" before attempting to sell the solution. Few people are interested in hearing about solutions to problems they don't know about or don't believe exist. His interest section introduces an additional, unforeseen problem with plastic product containers.

success, *prestige*, *compassion*, *free*, and *comfort*. Such words put your audience in a certain frame of mind and help people accept your message.

For most business situations, the best use of emotion is working in tandem with logic. Even if your audience reaches a conclusion based on emotions, they'll look to you to provide logical support as well. A **logical appeal** uses one of three types of reasoning:

> Logical appeals are based on the reader's notions of reason; these appeals can use analogy, induction, or deduction.

- **Analogy.** With analogy, you reason from specific evidence to specific evidence. For instance, to persuade reluctant employees to attend a planning session, you might use a town meeting analogy, comparing your company to a small community and your employees to valued members of that community.

- **Induction.** With inductive reasoning, you work from specific evidence to a general conclusion. To convince your boss to change a certain production process, you could point out that every company that has adopted it has increased profits.

- **Deduction.** With deductive reasoning, you work from a generalization to a specific conclusion. To persuade your boss to hire additional customer support staff, you might point to industry surveys that show how crucial customer satisfaction is to corporate profits.

Every method of reasoning is vulnerable to misuse. To avoid faulty logic, practice the following guidelines:[10]

Using logical appeals carries with it the ethical responsibility to avoid faulty logic.

- **Avoid hasty generalizations.** Make sure you have plenty of evidence before drawing conclusions.

- **Avoid circular reasoning.** *Circular reasoning* is a logical fallacy in which you try to support your claim by restating it in different words. The statement "We know temporary workers cannot handle this task because temps are unqualified for it" doesn't prove anything because the claim and the supporting evidence are essentially identical.

- **Avoid attacking an opponent.** Attack the argument your opponent is making, not your opponent's character.

- **Avoid oversimplifying a complex issue.** For example, don't reduce a complex situation to a simple "either/or" statement if the situation isn't that simple or clear-cut.

- **Avoid mistaken assumptions of cause and effect.** If you can't isolate the impact of a specific factor, you can't assume that it's the cause of whatever effect you're discussing. You lowered prices, and sales went up. Were lower prices the cause? Maybe, but the sales increase might have been caused by a better advertising campaign or some other factor.

- **Avoid faulty analogies.** Be sure that the two objects or situations being compared are similar enough for the analogy to hold.

Reinforcing Your Position

Choose your words carefully to trigger the desired responses.

After you've worked out the basic elements of your argument, step back and look for ways to bolster the strength of your position. Can you find more powerful words to convey your message? For example, if your company is in serious financial trouble, talking about *survival* is more powerful than talking about *continued operations*. As with any other powerful tool, though, use vivid language and abstractions carefully and honestly.

In addition to examining individual word choices, consider using *metaphors* and other figures of speech. If you want to describe a quality-control system as being designed to detect every possible product flaw, you might call it a "spider web" to imply that it catches everything that comes its way.

Anticipating Objections

Even powerful persuasive messages can encounter audience resistance.

Anticipate as many objections as you can and address them before your audience can even bring them up. By doing so, you can remove these potentially negative elements from the conversation and keep the focus on positive communication. Note that you don't need to explicitly mention a particular concern. For instance, if your proposal to switch to lower-cost materials is likely to raise concerns about quality, simply emphasize that the new materials are just as good as existing materials. You'll not only get this issue out of the way sooner, you'll demonstrate a broad appreciation of the issue and imply confidence in your message.[11]

If you expect to encounter strong resistance, present all sides of an issue.

If you expect a hostile audience that is biased against your plan, be sure to present all sides of the situation. As you cover each option, explain the pros and cons. You'll gain additional credibility if you present these options before presenting your recommendation or decision.[12] If you can, involve your audience in the design of the solution; people are more likely to support ideas they help create.

When putting together persuasive arguments, avoid these common mistakes:[13]

Avoid the common mistakes of using a hard sell, resisting compromise, relying solely on argumentation, and assuming that persuasion is a one-time event.

- **Using a hard sell.** Don't push. No one likes being pressured into making a decision, and communicators who take this approach can come across as being more concerned with meeting their own goals than with satisfying the needs of their audiences. In contrast, a "soft sell" is more like a comfortable conversation that uses calm, rational persuasion to help the recipient make a smart choice.

- **Resisting compromise.** Successful persuasion is often a process of give-and-take.
- **Relying solely on great arguments.** Great arguments are important, but connecting with your audience on the right emotional level and communicating through vivid language are just as vital. Sometimes a well-crafted story can be even more compelling than dry logic.
- **Assuming that persuasion is a one-shot effort.** Persuasion is often a process, not a one-time event. In many cases, you need to move your audience members along one small step at a time rather than try to convince them to say "yes" in one huge step.

Common Examples of Persuasive Business Messages

Throughout your career, you'll have numerous opportunities to write persuasive messages within your organization—for example, when selling a supervisor on more efficient operating procedures, eliciting cooperation from other departments, soliciting investment funds, or requesting adjustments that go beyond a supplier's contractual obligations. In addition, many of the routine requests you studied in Chapter 7 can become persuasive messages if you want a nonroutine result or believe that you haven't received fair treatment. Most of these messages can be divided into persuasive requests for action, persuasive presentation of ideas, and persuasive claims and requests for adjustment.

Persuasive Requests for Action

The bulk of your persuasive business messages will involve requests for action. In some cases, your request will be anticipated, so the direct approach is fine. In others, you'll need to introduce your intention indirectly, and the AIDA model or a similar approach is ideal for this purpose.

Open with an attention-getting device and show readers that you understand their concerns. Use the interest and desire sections of your message to demonstrate that you have good reason for making such a request and to cover what you know about the situation: the facts and figures, the benefits of helping, and any history or experience that will enhance your appeal. Your goals are (1) to gain credibility (for yourself and your request) and (2) to make your readers believe that helping you will indeed help solve a significant problem. Once you've demonstrated that your message is relevant to your reader, you can close with a request for some specific action (see Figure 9.3).

Most persuasive business messages involve a request for action.

Persuasive Presentation of Ideas

You may encounter situations in which you simply want to change attitudes or beliefs about a particular topic, without asking the audience to decide or do anything—at least not yet. The goal of your first message might be nothing more than convincing your audience to reexamine long-held opinions or admit the possibility of new ways of thinking.

For instance, suppose you think your company is spending too much time processing payroll, and you've found an outside firm that can do it for less money than you now spend on internal staff and systems (a practice known as *outsourcing*). However, your company president is philosophically opposed to outsourcing any critical business function. Until and unless you can bring about a change in the president's way of thinking, there is no point in pushing for a decision about outsourcing.

Sometimes the objective of persuasive messages is simply to encourage people to consider a new idea.

Persuasive Claims and Requests for Adjustments

Most claim letters are routine messages and use the direct approach discussed in Chapter 7. However, at times you want someone to consider an unusual claim or request. For instance, say that you signed off on a project done by an outside contractor and then discovered problems with the work later. You previously said the work was acceptable, so you'll need to build a persuasive case to ask for additional work or perhaps a refund.

The key ingredients of a good persuasive claim are a complete and specific review of the facts and a confident and positive tone. Remember that you have the right to be satisfied

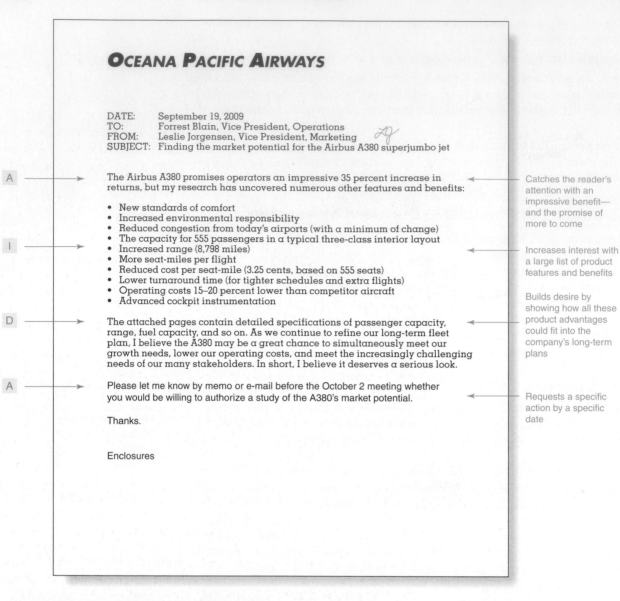

Figure 9.3   Using the AIDA Model to Request Action
Leslie Jorgensen believes the new Airbus A380 could help Oceana Pacific Airways meet its growth needs while lowering its operating costs. Here she uses the AIDA model to solicit her boss's approval for a study of the plane's market potential. Note that because she also wants to provide some printed materials to support her argument, she opted to create a printed memo rather than an e-mail message.

with every transaction. Begin persuasive claims by stating the basic problem or reviewing what has been done about it so far. Include a statement that both you and your audience can agree with or that clarifies what you want to convince your audience about. Be as specific as possible about what you want to happen.

Next, give your reader a good reason for granting your claim. Show how your audience is responsible for the problem and appeal to your reader's sense of fair play, goodwill, or moral responsibility. Explain how you feel about the problem but don't get carried away, don't complain too much, and don't make threats. People generally respond most favorably to requests that are both calm and reasonable.

DEVELOPING MARKETING AND SALES MESSAGES

Marketing and sales messages use many of the same techniques as persuasive business messages.

Marketing and sales messages use the same basic techniques as other persuasive messages, with the added emphasis of encouraging someone to participate in a commercial transaction. Although the terms *marketing message* and *sales message* are often used interchangeably, they are slightly different: Marketing messages usher potential buyers through the purchasing process without asking them to make an immediate decision; that's when sales messages take over. Marketing messages focus on such tasks as introducing new brands to the public, providing competitive comparisons, encouraging customers to visit websites for more information, and reminding buyers that a particular product or service is available. In contrast, a sales message makes a specific request for people to place an order for a particular product or service.

Strategies for Marketing and Sales Messages

Most marketing and sales messages, particularly in larger companies, are created and delivered by professionals with specific training in marketing, advertising, sales, or public relations. However, you may be called on to review the work of these specialists or even to write such messages in smaller companies, and having a good understanding of how these messages work will help you be a more effective manager. The basic strategies to consider include assessing audience needs; analyzing your competition; determining key selling points and benefits; anticipating purchase objections; applying the AIDA model; adapting your writing to social media, if appropriate; and maintaining high standards of ethics, legal compliance, and etiquette.

Assessing Audience Needs

As with every other business message, successful marketing and sales messages start with an understanding of audience needs. For some products and services, this assessment is a simple matter. For instance, customers compare only a few basic attributes when purchasing copy or printer paper, including weight, brightness, color, and finish. In contrast, they might consider dozens of features when shopping for real estate, cars, professional services, and other complex purchases. In addition, customer needs often extend beyond the basic product or service. For example, clothes do far more than simply keep you warm. What you wear makes a statement about who you are, which social groups you want to be associated with (or not), and how you view your relationship with the people around you.

> Purchasing decisions often involve more than just the basic product or service.

Analyzing Your Competition

Marketing and sales messages nearly always compete with messages from other companies trying to reach the same audience. When Chrysler plans a sales letter to introduce a new model to current customers, the company knows that its audience has also been exposed to messages from Ford, Honda, Volkswagen, and numerous other car companies. In crowded markets, writers sometimes have to search for words and phrases that other companies aren't already using. They might also want to avoid themes, writing styles, or creative approaches that are too similar to those of competitors' messages.

> Marketing and sales messages have to compete for the audience's attention.

Determining Key Selling Points and Benefits

With some insight into audience needs and existing messages from the competition, you're ready to decide which benefits and features of your product or service to highlight. For all but the simplest products, you'll want to prioritize the items you plan to discuss. You'll also want to distinguish between selling points and benefits. As Table 9.2 shows, **selling points** are the most attractive features of an idea or product, whereas **benefits** are the particular advantages that readers will realize from those features. Selling points focus on the *product*. Benefits focus on the *user*.

> Selling points focus on the product; benefits focus on the user.

For example, if you say that your snow shovel has "an ergonomically designed handle," you've described a good feature. But to persuade someone to buy that shovel, say "the ergonomically designed handle will reduce your risk of back injury." That's a benefit. Moreover, as much as possible, try to personalize the benefits to each segment of your audience. Some products have dozens of major and minor benefits, but you'll exhaust readers if you simply hit them with a long list. Identify the few that really matter.[14]

TABLE 9.2 Selling Points Versus Benefits

Selling Points	Customer Benefit
Our easy financing plan includes no money down, no interest, and no payments for 24 months.	Buy what you want right now, even if you have limited cash on hand.
Our marketing communication audit accurately measures the impact of your advertising and public relations efforts.	Determine whether your message is reaching the target audience and whether you're spending your marketing budget in the best possible manner.
The spools in our fly fishing reels are machined from solid blocks of aircraft-grade aluminum.	Go fishing with confidence: These lightweight reels will stand up to the toughest conditions.

Anticipating Purchase Objections

Anticipating objections is crucial to effective marketing and sales messages.

Marketing and sales messages usually encounter objections, and as with persuasive business messages, the best way to handle them is to identify them up front and address as many as you can. Keep in mind that with marketing and sales messages, you often don't get a second chance to present your case. If your website for fashion jewelry aimed at college-age consumers strikes visitors as too juvenile, for instance, they'll click away to another site and never come back.

Objections can range from high price or low quality to a lack of compatibility with existing products or a perceived risk involved with the product. Consumers might worry that a car won't be safe enough for a family or that a jacket will make them look unattractive. Business buyers might worry about disrupting operations or failing to realize the financial returns on a purchase.

Price can be a particularly tricky issue in any promotional message. Whether you highlight or downplay the price of your product, prepare your readers for it with words such as *luxurious* and *economical*.

If price is a major selling point, give it a position of prominence, such as in the headline or as the last item in a paragraph. If price is not a major selling point, you can handle it in several ways. You could leave the price out altogether or deemphasize it by putting the figure in the middle of a paragraph that comes well after you've presented the benefits and selling points:

Opens with other benefit-oriented information, such as the exclusivity of the product

Doesn't mention price until midway through the paragraph, after reader interest has been raised

Only 100 prints of this exclusive, limited-edition lithograph will be created. On June 15, they will be made available to the general public, but you can reserve one now for only $3,500, the special advance reservation price. Simply rush the enclosed reservation card back today so that your order is in before the June 15 publication date.

If price is likely to be a major objection, look for persuasive ways to minimize customer resistance. Comparing your price with that of a comparable product or service is a common tactic: "The cost of owning your own exercise equipment is less than you'd pay for a health club membership." In some cases, you can also compare the costs of *not* buying the product or service: "Ignoring small repairs now increases the risks of major repairs in the future."

Applying the AIDA Model

Conventional marketing and sales messages are often prepared using the AIDA model or some variation of it. (But compare this approach with how *conversation marketing* messages are prepared in "Writing Persuasive Messages for Social Media" on page 213.) Begin with an attention-getting device, generate interest by describing some of the product or service's unique features, increase desire by highlighting the benefits that are most appealing to your audience, and close by suggesting the action you want the audience to take.

Getting Attention   Professionals use a wide range of techniques to attract an audience's attention:

- **Your product's strongest feature or benefit.** "A little video for everyone" (promoting Apple's iPod nano with improved video-playing capabilities).[15]

- **A piece of genuine news.** "HealthGrades Reveals America's Best Hospitals."[16]

- **A point of common ground with the audience.** "An SUV adventurous enough to accommodate your spontaneity and the gear that comes with it."[17]

- **A personal appeal to the reader's emotions and values.** "Elastin Renewal: Our latest weapon in the fight against wrinkles."[18]

- **The promise of insider information.** "France may seem familiar, but nearly everything—from paying taxes to having a baby—is done quite differently. Get the practical answers to nearly 300 questions about making a life in France."[19]

- **The promise of savings.** "Through Save Energy Now, DOE's Industrial Technologies Program (ITP) helps industrial plants operate more efficiently and profitably by identifying ways to reduce energy use in key industrial process systems."[20]

- **A sample or demonstration of the product.** "In this real-time, online test drive, you'll be exploring the 2007 Microsoft Office release through your Web browser within minutes—with no product installation or download required!"[21]

- **A solution to a problem.** "This backpack's designed to endure all a kid's dropping and dragging."[22]

> You can employ a variety of attention-getting devices in marketing and sales messages.

Of course, words aren't the only attention-getting device at your disposal. Strong, evocative images are common attention-getters. With online messages, you have even more options, including audio, animation, and video. Even more so than in persuasive business messages, it's important to carefully balance emotion and logic in marketing and sales messages (see Figure 9.4).

Building Interest   Use the interest section of your message to build on the intrigue you created with your opening. This section should also offer support for any claims or promises you made in the opening. For instance, after opening with the headline that offers "A little video for everyone," the Apple iPod nano webpage continues with the following:[23]

> To build interest, expand on and support the promises in your attention-getting opening.

It's the small iPod with one very big idea: Video. Now the world's most popular music player lets you enjoy TV shows, movies, video podcasts, and more. The larger, brighter display means amazing picture quality. In six eye-catching colors, iPod nano is stunning all around. And with 4GB and 8GB models starting at just $149, little speaks volumes.

> Explains the headline message of "a little video"
>
> After establishing the key selling point (video), continues with other product features and benefits

At this point in the message, Apple has offered enough information to help people understand how they might use the product, and it has answered a couple potential objections as well (the quality of the video experience on such a small display and the price). Anyone interested in a digital music player with video capability is probably intrigued enough to keep reading.

Increasing Desire   To build desire for a product, a service, or an idea, continue to expand on and explain how accepting it will benefit the recipient. Think carefully about the sequence of support points and use plenty of subheadings, hyperlinks, and other devices to help people quickly find the information they need. For example, after reading this much about the iPod, some users might want to know more about the iTunes media store, whereas others will want technical specifications. The iPod product page continues with detailed discussions of various product features and benefits, and it also offers numerous links to pages with other kinds of support information. The ability to provide flexible access to information is just one of the reasons the web is such a powerful medium for marketing and sales.

> Add details and audience benefits to increase desire for the product or service.

Throughout the body of your message, remember to keep the focus on the audience, not on your company or your product. When you talk about product features, remember to stress the benefits and talk in terms that make sense to users. For instance, after stating that the maximum memory capacity of the iPod nano is 8 GB, Apple "translates" that technical

To help convince home builders to use its innovative panel system instead of traditional frame construction, Premier Building Systems focuses on logical factors such as cost, efficiency, and quality.

Gladiator GarageWorks uses a combination of logical and emotional appeals by promising to make your garage "a place to work, entertain and show off to your friends and neighbors."

Website photograph used with permission of Whirlpool Corporation

Figure 9.4   Balancing Emotional and Logical Appeals
All marketing and sales messages strike a balance between logical and emotional appeals. Premier Building Systems, a maker of building materials, relies almost entirely on logical appeals. In contrast, Gladiator GarageWorks mixes strong emotional appeals (such as showing off) with the logical appeal of functional storage solutions.

specification into various media storage capacities that have practical meaning to users, such as 2,000 songs, 7,000 photos, or 8 hours of video.[24]

To keep readers interested, use strong, colorful language without overdoing it.

As you work to build reader interest, be careful not to get so enthusiastic that you lose credibility. If Apple said that the video viewing experience on the iPod nano was as "satisfying as watching a full-size TV," most people would scoff at the notion of comparing a 2-inch display with a full-size television.

To increase desire, as well as boost your credibility, provide support for your claims. Creative writers find many ways to provide support, including testimonials from satisfied

In the United States, the Federal Trade Commission (FTC) has the authority to impose penalties against advertisers that violate federal standards for truthful advertising. Other federal agencies have authority over advertising in specific industries, such as transportation and financial services. Individual states have additional laws that apply. Pay close attention to the following legal aspects of marketing and sales communication:[27]

Marketing and sales messages are covered by a wide range of laws and regulations.

- Marketing and sales messages must be truthful and nondeceptive.
- You must back up your claims with evidence.
- Marketing and sales messages are considered binding contracts in many states.
- In most cases, you can't use a person's name, photograph, or other identifying information without permission.

Before you launch any marketing or sales campaign, make sure you're up to date on the latest regulations affecting customer privacy and data security.

Even after meeting your ethical and legal obligations, you may still face decisions regarding communication etiquette. For instance, you can produce a marketing campaign that complies with all applicable laws and yet is still offensive, insulting, or just plain annoying to your audience. Using an audience-centered approach, involving respect for your readers and their values, should help you avoid any such etiquette missteps.

Maintaining high ethical standards is a key aspect of good communication etiquette.

Many companies demonstrate their sensitivity to audiences through **permission-based marketing**, in which messages are sent only to recipients who have given the marketer permission to contact them. The newsfeeds from blogs are a form of permission-based marketing because recipients must sign up for the feeds in order to receive them. *Opt-in* e-mail newsletters, in which recipients actively choose to receive messages, are another popular technique. For example, readers of the *Milwaukee Journal Sentinel* newspaper can opt in to receive e-mail newsletters on a dozen different subjects.[28] ■

DOCUMENT MAKEOVER

Improve This E-Mail Message

To practice correcting drafts of actual documents, visit the "Document Makeovers" section in either MyBCommLab.com or the Companion Website for this text.

If MyBCommLab.com is being used in your class, see your User Guide for specific instructions on how to access the content for this chapter.

If you are accessing this feature through the Companion Website, click on "Document Makeovers" and then select Chapter 9. You will find an e-mail message that contains problems and errors related to what you've learned in this chapter about writing persuasive business messages. Use the Final Draft decision tool to create an improved version of this e-mail. Check the message for its effectiveness at gaining attention, building interest, stimulating desire, motivating action, focusing on the primary goal, and dealing with resistance. ●

❝ CHAPTER REVIEW AND ACTIVITIES

Chapter Summary

To plan persuasive messages successfully, carefully clarify your purpose to make sure you focus on a single goal. Most persuasive messages use the indirect approach to establish awareness and interest before asking the audience to take action. The "you" attitude is critical in persuasive messages, and successful writers work hard to establish credibility.

Seven common ways to establish credibility in persuasive messages are using simple language, supporting your claims, identifying your sources, establishing common ground, being objective, displaying good intentions, and avoiding the hard sell.

When using the AIDA model, you open your message by getting the audience's *attention*; build *interest* with facts, details, and additional benefits; increase *desire* by providing more evidence answering possible objections; and motivate a specific *action*.

Emotional appeals call on human feelings and sympathies. However, these appeals usually aren't effective by themselves. Logical appeals call on human reason (using analogy, induction, or deduction). You can use logic together with emotion, thereby supplying rational support for an idea that readers have already embraced emotionally.

By identifying potential objections and addressing them as you craft your message, you can help prevent audience members from gravitating toward negative answers before you have the opportunity to ask them for a positive response. You can often resolve these issues before the audience has a chance to go on the defensive.

To engage audiences in conversation marketing, start with efforts to build networked communities of potential buyers and other interested parties. Initiate and respond to conversations within these communities, being sure to use an objective, conversational style. Identify and support the enthusiastic product champions who want to help spread your message. Speak directly to customers so you don't have to rely on the news media. Finally, continue to use the AIDA model or similar approaches, but only at specific times and places.

Effective and ethical persuasive communicators maintain a "you" attitude, with honest concern for the audience's needs and interests. They help audiences understand how their proposals will provide benefits to the audience, using language that is persuasive without being manipulative.

Test Your Knowledge

1. What are some questions to ask when gauging the audience's needs during the planning of a persuasive message?

2. What role do demographics and psychographics play in audience analysis during the planning of a persuasive message?

3. How do emotional appeals differ from logical appeals?

4. What three types of reasoning can you use in logical appeals?

5. What is the AIDA model, and what are its limitations?

Apply Your Knowledge

1. When writing persuasive messages, why is it so important to give special attention to the analysis of your purpose and audience?

2. How are persuasive messages different from routine messages?

3. Can any company afford to avoid conversation marketing? Why or why not?

4. Imagine yourself working as an engineer for a high-tech company, a graphic designer for an advertising agency, or a sales representative for a company that sells building supplies to homebuilders. Now try to imagine what daily tasks would require persuasion. Who are your audiences, and how do their needs and characteristics affect the way you develop your persuasive messages at work?

5. **Ethical Choices**   Are emotional appeals ethical? Why or why not?

Practice Your Knowledge

Exercises for Perfecting Your Writing

Analyzing Persuasive Messages: Teamwork   With another student, analyze the persuasive e-mail message at Host Marriott (Figure 9.2 on page 205) by answering the following questions.

1. What techniques are used to capture the reader's attention?

2. Does the writer use the direct or indirect organizational approach? Why?

3. Is the subject line effective? Why or why not?

4. Does the writer use an emotional appeal or a logical appeal? Why?

5. What reader benefits are included?

6. How does the writer establish credibility?

7. What tools does the writer use to reinforce his position?

Persuasive Messages: Subject Lines   Compose effective subject lines for the following e-mail messages.

8. A recommendation to your branch manager to install wireless networking throughout the facility. Your primary reason is that management has encouraged more teamwork, and the teams often congregate in meeting rooms, the cafeteria, and other places that lack network access, without which they can't do much of the work they are expected to do.

9. A sales brochure to be sent to area residents, soliciting customers for your new business, "Meals à la Car," a carryout dining service that delivers from most local restaurants. Diners place orders online, and individual households can order from up to three restaurants at a time to accommodate different tastes. The price is equal to the standard menu prices plus a 10 percent delivery charge.

10. A special request to the company president to allow managers to carry over their unused vacation days to the following year. Apparently, many managers canceled their fourth-quarter vacation plans to work on the installation of a new company computer system. Under their current contract, vacation days not used by December 31 can't be carried over to the following year.

Marketing and Sales Messages: Features and Benefits   Determine whether the following sentences focus on features or benefits; rewrite them as necessary to focus on benefits.

11. All-Cook skillets are coated with a durable, patented nonstick surface.

12. You can call anyone and talk as long you like on Saturdays and Sundays with this new mobile phone plan.

13. With 8-millisecond response time, the Samsung LN-S4095D 40" LCD TV delivers fast video action that is smooth and crisp.[29]

Activities

Active links for all websites in this chapter can be found online. If MyBCommLab.com is being used in your class, see your User Guide for instructions on accessing the content for this chapter. Otherwise, visit www.pearsonhighered.com/bovee, locate *Business Communication Essentials*, Fourth Edition, click the Companion Website link, select Chapter 9, and then click on "Featured Websites." Please note that links to sites that become inactive after publication of the book will be removed from the Featured Websites section.

1. **Analyze This Message**   Read the following document and (1) analyze the strengths and weaknesses of each sentence and (2) revise the document so that it follows this chapter's guidelines.

    At Tolson Auto Repair, we have been in business for over 25 years. We stay in business by always taking into account what the customer wants. That's why we are writing. We want to know your opinions to be able to better conduct our business.

Take a moment right now and fill out the enclosed questionnaire. We know everyone is busy, but this is just one way we have of making sure our people do their job correctly. Use the enclosed envelope to return the questionnaire.

And again, we're happy you chose Tolson Auto Repair. We want to take care of all your auto needs.

2. Analyze This Message   Read the following document and (1) analyze the strengths and weaknesses of each sentence and (2) revise the document so that it follows this chapter's guidelines.

Dear TechStar Computing:

I'm writing to you because of my disappointment with my new multimedia PC display. The display part works all right, but the audio volume is also set too high and the volume knob doesn't turn it down. It's driving us crazy. The volume knob doesn't seem to be connected to anything but simply spins around. I can't believe you would put out a product like this without testing it first.

I depend on my computer to run my small business and want to know what you are going to do about it. This reminds me of every time I buy electronic equipment from what seems like any company. Something is always wrong. I thought quality was supposed to be important, but I guess not.

Anyway, I need this fixed right away. Please tell me what you want me to do.

3. Analyze This Message   Read the following document and (1) analyze the strengths and weaknesses of each sentence and (2) revise the document so that it follows this chapter's guidelines.

I am considered the country's foremost authority on employee health insurance programs. My clients offer universally positive feedback on the programs I've designed for them. They also love how much time I save them—hundreds and hundreds of hours. I am absolutely confident that I can thoroughly analyze your needs and create a portfolio that realizes every degree of savings possible. I invite you to experience the same level of service that has generated such comments as "Best advice ever!" and "Saved us an unbelievable amount of money."

4. Ethical Choices   Your boss has asked you to post a message on the company's internal blog, urging everyone in your department to donate money to the company's favorite charity, an organization that operates a summer camp for physically challenged children. You wind up writing a lengthy posting packed with facts and heartwarming anecdotes about the camp and the children's experiences. When you must work that hard to persuade your audience to take an action such as donating money to a charity, aren't you being manipulative and unethical? Explain.

5. Internet   Visit the Federal Trade Commission website and read the "Catch the Bandit in Your Mailbox" consumer warning at www.ftc.gov/bcp/conline/pubs/ tmarkg/bandit.htm. Select one or two marketing or sales letters you've recently received and see whether they contain any of the suspicious content mentioned in the FTC warning. What does the FTC suggest you do with any materials that don't sound legitimate?

6. Revising a Letter: Request for a Rent Refund from Kukyendahl Joint, Inc.   The following persuasive request for adjustment contains many flaws. Using what you've learned in the chapter, read the message carefully and analyze its faults. Then use the following steps to outline and write an improved message.

   a. Describe the flaws in this persuasive request for adjustment.

   b. Develop a plan for rewriting the letter. The following steps will help you organize your thoughts before you begin writing:

   1. Determine whether to use the direct or indirect approach.

   2. Use the "you" attitude to gain attention in the opening.

March 22, 2009

Mr. Robert Bechtold, Manager
Kukyendahl Joint, Inc.
88 North Park Road
Houston, TX 77005

Re: Last Warning

Dear Mr. Bechtold:

Enclosed is a summary of recent ETS-related court cases in which landlords and owners were held responsible for providing toxin-free air for their tenants. In most of these cases, owners were also required to reimburse rents and pay damages for the harm done before the environmental tobacco smoke problem was remedied.

We've been plagued with this since we moved in on January 2, 2008. You haven't acted on our complaints, or responded to our explanations that secondhand smoke is making us sick, filtering in from nearby offices. You must act now or you will be hearing from our lawyers. We've told you that we were forced to hire contractors to apply weather stripping and seal openings. This cost us $3,000 (bills attached) and we expect reimbursement. But the smoke is still coming in. We also want a refund for the $9,000 we've paid you in rent since January. Call us immediately at (832) 768-3899, or our attorneys will be calling you.

Cigarette smoke from tenants on either side of us, and perhaps above and below as well, has been infiltrating our space and you have done nothing, despite our pleas, to stop it. This is unacceptable. This is a known human carcinogen. Ask the Environmental Protection Agency, which classified it as this Group A toxin. It causes lung, breast, cervical, and endocrine cancer in nonsmokers. You wouldn't want to breathe it, either.

One employee already quit who suffered from asthma. Another is threatening because he's a high risk for heart attack. Migraines, bronchitis, respiratory infections—all caused by the 4,600 chemicals in ETS, including poisons such as cyanide, arsenic, formaldehyde, carbon monoxide, and ammonia. We've had them all—the illnesses, that is.

Secondhand smoke is even more dangerous than what smokers inhale, since the inhalation process burns off some of the toxins. Sick time has already cost CMSI valuable business and lowered productivity. Plus many of us are considering finding other jobs unless our office air becomes safe to breathe again. But as the court cases prove, the responsibility for fixing this problem is yours. We expect you to live up to that responsibility immediately. Frankly, we're fed up with your lack of response.

Kathleen Thomas
Manager

> 3. Find a way to establish your credibility.
> 4. Improve the order of material presented in the body of the letter.
> 5. Create an appropriate closing.
>
> c. Now rewrite the letter. Don't forget to leave ample time for revision of your work before you turn it in.

7. **Revising a Sales Brochure From ScrubaDub About Its Car Care Club** The following sales brochure falls short of its objectives. Use what you know about sales messages to analyze its flaws. Then use the steps that follow to produce a better version.

11 locations in Massachusetts and Rhode Island
Bob and Dan Paisner, Owners

We are pleased to announce that ScrubaDub has added a new service, the Car Care Club.

It costs $5.95 for a lifetime membership (your car's lifetime) and features our computer automation. You'll be given a bar-coded sticker for your windshield so our computers can identify you as a club member when you pull in. If you sign up within the next 30 days, we will grant you a SuperWash for free.

The new club offers the standard ScrubaDub Touch-less systems to protect your finishes, our private formula Superglo detergent to clean your car safely and thoroughly, wheel sensors to prescribe the right treatment for whitewalls, wire, or chrome, soft, heated well water to eliminate spots, soft-cloth drying for final gloss. We also recycle our water and grant you a free wash on your birthday.

In addition, club members only will have access to a 48-hour guarantee (free rewashes) or 4 days if you purchased the premium Super Wash, Luxury Wash, Special or Works Wash. After ten washes, our computer will award you a free wash. Also available only to club members are $5 rebates for foam waxes (Turtle Wax, Simonize, or Blue Coral). Some additional specials will be granted by us to car club members, on an unplanned basis.

We can handle special requests if you inquire of our Satisfaction Supervisors. We honor our customers with refunds if they remain unsatisfied after a rewash. This is our Bumper-to-Bumper Guarantee.

   a. Describe the mistakes made by the writers of this brochure.

   b. Develop a plan for improving the brochure. The following questions will help you organize your thinking:

      1. What can you assume about the audience, which is made up of regular customers?

      2. How can you use this information to develop a better opening?

      3. Given that customers already know ScrubaDub, what can you do to improve the body of the brochure? Can you identify selling points versus benefits? What about the use of language and the tone of the text?

      4. Does this brochure make effective use of the AIDA model?

      5. How would you improve the "call to action," the point in the message that asks the reader to make a purchase decision?

   c. Now rewrite the sales letter. Don't forget to leave ample time for revision of your work before you turn it in.

8. Revising a Persuasive E-Mail Message: E-Cruiting at Boulder Construction This "persuasive" e-mail message, from Shelby Howard to Sheila Young, probably won't work effectively. Can you identify the mistakes the writer has made? Use the steps that follow to analyze and improve on this persuasive request for action.

To: sryoung@sprenco.com
Subject: Recruiting tactics

Dear Sheila: I think we should try e-cruiting. I want you to use the huge websites of résumés now listed on the Internet. They provide the software for your searches through these thousands of résumés they receive, so it shouldn't be too difficult. But you will have to define the qualifications you want first. Then they'll supply the résumés that fit.

Eventually, you can develop a website for our company that will post job listings. Then you'll get replies from the kinds of people who might not otherwise post their résumés online. Some of them may be good employees we've been looking for.

Costs breakdowns are: About $1,300 apiece per candidate for traditional (newspaper ad) hiring. Plus your time for prescreening. For e-cruiting, approximately $183 per candidate, with prescreening supplied by jobsearch databases such as monster.com, hotjobs.com, or careermosaic.com. They will, however, charge us about $100–300 per month to list our jobs, rather than the $1,000 the local paper charges us for a Sunday ad. Online job posting word length: unlimited.

You might have to wade through the 30,000 to 100,000 Internet sites now devoted to recruiting. Better stick with the names I've already mentioned. You'll be accessing about 150 million Internet users in the United States, 74 percent of them over the age of 18 looking for jobs.

Right now, our competitors aren't using this method and I can't figure out why. I'm thinking it could be a way to reach talent we might otherwise miss. Maybe they just haven't figured this out yet. You know the ones I mean—the talented individuals we compete for with other construction companies, even though we offer good jobs and benefits.

I read that Bank of Montreal relied on e-cruiting this year. They say they saved $1 million, but we'll have to see how accurate that is with our own trial. Only two percent of building industry employers use e-cruiting. Sixty percent of computer companies use it, probably because surfing the Internet is no hassle for them. They insist hiring time per candidate is reduced from six weeks to one hour, but I'll have to see that to believe it! Something about not having to wait for snail mail résumés. But then they also don't get to screen candidates by sight first, so maybe it's a toss-up. On the other hand, they can e-mail questions back and forth.

Well, why don't we give it a go anyway?

a. Describe the flaws in approach and execution of this persuasive request for action.

b. Develop a plan for improving the message. The following questions should help to stimulate your ideas:

1. Starting with the subject line, how can you focus on your audience's needs?
2. What would be a better opening? Why?
3. How can you reorganize the body of the message to improve the reader's interest and receptivity to the new idea?
4. How can you handle facts, statistics, benefits, and appeals more skillfully?
5. What should be included in the conclusion?

c. Now rewrite this persuasive request for action.

9. **Analyzing a Sales Package: Learning from the Direct-Mail Pros** The daily mail often brings a selection of sales messages to your front door. Find a direct-mail package from your mailbox that includes a sales letter. Then answer the following questions to help analyze and learn from the approach used by the communication professionals who prepare these glossy sales messages. Your instructor might also ask you to share the package and your observations in a class discussion.

a. Who is the intended audience?

b. What are the demographic and psychographic characteristics of the intended audience?

c. What is the purpose of the direct-mail package? Has it been designed to solicit a phone response, make a mail-order sale, obtain a charitable contribution, or do something else?

d. What, if any, technique was used to encourage you to open the envelope?

e. What kind of letter is included? Is it fully printed, printed with a computer fill-in of certain specific information, or fully computer typed? Is the letter personalized with your name or your family's name? If so, how many times?

f. Did the letter writer follow the AIDA model? If not, explain the letter's organization.

g. What needs does the letter appeal to?

h. What emotional appeals and logical arguments does the letter use?

i. What selling points and consumer benefits does the letter offer?

j. How many and what kinds of enclosures (such as brochures or CD-ROMs) are included for support?

k. Does the letter or package have an unusual format? Does it use eye-catching graphics?

l. Is the message in the letter and on the supporting pieces believable? Would the package sell the product or service to you? Why or why not?

Expand Your Knowledge

Exploring the Best of the Web

Influence an Official and Promote Your Cause   At the Thomas site compiled by the Library of Congress, http://thomas.loc.gov, you'll discover voluminous information about federal legislation, congressional members, and committee reports. You can also access committee home-pages and numerous links to government agencies, current issues, and historical documents. You'll find all kinds of regulatory information, including laws and relevant issues that might affect you in the business world. Visit the site and stay informed. Maybe you'll want to convince a government official to support a business-related issue that affects you. Explore the data at the Thomas site and find an issue you can use to practice your skills at writing a persuasive message.

Exercises

1. What key ideas would you include in an e-mail message to persuade your congressional representative to support an issue that's important to you?

2. In a letter to a senator or member of Congress, what information would you include to convince the reader to vote for an issue supporting small business?

3. When sending a message to someone who receives hundreds of written appeals each day, what attention-getting techniques can you use? How can you get support for a cause that concerns you as a businessperson?

Surfing Your Way to Career Success

Bovée and Thill's Business Communication Headline News offers links to hundreds of online resources that can help you with this course, your other college courses, and your career. Visit http://businesscommunicationblog.com and click on "Web Directory." The Special Types of Communication section offers links to websites covering crisis management, organizational communication, public and media relations, and advertising and promotion. Identify three websites from this section that could be useful in your business career. For each site, write a two-sentence summary of what the site offers and how it could help you launch and build your career.

MyBCommLab.com

Use MyBCommLab.com to test your understanding of the concepts presented in this chapter and explore additional materials that will bring the ideas to life in video, activities, and an online multimedia e-book. Additionally, you can continue to improve your skill with commas, semicolons, and colons by using the "Peak Performance Grammar and Mechanics" module within the lab. Take the Pretest to determine whether you have any weak areas. Then review those areas in the Refresher Course. Take the Follow-Up Test to check your grasp of commas, semicolons, and colons. For an extra challenge, take the Advanced Test. Finally, for even more reinforcement, go to the "Improve Your Grammar, Mechanics, and Usage" section that follows the cases, and complete the "Level 1: Self-Assessment" exercises.

CASES

▼Apply the three-step writing process to the following cases, as assigned by your instructor.

[E-MAIL SKILLS]

1. That's the Point: E-Mail Encouraging Your Boss to Blog
You've been trying for months to convince your boss, Will Florence, to start blogging. You've told him that top executives in numerous industries now use blogging as a way to connect with customers and other stakeholders without going through the filters and barriers of formal corporate communications. He was just about convinced—until he read the blog by Bob Lutz, the co-chair and design chief of General Motors.

"Look at this!" he calls from his office. "Bob Lutz is one of the most respected executives in the world, and all these people are criticizing him on his own blog. Sure, a lot of the responses are positive, but quite a few are openly hostile, disagreeing with GM strategy, criticizing the products, criticizing the subjects he chooses for his blog—you name it. If blogging is all about opening yourself up to criticism from every bystander with a keyboard, no way am I going to start a blog."

Your task   Write Florence an e-mail (w_florence@sprenco.com), persuading him that the freewheeling nature of blog communication is its key advantage, not a disadvantage at all. While they may not always agree with what he has to say, automotive enthusiasts and car buyers respect Lutz for communicating in his own words—and for giving them the opportunity to respond. For background information, read some of the postings from Lutz and other GM executives at http://fastlane.gmblogs.com.[30]

[PODCASTING SKILLS]

2. Listen Up: Promoting a Podcast Channel   Podcasting, the technique of recording individual sound files that people download from the Internet to listen to on their computers or music players, is quickly redefining the concept of radio. A growing crowd of musicians, essayists, journalists, and others with compelling content are using podcasting to reach audiences they can't get to through traditional broadcast radio. The good news is that anyone with a microphone and a computer can record podcasts. That's also the bad news, at least from your perspective as a new podcaster: With so many podcasts now on the Internet, potential listeners have thousands and thousands of audio files to select from.

Your new podcast, School2Biz, offers advice to business students making the transition from college to career. You provide information on everything from preparing résumés to interviewing to finding a place in the business world and building a successful career. As you expand your audience, you'd eventually like to turn School2Biz into a profitable operation (perhaps by selling advertising time during your podcasts). For now, you're simply offering free advice.

Your task You've chosen Podcast Bunker (www.podcastbunker.com) as the first website on which to promote School2Biz. This site lets podcasters promote their feeds with brief text listings, such as this description of Pet Talk Radio: "A weekly lifestyle show for people with more than a passing interest in pets. Hosted by Brian Pickering & Kaye Browne with Australia's favourite vet Dr Harry Cooper & animal trainer Steve Austin."

As your instructor directs, either write a 50-word description of your new podcast that can be posted on Podcast Bunker or record a 30-second podcast describing the new service. Make up any information you need to describe School2Biz. Be sure to mention who you are and why the information you present is worth listening to.[31]

[PORTFOLIO BUILDER]

3. Your New Kentucky Home: Letter Promoting the Bluegrass State
Like all other states, Kentucky works hard to attract businesses that are considering expanding into the state or relocating entirely from another state. The Kentucky Cabinet for Economic Development is responsible for reaching out to these companies and overseeing the many incentive programs the state offers to both new and established businesses.

Your task As the communication director of the Kentucky Cabinet for Economic Development, you play the lead role in reaching out to companies that want to expand or relocate to Kentucky. Visit www.thinkkentucky.com and download the *Kentucky Facts* brochure (look under the "Why Kentucky" link). Identify the major benefits the state uses to promote Kentucky as a great place to locate a business. Summarize these reasons in a form letter that will be sent to business executives throughout the country. Be sure to introduce yourself and your purpose in the letter and close with a compelling call to action (have them reach you by telephone at 800-626-2930 or by e-mail at econdev@ky.gov). As you plan your letter, try to imagine yourself as the CEO of a company and consider what a complex choice it would be to move to another state.

[WEB WRITING SKILLS]   [PORTFOLIO BUILDER]

4. Don't Forget Print: Using the Web to Promote Time Inc.'s Magazine Advertising
After a shaky start as the technology matured and advertisers tried to figure out this new medium,

online advertising has finally become a significant force in both consumer and business marketing. Companies in a wide variety of industries are shifting some of the ad budgets from traditional media such as TV and magazines to the increasing selection of advertising possibilities online—and more than a few companies now advertise almost exclusively online. That's fine for companies that sell advertising time and space online, but your job involves selling advertising in print magazines that are worried about losing market share to online publishers.

Online advertising has two major advantages that you can't really compete with: interactivity and the ability to precisely target individual audience members. On the other hand, you have several advantages going for you, including the ability to produce high-color photography, the physical presence of print (such as when a magazine sits on a table in a doctor's waiting room), portability, guaranteed circulation numbers, and close reader relationships that go back years or decades.

Your task You work as an advertising sales specialist for the Time Inc. division of Time Warner, which publishes more than 150 magazines around the world. Write a brief persuasive message about the benefits of magazine advertising; the statement will be posted on the individual websites of Time Inc.'s numerous magazines, so you can't narrow in on any single publication. Also, Time Inc. coordinates its print publications with an extensive online presence (including thousands of paid online ads), so you can't bash online advertising, either.[32]

[E-MAIL SKILLS]

5. Give a Little to Get a Lot: Suggesting Free Wireless at Starbucks
Like many other students at the University of Wisconsin, Madison, you like to escape from your cramped apartment to work on school projects at local coffee shops. With your wireless-equipped laptop, you hunt for places that offer free wireless so you can access course websites, do research, and occasionally see how Badger athletic teams are doing. But there's a problem: At the Starbucks right around the corner, you have to pay for wireless access through the service offered by T-Mobile. Several of the locally owned coffee houses offer free wireless, but the closest one is a mile from your apartment. That's a long walk in the Wisconsin winter.

Your task Write a persuasive message to Starbucks, suggesting that the company drop its agreement with T-Mobile and offer free wireless instead. Try to convince the firm that free wireless will attract enough additional coffee-buying customers to offset the loss of revenue from wireless—and help Starbucks overcome the "big corporation" image that prompts some coffee drinkers to patronize locally owned establishments instead. Although you don't have the data to prove that the cost of offering free wireless would be more than offset by increased coffee sales, at least make a convincing argument that Starbucks should consider making the change. You'll post your message to the Starbucks website, www.starbucks.com, which has a limit of 2,600 characters for such messages.[33]

[PORTFOLIO BUILDER]

6. Outsourcing: Letter from Kelly Services Offering Solutions

Kelly Services is a global Fortune 500 company that offers staffing solutions, including temporary services, staff leasing, outsourcing, and vendor on-site and full-time placement. Kelly provides employees who have a wide range of skills across many disciplines, including office services, accounting, engineering, information technology, law, science, marketing, light industrial, education, health care, and home care.

Companies use Kelly Services to strategically balance workload and workforce during peaks and valleys of demand, to handle special projects, and to evaluate employees prior to making a full-time hiring decision. Many individuals are choosing the flexibility of personal career management, increasing options of where, when, and how to work. Therefore, more and more workers are becoming receptive to being contract, temporary, or consulting employees.

The flexibility of Kelly Services offers advantages to both the company and the employee. Both have the opportunity to evaluate one another prior to making a long-term commitment. Kelly Services earns a fee when its employees are hired permanently, but employers find that it's a small price to pay for such valuable preview time, which saves everyone the cost and pain of a bad hiring decision.

With 2,500 offices in 26 countries, Kelly provides its customers nearly 700,000 employees annually. The company provides staffing solutions to more than 90 percent of the Fortune 500 companies. Kelly has received many supplier awards for providing outstanding and cost-efficient staffing services, including Chrysler's Gold Award, Ford Motor Company's Q1 Preferred Quality Award, Intel Corporation's Supplier Continuous Quality Improvement (SCQI) Award, and DuPont Legal's Challenge Award.

As companies increasingly face new competitive pressures to provide better service and quality at lower prices, many are turning to outsourcing suppliers to deliver complete operational management of specific functions or support departments, allowing a company the necessary time to focus on its core competencies. One solution is to choose a single supplier such as the Kelly Management Services (KMS) division to deliver "full-service" outsourcing.

KMS combines management experience, people process improvements, technology enhancements, and industry expertise to optimize customer operations and reduce cost. KMS understands the unique challenges companies are facing in today's increasingly fast-paced business world and can provide customers with services across multiple functional offerings, including call center operations, warehousing, distribution and light assembly, back office and administrative functions, and mail and reprographic services.

Your task Write a sales letter to companies similar to Chrysler, Ford, Intel, and DuPont, explaining what Kelly has to offer. For current information, visit the Kelly website, at www.kellyservices.com.[34]

7. Always Urgent: Memo Pleading Case for Hosting a Red Cross Blood Drive

This morning as you drove to your job as food services manager at the Pechanga Casino Entertainment Center in Temecula, California, you were concerned to hear on the radio that the local Red Cross chapter put out a call for blood because national supplies have fallen dangerously low. During highly publicized disasters, people are emotional and eager to help out by donating blood. But in calmer times, only 5 percent of eligible donors think of giving blood. You're one of those few.

Not many people realize that donated blood lasts only 72 hours. Consequently, the mainstay of emergency blood supplies must be replenished in an ongoing effort. No one is more skilled, dedicated, or efficient in handling blood than the American Red Cross, which is responsible for half the nation's supply of blood and blood products.

Donated blood helps victims of accidents and disease, as well as surgery patients. Just yesterday you were reading about a girl named Melissa, who was diagnosed with multiple congenital heart defects and underwent her first open-heart surgery at 1 week old. Now 5, she's used well over 50 units of donated blood, and she wouldn't be alive without them. In a thank-you letter, her mother lauded the many strangers who had "given a piece of themselves" to save her precious daughter—and countless others. You also learned that a donor's pint of blood can benefit up to four other people.

Today, you're going to do more than just roll up your own sleeve. You know the local Red Cross chapter takes its Blood Mobile to corporations, restaurants, beauty salons—anyplace willing to host public blood drives. What if you could convince the board of directors to support a blood drive at the casino? The slot machines and gaming tables are usually full, hundreds of employees are on hand, and people who've never visited before might come down to donate blood. The positive publicity certainly couldn't hurt Pechanga's community image. With materials from the Red Cross, you're confident you can organize Pechanga's hosting effort and handle the promotion. (Last year, you headed the casino's successful Toys for Tots drive.)

To give blood, one must be healthy, be at least 17 years old (with no upper age limit), and weigh at least 110 pounds. Donors can give every 56 days. You'll be urging Pechanga donors to eat well, drink water, and be rested before the Blood Mobile arrives.[35]

Your task Write a memo persuading the Pechanga board of directors to host a public Red Cross blood drive. You can learn more about what's involved in hosting a blood drive at www.givelife.org (click on "Sponsor a Drive"). Ask the board to provide bottled water, orange juice, and snacks for donors. You'll organize food service workers to handle the distribution, but you'll need the board's approval to let your team volunteer during work hours. Use a combination of logical and emotional appeals.

8. Selling Your Idea: Sales Letter Promoting a Product of Your Own Invention

You never intended to become an inventor, but you saw a way to make something work more easily, so you set to work. You developed a model, found a way to mass-produce it, and set up a small manufacturing studio in your home. You know that other people are going to benefit from your invention. Now all you need to do is reach that market.

Your task Imagine a useful product that you have invented—perhaps something related to a hobby or sporting activity. List the benefits and features of your imaginary product. Then write a sales letter for it, using what you've learned in this chapter and making up details as you need them.

[TEXT MESSAGING SKILLS

9. Instant Promotion: Text Message from Hilton Hotels to Frequent Guests
Hilton Hotels uses SMS (short messaging service) to send text messaging promotions to customers who've signed up as HHonors members. You work in Hilton's marketing department, and you often struggle to condense elaborate travel packages into the system maximum of 65 enticing words.

For example, today's promotion offers "A Golfer's Dream Come True: 'I just played a round of golf by the pyramids!'" For $575 per person per day (double room), valid through January 15, 2010, travelers can stay in the Hilton Pyramids Golf Resort in Cairo, Egypt, for 7 nights/8 days, including breakfast, service charge, and tax. They'll be met at the airport, given transportation to the resort, plus two rounds of golf per person at Dreamland Golf course and two rounds of golf per person at Soleimaneia Pyramids Golf & Country Club course. That's almost 90 words.

But you also need to convey that the Dreamland course wraps like a serpent around the Hilton resort. Its lush greens and lakes, designed by Karl Litten, contrast sharply with the golden desert, culminating in a stunning view of the great Pyramids of Giza, one of the seven wonders of the world. The Soleimaneia course features the "biggest floodlit driving course in Egypt." The travel package provides free transportation to this nearby course.

Rates, of course, are subject to availability, and other restrictions may apply. But interested travelers should mention code G7 Pyramids Golf Special when they call Hilton Reservations Worldwide. They can also e-mail RM_PYRA-MIDS_GOLF@hilton.com or call the Cairo hotel directly at 20 2 8402402.[36]

Your task Write the persuasive text message; your space limit is 65 words.

[IM SKILLS

10. Helping Children: Instant Message Holiday Fund Drive at IBM
At IBM, you're one of the coordinators for the annual Employee Charitable Contributions Campaign. Since 1978, the company has helped employees contribute to more than 2,000 health and human service agencies. These groups may offer child care, treat substance abuse, provide health services, or fight illiteracy, homelessness, and hunger. Some offer disaster relief or care for the elderly. All deserve support. They're carefully screened by IBM, one of the largest corporate contributors of cash, equipment, and people to nonprofit organizations and educational institutions, both in the United States and elsewhere around the world. As your literature states, the program "has engaged our employees more fully in the important mission of corporate citizenship."

During the winter holidays, you target agencies that cater to the needs of displaced families, women, and children. It's not difficult to raise enthusiasm. The prospect of helping children enjoy the holidays—children who otherwise might have nothing—usually awakens the spirit of your most distracted workers. But some of them wait until the last minute and then forget.

Employees have until Friday, December 16, to come forth with cash contributions. To make it in time for holiday deliveries, they can also bring in toys, food, and blankets through Tuesday, December 20. They shouldn't have any trouble finding the collection bins; they're everywhere, marked with bright red banners. But some people will want to call you with questions or (you hope) to make credit card contributions: 800-658-3899, ext. 3342.[37]

Your task It's December 14. Write a 75- to 100-word instant message encouraging last-minute gifts.

[E-MAIL SKILLS

11. Helping Out: Message to Whole Foods Market Managers
Whole Foods Market has grown into a nationwide chain by catering to consumer desires for healthier foods and environmentally sensitive household products. For instance, meats come from animals that were never fed antibiotics, and the cheese is from cows said to be raised on small farms and treated humanely.

Along with selling these products, the company makes a commitment "to the neighborhood and larger community that we serve and in which we live." Whole Foods not only donates 5 percent of after-tax profits to not-for-profit organizations but also financially supports employees who volunteer their time for community service projects. Many Whole Foods stores donate goods and supplies to soup kitchens in their local communities. Company executives want to encourage this type of activity, which reflects the "Whole Foods, Whole People, Whole Planet" corporate motto.

You are the manager of the Whole Foods Market on Ponce de Leon Avenue in Atlanta. You developed a program for donating surplus food to local food banks. Because of the success of that program, top executives have asked you to help other Whole Foods stores coordinate this effort into a chainwide food donation program, "Whole Foods for Life." Ideally, by streamlining the process chainwide, the company would be able to increase the number of people it helps and to get more of its employees involved.

You don't have a great deal of extra money for the program, so the emphasis has to be on using resources already available to the stores. One idea is to use trucks from suburban stores to make the program "mobile." Another idea is to join forces with a retailing chain to give food and clothing to individuals. You've decided that the key will be to solicit input from the other stores so that they'll feel more involved in the final outcome as the larger food-donation program takes shape.[38]

Your task Send a persuasive e-mail message to all managers at Whole Foods Market, explaining the new program and requesting that they help by pooling ideas they've gleaned from their local experience. Even if they don't have food-donation programs currently in place, you want to hear ideas from them and their employees for this charitable project. With their help, you'll choose the best ideas to develop the new Whole Foods for Life program.

[E-MAIL SKILLS] **[PORTFOLIO BUILDER]**

12. Message to an Angel: Introducing Your Company to an Investor

Your new company, WorldConnect Language Services, started well and is going strong. However, to expand beyond your Memphis, Tennessee, home market, you need a one-time infusion of cash to open branch offices in other cities around the Southeast. At the Entrepreneur's Lunch Forum you attended yesterday, you learned about several *angels*, as they are called in the investment community—private individuals who invest money in small companies in exchange for a share of ownership. One such angel, Melinda Sparks, told the audience that she is looking for investment opportunities outside high technology, where angels often invest their money. She also indicated that she looks for entrepreneurs who know their industries and markets well, who are passionate about the value they bring to the marketplace, who are committed to growing their businesses, and who have a solid plan for how they will spend an investor's money. Fortunately, you meet all of her criteria.

Your task Draft an e-mail message to Sparks, introducing yourself and your business and asking for a meeting at which you can present your business plan in more detail. Explain that your Memphis office was booked to capacity within two months of opening, thanks to the growing number of international business professionals looking for translators and interpreters. You've researched the entire Southeast region and identified at least 10 other cities that could support language services offices such as yours. Making up whatever other information you need, draft a four-paragraph message following the AIDA model, ending with a request for a meeting within the next four weeks.

[BLOGGING SKILLS] **[PORTFOLIO BUILDER]**

13. Web Accessibility Advocacy: It's Not "World Wide" if It Doesn't Include Everybody

Like most other companies today, your firm makes extensive use of the web for internal and external communication. However, after reading about the Web Accessibility Initiative (WAI), you've become concerned that your company's various websites haven't been designed to accommodate people with disabilities or age-related limitations. Fortunately, as one of the company's top managers, you

have a perfect forum for letting everyone in the company know how important accessible web design is: Your internal blog is read by the vast majority of employees and managers throughout the company.

Your task Visit the WAI website, at www.w3.org/WAI, and read the two articles "Introduction to Web Accessibility" (look in the "Introducing Accessibility" section) and "Developing a Web Accessibility Business Case for Your Organization: Overview" (in the "Managing Accessibility" section). Using the information you learn in these articles, write a post for your blog that emphasizes how important it is for your company's websites to become more accessible. You don't have direct authority over the company's web developers, so it would be inappropriate for you to request them to take any specific action. Your goal is simply to raise awareness and encourage everyone to consider the needs of the company's online audiences. Don't worry about the technical aspects of web accessibility; focus instead on the benefits of improving accessibility.[39]

[E-MAIL SKILLS]

14. Time to Lose: Promoting the 6 Week Solution at Curves

The Curves franchise has grown quickly over the past several years by catering to women who may not feel at home in traditional gyms. As the owner of a successful Curves health club, you know that information and motivation are often the keys to healthy living in general and weight management in particular. You're excited about a new program the company offers called the Curves 6 Week Solution, a series of classes that help women make better nutrition choices.

Your task The corporate website offers a nice description of the Curves 6 Week Solution, but it's over 600 words long, and you'd like a shorter version to e-mail to current and prospective clients. Visit that page on the Curves website, www.curves.com/weight_loss, and summarize the description. Aim for no more than 300 words.

[PORTFOLIO BUILDER]

15. Try It—You Just Might Like It: Convincing Consumers to Sample Beefalo

You know enough about human nature to know that people tend to resist new ideas when it comes to food. In your job as public communications director for American Beefalo International, this knowledge presents a professional challenge as you try to convince people to give beefalo a try. The beefalo is a cross between bison (American buffalo) and beef cattle, and even though these animals are primarily cattle (genetically speaking), many consumers are reluctant to give up their familiar beef for something most have never tried.

But here's the good news: Many people are looking for healthier foods, and according to government tests, beefalo is lower than many other meats in cholesterol, saturated fat, total fat, and calories. Here's a comparison table published on your organization's website:

Meat	Protein (g)	Cholesterol (mg)	Saturated Fats (g)	Total Fat (g)	Calories	Percentage of Calories from Fat
Fish	22.9	47	0.104	0.81	105	6.9
Chicken	31.0	85	1.0	3.5	165	19.5
Pork	29.3	86	3.4	9.7	212	41.0
Beef	25.9	88	8.5	21.5	305	63.6
Beefalo	30.7	58	2.7	6.3	188	30.3

Your task Write a small flier to be displayed in food stores that sell beefalo cuts. The page size will be 8 1/2 inches tall by 3 3/4 inches wide, so format your word-processing page accordingly. Allow room for a photograph, and don't try to cram too much text on the page. Emphasize beefalo as a healthy alternative for people who want to continue enjoying meat in their diets.[40]

Improve Your Grammar, Mechanics, and Usage

Level 1: Self-Assessment—Commas

Review Section 2.6 in the Handbook of Grammar, Mechanics, and Usage, and then complete the following 15 items.

In items 1–15, insert required commas.

1. Please send us four cases of filters two cases of wing nuts and a bale of rags.

2. Your analysis however does not account for returns.

3. As a matter of fact she has seen the figures.

4. Before May 7 1999 they wouldn't have minded either.

5. After Martha has gone talk to me about promoting her.

6. Stoneridge Inc. will go public on September 9 2009.

7. We want the new copier not the old model.

8. "Talk to me" Sandra said "before you change a thing."

9. Because of a previous engagement Dr. Stoeve will not be able to attend.

10. The company started attracting attention during the long hard recession of the mid-1970s.

11. You can reach me at this address: 717 Darby Place Scottsdale Arizona 85251.

12. Transfer the documents from Fargo North Dakota to Boise Idaho.

13. Sam O'Neill the designated representative is gone today.

14. With your help we will soon begin.

15. She may hire two new representatives or she may postpone filling those territories until spring.

Level 2: Workplace Applications

The following items contain numerous errors in grammar, capitalization, punctuation, abbreviation, number style, word division, and vocabulary. Rewrite each sentence correcting all errors. Write *C* for any sentence that is already correct.

1. A pitfall of internal promotions is, that a person may be given a job beyond their competence.

2. What makes this development possible is the technological advances in todays workplace.

3. We have up to date physical safeguards, such as secure areas in buildings, electronic safeguards, such as passwords and encryption, and we have procedural safeguards, such as customer authentication procedures.

4. When asked why BASF need to bring in a consultant after so many years, process development quality assurance manager Merritt Sink says that experience is extremely important on these type of projects.

5. Looking at just one growth indicator imports to the United States from China "ballooned" to $102 billion in 2005; compared with 15 billion in 1994.

6. Levi Strauss was the first major manufacturer to develop and do publicity about a formal Code of Conduct for it's contract manufacturers.

7. In foreign countries, while the local labor laws may be comparable or even more stringent than in the United States, law enforcement mechanisms are weak or nonexistent often.

8. Hyundai Motor Co., South Koreas' largest-automotive producer are building a $1 billion assembly and manufacturing plant in Montgomery, Alabama.

9. The long term success of some Internet products rest heavily on broadbands wide acceptance.

10. Being creative, flexibility, and dynamic planning are the critical elements of any successful, manufacturing process.

11. "Starbucks expanded the Frappucciono family to satisfy customers by offering a broader array of blended beverages," said Howard Behar, Starbucks president, North American Operations.

12. Internationally-renowned interior designer, Jacques Garcia will be designing the hotel's interiors; the gardens will also be designed by him.

13. Anyone who thinks they know what a CEO does is probably wrong, according to Eric Kriss; a professional Chief Executive.

14. Doctor Ichak Adizes, who founded the Adizes institute, headquartered in Santa Barbara, Calif. has spent decade's studying the life cycle of businesses.

15. The best job-description in the world wont provide you with a trusted executive, finely-honed interviewing skills only will help one do that.

Level 3: Document Critique

The following document may contain errors in grammar, capitalization, punctuation, abbreviation, number style, vocabulary, and spelling. You may also discover problems with wordiness, usage, organization, and tone for a sales message. Correct all errors using standard proofreading marks (see Appendix C).

To:　　　　　　　<Promotional Customer List2>

From:　　　　　Sasha Morgenstern <smorgenstern@insure.com>

Subject:　　　Insurence Service

Dear potential buyers:

You will be able to compare prices from more than three hundredinsurance companies'. Or find the lower rates for any insurance, such as Term life Automobile; Medical. dental. "No-exam" whole life, workers' compensation, Medicare supplements; Fixed annuities

$500 Dollar Guaranttes

We'll find you the lowest U.S. rates for term life insurance, or we'll deliver $500 to you overnight.

Plus, every quote will carry a $five hundred dollar guarrantee of uptotheday accurracy.

"Insure.com provides rock-bottom quotes." —Forbes

All quotes are free and accurrate; We offer Lightning-Fast Service

What their saying about us can be found at www.insure.com. Our speedy service is being talked about by everyone, which has received high ratings and postive reviews from every major business publication "Nation's Business" "Kiplinger's Personal Finance" Good Housekeeping, The Los Angeles Times, "Money" "U.S. News & World Report"

Expert AdviSe Will be provided with No Sales Pitch:

You will not be dealing with insurance agents to save you time and monoy. But if you want advise our saleried insurance experts are available at our toll-free customer service number. We hope you will take a moment to peruse our webstie, www.insure.com today if possible.

Very truly yours,

Sasha Morgenstern

Longer Business Messages

CHAPTER 10: Understanding and Planning Reports and Proposals

CHAPTER 11: Writing and Completing Reports and Proposals

CHAPTER 12: Developing Oral and Online Presentations

Understanding and Planning Reports and Proposals

[from the real world]

"I think we'll have fewer legal problems with plain English and common sense than with pages and pages of rules."

—*Randy Michaels, CEO for Interactive & Broadcasting, Tribune Company*

www.tribune.com

In these days of complex regulations and rampant litigation, many employee handbooks have become long legal documents that specify acceptable employee behavior in minute detail. These comprehensive policy reports are designed in large part to reduce the number of lawsuits against employers, but Tribune's Randy Michaels claims that "the more policies you have, the more opportunities there are for someone who is very unhappy to sue." The latest edition of Tribune's employee handbook is only one-third the length of the previous edition, and instead of dense, legalistic language, it features such directives as "Rule 1: Use your best judgment." and "Question authority and push back if you do not like the answer." Whether the new approach will work in the long run is yet to be seen. At least one legal expert says the company is asking for trouble by not specifying exactly what employees may and may not do on the job.[1]

APPLYING THE THREE-STEP WRITING PROCESS TO REPORTS AND PROPOSALS

As the Tribune story illustrates, reports such as employee handbooks play a vital role in business, and they'll play a vital role in your career as well. In previous chapters, you learned to use the three-step writing process when developing shorter business messages; now it's time to apply those skills to longer messages. Reports fall into three basic categories (see Figure 10.1):

Reports can be classified as informational reports, analytical reports, and proposals.

- **Informational reports** offer data, facts, feedback, and other types of information, without analysis or recommendations.

- **Analytical reports** offer both information and analysis, and they can also include recommendations.

- **Proposals** offer structured persuasion for internal or external audiences.

Try to view every business report as an opportunity to demonstrate your understanding of your audience's challenges and your ability to contribute to your organization's success.

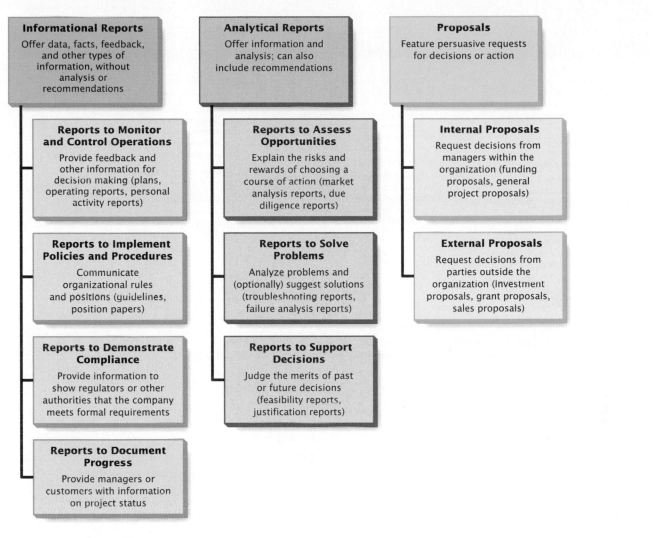

Figure 10.1 Common Business Reports and Proposals
You will have the opportunity to read and write many types of reports in your career; here are some of the most common.

The three-step process (see Figure 10.2) is easily adapted to reports and, in fact, makes these larger projects much easier by ensuring a methodical, efficient approach to planning, writing, and completing.

Analyzing the Situation

Reports can be complex, time-consuming projects, so be sure to analyze the situation carefully before you begin to write. Pay special attention to your **statement of purpose**, which explains *why* you are preparing the report and what you plan to deliver.

Define your purpose clearly so you don't waste time with unnecessary rework.

The most useful way to phrase your purpose statement is to begin with an infinitive phrase (*to* plus a verb), which helps pin down your general goal (*to inform*, *to identify*, *to analyze*, and so on). For instance, in an informational report, your statement of purpose can be as simple as one of these:

To identify potential markets for our new phone-based videogames

To update the board of directors on the progress of the research project

To submit required information to the Securities and Exchange Commission

The statement of purpose for an analytical report often needs to be more comprehensive. When Linda Moreno, the cost accounting manager for Electrovision, a high-tech

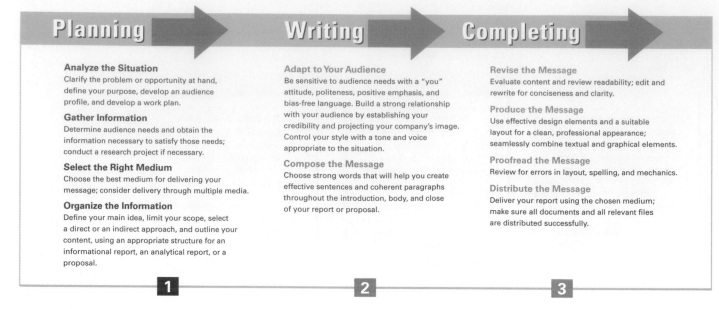

Figure 10.2   Three-Step Writing Process for Reports and Proposals
The three-step writing process is especially valuable with lengthy documents such as reports and
proposals. By guiding your work at each step, the process helps you make the most of the time and energy
you invest.

company based in Los Gatos, California, was asked to find ways of reducing employee travel
and entertainment (T&E) costs, she phrased her statement of purpose accordingly:

> To analyze the T&E budget, evaluate the impact of recent changes in airfares and hotel
> costs, and suggest ways to tighten management's control over T&E expenses.

Because Moreno was assigned an analytical report rather than an informational report,
she had to go beyond merely collecting data; she had to draw conclusions and make recommendations. You'll see her complete report in Chapter 11.

A proposal must also be guided by a clear statement of purpose to help you focus on
crafting a persuasive message. Here are several examples:

> To secure funding in next year's budget for new conveyor systems in the warehouse
>
> To get management approval to reorganize the North American salesforce
>
> To secure $2 million from outside investors to start production of the new titanium
> mountain bike

In addition to considering your purpose carefully, you will want to prepare a *work plan*
for most reports and proposals in order to make the best use of your time. For simpler
reports, the work plan can be an informal list of tasks and a simple schedule. However, if
you're preparing a lengthy report, particularly when you're collaborating with others, you'll
want to develop a more detailed work plan (see Figure 10.3).

Gathering Information

Obtaining the information needed for many reports and proposals requires careful planning, and you may even need to do a separate research project just to acquire the data and
information you need. To stay on schedule and on budget, be sure to review both your statement of purpose and your audience's needs so that you collect all the information you
need—and only the information you need. In some cases, you won't be able to collect every
piece of information you'd like, so prioritize your needs up front and focus on the most
important questions.

*The statement of purpose for a
proposal should help guide you in
developing a persuasive message.*

*A detailed work plan saves time and
often produces more effective
reports.*

*Some reports require formal research
projects in order to gather all the
necessary information.*

STATEMENT OF THE PROBLEM

The rapid growth of our company over the past five years has reduced the sense of community among our staff. People no longer feel like part of an intimate organization that values teamwork.

States the problem clearly enough for anyone to understand without additional research

PURPOSE AND SCOPE OF WORK

The purpose of this study is to determine whether a company newsletter would help rebuild a sense of community within the workforce. The study will evaluate the impact of newsletters in other companies and will attempt to identify features that may be desirable in our own newsletter. Such variables as length, frequency of distribution, types of articles, and graphic design will be considered. Costs will be estimated for several approaches, including print and electronic versions. In addition, the study will analyze the personnel and procedures required to produce a newsletter.

Explains exactly what will be covered by the research and included in the final report

SOURCES AND METHODS OF DATA COLLECTION

Sample newsletters will be collected from 10 to 20 companies similar to ours in size, growth rate, and types of employees. The editors will be asked to comment on the impact of their publications on employee morale. Our own employees will be surveyed to determine their interest in a newsletter and their preferences for specific features. Production procedures and costs will be analyzed through conversations with newsletter editors, printers, and our website development team.

Identifies the tasks to be accomplished and does so in clear, simple terms

PRELIMINARY OUTLINE

The preliminary outline for this study is as follows:

I. Do newsletters affect morale?
   A. Do people read them?
   B. How do employees benefit?
   C. How does the company benefit?
II. What are the features of good newsletters?
   A. How long are they?
   B. What do they contain?
   C. How often are they published?
   D. How are they designed?
III. How should a newsletter be produced?
   A. Should it be written and edited internally or externally?
   B. Should it be printed or produced electronically?
   C. If electronic, should it be formatted as e-mail, a blog, or regular web content?
IV. What would a newsletter cost?
   A. What would the personnel cost be?
   B. What would the material cost be?
   C. What would outside services cost?
V. Should we publish a company newsletter?
VI. If so, what approach should we take?

Offers a preliminary outline to help readers understand the issues that will be addressed in the report

TASK ASSIGNMENTS AND SCHEDULE

Each phase of this study will be completed by the following dates:

Task	Person	Date
Collect/analyze newsletters	Hank Waters	September 15, 2009
Interview editors by phone	Hank Waters	September 22, 2009
Survey employees	Julienne Cho	September 29, 2009
Develop sample	Hank Waters	October 6, 2009
Develop cost estimates	Julienne Cho	October 13, 2009
Prepare report	Hank Waters	October 20, 2009
Submit final report	Hank Waters	October 24, 2009

Identifies who is responsible for each task and when it will be completed

Figure 10.3 Work Plan for a Report

A formal work plan such as this is a vital tool for planning and managing complex writing projects. The preliminary outline here helps guide the research; the report writers may well modify the outline when they begin writing the report.

Selecting the Right Medium

In addition to the general media selection criteria discussed in Chapter 3, consider several points for reports and proposals. First, for many reports and proposals, audiences have specific media requirements, and you might not have a choice. For instance, executives in many corporations now expect to review many reports via their in-house intranets, sometimes in conjunction with an *executive dashboard*, a customized online presentation of highly summarized business information. Second, consider how your audience members want to provide feedback on your report or proposal. Do they prefer to write comments on a printed document or edit a wiki article? Third, will people need to search through your document electronically or update it in the future? Fourth, bear in mind that your choice of medium sends a message. For instance, a routine sales report dressed up in expensive multimedia will look like a waste of valuable company resources.

The best medium for any given report might be anything from a professionally printed and bound document to an online executive dashboard that displays nothing but report highlights.

DIRECT APPROACH

Since the company's founding 25 years ago, we have provided regular repair service for all our electric appliances. This service has been an important selling point as well as a source of pride for our employees. However, rising labor costs have made it impossible to maintain profitability while offering competitive service rates. Last year, we lost $500,000 on our repair business.

Because of your concern over these losses, you asked me to study whether we should discontinue our repair service. After analyzing the situation in depth, I have concluded that the repair service is an expensive, impractical tradition, and I recommend that the service be discontinued.

By withdrawing from the electric appliance repair business, we can substantially improve our financial performance without damaging our reputation with customers. This conclusion is based on three basic points that are covered in the following pages:

• It is highly unlikely that we will ever be able to make a profit in the repair business.

• We can refer customers to a variety of qualified repair firms without significantly reducing customer satisfaction.

• Closing down the service operation will create few internal problems.

— Summarizes the situation

— Immediately introduces one of the report's major conclusions

— Reminds the audience why the report was prepared

— Presents the report's key recommendation, that the repair service should be discontinued

— Emphasizes the benefits of acting on the recommendation and addresses any fears about possible negative consequences

— Lists three important conclusions that led to the recommendation to end the service (notice how the indirect approach that follows presents these same three points as questions to be considered)

Summarizes the situation ——————

Reminds the audience why the report ———— was prepared

Indicates that conclusions and a ———— recommendation will be presented later in the report

Introduces the three points that will ———— eventually lead to the conclusions and ultimately to the recommendation

INDIRECT APPROACH

Since the company's founding 25 years ago, we have provided regular repair service for all our electric appliances. This service has been an important selling point as well as a source of pride for our employees. However, rising labor costs have made it impossible to maintain profitability while offering competitive service rates.

Because of your concern over these losses, you have asked me to study whether we should discontinue our repair service. I have analyzed the situation in depth, and the following pages present my findings and recommendations for your review. The analysis addressed three basic questions:

• What is the extent of our losses, and what can we do to turn the business around?

• Would withdrawal hurt our sales of electrical appliances?

• What would be the internal repercussions of closing down the repair business?

Figure 10.4 **Direct Approach Versus Indirect Approach in an Introduction**
In the direct version of this introduction, the writer quickly presents the report's recommendation, followed by the conclusions that led to that recommendation. In the indirect version, the same topics are introduced in the same order, but no conclusions are drawn about them; the conclusions and the ultimate recommendation appear later, in the body of the report.

Organizing Your Information

The direct approach is popular with reports, but some situations call for the indirect approach.

The direct approach is by far the most popular and convenient for business reports; it saves time, makes the rest of the report easier to follow, and produces a more forceful document. However, the confidence implied by the direct approach may be misconstrued as arrogance, especially if you're a junior member of a status-conscious organization. In contrast, the indirect approach gives you a chance to prove your points and gradually overcome your audience's reservations. However, the indirect approach can become unwieldy with long reports, so carefully consider report length before deciding on the direct or indirect approach. Both approaches have merit, and businesspeople often combine them, revealing their conclusions and recommendations as they go along, rather than putting them first or last (see Figure 10.4).

SUPPORTING YOUR MESSAGES WITH RELIABLE INFORMATION

Researching without a plan wastes time and usually produces unsatisfactory results.

Effective research involves a lot more than simply typing a few terms into a search engine. Save time and get better results by using a clear process:

1. **Plan your research.** Planning is the most important step of any research project; a solid plan yields better results in less time.

2. **Locate the data and information you need.** Your next step is to figure out *where* the data and information are and *how* to access them.

3. **Process the data and information you located.** The data and information you find probably won't be in a form you can use immediately and may require statistical analysis or other processing.

4. **Apply your findings.** You can apply your research findings in three ways: summarizing information, drawing conclusions, and developing recommendations.

5. **Manage information efficiently.** Many companies today are trying to maximize the return on the time and money they invest in business research by collecting and sharing research results in a variety of computer-based systems, known generally as **knowledge management systems**.

Planning Your Research

Start by developing a **problem statement** that defines the purpose of your research—the decision you need to make or the conclusion you need to reach at the end of the process. Next, identify the information you need in order to make that decision or reach that conclusion. You can then begin to generate the questions that will constitute your research. Chances are you will have more questions than you have time or money to answer, so prioritize your information needs.

The problem statement guides your research by focusing on the decision you need to make or the conclusion you need to reach.

Before beginning any research project, remember that research carries some significant ethical responsibilities. Your research tactics affect the people from whom you gather data and information, the people who read your results, and the people who are affected by the way you present those results. To avoid ethical lapses, follow these guidelines:

- Keep an open mind so that you don't skew the research toward answers you want or expect to see.
- Respect the privacy of your research participants and don't mislead people about the purposes of your research.[2]
- Document sources and give appropriate credit.
- Respect your sources' *intellectual property rights* (the ownership of unique ideas that have commercial value in the marketplace).[3]

In addition to ethics, research etiquette deserves careful attention, too. For example, respect the time of anyone who agrees to be interviewed or to be a research participant and maintain courtesy throughout the interview or research process.

Locating Data and Information

The range of sources available to business researchers today can be overwhelming. The good news is that if you have a question about an industry, a company, a market, a new technology, or a financial topic, somebody else has probably already researched the subject. Research done previously for another purpose is considered **secondary research**; sources for such research information include magazines, newspapers, public websites, books, and other reports. Don't let the name *secondary* fool you, though. You want to start with secondary research because it can save you considerable time and money for many projects. In contrast, **primary research** is new research done specifically for the current project.

Primary research contains information that you gather specifically for a new research project; secondary research contains information that others have gathered (and published, in many cases).

Evaluating Sources

In every research project, you have the responsibility to verify the quality of the sources you use. To avoid tainting your results and damaging your reputation, ask the following questions about each piece of material:

Evaluate your sources carefully to avoid embarrassing and potentially damaging mistakes.

- **Does the source have a reputation for honesty and reliability?** For example, try to find out how the source accepts articles and whether it has an editorial board, conducts peer review, or follows fact-checking procedures.
- **Is the source potentially biased?** To interpret an organization's information, you need to know its point of view.

- **What is the purpose of the material?** For instance, was the material designed to inform others of new research, advance a political position, or promote a product?

- **Is the author credible?** Is the author a professional journalist or merely someone with an opinion?

- **Where did the source get *its* information?** Try to find out who collected the data and the methods they used.

- **Can you verify the material independently?** Verification is particularly important when the information goes beyond simple facts to include projections, interpretations, and estimates.

- **Is the material current?** Make sure you are using the most current information available.

- **Is the material complete?** Have you accessed the entire document or only a selection from it?

- **Do the source's claims stand up to scrutiny?** Step back and determine whether the information makes sense.

You probably won't have time to conduct a thorough background check on all your sources, so focus your efforts on the most important or most suspicious pieces of information.

Conducting Secondary Research

You'll want to start most projects by conducting secondary research first.

Even if you intend to eventually conduct primary research, most projects start with a review of secondary research. Inside your company, you might be able to find a variety of reports, memos, and other documents that could help. Outside the company, business researchers can choose from a wide range of print and online resources, both in libraries and online.

Even in the Internet age, libraries offer information and resources you can't find anywhere else—including experienced research librarians.

Finding Information at a Library   Public and university libraries offer an enormous array of business books, electronic databases, newspapers, periodicals, directories, almanacs, and government publications. Many of these may be unavailable through a standard web search or may be available only with a subscription. Libraries are also where you'll find one of your most important resources: librarians. Reference librarians are trained in research techniques and can often help you find obscure information you can't find on your own. They can also direct you to the typical library's many sources of business information:

- **Newspapers and periodicals.** Libraries offer access to a wide variety of popular magazines, general business magazines, *trade journals* (which provide information about specific professions and industries), and *academic journals* (which provide research-oriented articles from researchers and educators).

- **Business books.** Although less timely than newspapers and periodicals, business books provide in-depth coverage of a variety of business topics.

- **Directories.** Thousands of directories are published in print and electronic formats in the United States, and many include membership information for all kinds of professions, industries, and special-interest groups.

- **Almanacs and statistical resources.** Almanacs are handy guides to factual and statistical information about countries, politics, the labor force, and so on. One of the most extensive is the *Statistical Abstract of the United States* (available at www.census.gov).

Local, state, and federal government agencies publish a huge array of information that is helpful to business researchers.

- **Government publications.** Information on laws, court decisions, tax questions, regulatory issues, and other governmental concerns can often be found in collections of government documents.

- **Electronic databases.** Databases offer vast collections of computer-searchable information, often in specific areas such as business, law, science, technology, and education. Some libraries offer remote online access to some or all databases; for others, you'll need to visit in person.

Finding Information Online   The Internet can be a tremendous source of business information, provided that you know where to look and how to use the tools available. **Search engines** scan millions of websites to identify individual webpages that contain a specific word or phrase you've asked for. For all their ease and power, search engines have three disadvantages: (1) No human editors are involved to evaluate the quality of the results; (2) various engines use different search techniques, so they often find different material; and (3) search engines can't reach all the content on some websites (this part of the Internet is sometimes called the *hidden Internet* or the *deep Internet*).

Web directories address the first major shortcoming of search engines by using human editors to categorize and evaluate websites. *Metacrawlers* or *metasearch* engines (such as Bovée and Thill's Web Search, at http://businesscommunicationblog.com/websearch) address the second shortcoming by formatting your search request for the specific requirements of multiple search engines. **Online databases** help address the third shortcoming of search engines by offering access to the newspapers, magazines, and journals that you're likely to need for many research projects.

Search engines, web directories, and databases work in different ways, so make sure you understand how to optimize your search and interpret the results. With a *keyword search*, the engine or database attempts to find items that include all the words you enter. A *Boolean search* lets you define a query with greater precision, using such operators as AND (the search must include two terms linked by AND), OR (it can include either or both words), or NOT (the search ignores items with whatever word comes after NOT). *Natural language searches* let you ask questions in everyday English. *Forms-based searches* help you create powerful queries by simply filling out an online form.[4]

To make the best use of any search engine or database, keep the following points in mind:

- Read the instructions and pay attention to the details.

- Review the search and display options carefully so you don't misinterpret the results.

- Try variations of your terms, such as *child*, *adolescent*, and *youth* or *management* and *managerial.*

- User fewer search terms to find more results; use more search terms to find fewer results.

If you want to monitor a particular information source over time, see whether it offers a newsfeed subscription. You can easily manage dozens or hundreds of newsfeeds by using a newsreader such as FeedDemon (www.feeddemon.com) or Google Reader (www.google .com/reader).[5] Also, keep an eye out for new advances in online research tools, such as *social bookmarking* sites (www.digg.com and http://delicious.com, for example), *desktop search engines* and *enterprise search engines* (which search your computer or your entire company's network, respectively), and a variety of software tools known as *research managers* or *content managers* that help organize information sources and research materials.[6] For information on the latest online research tools and techniques, visit http://real-timeupdates.com/bce and click on Chapter 10.

Documenting Your Sources   Documenting your sources serves three important functions: It properly and ethically credits the person who created the original material, it shows your audience that you have sufficient support for your message, and it helps readers explore your topic in more detail, if desired. Be sure to take advantage of the source documentation tools in your software, such as automatic endnote or footnote tracking. Also, tools such as Microsoft OneNote and Google Notebook can help you collect and organize your notes.[7]

Appendix B discusses the common methods of documenting sources. Whatever method you choose, documentation is necessary for books, articles, tables, charts, diagrams, song lyrics, scripted dialogue, letters, speeches—anything that you take from someone else, including ideas and information that you've re-expressed through paraphrasing or summarizing. However, you do not have to cite a source for knowledge that's generally known among your readers, such as the fact that Microsoft is a large software company and that computers are pervasive in business today.

Conducting Primary Research

If secondary research can't provide the information and insights you need, your next choice is to gather the information yourself with primary research. Primary research encompasses a variety of methods, from observations to experiments such as test marketing, but the two tools most commonly used for business research are surveys and interviews.

Marginal notes:

Conduct online research with extreme care; much of the information online has not been subjected to the same quality controls common in traditional offline publishing.

Web directories rely on human editors to evaluate and select websites.

Search engines, web directories, databases, and metacrawlers work in different ways, and you can get unpredictable results if you don't know how each one operates.

Proper documentation of the sources you use is both ethical and an important resource for your readers.

Surveys and interviews are the most common primary research techniques.

Conducting Surveys   A carefully prepared and conducted survey can provide invaluable insights, but only if it is *reliable* (would produce identical results if repeated) and *valid* (measures what it's supposed to measure). For important surveys, consider hiring a research specialist to avoid errors in design and implementation. To develop an effective survey questionnaire, follow these tips:[8]

> *For a survey to produce valid results, it must be based on a representative sample of respondents.*

- Provide clear instructions to make sure people can answer every question correctly.
- Don't ask for information that people can't be expected to remember, such as how many times they went grocery shopping in the past year.
- Keep the questionnaire short and easy to answer; don't expect people to give you more than 10 or 15 minutes of their time.
- Whenever possible, formulate questions to provide answers that are easy to analyze. Numbers and facts are easier to summarize than opinions, for instance.
- Avoid *leading questions* that could bias your survey. If you ask, "Do you prefer that we stay open in the evenings for customer convenience?" you'll no doubt get a "yes." Instead, ask, "What time of day do you normally do your shopping?"
- Avoid ambiguous descriptors such as "often" or "frequently." Such terms mean different things to different people.
- Avoid compound questions such as "Do you read books and magazines?"

> *Provide clear instructions to prevent mistaken answers.*

The Internet has become a preferred survey mechanism for many researchers, and dozens of companies now offer online survey services.[9] Compared to traditional mail and in-person techniques, online surveys are usually faster to create, easier to administer, quicker to analyze, and less expensive overall. However, online surveys require the same care as any other type of survey.[10]

Conducting Interviews   Like surveys, interviews require careful planning to get the best results. The answers you receive are influenced by the types of questions you ask and the way you ask them. Ask **open-ended questions** to invite an expert to offer opinions, insights, and information, such as "Why do you believe that South America represents a better opportunity than Europe for this product line?" Ask **closed questions** to elicit a specific answer, such as yes or no. Note that including too many closed questions in an interview makes the experience feel more like a simple survey and doesn't take full advantage of the interview setting.

> *Interviews are easy to conduct but require careful planning to produce useful results.*

Think carefully about the sequence of your questions and the potential answers so you can arrange them in an order that helps uncover layers of information. Also consider providing each subject with a list of questions at least a day or two before the interviews, especially if you'd like to quote your subjects in writing or if your questions might require people to conduct research or think extensively about the answers. If you want to record interviews, ask ahead of time; never record without permission.

> *Choose question types that will generate the specific information you need.*

Face-to-face interviews give you the opportunity to gauge reactions to your questions and observe the nonverbal signals that accompany the answers, but interviews don't necessarily have to take place in person. E-mail interviews are becoming more common, partly because they give subjects a chance to think through their responses thoroughly rather than rushing to fit the time constraints of a face-to-face interview.[11] Disadvantages of e-mail interviews include the inability to observe nonverbal signals and the extra messages required to follow up on answers or pursue new lines of questioning.

> *Face-to-face interviews give you the opportunity to gauge nonverbal responses.*

Using Your Research Results

After you've collected your data and information, the next step is to transform this raw material into the specific content you need. This step can involve quoting, paraphrasing, or summarizing textual material; drawing conclusions; and making recommendations.

> *After you collect data, the next step is to convert it into usable information.*

Quoting, Paraphrasing, and Summarizing Information

You can use textual information from secondary sources in three ways. *Quoting* a source means you reproduce the material exactly as you found it. Use direct quotations when the original language will enhance your argument or when rewording the passage would

> *Quoting a source means reproducing the content exactly and indicating who originally created the information.*

TABLE 10.1 Summarizing Effectively		
Original Material (116 Words)	**45-Word Summary**	**22-Word Summary**
Our facilities costs spiraled out of control last year. The 23 percent jump was far ahead of every other cost category in the company and many times higher than the 4 percent average rise for commercial real estate in the Portland metropolitan area. The rise can be attributed to many factors, but the major factors include repairs (mostly electrical and structural problems at the downtown office), energy (most of our offices are heated by electricity, the price of which has been increasing much faster than for oil or gas), and last but not least, the loss of two sublease tenants whose rent payments made a substantial dent in our cost profile for the past five years.	Our facilities costs jumped 23 percent last year, far ahead of every other cost category in the company and many times higher than the 4 percent local average. The major factors contributing to the increase are repairs, energy, and the loss of two sublease tenants.	Our facilities costs jumped 23 percent last year, due mainly to rising repair and energy costs and the loss of sublease income.

Main idea

Major support points

Details

reduce its impact. However, be careful with direct quotes: Using too many creates a choppy patchwork of varying styles and gives the impression that all you've done is piece together the work of other people. When quoting sources, set off shorter passages with quotation marks and set longer passages (generally, five lines or more) as separate, indented paragraphs.

You can often maximize the impact of secondary material in your own writing by *paraphrasing* it: restating it in your own words and with your own sentence structures.[12] Paraphrasing helps you maintain consistent tone while using vocabulary that's familiar to your audience. Of course, you still need to credit the originator of the information, but you don't need quotation marks or indented paragraphs.

Paraphrasing is expressing someone else's ideas in your own words.

Summarizing is similar to paraphrasing but presents the gist of the material in fewer words than the original by leaving out details, examples, and less-important information (see Table 10.1). Like quotations and paraphrases, summaries also require complete documentation of sources. Summarizing is not always a simple task, and your audience will judge your ability to separate significant issues from less significant details.

Summarizing is similar to paraphrasing but distills the content into fewer words.

Of course, all three approaches require careful attention to ethics. When quoting directly, take care not to distort the original intent of the material by quoting selectively or out of context. And never succumb to **plagiarism**—presenting someone else's words as your own.

Drawing Conclusions

A **conclusion** is a logical interpretation of facts and other information. In addition to being logically sound, a conclusion should be based only on the information provided or at least referred to in the report. Reaching good conclusions is one of the most important skills you can develop in your business career. In fact, the ability to see patterns and possibilities that others can't see is one of the hallmarks of innovative business leaders.

Making Recommendations

Whereas a conclusion interprets information, a **recommendation** suggests what to do about the information. The following example shows the difference between a conclusion and a recommendation:

Conclusion	**Recommendation**
On the basis of its track record and current price, I believe that this company is an attractive buy.	I recommend that we write a letter to the board of directors offering to buy the company at a 10 percent premium over the current market value of its stock.

To be credible, recommendations must be practical and based on sound logical analysis. Also, when making a recommendation, be certain that you have adequately described the recommended course of action so that readers aren't left wondering what happens next.

PLANNING INFORMATIONAL REPORTS

Informational reports provide the feedback that employees, managers, and others need in order to make decisions, take action, and respond to changes. As Figure 10.1 on page 233 indicates, informational reports can be grouped into four general categories:

Informational reports are used to monitor and control operations, to implement policies and procedures, to demonstrate compliance, and to document progress.

- **Reports to monitor and control operations.** Managers rely on a wide range of reports to see how well their companies are functioning. *Plans* establish expectations and guidelines to direct future action. The most important of these are *business plans*, which summarize a proposed business venture and describe the company's goals and plans for each major functional area. *Operating reports* provide feedback on a wide variety of an organization's functions, including sales, inventories, expenses, shipments, and so on. *Personal activity reports* provide information regarding an individual's experiences during sales calls, industry conferences, and other activities.

- **Reports to implement policies and procedures.** *Policy reports* range from brief descriptions of business procedures to manuals that run dozens or hundreds of pages. *Position papers* outline an organization's official position on issues that affect the company's success.

- **Reports to demonstrate compliance.** Businesses are required to submit a variety of *compliance reports*, from tax returns to reports describing the proper handling of hazardous materials.

- **Reports to document progress.** Supervisors, investors, and customers frequently expect to be informed of the progress of projects and other activities. *Progress reports* range from simple updates in memo form to comprehensive status reports.

Organizing Informational Reports

The messages conveyed by informational reports can range from extremely positive to extremely negative, so the approach you take warrants careful consideration.

In most cases, the direct approach is the best choice for informational reports because you are simply conveying information. However, if the information is disappointing, such as a project being behind schedule or over budget, you might consider using the indirect approach to build up to the bad news. Most informational reports use a **topical organization**, arranging material in one of the following ways (see Figure 10.5):

- **Comparison.** Showing similarities and differences (or advantages and disadvantages) between two or more entities
- **Importance.** Building up from the least important item to the most important (or from most important to the least, if you don't think your audience will read the entire report)
- **Sequence.** Organizing the steps or stages in a process or procedure
- **Chronology.** Organizing a chain of events in order from oldest to newest or vice versa
- **Geography.** Organizing by region, city, state, country, or other geographic unit
- **Category.** Grouping by topical category, such as sales, profit, cost, or investment

Organizing Website Content

Most of what you've already learned about informational reports applies to website writing, but the online environment requires some special considerations:

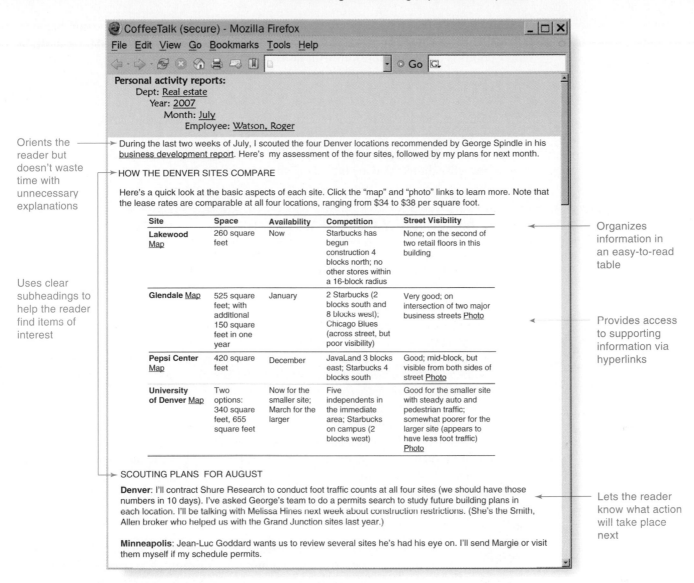

Orients the reader but doesn't waste time with unnecessary explanations

Uses clear subheadings to help the reader find items of interest

Organizes information in an easy-to-read table

Provides access to supporting information via hyperlinks

Lets the reader know what action will take place next

Figure 10.5 Effective Informational Report
Roger Watson's personal activity report for July is a good example of a report that efficiently conveys key information points. Note the use of hyperlinks to maps, photos, and a related report, all of which are stored on the same secure intranet site.

- **Web readers are demanding.** If they can't find what they're looking for in a few minutes, most site visitors will click away to another site.[13]

- **Reading online can be difficult.** Studies show that reading speeds are about 25 percent slower on a monitor than on paper.[14] Reading from computer screens can also be exhausting and a source of physical discomfort.[15]

- **The web is a nonlinear, multidimensional medium.** Readers of online material move around in any order they please; there often is no beginning, middle, or end.

When planning online reports or other website content, remember that the online reading experience differs from offline reading in several important ways.

In addition, many websites have to perform more than one communication function and therefore have more than one purpose. Each of these individual purposes needs to be carefully defined and then integrated into an overall statement of purpose for the entire website.[16]

Moreover, many websites also have multiple target audiences, such as potential employees, customers, investors, and the news media. You need to analyze each group's unique information needs and find a logical way to organize all that material. Website designers use the term **information architecture** to describe the structure and navigational

The information architecture of a website is the equivalent of an outline for a paper report.

flow of all the parts of a website. As you develop the site architecture, you can begin to simulate how various audiences will enter and explore the site. Accommodating multiple entry points is one of the most difficult tasks in site design.[17]

To organize your site effectively, keep the following advice in mind:

- Plan your site structure and navigation before you write.[18]
- Let your readers be in control by creating links and pathways that let them explore on their own.
- Help online readers scan and absorb information by breaking it into self-contained, easily readable chunks that are linked together logically.

PLANNING ANALYTICAL REPORTS

The purpose of analytical reports is to analyze, to understand, or to explain—to think through a problem or an opportunity and explain how it affects the company and how the company should respond. As you also saw in Figure 10.1, analytical reports fall into three basic categories:

Analytical reports are used to assess opportunities, solve problems, and support decisions.

- **Reports to assess opportunities.** Every business opportunity carries some degree of risk and requires a variety of decisions and actions in order to capitalize on the opportunity. You can use analytical reports to assess both risk and required decisions and actions. For instance, *market analysis reports* are used to judge the likelihood of success for new products or sales. *Due diligence reports* examine the financial aspects of a proposed decision, such as acquiring another company.
- **Reports to solve problems.** Managers often assign *troubleshooting reports* when they need to understand why something isn't working properly and how to fix it. A variation, the *failure analysis report*, studies events that happened in the past, with the hope of learning how to avoid similar failures in the future.
- **Reports to support decisions.** *Feasibility reports* explore the potential ramifications of a decision that managers are considering, and *justification reports* explain a decision that has already been made.

Writing analytical reports presents a greater challenge than writing informational reports, for three reasons. First, you're doing more than simply delivering information—you're also analyzing a situation and presenting your conclusions. Second, when your analysis is complete, you need to present your thinking in a compelling and persuasive manner. Third, analytical reports often convince other people to make significant financial and personnel decisions, and these reports carry the added responsibility of the consequences of such decisions.

Focusing on Conclusions

Focusing on conclusions is often the best approach when you're addressing a receptive audience.

When writing for audiences that are likely to accept your conclusions—either because they've asked you to perform an analysis or they trust your judgment—consider using the direct approach, focusing immediately on your conclusions. This structure communicates the main idea quickly, but it does present some risks. Even if audiences trust your judgment, they may have questions about your data or the methods you used. Moreover, starting with a conclusion may create the impression that you have oversimplified the situation. To give readers the opportunity to explore the thinking behind your conclusion, support that conclusion with solid reasoning and evidence (see Figure 10.6).

Focusing on Recommendations

When readers want to know what you think they should do, organize your report to focus on recommendations.

A slightly different approach is useful when your readers want to know what they ought to do in a given situation (as opposed to what they ought to conclude). The actions you want your readers to take become the main subdivisions of your report.

Opens with the conclusion that the program is a success

Supports the conclusion with evidence from two key areas

Completes the story by highlighting areas that still need improvement

MEASURING QUALITY IMPROVEMENTS

I. Introduction

II. Conclusion: Outsourcing employee training has reduced costs and improved quality

III. Cost reductions

    A. Exceeded 15 percent cost-reduction goal with 22 percent savings in first year

    B. Achieved actual reduction of 22 percent

    C. Reassigned three staffers who used to work on training full-time

    D. Reduced management time needed to oversee training

    E. Sold the computers that used to be reserved for training

IV. Quality improvements

    A. Employees say they are more confident in 7 out of 10 key skill areas

    B. Measurable mistakes have dropped by 12 percent

V. Areas needing improvement

    A. Three skill areas still need improvement

    B. Two trainers received approval ratings below 80 percent

    C. Outside trainers aren't always aware of internal company issues

    D. We have lost some flexibility for scheduling courses

VI. Summary

Figure 10.6   Preliminary Outline of a Research Report Focusing on Conclusions
Cynthia Zolonka works on the human resources staff of a bank in Houston, Texas. Her company decided to have an outside firm handle its employee training, and a year after the outsourcing arrangement was established, Zolonka was asked to evaluate the results. Her analysis shows that the outsourcing experiment was a success, and she opens with that conclusion and then supports it with clear evidence. Readers who accept the conclusion can stop reading, and those who desire more information can continue.

When structuring a report around recommendations, use the direct approach, as you would for a report that focuses on conclusions. Then unfold your recommendations using a series of five steps:

1. Establish the need for action in the introduction by briefly describing the problem or opportunity.
2. Introduce the benefit(s) that can be achieved if the recommendation is adopted, along with any potential risks.
3. List the steps (recommendations) required to achieve the benefit, using action verbs for emphasis.
4. Explain each step more fully, giving details on procedures, costs, and benefits; if necessary, also explain how risks can be minimized.
5. Summarize your recommendations.

Focusing on Logical Arguments

When readers are potentially skeptical or hostile, consider using the indirect approach to logically build toward your conclusion or recommendation. If you guide readers along a rational path toward the answer, they are more likely to accept it when they encounter it. The two most common logical approaches are known as the 2 + 2 = 4 approach, in which you convince readers by demonstrating that everything adds up to your conclusion, and the yardstick approach, in which you use a number of criteria to decide which option to select from two or more possibilities (see Figure 10.7).

Logical arguments can follow two basic approaches: 2 + 2 = 4 (adding everything up) and the yardstick method (comparing ideas against a predetermined set of standards).

MEMO

TO:	Robert Mendoza, Vice President of Marketing
FROM:	Binh Phan, National Sales Manager
DATE:	September 14, 2009
SUBJECT:	Major accounts sales problems

BP

As you requested on August 20, this report outlines the results of my investigation into the recent slowdown in sales to major accounts and the accompanying rise in sales- and service-related complaints from some of our largest customers.

Over the last four quarters, major account sales dropped 12%, whereas overall sales were up 7%. During the same time, we've all noticed an increase in both formal and informal complaints from larger customers, regarding how confusing and complicated it has become to do business with us.

My investigation started with in-depth discussions with the four regional sales managers, first as a group and then individually. The tension I felt in the initial meeting eventually bubbled to the surface during my meetings with each manager. Staff members in each region are convinced that other regions are booking orders they don't deserve, with one region doing all the legwork only to see another region get the sale, the commission, and the quota credit.

I followed up these formal discussions by talking informally and exchanging e-mail with several sales representatives from each region. Virtually everyone who is involved with our major national accounts has a story to share. No one is happy with the situation, and I sense that some reps are walking away from major customers because the process is so frustrating.

The decline in sales to our major national customers and the increase in their complaints stem from two problems: (1) sales force organization and (2) commission policy.

ORGANIZATIONAL PROBLEMS

When we divided the national sales force into four geographical regions last year, the idea was to focus our sales efforts and clarify responsibilities for each prospective and current customer. The regional managers have gotten to know their market territories very well, and sales have increased beyond even our most optimistic projections.

However, while solving one problem, we have created another. In the past 12 to 18 months, several regional customers have grown to national status, and a few retailers have taken on (or expressed interest in) our products. As a result, a significant portion of both current sales and future opportunities lies with these large national accounts.

I uncovered more than a dozen cases in which sales representatives from two or more regions found themselves competing with each other by pursuing the same customers from different locations. Moreover, the complaints from our major accounts about overlapping or nonexistent account coverage are a direct result of the regional organization. In some cases, customers aren't sure which of our representatives they're supposed to call with problems and orders. In other cases, no one has been in contact with them for several months.

Clarifies who requested the report, when it was requested, and who wrote it

Explains how the information used in the analysis was collected

Describes the first problem and explains how it occurred, without blaming anyone personally

Highlights the serious nature of the problem

Organizational problems are the first "2" in Phan's 2 + 2 = 4 approach

(continued)

Figure 10.7   Analytical Report Focusing on Logical Arguments
As national sales manager of a New Hampshire sporting goods company, Binh Phan was concerned about his company's ability to sell to its largest customers. His boss, the vice president of marketing, shared these concerns and asked Phan to analyze the situation and recommend a solution. In this troubleshooting report, his main idea is that the company should establish separate sales teams for these major accounts rather than continue to service them through the company's four regional divisions. However, Phan knew his plan would be controversial because it required a big change in the company's organization and in the way sales reps are paid. His thinking had to be clear and easy to follow, so he focused on logical argumentation.

PLANNING PROPOSALS

The specific formats for proposals are innumerable, but they can be grouped into two general categories. *Internal proposals* (see Figure 10.8) request decisions from managers within the organization. *External proposals* request decisions from parties outside the organization. For example, *investment proposals* request funding from outside investors, *grant proposals* request funds from government agencies and other sponsoring organizations, and *sales proposals* present solutions for potential customers and request purchase decisions.

2

Brings the first problem to life by complementing the general description with a specific example

For example, having retail outlets across the lower tier of the country, AmeriSport received pitches from reps out of our West, South, and East regions. Because our regional offices have a lot of negotiating freedom, the three were offering different prices. But all AmeriSport buying decisions were made at the Tampa headquarters, so all we did was confuse the customer. The irony of the current organization is that we're often giving our weakest selling and support efforts to the largest customers in the country.

COMMISSION PROBLEMS

Commission problems are the second "2" in Phan's 2 + 2 = 4 approach

The regional organization problems are compounded by the way we assign commissions and quota credit. Salespeople in one region can invest a lot of time in pursuing a sale, only to have the customer place the order in another region. So some sales rep in the second region ends up with the commission on a sale that was partly or even entirely earned by someone in the first region. Therefore, sales reps sometimes don't pursue leads in their regions, thinking that a rep in another region will get the commission.

Simplifies the reader's task by maintaining a parallel structure for the discussion of the second problem: a general description followed by a specific example

For example, Athletic Express, with outlets in 35 states spread across all four regions, finally got so frustrated with us that the company president called our headquarters. Athletic Express has been trying to place a large order for tennis and golf accessories, but none of our local reps seem interested in paying attention. I spoke with the rep responsible for Nashville, where the company is headquartered, and asked her why she wasn't working the account more actively. Her explanation was that last time she got involved with Athletic Express, the order was actually placed from its L.A. regional office, and she didn't get any commission after more than two weeks of selling time.

RECOMMENDATIONS

Phan concludes the 2 + 2 = 4 approach: organizational problems + commission problems = the need for a new sales structure

Our sales organization should reflect the nature of our customer base. To accomplish that goal, we need a group of reps who are free to pursue accounts across regional borders—and who are compensated fairly for their work. The most sensible answer is to establish a national account group. Any customers whose operations place them in more than one region would automatically be assigned to the national group.

Explains how the new organizational structure will solve both problems

Acknowledges that the recommended solution does create a temporary compensation problem, but expresses confidence that a solution to that can be worked out

In addition to solving the problem of competing sales efforts, the new structure will also largely eliminate the commission-splitting problem because regional reps will no longer invest time in prospects assigned to the national accounts team. However, we will need to find a fair way to compensate regional reps who are losing long-term customers to the national team. Some of these reps have invested years in developing customer relationships that will continue to yield sales well into the future, and everyone I talked to agrees that reps in these cases should receive some sort of compensation. Such a "transition commission" would also motivate the regional reps to help ensure a smooth transition from one sales group to the other. The exact nature of this compensation would need to be worked out with the various sales managers.

3

SUMMARY

Neatly summarizes both the problem and the recommended solution

The regional sales organization is effective at the regional and local levels but not at the national level. We should establish a national accounts group to handle sales that cross regional boundaries. Then we'll have one set of reps who are focused on the local and regional levels and another set who are pursuing national accounts.

To compensate regional reps who lose accounts to the national team, we will need to devise some sort of payment to reward them for the years of work invested in such accounts. This can be discussed with the sales managers once the new structure is in place.

Figure 10.7   Continued

The most significant factor in planning a proposal is whether the recipient has asked you to submit a proposal. *Solicited proposals* are generally prepared at the request of external parties that require a product or a service, but they may also be requested by such internal sources as management or the board of directors. Some organizations prepare a formal invitation to bid on their contracts, called a **request for proposals (RFP)**, which includes instructions that specify exactly the type of work to be performed or products to be delivered, along with budgets, deadlines, and other requirements. Other companies then respond

Organizations solicit proposals by publishing a request for proposals (RFP).

MEMO

TO: Jamie Engle
FROM: Shandel Cohen   SC
DATE: July 8, 2009
SUBJECT: Saving $145k/year with an automated e-mail response system

THE PROBLEM:
Expensive and Slow Response to Customer Information Requests

Our new product line has been very well received, and orders have surpassed our projections. This very success, however, has created a shortage of printed brochures, as well as considerable overtime for people in the customer response center. As we introduce upgrades and new options, our printed materials quickly become outdated. If we continue to rely on printed materials for customer information, we have two choices: Distribute existing materials (even though they are incomplete or inaccurate) or discard existing materials and print new ones.

THE SOLUTION:
Automated E-Mail Response System

With minor additions and modifications to our current e-mail system, we can set up an automated system to respond to customer requests for information. This system can save us time and money and can keep our distributed information current.

Automated e-mail response systems have been tested and proven effective. Many companies already use this method to respond to customer information requests, so we won't have to worry about relying on untested technology. Using the system is easy, too: Customers simply send a blank e-mail message to a specific address, and the system responds by sending an electronic copy of the requested brochure.

Benefit #1: Always-Current Information

Rather than discard and print new materials, we would only need to keep the electronic files up to date on the server. We could be able to provide customers and our field sales organization with up-to-date, correct information as soon as the upgrades or options are available.

Benefit #2: Instantaneous Delivery

Almost immediately after requesting information, customers would have that information in hand. Electronic delivery would be especially advantageous for our international customers. Regular mail to remote locations sometimes takes weeks to arrive, by which time the information may already be out of date. Both customers and field salespeople will appreciate the automatic mail-response system.

Benefit #3: Minimized Waste

With our current method of printing every marketing piece in large quantities, we discard thousands of pages of obsolete catalogs, data sheets, and other materials every year. By maintaining and distributing the information electronically, we would eliminate this waste. We would also free up a considerable amount of expensive floor space and shelving that is required for storing printed materials.

(continued)

Catches the reader's attention with a compelling promise in subject line

Describes the current situation and explains why it should be fixed

Explains the proposed solution in enough detail to make it convincing, without burdening the reader with excessive detail

Builds reader interest in the proposed solution by listing a number of compelling benefits

Figure 10.8   Internal Proposal
Shandel Cohen's internal proposal seeks management's approval to install an automatic mail-response system. Because the company manufactures computers, Cohen knows that her boss won't object to a computer-based solution. Also, because profits are always a concern, her report emphasizes the financial benefits of her proposal. Her report describes the problem, her proposed solutions, the benefits to the company, and the projected costs.

by preparing proposals that show how they would meet those needs. In most cases, organizations that issue RFPs also provide strict guidelines on what the proposals should include, and you need to follow these guidelines carefully in order to be considered. RFPs can seem surprisingly picky, even to the point of specifying the size of paper to use, but you must follow every detail.

Unsolicited proposals offer more flexibility but a completely different sort of challenge because recipients aren't expecting to receive them. In fact, your audience may not be aware of the problem or opportunity you are addressing, so before you can propose a solution, you

2

Of course, some of our customers may still prefer to receive printed materials, or they may not have access to electronic mail. For these customers, we could simply print copies of the files when we receive such requests. The new Xerox DocuColor printer just installed in the Central Services building would be ideal for printing high-quality materials in small quantities.

Benefit #4: Lower Overtime Costs

Acknowledges one potential shortcoming with the new approach but provides a convincing solution to that as well →

In addition to saving both paper and space, we would also realize considerable savings in wages. Because of the increased interest in our new products, we must continue to work overtime or hire new people to meet the demand. An automatic mail-response system would eliminate this need, allowing us to deal with fluctuating interest without a fluctuating workforce.

Cost Analysis

The necessary equipment and software costs approximately $15,000. System maintenance and upgrades are estimated at $5,000 per year. However, those costs are offset many times over by the predicted annual savings:

Itemizes the cost savings in order to support the $145k/year claim made in the subject line →

Printing	$100,000
Storage	25,000
Postage	5,000
Wages	20,000
Total	$150,000

Based on these figures, the system would save $130,000 the first year and $145,000 every year after that.

CONCLUSION

Summarizes the benefits and invites further discussion →

An automated e-mail response system would yield considerable benefits in both customer satisfaction and operating costs. If you approve, we can have it installed and running in 6 weeks. Please give me a call if you have any questions.

Figure 10.8   Continued

might first need to convince your readers that a problem or an opportunity exists. Consequently, the indirect approach is often the wise choice for unsolicited proposals.

Regardless of its format and structure, a good proposal explains what a project or course of action will involve, how much it will cost, and how the recipient and his or her organization will benefit. ■

DOCUMENT MAKEOVER

Improve This Report

To practice correcting drafts of actual documents, visit the "Document Makeovers" section in either MyBCommLab.com or the Companion Website for this text.

If MyBCommLab.com is being used in your class, see your User Guide for specific instructions on how to access the content for this chapter.

If you are accessing this feature through the Companion Website, click on "Document Makeovers" and then select Chapter 10. You will find a personal activity report that contains problems and errors related to what you've learned in this chapter about planning business reports and proposals. Use the Final Draft decision tool to create an improved version of this personal activity report. Check the report for parallel construction, appropriate headings, suitable content, positive and bias-free language, and use of the "you" attitude. ●

❝ CHAPTER REVIEW AND ACTIVITIES

Chapter Summary

To adapt the three-step process to reports and proposals, apply what you learned in Chapters 3 through 5, with particular emphasis on clearly identifying your purpose, preparing a work plan, determining whether a separate research project might be needed, choosing the medium, and selecting the best approach for the specific type of report.

Informational reports focus on the delivery of facts, figures, and other types of information. Analytical reports assess a situation or problem and recommend a course of action in response. Proposals offer a solution to a problem or opportunity.

When developing online reports and websites in general, start by planning the structure and navigation paths before writing the content. Next, make sure you let readers be in control by giving them navigational flexibility. Finally, break your information in chunks that can be scanned and absorbed quickly.

Begin the research process with careful planning to make sure you focus on the most important questions. Then locate the data and information, using primary and secondary research as needed. Process the results of your research and apply your findings by summarizing information, drawing conclusions, or developing recommendations. Finally, manage information effectively so that you and others can retrieve it later and reuse it in other projects.

Primary research is research that is being conducted for the first time, whereas secondary research involves information that was originally gathered for another project or by other sources. Secondary research is generally used first, both to save time in case someone else has already gathered the information needed and to offer additional insights into your research questions.

Information should come from a reliable, unbiased source. The purpose of the material should be known, and the author should be credible. The information should include references to sources (if obtained elsewhere), and it should be independently verifiable. Finally, the material should be current, complete, and logical.

The three most common ways to organize analytical reports are by focusing on conclusions, focusing on recommendations, and focusing on logical arguments.

Test Your Knowledge

1. How are reports for monitoring and controlling operations used?

2. How does primary research differ from secondary research?

3. What makes a survey reliable and valid?

4. How does a conclusion differ from a recommendation?

5. How do proposal writers use an RFP?

Apply Your Knowledge

1. Why must you be careful when using information from the Internet in a business report?

2. Can you use the same approach for planning website content as you use for planning printed reports? Why or why not?

3. If you were writing a recommendation report for an audience that doesn't know you, would you use the direct approach, focusing on the recommendation, or the indirect approach, focusing on logic? Why?

4. Why are unsolicited proposals more challenging to write than solicited proposals?

5. Ethical Choices Companies occasionally make mistakes that expose confidential information, such as when employees lose laptop computers containing sensitive data files or webmasters forget to protect confidential webpages from search engine indexes. If you conducted an online search that turned up competitive information on webpages that were clearly intended to be private, what would you do? Explain your answer.

Practice Your Knowledge

Activities

Active links for all websites in this chapter can be found online. If MyBCommLab.com is being used in your class, see your User Guide for instructions on accessing the content for this chapter. Otherwise, visit www.pearsonhighered.com/bovee, locate *Business Communication Essentials*, Fourth Edition, click the Companion Website link, select Chapter 10, and then click on "Featured Websites." Please note that links to sites that become inactive after publication of the book will be removed from the Featured Websites section.

1. Analyze This Message The Securities and Exchange Commission (SEC) requires all public companies to file a comprehensive annual report (form 10-K) electronically. Many companies post links to these reports on their websites, along with links to other company reports. Visit Dell's website, at www.dell.com, and find the company's most recent annual reports: 10-K and Year in Review (under "About Dell" on the homepage, click on the "Investor Relations" link). Compare the style and format of the two reports. For which audience(s) is the Year in Review targeted? Who besides the SEC might be interested in form 10-K? Which report do you find easier to read? More interesting? More detailed?

2. Finding Information: Surveys You work for a movie studio that is producing a young director's first motion picture, the story of a group of unknown musicians finding work and making a reputation in a competitive industry. Unfortunately, some of your friends leave the screening saying that the 182-minute movie is simply too long. Others say they can't imagine any sequences to cut out. Your boss wants to test the movie on a typical audience and ask viewers to complete a questionnaire that will help the director decide whether edits are needed and, if so, where. Design a questionnaire that you can use to solicit valid answers for a report to the director about how to handle the audience's reaction to the movie.

3. Internet Read the step-by-step hints and examples for writing a funding proposal at www.learnerassociates.net/proposal. Review the entire sample proposal online. What details did the writer decide to include in the appendixes? Why was this material placed in the appendixes and not the main body of the report? According to the writer's tips, when is the best time to prepare a project overview?

4. Informational Reports: Policy Report You're the vice president of operations for a Florida fast-food chain. In the aftermath of a major hurricane, you're drafting a report on the emergency procedures to be followed by personnel in each restaurant when storm warnings are in effect. Answer who, what, when, where, why, and how and then prepare a one-page outline of your report. Make up any details you need.

5. Teamwork: Planning an Unsolicited Proposal Break into small groups and identify an operational problem occurring at your campus—perhaps involving registration, university housing, food services, parking, or library services. Then develop a workable solution to that problem. Finally, develop a list of pertinent facts that your team will need to gather to convince readers that the problem exists and that your solution will work.

6. Preparing the Work Plan South by Southwest (SXSW) is a family of conferences and festivals in Austin, Texas, that showcase some of the world's most creative talents in music, interactive media, and film. In addition to being a major entertainment venue for a week every March, SXSW is also an increasingly important *trade show*, an opportunity for companies to present products and services to potential customers and business partners. You work for a company that makes music training equipment, such as an electronic keyboard with an integrated computer screen that guides learners through every step of learning to play the keyboard. Your manager has asked you to look into whether the company should rent an exhibition booth at SXSW next year. Prepare a work plan for an analytical report that will assess the promotional opportunities at SXSW and make a recommendation on exhibiting. Include the statement of purpose, a problem statement for any research you will conduct, a description of what will result from your investigation, the sources and methods of data collection, and a preliminary outline. Visit the SXSW website, at http://sxsw.com, for more information.[19]

7. **Finding Secondary Information**   Using online, database, or printed sources, find the following information. Be sure to properly cite your sources, using the formats discussed in Appendix B.

   a. Contact information for the American Management Association

   b. Median weekly earnings of men and women by occupation

   c. Current market share for Perrier water

   d. Performance ratios for office supply retailers

   e. Annual stock performance for Hewlett-Packard (HP)

   f. Number of franchise outlets in the United States

   g. Composition of the U.S. workforce by profession

8. **Finding Information: Company Information**   Select any public company and find the following information.

   a. Names of the company's current officers

   b. List of the company's products or services (or, if the company has a large number of products, the product lines or divisions)

   c. Some important current issues in the company's industry

   d. The outlook for the company's industry as a whole

9. **Finding Information: Interviews**   You're conducting an information interview with a manager in another division of your company. Partway through the interview, the manager shows clear signs of impatience. How should you respond? What might you do differently to prevent this from happening in the future? Explain your answers.

10. **Processing Information: Documenting Sources**   Select five business articles from sources such as journals, books, newspapers, or websites. Develop a resource list, using Appendix B as a guideline.

11. **Organizing Reports: Deciding on Format**   Go to the library or visit www.annualreport service.com and review the annual reports recently released by two corporations in the same industry. Analyze each report and be prepared to discuss the following questions in class.

   a. What organizational differences, if any, do you see in the way each corporation discusses its annual performance? Are the data presented clearly so that shareholders can draw conclusions about how well the company performed?

   b. What goals, challenges, and plans do top managers emphasize in their discussion of results?

   c. How do the format and organization of each report enhance or detract from the information being presented?

12. **Organizing Reports: Choosing the Direct or Indirect Approach**   Of the organizational approaches introduced in the chapter, which is best suited for writing a report that answers the following questions? Briefly explain why.

   a. In which market segment—energy drinks or traditional soft drinks—should Fizz Drinks, Inc., introduce a new drink to take advantage of its enlarged research and development budget?

b. Should Major Manufacturing, Inc., close down operations of its antiquated Bellville, Arkansas, plant despite the adverse economic impact on the town that has grown up around the plant?

c. Should you and your partner adopt a new accounting method to make your financial statements look better to potential investors?

d. Should Grand Canyon Chemicals buy disposable test tubes to reduce labor costs associated with cleaning and sterilizing reusable test tubes?

e. What are some reasons for the recent data loss at the college computer center, and how can we avoid similar problems in the future?

13. **Teamwork: Report Structure** You and a classmate are helping Linda Moreno prepare her report on Electrovision's travel and entertainment costs (see pages 279–292). This time, however, the report is to be informational rather than analytical, so it will not include recommendations. Review the existing report and determine what changes would be needed to make it an informational report. Be as specific as possible. For example, if your team decides the report needs a new title, what title would you use? Draft a transmittal memo for Moreno to use in conveying this informational report to Dennis McWilliams, Electrovision's vice president of operations.

14. **Organizing Reports: Structuring Informational Reports** Assume that your college president has received many student complaints about campus parking problems. You are appointed to chair a student committee organized to investigate the problems and recommend solutions. The president gives you a file labeled "Parking: Complaints from Students," and you jot down the essence of the complaints as you inspect the contents. Your notes look like this:

- Inadequate student spaces at critical hours
- Poor night lighting near the computer center
- Inadequate attempts to keep resident neighbors from occupying spaces
- Dim marking lines
- Motorcycles taking up full spaces
- Discourteous security officers
- Spaces (usually empty) reserved for college officials
- Relatively high parking fees
- Full fees charged to night students even though they use the lots only during low demand periods
- Vandalism to cars and a sense of personal danger
- Inadequate total space
- Harassment of students parking on the street in front of neighboring house

Now prepare an outline for an informational report to be submitted to committee members. Use a topical organization for your report that categorizes this information.

Expand Your Knowledge

Exploring the Best of the Web

The Library That Never Closes Start your business research by visiting the Internet Public Library, at **www.ipl.org**. Visit the reference center and explore the many online references available. These cover topics such as business, economics, law, government, science, technology, computers, education, and more. You can even submit questions for the IPL staff. Explore the site to perform these tasks.

Exercises

1. Click on "Ready Reference" (left side of the page) and follow some of the reference links. How might these links help you when performing business research?

2. Click on "Business" under "Subject Collections" and locate the "Consumer Issues & Services" subheading. Find three sites that help consumers make better-informed decisions.

3. Click on "Business," find "Business Directories," and use one of the sites listed to select five companies. Find contact information (address, phone, website, officers' names, and so on) for each company. What kinds of contact information did you find at the company websites?

Surfing Your Way to Career Success

Bovée and Thill's Business Communication Headline News offers links to hundreds of online resources that can help you with this course, your other college courses, and your career. Visit http://businesscommunicationblog.com and click on "Web Directory." The Research section connects you to a variety of websites and articles on such important topics as using research tools, analyzing and evaluating research materials, checking facts, interviewing, and using online research tools. Identify three websites from this section that could be useful in your business career. For each site, write a two-sentence summary of what the site offers and how it could help you launch and build your career.

MyBCommLab.com ....

Use MyBCommLab.com to test your understanding of the concepts presented in this chapter and explore additional materials that will bring the ideas to life in video, activities, and an online multimedia e-book. Additionally, you can improve your skill with periods, question marks, and other punctuation by using the "Peak Performance Grammar and Mechanics" module within the lab. Take the Pretest to determine whether you have any weak areas. Then review those areas in the Refresher Course. Take the Follow-Up Test to check your grasp of periods, question marks, and other punctuation. For an extra challenge, take the Advanced Test. Finally, for even more reinforcement, go to the "Improve Your Grammar, Mechanics, and Usage" section that follows the cases, and complete the "Level 1: Self-Assessment" exercises.

CASES

▼ *Apply the three-step writing process to the following cases, as assigned by your instructor.*

Informational Reports

1. My Progress to Date: Interim Progress Report on Your Academic Career As you may know, the paperwork involved in getting a degree or certificate is nearly as challenging as any course you could take.

Your task   Prepare an interim progress report that details the steps you've taken toward completing your graduation or certification requirements. After examining the requirements listed in your college catalog, indicate a realistic schedule for completing those that remain. In addition to course requirements, include steps such as completing the residency requirement, filing necessary papers, and paying necessary fees. Use a memo format for your report and address it to anyone who is helping or encouraging you through school.

2. Who Said What: Personal Activity Report of a Meeting Meetings, conferences, and conventions abound in the academic world, and you have probably attended your share.

Your task   Prepare a personal activity report on a meeting, convention, or conference that you recently attended. Use a memo format and direct the report to other students in your field who were not able to attend.

3. Check That Price Tag: Informational Report on Trends in College Costs Your college's administration has asked you to compare your college's tuition costs with those of a nearby college and determine which college's costs have risen more quickly. Research the trend by checking your college's annual tuition costs for each of the most recent four years. Then research the four-year tuition trends for a neighboring college. For both colleges, calculate the percentage change in tuition costs from year to year and between the first and fourth years.

Your task   Prepare an informal report (using the letter format) that presents your findings and conclusions to the president of your college. Include graphics to explain and support your conclusions.

4. Get a Move on It: Lasting Guidelines for Moving into College Dormitories Moving into a college dormitory is one experience you weren't quite prepared for. In addition to lugging all your earthly belongings up four flights of stairs in 90-degree heat, channeling electrical cords to the one room outlet tucked in the corner of the room, lofting your beds, and negotiating with your roommate over who gets the bigger closet, you had to hug your parents goodbye in the parking lot in front of the entire freshman class—or so it seemed. Now that you are a pro, you've offered to write some lasting guidelines for future freshmen so they know what is expected of them on moving day.

Your task   Prepare an informational report for future freshmen classes, outlining the rules and procedures to follow when moving into a college dorm. Lay out the rules, such as starting time, handling of trash and empty boxes, items permitted and not permitted in dorm rooms, common courtesies, parking, and so on. Be sure to mention what the policy is for removing furniture from the room, lofting beds, and overloading electrical circuits. Of course, any recommendations on how to handle disputes with roommates would be helpful. So would some brief advice on how to cope with anxious parents. Direct your memo report to the college dean.

Analytical Reports

5. My Next Career Move: Feasibility Report Organized Around Recommendations If you've ever given yourself a really good talking-to, you'll be quite comfortable with this project.

Your task Write a memo report directed to yourself and signed with a fictitious name. Indicate a possible job that your college education will qualify you for, mention the advantages of the position in terms of your long-range goals, and outline the actions you must take to get the job.

6. Staying the Course: Unsolicited Proposal Think of a course you would love to see added to the curriculum at your school. Conversely, if you would like to see a course offered as an elective rather than being required, write your e-mail report accordingly. Construct a sequence of logical reasons to support your choice. (This is the 2 + 2 = 4 approach mentioned in the chapter.)

Your task Plan and draft a short e-mail proposal to be submitted to the academic dean by e-mail. Be sure to include all the reasons supporting your idea.

7. Planning My Program: Problem-Solving Report Assume that you will have time for only one course next term. Identify the criteria you will use to decide which of several courses to take. (This is the yardstick approach mentioned in the chapter.)

Your task List the pros and cons of four or five courses that interest you and use the selection criteria you identified to choose the one course that is best for you to take at this time. Write your report in memo format, addressing it to your academic adviser.

8. Restaurant Review: Troubleshooting Report on a Restaurant's Food and Operations Visit any restaurant, possibly your school cafeteria. The workers and fellow customers will assume that you are an ordinary customer, but you are really a spy for the owner.

Your task After your visit, write a short letter to the owner explaining (a) what you did and what you observed, (b) any possible violations of policy that you observed, and (c) your recommendations for improvement. The first part of your report (what you did and what you observed) will be the longest. Include a description of the premises, inside and out. Tell how long it took for each step of ordering and receiving your meal. Describe the service and food thoroughly. You are interested in both the good and bad aspects of the establishment's décor, service, and food. For the second section (violations of policy), use some common sense: If all the servers but one have their hair covered, you may assume that policy requires hair to be covered; a dirty window or restroom obviously violates policy. The last section (recommendations for improvement) involves professional judgment. What management actions will improve the restaurant?

9. On the Books: Troubleshooting Report on Improving the Campus Bookstore Imagine that you are a consultant hired to improve the profits of your campus bookstore.

Your task Visit the bookstore and look critically at its operations. Then draft a letter to the bookstore manager, offering recommendations that would make the store more profitable, perhaps suggesting products it should carry, hours that it should remain open, or added services that it should make available to students. Be sure to support your recommendations.

10. Day and Night: Problem-Solving Report on a 24-Hour Convenience Store When a store is open all day, every day, when's the best time to restock the shelves? That's the challenge at Store 24, a retail chain that never closes. Imagine that you're the assistant manager of a Store 24 branch that just opened near your campus. You want to set up a restocking schedule that won't conflict with prime shopping hours. Think about the number of customers you're likely to serve in the morning, afternoon, evening, and overnight hours. Consider, too, how many employees you might have during these four periods.

Your task Write a problem-solving report in letter form to the store manager (Isabel Chu) and the regional manager (Eric Angstrom), who must agree on a solution to this problem. Discuss the pros and cons of each of the four periods and include your recommendation for restocking the shelves.

PORTFOLIO BUILDER

11. Building a New Magazine: Finding Opportunity in the Remodeling Craze Spurred in part by the success of such hit shows as *This Old House*, *Trading Spaces*, and *Sweat Equity*, homeowners across the country are redecorating, remodeling, and rebuilding. Many people are content with superficial changes, such as new paint or new accessories, but some are more ambitious. These homeowners want to move walls, add rooms, redesign kitchens, convert garages to home theaters—the big stuff.

Publishers try to create magazines that appeal to carefully identified groups of potential readers and the advertisers who'd like to reach them. The do-it-yourself (DIY) market is already served by numerous magazines, but you see an opportunity in the homeowners who tackle the heavy-duty projects. Tables 1 through 3 on the next page summarize the results of some preliminary research you asked your company's research staff to conduct.

TABLE 1   Rooms Most Frequently Remodeled by DIYers

Room	Percentage of Homeowners Surveyed Who Have Tackled or Plan to Tackle at Least a Partial Remodel
Kitchen	60
Bathroom	48
Home office/study	44
Bedroom	38
Media room/home theater	31
Den/recreation room	28
Living room	27
Dining room	12
Sun room/solarium	8

TABLE 2   Average Amount Spent on Remodeling Projects

Estimated Amount	Percentage of Surveyed Homeowners
Under $5k	5
$5k–$10k	21
$10k–$20k	39
$20k–$50k	22
More than $50k	13

TABLE 3   Tasks Performed by Homeowner on a Typical Remodeling Project

Task	Percentage of Surveyed Homeowners Who Perform or Plan to Perform Most or All of This Task Themselves
Conceptual design	90
Technical design/architecture	34
Demolition	98
Foundation work	62
Framing	88
Plumbing	91
Electrical	55
Heating/cooling	22
Finish carpentry	85
Tile work	90
Painting	100
Interior design	52

Your task   You think the data show a real opportunity for a "big projects" DIY magazine, although you'll need more extensive research to confirm the size of the market and refine the editorial direction of the magazine. Prepare a brief analytical report that presents the data you have, identifies the opportunity or opportunities you've found (suggest your own ideas, based on the data in the tables), and requests funding from the editorial board to pursue further research.

Proposals

12. "Would You Carry It?" Unsolicited Sales Proposal Recommending a Product to a Retail Outlet   Select a product you are familiar with and imagine that you are the manufacturer, trying to get a local retail outlet to carry it. Use the Internet and other resources to gather information about the product.

Your task   Write an unsolicited sales proposal in letter format to the owner (or manager) of the store, proposing that the item be stocked. Use the information you gathered to describe some of the product's features and benefits. Then make up some reasonable figures, highlighting what the item costs, what it can be sold for, and what services your company provides (return of unsold items, free replacement of unsatisfactory items, necessary repairs, and so on).

[PORTFOLIO BUILDER]

13. Where Is Everybody? Proposal to Sell GPS Fleet Tracking System   You are a sales manager for Air-Trak, and one of your responsibilities is writing sales proposals for potential buyers of your company's Air-Trak tracking system. The system uses the global positioning system (GPS) to track the location of vehicles and other assets. For example, the dispatcher for a trucking company can simply click a map display on a computer screen to find out where all the company's trucks are at that instant. Air-Trak lists the following as benefits of the system:

- Making sure vehicles follow prescribed routes, with minimal loitering time
- "Geofencing," in which dispatchers are alerted if vehicles leave assigned routes or designated service areas
- Route optimization, in which fleet managers can analyze routes and destinations to find the most time- and fuel-efficient path for each vehicle
- Comparisons between scheduled and actual travel
- Enhanced security, protecting both drivers and cargos

Your task   Write a brief proposal to Doneta Zachs, fleet manager for Midwest Express, 338 S.W. 6th, Des Moines, Iowa, 50321. Introduce your company, explain the benefits of the Air-Trak system, and propose a trial deployment in which you would equip five Midwest Express trucks. For the purposes of this assignment, you don't need to worry about the technical details of the system; focus on promoting the benefits and asking for a decision regarding the test project. (You can learn more about the Air-Trak system at www. air-trak.com.)[20]

Improve Your Grammar, Mechanics, and Usage

Level 1: Self-Assessment—Dashes and Hyphens

Review Sections 2.7 and 2.8 in the Handbook of Grammar, Mechanics, and Usage and then complete the following 15 items.

In items 1–15, insert the required dashes (—) and hyphens (-).

1. Three qualities speed, accuracy, and reliability are desirable in any applicant to the data entry department.

2. A highly placed source explained the top secret negotiations.

3. The file on Marian Gephardt yes, we finally found it reveals a history of late payments.

4. They're selling a well designed machine.

5. A bottle green sports jacket is hard to find.

6. Argentina, Brazil, Mexico these are the countries we hope to concentrate on.

7. Only two sites maybe three offer the things we need.

8. How many owner operators are in the industry?

9. Your ever faithful assistant deserves without a doubt a substantial raise.

10. Myrna Talefiero is this organization's president elect.

11. Stealth, secrecy, and surprise those are the elements that will give us a competitive edge.

12. The charts are well placed on each page unlike the running heads and footers.

13. We got our small business loan an enormous advantage.

14. Ron Franklin do you remember him? will be in town Monday.

15. Your devil may care attitude affects everyone involved in the decision making process.

Level 2: Workplace Applications

The following items contain numerous errors in grammar, capitalization, punctuation, abbreviation, number style, word division, and vocabulary. Rewrite each sentence, correcting all errors. Write *C* for any sentence that is already correct.

1. Commerce One helps its customer's to more efficiently lower administrative costs, improve order times, and to manage contract negotiations.

2. The intermodal bus vehicle seats up to 35 passengers, but is equipped with a 20 feet standardized container in the rear. The same container one sees on ships, trains and on planes.

3. "The American Dream of innovation, persistence, and a refusal to except the status quo has just created, in our opinion, Americas newest and most exciting company to watch," said James Gaspard President of Neoplan USA.

4. This new, transportation paradigm may have a global affect and the barriers to entry will be extremely costly too overcome.

5. Autobytel also owns and operates Carsmart.com and Autosite.com as well as AIC Automotive Information Center] a provider of automotive marketing data and technology.

6. Mymarket.com offers a low cost high reward, entry into e-commerce not only for buyers but also suppliers.

7. Eclipse Aviation's main competitor are another start-up Safire Aircraft of west Palm Beach, Fl.

8. After identifying the factors that improve a industrial process, additional refining experiments must be conducted to confirm the results.

9. The fair labor standards Act regulates minimum wages, establishes overtime compensation, and it outlaws labor for children.

10. The Chinese government are supporting use of the Internet as a business tool because it is seen by it as necessary to enhance competitiveness.

11. At a certain point in a company's growth, the entrepreneur, who wants to control everything, can no longer keep up so they look mistakenly for a better manager and call that person a CEO.

12. City Fresh foods is paid by City health agencies to provide Ethnic food to the homebound "elderly" in the Boston Area.

13. Being in business since 1993, Miss Rosen has boiled down her life story into a 2-minute sound bight for sales prospects.

14. Anyone that wants to gain a new perspective on their product or service must cast aside one's own biases.

15. If I was Microsoft's Steve Ballmer, I'd handle the Federal government's antitrust lawsuit much different.

Level 3: Document Critique

The following document may contain errors in grammar, capitalization, punctuation, abbreviation, number style, vocabulary, and spelling. You may also find problems with organization, format, and word use. Correct all errors using standard proofreading marks (see Appendix C).

Memo

DATE	March 14 2009
TO	Jeff Black and HR staff
FROM:	Carrie andrews
SUBJECT:	Recruiting and hiring Seminar

As you all know the process of recruiting screening and hiring new employees might be a legal minefield. Because we don't have an inhouse lawyer to help us make every decision, its important for all of us to be aware of what actions are legally acceptible and what isn't. Last week I attended a American management Association seminar on this subject. I given enough useful information to warrant updating our online personnel handbook and perhaps developing a quick training session for all interviewing teams. First, heres a quick look at the things I learned.

Avoiding Legal Mistakes

- How to write recruiting ads that accurately portray job openings and not discriminate.
- Complying with the Americans with Disabilities Act
- How to use an employment agency effectively and safe (without risk of legal entanglements)

How to Screen and Interview More Effectively

- How to sort through résumés more efficient (including looking for telltale signs of false information)
- We can avoid interview questions that could get us into legal trouble
- When and how to check criminal records

Measuring Applicants

- Which type of preemployment tests have been proven most effective?
- Which drug-testing issues and recommendations effect us

as you can see the seminar addressed alot of important information. We covering the basic guidelines for much of this already; but a number of specific recommendations and legal concepts should be emphisized and underline.

It will take me a couple of weeks to get the personel handbook updated: but we don't have any immediate hiring plans anyway so that shouldn't be too much of a problem unless you think I should ocmplete it sooner and then we can talk about that.

I'll keep the seminar handouts and my notes on my desk in case you want to peruse them.

After the handbook is updated by me, we can get together and decide whether we need to train the interviewing team members.

Although we have a lot of new information, what people need to be aware of can be highlighted and the new sections can be read as schedules allow, although they might be reluctant to do this and we can also talk about that later, at a time of your conveinence that you can select later.

If you have any questions in the mean-time; don't hesitate to e-mail me or drop by for a chat.

Writing and Completing Reports and Proposals

[from the real world]

"It is easy to slip into unnatural corporate-speak, particularly when under pressure to communicate a complex issue quickly. This language is an immediate turn-off. Even if you have to explain a technical issue, don't forget you are communicating to fellow human beings."
—*Tania Menegatti,*
Senior consultant, CHA
www.chapr.co.uk

Focusing on the content of your longer business documents is not only natural but necessary because doing so helps ensure complete, correct information. However, once you have the technical content in place, you need to stand back and view the document from the perspective of your audience—the people you expect to read and act on the information. Is your message clear, compelling, and concise? Is it something a real, living, breathing person could be expected to read and understand? Remember Tania Menegatti's advice whenever you're writing and completing reports and proposals: Even with the most complex or technical documents, another human being is at the receiving end of your communication efforts.[1]

WRITING REPORTS AND PROPOSALS

This chapter builds on the writing techniques and ideas you learned in Chapter 4, addressing issues that are particularly important when preparing longer message formats. In addition, the chapter provides an introduction to creating effective visuals, which are a vital aspect of many reports and proposals.

Adapting to Your Audience

Long or complex reports demand a lot from readers, making the "you" attitude especially important in such writing.

You can adjust the formality of your writing through your word choices and writing style.

Reports and proposals can put heavy demands on your readers, so the "you" attitude is especially important with these long messages. Many companies have specific guidelines for communicating with public audiences, so make sure you're aware of these preferences before you start writing.

In general, try to strike a balance between overly informal (which can be perceived as trivializing important issues) and overly formal (which can put too much distance between writer and reader). If you know your readers reasonably well and your report is likely to meet with their approval, you can generally adopt an informal tone. To make your tone less formal, speak to readers in the first person, refer to them as *you*, and refer to yourself as *I* (or *we* if there are multiple report authors).

To make your tone more formal, use the impersonal journalism style: Emphasize objectivity, avoid personal opinions, and build your argument on provable facts. Eliminate all personal pronouns (including *I*, *you*, *we*, *us*, and *our*). Be careful to avoid jokes, similes, and metaphors, and try to minimize the use of colorful adjectives or adverbs.

Take into account that communicating with people in other cultures often calls for more formality in reports, both to respect cultural preferences and to reduce the risk of miscommunication. Informal elements such as humor and casual language tend to translate poorly from one culture to another.

Composing Reports and Proposals

When you compose reports and proposals, follow the writing advice offered in Chapter 4: Select the best words, create the most effective sentences, and develop coherent paragraphs. Like other written business communications, reports and proposals have three main sections: an introduction (or *opening*), a body, and a close.

An effective *introduction* accomplishes at least four tasks:

- It puts the report or proposal in context by tying it to a problem or an assignment.
- It introduces the subject or purpose of the report or proposal and indicates why the subject is important.
- It previews the main ideas and the order in which they'll be covered.
- It establishes the tone of the document and the writer's relationship with the audience.

The introduction needs to put the report in context for the reader, introduce the subject, preview main ideas, and establish the tone of the document.

The *body* presents, analyzes, and interprets the information gathered during your investigation and supports your recommendations or conclusions (see Figure 11.1).

The *close* is the final section in the text of your report or proposal. It has four important functions:

The body of your report presents, analyzes, and interprets the information you gathered during your investigation.

- It emphasizes your main points.
- It summarizes the benefits to the reader if the document suggests a change or some other course of action.
- It refers to all the pieces and reminds readers how those pieces fit together.
- It brings all the action items together in one place.

The close gives you one last chance to make sure that your report says what you intended, so make sure it carries a strong, clear message.[2]

Your close is often the last opportunity to get your message across, so make it clear and compelling.

Drafting Report Content

Your credibility and career advancement are on the line with every business report you write, so make sure your content is

- **Accurate.** If readers suspect that your information is shaky, they'll start to view all your work with skepticism.
- **Complete.** Include everything necessary for readers to understand the situation, problem, or proposal. Support all key assertions, using an appropriate combination of examples, explanations, and facts.[3]
- **Balanced.** Present all sides of the issue fairly and equitably and include all the essential information, even if some of the information doesn't support your line of reasoning.
- **Clear and logical.** Reports often contain large amounts of information and involved reasoning, so make sure your writing is easy to follow.
- **Documented properly.** Properly document and give credit to your sources.

Report Introduction The specific elements to include in an introduction depend on the nature and length of the report, the circumstances under which you're writing it, and your relationship with the audience. Choose from these elements for each report:

Keep the introduction as brief as possible while providing enough information to help readers use the report effectively.

- **Authorization.** When, how, and by whom the report was authorized; who wrote it; and when it was submitted.

MEMO

TO: Board of Directors, Executive Committee members
FROM: Alycia Jenn, Business Development Manager
DATE: July 7, 2009
SUBJECT: Website expansion

Reminds readers of the origin and purpose of the report

In response to your request, my staff and I investigated the potential for expanding our website from its current "brochureware" status (in which we promote our company and its products but don't provide any way to place orders online) to full e-commerce capability (including placing orders and checking on order delivery status). After analyzing the behavior of our customers and major competitors and studying the overall development of electronic retailing, we have three recommendations:

1. We should expand our online presence from "brochureware" to e-commerce capability within the next 6 months.

2. We should engage a firm that specializes in online retailing to design and develop the new e-commerce capabilities.

3. We must take care to integrate online retailing with our store-based and mail-order operations.

Clarifies the recommendation by listing the necessary actions in clear, direct language

1. WE SHOULD EXPAND THE WEBSITE TO FULL E-COMMERCE CAPABILITY

Presents logical reasons for recommending that the firm expand its website to include e-commerce

First, does e-commerce capability make sense today for a small company that sells luxury housewares? Even though books and many other products are now commonly sold online, in most cases, this enterprise involves simple, low-cost products that don't require a lot of hands-on inspection before purchasing. As we've observed in our stores, shoppers like to interact with our products before purchasing them. However, a small but growing number of websites do sell specialty products, using such tactics as "virtual product tours" (in which shoppers can interactively view a product in three dimensions, rather than simply looking at a static photograph) and generous return policies (to reduce the perceived risk of buying products online).

Second, do we need to establish a presence now in order to remain competitive in the future? The answer is an overwhelming "yes." The initial steps taken by our competitors are already placing us at a disadvantage among those shoppers who are already comfortable buying online, and every trend indicates our minor competitive weakness today will turn into a major weakness in the next few years:

• Several of our top competitors are beginning to implement full e-commerce, including virtual product tours. Our research suggests that these companies aren't yet generating significant financial returns from these online investments, but their online sales are growing.

• Younger consumers who grew up with the World Wide Web will soon be reaching their peak earning years (ages 35–54). This demographic segment expects e-commerce in nearly every product category, and we'll lose them to the competition if we don't offer it.

Supports the reasoning with evidence

• The web is erasing geographical shopping limits, presenting both a threat and an opportunity. Even though our customers can now shop websites anywhere in the world (so that we have thousands of competitors instead of a dozen), we can now target customers anywhere in the world.

(continued)

Figure 11.1   Effective Problem-Solving Report Focusing on Recommendations
In this report recommending that her firm expand its website to full e-commerce capability, Alycia Jenn uses the body of her report to provide enough information to support her argument without burdening her high-level readership with a lot of tactical details.

- **Problem/opportunity/purpose.** The reason the report was written and what is to be accomplished as a result of your having written it.
- **Scope.** What is and what isn't covered in the report.
- **Background.** The historical conditions or factors that led up to the report.
- **Sources and methods.** The primary and secondary research that provided information for the report.
- **Definitions.** A list of terms that might be unfamiliar to your audience, along with brief definitions.
- **Limitations.** Factors beyond your control that affect report quality, such as budgets, schedule constraints, or limited access to information or people. (However, don't apologize or try to explain away personal shortcomings.)

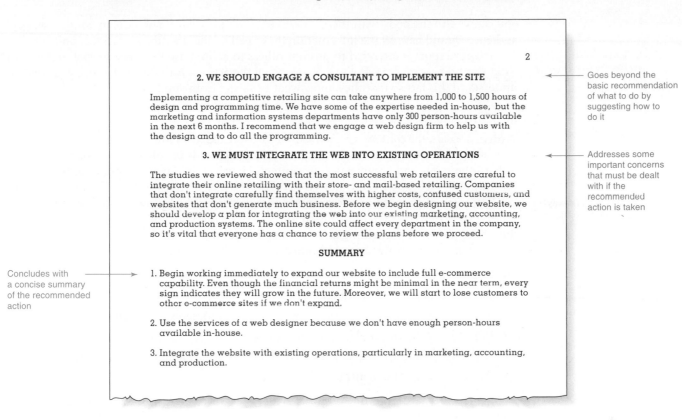

Figure 11.1 **Continued**

- **Report organization.** The organization of the report. This "road map" helps readers understand what's coming in the report and why this information is included.

Report Body The body of your report can require some tough decisions about which elements to include and how much detail to offer. Provide only enough detail in the body to support your conclusions and recommendations; you can put additional information in appendixes. The following topics are commonly covered in a report body:

The report body should contain only enough information to convey your message in a convincing fashion; use an appendix for less-important details.

- Explanations of a problem or an opportunity
- Facts, statistical evidence, and trends
- Results of studies or investigations
- Discussion and analyses of potential courses of action
- Advantages, disadvantages, costs, and benefits of a particular course of action
- Procedures or steps in a process
- Methods and approaches
- Criteria for evaluating alternatives and options
- Conclusions and recommendations
- Supporting reasons for conclusions or recommendations

For analytical reports using the direct organizational approach, you'll generally state your conclusions or recommendations in the introduction and use the body of your report to provide your evidence and support. If you're using the indirect approach, you're likely to use the body to discuss your logic and reserve your conclusions or recommendations until the very end.

Report Close The content and length of the close depend primarily on your choice of direct or indirect order. If you're using the direct approach, you can end with a summary of key points, listed in the order in which they appear in the report body. If you're using the indirect approach, you can use the close to present your conclusions or recommendations if

The nature of your close depends on the type of report (informational or analytical) and the approach (direct or indirect).

you didn't end the body with them. However, don't introduce new facts in your close; your audience should have all the information they need by the time they reach this point.

If your report is intended to prompt others to action, use the close to spell out exactly what should happen next. If you'll be taking all the actions yourself, make sure your readers understand this fact so that they know what to expect from you.

Drafting Proposal Content

With proposals, the content for each section is governed by many variables, the most important of which is the nature of the proposal. If a proposal is unsolicited, you have some latitude in the scope and organization of content. However, if you are responding to a request for proposals (see page 247), you need to follow the instructions in the RFP in every detail.

The general purpose of any proposal is to persuade readers to do something, so your writing approach is similar to that used for persuasive messages, perhaps including the use of the AIDA model or something similar to gain attention, build interest, create desire, and motivate action. Here are some additional strategies to strengthen your argument:[4]

- Demonstrate your knowledge.
- Provide concrete information and examples.
- Research the competition so you know what other proposals your audience is likely to read.
- Prove that your proposal is appropriate and feasible for your audience.
- Relate your product, service, or personnel to the reader's exact needs.
- Package your proposal attractively.

Moreover, make sure your proposal is letter perfect, inviting, and readable. Readers will prejudge the quality of your products, services, and capabilities by the quality of the proposal you submit. Errors, omissions, and inconsistencies will work against you—and might even cost you important career and business opportunities.

Proposal Introduction   The introduction of a proposal describes the problem you intend to solve or the opportunity you want to pursue, along with your suggested solution. If your proposal is solicited, follow the RFP's instructions about indicating the specific RFP to which you're responding. If your proposal is unsolicited, mention any factors that led you to submit your proposal. The following topics are commonly covered in a proposal introduction:

- **Background or statement of the problem.** Briefly reviews the reader's situation and establishes a need for action. In unsolicited proposals, you may need to convince readers that a problem or an opportunity exists before you can convince them to consider and accept your solution.
- **Solution.** Briefly describes the change you propose and highlights your key selling points and their benefits to your audience.
- **Scope.** States the boundaries of the proposal—what you will and will not do. Sometimes called "Delimitations."
- **Organization.** Orients the reader to the remainder of the proposal and calls attention to the major divisions of information.

In short proposals, your discussion of these topics will be brief—perhaps only a sentence or two for each one. For long, formal proposals, each of these topics may warrant separate subheadings and several paragraphs of discussion.

Proposal Body   The proposal's body gives complete details on the proposed solution and describes the anticipated results. Because a proposal is by definition a persuasive message, your audience expects you to promote your offering in a confident but professional and objective manner.

The body of a proposal typically includes these sections:

- **Proposed solution.** Describes what you have to offer: your concept, product, or service. This section may also be titled "Technical Proposal," "Research Design," "Issues for Analysis," or "Work Statement."

Margin notes:

If a report calls for follow-up action of any kind, clearly identify who is going to do what.

Approach proposals the same way you approach persuasive messages.

Business proposals need to provide more than just attractive ideas; readers look for evidence of practical, achievable solutions.

In an unsolicited proposal, your introduction needs to convince readers that a problem or an opportunity exists.

Readers understand that a proposal is a persuasive message, so they're willing to accommodate a degree of promotional emphasis in your writing—as long as it is professional and focused on their needs.

JWS Remodeling Solutions

1701 Lake Street • Traverse City, Michigan 49685
(231) 946-8845 • Fax: (231) 946-8846 • E-mail: jws@worldnet.att.net

October 29, 2009

Mr. Daniel Yurgren
Data Dimensions
15 Honeysuckle Lane
Traverse City, Michigan 49686

Dear Mr. Yurgren:

Subject: Proposal for Home Office Construction

JWS Remodeling Solutions would be happy to convert your existing living room area into a home office according to the specifications discussed during our October 14 meeting. We can schedule the project for the week beginning November 12, 2009 (two weeks from today). The project will take roughly 3 weeks to complete.

Our construction approach is unique. We provide a full staff of licensed tradespeople and schedule our projects so that when one trade finishes, the next trade is ready to begin. To expedite this project, as you requested, we have agreed to overlap several trades whose work can be done concurrently.

JWS Remodeling Solutions will provide the following work:

- Remove baseboard, door casing, fluted casing, and sheetrock to prepare for construction of new partition wall at north end of living room.
- Partition and finish walls to create two separate storage closets at north end of living room with access through two 36" six-panel door units. Replace all disturbed sheetrock.
- Hang and trim new door units and replace all disturbed baseboards and door casings.
- Install 60" double French door unit in location of current cased opening at the SW entrance to living room adjacent to foyer. Trim appropriately.
- Provide all rough and finished electrical, using recessed lighting in the ceiling and appropriate single pole switches and duplex outlets.
- Move cold air return from west wall to east wall of living room.
- Paint or finish all surfaces/trim to match specs used throughout house.

The work does *not* include custom office cabinetry, carpeting, or phone or cable wiring. We would be happy to bid on these projects in the future.

Margin annotations (left):
- Acknowledges the scope of project
- Itemizes the specific tasks to be performed
- Avoids confusion by identifying work that is outside the scope of the proposal

Margin annotations (right):
- Uses the introduction to grab the reader's attention with expedited completion date—a key selling point
- Uses the body to explain how the company will expedite the schedule, outline the approach, provide a work plan, and (on the next page) list qualifications and state costs

(continued)

Figure 11.2 Solicited Proposal
This informal solicited proposal in letter format provides the information the customer needs to make a purchase. Note that by signing the proposal and returning it, the customer enters into a legal contract to pay for the services described.

- **Work plan.** Explains the steps you'll take, their timing, the methods or resources you'll use, and the person(s) responsible. Specifically includes when the work will begin, how it will be divided into stages, when you will finish, and whether any follow-up is involved. The work plan is contractually binding if your proposal is accepted, so don't promise more than you can deliver. (Note that *work plan* here is different from the work plan discussed on page 234.)

- **Statement of qualifications.** Describes your organization's experience, personnel, and facilities as they relate to audience needs.

- **Costs.** Covers pricing, reimbursable expenses, discounts, and so on. If you're responding to an RFP, follow the instructions it contains.

In an informal proposal, discussion of some or all of these elements may be grouped together and presented in a letter format, as shown in the proposal in Figure 11.2. In a formal proposal, each of these elements is given its own section.

Margin note: A work plan indicates exactly how you will accomplish the solution presented in the proposal.

Mr. Daniel Yurgren   Page 2   October 29, 2009

JWS Remodeling Solutions has been in business in the Michigan area for over 17 years. We have a strong reputation for being a quality builder. We take great pride in our work and we treat all projects with the same high-level attention, regardless of their size or scope. Our tradespeople are all licensed, insured professionals with years of experience in their respective crafts. Enclosed is a copy of our company brochure discussing our qualifications in greater detail, along with a current client list. Please contact any of the names on this list for references.

Increases desire by highlighting qualifications

Helps reader accept the cost total by breaking it down into specific categories

The total cost for this project is $6,800, broken down as follows:

Materials and supplies	$3,800
Labor	2,700
Disposal fees	300
Total	$6,800

An initial payment of $3,800 is due upon acceptance of this proposal. The remaining $3,000 is due upon completion of the work.

If you would like to have JWS Remodeling Solutions complete this work, please sign one copy of this letter and return it to us with your deposit in the enclosed envelope. We currently anticipate no construction delays, since the materials needed for your job are in stock and our staff of qualified workers is available during the period mentioned. If you have any questions regarding the terms of this proposal, please call me.

Sincerely,

Jordan W. Spurrier

Jordan W. Spurrier
President

Enclosures (3)

Makes letter a binding contract, if signed

Accepted by:

_____   _____
Daniel Yurgren   Date

Pointers for Developing Proposals
- Carefully review and follow all requirements listed in the RFP (if applicable).
- Define the scope of work you intend to complete.
- Determine the methods and procedures to be used.
- Carefully estimate requirements for time, personnel, and costs.
- Write, format, and deliver the proposal exactly as the RFP specifies.
- Open by stating the purpose of the proposal, defining the scope of work, presenting helpful background information, and explaining any relevant restrictions or limitations.
- In the body, provide details and specify anticipated results, including methods, schedule, facilities, quantities, equipment, personnel, and costs.
- Close by summarizing key selling points and benefits, then ask for a decision from the audience.

Figure 11.2   Continued

The close is your last chance to convince the reader of the merits of your proposal, so make doubly sure it's clear, compelling, and audience oriented.

Proposal Close   The final section of a proposal summarizes the key points, emphasizes the benefits that readers will realize from your solution, summarizes the merits of your approach, restates why you and your firm are a good choice, and asks for a decision from the reader. Keep this section brief and use a confident, optimistic tone.

Table 11.1 summarizes the items to consider in the introduction, body, and close of a report or proposal.

TABLE 11.1   Report and Proposal Contents

Report Contents	Proposal Contents

Report Contents

Introduction

- **Authorization.** Reiterate who authorized the report (when, how), who wrote it, and when it was submitted.
- **Problem/purpose.** Explain the reason for the report's existence and what the report will achieve.
- **Scope.** Describe what will and won't be covered in the report—indicating size and complexity.
- **Background.** Review historical conditions or factors that led up to the report.
- **Sources and methods.** Discuss the primary and secondary sources consulted and methods used.
- **Definitions.** List terms and their definitions, including any terms that might be misinterpreted. Terms may also be defined in the body, explanatory notes, or glossary.
- **Limitations.** Discuss factors beyond your control that affect report quality—but note that this not an excuse for poor research or a poorly written report.
- **Report organization.** Tell what topics are covered, in what order.

Body

- **Explanations.** Give complete details of the problem, project, or idea.
- **Facts, statistical evidence, and trends.** Lay out the results of studies or investigations.
- **Analysis of action.** Discuss potential courses of action.
- **Pros and cons.** Explain advantages, disadvantages, costs, and benefits of a particular course of action.
- **Procedures.** Outline steps for a process.
- **Methods and approaches.** Discuss how you've studied a problem (or gathered evidence) and arrived at your solution (or collected your data).
- **Criteria.** Describe the benchmarks for evaluating options and alternatives.
- **Conclusions and recommendations.** Discuss what you believe the evidence reveals and what you propose should be done about it.
- **Support.** Give the reasons behind your conclusions or recommendations.

Close

- **For direct order.** Summarize key points (except in short memos), listing them in the order in which they appear in the body. Briefly restate your conclusions or recommendations, if appropriate.
- **For indirect order.** You may use the close to present your conclusions or recommendations for the first time—just be sure not to present any new facts.
- **For motivating action.** Spell out exactly what should happen next and provide a schedule with specific task assignments.

Proposal Contents

Introduction

- **Background or statement of the problem.** Briefly review the reader's situation, establish a need for action, and explain how things could be better. In unsolicited proposals, convince readers that a problem or an opportunity exists.
- **Solution.** Briefly describe the change you propose, highlighting your key selling points and their benefits to show how your proposal will solve the reader's problem.
- **Scope.** State the boundaries of the proposal—what you will and will not do.
- **Report organization.** Orient the reader to the remainder of the proposal and call attention to the major divisions of thought.

Body

- **Facts and evidence to support your conclusions.** Give complete details of the proposed solution and anticipated results.
- **Proposed approach.** Describe your concept, product, or service. Stress reader benefits and emphasize any advantages you have over your competitors.
- **Work plan.** Describe how you'll accomplish what must be done (unless you're providing a standard, off-the-shelf item). Explain the steps you'll take, their timing, the methods or resources you'll use, and the person(s) responsible. State when work will begin, how it will be divided into stages, when you'll finish, and whether follow-up will be needed.
- **Statement of qualifications.** Describe your organization's experience, personnel, and facilities—relating it all to readers' needs. Include a list of client references.
- **Costs.** Prove that your costs are realistic—break them down so that readers can see the costs of labor, materials, transportation, travel, training, and other categories.

Close

- **Review of argument.** Briefly summarize the key points.
- **Review of reader benefits.** Briefly summarize how your proposal will help the reader.
- **Review of the merits of your approach.** Briefly summarize why your approach will be more effective than that of competitors.
- **Restatement of qualifications.** Briefly reemphasize why you and your firm should do the work.
- **Request.** Ask for a decision from the reader.

Drafting Online Content

The basic principles of report writing apply to online content, but keep these five additional points in mind as well:

Composing effective online content requires some unique considerations.

- Take special care to build trust with your intended audiences because careful readers can be skeptical of online content. Make sure your content is accurate, current, complete, and authoritative.

- As much as possible, adapt your content for a global audience. Translating content is expensive, so some companies compromise by *localizing* the homepage while keeping the deeper, more detailed content in its original language.

- In an environment that presents many reading challenges, compelling, reader-oriented content is key to success.[5] Wherever you can, use the *inverted pyramid* style, in which you cover the most important information briefly at first and then gradually reveal successive layers of detail—letting readers choose to see those additional layers if they want to.

- Present your information in a concise, skimmable format. Effective websites use a variety of means to help readers skim pages quickly, including lists, careful use of color and boldface, informative headings, and helpful summaries that give readers a choice of learning more if they want to.

- Write effective links that serve for both site navigation and content skimming. Above all else, clearly identify where a link will take readers; don't force them to click through and try to figure out where they're going.

Helping Readers Find Their Way

To help today's time-pressed readers find what they're looking for and stay on track as they navigate through your documents, learn to make good use of headings and links, smooth transitions, and previews and reviews:

Help your readers find what they want and stay on track with headings or links, transitions, previews, and reviews.

- **Headings or links.** Readers should be able to follow the structure of your document and pick up the key points of your message from the headings and subheadings. For online reports, make generous use of hyperlinks to help your readers navigate the reports and access additional information.

- **Transitions.** Chapter 4 defines *transitions* as words or phrases that tie together ideas and show how one thought is related to another. In a long report, an entire paragraph might be used to highlight transitions from one section to the next.

- **Previews and reviews.** *Preview sections* introduce important topics by helping readers get ready for new information. *Review sections* come after a body of material and summarize the information for your readers, helping them absorb details.

Using Technology to Craft Reports and Proposals

Creating lengthy reports and proposals can be a huge task, so take advantage of technological tools that can help throughout the process:

Look for ways to utilize technology to reduce the mechanical work involved in writing long reports.

- **Templates.** Templates can identify the specific sections required for each type of report and can automatically insert headings for each section.

- **Linked and embedded documents.** In many reports and proposals, you'll include graphics, spreadsheets, databases, and other elements produced in other software programs. Make sure you know how your software handles the files. For instance, in Microsoft Office, *linking* to a file maintains a "live" connection to it (so changes in the original file will show up in the document you're working on), but *embedding* a file doesn't. If you send readers a Word document that contains links to other files, be sure to include those files as well.

- **Electronic forms.** For recurring reports such as sales reports and compliance reports, consider creating a word processor file that uses *form tools* such as text boxes (in which users can type new text) and check boxes (which can be used to select from a set of predetermined choices).

- **Electronic documents.** Portable document format (PDF) files have become a universal replacement for printed reports and proposals. Using Adobe Acrobat or similar products, you can quickly convert reports and proposals to PDF files that are easy and safe to share electronically.

- **Multimedia documents.** When the written word isn't enough, combine your report with video clips, animation, presentation software slides, screencasts (recordings of on-screen activity), and other elements.

- **Proposal-writing software.** Proposal-writing software can automatically personalize proposals, ensure proper structure (making sure you don't forget any sections, for instance), organize storage of all your boilerplate text, and scan RFPs to identify questions and requirements and fill in potential answers from a centralized knowledge base.[6]

ILLUSTRATING YOUR REPORTS WITH EFFECTIVE VISUALS

Well-designed visual elements can enhance the communication power of textual messages and, in some instances, even replace textual messages. Generally speaking, in a given amount of time, well-designed images can convey much more information than text.[7] Using pictures is also an effective way to communicate with diverse audiences.

Carefully crafted visuals enhance the power of your words.

Given the importance of visuals in today's business environment, **visual literacy**—the ability (as a sender) to create effective images and (as a receiver) to correctly interpret visual messages—has become a key business skill.[8] Even without any formal training in design, being aware of the following six principles will help you be a more effective visual communicator:

Visual literacy is the ability to create effective images and to interpret images correctly.

- **Consistency.** Think of consistency as *visual parallelism*, similar to textual parallelism that helps audiences understand and compare a series of ideas.[9] You can achieve visual parallelism through the consistent use of color, shape, size, texture, position, scale, or typeface.

Pay close attention to consistency, contrast, balance, emphasis, convention, and simplicity.

- **Contrast.** To emphasize differences, depict items in contrasting colors, such as red and blue or black and white. To emphasize similarities, make color differences more subtle.

- **Balance.** Balance can be either *formal*, in which the elements in the images are arranged symmetrically around a central point or axis, or *informal*, in which elements are not distributed evenly, but stronger and weaker elements are arranged in a way that achieves an overall effect of balance.[10]

- **Emphasis.** Audiences usually assume that the dominant element in a design is the most important, so make sure that the visually dominant element really does represent the most important information.

- **Convention.** Just as written communication is guided by an array of spelling, grammar, punctuation, and usage conventions, visual communication is guided by a variety of generally accepted rules or conventions that dictate virtually every aspect of design.[11] In any given culture, for example, certain colors and shapes have specific meanings.

- **Simplicity.** When you're designing graphics for your documents, limit the number of colors and design elements and take care to avoid *chartjunk*—decorative elements that clutter documents without adding any relevant information.[12]

Choosing the Right Visual for the Job

Once you've identified which points would benefit most from visual presentation, your next decision is to choose what types of visuals to use. As you can see in Figure 11.3, you have many choices for business graphics. For certain types of information, the decision is usually obvious. If you want to present a large set of numeric values or detailed textual information, for example, a table is the obvious choice in most cases. Also, certain visuals are commonly used for certain applications, so, for example, your audience is likely to expect line charts and bar charts to show trends.

You have many types of visuals to choose from, and each is best suited to particular communication tasks.

Communication Challenge	Effective Visual Choice
Presenting Data	
To present individual, exact values	Table
To show trends in one or more variables, or the relationship between those variables, over time	Line chart, bar chart
To compare two or more sets of data	Bar chart, line chart
To show frequency or distribution of parts in a whole	Pie chart
To show massive data sets, complex quantities, or dynamic data	Data visualization
Presenting Information, Concepts, and Ideas	
To show geographic relationships or comparisons	Map
To illustrate processes or procedures	Flowchart, diagram
To show conceptual or spatial relationships (simplified)	Drawing
To show spatial relationships (realistic)	Photograph
To show processes, transformations, and so on in action	Animation, video

Station	Pretest	Posttest	Change
Bark peeler	0.08	0.07	+13%
Slab saw	1.12	1.18	-5%
Edger	0.45	0.30	+33%
Trim saw	2.27	2.07	+9%
Chop saw	3.62	3.68	-2%

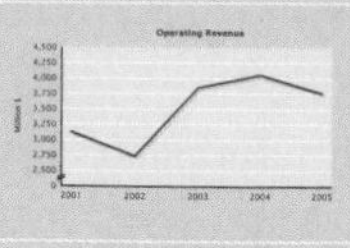

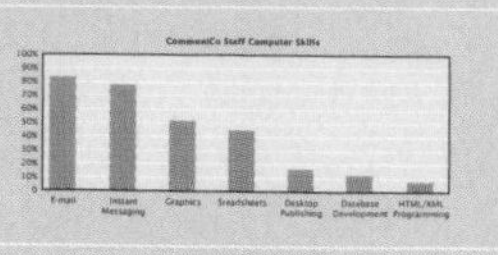

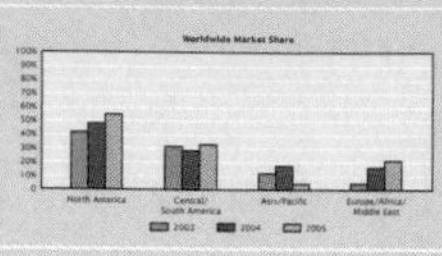

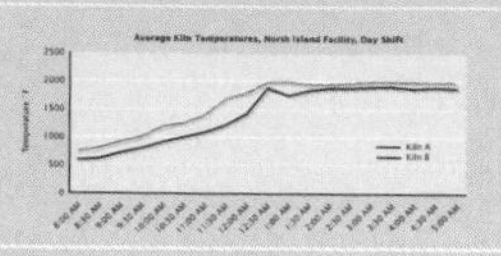

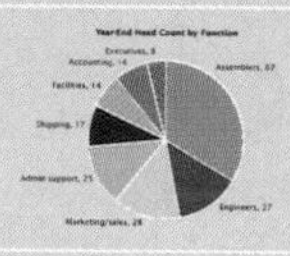

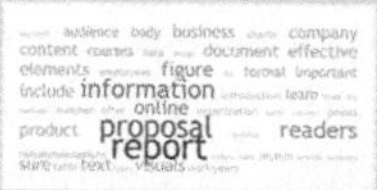

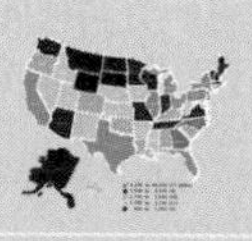

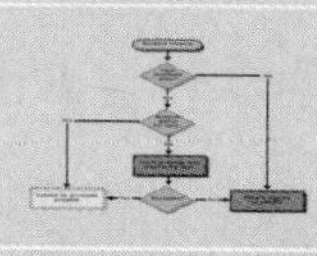

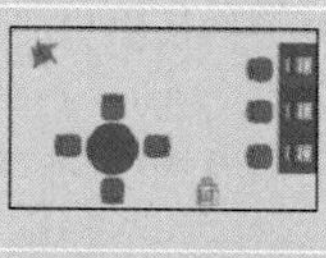

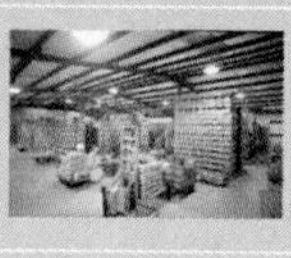

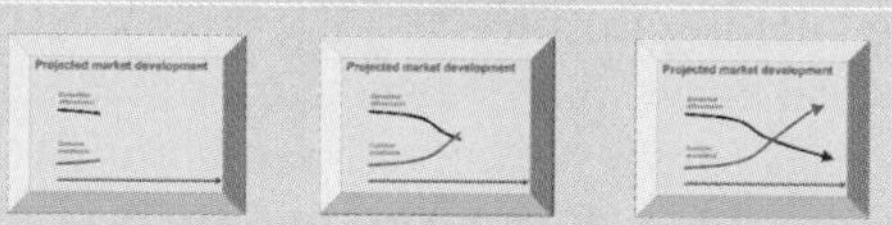

Figure 11.3 **Selecting the Best Visual**
Choose your visuals carefully for maximum communication effectiveness.

Tables

Printed tables can display extensive amounts of data, but tables for online display and electronic presentations need to be simpler.

When you need to present detailed, specific information, choose a **table**, a systematic arrangement of data in columns and rows. Tables are ideal when your audience needs information that would be either difficult or tedious to handle in the main text. Most tables contain the standard parts illustrated in Figure 11.4. Follow these guidelines to create clear, effective tables:

- Use common, understandable units and clearly identify them: dollars, percentages, price per ton, and so on.
- Express all items in a column in the same unit and round off for simplicity.

Multicolumn Heading				
Subheading	**Subheading**	**Subheading**	**Subheading**	**Single-Column Heading**
Row heading	xxx	xxx	xxx	xxx
Row heading	xxx	xxx	xxx	xxx
Subheading	xxx	xxx	xxx	xxx
Subheading	xxx	xxx	xxx	xxx
Total	xxx	xxx	xxx	xxx

Source: (In the same format as a text footnote; see Appendix B)

*Footnote (For an explanation of elements in the table, a superscript number or small letter may be used instead of an asterisk or other symbol.)

Figure 11.4   Parts of a Table
Here are the standard parts of a table. No matter which design you choose, make sure the layout
is clear and that individual rows and columns are easy to follow.

- Label column headings clearly and use subheads if necessary.
- Separate columns or rows with lines or extra space to make the table easy to follow.
- Don't cram so much information into a table that it becomes difficult to read.
- Keep online tables small enough to read comfortably on-screen.
- Document the source of data using the same format as a text footnote (see Appendix B).

Line Charts and Surface Charts

A **line chart** (see Figure 11.5) illustrates trends over time or plots the relationship of two variables. In line charts that show trends, the vertical, or y, axis shows the amount, and the horizontal, or x, axis shows the time or other quantity against which the amount is being measured. You can plot just a single line or overlay multiple lines to compare different entities. (Note that *chart* and *graph* are used interchangeably for most of the display formats discussed here.)

A **surface chart**, also called an **area chart**, is a form of line chart that shows a cumulative effect; all the lines add up to the top line, which represents the total (see Figure 11.6). This type of chart helps you illustrate changes in the composition of something over time. When preparing a surface chart, put the most important segment against the baseline and restrict the number of strata to four or five.

Line charts are commonly used to show trends over time or the relationship between two variables.

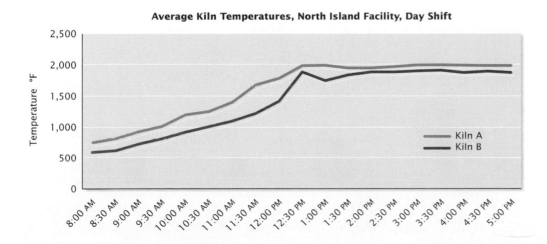

Average Kiln Temperatures, North Island Facility, Day Shift

Kiln A
Kiln B

Figure 11.5   Line Chart
This two-line line chart compares the temperatures measured inside two cement kilns from 8:00 A.M. to 5:00 P.M.

Figure 11.6 Surface Chart
Surface, or area, charts can show a combination of trends over time and the individual contributions of the components of a whole.

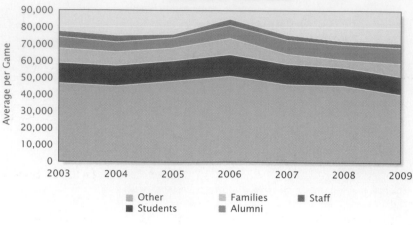

Bar Charts and Pie Charts

Bar charts can show a variety of relationships among two or more variables.

A bar chart (see Figure 11.7) portrays numbers with the height or length of its rectangular bars, making a series of numbers easy to grasp quickly. Bar charts are particularly valuable when you want to do the following:

- Compare the size of several items at one time
- Show changes in one item over time
- Indicate the composition of several items over time
- Show the relative size of components of a whole

Figure 11.7 The Versatile Bar Chart
These charts show just four of the many variations available for bar charts: *singular* (11.7a: "CommuniCo Staff Computer Skills"), *grouped* (11.7b: "Worldwide Market Share"), *segmented* (11.7c: "CommuniCo Preferred Communication Media"), and *combination* (11.7d: "CommuniCo Employee Training Costs").

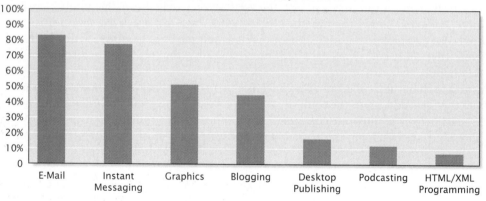

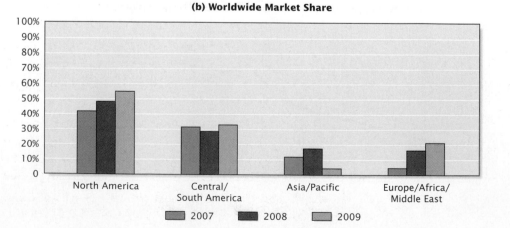

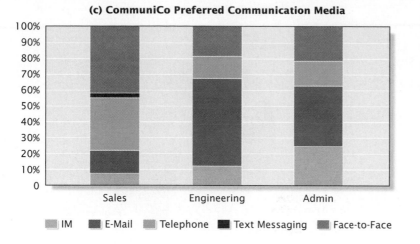

Figure 11.7   **Continued**

(c) CommuniCo Preferred Communication Media

IM   E-Mail   Telephone   Text Messaging   Face-to-Face

(d) CommuniCo Employee Training Costs

Headcount   Training Costs

Grouped bar charts compare more than one set of data, using a different color or pattern for each set. *Segmented* bar charts, also known as stacked bar charts, show how individual components contribute to a total number, using a different color or pattern for each component. *Combination* bar and line charts compare quantities that require different intervals.

A **pie chart** is the primary visual for showing how the parts of a whole are distributed (see Figure 11.8). When creating pie charts, limit the number of slices to keep the chart from getting cluttered. If necessary, combine the smallest quantities in a "miscellaneous" category. Remember that the segments must add up to 100 percent if percentages are used or to the total number if numbers are used.

Most readers expect pie charts to show the distribution of parts within a whole.

Data Visualization

Conventional charts and graphs are limited in two ways: They can represent only numeric data, and most types show only a limited number of data points before the display becomes too cluttered to interpret. A diverse class of display capabilities known as **data visualization** overcomes both of these drawbacks. First, some types of data visualization displays can show hundreds or even thousands of data points, using a variety of graphical presentations. For instance, regional sales data can be displayed as three-dimensional "topography" maps to quickly show strong and weak areas. Second, other kinds of visualization tools combine data with textual information to communicate complex or dynamic data much faster than conventional presentations can. For example, a *tag cloud* shows the relative frequency of terms, or *tags* (user-applied content labels), in an article, a blog, a website, survey data, or another collection of text (see Figure 11.9).[13]

Data visualization tools can overcome the limitations of conventional charts and other display types.

Figure 11.8 Pie Chart
When creating pie charts, use different colors or patterns to distinguish the various pieces. Label all the segments and indicate the value of each in either percentage or unit of measure so that your readers will be able to judge the values of the wedges.

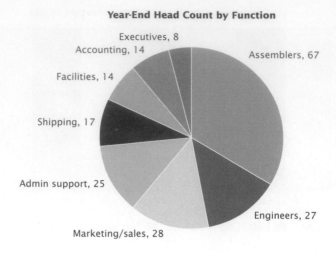

Year-End Head Count by Function

Executives, 8
Accounting, 14
Facilities, 14
Assemblers, 67
Shipping, 17
Admin support, 25
Engineers, 27
Marketing/sales, 28

Figure 11.9   Data Visualization Using a Tag Cloud
This simple tag cloud shows the relative frequency of the 50 most commonly used words in this chapter (not including common words such as *the*). On a blog or website, such a tag cloud could display the most frequently entered content labels, allowing visitors to see which topics are most popular. Moreover, each word can be a hyperlink that connects to all the articles or pages tagged with that term. The range of data visualization tools is vast, with creative communicators constantly searching for more effective ways to display complex sets of data and information.

Flowcharts and Organization Charts

Be aware that there is a formal symbolic "language" in flowcharting; each shape has a specific meaning.

A **flowchart** (see Figure 11.10) illustrates a sequence of events from start to finish; it is indispensable when illustrating processes, procedures, and sequential relationships. For general business purposes, you don't need to be too concerned about the specific shapes on a flowchart; just be sure to use them consistently. However, you should be aware that there is a formal flowchart "language," in which each shape has a specific meaning (diamonds are decision points, rectangles are process steps, and so on). If you're communicating with computer programmers and others who are accustomed to formal flowcharting, make sure you use the correct symbols in each case to avoid confusion.

As the name implies, an **organization chart** illustrates the positions, units, or functions in an organization and the ways they interrelate. An organization's normal communication channels are almost impossible to describe without the benefit of a chart like the one in Figure 11.11.

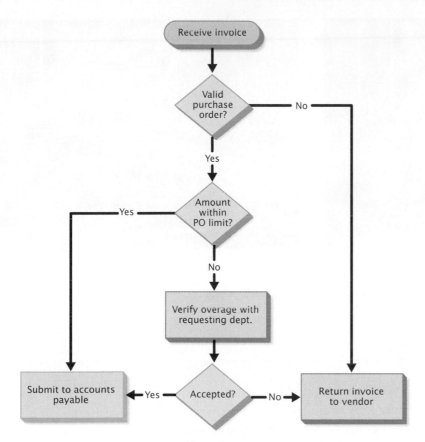

Figure 11.10 Flowchart
Flowcharts show sequences of events and are most valuable when a process or procedure has a number of decision points and variable paths.

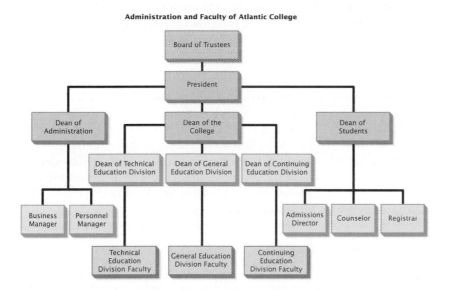

Figure 11.11 Organization Chart
An organization chart illustrates the hierarchy of positions in an organization.

Maps, Drawings, Diagrams, and Photographs

Maps are useful for showing territories, routes, and locations. Simple maps are available via clip art libraries, but more powerful uses (such as automatically generating color-coded maps based on data inputs) usually require the specialized capabilities of *geographic information systems.*

Drawings can show an endless variety of business concepts, such as the network of suppliers in an industry, the flow of funds through a company, or the process for completing payroll each week. More complex diagrams can convey technical topics such as the operation of a machine or repair procedures.

Use maps to represent statistics by geographic area and to show spatial relationships.

Drawings are sometimes better than photographs because they let you focus on the most important details.

Figure 11.12   **Digital Image Manipulation**
To show investors what a new building would look like in its environment, an artist combined a photograph of a scale model of the building with a photograph of the actual street scene. Because the target audience clearly understands that the building doesn't exist, the image manipulation in this instance is not unethical. However, deceiving viewers by altering images can be considered unethical, particularly if doing so affects decision making.

Use photographs for visual appeal and to show exact appearances.

Photographs offer both functional and decorative value, and nothing can top a photograph when you need to show exact appearances. However, in some situations, a photograph can show too much detail, which is one reason repair manuals frequently use drawings instead of photos, for instance. Because audiences expect photographs to show literal visual truths, you must take care when using image processing tools such as Adobe Photoshop (see Figure 11.12).

Animation and Video

Computer animation and video are among the most specialized forms of business visuals. When they are appropriate and done well, they offer unparalleled visual impact. At a simple level, you can animate shapes and text within Microsoft PowerPoint, although its possibilities are somewhat limited. At a more sophisticated level, software programs such as Adobe Flash enable the creation of multimedia files that include computer animation, digital video, and other elements. A wide variety of tools are also available for digital video production. Chances are, you won't have to use these tools yourself, but if you employ a specialist to create animation or video for websites or presentations, make sure the results follow all the guidelines for designing effective business messages.

Designing Effective Visuals

Computers make it easy to create visuals, but they also make it easy to create ineffective, distracting, and even downright ugly visuals. However, by following the design principles discussed on page 269, you can create basic visuals that are attractive and effective. If possible, have a professional designer set up a *template* for the various types of visuals you and your colleagues need to create. By specifying color palettes, font selections, slide layouts, and other choices, design templates have three important benefits: They help ensure better designs, they promote consistency across the organization, and they save everyone time by eliminating repetitive decision making.

Remember that the style and quality of your visuals communicates a subtle message about your relationship with the audience. A simple sketch might be fine for a working meeting but inappropriate for a formal presentation or report. On the other hand, elaborate, full-color visuals may be viewed as extravagant for an informal report but may be entirely appropriate for a message to top management or influential outsiders.

In addition to being well designed, visuals need to be well integrated with text. First, try to position your visuals so that your audience won't have to flip back and forth (in printed documents) or scroll (on-screen) between the visuals and the text. Second, clearly refer to visuals by number in the text of your report and help your readers understand the significance of visuals by referring to them before readers encounter them in the document or on-screen. Third, write effective *titles*, *captions*, and *legends* to complete the integration of your text and visuals. A **title** provides a short description that identifies the content and purpose of the visual. A **caption** usually offers additional discussion of the visual's content and can be several sentences long, if appropriate. A **legend** helps readers "decode" the visual by explaining what various colors, symbols, or other design choices mean.

> To tie visuals to the text, introduce them in the text and place them near the points they illustrate.

Finally, check your visuals carefully for accuracy. Check for mistakes such as typographical errors, inconsistent color treatment, confusing or undocumented symbols, and misaligned elements. Make sure that your computer hasn't done something unexpected, such as arranging pie chart slices in an order you don't want or plotting line charts in unusual colors. Make sure your visuals are properly documented. Most importantly, make sure your visuals are honest—that they don't intentionally or unintentionally distort the truth.

> Proof visuals as carefully as you proof text.

For more information on visual communication, including design principles, ethical matters, and the latest tools for creating and displaying visuals, visit http://real-timeupdates .com/bce and click on Chapter 11.

COMPLETING REPORTS AND PROPOSALS

As with shorter messages (Chapter 5), when you have finished your first draft, you need to perform four tasks to complete your document: revise, produce, proofread, and distribute.

Revising Reports and Proposals

The revision process is essentially the same for reports as for other business messages, although it may take considerably longer, depending on the length of your document. Evaluate your organization, style, and tone, making sure that your content is clear, logical, and reader oriented. Then work to improve the report's readability by varying sentence length, keeping paragraphs short, using lists and bullets, and adding headings and subheadings. Keep revising the content until it is clear, concise, and compelling. Remember that even minor mistakes can affect your credibility.

> The revision process for long reports can take considerable time, so be sure to plan ahead.

Tight, efficient writing that is easy to skim is always a plus, but it's especially important for impatient online audiences.[14] Review online content carefully; strip out all information that doesn't meet audience needs and condense everything else as much as possible. Audiences will gladly return to sites that deliver quality information quickly—and they'll avoid sites that don't.

> Tight, efficient writing is especially important with online content.

Producing a Formal Report

The parts included in a report depend on the type of report you are writing, the requirements of your audience, the organization you're working for, and the length of your report (see Figure 11.13). The instructions here pertain primarily to printed reports, but you can adapt many of these elements to reports delivered electronically.

> The number and variety of parts you include in a report depend on the type of report, audience requirements, organizational expectations, and report length.

Most prefatory parts (such as the table of contents) should be placed on their own pages. However, the various parts in the report text are often run together. If your introduction is only a paragraph long, don't bother with a page break before moving into the body of your report. If the introduction runs longer than a page, however, a page break can signal the reader that a major shift is about to occur.

For an illustration of how the various parts fit together in a report, see Figure 11.14, beginning on page 279. This report was prepared by Linda Moreno, manager of the cost accounting department at Electrovision, a high-tech company based in Los Gatos,

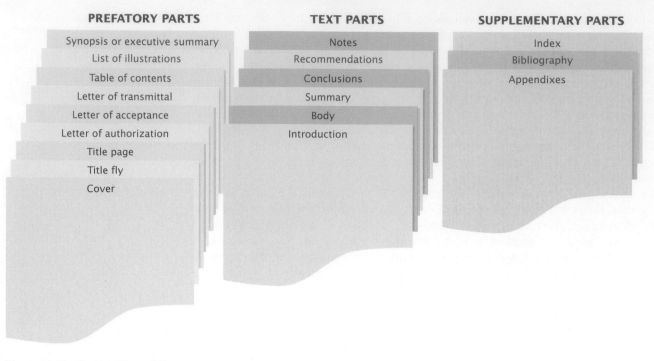

PREFATORY PARTS	TEXT PARTS	SUPPLEMENTARY PARTS
Synopsis or executive summary	Notes	Index
List of illustrations	Recommendations	Bibliography
Table of contents	Conclusions	Appendixes
Letter of transmittal	Summary	
Letter of acceptance	Body	
Letter of authorization	Introduction	
Title page		
Title fly		
Cover		

Figure 11.13 Parts of Formal Report
Formal reports can contain a variety of prefatory and supplemental parts in addition to the main text.

California. Electrovision's main product is optical character recognition equipment, which the U.S. Postal Service uses for sorting mail. Moreno's job is to help analyze the company's costs. Moreno used the direct approach and organized her report based on conclusions and recommendations.

Prefatory Parts of a Formal Report

Formal reports can contain a variety of prefatory parts; choose the elements that will make your report most successful.

Prefatory parts come before the main text of your report and help readers decide whether and how to read the report:[15]

- **Cover.** The cover should start with a concise title that gives readers the information they need to grasp the purpose and scope of the report. For a formal report, choose high-quality *cover stock* (heavy, high-quality paper).
- **Title fly.** Many formal reports begin with a plain sheet of paper that has only the title of the report on it.
- **Title page.** The title page typically includes the report title; the name, job title, and address of the person, group, or organization that authorized the report; the name, job title, and address of the person, group, or organization that prepared the report; and the date on which the report was submitted.
- **Letter of authorization.** If you received written authorization to prepare the report, you may want to include that letter or memo in your report.
- **Letter of transmittal.** The letter or memo of transmittal introduces the report on your behalf. The opening discusses scope, methods, and limitations. The body can highlight important sections of the report, suggest follow-up studies, offer details to help readers use the report, and acknowledge help from others. The close can include a note of thanks for the assignment, an expression of willingness to discuss the report, and an offer to assist with future projects (see Figure 11.14 on page 280).

(*continued on page 293*)

Puts the title all in capital letters →

Puts all lines other than title in uppercase and lowercase letters

**REDUCING ELECTROVISION'S
TRAVEL AND ENTERTAINMENT COSTS**

← Centers lines horizontally (if this report were left-bound, you would allow an extra half-inch margin on the left side)

Prepared for
Dennis McWilliams,
Vice President of Operations
Electrovision, Inc.

← Follows the title with the name, title, and organization of the recipient

← Balances the white space between the items on the page

Prepared by
Linda Moreno, Manager
Cost Accounting Services
Electrovision, Inc.

February 16, 2009

← Includes the report's publication date for future reference

The "how-to" tone of Moreno's title is appropriate for an action-oriented report that emphasizes recommendations. A more neutral title, such as "An Analysis of Electrovision's Travel and Entertainment Costs," would be more suitable for an informational report.

Figure 11.14   Analyzing an Effective Formal Report

MEMORANDUM

TO: Dennis McWilliams, Vice President of Operations
FROM: Linda Moreno, Manager of Cost Accounting Services   *LM*
DATE: February 16, 2009
SUBJECT: Reducing Electrovision's Travel and Entertainment Costs

Here is the report you requested January 28 on Electrovision's travel and entertainment costs.

Your suspicions were right. We are spending far too much on business travel. Our unwritten policy has been "anything goes," leaving us with no real control over T&E expenses. Although this hands-off approach may have been understandable when Electrovision's profits were high, we can no longer afford the luxury of going first class.

The solutions to the problem seem rather clear. We need to have someone with centralized responsibility for travel and entertainment costs, a clear statement of policy, an effective control system, and a business-oriented travel service that can optimize our travel arrangements. We should also investigate alternatives to travel, such as videoconferencing. Perhaps more important, we need to change our attitude. Instead of viewing travel funds as a bottomless supply of money, all traveling employees need to act as if they were paying the bills themselves.

Getting people to economize is not going to be easy. In the course of researching this issue, I've found that our employees are deeply attached to their generous travel privileges. I think some would almost prefer a cut in pay to a loss in travel status. We'll need a lot of top management involvement to sell people on the need for moderation. One thing is clear: People will be very bitter if we create a two-class system in which top executives get special privileges while the rest of the employees make the sacrifices.

I'm grateful to Mary Lehman and Connie McIllvain for their help in rounding up and sorting through five years' worth of expense reports. Their efforts were truly Herculean.

Thanks for giving me the opportunity to work on this assignment. It's been a real education. If you have any questions about the report, please give me a call.

Margin annotations (left):
- Uses memo format for transmitting this internal report; otherwise, letter format would be used for transmitting external reports
- Uses a conversational style
- Acknowledges help that has been received

Margin annotations (right):
- Presents the main conclusion right away (because Moreno expects a positive response)
- Closes with thanks and an offer to discuss results (when appropriate, you could also include an offer to help with future projects)

In this report, Moreno decided to write a brief memo of transmittal and include a separate executive summary. Short reports (fewer than 10 pages) often combine the synopsis or executive summary with the memo or letter of transmittal.

Figure 11.14   Continued

CONTENTS

PAGE

Executive Summary iv

Introduction 1

The High Cost of Travel and Entertainment 1
  $16 Million per Year Spent on Travel and Entertainment 2
  Electrovision's Travel Expenses Exceed National Averages 3
  Spending Has Been Encouraged 3

Growing Impact on the Bottom Line 4
  Lower Profits Underscore the Need for Change 4
  Airfares and Hotel Rates Are Rising 5

Methods For Reducing T&E costs.. 5
  Four Ways to Trim Expenses 5
  The Impact of Reforms 8

Conclusions and Recommendations 9

Works Cited 10

LIST OF ILLUSTRATIONS

FIGURES   PAGE

1. Airfares and Lodging Account for Over Two-Thirds of
   Electrovision's T&E Budget 2

2. T&E Expenses Continue to Increase
   as a Percentage of Sales 2

3. Electrovision Employees Spend Over Twice as Much as
   the Average Business Traveler... 3

TABLE

1. Electrovision Can Trim Travel and Entertainment Costs
   by an Estimated $6 Million per Year....................................... 8

iii

Doesn't include any elements that appear before the "Contents" page

Words the headings exactly as they appear in the text

Includes only the page numbers where sections begin

Numbers figures consecutively throughout the report

Numbers the contents page with lowercase Roman numerals centered at the bottom margin

Moreno included only first- and second-level headings in her table of contents, even though the report contains third-level headings. She prefers a shorter table of contents that focuses attention on the main divisions of thought. She used informative titles, which are appropriate for a report to a receptive audience.

Figure 11.14   Continued

Begins by stating the purpose of the report

Presents the points in the executive summary in the same order as they appear in the report, using subheadings that summarize the content of the main sections of the report

Continues numbering the executive summary pages with lowercase Roman numerals

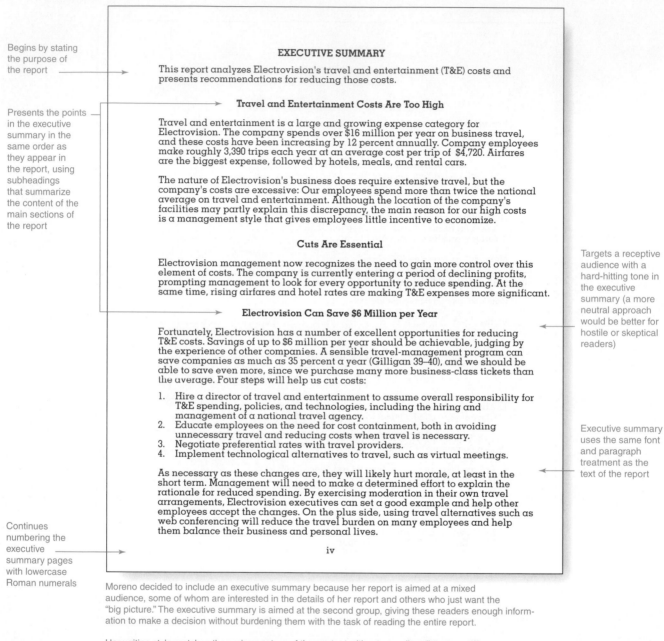

EXECUTIVE SUMMARY

This report analyzes Electrovision's travel and entertainment (T&E) costs and presents recommendations for reducing those costs.

Travel and Entertainment Costs Are Too High

Travel and entertainment is a large and growing expense category for Electrovision. The company spends over $16 million per year on business travel, and these costs have been increasing by 12 percent annually. Company employees make roughly 3,390 trips each year at an average cost per trip of $4,720. Airfares are the biggest expense, followed by hotels, meals, and rental cars.

The nature of Electrovision's business does require extensive travel, but the company's costs are excessive: Our employees spend more than twice the national average on travel and entertainment. Although the location of the company's facilities may partly explain this discrepancy, the main reason for our high costs is a management style that gives employees little incentive to economize.

Cuts Are Essential

Electrovision management now recognizes the need to gain more control over this element of costs. The company is currently entering a period of declining profits, prompting management to look for every opportunity to reduce spending. At the same time, rising airfares and hotel rates are making T&E expenses more significant.

Electrovision Can Save $6 Million per Year

Fortunately, Electrovision has a number of excellent opportunities for reducing T&E costs. Savings of up to $6 million per year should be achievable, judging by the experience of other companies. A sensible travel-management program can save companies as much as 35 percent a year (Gilligan 39–40), and we should be able to save even more, since we purchase many more business-class tickets than the average. Four steps will help us cut costs:

1. Hire a director of travel and entertainment to assume overall responsibility for T&E spending, policies, and technologies, including the hiring and management of a national travel agency.
2. Educate employees on the need for cost containment, both in avoiding unnecessary travel and reducing costs when travel is necessary.
3. Negotiate preferential rates with travel providers.
4. Implement technological alternatives to travel, such as virtual meetings.

As necessary as these changes are, they will likely hurt morale, at least in the short term. Management will need to make a determined effort to explain the rationale for reduced spending. By exercising moderation in their own travel arrangements, Electrovision executives can set a good example and help other employees accept the changes. On the plus side, using travel alternatives such as web conferencing will reduce the travel burden on many employees and help them balance their business and personal lives.

iv

Targets a receptive audience with a hard-hitting tone in the executive summary (a more neutral approach would be better for hostile or skeptical readers)

Executive summary uses the same font and paragraph treatment as the text of the report

Moreno decided to include an executive summary because her report is aimed at a mixed audience, some of whom are interested in the details of her report and others who just want the "big picture." The executive summary is aimed at the second group, giving these readers enough information to make a decision without burdening them with the task of reading the entire report.

Her writing style matches the serious nature of the content without sounding distant or stiff. Moreno chose the formal approach because several members of her audience are considerably higher up in the organization, and she did not want to sound too familiar. In addition, her company prefers the impersonal style for formal reports.

Figure 11.14   Continued

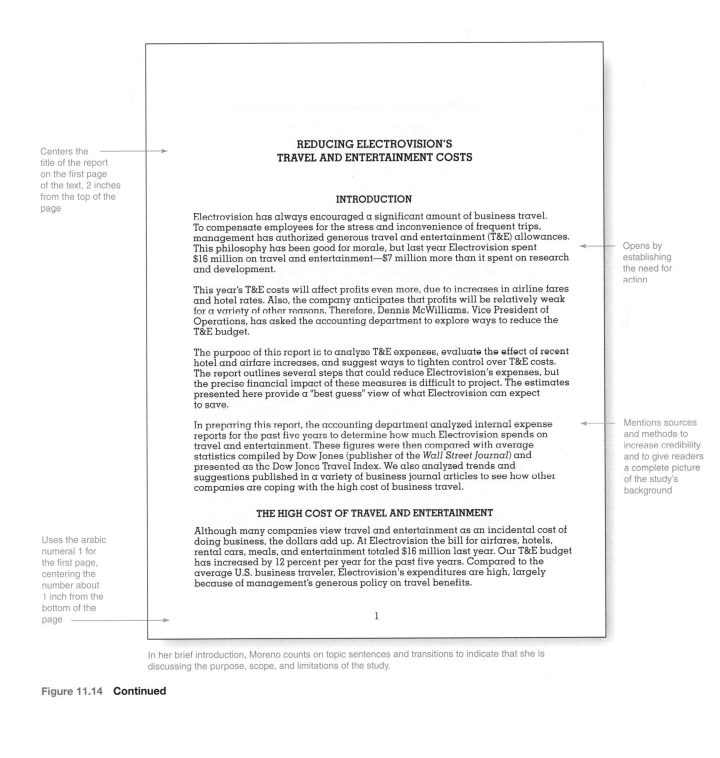

Centers the title of the report on the first page of the text, 2 inches from the top of the page

Uses the arabic numeral 1 for the first page, centering the number about 1 inch from the bottom of the page

Opens by establishing the need for action

Mentions sources and methods to increase credibility and to give readers a complete picture of the study's background

REDUCING ELECTROVISION'S TRAVEL AND ENTERTAINMENT COSTS

INTRODUCTION

Electrovision has always encouraged a significant amount of business travel. To compensate employees for the stress and inconvenience of frequent trips, management has authorized generous travel and entertainment (T&E) allowances. This philosophy has been good for morale, but last year Electrovision spent $16 million on travel and entertainment—$7 million more than it spent on research and development.

This year's T&E costs will affect profits even more, due to increases in airline fares and hotel rates. Also, the company anticipates that profits will be relatively weak for a variety of other reasons. Therefore, Dennis McWilliams, Vice President of Operations, has asked the accounting department to explore ways to reduce the T&E budget.

The purpose of this report is to analyze T&E expenses, evaluate the effect of recent hotel and airfare increases, and suggest ways to tighten control over T&E costs. The report outlines several steps that could reduce Electrovision's expenses, but the precise financial impact of these measures is difficult to project. The estimates presented here provide a "best guess" view of what Electrovision can expect to save.

In preparing this report, the accounting department analyzed internal expense reports for the past five years to determine how much Electrovision spends on travel and entertainment. These figures were then compared with average statistics compiled by Dow Jones (publisher of the *Wall Street Journal*) and presented as the Dow Jones Travel Index. We also analyzed trends and suggestions published in a variety of business journal articles to see how other companies are coping with the high cost of business travel.

THE HIGH COST OF TRAVEL AND ENTERTAINMENT

Although many companies view travel and entertainment as an incidental cost of doing business, the dollars add up. At Electrovision the bill for airfares, hotels, rental cars, meals, and entertainment totaled $16 million last year. Our T&E budget has increased by 12 percent per year for the past five years. Compared to the average U.S. business traveler, Electrovision's expenditures are high, largely because of management's generous policy on travel benefits.

1

In her brief introduction, Moreno counts on topic sentences and transitions to indicate that she is discussing the purpose, scope, and limitations of the study.

Figure 11.14   Continued

2

Uses arabic numerals to number the second and succeeding pages of the text in the upper right-hand corner where the top and right-hand margins meet

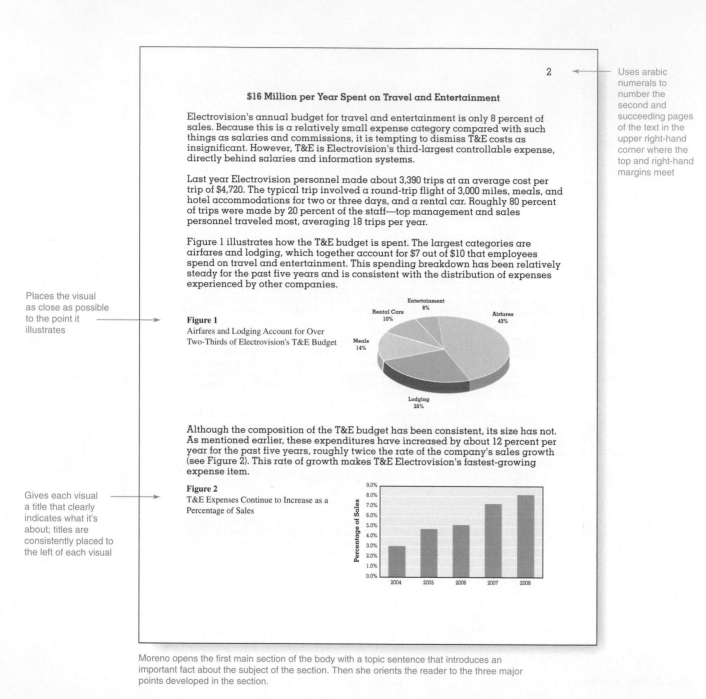

$16 Million per Year Spent on Travel and Entertainment

Electrovision's annual budget for travel and entertainment is only 8 percent of sales. Because this is a relatively small expense category compared with such things as salaries and commissions, it is tempting to dismiss T&E costs as insignificant. However, T&E is Electrovision's third-largest controllable expense, directly behind salaries and information systems.

Last year Electrovision personnel made about 3,390 trips at an average cost per trip of $4,720. The typical trip involved a round-trip flight of 3,000 miles, meals, and hotel accommodations for two or three days, and a rental car. Roughly 80 percent of trips were made by 20 percent of the staff—top management and sales personnel traveled most, averaging 18 trips per year.

Figure 1 illustrates how the T&E budget is spent. The largest categories are airfares and lodging, which together account for $7 out of $10 that employees spend on travel and entertainment. This spending breakdown has been relatively steady for the past five years and is consistent with the distribution of expenses experienced by other companies.

Figure 1
Airfares and Lodging Account for Over
Two-Thirds of Electrovision's T&E Budget

Entertainment 8%
Rental Cars 10%
Airfares 43%
Meals 14%
Lodging 25%

Although the composition of the T&E budget has been consistent, its size has not. As mentioned earlier, these expenditures have increased by about 12 percent per year for the past five years, roughly twice the rate of the company's sales growth (see Figure 2). This rate of growth makes T&E Electrovision's fastest-growing expense item.

Figure 2
T&E Expenses Continue to Increase as a
Percentage of Sales

Percentage of Sales
9.0%
8.0%
7.0%
6.0%
5.0%
4.0%
3.0%
2.0%
1.0%
0.0%
2004 2005 2006 2007 2008

Places the visual as close as possible to the point it illustrates

Gives each visual a title that clearly indicates what it's about; titles are consistently placed to the left of each visual

Moreno opens the first main section of the body with a topic sentence that introduces an important fact about the subject of the section. Then she orients the reader to the three major points developed in the section.

Figure 11.14 **Continued**

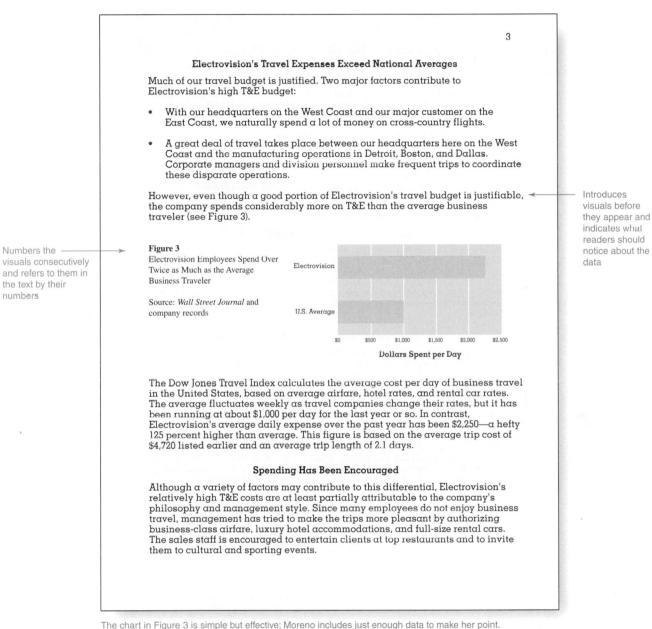

3

Electrovision's Travel Expenses Exceed National Averages

Much of our travel budget is justified. Two major factors contribute to Electrovision's high T&E budget:

- With our headquarters on the West Coast and our major customer on the East Coast, we naturally spend a lot of money on cross-country flights.

- A great deal of travel takes place between our headquarters here on the West Coast and the manufacturing operations in Detroit, Boston, and Dallas. Corporate managers and division personnel make frequent trips to coordinate these disparate operations.

However, even though a good portion of Electrovision's travel budget is justifiable, the company spends considerably more on T&E than the average business traveler (see Figure 3).

Figure 3
Electrovision Employees Spend Over Twice as Much as the Average Business Traveler

Source: *Wall Street Journal* and company records

Electrovision

U.S. Average

$0 $500 $1,000 $1,500 $2,000 $2,500

Dollars Spent per Day

The Dow Jones Travel Index calculates the average cost per day of business travel in the United States, based on average airfare, hotel rates, and rental car rates. The average fluctuates weekly as travel companies change their rates, but it has been running at about $1,000 per day for the last year or so. In contrast, Electrovision's average daily expense over the past year has been $2,250—a hefty 125 percent higher than average. This figure is based on the average trip cost of $4,720 listed earlier and an average trip length of 2.1 days.

Spending Has Been Encouraged

Although a variety of factors may contribute to this differential, Electrovision's relatively high T&E costs are at least partially attributable to the company's philosophy and management style. Since many employees do not enjoy business travel, management has tried to make the trips more pleasant by authorizing business-class airfare, luxury hotel accommodations, and full-size rental cars. The sales staff is encouraged to entertain clients at top restaurants and to invite them to cultural and sporting events.

Numbers the visuals consecutively and refers to them in the text by their numbers

Introduces visuals before they appear and indicates what readers should notice about the data

The chart in Figure 3 is simple but effective; Moreno includes just enough data to make her point. Notice how she is as careful about the appearance of her report as she is about the quality of its content.

Figure 11.14 Continued

4

The cost of these privileges is easy to overlook, given the weakness of Electrovision's system for keeping track of T&E expenses:

- The monthly financial records do not contain a separate category for travel and entertainment; the information is buried under Cost of Goods Sold and under Selling, General, and Administrative Expenses.

- Each department head is given authority to approve any expense report, regardless of how large it may be.

- Receipts are not required for expenditures of less than $100.

- Individuals are allowed to make their own travel arrangements.

- No one is charged with the responsibility for controlling the company's total spending on travel and entertainment.

GROWING IMPACT ON THE BOTTOM LINE

During the past three years, the company's healthy profits have resulted in relatively little pressure to push for tighter controls over all aspects of the business. However, as we all know, the situation is changing. We're projecting flat to declining profits for the next two years, a situation that has prompted all of us to search for ways to cut costs. At the same time, rising airfares and hotel rates have increased the impact of T&E expenses on the company's financial results.

Lower Profits Underscore the Need for Change

The next two years promise to be difficult for Electrovision. After several years of steady increases in spending, the Postal Service is tightening procurement policies for automated mail-handling equipment. Funding for the A-12 optical character reader has been canceled. As a consequence, the marketing department expects sales to drop by 15 percent. Although Electrovision is negotiating several other promising R&D contracts, the marketing department does not foresee any major procurements for the next two to three years.

At the same time, Electrovision is facing cost increases on several fronts. As we have known for several months, the new production facility now under construction in Salt Lake City, Utah, is behind schedule and over budget. Labor contracts in Boston and Dallas will expire within the next six months, and plant managers there anticipate that significant salary and benefits concessions may be necessary to avoid strikes.

Moreover, marketing and advertising costs are expected to increase as we attempt to strengthen these activities to better cope with competitive pressures. Given the expected decline in revenues and increase in costs, the Executive Committee's prediction that profits will fall by 12 percent in the coming fiscal year does not seem overly pessimistic.

Moreno designed her report to include plenty of white space so even those pages that lack visuals are still attractive and easy to read.

Figure 11.14 Continued

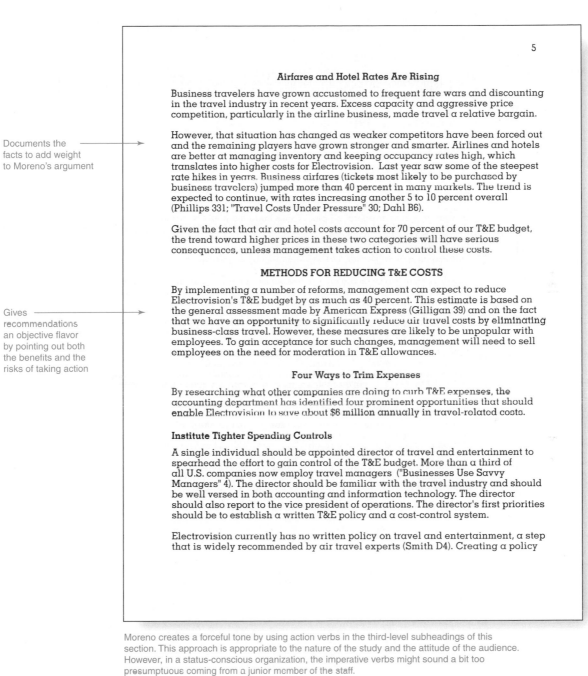

5

Airfares and Hotel Rates Are Rising

Business travelers have grown accustomed to frequent fare wars and discounting in the travel industry in recent years. Excess capacity and aggressive price competition, particularly in the airline business, made travel a relative bargain.

However, that situation has changed as weaker competitors have been forced out and the remaining players have grown stronger and smarter. Airlines and hotels are better at managing inventory and keeping occupancy rates high, which translates into higher costs for Electrovision. Last year saw some of the steepest rate hikes in years. Business airfares (tickets most likely to be purchased by business travelers) jumped more than 40 percent in many markets. The trend is expected to continue, with rates increasing another 5 to 10 percent overall (Phillips 331; "Travel Costs Under Pressure" 30; Dahl B6).

Given the fact that air and hotel costs account for 70 percent of our T&E budget, the trend toward higher prices in these two categories will have serious consequences, unless management takes action to control these costs.

METHODS FOR REDUCING T&E COSTS

By implementing a number of reforms, management can expect to reduce Electrovision's T&E budget by as much as 40 percent. This estimate is based on the general assessment made by American Express (Gilligan 39) and on the fact that we have an opportunity to significantly reduce air travel costs by eliminating business-class travel. However, these measures are likely to be unpopular with employees. To gain acceptance for such changes, management will need to sell employees on the need for moderation in T&E allowances.

Four Ways to Trim Expenses

By researching what other companies are doing to curb T&E expenses, the accounting department has identified four prominent opportunities that should enable Electrovision to save about $6 million annually in travel-related costs.

Institute Tighter Spending Controls

A single individual should be appointed director of travel and entertainment to spearhead the effort to gain control of the T&E budget. More than a third of all U.S. companies now employ travel managers ("Businesses Use Savvy Managers" 4). The director should be familiar with the travel industry and should be well versed in both accounting and information technology. The director should also report to the vice president of operations. The director's first priorities should be to establish a written T&E policy and a cost-control system.

Electrovision currently has no written policy on travel and entertainment, a step that is widely recommended by air travel experts (Smith D4). Creating a policy

---

Documents the facts to add weight to Moreno's argument

Gives recommendations an objective flavor by pointing out both the benefits and the risks of taking action

---

Moreno creates a forceful tone by using action verbs in the third-level subheadings of this section. This approach is appropriate to the nature of the study and the attitude of the audience. However, in a status-conscious organization, the imperative verbs might sound a bit too presumptuous coming from a junior member of the staff.

Figure 11.14 Continued

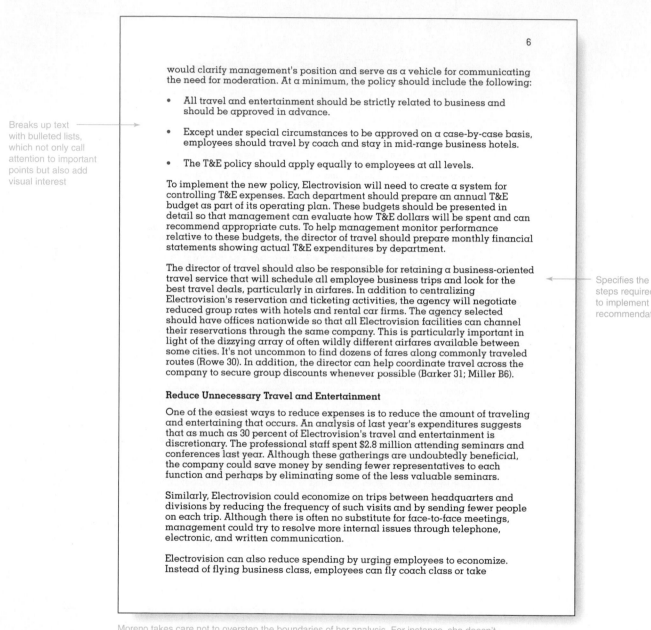

6

would clarify management's position and serve as a vehicle for communicating the need for moderation. At a minimum, the policy should include the following:

- All travel and entertainment should be strictly related to business and should be approved in advance.

- Except under special circumstances to be approved on a case-by-case basis, employees should travel by coach and stay in mid-range business hotels.

- The T&E policy should apply equally to employees at all levels.

To implement the new policy, Electrovision will need to create a system for controlling T&E expenses. Each department should prepare an annual T&E budget as part of its operating plan. These budgets should be presented in detail so that management can evaluate how T&E dollars will be spent and can recommend appropriate cuts. To help management monitor performance relative to these budgets, the director of travel should prepare monthly financial statements showing actual T&E expenditures by department.

The director of travel should also be responsible for retaining a business-oriented travel service that will schedule all employee business trips and look for the best travel deals, particularly in airfares. In addition to centralizing Electrovision's reservation and ticketing activities, the agency will negotiate reduced group rates with hotels and rental car firms. The agency selected should have offices nationwide so that all Electrovision facilities can channel their reservations through the same company. This is particularly important in light of the dizzying array of often wildly different airfares available between some cities. It's not uncommon to find dozens of fares along commonly traveled routes (Rowe 30). In addition, the director can help coordinate travel across the company to secure group discounts whenever possible (Barker 31; Miller B6).

Reduce Unnecessary Travel and Entertainment

One of the easiest ways to reduce expenses is to reduce the amount of traveling and entertaining that occurs. An analysis of last year's expenditures suggests that as much as 30 percent of Electrovision's travel and entertainment is discretionary. The professional staff spent $2.8 million attending seminars and conferences last year. Although these gatherings are undoubtedly beneficial, the company could save money by sending fewer representatives to each function and perhaps by eliminating some of the less valuable seminars.

Similarly, Electrovision could economize on trips between headquarters and divisions by reducing the frequency of such visits and by sending fewer people on each trip. Although there is often no substitute for face-to-face meetings, management could try to resolve more internal issues through telephone, electronic, and written communication.

Electrovision can also reduce spending by urging employees to economize. Instead of flying business class, employees can fly coach class or take

Breaks up text with bulleted lists, which not only call attention to important points but also add visual interest

Specifies the steps required to implement recommendations

Moreno takes care not to overstep the boundaries of her analysis. For instance, she doesn't analyze the value of the seminars that employees attend every year, so she avoids any absolute statements about reducing travel to seminars.

Figure 11.14 Continued

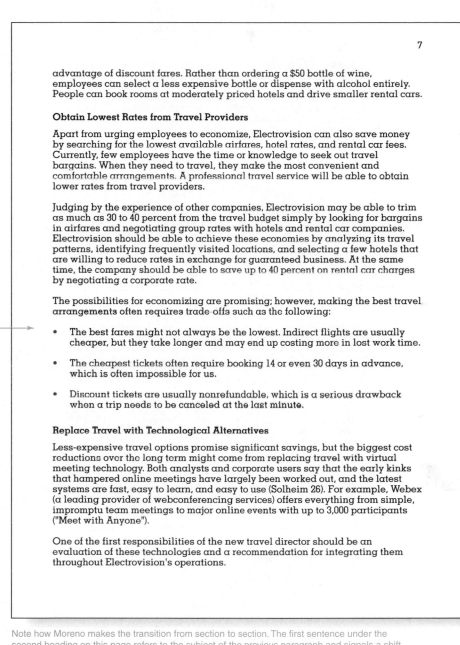

7

advantage of discount fares. Rather than ordering a $50 bottle of wine, employees can select a less expensive bottle or dispense with alcohol entirely. People can book rooms at moderately priced hotels and drive smaller rental cars.

Obtain Lowest Rates from Travel Providers

Apart from urging employees to economize, Electrovision can also save money by searching for the lowest available airfares, hotel rates, and rental car fees. Currently, few employees have the time or knowledge to seek out travel bargains. When they need to travel, they make the most convenient and comfortable arrangements. A professional travel service will be able to obtain lower rates from travel providers.

Judging by the experience of other companies, Electrovision may be able to trim as much as 30 to 40 percent from the travel budget simply by looking for bargains in airfares and negotiating group rates with hotels and rental car companies. Electrovision should be able to achieve these economies by analyzing its travel patterns, identifying frequently visited locations, and selecting a few hotels that are willing to reduce rates in exchange for guaranteed business. At the same time, the company should be able to save up to 40 percent on rental car charges by negotiating a corporate rate.

The possibilities for economizing are promising; however, making the best travel arrangements often requires trade-offs such as the following:

- The best fares might not always be the lowest. Indirect flights are usually cheaper, but they take longer and may end up costing more in lost work time.

- The cheapest tickets often require booking 14 or even 30 days in advance, which is often impossible for us.

- Discount tickets are usually nonrefundable, which is a serious drawback when a trip needs to be canceled at the last minute.

Replace Travel with Technological Alternatives

Less-expensive travel options promise significant savings, but the biggest cost reductions over the long term might come from replacing travel with virtual meeting technology. Both analysts and corporate users say that the early kinks that hampered online meetings have largely been worked out, and the latest systems are fast, easy to learn, and easy to use (Solheim 26). For example, Webex (a leading provider of webconferencing services) offers everything from simple, impromptu team meetings to major online events with up to 3,000 participants ("Meet with Anyone").

One of the first responsibilities of the new travel director should be an evaluation of these technologies and a recommendation for integrating them throughout Electrovision's operations.

Points out possible difficulties to show that all angles have been considered and to build confidence in her judgment

Note how Moreno makes the transition from section to section. The first sentence under the second heading on this page refers to the subject of the previous paragraph and signals a shift in thought.

Figure 11.14 Continued

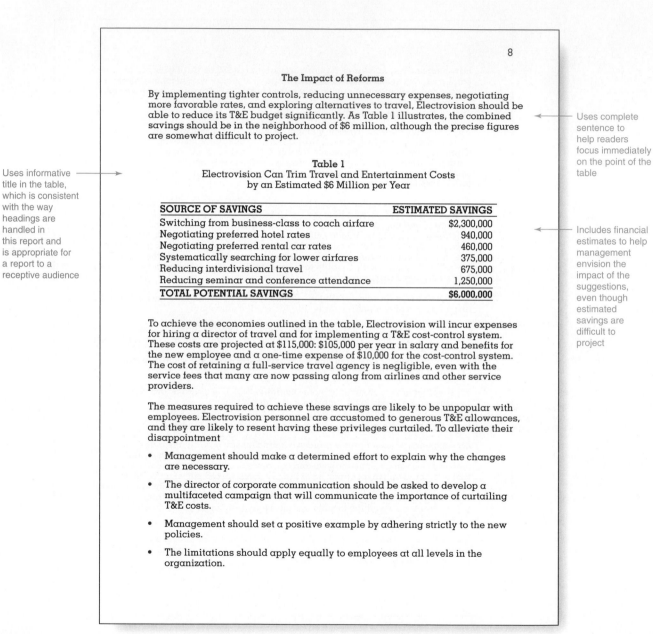

Uses informative title in the table, which is consistent with the way headings are handled in this report and is appropriate for a report to a receptive audience

Uses complete sentence to help readers focus immediately on the point of the table

Includes financial estimates to help management envision the impact of the suggestions, even though estimated savings are difficult to project

The Impact of Reforms

By implementing tighter controls, reducing unnecessary expenses, negotiating more favorable rates, and exploring alternatives to travel, Electrovision should be able to reduce its T&E budget significantly. As Table 1 illustrates, the combined savings should be in the neighborhood of $6 million, although the precise figures are somewhat difficult to project.

Table 1
Electrovision Can Trim Travel and Entertainment Costs
by an Estimated $6 Million per Year

SOURCE OF SAVINGS	ESTIMATED SAVINGS
Switching from business-class to coach airfare	$2,300,000
Negotiating preferred hotel rates	940,000
Negotiating preferred rental car rates	460,000
Systematically searching for lower airfares	375,000
Reducing interdivisional travel	675,000
Reducing seminar and conference attendance	1,250,000
TOTAL POTENTIAL SAVINGS	**$6,000,000**

To achieve the economies outlined in the table, Electrovision will incur expenses for hiring a director of travel and for implementing a T&E cost-control system. These costs are projected at $115,000: $105,000 per year in salary and benefits for the new employee and a one-time expense of $10,000 for the cost-control system. The cost of retaining a full-service travel agency is negligible, even with the service fees that many are now passing along from airlines and other service providers.

The measures required to achieve these savings are likely to be unpopular with employees. Electrovision personnel are accustomed to generous T&E allowances, and they are likely to resent having these privileges curtailed. To alleviate their disappointment

- Management should make a determined effort to explain why the changes are necessary.

- The director of corporate communication should be asked to develop a multifaceted campaign that will communicate the importance of curtailing T&E costs.

- Management should set a positive example by adhering strictly to the new policies.

- The limitations should apply equally to employees at all levels in the organization.

Note how Moreno calls attention in the first paragraph to items in the following table, without repeating the information in the table.

Figure 11.14   Continued

9

Uses a descriptive heading for the last section of the text (in informational reports, this section is often called "Summary"; in analytical reports, it is called "Conclusions" or "Conclusions and Recommendations")

Summarizes conclusions in the first two paragraphs—a good approach because Moreno organized her report around conclusions and recommendations, so readers have already been introduced to them

Emphasizes the recommendations by presenting them in list format

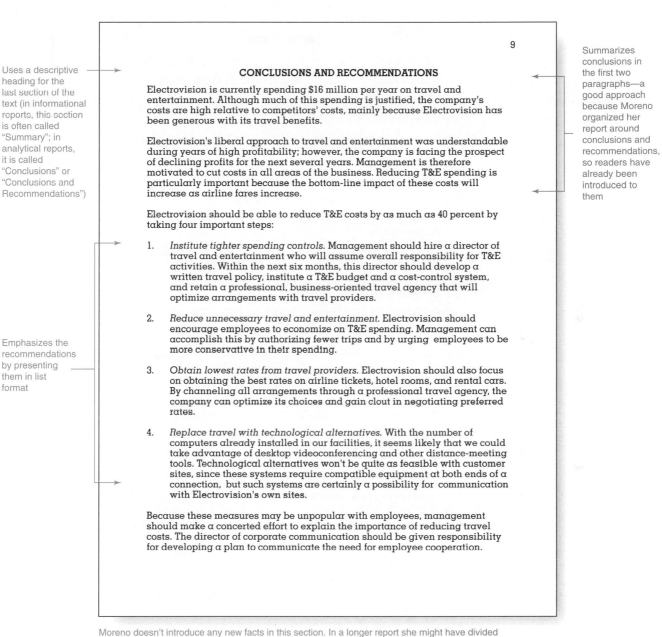

CONCLUSIONS AND RECOMMENDATIONS

Electrovision is currently spending $16 million per year on travel and entertainment. Although much of this spending is justified, the company's costs are high relative to competitors' costs, mainly because Electrovision has been generous with its travel benefits.

Electrovision's liberal approach to travel and entertainment was understandable during years of high profitability; however, the company is facing the prospect of declining profits for the next several years. Management is therefore motivated to cut costs in all areas of the business. Reducing T&E spending is particularly important because the bottom-line impact of these costs will increase as airline fares increase.

Electrovision should be able to reduce T&E costs by as much as 40 percent by taking four important steps:

1. *Institute tighter spending controls.* Management should hire a director of travel and entertainment who will assume overall responsibility for T&E activities. Within the next six months, this director should develop a written travel policy, institute a T&E budget and a cost-control system, and retain a professional, business-oriented travel agency that will optimize arrangements with travel providers.

2. *Reduce unnecessary travel and entertainment.* Electrovision should encourage employees to economize on T&E spending. Management can accomplish this by authorizing fewer trips and by urging employees to be more conservative in their spending.

3. *Obtain lowest rates from travel providers.* Electrovision should also focus on obtaining the best rates on airline tickets, hotel rooms, and rental cars. By channeling all arrangements through a professional travel agency, the company can optimize its choices and gain clout in negotiating preferred rates.

4. *Replace travel with technological alternatives.* With the number of computers already installed in our facilities, it seems likely that we could take advantage of desktop videoconferencing and other distance-meeting tools. Technological alternatives won't be quite as feasible with customer sites, since these systems require compatible equipment at both ends of a connection, but such systems are certainly a possibility for communication with Electrovision's own sites.

Because these measures may be unpopular with employees, management should make a concerted effort to explain the importance of reducing travel costs. The director of corporate communication should be given responsibility for developing a plan to communicate the need for employee cooperation.

Moreno doesn't introduce any new facts in this section. In a longer report she might have divided this section into subsections, labeled "Conclusions" and "Recommendations," to distinguish between the two.

Figure 11.14 Continued

10

WORKS CITED

Barker, Julie. "How to Rein in Group Travel Costs." *Successful Meetings* Feb. 2008: 31.

"Businesses Use Savvy Managers to Keep Travel Costs Down." *Christian Science Monitor* 17 July 2008: 4.

Dahl, Jonathan. "2000: The Year Travel Costs Took Off." *Wall Street Journal* 29 Dec. 2007: B6.

Gilligan, Edward P. "Trimming Your T&E Is Easier Than You Think." *Managing Office Technology* Nov. 2008: 39–40.

"Meet With Anyone, Anywhere, Anytime, "*Webex.com.* 2009. WebEx, 2 February 2009, <http://www.webex.com/solutions/online-meeting-suc.html>.

Miller, Lisa. "Attention, Airline Ticket Shoppers." *Wall Street Journal* 7 July 2007: B6.

Phillips, Edward H. "Airlines Post Record Traffic." *Aviation Week & Space Technology* 8 Jan. 2007: 331.

Rowe, Irene Vlitos. "Global Solution for Cutting Travel Costs." *European* 12 Oct. 2008: 30.

Smith, Carol. "Rising, Erratic Airfares Make Company Policy Vital." *Los Angeles Times* 2 Nov. 2007: D4.

Solheim, Shelley. "Web Conferencing Made Easy." *eWeek* 22 Aug. 2008: 26.

"Travel Costs Under Pressure." *Purchasing* 15 Feb. 2007: 30.

Lists references alphabetically by the author's last name, and when the author is unknown, by the title of the reference (see Appendix B for additional details on preparing reference lists)

Moreno's list of references follows the style recommended in The MLA Style Manual. The box below shows how these sources would be cited following APA style.

10

REFERENCES

Barker, J. (2008, February). How to rein in group travel costs. *Successful Meetings*, 31.

Businesses use savvy managers to keep travel costs down. (2008, July 17). *Christian Science Monitor*, 4.

Dahl, J. (2007, December 29). 2000: The year travel costs took off. *Wall Street Journal*, B6.

Gilligan, E. (2008, November). Trimming your T&E is easier than you think. *Managing Office Technology*, 39–40.

Miller, L. (2007, July 7). Attention, airline ticket shoppers. *Wall Street Journal*, B6.

Phillips, E. (2007, January 8). Airlines post record traffic. *Aviation Week & Space Technology*, 331.

Rowe, I. (2008, October 12). Global solution for cutting travel costs. *European*, 30.

Smith, C. (2007, November 2). Rising, erratic airfares make company policy vital. *Los Angeles Times*, D4.

Solheim, S. (2008, August 22). Web conferencing made easy. *eWeek*, 26.

Travel costs under pressure. (2007, February 15). *Purchasing*, 30.

Webex.com. (2009). *Meet With Anyone, Anywhere, Anytime.* Retrieved 2 February 2009, from http://www.webex.com/solutions/online-meeting-suc.html.

Figure 11.14   Continued

- **Table of contents.** The contents page lists report parts and text headings to indicate the location and hierarchy of the information in the report. List all prefatory parts that come after the contents page and all supplementary parts (see Figure 11.14 on page 281).

- **List of illustrations.** Not all reports include a list of illustrations, but consider including one if the illustrations are particularly important.

- **Synopsis.** A **synopsis**—sometimes called an **abstract**—is a brief overview (one page or less) of a report's most important points. The phrasing of a synopsis can be informative (presenting the main points in the order in which they appear in the text) if you're using the direct approach or descriptive (simply telling what the report is about) if you're using the indirect approach.

- **Executive summary.** Instead of a synopsis or an abstract, a longer report may include an **executive summary**—a fully developed "mini" version of the report—for readers who lack the time or motivation to read the entire document.

Text of a Report

The heart of a report is the text, with its introduction, body, and close. If you have a synopsis or an executive summary, minimize redundancy by balancing your introduction with the material in your summary, as Moreno does in her report (Figure 11.14). Moreno's executive summary is fairly detailed, so she makes her introduction relatively brief.

If you include a synopsis or an executive summary, keep your introduction brief.

Moreno's report also gives you a good idea of the types of supporting detail commonly included in the text body. Include only the essential supporting data in the body; put any additional detail in an appendix. Notice her effective use of visuals.

In a long report, the close may be labeled "Summary" or "Conclusions and Recommendations." Because Moreno organized her report with the direct approach (so her audience has read the key message points in the body), her close is relatively brief. When using the indirect approach, you may use the close to present your recommendations and conclusions for the first time, in which case this section could be more extensive.

Supplementary Parts of a Report

Supplementary parts follow the text of a report and provide information for readers who seek more detailed discussion. Supplements are more common in long reports than in short ones. They typically include the following:

Supplementary parts provide additional detail and reference materials.

- **Appendixes.** An appendix contains additional information for readers who want it—information related to the report but not included in the text because it is too lengthy, is too bulky, or lacks direct relevance. Be sure to list appendixes in your table of contents and refer to them as appropriate in the text.

- **Bibliography.** The bibliography lists the secondary sources you consulted. For more on citing sources, see Appendix B.

- **Index.** An index is an alphabetical list of names, places, and subjects mentioned in the report, along with the pages on which they occur. (See the index of this book for an example.)

Producing a Formal Proposal

Formal proposals contain many of the same components as other formal reports, but the special nature of proposals does require some unique elements (see Figure 11.15).

Prefatory Parts of a Formal Proposal

The cover, title fly, title page, table of contents, and list of illustrations are handled the same in formal proposals as in formal reports. However, other prefatory parts are handled quite differently:

- **Copy of or reference to the RFP.** Instead of having a letter of authorization, a solicited proposal should follow the instructions in the RFP. Some will instruct you to include the entire RFP in your proposal; others may want you to simply identify it by a name and tracking number.

Follow an RFP's instructions for referring to the RFP in your introduction.

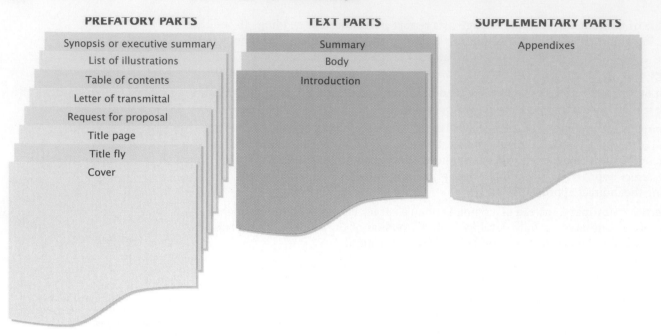

PREFATORY PARTS	TEXT PARTS	SUPPLEMENTARY PARTS
Synopsis or executive summary	Summary	Appendixes
List of illustrations	Body	
Table of contents	Introduction	
Letter of transmittal		
Request for proposal		
Title page		
Title fly		
Cover		

Figure 11.15   Parts of a Formal Proposal
Like formal reports, formal proposals can contain a wide variety of elements in addition to the main text.

- **Synopsis or executive summary.** Although you may include a synopsis or an executive summary, these components are often less useful in a formal proposal than in a report. In an unsolicited proposal, your transmittal letter will catch the reader's interest. In a solicited proposal, the introduction would provide an adequate preview of the contents.
- **Letter of transmittal.** If the proposal is solicited, the transmittal letter follows the pattern for positive messages, highlighting those aspects of your proposal that may give you a competitive advantage. If the proposal is unsolicited, the transmittal letter should follow the advice for persuasive messages (see Chapter 9). The letter must persuade the reader that you have something worthwhile to offer that justifies reading the entire proposal.

Text of a Proposal

> The introduction of a proposal needs to summarize the problem or opportunity that your proposal intends to address.

Just as with reports, the text of a proposal is composed of an introduction, a body, and a close. The introduction presents and summarizes the problem you intend to solve and your solution. It highlights the benefits the reader will receive from the solution. The body explains the complete details of the solution: how the job will be done, how it will be broken into tasks, what method will be used to do it (including the required equipment, material, and personnel), when the work will begin and end, how much the entire job will cost (including a detailed breakdown), and why your company is qualified. The close emphasizes the benefits readers will realize from your solution and urges readers to act (see Figure 11.16).

Proofreading Your Reports and Proposals

After assembling your report or proposal in its final form, review it thoroughly one last time, looking for inconsistencies, errors, and missing components. By proofreading, you can catch minor flaws that might diminish your credibility and major flaws that might damage your career. Don't forget to proof your visuals thoroughly and make sure they are positioned correctly. For online reports, make sure all links work as expected and all necessary files are active and available. If you need specific tips on proofreading documents, look back at Chapter 5.

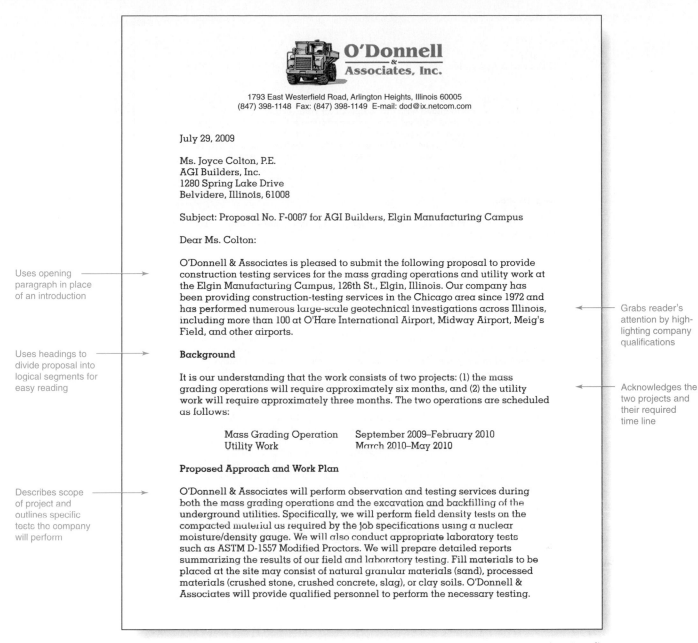

Uses opening paragraph in place of an introduction

Uses headings to divide proposal into logical segments for easy reading

Describes scope of project and outlines specific tests the company will perform

Grabs reader's attention by high-lighting company qualifications

Acknowledges the two projects and their required time line

(continued)

Figure 11.16 Solicited Proposal
This proposal was submitted by Dixon O'Donnell, vice president of O'Donnell & Associates, a geotechnical engineering firm that conducts a variety of environmental testing services. The company is bidding on the mass grading and utility work specified by AGI Builders. As you review this document, pay close attention to the specific items addressed in the proposal's introduction, body, and closing.

Be aware that at this point in the process, you are so familiar with the content of your report or proposal that your mind will fill in missing words, fix misspelled words, and subconsciously compensate for other flaws. Whenever possible, arrange for someone with "fresh eyes" to proofread the report or proposal. Someone who hasn't read the report or proposal yet will be better able to spot flaws. An ideal approach is to have two people review it, one who is an expert in the subject matter and one who isn't. The first person can ensure its technical accuracy, and the second can ensure that a wide range of readers will understand it.[16]

If possible, have someone who hasn't seen the report before proofread it for you.

O'Donnell & Associates, Inc.   Page 2   July 28, 2009

Kevin Patel will be the lead field technician responsible for the project. A copy of Mr. Patel's résumé is included with this proposal for your review. Kevin will coordinate field activities with your job site superintendent and make sure that appropriate personnel are assigned to the job site. Overall project management will be the responsibility of Joseph Proesel. Project engineering services will be performed under the direction of Dixon O'Donnell, P.E. All field personnel assigned to the site will be familiar with and abide by the Project Site Health and Safety Plan prepared by Carlson Environmental, Inc., dated April 2009.

Qualifications

O'Donnell & Associates has been providing quality professional services since 1972 in the areas of

- Geotechnical engineering
- Materials testing and inspection
- Pavement evaluation
- Environmental services
- Engineering and technical support (CADD) services

The company provides Phase I and Phase II environmental site assessments, preparation of LUST site closure reports, installation of groundwater monitoring wells, and testing of soil/groundwater samples for environmental contaminants. Geotechnical services include all phases of soil mechanics and foundation engineering, including foundation and lateral load analysis, slope stability analysis, site preparation recommendations, seepage analysis, pavement design, and settlement analysis.

O'Donnell & Associates materials testing laboratory is certified by AASHTO Accreditation Program for the testing of Soils, Aggregate, Hot Mix Asphalt and Portland Cement Concrete. A copy of our laboratory certification is included with this proposal. In addition to in-house training, field and laboratory technicians participate in a variety of certification programs, including those sponsored by the American Concrete Institute (ACI) and Illinois Department of Transportation (IDOT).

Costs

On the basis of our understanding of the scope of the work, we estimate the total cost of the two projects to be $100,260.00, as follows:

(continued)

Explains who will be responsible for the various tasks

Encloses résumé rather than listing qualifications in the document

Grabs attention by mentioning compelling qualifications

Gains credibility by describing certifications (approvals by recognized industry associations or government agencies)

Figure 11.16   Continued

Distributing Your Reports and Proposals

For physical distribution of important reports or proposals, consider spending the extra money for a professional courier or package delivery service. Doing so can help you stand out in a crowd, and it lets you verify receipt. Alternatively, if you've prepared the document for a single person or small group in your office or the local area, delivering it in person will give you the chance to personally "introduce" the report and remind readers why they're receiving it.

For electronic distribution, unless your audience specifically requests a word processor file, provide documents in PDF format. PDF files aren't as vulnerable to viruses as word processor files, and they let you control how your document is displayed on your audience's computer.

Many businesses use the Adobe portable document format (PDF) to distribute reports electronically.

If your company or client expects you to distribute your reports via a web-based content management system, an intranet, or an extranet, be sure to upload the correct file(s) to the correct online location. Verify the on-screen display of your report after you've posted it, too; make sure graphics, charts, links, and other elements are in place and operational. ■

O'Donnell & Associates, Inc.   Page 3   July 28, 2009

Cost Estimates

Cost Estimate: Mass Grading	Units	Rate ($)	Total Cost ($)
Field Inspection			
Labor	1,320 hours	$38.50	$ 50,820.00
Nuclear Moisture Density Meter	132 days	35.00	4,620.00
Vehicle Expense	132 days	45.00	5,940.00
Laboratory Testing			
Proctor Density Tests (ASTM D-1557)	4 tests	130.00	520.00
Engineering/Project Management			
Principal Engineer	16 hours	110.00	1,760.00
Project Manager	20 hours	80.00	1,600.00
Administrative Assistant	12 hours	50.00	600.00
Subtotal			$ 65,860.00

Cost Estimate: Utility Work	Units	Rate ($)	Total Cost ($)
Field Inspection			
Labor	660 hours	$ 38.50	$ 25,410.00
Nuclear Moisture Density Meter	66 days	5.00	2,310.00
Vehicle Expense	66 days	45.00	2,970.00
Laboratory Testing			
Proctor Density Tests (ASTM D-1557)	2 tests	130.00	260.00
Engineering/Project Management			
Principal Engineer	10 hours	110.00	1,100.00
Project Manager	20 hours	80.00	1,600.00
Administrative Assistant	15 hours	50.00	750.00
Subtotal			$ 34,400.00

Total Project Costs			**$100,260.00**

This estimate assumes full-time inspection services. However, our services may also be performed on an as-requested basis, and actual charges will reflect time associated with the project. We have attached our standard fee schedule for your review. Overtime rates are for hours in excess of 8.0 hours per day, before 7:00 a.m., after 5:00 p.m., and on holidays and weekends.

Itemizes costs by project and gives supporting details

Provides alternative option in case full-time service costs exceed client's budget

(continued)

Figure 11.16 **Continued**

DOCUMENT MAKEOVER

Improve This Report

To practice correcting drafts of actual documents, visit the "Document Makeovers" section in either MyBCommLab.com or the Companion Website for this text.

If MyBCommLab.com is being used in your class, see your User Guide for specific instructions on how to access the content for this chapter.

If you are accessing this feature through the Companion Website, click on "Document Makeovers" and then select Chapter 11. You will find a policy report that contains problems and errors related to what you've learned in this chapter about composing business reports and proposals. Use the Final Draft decision tool to create an improved version of this report. Check the message for an effective opening, consistent levels of formality or informality, and the use of headings, transitions, previews, and reviews to help orient readers. ●

O'Donnell & Associates, Inc.   Page 4   July 28, 2009

Authorization

With a staff of over 30 personnel, including registered professional engineers, resident engineers, geologists, construction inspectors, laboratory technicians, and drillers, we are convinced that O'Donnell & Associates is capable of providing the services required for a project of this magnitude.

Uses brief close to emphasize qualifications and ask for client decision

If you would like our firm to provide the services as outlined in this proposal, please sign this letter and return it to us along with a certified check in the amount of $10,000 (our retainer) by August 14, 2009. Please call me if you have any questions regarding the terms of this proposal or our approach.

Provides deadline and makes response easy

Sincerely,

Dixon O'Donnell

Dixon O'Donnell
Vice President

Enclosures

Accepted for AGI BUILDERS, INC.

Makes letter a binding contract, if signed

By_____   Date _____

Figure 11.16   Continued

❝ CHAPTER REVIEW AND ACTIVITIES

Chapter Summary

The introduction of a report highlights who authorized the report, the purpose and scope, the sources or methods used to gather information, important definitions, any limitations, and the order in which the various topics are covered. The body provides enough information to support your conclusion and recommendations, which can range from explanations of problems or opportunities to facts and trends to results of studies or investigations. The close summarizes key points, restates conclusions and recommendations if appropriate, and lists action items.

Follow these five guidelines to draft effective online content: (1) Build trust by being accurate, current, complete, and authoritative; (2) adapt content to global audiences; (3) write web-friendly content that is compact and efficient; (4) present information in a concise, skimmable format; and (5) make effective use of links.

An effective report helps readers navigate the document by using headings or links that set off important ideas and provides the reader with clues to the report's organization, transitions that tie together ideas and keep readers moving along, and previews and reviews that prepare readers for new information and summarize previously discussed information.

When preparing visuals, (1) use elements of design consistently; (2) use color and other elements to show contrast effectively; (3) strive for visual balance, either formal or informal, that creates a feel that is appropriate for your overall message; (4) use design choices to draw attention to key elements; (5) understand and follow design conventions; and (6) strive for simplicity in your visuals.

Make sure every visual you use is accurate (there are no mistakes or missing information), properly documented (the creator of any underlying data used in the visual has been given complete credit), and honest (the visual honestly reveals the real meaning of the underlying data or information).

A synopsis is a brief overview of an entire report and may either highlight the main points as they appear in the text or simply tell the reader what the report is about. In contrast, an executive summary is essentially a miniature version of the report.

To complete a business report or proposal, you first need to revise, produce, and proofread the document just as you would any other business message. Revising reports and proposals involves evaluating content, style, organization, and tone; reviewing for readability; and editing for clarity and conciseness. After you've verified a report's quality, the fourth step is distributing the report and all supporting materials to the intended audience.

Test Your Knowledge

1. Why must the introduction of an unsolicited proposal include a statement of the problem or opportunity that the proposal addresses?

2. What navigational elements can you use to help readers follow the structure and flow of information in a long report?

3. Both bar charts and pie charts can show the relative size of related variables; when would you use a pie chart rather than a bar chart?

4. What is the purpose of adding titles, captions, and legends to visuals?

5. What is the equivalent of a letter of authorization for a proposal?

Apply Your Knowledge

1. Should a report always explain the writer's method of gathering evidence or solving a problem? Why or why not?

2. When you read a graph, how can you be sure that the visual impression you are receiving is an accurate reflection of reality? Explain.

3. How is consistency in visual design analogous to parallelism in textual elements?

4. You're writing a report to the director of human resources on implementing teams throughout your company. You want to emphasize that since the new approach was implemented six months ago, absenteeism and turnovers have been sharply reduced in all but two departments. How do you visually present your data in the most favorable light? Explain.

5. **Ethical Choices**   If a company receives a solicited formal proposal outlining the solution to a particular problem, is it ethical for the company to adopt the proposal's recommendations without hiring the firm that submitted the proposal? Why or why not?

Practice Your Knowledge

Activities

Active links for all websites in this chapter can be found online. If MyBCommLab.com is being used in your class, see your User Guide for instructions on accessing the content for this chapter. Otherwise, visit www.pearsonhighered.com/bovee, locate *Business Communication Essentials*, Fourth Edition, click the Companion Website link, select Chapter 11, and then click on "Featured Websites." Please note that links to sites that become inactive after publication of the book will be removed from the Featured Websites section.

1. **Teamwork**   You and a classmate are helping Linda Moreno prepare her report on Electrovision's travel and entertainment costs (see Figure 11.14). This time, however, the report is to be informational rather than analytical, so it will not include recommendations. Review the existing report and determine what changes would be needed to make it an informational report. Be as specific as possible. For example, if your team decides the report needs a new title, what title would you use? Draft a transmittal memo for Moreno to use in conveying this informational report to Dennis McWilliams, Electrovision's vice president of operations.

2. **Improve a Wiki Article**   To access this wiki article, go to http://real-timeupdates.com/bce, click on "Student Assignments," and select Chapter 11, Page 300, Activity 2. Revise the article using the editing and revising guidelines in Chapter 5 (page 99), the wiki writing guidelines in Chapter 6 (pages 128–129), and the information in this chapter.

3. **Choosing the Right Visual**   You're preparing the annual report for FretCo Guitar Corporation. For each of the following types of information, select the appropriate chart or visual to illustrate the text. Explain your choices.

   a. Data on annual sales for the past 20 years

   b. Comparison of FretCo sales, product by product (electric guitars, bass guitars, amplifiers, acoustic guitars), for this year and last year

   c. Explanation of how a FretCo acoustic guitar is manufactured

   d. Explanation of how the FretCo Guitar Corporation markets its guitars

   e. Data on sales of FretCo products in each of 12 countries

   f. Comparison of FretCo sales figures with sales figures for three competing guitar makers over the past 10 years

4. **Creating Maps**   You work for C & S Holdings, a company that operates coin activated, self-service car washes. Research shows that the farther customers live from a car wash, the less likely they are to visit. You know that 50 percent of customers at each of your car washes live within a 4-mile radius of the location, 65 percent live within 6 miles, 80 percent live within 8 miles, and 90 percent live within 10 miles. C & S's owner wants to open two new car washes in your city and has asked you to prepare a report recommending locations. Using a map of your city from an online or printed source, choose

two possible locations for car washes and create a visual that depicts the customer base surrounding each location (make up whatever population data you need).

5. **Composing Reports: Navigational Clues**   Review a long business article in a journal or newspaper. Highlight examples of how the article uses headings, transitions, previews, and reviews to help the readers find their way.

6. **Ethical Choices**   Your boss has asked you to prepare a feasibility report to determine whether the company should advertise its custom-crafted cabinetry in the weekly neighborhood newspaper. Based on your primary research, you think it should. As you draft the introduction to your report, however, you discover that the survey administered to the neighborhood newspaper subscribers was flawed. Several of the questions were poorly written and misleading. You used the survey results, among other findings, to justify your recommendation. The report is due in three days. What actions might you want to take, if any, before you complete your report?

7. **Producing Reports: Letter of Transmittal**   You are president of the Friends of the Library, a not-for-profit group that raises funds and provides volunteers to support your local library. Every February, you send a report of the previous year's activities and accomplishments to the County Arts Council, which provides an annual grant of $1,000 toward your group's summer reading festival. Now it's February 6, and you've completed your formal report. Here are the highlights:

- Back-to-school book sale raised $2,000.
- Holiday craft fair raised $1,100.
- Promotion and prizes for summer reading festival cost $1,450.
- Materials for children's program featuring local author cost $125.
- New reference databases for library's career center cost $850.
- Bookmarks promoting library's website cost $200.

Write a letter of transmittal to Erica Maki, the council's director. Because she is expecting this report, you can use the direct approach. Be sure to express gratitude for the council's ongoing financial support.

8. **Executive Summaries**   Visit the website of the U.S. Citizenship and Immigration Services (a division of the U.S. Department of Homeland Security), at http://uscis.gov. Click on "About USCIS," followed by "Reports and Studies" and then find the report titled "The Triennial Comprehensive Report on Immigration." Open this file and read the executive summary. Using the information in this chapter, analyze the executive summary and offer specific suggestions for revising it.

Expand Your Knowledge

Exploring the Best of the Web

Brush Up on Your Computer Graphics Skills   Need some help using graphics software? Get started at the About.com graphics software website, http://graphicssoft.about.com. Take the tutorials and learn how to manage fonts and images and how to accomplish a variety of graphics-related tasks. View the illustrated demonstrations. Read the instructional articles. Learn how to use the most common file formats for graphics. Expand your knowledge of the basic principles of graphic design and master some advanced color tips and theory. Don't leave without following the links to recommended books and magazines. Then answer the following questions.

Exercises

1. What are the most common file formats for online visuals?

2. What does color depth mean in computer visuals?

3. What is dithering, and how can it affect your visuals?

Surfing Your Way to Career Success

Bovée and Thill's Business Communication Headline News offers links to hundreds of online resources that can help you with this course, your other college courses, and your career. Visit http://businesscommunicationblog.com and click on

"Web Directory." The Search Engines and Directories section connects you to a variety of search and metasearch engines, online directories and libraries, specialized search engines for multimedia content, newsfeed aggregators, and other helpful tools. Identify three websites from this section that could be useful in your business career. For each site, write a two-sentence summary of what the site offers and how it could help you launch and build your career.

MyBCommLab.com

Use MyBCommLab.com to test your understanding of the concepts presented in this chapter and explore additional materials that will bring the ideas to life in video, activities, and an online multimedia e-book. Additionally, you can improve your skill with quotation marks, parentheses, ellipses, underscores, and italics by using the "Peak Performance Grammar and Mechanics" module within the lab. Take the Pretest to determine whether you have any weak areas. Then review those areas in the Refresher Course. Take the Follow-Up Test to check your grasp of quotation marks, parentheses, ellipses, underscores, and italics. For an extra challenge, take the Advanced Test. Finally, for even more reinforcement, go to the "Improve Your Grammar, Mechanics, and Usage" section that follows the cases, and complete the "Level 1: Self-Assessment" exercises.

CASES

▼ *Apply the three-step writing process to the following cases, as assigned by your instructor.*

Short Reports

1. Grumbling in the Ranks: When Departments Can't Agree on the Value of Work You've been in your new job as human resources director for only a week, and already you have a major personnel crisis on your hands. Some employees in the marketing department got their hands on a confidential salary report and learned that, on average, marketing employees earn less than engineering employees. In addition, several top performers in the engineering group make significantly more than anybody in marketing. The report was instantly passed around the company by e-mail, and now everyone is discussing the situation. You'll deal with the data security issue later; for now, you need to address the dissatisfaction in the marketing group.

Table 1 on page 303 lists the salary and employment data you were able to pull from the employee database. You also had the opportunity to interview the engineering and marketing directors to get their opinions on the pay situation; their answers are listed in Table 2.

Your task The CEO has asked for a short report, summarizing whatever data and information you have on engineering and marketing salaries. Feel free to offer your own interpretation of the situation as well (make up any information you need), but keep in mind that because you are a new manager with almost no experience in the company, your opinion might not have a lot of influence.

2. Selling Overseas: Research Report on the Prospects for Marketing a Product in Another Country Select a fairly inexpensive product that you currently own and a country that you're not very familiar with. The product could be a moderately priced watch, radio, or other device. Now imagine that you are with the international sales department of the company that manufactures and sells the item and that you are proposing to make it available in the country you have selected.

The first step is to learn as much as possible about the country where you plan to market the product. Check almanacs, encyclopedias, the Internet, and library databases for the most recent information, paying particular attention to descriptions of the social life of the inhabitants, their economic conditions, and cultural traditions that would encourage or discourage use of the product.

Your task Write a short report that describes the product you plan to market abroad, briefly describes the country you have selected, indicates the types of people in this country who would find the product attractive, explains how the product would be transported into the country (or possibly manufactured there, if materials and labor are available), recommends a location for a regional sales center, and suggests how the product should be sold. Your report is to be submitted to the chief operating officer of the company, whose name you can either make up or find in a corporate directory. The report should include your conclusions (how the product will do in this new environment) and your recommendations for marketing (steps the company should take immediately and those it should develop later).

3. A Ready-Made Business: Finding the Right Franchise Opportunity After 15 years in the corporate world, you're ready to strike out on your own. Rather than building a business from the ground up, however, you think that buying a franchise is a better idea. Unfortunately, some of the most lucrative franchise opportunities, such as the major fast-food chains, require significant

TABLE 1 Selected Employment Data for Engineers and Marketing Staff

Employment Statistic	Engineering Department	Marketing Department
Average number of years of work experience	18.2	16.3
Average number of years of experience in current profession	17.8	8.6
Average number of years with company	12.4	7.9
Average number of years of college education	6.9	4.8
Average number of years between promotions	6.7	4.3
Salary range	$58k–$165k	$45k–$85k
Median salary	$77k	$62k

TABLE 2 Summary Statements from Department Director Interviews

Question	Engineering Director	Marketing Director
Should engineering and marketing professionals receive roughly similar pay?	In general, yes, but we need to make allowances for the special nature of the engineering profession. In some cases, it's entirely appropriate for an engineer to earn more than a marketing person.	Yes.
Why or why not?	Several reasons: (1) Top engineers are extremely hard to find, and we need to offer competitive salaries; (2) the structure of the engineering department doesn't provide as many promotional opportunities, so we can't use promotions as a motivator the way marketing can; (3) many of our engineers have advanced degrees, and nearly all pursue continuous education to stay on top of the technology.	Without marketing, the products the engineers create wouldn't reach customers, and the company wouldn't have any revenue. The two teams make equal contributions to the company's success.
If we decide to balance pay between the two departments, how should we do it?	If we do anything to cap or reduce engineering salaries, we'll lose key people to the competition.	If we can't increase payroll immediately to raise marketing salaries, the only fair thing to do is freeze raises in engineering and gradually raise marketing salaries over the next few years.

start-up costs—some more than a half million dollars. Fortunately, you've met several potential investors who seem willing to help you get started in exchange for a share of ownership. Between your own savings and these investors, you estimate that you can raise from $350,000 to $600,000, depending on how much ownership share you want to concede to the investors.

You've worked in several functional areas already, including sales and manufacturing, so you have a fairly well-rounded business résumé. You're open to just about any type of business, too, as long as it provides the opportunity to grow; you don't want to be so tied down to the first operation that you can't turn it over to a hired manager and expand into another market.

Your task To convene a formal meeting with the investor group, you need to first draft a report that outlines the types of franchise opportunities you'd like to pursue. Write a brief report, identifying five franchises that you would like to explore further. (Choose five based on your own personal interests and the criteria identified above.) For each possibility, identify the nature of the business, the financial requirements, the level of support the company provides, and a brief statement of why you could run such a business successfully (make up any details you need). Be sure to carefully review the information you find about each franchise company to make sure you can qualify for it. For instance, McDonald's doesn't allow investment partnerships to buy franchises, so you won't be able to start up a McDonald's outlet until you have enough money to do it on your own.

For a quick introduction to franchising, see How Stuff Works (www.howstuffworks.com/franchising). You can learn more about the business of franchising at Franchising.com (www.franchising.com) and search for specific franchise opportunities at FranCorp Connect (www.francorpconnect .com). In addition, many companies that sell franchises, such as Subway, offer additional information on their websites.

Long Reports

[PORTFOLIO BUILDER]

4. Moving the Workforce: Understanding Commute Patterns

Your company is the largest private employer in your metropolitan area, and the 43,500 employees in your workforce have a tremendous impact on local traffic. A group of city and county transportation officials recently approached your CEO with a request to explore ways to reduce this impact. The CEO has assigned you the task of analyzing the workforce's transportation habits and attitudes as a first step toward identifying potential solutions. He's willing to consider anything from subsidized bus passes to company-owned shuttle buses to telecommuting, but the decision requires a thorough understanding of employee transportation needs. Tables 1 through 5 summarize data you collected in an employee survey.

TABLE 1 Employee Carpool Habits

Frequency of Use: Carpooling	Portion of Workforce
Every day, every week	10,138 (23%)
Certain days, every week	4,361 (10%)
Randomly	983 (2%)
Never	28,018 (64%)

TABLE 2 Use of Public Transportation

Frequency of Use: Public Transportation	Portion of Workforce
Every day, every week	23,556 (54%)
Certain days, every week	2,029 (5%)
Randomly	5,862 (13%)
Never	12,053 (28%)

TABLE 3 Effect of Potential Improvements to Public Transportation

Which of the Following Would Encourage You to Use Public Transportation More Frequently? (Check all that apply.)*	Portion of Respondents
Increased perceptions of safety	4,932 (28%)
Improved cleanliness	852 (5%)
Reduced commute times	7,285 (41%)
Greater convenience: fewer transfers	3,278 (18%)
Greater convenience: more stops	1,155 (6%)
Lower (or subsidized) fares	5,634 (31%)
Nothing could encourage me to take public transportation	8,294 (46%)

*Note: This question was asked of respondents who use public transportation randomly or never, a subgroup that represents 17,915 employees, or 41 percent of the workforce.

TABLE 4 Distance Traveled to/from Work

Distance You Travel to Work (one way)	Portion of Workforce
Less than 1 mile	531 (1%)
1–3 miles	6,874 (16%)
4–10 miles	22,951 (53%)
11–20 miles	10,605 (24%)
More than 20 miles	2,539 (6%)

TABLE 5 Is Telecommuting an Option?

Does the Nature of Your Work Make Telecommuting a Realistic Option?	Portion of Workforce
Yes, every day	3,460 (8%)
Yes, several days a week	8,521 (20%)
Yes, random days	12,918 (30%)
No	18,601 (43%)

Your task Present the results of your survey in an informational report, using the data provided in the tables.

[PORTFOLIO BUILDER]

5. You Can Get Anything Online These Days: Shopping for Automobiles on the Internet

As a researcher in your state's consumer protection agency, you're frequently called on to investigate consumer topics and write reports for the agency's website. Thousands of consumers have arranged the purchase of cars online, and millions more do at least some of their research online before heading to a dealership. Some want to save time and money, some want to be armed with as much information as possible before talking to a dealer, and others want to completely avoid the often-uncomfortable experience of negotiating prices with car salespeople. In response, a variety of online services have emerged to meet these consumer needs. Some let you compare information on various car models, some connect you to local dealers to complete the transaction, and some complete nearly all the transaction details for you, including negotiating the price. Some search the inventory of thousands of dealers, whereas others search only a single dealership or a network of affiliated dealers. In other words, a slew of new tools are available for car buyers, but it's not always easy to figure out where to go and what to expect. That's where your report will help.

By visiting a variety of car-related websites and reading magazine and newspaper articles on the car-buying process, you've compiled a variety of notes related to the subject:

- **Process overview.** The process is relatively straightforward and fairly similar to other online shopping experiences, with two key differences. In general, a consumer identifies the make and model of car he or she wants, and then the online car buying service searches the inventories of car dealers nationwide and presents the available choices. The consumer chooses a particular car from that list, and then the service handles the communication and purchase details with the dealer. When the paperwork is finished, the consumer visits the dealership and picks up the car. The two biggest differences with online auto buying are that (1) you can't actually complete the purchase over the Internet (in most cases, you must visit a local dealer to pick up the car and sign the papers, although in some cities, a dealer or a local car buying service will deliver it to your home) and (2) in most states, it's illegal to purchase a new car from anyone other than a franchise dealer (that is, you can't buy directly from the manufacturer, the way you can buy a Dell computer directly from Dell, for instance).

- **Information you can find online (not all information is available at all sites).** You can find information on makes, models, colors, options, option packages (often, specific options are available only as part of a package; you need to know these constraints before you select your options), photos, specifications (everything from engine size to interior space), mileage estimates, performance data, safety information, predicted resale value, reviews, comparable models, insurance costs, consumer ratings, repair and reliability histories, available buyer incentives and rebates, true ownership costs (including costs for fuel, maintenance, repair, and so on), warranty, loan and lease payments, and maintenance requirements.

- **Advantages of shopping online.** Advantages of shopping online include shopping from the comfort and convenience of home, none of the dreaded negotiating at the dealership (in many cases), the ability to search far and wide for a specific car (even nationwide, on many sites), rapid access to considerable amounts of data and information, and reviews from both professional automotive journalists and other consumers. In general, online auto shopping reduces a key advantage that auto dealers used to have, which was control of most of the information in the purchase transaction. Now consumers can find out how reliable each model is, how quickly it will depreciate, how often it is likely to need repairs, what other drivers think of it, how much the dealer paid the manufacturer for it, and so on.

- **Changing nature of the business.** The relationship between dealers and third-party websites (such as CarsDirect.com and Vehix.com) continues to evolve. At first, the relationship was more antagonistic, as some third-party sites and dealers frequently competed for the same customers, and each side made bold proclamations about driving the other out of business. However, the relationship is more collaborative in many cases now, with dealers realizing that some third-party sites already have wide brand awareness and nationwide audiences. As the percentage of new car sales that originate via the Internet continues to increase, dealers are more receptive to working with third-party sites.

- **Comparing information from multiple sources.** Consumers shouldn't rely solely on information from a single website. Each site has its own way of organizing information, and many sites have their own ways of evaluating car models and connecting buyers with sellers.

- **Understanding what each site is doing.** Some sites search thousands of dealers, regardless of ownership connections. Others, such as AutoNation, search only affiliated dealers. A search for a specific model might yield only a half dozen cars on one site but dozens of cars on another site. Find out who owns the site and what their business objectives are, if you can; this will help you assess the information you receive.

- **Leading websites.** Consumers can check out a wide variety of websites, some of which are full-service operations, offering everything from research to negotiation; others provide more specific and limited services. For instance, CarsDirect (www.carsdirect.com) provides a full range of services, whereas Carfax (www.carfax.com) specializes in uncovering the repair histories of individual used cars. Table 1 on page 306 lists some of the leading car-related websites.

Your task Write an informational report based on your research notes. The purpose of the report is to introduce consumers to the basic concepts of integrating the Internet into their car-buying activities and to educate them about important issues.[17]

[PORTFOLIO BUILDER]

6. Secondary Sources: Report Based on Library and Online Research
As a college student and an active consumer, you may have considered one or more of the following questions at some point in the past few years:

a. What criteria distinguish the top-rated MBA programs in the country? How well do these criteria correspond to the needs and expectations of business? Are the criteria fair for students, employers, and business schools?

TABLE 1 Leading Automotive Websites

Site	URL
AutoAdvice	www.autoadvice.com
Autobytel	www.autobytel.com
Autos.com	www.autos.com
AutoVantage	www.autovantage.com
Autoweb	www.autoweb.com
CarBargains	www.carbargains.com
Carfax	www.carfax.com
CarPrices.com	www.carprices.com
Cars.com	www.cars.com
CarsDirect	www.carsdirect.com
CarSmart	www.carsmart.com
Consumer Reports	www.consumerreports.org
eBay Motors	www.motors.ebay.com
Edmunds	www.edmunds.com
iMotors	www.imotors.com
IntelliChoice	www.intellichoice.com
InvoiceDealers	www.invoicedealers.com
J.D. Power	www.jdpower.com
Kelly Blue Book	www.kbb.com
MSN Autos	http://autos.msn.com
PickupTrucks.com	www.pickuptrucks.com
The Car Connection	www.thecarconnection.com
Vehix.com	www.vehix.com
Yahoo! Autos	http//autos.yahoo.com

b. Which of three companies you might like to work for has the strongest corporate ethics policies?

c. What will the music industry look like in the future? What's next after online stores such as Apple iTunes and digital players such as the iPod?

d. Which industries and job categories are forecast to experience the greatest growth—and therefore the greatest demand for workers—in the next 10 years?

e. What has been the impact of Starbucks's aggressive growth on small, independent coffee shops? On midsized chains or franchises? In the United States or in another country?

f. How large is the "industry" of major college sports? How much do the major football or basketball programs contribute—directly or indirectly—to other parts of a typical university?

g. How much have minor league sports—baseball, hockey, arena football—grown in small- and medium-market cities? What is the local economic impact when these municipalities build stadiums and arenas?

Your task   Answer one of the preceding questions using secondary research sources for information. Be sure to document your sources in the correct form. Give conclusions and offer recommendations where appropriate.

Proposals

7. Polishing the Presenters: Offering Your Services as a Presentation Trainer   Presentations can make—or break—both careers and businesses. A good presentation can bring in millions of dollars in new sales or fresh investment capital. A bad presentation might cause any number of troubles, from turning away potential customers to upsetting fellow employees to derailing key projects. To help business professionals plan, create, and deliver more effective presentations, you offer a three-day workshop that covers the essentials of good presentations:

- Understanding your audience's needs and expectations
- Formulating your presentation objectives
- Choosing an organizational approach
- Writing openings that catch your audience's attention
- Creating effective graphics and slides
- Practicing and delivering your presentation
- Leaving a positive impression on your audience
- Avoiding common mistakes with Microsoft PowerPoint
- Making presentations online using webcasting tools
- Handling questions and arguments from the audience
- Overcoming the top 10 worries of public speaking (including *How can I overcome stage fright?* and *I'm not the performing type; can I still give an effective presentation?*)

Workshop benefits: Students will learn how to prepare better presentations in less time and deliver them more effectively.
Who should attend: Top executives, project managers, employment recruiters, sales professionals, and anyone else who gives important presentations to internal or external audiences.
Your qualifications: 18 years of business experience, including 14 years in sales and 12 years of public speaking. Experience speaking to audiences as large as 5,000 people. More than a dozen speech-related articles published in professional journals. Have conducted successful workshops for nearly 100 companies.
Workshop details: Three-day workshop (9 A.M. to 3:30 P.M.) that combines lectures, practice presentations, and both individual and group feedback. Minimum number of students: 6. Maximum number of students per workshop: 12.
Pricing: The cost is $3,500, plus $100 per student; 10 percent discount for additional workshops.
Other information: Each attendee will have the opportunity to give three practice presentations that will last from 3 to 5 minutes. Everyone is encouraged to bring PowerPoint files containing slides from actual business presentations. Each attendee will also receive a workbook and a digital video recording of his or her final class presentation on DVD. You'll also be available for phone or e-mail coaching for six months after the workshop.

Your task Identify a company in your local area that might be a good candidate for your services. Learn more about the company by visiting its website so you can personalize your proposal. Using the information listed above, prepare a sales proposal that explains the benefits of your training and what students can expect during the workshop.

[PORTFOLIO BUILDER]

8. Healthy Alternatives: Proposal to Sell Snacks and Beverages at Local Schools For years, a controversy has been brewing over the amount of junk food and soft drinks being sold through vending machines in local schools. Schools benefit from revenue-sharing arrangements, but many parents and health experts are concerned about the negative effects of these snacks and beverages. You and your brother have almost a decade of experience running espresso and juice stands in malls and on street corners, and you'd love to find some way to expand your business into schools. After a quick brainstorming session, the two of you craft a plan that makes good business sense while meeting the financial concerns of school administrators and the nutritional concerns of parents and dietitians. Here are the notes from your brainstorming session:

- Set up portable juice bars on school campuses, offering healthy fruit and vegetable drinks along with simple, healthy snacks
- Offer schools 30 percent of profits in exchange for free space and long-term contracts
- Provide job-training opportunities for students (during athletic events, etc.)
- Provide detailed dietary analysis of all products sold
- Establish a nutritional advisory board composed of parents, students, and at least one certified health professional
- Assure schools and parents that all products are safe (e.g., no stimulant drinks, no dietary supplements, and so on)
- Support local farmers and specialty food preparers by buying locally and giving these vendors the opportunity to test-market new products at your stands

Your task Based on the ideas listed, draft a formal proposal to the local school board, outlining your plan to offer healthier alternatives to soft drinks and prepackaged snack foods. Invent any details you need to complete your proposal.

[PORTFOLIO BUILDER]

9. Career Connections: Helping Employees Get the Advice They Need to Move Ahead It seems like everybody in your firm is frustrated. On the one hand, top executives complain about the number of lower-level employees who want promotions but just don't seem to "get it" when it comes to dealing with customers and the public, recognizing when to speak out and when to be quiet, knowing how to push new ideas through the appropriate channels, and performing other essential but difficult-to-teach tasks. On the other hand, ambitious employees who'd like to learn more feel that they have nowhere to turn for career advice from people who've been there. In between, a variety of managers and midlevel executives are overwhelmed by the growing number of mentoring requests they're getting, sometimes from employees they don't even know.

You've been assigned the challenge of proposing a formal mentoring program—and a considerable challenge it is:

- The number of employees who want mentoring relationships far exceeds the number of managers and executives willing and able to be mentors; how will you select people for the program?
- The people most in demand for mentoring also tend to be some of the busiest people in the organization.
- After several years of belt tightening and staff reductions, the entire company feels overworked; few people can imagine adding another recurring task to their seemingly endless to-do lists.
- What's in it for the mentors? Why would they be motivated to help lower-level employees?
- How will you measure the success or failure of the mentoring effort?

Your task Identify potential solutions to the issues (make up any information you need) and draft a proposal to the executive committee for a formal, companywide mentoring program that would match selected employees with successful managers and executives.

Improve Your Grammar, Mechanics, and Usage

Level 1: Self-Assessment—Quotation Marks, Parentheses, Ellipses, Underscores, and Italics

Review Sections 2.10, 2.11, 2.12, and 3.2 in the Handbook of Grammar, Mechanics, and Usage and then complete the following 15 items.

In items 1–15, insert quotations marks, parentheses, ellipses, and underscores (for italics) wherever necessary.

1. Be sure to read How to Sell by Listening in this month's issue of Fortune.

2. Her response see the attached memo is disturbing.

3. Contact is an overused word.

4. We will operate with a skeleton staff during the holiday break December 21 through January 2.

5. The SBP's next conference, the bulletin noted, will be held in Minneapolis.

6. Sara O'Rourke a reporter from The Wall Street Journal will be here on Thursday.

7. I don't care why you didn't fill my order; I want to know when you'll fill it.

8. The term up in the air means undecided.

9. Her assistant the one who just had the baby won't be back for four weeks.

10. Ask not what your country can do for you is the beginning of a famous quotation from John F. Kennedy.

11. Whom do you think Time magazine will select as its Person of the year?

12. Do you remember who said And away we go?

13. Refinements in robotics may prove profitable. More detail about this technology appears in Appendix A.

14. The resignation letter begins Since I'll never regain your respect and goes on to explain why that's true.

15. You must help her distinguish between i.e. which means that is and e.g. which means for example.

Level 2: Workplace Applications

The following items contain numerous errors in grammar, capitalization, punctuation, abbreviation, number style, word division, and vocabulary. Rewrite each sentence, correcting all errors. Write *C* for any sentence that is already correct.

1. For the lst time, thank's to largely deals with the big chains like Stop & Shop, Sheila's Snak Treetz are showing a profit.

2. The premise for broadband, sometimes called simply 'high speed Internet', is that consumers need a more fast pipeline for getting digital information in our homes.

3. After moving into they're own factory, the Anderson's found theirselves in the market for an oven with airflow controls.

4. Cash-strapped entrepreneurs have learned penny-pinching, cost-cutting, credit-stretching techniques.

5. Designs in the Rough send out some 7 million catalogs a year yet until recently the company did'nt need a warehouse and they hadn't hardly any carrying costs.

6. Blockbuster estimates that 70 percent of the US population live within a 10 minute drive of a Blockbuster store.

7. Nestle Waters North America are the exclusive importer of globally-recognized brands such as: Perrier and Vittel from France and, S. Pelligrino from Italy,

8. The U.S. hispanic community; the largest Minority Group in the country; commands a impressive total purchasing power estimated at more than $500 billion dollars.

9. We conducted a six-month pilot in Chicago, to insure the affectiveness of the program.

10. A series of 7-Eleven television spots help make the term brain freeze part of every day American language.

11. The ad agencies accounts include the following consumer-brands; Wal-Mart, Southwest airlines, Kinko's, Land Rover, and Krispy Kreme.

12. PETsMART allows pets and their humans to together stroll the aisles of its stores; the number one Specialty Retailer of pet supplies.

13. Signature Fruit Co. has confirmed its closing it's Gridley, CA peach plant this Fall.

14. To unite the company's 91 franchisees around a common corporate identity WingsToGo have setup a corporate intranet.

15. It would be well for you to contract with an Internet service provider—a ISP - to both run and to maintain your website.

Level 3: Document Critique

The following document may contain errors in grammar, capitalization, punctuation, abbreviation, number style, vocabulary, and spelling. You may also find problems with organization, format, and word use. Correct all errors using standard proofreading marks (see Appendix C).

Proposal

From: Kris Beiersdorf

Date: 18 April 2009

RE PROJECT: Contract no. 79371 DuPage county

To: Ken Estes, Northern Illinois concrete

Memco Construction is pleased to submit a road construction proposal for the above project. Our company has been providing quality materials and subcontracting services for highway reconstruction projects for over twenty-three years. Our most recent jobs in Illinois have included Illinois State Route 60 resurfacing, and reconstructing Illinois tollway 294.

Should you have any questions about this proposal please contact me at the company 847-672-0344, direct extension #30) or by e-mail at kbeirsdorf@memcocon.com.

Based on the scope of the work outlined: the total cost of this job is projected by us to run ninety-nine thousand, two hundred eighty-three dollars. Because material quantities can vary once a project gets underway a separate page will be attached by us to this memorandum detailing our per-unit fees. Final charges will be based on the exact quantity of materials used for the job, and anything that accedes this estimate will be added of course.

Our proposal assumes that the following items will be furnished by other contractors (at no cost to Memco). All forms, earthwork and clearing; All prep work; Water at project site; Traffic control setup, devices, and maintenance—Location for staging, stockpiling, and storing material and equipment at job sight.

If we win this bid, we are already to begin when the apropriate contracts have been signed by us and by you.

Developing Oral and Online Presentations

LEARNING OBJECTIVES

After studying this chapter, you will be able to

1. Explain the importance of presentations to your career success

2. Explain how to adapt the three-step writing process to presentations

3. Discuss the three functions of an effective introduction

4. Identify ways to get and keep your audience's attention during your presentation

5. Explain how visuals enhance oral presentations and list several popular types of visuals

6. Explain the importance of design consistency in electronic slides and other visuals

7. Highlight six major issues to consider when you're preparing to give a presentation online

8. Identify six methods that effective speakers use to handle questions responsively

With more than 30 years of experience in public speaking, teaching, and training, Marc Friedman has witnessed many technological changes that have transformed oral presentations. While the right tools used in the right way can help a speaker build a strong connection with the audience, too often the technology gets in the way. Friedman says that holding an audience's attention is challenging enough in the best of circumstances, so any kind of barrier that gets in the way—from poorly designed slides to distracting laser pointers to excessive reliance on visual aids—makes the challenge that much greater. By all means, use the latest presentation tools whenever they can help, but don't let them interfere with the conversation you want to have with your audience.[1]

BUILDING YOUR CAREER WITH ORAL PRESENTATIONS

Oral presentations involve all your communication skills, from research through nonverbal communication.

Oral presentations, delivered in person or online, offer important opportunities to put all your communication skills on display, including research, planning, writing, visual design, and interpersonal and nonverbal communication. Presentations also let you demonstrate your ability to think on your feet, grasp complex business issues, and handle challenging situations—all attributes that executives look for when searching for talented employees to promote.

The three-step writing process can help you create more effective presentations and turn your public speaking anxiety into positive energy.

If the thought of giving a speech or presentation makes you nervous, try to keep three points in mind. First, everybody gets nervous when speaking in front of groups. Second, being nervous is actually a good thing; it means you care about the topic, your audience, and your career success. Third, with practice, you can convert those nervous feelings into positive energy that helps you give more compelling presentations. You can take control of the situation by using the three-step writing process to prepare for successful presentations (see Figure 12.1).

Planning

Writing

Completing

Analyze the Situation
Define your purpose and develop a profile of your audience members, including their emotional states and language preferences.

Gather Information
Determine audience needs and obtain the information necessary to satisfy those needs.

Select the Right Medium
Choose the best medium or combination of media for delivering your presentation, including handouts and other support materials.

Organize the Information
Define your main idea, limit your scope and verify timing, select the direct or indirect approach, and outline your content.

Adapt to Your Audience
Be sensitive to audience needs and expectations with a "you" attitude, politeness, positive emphasis, and bias-free language. Build a strong relationship with your audience by establishing your credibility and projecting your company's image. Adjust your delivery style to fit the situation, from casual to formal.

Compose Your Presentation
Outline an effective introduction, body, and close. Consider drafting vital sections such as your opening statement. Prepare supporting visuals and speaking notes.

Revise the Message
Evaluate your content and speaking notes.

Master Your Delivery
Choose your delivery mode and practice your presentation.

Prepare to Speak
Verify facilities, seating arrangements, and equipment, including online connections and software setups. Hire an interpreter if necessary.

Overcome Anxiety
Take steps to feel more confident and appear more confident on stage.

1 **2** **3**

Figure 12.1 **The Three-Step Process for Developing Oral and Online Presentations**
Although you rarely "write" a presentation or speech in the sense of composing every word ahead of time, the tasks in the three-step writing process adapt quite well to the challenge of planning, creating, and delivering oral and online presentations.

PLANNING YOUR PRESENTATION

Planning oral presentations is much like planning any other business message: You analyze the situation, gather information, select the right medium, and organize the information. Gathering information for oral presentations is essentially the same as for written communication projects (see Chapter 10). Be sure to provide full credit for any sources you use, too. Work these credits into your talk, when appropriate, and add citations to your presentation slides, handouts, and other materials. The other three planning tasks have some special applications when it comes to oral presentations; they are covered in the following sections.

Analyzing the Situation

As with written communications, analyzing the situation involves defining your purpose and developing an audience profile (see Table 12.1). The purpose of most of your presentations will be to inform or to persuade, although you may occasionally need to make a collaborative presentation, such as when you're leading a problem-solving or brainstorming session.

In addition to following the audience analysis advice in Chapter 3, try to anticipate the likely emotional state of your audience members. Here are some tips for dealing with a variety of audience mindsets:

Knowing your audience's state of mind will help you adjust both your message and your delivery.

- **Supportive.** Whenever you're fortunate enough to be speaking to people who welcome both you and your message, reward their goodwill with a presentation that is clear, concise, and upbeat. Speak in a relaxed, confident manner and provide just enough information to confirm their belief in you and your message.

311

TABLE 12.1	Analyzing Audiences for Oral Presentations
Task	**Actions**
Determine audience size and composition	1. Estimate how many people will attend.
	2. Identify what they have in common and how they differ.
	3. Analyze the mix of men and women, age ranges, socioeconomic and ethnic groups, occupations, and geographic regions represented.
Predict the audience's probable reaction	1. Analyze why audience members are attending the presentation.
	2. Determine the audience's general attitude toward the topic: interested, moderately interested, unconcerned, open-minded, or hostile.
	3. Analyze the mood that people will be in when you speak to them.
	4. Find out what kind of backup information will most impress the audience: technical data, historical information, financial data, demonstrations, samples, and so on.
	5. Consider whether the audience has any biases that might work against you.
	6. Anticipate possible objections or questions.
Gauge the audience's experience	1. Analyze whether everybody in the audience has the same background and level of understanding.
	2. Determine what the audience already knows about the subject.
	3. Decide what background information the audience will need to better understand the subject.
	4. Consider whether the audience is familiar with the vocabulary you intend to use.
	5. Analyze what the audience expects from you.
	6. Think about the mix of general concepts and specific details you will need to present.

- **Interested but neutral.** Plan to build your credibility as you present your main idea and key support points. Address possible objections as you move along to show that you've considered all sides of the issue. Be confident in what you have to say but remain open to questions and challenges.

- **Uninterested.** In some respects, an uninterested audience can be even more challenging than an apprehensive or hostile audience. If people don't care, it doesn't matter how good your presentation is. Think creatively to find a way to connect your message with some aspect of their personal or professional lives (see Table 12.2 on page 317).

- **Apprehensive.** If listeners are worried about your message, treat their emotions with respect. Don't try to defuse the situation with humor or trivialize their concerns. If your message will calm their fears, use the direct approach to share the good news immediately. If your message will confirm their fears, consider using the indirect approach to build up rational support for the negative message.

- **Hostile.** No one looks forward to addressing an angry audience, but with such an audience, you do have one major factor working in your favor: People definitely care about your message. As with an apprehensive audience, treat hostile audience members' emotions with respect and avoid humor. Prepare thoroughly so you can provide complete information in a calm, rational manner. Consider using the indirect approach to build support for your message while addressing points of concern along the way. Remain calm and don't engage in emotional exchanges with the audience.

Try to learn as much as you can about the setting and circumstances of your presentation, from the size of the audience to seating arrangements.

As you analyze the situation, also consider the circumstances. Is the audience in the room or online? How many people will be present, and how will they be seated? Can you control the environment to minimize distractions? What equipment will you need? Such variables can influence not only the style of your presentation but the content itself.

Selecting the Right Medium

The task of selecting the right medium might seem obvious—after all, you are speaking, so it's an oral medium. However, you have an array of choices these days, ranging from live, in-person presentations to **webcasts** (online presentations that people either view live or download later from your website) or **screencasts** (recordings of activity on computer displays with audio voiceover).

Organizing Your Presentation

Organizing a presentation involves the same tasks as organizing a written message: Define your main idea, limit your scope, select the direct or indirect approach, and outline your content. Remember that when people read written reports, they can skip back and forth if they're confused or don't need certain information. However, in an oral presentation, audiences are more or less trapped in your time frame and sequence. For some presentations, you should plan to be flexible and respond to audience feedback, such as skipping over sections the audience doesn't need to hear and going into more detail in other sections.

Defining Your Main Idea

If you've ever heard a speaker struggle to get his or her main point across ("What I really mean to say is . . ."), you know how frustrating such an experience can be for an audience. To avoid that struggle, figure out the one key message you want audience members to walk away with. Then compose a one-sentence summary that links your subject and purpose to your audience's frame of reference. Here are some examples:

- Convince management that reorganizing the technical support department will improve customer service and reduce employee turnover.
- Convince the board of directors that we should build a new plant in Texas to eliminate manufacturing bottlenecks and improve production quality.
- Address employee concerns regarding a new health-care plan by showing how the plan will reduce costs and improve the quality of their care.

Each of these statements puts a particular slant on the subject, one that directly relates to the audience's interests. By focusing on your audience's needs and using the "you" attitude, you help keep their attention and convince them that your points are relevant.

> If you can't express your main idea in a single sentence, you probably haven't defined it clearly enough.

Limiting Your Scope

For many business presentations, you will be expected to stay within a fixed time frame, so matching the scope of your material to these length expectations is essential. You don't want to get stuck with 10 more minutes of material but only 2 minutes left in your time slot.

Even when you don't have a time limit, audiences appreciate shorter presentations. Studies show that audience attention levels and retention rates drop sharply after 20 minutes, and venture capitalists (investors who fund many new companies) expect entrepreneurs to get to the point within 15 minutes.[2]

The only sure way to know how much material you can cover in a given time is to practice your presentation after you complete it. However, during the planning stage, you can use two techniques to estimate time requirements. First, if you will be using overhead transparencies or electronic slides, figure on 3 or even 4 minutes per slide.[3] For instance, if you have 20 minutes, plan on roughly six or seven slides. Second, most people speak between 125 and 150 words per minute, so you can practice a small portion of your presentation while recording it and then go back and count how many words you used. From that test sample, you can estimate how much material you can cover in a given time frame.

Of course, always be sure to factor in time for introductions, coffee breaks, demonstrations, question-and-answer sessions, and anything else that takes away from your speaking time.

> Limiting your scope ensures that your presentation fits the allotted time and your content meets audience needs and expectations.

> The only sure way to measure the length of your presentation is to complete a practice run.

Choosing Your Approach

With a well-defined main idea to guide you and a clear idea about the scope of your presentation, you can begin to arrange your message. If you have 10 minutes or less to deliver your message, organize your presentation much as you would a letter or a brief memo: Use the direct approach if the subject involves routine information or good news and use the

> Organize short presentations the same way you would a letter or brief memo; organize long presentations as you would a report or proposal.

Figure 12.2 Effective Outline for a 10-Minute Progress Report
Here is an outline of a short presentation that updates management on the status of a key project. The presenter has some bad news to deliver, so she opted for the indirect approach to lay out the reasons for the delay before sharing the news of the schedule slip.

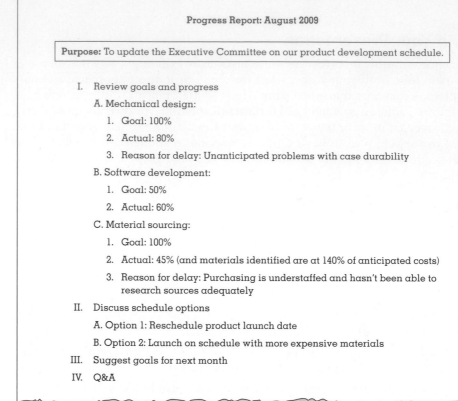

Progress Report: August 2009

Purpose: To update the Executive Committee on our product development schedule.

I. Review goals and progress
   A. Mechanical design:
      1. Goal: 100%
      2. Actual: 80%
      3. Reason for delay: Unanticipated problems with case durability
   B. Software development:
      1. Goal: 50%
      2. Actual: 60%
   C. Material sourcing:
      1. Goal: 100%
      2. Actual: 45% (and materials identified are at 140% of anticipated costs)
      3. Reason for delay: Purchasing is understaffed and hasn't been able to research sources adequately
II. Discuss schedule options
   A. Option 1: Reschedule product launch date
   B. Option 2: Launch on schedule with more expensive materials
III. Suggest goals for next month
IV. Q&A

indirect approach if the subject involves bad news or persuasion. Plan your introduction to arouse interest and to give a preview of what's to come. For the body of the presentation, be prepared to explain the who, what, when, where, why, and how of your subject. In the final section, review the points you've made and close with a statement that will help your audience remember the subject of your speech (see Figure 12.2).

Longer presentations are organized like reports. If the purpose is to motivate or inform, you'll typically use the direct approach and a structure imposed naturally by the subject: comparison, importance, sequence, chronology, geography, or category (as discussed in Chapter 10). If your purpose is to analyze, persuade, or collaborate, organize your material around conclusions and recommendations or around a logical argument. Use the direct approach if the audience is receptive and the indirect approach if you expect resistance.

Using the three-act storytelling model can be a great way to hold the audience's attention.

Finally, remind yourself that like every other good business message, an effective presentation has a clear introduction, body, and close. In fact, one noted presentation expert even advises a three-act storytelling structure (the approach used in many novels, plays, movies, and TV shows), where Act I introduces the "story" you're about to tell and grabs the audience's attention; Act II explores the complications, evidence, support points, and other information needed to understand the story and its conclusion; and Act III resolves all the complications and presents a solution that addresses the problem introduced in Act I and that is strongly supported by all the evidence introduced in Act II.[4]

Preparing Your Outline

In addition to helping you plan your speech, a presentation outline helps you plan your speaking notes.

A presentation outline performs the same all-important function as an outline for a written report: It helps you organize the message in a way that maximizes its impact on your audience. Prepare your outline in several stages:[5]

- State your purpose and main idea and then use these to guide the rest of your planning.
- Organize your major points and subpoints in logical order, expressing each major point as a single, complete sentence.

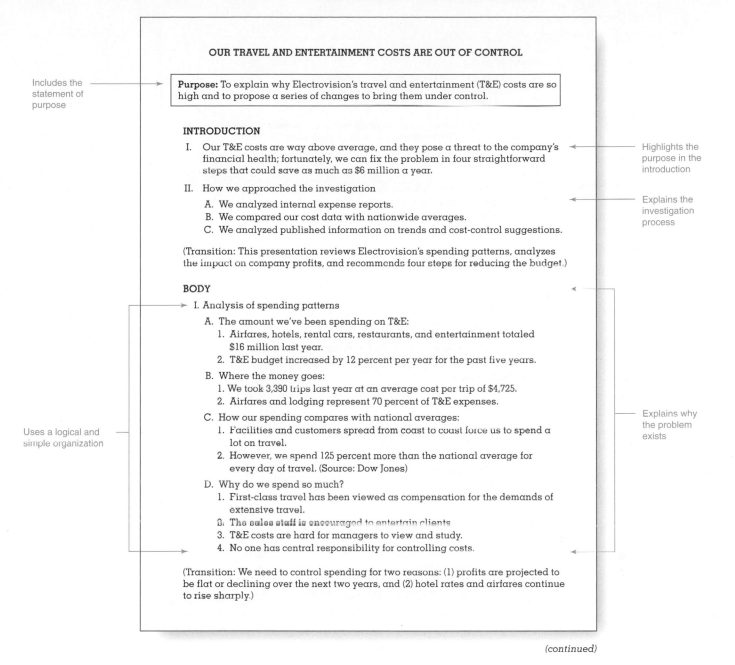

Includes the statement of purpose →

OUR TRAVEL AND ENTERTAINMENT COSTS ARE OUT OF CONTROL

Purpose: To explain why Electrovision's travel and entertainment (T&E) costs are so high and to propose a series of changes to bring them under control.

INTRODUCTION

I. Our T&E costs are way above average, and they pose a threat to the company's financial health; fortunately, we can fix the problem in four straightforward steps that could save as much as $6 million a year.   ← Highlights the purpose in the introduction

II. How we approached the investigation   ← Explains the investigation process
    A. We analyzed internal expense reports.
    B. We compared our cost data with nationwide averages.
    C. We analyzed published information on trends and cost-control suggestions.

(Transition: This presentation reviews Electrovision's spending patterns, analyzes the impact on company profits, and recommends four steps for reducing the budget.)

BODY

I. Analysis of spending patterns
    A. The amount we've been spending on T&E:
        1. Airfares, hotels, rental cars, restaurants, and entertainment totaled $16 million last year.
        2. T&E budget increased by 12 percent per year for the past five years.
    B. Where the money goes:
        1. We took 3,390 trips last year at an average cost per trip of $4,725.
        2. Airfares and lodging represent 70 percent of T&E expenses.
    C. How our spending compares with national averages:
        1. Facilities and customers spread from coast to coast force us to spend a lot on travel.
        2. However, we spend 125 percent more than the national average for every day of travel. (Source: Dow Jones)
    D. Why do we spend so much?
        1. First-class travel has been viewed as compensation for the demands of extensive travel.
        2. The sales staff is encouraged to entertain clients
        3. T&E costs are hard for managers to view and study.
        4. No one has central responsibility for controlling costs.

Explains why the problem exists →

Uses a logical and simple organization →

(Transition: We need to control spending for two reasons: (1) profits are projected to be flat or declining over the next two years, and (2) hotel rates and airfares continue to rise sharply.)

(continued)

Figure 12.3   Effective Outline for a 30-Minute Presentation
This outline clearly identifies the purpose and the distinct points to be made in the introduction, body, and close. Notice also how the speaker has written her major transitions in full-sentence form to be sure she can clearly phrase these critical passages when it's time to speak.

- Identify major points in the body first and then outline the introduction and close.
- Identify transitions between major points or sections and then write these transitions in full-sentence form.
- Prepare your bibliography or source notes; highlight those sources you want to identify by name during your talk.
- Choose a compelling title. Make it brief, action oriented, and focused on what you can do for the audience.[6]

Many speakers like to prepare both a detailed *planning outline* (see Figure 12.3) and a simpler *speaking outline* that provides all the cues and reminders they need to present their material. To prepare an effective speaking outline, follow these steps:[7]

You may find it helpful to create a simpler speaking outline from your planning outline.

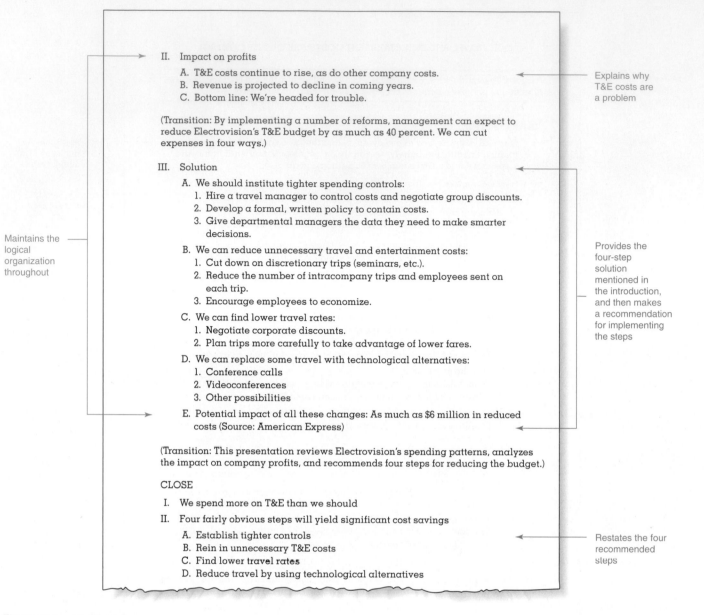

Maintains the logical organization throughout

II.   Impact on profits
    A. T&E costs continue to rise, as do other company costs.
    B. Revenue is projected to decline in coming years.
    C. Bottom line: We're headed for trouble.

(Transition: By implementing a number of reforms, management can expect to reduce Electrovision's T&E budget by as much as 40 percent. We can cut expenses in four ways.)

III. Solution
    A. We should institute tighter spending controls:
      1. Hire a travel manager to control costs and negotiate group discounts.
      2. Develop a formal, written policy to contain costs.
      3. Give departmental managers the data they need to make smarter decisions.
    B. We can reduce unnecessary travel and entertainment costs:
      1. Cut down on discretionary trips (seminars, etc.).
      2. Reduce the number of intracompany trips and employees sent on each trip.
      3. Encourage employees to economize.
    C. We can find lower travel rates:
      1. Negotiate corporate discounts.
      2. Plan trips more carefully to take advantage of lower fares.
    D. We can replace some travel with technological alternatives:
      1. Conference calls
      2. Videoconferences
      3. Other possibilities
    E. Potential impact of all these changes: As much as $6 million in reduced costs (Source: American Express)

(Transition: This presentation reviews Electrovision's spending patterns, analyzes the impact on company profits, and recommends four steps for reducing the budget.)

CLOSE

I.   We spend more on T&E than we should
II. Four fairly obvious steps will yield significant cost savings
    A. Establish tighter controls
    B. Rein in unnecessary T&E costs
    C. Find lower travel rates
    D. Reduce travel by using technological alternatives

Explains why T&E costs are a problem

Provides the four-step solution mentioned in the introduction, and then makes a recommendation for implementing the steps

Restates the four recommended steps

Figure 12.3   Continued

- Start with the planning outline and then strip away anything you don't plan to say directly to your audience.
- Condense points and transitions to key words or phrases.
- Add delivery cues, such as places where you plan to pause for emphasis or use visuals.
- Arrange your notes on numbered cards or sheets of paper. If you plan to use PowerPoint or other presentation software, you can also use the "notes" field on each slide for speaking notes.

WRITING YOUR PRESENTATION

Although you usually don't write out a presentation word for word, you still engage in the writing process—developing your ideas, structuring support points, phrasing your transitions, and so on. Depending on the situation and your personal style, the eventual presentation might follow your initial words closely, or you might express your thoughts in fresh, spontaneous language.

Adapting to Your Audience

Your audience's size, your subject, your purpose, your budget, and the time available for preparation all influence the style of your presentation. If you're speaking to a small group, particularly people you already know, you can use a casual style that encourages audience participation. A small conference room, with your audience seated around a table, may be appropriate. Use simple visuals and invite your audience to interject comments. Deliver your remarks in a conversational tone, using notes to jog your memory if necessary.

Adapting to your audience involves a number of issues, from speaking style to technology choices.

If you're addressing a large audience or if the event is important, establish a more formal atmosphere. During formal presentations, speakers are often on a stage or platform, standing behind a lectern and using a microphone so that their remarks can be heard throughout the room or captured for broadcasting or webcasting.

Composing Your Presentation

Like written documents, oral presentations are composed of distinct elements: the introduction, the body, and the close.

Presentation Introduction

A good introduction arouses the audience's interest in your topic, establishes your credibility, and prepares the audience for what will follow. That's a lot to pack into the first few minutes of your presentation, so give yourself plenty of time to develop the words and visuals you'll use to get your presentation off to a great start.

An effective introduction arouses interest in your topic, establishes your credibility, and prepares the audience for the body of your presentation.

Arousing Audience Interest If your audience members aren't already interested in your subject, your introduction needs to grab their attention. For example, if you wanted to interest younger employees in the company pension plan—which they won't benefit from until many years in the future—you might begin like this:

> If somebody offered to give you $200,000 in exchange for $40 a week, would you be interested? That's the amount you can expect to collect during your retirement years if you choose to contribute to the voluntary pension plan. Although retirement is many years away for most of you, it is an important financial decision that you should consider now. During the next 20 minutes, I'll give you the information you need to make the choice that's best for you and your family.

Table 12.2 suggests six techniques you can use to arouse audience interest during your introduction, and "Holding Your Audience's Attention" on page 318 lists six ways to keep

TABLE 12.2 Six Ways to Get Attention During Your Introduction

Unite the audience around a common goal	Invite the audience to help solve a problem, capitalize on an opportunity, or otherwise engage in the topic of your presentation.
Tell a story	Slice-of-life stories are naturally interesting and can be compelling. Be sure your story illustrates an important point.
Pass around a sample	Physically interacting with objects helps get people involved. If your company is in the textile business, let the audience handle some of your fabrics. If you sell chocolates, give everybody a taste.
Ask a question	Asking questions will get audience members actively involved in your presentation and help you respond to their needs and expectations.
State a startling statistic	People love unusual details and intriguing information.
Use humor	Including a light comment now and then can perk up the audience. Just be sure the humor is relevant to the presentation and not offensive to the audience. In general, avoid humor when you and the audience don't share the same native language.

audience members' attention throughout your presentation. Regardless of which technique you choose, make sure you can give audience members a reason to care and to believe that the time they're about to spend listening to you will be worth their while.[8]

Building Your Credibility   Audiences tend to decide within a few minutes whether you're worth listening to, so establishing your credibility quickly is vital.[9] If you're not a well-known expert or haven't already earned your audience's trust in other situations, you'll need to build credibility in your introduction. If someone else will introduce you, he or she can present your credentials. If you will be introducing yourself, keep your comments brief but don't be afraid to mention your accomplishments. Your listeners will be curious about your qualifications, so tell them briefly who you are, why you're there, and how they'll benefit from listening to you. You might say something like this:

> I'm Karen Whitney, a market research analyst with Information Resources Corporation. For the past five years, I've specialized in studying high-technology markets. Your director of engineering, John LaBarre, asked me to talk about recent trends in computer-aided design so that you'll have a better idea of how to direct your research efforts.

This speaker establishes credibility by tying her credentials to the purpose of her presentation. By mentioning her company's name, her specialization and position, and the name of the audience's boss, she lets her listeners know immediately that she is qualified to tell them something they need to know.

Previewing Your Message   A good introduction gives your listeners a preview of what's ahead, just as the introduction in a report helps readers understand what is coming. Summarize the main idea of your presentation, identify major supporting points, and indicate the order in which you'll develop those points. Of course, if you're building up to a conclusion or recommendation indirectly, you'll need to consider how much to reveal during your introduction.

Presentation Body

The bulk of your speech or presentation is devoted to a discussion of the main points in your outline. No matter what organizational pattern you're using, your goals are to make sure that (1) the organization of your presentation is clear and (2) your presentation holds the audience's attention.

Connecting Your Ideas   In written documents, you can show how ideas are related with a variety of design clues: headings, paragraph indentions, white space, and lists. However, with oral communication—particularly when you aren't using visuals for support—you have to rely primarily on spoken words to link various parts and ideas.

For the links between sentences and paragraphs, use one or two transitional words: *therefore, because, in addition, in contrast, moreover, for example, consequently, nevertheless,* or *finally*. To link major sections of a presentation, use complete sentences or paragraphs, such as "Now that we've reviewed the problem, let's take a look at some solutions." Every time you shift topics, be sure to stress the connection between ideas by summarizing what's been said and previewing what's to come. The longer your presentation, the more important your transitions. Your listeners need clear transitions to guide them to the most important points. Furthermore, they'll appreciate brief interim summaries to pick up any ideas they may have missed.

Holding Your Audience's Attention   A successful introduction will have grabbed your audience's attention; now the body of your presentation needs to hold that attention. Here are a few helpful tips for keeping the audience tuned into your message:

- Keep relating your subject to your audience's needs.
- Anticipate—and answer—your audience's questions as you move along so people don't get confused or distracted.

Margin notes:

If someone else will be introducing you, ask that person to present your credentials.

Offer a preview to help your audience understand the importance, structure, and content of your message.

Use transitions to repeat key ideas, particularly in longer presentations.

- Use clear, vivid language and throw in some variety; repeating the same words and phrases over and over puts people to sleep.

- Show how your subject is related to ideas that audience members already understand and give people a way to categorize and remember your points.[10]

- If appropriate, encourage participation by asking for comments or questions.

- Illustrate your ideas with visuals, which enliven your message, help you connect with audience members, and help them remember your message more effectively (see "Enhancing Your Presentation with Effective Visuals," pages 320–325).

> The most important way to hold an audience's attention is to show how your message relates to their individual needs and concerns.

Presentation Close

Your close is critical because audiences tend to focus more carefully as they wait for you to wrap up, and they will leave with your final words ringing in their ears. Before closing your presentation, tell listeners that you're about to finish so that they'll make one final effort to listen intently. Don't be afraid to sound obvious. Consider saying something such as "In conclusion" or "To sum it all up." You want people to know that this is the final segment of your presentation.

> Plan your close carefully so that your audience leaves with a clear summary of your main idea.

Restating Your Main Points   Repeat your main idea, emphasizing what you want your audience to do or to think, and stress the key motivating factor that will encourage them to respond that way. Reinforce your theme by restating your main supporting points, as this speaker did in a presentation on the company's executive compensation program:

> We can all be proud of the way our company has grown. However, if we want to continue that growth, we need to take four steps to ensure that our best people don't start looking for opportunities elsewhere:
>
> - First, increase the overall level of compensation
> - Second, establish a cash bonus program
> - Third, offer a variety of stock-based incentives
> - Fourth, improve our health insurance and pension benefits
>
> By taking these steps, we can ensure that our company retains the management talent it needs to face our industry's largest competitors.

Repetition of key ideas, as long as you don't overdo it, greatly improves the chance that your audience will hear your message in the way you intended.

Describing Next Steps   Some presentations require the audience to reach a decision or an agreement. If the people agree, verify that consensus. If they don't agree, acknowledge the lack of consensus and then be ready to suggest a method of resolving the differences. If you're not sure how your audience will respond, prepare two closes—one that acknowledges the agreement reached and one that accommodates the fact that the audience didn't reach agreement (such as laying out a timetable for reaching a decision).

If you expect any action to occur as a result of your speech, be sure to explain who is responsible for doing what. List each action item with an estimated completion date and the name of the person or team responsible. This public commitment to action is good insurance that something will happen.

> If you need to have the audience make a decision or agree to take action, make sure the responsibilities for doing so are clear.

Ending on a Strong Note   Be sure to spend plenty of time composing your closing remarks so that you can leave on a strong note. You don't want to wind up on stage with nothing to say but "Well, I guess that's it." Even if the presentation raised tough questions or the audience is in disagreement about some key issues, make sure your final remarks are upbeat and memorable. Conclude with a call to action or some encouraging words. For instance, you might stress the benefits of action or express confidence in the listeners' ability to accomplish the work ahead. An alternative is to end with a question or a statement that will leave your audience thinking.

> Plan your final statement carefully so you can end on a strong, positive note.

Enhancing Your Presentation with Effective Visuals

Thoughtfully designed visuals create interest, illustrate complex points in your message, add variety, and help the audience absorb and remember information.

Visuals can improve the quality and impact of your oral presentation by creating interest, illustrating points that are difficult to explain in words alone, adding variety, and increasing the audience's ability to absorb and remember information. Behavioral research has shown that visuals can improve learning by up to 400 percent because humans can process visuals 60,000 times faster than text.[11]

You can select from a variety of visuals to enhance oral presentations, each with unique advantages and disadvantages:

In most businesses, electronic presentations are now the presentation technology of choice, although they're certainly not the only option.

- **Electronic presentations. Electronic presentations**, or *slide shows*, consist of a series of slides composed using computer software such as Microsoft PowerPoint or Apple Keynote and displayed through a projector. Electronic presentations are easy to edit and update; you can add sound, photos, video, animation, and web links; you can incorporate them into online meetings, webcasts, and *webinars* (web-based seminars); and you can record self-running presentations for trade shows, websites, and other uses. The primary disadvantage is complexity because you must rely on a computer and a projector.

- **Overhead transparencies.** Some professionals still prefer transparencies to electronic presentations. Transparencies don't require the latest computer or projection equipment, you can write on them during a presentation, and they never crash on you—as computers have been known to do. However, they're limited to static displays, and they're impossible to edit once you've printed them.

- **Chalkboards and whiteboards.** Chalkboards and whiteboards are effective tools for the flexible, spontaneous nature of workshops and brainstorming sessions. Electronic whiteboards let you capture and e-mail the information written on them.

- **Flip charts.** Flip charts are great for recording comments and questions during your presentation or for keeping track of ideas during a brainstorming session.

- **Other visuals.** Be creative when choosing visuals to support your presentation. A video recording of a group of customers talking about your company can have a lot more impact than a series of slides that summarize what they said. Samples of products and materials let your audience experience your subject directly. Designers and architects use mock-ups and models to help people envision what a final creation will look like.

This chapter focuses on electronic presentations, but most of these design tips apply to overhead transparencies as well.

Think through your presentation outline carefully before designing your visuals.

Once you've decided on the form your visuals will take, think through your presentation plan carefully before you start creating anything. Visuals are powerful devices, and that power can just as easily harm your efforts as help. Above all, remember that visuals support your spoken message; they should never replace it or overshadow it.

Creating Effective Slides

When creating slides or other visuals, let accuracy and simplicity guide you. First, simple materials take less time to create than complex materials. Second, simple visuals reduce the chances of distraction and misinterpretation. Third, the more "bells and whistles" you have in your presentation, the more likely it is that something will go wrong.

Use slide text to emphasize key points, not to convey your entire message.

Writing Readable Content　Slides that contain too much text are one of the most common complaints voiced by presentation audiences.[12] Use text sparingly and only to support your spoken message, not to replace it (see Figure 12.4). Text-heavy slides exhaust audience members and pull their attention away from your spoken message. Follow these guidelines for effective text slides:

- Limit each slide to one thought, concept, or idea.
- Limit the content of each slide to 20 or 25 words—with no more than five or six lines of text containing about 3 or 4 words per line.
- Avoid full sentences or blocks of text.
- Phrase items in parallel form to simplify reading.

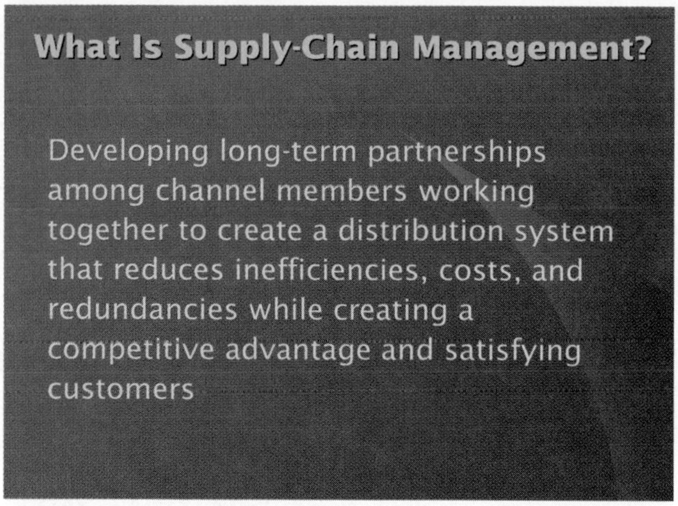

What Is Supply-Chain Management?

Developing long-term partnerships among channel members working together to create a distribution system that reduces inefficiencies, costs, and redundancies while creating a competitive advantage and satisfying customers

(a) Inefficient Paragraph Style

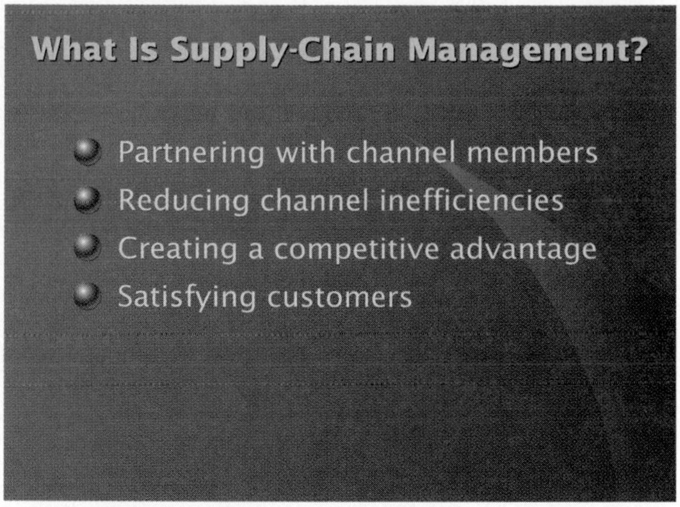

What Is Supply-Chain Management?

- Partnering with channel members
- Reducing channel inefficiencies
- Creating a competitive advantage
- Satisfying customers

(b) Efficient Bullet Style

The paragraph style in Figure 12.4a is much more difficult to read, particularly from a distance, than the bulleted style in Figure 12.4b. The speaker will explain these bullet points while showing the slide.

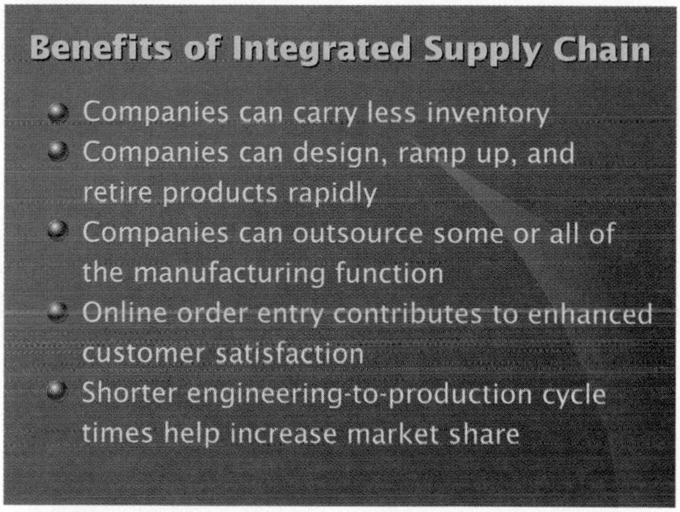

Benefits of Integrated Supply Chain

- Companies can carry less inventory
- Companies can design, ramp up, and retire products rapidly
- Companies can outsource some or all of the manufacturing function
- Online order entry contributes to enhanced customer satisfaction
- Shorter engineering-to-production cycle times help increase market share

(c) Wordy Bullets

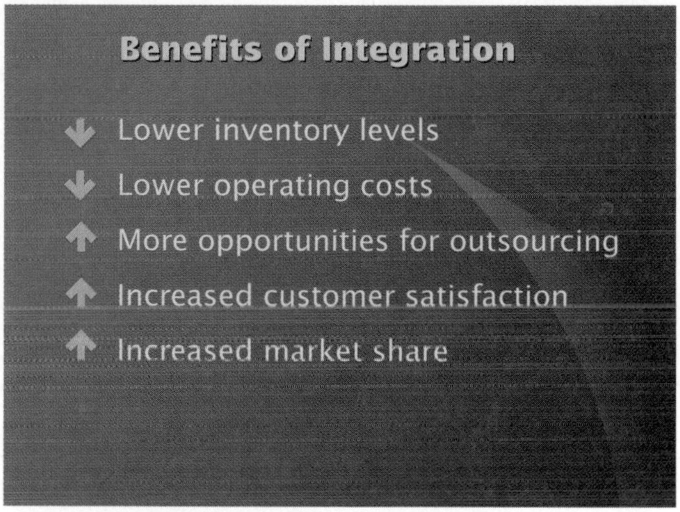

Benefits of Integration

- Lower inventory levels
- Lower operating costs
- More opportunities for outsourcing
- Increased customer satisfaction
- Increased market share

(d) Concise Bullets

Unnecessary words in Figure 12.4c make these bullets harder to read. With the concise bullets in Figure 12.4d, the audience can quickly grasp key message points as the speaker provides additional information. Note also how the phrases in Figure 12.4d are parallel and the font is larger, both of which make this slide easier to read.

Figure 12.4   **Writing Readable Content**

- Use active voice.
- Avoid long sequences of text-only slides; mix in visuals to hold viewer attention.

Designing Graphics for Slides   Like text, graphics also need to be simplified for use on slides. Remember that your audience members will view your visuals from across the room—not from a foot or two away, as you do while you create them. Start by reducing the level of detail, eliminating anything that is not absolutely essential. If necessary, break information into more than one illustration. Look for shorter variations of text elements and numeric values. For instance, on a graph, round off a number such as $12,500.72 to $12 or $12.5 and then label the axis to indicate thousands.

As much as possible, design visuals in a way that gives the viewer's eyes a clear path to follow, such as from right to left or from top to bottom. Avoid jumbled layouts that force the eye to traverse all over the screen to assemble the meaning of the visual. With the basic design in place, use design elements such as arrows, contrasting accent colors, and text labels to highlight key points.

Selecting Design Elements   Chapter 11 highlights the six design principles: consistency, contrast, balance, emphasis, convention, and simplicity (see page 269). Also pay close attention to the following principles as you create your slides:

Color is more than just decoration; colors themselves have meanings, based on both cultural experience and the relationships established between the colors in your designs.

- **Color.** Research shows that color visuals can account for 60 percent of an audience's acceptance or rejection of an idea. Color can increase willingness to read by up to 80 percent, and it can enhance learning and improve retention by more than 75 percent.[13] Your color choices can also stimulate various emotions, as Table 12.3 suggests. Also, keep in mind that contrasting colors increase readability, whereas colors closer in hue, such as brown on green or blue on purple, decrease readability.[14] Finally, remember that colors may have different meanings in different cultures, so research these variations if needed.

- **Background designs and artwork.** All visuals have two layers of design: the background and the foreground. The *background* is the equivalent of paper in a printed report. Generally speaking, the simpler and "quieter" your background, the better.

Artwork in the foreground of your slides can be either decorative or functional; use decorative artwork sparingly.

- **Foreground designs and artwork.** The *foreground* contains the unique text and graphic elements that make up each individual slide. In the foreground, artwork can be either functional or decorative. *Functional artwork* includes photos, drawings, charts, and other visual elements with information that's part of your message. In contrast, *decorative artwork* simply enhances the look of your slides. Used sparingly and unobtrusively, such artwork can make your slides more inviting to view. However, decorative artwork that is misused, overused, or inappropriate is distracting.

Many of the fonts available on your computer are difficult to read on-screen, so they aren't good choices for presentation slides.

- **Fonts and type styles.** Type is harder to read on-screen than on the printed page because projectors have lower *resolution* (the ability to display fine details) than typical office printers. Consequently, you need to choose fonts and type styles with care. Sans serif fonts are usually easier to read than serif fonts (see Figure 12.5). Use both uppercase and lowercase letters, with extra white space between lines of text, and limit the number of fonts to one or two per slide. Choose font sizes that are easy to read from anywhere in the room, usually between 24 and 36 points, and test them in the room if possible.

Design inconsistencies confuse and annoy audiences; don't change colors and other design elements randomly throughout your presentation.

With so many choices at your fingertips, maintaining consistency in your design is critical. If you use colors, shapes, fonts, and other design elements inconsistently from slide to slide, you force audience members to keep reinterpreting your design scheme—and this effort hinders their ability to focus on your message. Fortunately, software designed specifically for presentations makes consistency easy to achieve. You simply create a *slide master*,

TABLE 12.3   Color and Emotion

Color	Emotional Associations	Best Uses
Blue	Peaceful, soothing, tranquil, cool, trusting	Background for electronic business presentations (usually dark blue); safe and conservative
White	Neutral, innocent, pure, wise	Font color of choice for most electronic business presentations with a dark background
Yellow	Warm, bright, cheerful, enthusiastic	Text bullets and subheadings with a dark background
Red	Passionate, dangerous, active, painful	For promoting action or stimulating the audience; seldom used as a background ("in the red" specifically refers to financial losses)
Green	Assertive, prosperous, envious, relaxed	Highlight and accent color (green symbolizes money in the United States but not in other countries).

(a) Times New Roman font

(b) Arial font

Figure 12.5 **Selecting Readable Fonts and Type Styles**
Times New Roman is a standard font for many print documents; however, as Figure 12.5a demonstrates, the serifs at the end of each letter make the font difficult to read on-screen, and so does the italicized type. Sans serif fonts such as the Arial font shown in Figure 12.5b are a better choice for slides; they are cleaner and easier to read from a distance.

using the colors, fonts, and other design elements you've chosen, and then those choices automatically show up on every slide in the presentation (see Figure 12.6).

Adding Animation and Special Effects Today's presentation software offers many options for livening up your slides, including sound, animation, video clips, transition effects, and hyperlinks. However, use these elements with care and make sure they support your message.[15]

Functional animation involves motion that is directly related to your message, such as a highlight arrow that moves around the screen to emphasize specific points in a technical diagram. Using such animation is a great way to demonstrate sequences and procedures.

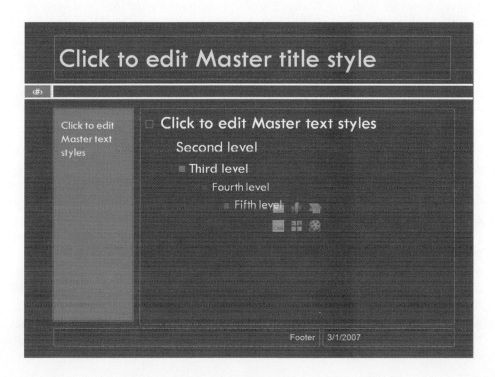

Figure 12.6 **Slide Master**
A *slide master* helps maintain consistency by ensuring that colors are used consistently and that bulleted lists, charts, graphics, and other elements show up in predictable places on each slide. The less readers have to work to interpret your slide designs, the more attention they can pay to your message.

In contrast, *decorative animation*, such as having a block of text cartwheel in from offscreen, doesn't have any communication value and can easily distract audiences.

Transitions control how one slide replaces another, such as having the current slide gently fade out before the next slide fades in. Subtle transitions can ease your viewers' gaze from one slide to the next, but many of the transition effects now available are visually distracting, so it's best to avoid them. **Builds** control the release of text, graphics, and other elements on individual slides. With builds, you can make bullet points and other elements appear one at a time, thereby making it easier for you and the audience to focus on each new point.

A **hyperlink** instructs your presentation software to jump to another slide in your presentation, to a website, or to another program entirely. Hyperlinks can also be assigned to preprogrammed icons known as **action buttons**. Action buttons let you perform such common tasks as jumping forward or backward to a specific slide or opening a document or spreadsheet. Using hyperlinks and action buttons is also a great way to build flexibility into your presentations so that you can instantly change the flow of your presentation in response to audience feedback.

Multimedia elements offer the ultimate in active presentations. For example, integrating short video clips can be a great way to add interest to your presentation. You can show anything from live webcam feeds to DVDs to clips from YouTube, as long as they support your message. However, keep these clips short, particularly if you are showing a "talking head" recording of a speech; audiences dislike being forced to sit through long recorded speeches.[16] If you will have a fast, reliable Internet connection during your presentation, you can *stream* online video directly from the web. Otherwise, store the video file on your computer and play it from your hard drive.

For the latest information on electronic presentation tools and techniques, visit http://real-timeupdates.com/bce and click on Chapter 12.

Giving Presentations Online

In some companies, online presentations have already become a routine matter, conducted via internal groupware, virtual meeting systems, or webcast systems designed specifically for online presentations. In most cases, you'll communicate through some combination of audio, video, and data presentations (for instance, PowerPoint slides). Your audience members will view your presentation either on their individual computer screens or via a projector in a conference room.

The benefits of online presentations are considerable, including the opportunity to communicate with a geographically dispersed audience at a fraction of the cost of travel and the ability for a project team or an entire organization to meet at a moment's notice. However, the challenges for a presenter can be significant, thanks to that layer of technology between you and your audience. Many of those "human moments" that guide and encourage you through an in-person presentation won't travel across the digital divide. For instance, it's often difficult to tell whether audience members are bored or confused because your view of them is usually confined to small video images (and sometimes not even that).

To ensure successful online presentations, keep the following advice in mind:

- **Consider sending preview study materials ahead of time.** Doing so lets your audience members familiarize themselves with any important background information.

- **Keep your presentation as simple as possible.** Break complicated slides down into multiple slides if necessary and keep the direction of your discussion clear so that no one gets lost.

- **Ask for feedback frequently.** You won't have as much of the visual feedback that alerts you when audience members are confused, and many online viewers will be reluctant to call attention to themselves by interrupting you to ask for clarification.

- **Consider the viewing experience from the audience members' point of view.** Will they be able to see what you think they can see? For instance, webcast video is typically displayed in a small window on-screen, so viewers may miss important details.

- **Make sure your audience can receive the sort of content you intend to use.** For instance, some corporate *firewalls* (network security devices) don't allow streaming media, so your webcast video might not survive the trip.[17]

- **Allow plenty of time for everyone to get connected and familiar with the screen they're viewing.** Build extra time into your schedule to ensure that everyone is connected and ready to start.

Last but not least, don't get lost in the technology. Use these tools whenever they'll help but remember that the most important aspect of any presentation is getting the audience to receive, understand, and embrace your message.

For the latest information on successful online presentations, visit http://real-timeup dates.com/bce and click on Chapter 12.

Once you master presentation technology, you can spend less time thinking about it and more time thinking about your message and your audience.

COMPLETING YOUR PRESENTATION

As with written communication, the completion step for a presentation starts with the all-important task of revising your message to ensure appropriate and effective content. Edit your presentation for clarity and conciseness as you would any other business message. If you're using electronic slides, make sure they are readable, concise, consistent from slide to slide, and fully operational (including transitions, builds, animations, and web links).

Finalizing Slides and Support Materials

Electronic presentation software can help you throughout the editing and revision process. As Figure 12.7 shows, the *slide sorter view* lets you see some or all of the slides in your presentation on a single screen. Use this view to add and delete slides, reposition

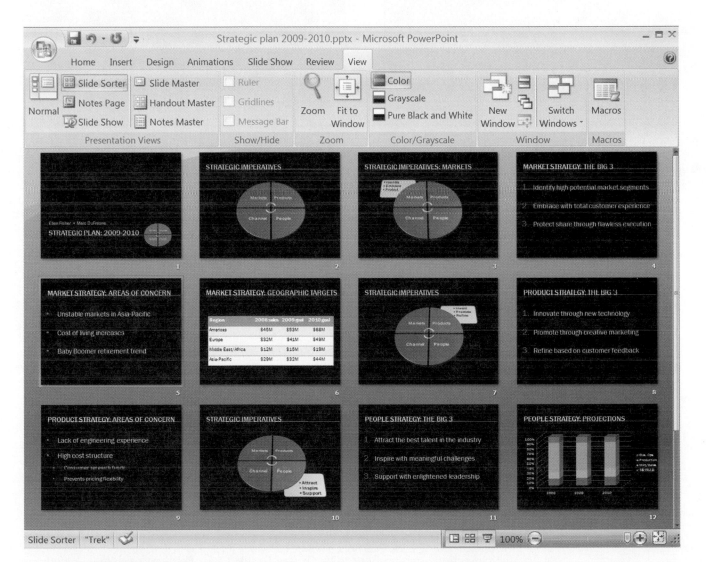

Figure 12.7 **Slide Sorter View**
Examining thumbnails of slides on one screen is the best way to check the overall design of your final product. The slide sorter also makes it easy to ponder the order and organization of your presentation; you can change the position of any slide simply by clicking and dragging it to a new position.

Making the Connection

New Media Options for
Managerial Communication

(a) Title Slide (1 of 2)

Today's presenter: Sara Flick

- VP Human Resources, RTL Properties
- 18 years management experience
- Author of more than 20 articles on leadership and communication
- Follow-up questions: sflick@rtlprops.com

(b) Title Slide (2 of 2)

Today's topics

- Understanding the techno-savvy workforce
- Exploring the new media options
- Creating and maintaining an executive blog
- Using podcasts to reach a mobile workforce
- Encouraging collaboration with wikis

(c) Agenda Slide

Program details

- Lunch will be served next door at 12:30
- Wireless connections
  - Log on to rtlpropnet
  - Network key in your handout packet
- CD in your handout packet
  - Free podcasting software
  - Blog templates
  - Copies of these slides

(d) Helpful Information for the Audience

Figure 12.8   Navigation and Support Slides
You can use a variety of navigation and support slides to introduce yourself and your presentation, to let the audience know what your presentation will cover, and to provide essential details.

slides, check slides for design consistency, and verify the operation of animation and transition effects.

In addition to using content slides, you can help your audience follow the flow of your presentation by creating slides for your title, agenda and program details, and navigation:

- **Title slide(s).** You can make a good first impression with one or two title slides, the equivalent of a report's cover and title page (see Figures 12.8a and 12.8b).

- **Agenda and program details.** These slides communicate the agenda for your presentation and any additional information the audience might need (see Figures 12.8c and 12.8d).

- **Navigation slides.** To tell your audience where you're going and where you've been, you can use a series of *navigation slides* based on your outline or agenda. As you complete each section, repeat the agenda slide but indicate which material has been covered and which section you are about to begin (see Figure 12.9). This sort of slide is sometimes referred to as a *moving blueprint.* As an alternative to the repeating agenda slide, you can insert a simple *bumper slide* at each major section break, announcing the title of the section you're about to begin.[18]

Navigational slides help your audience keep track of what you've covered already and what you plan to cover next.

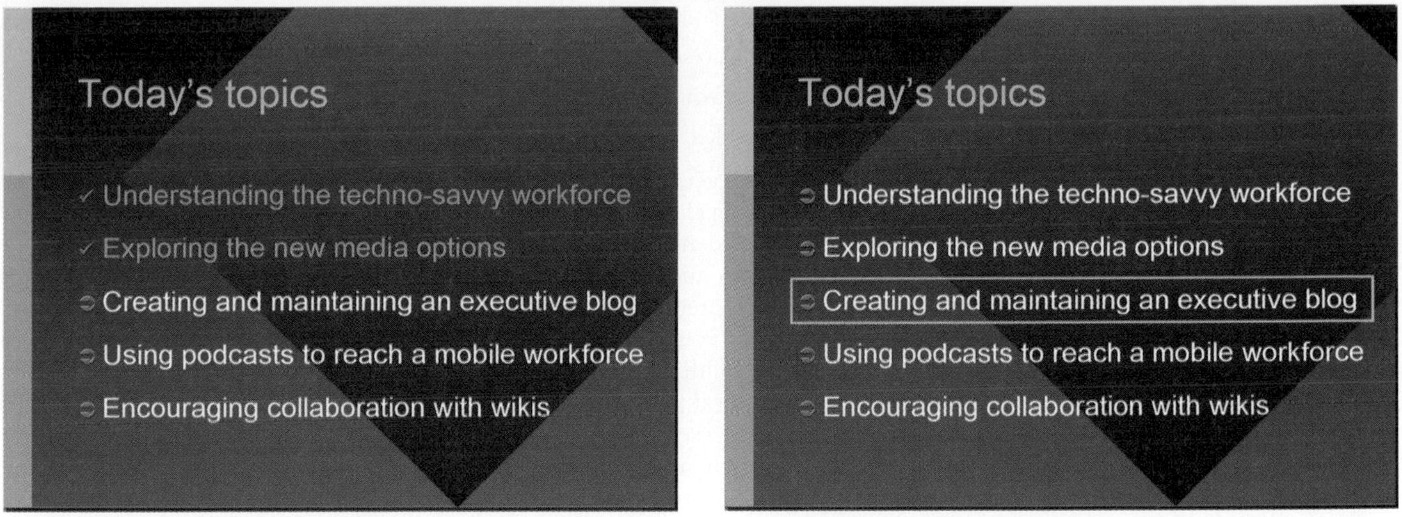

(a) "Muting" Sections Already Covered

(b) Highlighting the Next Section to Be Covered

Figure 12.9   Moving Blueprint Slides
Here are two of the ways you can use a *blueprint slide* as a navigational aid to help your audience stay on track with the presentation. Figure 12.9a visually "mutes" and checks off the sections of the presentation that have already been covered. In contrast, Figure 12.9b uses a sliding highlight box to indicate the next section to be covered.

With your slides working properly and in clear, logical order, consider whether printed handouts could help your audience during or after your presentation. Possibilities for good handout materials include complex charts and diagrams that are too unwieldy for the screen, articles and technical papers, case studies, lists of websites, and printed copies of your slides.[19]

> Use handout materials to support the points made in your presentation and to offer the audience additional information on your topic.

Preparing to Speak

With all your materials ready, your next step is to decide which method of speaking you want to use. You have three options: memorizing your material word for word, reading a printout of your material, or speaking from notes. Memorizing is usually not a good choice. In the best of circumstances, you'll probably sound stilted; in the worst, you might forget your lines. However, memorizing a quotation, an opening paragraph, or a few concluding remarks can bolster your confidence and strengthen your delivery.

Reading your speech is sometimes necessary, such as when delivering legal information, policy statements, or other messages that must be conveyed in an exact manner. However, for most business presentations, reading is a poor choice because it limits your interaction with the audience and lacks the fresh, dynamic feel of natural talking. (In any event, *never* stand in front of an audience and simply read the text on your slides.) If you do plan to read a prepared speech, practice enough so that you can still maintain eye contact with your audience. Print your speech with triple-spaced lines, wide margins, and large type.

Speaking from notes, with the help of an outline, note cards, or visuals, is usually the most effective and easiest delivery mode. This approach gives you something to refer to and still allows for plenty of eye contact, interaction with the audience, and improvisation in response to audience feedback.

> Speaking from carefully prepared notes is the easiest and most effective delivery mode for most speakers.

Practicing Your Delivery

Experienced speakers always practice important presentations. Practice helps ensure that you appear polished and confident, and it lets you verify the operation of visuals and equipment. A test audience can tell you if your slides are understandable and whether your delivery is effective. A day or two before you're ready to step on stage for an important talk, make sure you and your presentation are ready:

> The more you practice, the more confidence you'll have in yourself and your material.

- Can you present your material naturally, without reading your slides?
- Is the equipment working, and do you know how to work it?

- Is your timing on track?
- Can you easily pronounce all the words you plan to use?
- Have you decided how you're going to introduce your slides?
- Have you anticipated likely questions and objections?

With experience, you'll get a feel for how much practice is enough in any given situation. Practicing helps keep you on track, helps you maintain a conversational tone with your audience, and boosts your confidence and composure.

If you're addressing an audience that doesn't speak your language, consider using an interpreter. Send your interpreter a copy of your speech and visuals as far in advance of your presentation as possible. If your audience is likely to include persons with hearing impairments, be sure to team up with a sign-language interpreter as well.

When you deliver an oral presentation to people from other cultures, you may need to adapt the content of your presentation. It is also important to take into account any cultural differences in appearance, mannerisms, and other customs. Your interpreter or host will be able to suggest appropriate changes for a specific audience or occasion.

Overcoming Anxiety

Remember that nervousness is an indication that you care about your audience, your topic, and the occasion. These techniques will help you convert anxiety into positive energy:[20]

- **Prepare more material than necessary.** Combined with having a genuine interest in your topic, having extra knowledge will reduce your anxiety.
- **Practice.** The more familiar you are with your material, the less panic you'll feel.
- **Think positively.** See yourself as polished and professional, and your audience will, too.
- **Visualize your success.** Visualize mental images of yourself in front of the audience, feeling confident, prepared, and able to handle any situation that might arise.[21]
- **Take a few deep breaths.** Before you begin to speak, remember that your audience wants you to succeed, too.
- **Be ready.** Have your first sentence memorized and on the tip of your tongue.
- **Be comfortable.** Dress appropriately but as comfortably as possible. Drink plenty of water ahead of time to hydrate your voice (bring a bottle of water with you, too).
- **Don't panic.** If you sense that you're starting to race, pause and arrange your notes or perform some other small task while taking several deep breaths. Then start again at your normal pace. If you feel that you're losing your audience, try to pull them back by asking for comments or questions.
- **Concentrate on your message and your audience, not on yourself.** When you're busy thinking about your subject and observing your audience's response, you tend to forget your fears.
- **Maintain eye contact with friendly audience members.** Eye contact not only makes you appear sincere, confident, and trustworthy but can give you positive feedback as well.
- **Keep going.** Things usually get better as you move along, with each successful minute giving you more and more confidence.

Handling Questions Responsively

The question-and-answer (Q&A) period is one of the most important parts of an oral presentation. It gives you a chance to obtain important information, to emphasize your main idea and supporting points, and to build enthusiasm for your point of view. When you're speaking to high-ranking executives in your company, the Q&A period will often consume most of the time allotted for you presentation.[22]

Whether or not you can establish ground rules for Q&A depends on the audience and the situation. If you're presenting to a small group of upper managers or potential investors, for example, you will probably have no say in the matter: Audience members will ask as many questions as they want to get the information they need. On the other hand, if you are presenting to your peers or a large public audience, establish some guidelines, such as the number of questions allowed per person and the overall time limit for questions.

Don't assume that you can handle whatever comes up without some preparation.[23] Learn enough about your audience members to get an idea of their concerns and think through answers to potential questions.

When people ask questions, pay attention to nonverbal signals to help determine what each person really means. Repeat the question to confirm your understanding and to ensure that the entire audience has heard it. If the question is vague or confusing, ask for clarification; then give a simple, direct answer.

If you are asked a difficult or complex question, avoid the temptation to sidestep it or try to laugh it off without answering. Offer to meet with the questioner afterward if giving an adequate answer would take too long. If you don't know the answer, don't pretend that you do. Instead, offer to get a complete answer as soon as possible.

If you don't have the complete answer to an important question, offer to provide it after the presentation.

Be on guard for audience members who use questions to make impromptu speeches or to take control of your presentation. Without offending anyone, find a way to stay in control. You might admit that you and the questioner have differing opinions and, before calling on someone else, offer to get back to the questioner after you've done more research.[24]

If a question ever puts you on the hot seat, respond honestly but keep your cool. Look the person in the eye, answer the question as well as you can, and keep your emotions under control. Defuse hostility by paraphrasing the question and asking the questioner to confirm that you've understood it correctly. Maintain a businesslike tone of voice and a pleasant expression.[25]

If you ever face hostile questions, respond honestly and directly while keeping your cool.

When the time allotted for your presentation is almost up, prepare the audience for the end by saying something like, "Our time is almost up. Let's have one more question." After you reply to that last question, summarize the main idea of the presentation and thank people for their attention. Conclude the way you opened: by looking around the room and making eye contact. Then leave the podium with the same confident demeanor you've had from the beginning. ■

DOCUMENT MAKEOVER

Improve This Speech

To practice correcting drafts of actual documents, visit the "Document Makeovers" section in either MyBCommLab.com or the Companion Website for this text.

If MyBCommLab.com is being used in your class, see your User Guide for specific instructions on how to access the content for this chapter.

If you are accessing this feature through the Companion Website, click on "Document Makeovers" and then select Chapter 12. You will find a speech that contains problems and errors related to what you've learned in this chapter about preparing effective speeches and oral presentations. Use the Final Draft decision tool to create an improved version of this speech. Check the message for effective choices in scope, style, opening, use of transitions, and closing. ●

CHAPTER REVIEW AND ACTIVITIES

Chapter Summary

Oral and online presentations give the opportunity to use all your communication skills, from research to writing to speaking. Presentations also demonstrate your ability to think quickly, to adapt to challenging situations, and to handle touchy questions and complex issues.

The steps you take in planning oral presentations are generally the same as with any other business message. You don't actually "write" your presentation in most cases but rather plan key word and phrase choices and create whatever visual support materials you need. You revise and proofread all materials, practice your delivery, verify facilities and equipment, manage anxiety, and plan your approach to handling questions.

Remember the three goals of an effective introduction: arouse audience interest in your topic, build your credibility, and give your audience a preview of your message.

To grab your audience's attention, you can unite people around a common goal, tell a story, pass around a sample, ask a question, state a startling statistic, or use humor carefully.

To hold your audience's attention, continue to relate your subject to your audience's needs, anticipate audience questions, use clear and vivid language, connect your subject with familiar concepts, ask for questions or comments, and illustrate your ideas with visuals.

Visuals create interest, illustrate and clarify important points, add variety, and help listeners absorb information. Electronic presentations are the most common today, but you might also use overhead transparencies, chalkboards and whiteboards, flip charts, product samples, models, and video.

Consistency is important because your audience looks for patterns in the way you use color, font size, and other design elements. You'll lose viewers' attention if they must keep reinterpreting your design.

To ensure a successful online presentation, consider sending preview materials ahead of time, keep your content and presentation as simple as possible, ask for feedback frequently, consider the viewing experience from the audience's side, improve any sections of your presentation that might be slow or difficult, make sure your audience can receive the sort of content you intend to use, and give participants time to get connected.

To handle questions responsively, first determine whether you can set boundaries for the Q&A period. Prepare answers to potential questions. Pay attention to nonverbal signals and be sure to respond to all questions. Don't let questioners take control of the presentation. Face hostile questions head on without getting defensive. Finally, alert the audience when the Q&A period is almost over.

Test Your Knowledge

1. What skills do oral presentations give you the opportunity to practice and demonstrate?

2. What three goals should you accomplish during the introduction of an oral presentation?

3. What techniques can you use to get an audience's attention during your introduction?

4. What three tasks should you accomplish in the close of your presentation?

5. What steps can you take to ensure success with online presentations?

Apply Your Knowledge

1. Why is it important to limit the scope of oral presentations?

2. How might the audience's attitude affect the amount of audience interaction during or after a presentation? Explain your answer.

3. If you were giving an oral presentation on the performance of a company product, what three attention-getters might you use to enliven your talk?

4. From the speaker's perspective, what are the advantages and disadvantages of responding to questions from the audience throughout an oral presentation rather than just afterward? From the listener's perspective, which approach would you prefer? Why?

5. **Ethical Choices**   Is it ethical to use design elements and special effects to persuade an audience? Why or why not?

Practice Your Knowledge

Activities

Active links for all websites in this chapter can be found online. If MyBCommLab.com is being used in your class, see your User Guide for instructions on accessing the content for this chapter. Otherwise, visit www.pearsonhighered.com/bovee, locate *Business Communication Essentials*, Fourth Edition, click the Companion Website link, select Chapter 12, and then click on "Featured Websites." Please note that links to sites that become inactive after publication of the book will be removed from the Featured Websites section.

1. **Analyze This Message**   Locate the transcript of a speech, either online or through your school library. Good sources include Yahoo's directory of commencement speeches (http://dir.yahoo.com/Education/Graduation/Speeches) and the publication *Vital Speeches of the Day*. (Recent years of *Vital Speeches of the Day* are available in the ProQuest database; ask at your library.) Many corporate websites also have archives of executives' speeches; look in the "investor relations" section. Examine both the introduction and the close of the speech you've chosen and then analyze how these two sections work together to emphasize the main idea. What action does the speaker want the audience to take? Next, identify the transitional sentences or phrases that clarify the speech's structure for the listener, especially those that help the speaker shift between supporting points. Using these transitions as clues, list the main message and supporting points; then indicate how each transitional phrase links the current supporting point to the succeeding one. Prepare a two- to three-minute oral presentation summarizing your analysis for your class.

2. **Analyze This Message**   To access this PowerPoint presentation, go to http://real-time updates.com/bce, click on "Student Assignments," and select Chapter 12, Page 331, Activity 2. Download and watch the presentation in slide show mode. (After you select Slide Show from the View menu, simply click your mouse to advance through the slides.) After you've watched the presentation, identify at least three ways in which various animations, builds, and transitions either enhanced or impeded your understanding of the subject matter.

3. **Creating Effective Slides: Content**   Look through recent issues (print or online) of *BusinessWeek*, *Fortune*, or other business publications for articles discussing challenges that a specific company or industry is facing. Using the articles and the guidelines discussed in this chapter, create three to five slides summarizing these issues. If you don't have access to computer presentation software or a word processor, you can draw the slides on plain paper.

4. **Mastering Delivery: Analysis**   Attend a presentation at your school or in your town or watch a speech on television. Categorize the speech as one that motivates or entertains, one that informs or analyzes, or one that persuades or urges collaboration. Then compare the speaker's delivery with the concepts presented in this chapter. Write a two-page report analyzing the speaker's performance and suggesting improvements.

5. **Mastering Delivery: Nonverbal Signals**   Observe and analyze the delivery of a speaker in a school, work, or other setting. What type of delivery did the speaker use? Was this delivery appropriate for the occasion? What nonverbal signals did the speaker use to emphasize key points? Were these signals effective? Which nonverbal signals would you suggest to further enhance the delivery of this oral presentation? Why?

6. **Ethical Choices**   Think again about the oral presentation you observed and analyzed in the previous activity. How could the speaker have used nonverbal signals to unethically manipulate the audience's attitudes or actions?

7. **Teamwork**   You've been asked to give an informative 10-minute talk on vacation opportunities in your home state. Draft your introduction, which should last no more than 2 minutes. Then pair off with a classmate and analyze each other's introductions. How well do these two introductions arouse the audience's interest, build credibility, and preview the presentation? Suggest how these introductions might be improved.

8. **Delivering Oral Presentations: Possible Topics**   Perhaps one of the following topics interests you.

   a. What I expect to learn in this course

   b. Past public speaking experiences: the good, the bad, and the ugly

   c. I would be good at teaching _____.

   d. I am afraid of _____.

   e. It's easy for me to _____.

   f. I get angry when _____.

   g. I am happiest when I _____.

   h. People would be surprised if they knew that I _____.

   i. My favorite older person

   j. My favorite charity

   k. My favorite place

   l. My favorite sport

   m. My favorite store

   n. My favorite television show

   o. The town you live in suffers from a great deal of juvenile vandalism. Explain to a group of community members why juvenile recreational facilities should be built instead of a juvenile detention complex.

   p. You are speaking to the Humane Society. Support or oppose the use of animals for medical research purposes.

   q. You are talking to civic leaders of your community. Try to convince them to build an art gallery.

   r. You are speaking to a first-grade class at an elementary school. Explain why they should brush their teeth after meals.

   s. You are speaking to a group of traveling salespeople. Convince them that they should wear their seatbelts while driving.

   t. You are speaking to a group of elderly people. Convince them to adopt an exercise program.

   u. Energy issues (supply, conservation, alternative sources, national security, global warming, pollution, etc.)

   v. Financial issues (banking, investing, family finances, etc.)

   w. Government (domestic policy, foreign policy, Social Security taxes, welfare, etc.)

   x. Interesting new technologies (virtual reality, geographic information systems, nanotechnology, bioengineering, etc.)

   y. Politics (political parties, elections, legislative bodies and legislation, the presidency, etc.)

   z. Sports (amateur and professional, baseball, football, golf, hang gliding, hockey, rock climbing, tennis, etc.)

   Choose a topic and prepare a brief presentation (5–10 minutes) to be given to your class.

9. Oral Presentations: Self-Assessment   How good are you at planning, writing, and delivering oral presentations? Rate yourself on each of the following elements of the oral presentation process. Then examine your ratings to identify where you are strongest and where you can improve, using the tips in this chapter.

Elements of the Presentation Process	Always	Frequently	Occasionally	Never
1. I start by defining my purpose.	_____	_____	_____	_____
2. I analyze my audience before writing an oral presentation.	_____	_____	_____	_____
3. I match my presentation length to the allotted time.	_____	_____	_____	_____
4. I begin my oral presentations with an attention-getting introduction.	_____	_____	_____	_____
5. I look for ways to build credibility as a speaker.	_____	_____	_____	_____
6. I cover only a few main points in the body of my presentation.	_____	_____	_____	_____
7. I use transitions to help listeners follow my ideas.	_____	_____	_____	_____
8. I review main points and describe next steps in the close.	_____	_____	_____	_____
9. I practice my presentation beforehand.	_____	_____	_____	_____
10. I prepare in advance for questions and objections.	_____	_____	_____	_____
11. I conclude oral presentations by summarizing my main idea.	_____	_____	_____	_____

Expand Your Knowledge

Exploring the Best of the Web

Get Electronic Presentation Tips from the Pros   Visit the Epson Presenters Online website, at www.presentersonline .com, and follow the expert advice on creating and delivering effective presentations. Learn the basics of delivery, content, and visuals. Find out about some of the new hardware and software products for electronic presentations and access a variety of resources you can use in your presentations. After you learn the secrets from the pros, address the following questions.

Exercises

1. How can you avoid some of the mistakes that presenters commonly make?

2. How can you add a narration sound track to a PowerPoint presentation?

3. What are the advantages and disadvantages of three common seating arrangements?

Surfing Your Way to Career Success

Bovée and Thill's Business Communication Headline News offers links to hundreds of online resources that can help you with this course, your other college courses, and your career. Visit http://businesscommunicationblog.com and click on "Web Directory." The Oral Communication section connects you to a variety of websites and articles on speeches, stage fright, presentations, PowerPoint tips, podcasts, webcasts, and videoconferencing. Identify three websites from this section that could be useful in your business career. For each site, write a two-sentence summary of what the site offers and how it could help you launch and build your career.

MyBCommLab.com

Use MyBCommLab.com to test your understanding of the concepts presented in this chapter and explore additional materials that will bring the ideas to life in video, activities, and an online multimedia e-book. Additionally, you can improve your skill with vocabulary by using the "Peak Performance Grammar and Mechanics" module. Click "Vocabulary" and then "Vocabulary 1." Take the Pretest to assess your ability to recognize correct word choices. Review the list of frequently confused words in the Refresher Course and then take the Follow-Up Test to verify your grasp of these essential words.

CASES

▼ *Apply the three-step writing process to the following cases, as assigned by your instructor.*

[PORTFOLIO BUILDER] [PRESENTATION SKILLS]

1. Is Anybody Out There? Explaining Loopt's Social Mapping Service
How many times have you been out shopping or clubbing and wondered whether any of your friends were in the neighborhood? A new *social mapping* service from Loopt can provide the answer. It lets you put yourself on a map that your friends can see on their mobile phones, and you can see their locations as well. You can even get automatic alerts whenever friends are near.

Your task Create a brief presentation explaining the Loopt concept to someone who is comfortable using text messaging and other mobile phone features. Be sure to explain what type of phone is required and include one slide that discusses safety issues. You can learn more about it at www.loopt.com.[26]

[PORTFOLIO BUILDER] [PRESENTATION SKILLS]

2. I'll Find My Space Somewhere Else, Thanks: Promoting Alternatives to MySpace
With a user base well on its way toward 200 million people, MySpace is the king of social networking sites. However, it doesn't appeal to everyone. Some people want to be able to customize their online presence more than MySpace allows, while others want more control over who sees various aspects of their online profiles.

Your task Choose one of the lesser-known alternatives to MySpace, such as Ning (www.ning.com), Vox (www.vox.com), Esnips (www.esnips.com), or any other site that offers some degree of social networking. Compare its features and functions to those of MySpace and then prepare a brief presentation that highlights the similarities and differences of the two sites. In your presentation, identify the sort of people most likely to prefer the site you've chosen over MySpace.[27]

[PRESENTATION SKILLS]

3. Face to Face: Updating Management on Your Monthly Progress
Imagine that you've just completed the impressive-looking online progress report shown in Figure 10.5 (page 243), when your boss decides he'd like to hear a presentation from you instead.

Your task Adapt the information in Figure 10.5 to a brief electronic slide show. Your boss might want to see maps of the four locations listed, so have slides with maps ready. (Because you don't have the specific addresses, just capture an online map for each general area; Lakewood and Glendale are suburbs of Denver, and Pepsi Center is a sports arena in Denver.)

[PORTFOLIO BUILDER] [PRESENTATION SKILLS]

4. Hot Topics: Identifying Key Elements in an Important Business Issue
In your job as a business development researcher for a major corporation, you're asked to gather and process information on a wide variety of subjects. Management has gained confidence in your research and analysis skills and would now like you to begin making regular presentations at management retreats and other functions. Topics are likely to include the following:

- Offshoring of U.S. jobs
- Foreign ownership of U.S. firms
- Employment issues involving immigrants
- Tax breaks offered by local and state governments to attract new businesses
- Economic impact of environmental regulations

Your task Choose one of the topics from the list and conduct enough research to familiarize yourself with the topic. Identify at least three important issues that anyone involved with this topic should know about. Prepare a 10-minute presentation that introduces the topic, comments on its importance to the U.S. economy, and discusses the issues you've identified. Assume that your audience is a cross-section of business managers who don't have any particular experience in the topic you've chosen.

Improve Your Grammar, Mechanics, and Usage

Level 1: Self-Assessment—Capitals and Abbreviations

Review Sections 3.1 and 3.3 in the Handbook of Grammar, Mechanics, and Usage and then complete the following 15 items.

In items 1–15, indicate proper capitalization by underlining appropriate letters with three underscores. Circle abbreviations that should be spelled out and insert abbreviations where appropriate.

1. Dr. paul hansen is joining our staff.

2. New caressa skin cream should be in a position to dominate that market.

3. Send this report to MR h. k. danforth, rural route 1, warrensburg, new york 12885.

4. You are responsible for training my new assistant to operate the xerox machine.

5. She received her master of business administration degree from the university of michigan.

6. The building is located on the corner of madison and center streets.

7. Call me at 8 tomorrow morning, pacific standard time, and I'll have the information you need.

8. When jones becomes ceo next month, we'll need your input asap.

9. Address it to art bowers, chief of production.

10. Please rsvp to sony corp. just as soon as you know your schedule.

11. The data-processing department will begin work on feb. 2, just one wk. from today.

12. You are to meet him on friday at the un building in nyc.

13. Whenever you can come, professor, our employees will greatly enjoy your presentation.

14. At 50 per box, our std. contract forms are $9 a box, and our warranty forms are $7.95 a box.

15. We plan to establish a sales office on the west coast.

Level 2: Workplace Applications

The following items contain numerous errors in grammar, capitalization, punctuation, abbreviation, number style, word division, and vocabulary. Rewrite each sentence, correcting all errors. Write C for any sentence that is already correct.

1. Mc'Donalds and Sears' have partnered with the television program, "Its Showtime At The Apollo." To offer talented kids the opportunity too appear on national television.

2. Tiffany & Co., the internationally-renowned jeweler and specialty retailer plan to open a 5000 square feet store in Walnut Creek, CA next year.

3. If none of the solutions seem satisfying, pick the more easier one.

4. Ken Baker, the west coast bureau chief for Us magazine, will be responsible for overseeing all of magazine reporting in Hollywood, conducting high profile, celebrity interviews, for identifying news stories, and assist in the generation of cover concepts.

5. With experience managing numerous enthusiast brands, including "Kawasaki" and "Skechers," Juxt Interactive are cementing their role as a leader in strategic, integrated campaigns.

6. You're message, tone, and product positioning has to be right on to be excepted and successful.

7. As I begun to put the team together, it became apparent to myself that my idea was ahead of it's time.

8. Many think that the primary market for newspapers are the readers, however advertisers generate the majority of revenues.

9. REIs second website, www.rei-outlet.com, features items that are not available at REI's physical stores, catalog, or main website.

10. The company's C.E.O., who we had saw at the awards dinner wednesday night, was fired the next day.

11. A designer of high priced purses such as Kate Spade or Louis Vitton generally limit distribution to exclusive boutiques or high end retail stores: such as Neiman-Marcus.

12. There is many indications that an economic recovery is underway, and will continue to stabilize and build however modestly.

13. We bought the equipment at a second hand store which turned out to be shoddy and defective.

14. Experts site 2 principle reasons for Webvan's failure; consumer resistance and over expansion.

15. Implementation of the over time hours guidelines will be carried out by the Human Resources Staff members.

Level 3: Document Critique

The following document contains errors in grammar, punctuation, capitalization, abbreviation, number style, vocabulary, and spelling. You may also find problems with organization, format, and word use. Correct all errors using standard proofreading marks (see Appendix C).

DATE:	Thu, 25 April, 2009
FROM:	Steve Pendergrass <spender@manchcc.edu>
TO:	Gregory Hansford <gregory.hansford@manchcc.edu>
SUBJECT:	Library Hours

Dear Mr. Hansford,

There is a favorite place in which Manchester students study on our campus: the library because of the quiet atmosphere excellent resources, and helpful staff. With a ajustment in library hours there assets could be taken advantage of by more students.

In an informal survey of the students in my English class, a desire for the library to be open more hours on the weekends became evident. Many students find weekends best for researching term papers: because that's when large blocks of time can be found in their schedules.

I'd like to sight several reasons for the change I am about to propose to encourage your interest and desire for my suggestion. Understandable, librarians need a day off. Perhaps students and librarians could both be accomodated if the library closed at five p.m. on Friday night. Friday night is the time most students like to relax and attend sports events or parties. The libary could then be open on Saturdays from ten a.m. until 4:30 p.m. To make this arrangement fair to librarians; perhaps their schedules could be staggered so that nobody would have to work every Saturday or those scheduled to work on Saturdays could be given Mondays or Fridays off.

Consider implementing this new schedule this Fall. Another much-appreciated service for students will be performed if you do this.

Sincerely:

Steve Pendergrass, student

Employment Messages and Job Interviews

CHAPTER 13: Building Careers and Writing Résumés

CHAPTER 14: Applying and Interviewing for Employment

Building Careers and Writing Résumés

[from the real world]

"At our office, these résumés are rejected without even being read."

—Ed Tazzia,
Managing partner,
Gundersen Partners
www.gpllc.com

Taking a few simple precautions can help you avoid the regrettable fate that befalls too many job seekers: failing to even get to the interview stage because of some silly and avoidable error on your résumé. Ed Tazzia's comment refers specifically to the rejection of résumés with amateurish designs—too many type fonts and sizes, too much color, excessive boldface, and italics all over the place.[1] However, his observation also speaks to two larger truths about résumés and your job search in general. First, perceptions can make or break your job search, and no perception is more important than the first impression you make with your résumé and cover letter. Second, today's employers are frequently overwhelmed by the number of résumés they receive. To narrow the list of potential candidates to a manageable number, many are forced to aggressively filter all those incoming résumés, and, as Tazzia notes, poor design is enough to get a résumé eliminated from consideration.

SECURING EMPLOYMENT IN TODAY'S JOB MARKET

If you haven't already, read the Prologue, "Building a Career with Your Communication Skills," before studying this chapter.

Understanding how employers approach the hiring process is just one of many insights and skills you need in order to conduct a successful job search. Figure 13.1 shows the six most important tasks in the job search process. This chapter discusses the first two, and Chapter 14 explores the final four.

Understanding Employers' Approach to the Employment Process

The easiest way for you to find jobs (through company advertising) is the least-preferred channel for many companies to find new employees.

You can save considerable time and effort in your job search by understanding how employers approach the recruiting process. Looking at Figure 13.2, you'll notice that the easiest way for you to find out about new opportunities—through the employer's outside advertising—is the employer's *least-preferred* way of finding new employees. Some top employers find as many as 40 percent of new hires through employee referrals.[2] In fact, according to some estimates, up to 80 percent of all job openings are never advertised, a phenomenon known as the *hidden job market*.[3] In other words, employers have checked out quite a few other places

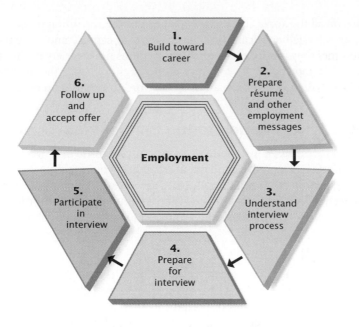

Figure 13.1 **The Employment Search**
Finding the ideal job opportunity is a six-step process that you might repeat a number of times during your career.

before they come looking for you. To find the best opportunities, it's up to you to take action to get yourself noticed.

Beyond personal referrals, employers use a variety of methods to identify potential employees. According to one recent survey of larger employers, companies' own websites were the number-one source of external hires.[4] Many employers also send representatives to college campuses and job fairs to interview students. Employers also recruit candidates through employment agencies, state employment services, temporary staffing services, the employment bureaus operated by some trade associations, and *headhunters* (recruiters who specialize in finding experienced executives and professionals for specific job openings). Employers advertise job openings in a variety of news media, through search-engine advertising, and on *job boards* such as Monster and CareerBuilder.

The major job boards have grown so popular that some employers feel deluged with résumés from these sources, and some job seekers fear it's becoming impossible to stand out from the crowd when hundreds or thousands of people are applying for the same jobs. As a result, many specialized websites are now springing up to focus on narrow parts of the job market or offer technology that promises to do a better job of matching employers and job searchers. For example, Jobfox, www.jobfox.com, uses in-depth questionnaires to match employers and employees.[5] Jobster, www.jobster.com, uses the latest social networking technologies to create a vast referral network that its corporate clients use to find potential employees.[6]

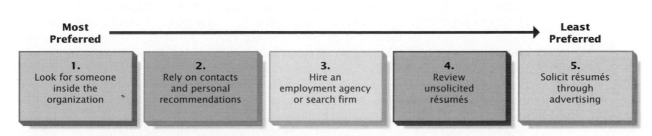

Figure 13.2 **How Organizations Prefer to Find New Employees**
Employers often prefer to look at their existing workforce to find candidates for new jobs and promotions. If no suitable candidates can be found, they begin to look outside the firm, starting with people whom company insiders already know.

To keep tabs on all the applicants in various stages of the recruiting process, many companies now use computerized **applicant tracking systems** to capture and store the hundreds or thousands of résumés they receive each year. These systems use a variety of filtering techniques to help recruiters find good prospects for current openings, so having the right terminology on your résumé is essential. (See the information on keyword summaries on page 354.)[7]

Organizing Your Approach to the Employment Process

The employment process can consume many hours of your time over weeks or months, and organizing your efforts in a logical, careful manner can help you save time. Begin by finding out where the job opportunities are, which industries are strong, which parts of the country are booming, and which specific job categories offer the best prospects for the future. From there you can investigate individual organizations, doing your best to learn as much about them as possible.

Staying Abreast of Business and Financial News

Thanks to the Internet, staying on top of business news is easy today. In fact, your biggest challenge will be selecting new material from the many available sources. To help you get started, here is a selection of websites of periodicals that offer business news (in some cases, you need to be a subscriber to access all the material, including archives):

- *Wall Street Journal*: http://online.wsj.com/public/us
- *New York Times*: www.nyt.com
- *USA Today*: www.usatoday.com
- *BusinessWeek*: www.businessweek.com
- *Business 2.0*: www.business2.com
- *Fast Company*: www.fastcompany.com
- *Fortune*: www.fortune.com
- *Forbes*: www.forbes.com

In addition, thousands of bloggers and podcasters offer news and commentary on the business world. To identify some that you might find helpful, start with directories such as Technorati (www.technorati.com/blogs/tag/business) for blogs or Podcast Alley (www.podcastalley.com; select the "Business" genre in the drop-down menu) for podcasts. For all these online resources, use a newsfeed aggregator to select the type of stories you're interested in and have them delivered to you automatically.

Of course, with all the business information available today, it's easy to get lost in the details. Try not to get too caught up in the daily particulars of business. Start by examining "big picture" topics—trends, issues, industrywide challenges, and careers—before delving into specific companies that look attractive.

Researching Specific Companies

After you've identified a promising industry and career field, consult directories of employers at your college library, at your career center, or on the Internet and compile a list of specific organizations that appeal to you. In addition to using the web to find detailed information about prospective employers, you can use it to look for and respond to job openings. On company websites, look for the "About Us" or "Company" part of the site to find a company profile, executive biographies, press releases, financial information, and information on employment opportunities. You'll often find information about an organization's mission, products, annual reports, and employee benefits. Plus, you can often download annual reports, brochures, and other materials. Any company's website is going to present the firm in the most positive light possible, of course, so look for outside sources as well, including the business sections of local newspapers and trade publications that cover the company's industries and markets.

Don't limit your research to easily available sources, however. Companies are likely to be impressed by creative research, such as interviewing their customers to learn more about how the firm does business. "Detailed research, including talking to our customers, is so rare it will almost guarantee you get hired," explains the recruiting manager at Alcon Laboratories.[8]

Table 13.1 lists some of the many websites where you can learn more about companies and find job openings. Start with The Riley Guide, www.rileyguide.com, which offers links to hundreds of specialized websites that post openings in specific industries and professions. Your college's career center probably maintains an up-to-date list as well.

Networking

Networking is the process of making informal connections with mutually beneficial business contacts. According to one recent survey, networking is the most common way that employees find jobs.[9] Networking takes place wherever and whenever people talk: at industry functions, at social gatherings, at sports events and recreational activities, at alumni reunions, and so on. Social networking technologies, particularly business-oriented websites such as www.linkedin.com, www.ryze.com, and www.spoke.com, have become powerful networking resources.[10] Read news sites, blogs, and other online sources. Participate in student business organizations, especially those with ties to professional organizations. Visit trade shows to learn about various industries and rub shoulders with people who work in those industries.[11] Don't overlook volunteering; you not only meet people but also demonstrate your ability to solve problems, plan projects, and so on. You can do some good while creating a network for yourself.

Start thinking like a networker now; your classmates could turn out to be some of your most important business contacts.

TABLE 13.1   Netting a Job on the Web

Website*	URL	Highlights
Riley Guide	www.rileyguide.com	Vast collection of links to both general and specialized job sites for every career imaginable; don't miss this one—it'll save you hours and hours of searching
CollegeRecruiter.com	www.collegerecruiter.com	A site focused on opportunities for graduates with less than three years of work experience
Monster	www.monster.com	One of the most popular job sites, with hundreds of thousands of openings, many from hard-to-find smaller companies; extensive collection of advice on the job search process
MonsterTrak	www.monstertrak.com	A site that focuses on job searches for new college grads; your school's career-center site probably links here
Yahoo! Hotjobs	http://hotjobs.yahoo.com	Another leading job board; like Monster and CareerBuilder, offers extensive advice for job seekers
CareerBuilder	www.careerbuilder.com	One of the largest job boards; affiliated with more than 150 newspapers around the country
Jobster	www.jobster.com	Newer site that uses social networking to link employers with job seekers
USA Jobs	www.usajobs.opm.gov	The official job search site for the U.S. government, featuring positions from economists to astronauts to border patrol agents
IMDiversity	www.imdiversity.com	Good resource on diversity in the workplace, with job postings from companies that have made a special commitment to promoting diversity in their workforces
Dice.com	www.dice.com	One of the best sites for high-technology jobs
Net-Temps	www.nettemps.com	Popular site for contractors and freelancers looking for short-term assignments
InternshipPrograms.com	http://internshipprograms.com	A site that posts listings from companies looking for interns in a wide variety of professions
Simply Hired Indeed	www.simplyhired.com www.indeed.com	Specialized search engines that look for job postings on hundreds of websites worldwide; they find many postings that aren't listed on job board sites such as Monster

*This list represents only a small fraction of the hundreds of job-posting sites and other resources available online; be sure to check with your college's career center for the latest information.

Remember that networking is about people helping each other, not just about other people helping you. Pay close attention to networking etiquette: Try to learn something about the people you want to connect with, don't overwhelm others with too many messages or requests, be succinct in all your communication efforts, don't give out other people's names and contact information without their permission, never e-mail your résumé to complete strangers, and remember to say thank you every time someone helps you.[12]

To become a valued network member, you need to be able to help others in some way. You may not have any influential contacts yet, but because you're actively researching a number of industries and trends in your own job search, you probably have valuable information you can share. Or you might simply be able to connect one person with another person who can help. The more you network, the more valuable you become in your network—and the more valuable your network becomes to you.

Seeking Career Counseling

Don't overlook the many resources available through your college's career center.

Your college's career center probably offers a wide variety of services, including individual counseling, job fairs, on-campus interviews, and job listings. Counselors can give you advice on résumé-writing software and provide workshops in job search techniques, résumé preparation, job readiness training, interview techniques, self-marketing, and more.[13]

You can also find job counseling online. You might begin your self-assessment, for example, with the Keirsey Temperament Sorter, an online personality test at www.advisorteam .com. For excellent job seeking pointers and counseling, visit college- and university-run online career centers. Major online job boards such as Monster also offer a variety of career planning resources.

PREPARING RÉSUMÉS

Some job searchers are intimidated by the prospect of writing a résumé, but your résumé is really just another specialized business message. Follow the three step writing process, and it'll be easier than you might think (see Figure 13.3).

Planning Your Résumé

As with other business messages, planning a résumé means analyzing your purpose and your audience, gathering information, choosing the best medium, and organizing your content.

Analyzing Your Purpose and Audience

When you view your résumé as a persuasive business message, it's easier to decide what should and shouldn't be in it.

A **résumé** is a structured, written summary of a person's education, employment background, and job qualifications. Before you begin writing a résumé, make sure you understand its true function—as a persuasive business message intended to stimulate an employer's interest in meeting you and learning more about you (see Table 13.2). A successful résumé inspires a prospective employer to invite you to interview with the company. In other words, your purpose in writing your résumé is to create interest—*not* to tell readers every little detail.[14]

Because you've already completed a good deal of research on specific companies, you should know quite a bit about the organizations you'll be applying to. Now learn as much as you can about the individuals who may be reading your résumé. For example, if you learned of an opportunity through networking, chances are you'll have both a contact name and some personalized advice to help fine-tune your writing. Search online using the person's name; you might find him or her mentioned in a news release, magazine article, or blog. Any bit of information can help you craft a more effective message. Even if you can't identify a specific hiring manager, try to put yourself in his or her shoes so that you can tailor your résumé to satisfy your audience's needs. Why would that person be interested in learning more about you?

By the way, if employers ask to see your "CV," they're referring to your *curriculum vitae*, the term used instead of *résumé* in some professions and in many countries outside the United States. Résumés and CVs are essentially the same, although CVs can be more detailed. If you need to adapt a U.S.-style résumé to CV format, or vice versa, go to Monster.com, which offers helpful guidelines on the subject.

Planning → Writing → Completing

1

Analyze the Situation
Recognize that the purpose of your résumé is to get an interview, not to get a job.

Gather Information
Research target industries and companies so that you know what they're looking for in new hires; learn about various jobs and what to expect; learn about the hiring manager, if possible.

Select the Right Medium
Start with a traditional paper résumé and develop scannable, electronic plain-text, HTML, or PDF versions as needed. Consider PowerPoint and video for your e-portfolio.

Organize the Information
Choose an organizational model that highlights your strengths and downplays your shortcomings; use the chronological approach unless you have a strong reason not to.

2

Adapt to Your Audience
Plan your wording carefully so that you can catch a recruiter's eye within seconds; translate your education and experience into attributes that target employers find valuable.

Compose the Message
Write clearly and succinctly, using active, powerful language that is appropriate to the industries and companies you're targeting; use a professional tone in all communications, even when using e-mail.

3

Revise the Message
Evaluate content, review readability, and then edit and rewrite for conciseness and clarity.

Produce the Message
Use effective design elements and suitable layout for a clean, professional appearance; seamlessly combine text and graphical elements.

Proofread the Message
Review for errors in layout, spelling, and mechanics; mistakes can cost you interview opportunities.

Distribute the Message
Deliver your résumé, following the specific instructions of each employer or job board website.

Figure 13.3 Three-Step Writing Process for Résumés
Following the three-step writing process will help you create a successful résumé in a short time. Remember to pay particular attention to the "you" attitude and presentation quality; your résumé will probably get tossed aside if it doesn't speak to audience needs or if it contains mistakes.

Gathering Pertinent Information

If you haven't been keeping a log or journal of your accomplishments so far, you may need to do some research on yourself. Gather all the information you need to document your work and education history, including all the specific dates, duties, and accomplishments from any previous jobs you've held. Itemize your educational experience, including degrees, skills certificates, academic awards, and scholarships. Also, gather any relevant information about personal endeavors such as offices held in nonprofit organizations or speeches given. You'll save time by having all this material at your fingertips before you begin composing your résumé.

TABLE 13.2 Fallacies and Facts About Résumés	
Fallacy	**Fact**
The purpose of a résumé is to list all your skills and abilities.	The purpose of a résumé is to kindle employer interest and generate an interview.
A good résumé will get you the job you want.	All a résumé can do is get you in the door.
Your résumé will always be read carefully and thoroughly.	In most cases, your résumé needs to make a positive impression within 30 or 45 seconds; only then will someone read it in detail. Moreover, it may be screened by a computer looking for keywords first—and if it doesn't contain the right keywords, a human being may never see it.
The more good information you present about yourself in your résumé, the better, so stuff your résumé with every positive detail you can think of.	Recruiters don't need that much information about you at the initial screening stage, and they probably won't read it.
If you want a really good résumé, have it prepared by a résumé service.	You have the skills needed to prepare an effective résumé, so prepare it yourself—unless the position is especially high level or specialized. Even then, you should check carefully before using a service.

Selecting the Best Medium

Selecting the medium for your résumé used to be a simple matter: You typed it on paper. These days, though, it may take various forms, including a Word document, a plain-text document that you can e-mail or paste into online forms, a PowerPoint presentation, or a multimedia résumé that is part of your online e-portfolio. Explore all your options and choose those that (a) meet the requirements of target employers and (b) allow you to present yourself in a compelling fashion. For instance, if you're applying for a sales position in which your personal communication skills would be a strong point, a vidcast showing you making a sales presentation (even a mock presentation) could be a strong persuader.

No matter how many different media you eventually use, it's always a good idea to prepare a basic paper résumé and keep copies on hand. You'll never know when someone might ask for it, and not all employers want to bother with electronic media when all they want to know is your basic profile. In addition, starting with a traditional paper résumé is a great way to organize your background information and identify your unique strengths.

Organizing Your Résumé Around Your Strengths

The key to organizing a résumé is aligning your personal strengths with both the general and specific qualities that your target employers are looking for.

The most successful résumés convey seven qualities that employers seek: They demonstrate that you (1) think in terms of results, (2) know how to get things done, (3) are well rounded, (4) show signs of career progress and professional development, (5) have personal standards of excellence, (6) are flexible and willing to try new things, and (7) communicate effectively.

Although you may want to include a little information in all categories, you'll naturally want to emphasize the information that does the best job of aligning your career objectives with the needs of your target employers—and that does so without misrepresenting the facts.[15] Do you have something in your history that might trigger an employer's red flag? Here are some common problems and some quick suggestions for overcoming them:[16]

Frequent job changes and gaps in your work history are two of the most common issues that employers may perceive as weaknesses.

- **Frequent job changes.** If you've had a number of short-term jobs of a similar type, such as independent contracting and temporary assignments, try to group them under a single heading. Also, if past job positions were eliminated as a result of layoffs or mergers, find a subtle way to convey that information (if not in your résumé, then in your cover letter). Reasonable employers understand that many otherwise stable employees have been forced to job hop in recent years.

- **Gaps in work history.** Mention relevant experience and education you gained during employment gaps, such as volunteer or community work.

- **Inexperience.** Mention related volunteer work. List relevant course work and internships. If appropriate for the position, offer hiring incentives such as "willing to work nights and weekends."

- **Overqualification.** Tone down your résumé, focusing exclusively on the experience and skills that relate to the position.

- **Long-term employment with one company.** Itemize each position held at the firm to show "interior mobility" and increased responsibilities.

- **Job termination for cause.** Be honest with interviewers. Show that you're a hard-working employee and counter their concerns with proof, such as recommendations and examples of completed projects.

- **Criminal record.** You don't necessarily need to disclose a criminal record or time spent incarcerated on your résumé, but you may be asked about it on job application forms. Laws regarding what employers may ask (and whether they can conduct a criminal background check) vary by state and profession, but if you are asked and the question applies to you, you must answer truthfully, or you risk being terminated later if the employer finds out. Use the interview process to explain any mitigating circumstances and to emphasize your rehabilitation and commitment to being a law-abiding, trustworthy employee.[17]

To focus attention on your strongest points, adopt the appropriate organizational approach—make your résumé chronological, functional, or a combination of the two. The right choice depends on your background and your goals.

The Chronological Résumé In a **chronological résumé**, the work experience section dominates and is placed immediately after the name and address and optional objective. You develop this section by listing your jobs sequentially in reverse order, beginning with the most recent position and working backward toward earlier jobs. Under each listing, describe your responsibilities and accomplishments, giving the most space to the most recent positions (see Figures 13.4 and 13.5 for examples of ineffective and effective approaches). If you're just graduating from college and have limited professional experience, you can vary this chronological approach by putting your educational qualifications before your experience.

The chronological approach is the most common way to organize a résumé, and many employers prefer it. This approach has three key advantages: (1) Employers are familiar with it and can easily find information, (2) it highlights growth and career progression, and (3) it highlights employment continuity and stability.[18] Recruiter Robert Nesbit speaks for many employers when he says, "Unless you have a really compelling reason, don't use any but the standard chronological format. Your résumé should not read like a treasure map, full of minute clues to the whereabouts of your jobs and experience. I want to be able to grasp quickly where a candidate has worked, how long, and in what capacities."[19]

> The chronological résumé is the most common approach, but it might not be right for you at a particular stage in your career.

The Functional Résumé A **functional résumé**, sometimes called a *skills résumé*, emphasizes your skills and capabilities, identifying employers and academic experience in subordinate sections. This pattern stresses individual areas of competence rather than job history.

> The functional résumé is often used by people with limited or spotty employment history, but many employers are suspicious of this format.

Roberto Cortez

5687 Crosswoods Drive, Falls Church, Virginia 22046
Home: (703) 987-0086   Office: (703) 549-6624
Email: rcortez@silvernet.com

Fails to provide an introductory statement of any kind, forcing the reader to piece together what this applicant is all about

I have been staff accountant/financial analyst at Inter-American Imports in Alexandria, Virginia, from March 2002 to present.

Organizes information chronologically but hides that fact with awkward format

- I have negotiated with major suppliers.

- I speak both Spanish and German fluently, and I was recently encouraged to implement an electronic funds transfer for vendor disbursements.

- In my current position, I am responsible for preparing accounting reports.

- I have audited financial transactions.

- I have also been involved in the design of a computerized model to adjust accounts for fluctuations in currency exchange rates.

Uses bulleted lists ineffectively: items are poorly organized, lack parallelism, use "I" too often, use too many words, and fail to highlight most important skills

- I am skilled in the use of Excel, Access, Microsoft Dynamics, and SAP business One.

- I am deeply knowledgeable regarding Sarbox reporting.

Fails to highlight skills and attributes that will be valuable to a future employer

Was staff accountant with Monsanto Agricultural Chemicals in Mexico City, Mexico (October 2001 to March 2005).

- While with Monsanto in Mexico City, I was responsible for budgeting and billing.

- I am responsible for credit-processing functions.

- I was also responsible for auditing the travel and entertainment expenses for the sales department.

- I launched an online computer system to automate all accounting functions.

- Also during this time, I was able to travel extensively in Latin America.

Fails to use headings, making it difficult to find key information

Uses too many words to describe education and lacks parallelism

I have my Master of Business Administration with emphasis on international business, which I earned while attending George Mason University in Fairfax, Virginia, from 1991 to 2001.

Bachelor of Business Administration, Accounting (1996–1999), earned while attending University of Texas in Austin, Texas.

Figure 13.4 Ineffective Chronological Résumé
This chronological résumé exhibits a wide range of problems. The language is self-centered and unprofessional, and the organization forces the reader to dig out essential details—and today's recruiters don't have the time or the patience for that. Compare this with the improved version in Figure 13.5.

"Brands" himself as a management candidate with this title for his qualifications summary—and also subtly expresses his career objective

Uses side heads to make major sections easy to find

Highlights a few special skills, focusing on talents that employers value in this position

ROBERTO CORTEZ
5687 Crosswoods Drive
Falls Church, Virginia 22046
Home: (703) 987-0086 Office: (703) 549-6624
E-mail: RCortez@silvernet.com

International Accounting Management

Experienced international accountant and financial analyst with proven leadership, planning, negotiating, and intercultural communication skills. Demonstrated ability to improve process efficiency and reduce operating costs.

Succinctly summarizes his qualifications for an international accounting management job; an employer can "get" who he is in a matter of seconds

Experience

3/2005 to present

Staff Accountant/Financial Analyst
Inter-American Imports: Alexandria, Virginia

- Prepare accounting reports for wholesale giftware importer ($15 million annual sales)
- Audit financial transactions with suppliers in 12 Latin American countries
- Verify Sarbanes-Oxley process and reporting standards
- Serve as project and team leader
- Created a computerized model to adjust accounts for fluctuations in currency exchange rates
- Negotiated joint-venture agreements with major suppliers in Mexico and Colombia
- Implemented electronic funds transfer for vendor disbursements, improving cash flow and eliminating payables clerk position

Presents specific skills and accomplishments in easy-to-skim bullet format

10/2001 to 3/2005

Staff Accountant
Monsanto Agricultural Chemicals: Mexico City, Mexico
- Handled budgeting, billing, and credit-processing functions for the Mexico City branch
- Audited travel & entertainment expenses for Monsanto's 30-member Latin American sales force
- Helped launch an onlinesystem to automate all accounting functions, improving reporting accuracy by 65%

Education

6/2001

Master of Business Administration with emphasis in international business
George Mason University, Fairfax, Virginia

Doesn't go into detail about education because he has been out of college for almost a decade

5/1999

Master of Business Administration Accounting
University of Texas, Austin, Texas

Special Skills   Cultural

- Fluent in Spanish and German
- Extensive business contacts in Latin America

Technical
- Proficient with a wide range of financial software and systems, including Excel, Access, Microsoft Dynamics, and SAP Business One

---

Planning → Writing → Completing

Planning

Analyze the Situation
Decide on the best way to combine finance and international experience.

Gather Information
Research target positions to identify key employer needs.

Select the Right Medium
Start with a traditional paper résumé and develop scannable or plain-text versions as needed.

Organize the Information
Open with a qualifications summary that also signals his career objective; choose the chronological format because it fits this strong employment history perfectly.

1

Writing

Adapt to Your Audience
Translate specific experience into general qualifications that all multinational companies will find valuable.

Compose Your Presentation
Write clearly and succinctly, using active, powerful language that is appropriate to the accounting management profession.

2

Completing

Revise the Message
Evaluate content and review readability, clarity, and accuracy.

Produce the Message
Use effective design elements and suitable layout for a clean, professional appearance.

Proofread the Message
Review for errors in layout, spelling, and mechanics.

Distribute the Message
Deliver the résumé and other employment messages following the specific instructions of each employer or job board website.

3

Figure 13.5   Effective Chronological Résumé
This version does a much better job than the résumé in Figure 13.4 of presenting the candidate's ability to contribute to a new employer. Notice in particular how easy it is to scan through this résumé to find sections of interest.

The functional approach also has three advantages: (1) Without having to read through job descriptions, employers can see what you can do for them, (2) you can emphasize earlier job experience, and (3) you can deemphasize any lengthy unemployment or lack of career progress. However, you should be aware that because the functional résumé can obscure your work history, many employment professionals are suspicious of it—and some assume that candidates who use it are trying to hide something. In fact, Monster.com lists the functional résumé as one of employers' "Top 10 Pet Peeves."[20] If you don't believe the chronological format will work for you, consider the combination résumé instead.

The Combination Résumé A **combination résumé** includes the best features of the chronological and functional approaches (see Figure 13.6). One approach is to group your strengths in *skills clusters* and then list your experience chronologically.[21] Be aware that the combination format is not as commonly used as the chronological format, and it has two major disadvantages: (1) It tends to be longer than a chronological résumé, and (2) it can be repetitious if you have to list your accomplishments and skills in both the functional section and the chronological job descriptions.[22]

If you don't have a lot of work history to show, consider using a combination résumé to highlight your skills while still providing a chronological history of your employment.

As you look at a number of sample résumés, you'll probably notice variations on the three basic formats presented here. Study these other options in light of effective communication principles; if you find one that seems like the best fit for your unique situation, by all means use it.

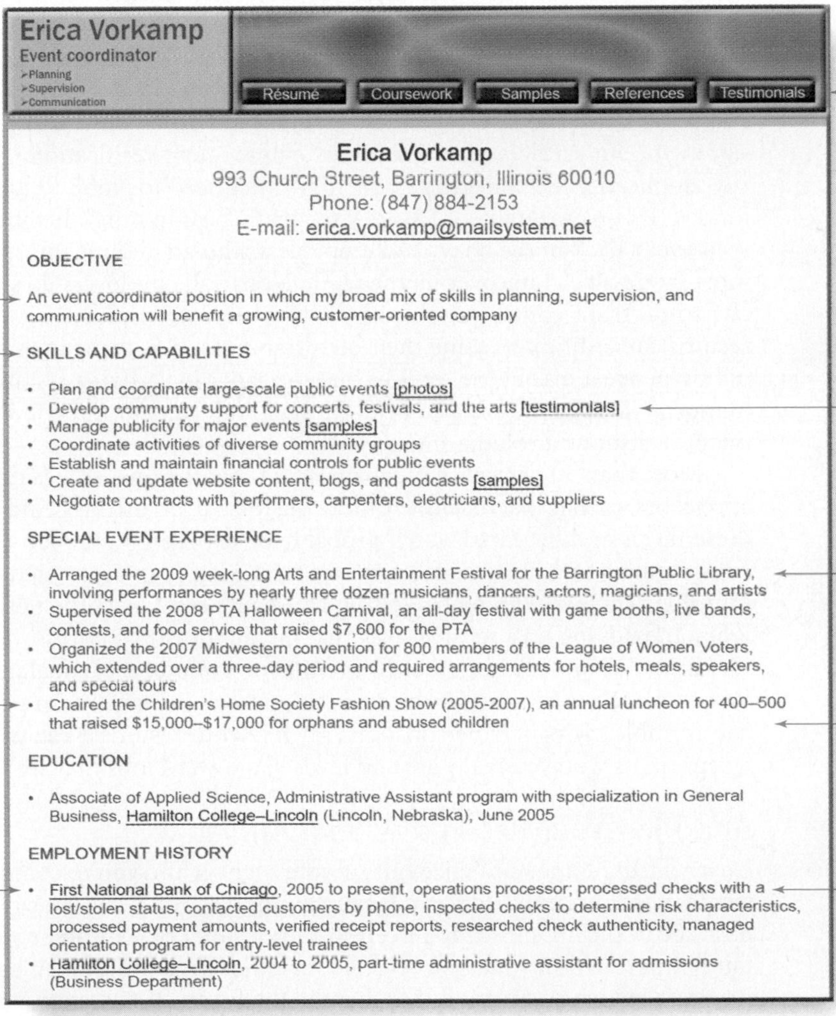
Erica Vorkamp
Event coordinator
>Planning
>Supervision
>Communication

Résumé | Coursework | Samples | References | Testimonials

Erica Vorkamp
993 Church Street, Barrington, Illinois 60010
Phone: (847) 884-2153
E-mail: erica.vorkamp@mailsystem.net

OBJECTIVE

An event coordinator position in which my broad mix of skills in planning, supervision, and communication will benefit a growing, customer-oriented company

SKILLS AND CAPABILITIES

- Plan and coordinate large-scale public events [photos]
- Develop community support for concerts, festivals, and the arts [testimonials]
- Manage publicity for major events [samples]
- Coordinate activities of diverse community groups
- Establish and maintain financial controls for public events
- Create and update website content, blogs, and podcasts [samples]
- Negotiate contracts with performers, carpenters, electricians, and suppliers

SPECIAL EVENT EXPERIENCE

- Arranged the 2009 week-long Arts and Entertainment Festival for the Barrington Public Library, involving performances by nearly three dozen musicians, dancers, actors, magicians, and artists
- Supervised the 2008 PTA Halloween Carnival, an all-day festival with game booths, live bands, contests, and food service that raised $7,600 for the PTA
- Organized the 2007 Midwestern convention for 800 members of the League of Women Voters, which extended over a three-day period and required arrangements for hotels, meals, speakers, and special tours
- Chaired the Children's Home Society Fashion Show (2005-2007), an annual luncheon for 400–500 that raised $15,000–$17,000 for orphans and abused children

EDUCATION

- Associate of Applied Science, Administrative Assistant program with specialization in General Business, Hamilton College–Lincoln (Lincoln, Nebraska), June 2005

EMPLOYMENT HISTORY

- First National Bank of Chicago, 2005 to present, operations processor; processed checks with a lost/stolen status, contacted customers by phone, inspected checks to determine risk characteristics, processed payment amounts, verified receipt reports, researched check authenticity, managed orientation program for entry-level trainees
- Hamilton College–Lincoln, 2004 to 2005, part-time administrative assistant for admissions (Business Department)

Figure 13.6 Combination Résumé
With her limited work experience in her field of interest, Erica Vorkamp opted for a combination résumé to highlight her skills. Her employment history is complete and easy to find, but it isn't featured to the same degree as the other elements. Note that even though this is a webpage, she mimicked a conventional résumé design to make her information easy to find. Having an HTML version as part of her e-portfolio also lets her provide instant links to other information, such as samples of her work and testimonials from people who have worked with her in the past.

Writing Your Résumé

As you follow the three-step process to develop your résumé, keep four points in mind. First, treat your résumé with the respect it deserves. Until you're able to meet with employers in person, you *are* your résumé, and a single mistake or oversight can cost you interview opportunities. Second, give yourself plenty of time. Don't put off preparing your résumé until the last second and then try to write it in one sitting. Third, learn from good models. You can find thousands of sample résumés online at college websites and job sites such as Monster.com. Fourth, don't get frustrated by the conflicting advice you'll read about résumés. Résumés are more art than science, and there is more than one way to be successful with them. Consider the alternatives and choose the approach that makes the most sense to you, given everything you know about successful business communication.

If you feel uncomfortable writing about yourself, you're not alone. Many people, even accomplished writers, find it difficult to write their own résumés. If you get stuck, find a classmate or friend who is also writing a résumé and swap projects for a while. By working on each other's résumés, you might be able to speed up the process for both of you.

Keeping Your Résumé Honest

Somehow, the idea that "everybody lies on their résumés" has crept into popular consciousness, and dishonesty in the job search process has reached epidemic proportions. Estimates vary, but one comprehensive study uncovered lies about work history in more than 40 percent of the résumés tested.[23] And it's not just the simple fudging of facts here and there. Dishonest applicants are getting bolder all the time—buying fake diplomas online, paying a computer hacker to insert their names into prestigious universities' graduation records, and signing up for services that offer phony employment verification.[24]

Applicants with integrity know they don't need to stoop to lying to compete in the job market. If you are tempted to stretch the truth, bear in mind that professional recruiters have seen every trick in the book, and employers who are fed up with the dishonesty are getting more aggressive at uncovering the truth. Nearly all employers do some form of background checking, from contacting references to verifying employment to checking for criminal records. In addition to using their own resources, U.S. companies now spend more than $2 billion per year on outside services that specialize in verifying résumés and application information.[25] Employers are also beginning to craft certain interview questions specifically to uncover dishonest résumé entries.[26]

More than 90 percent of companies that find lies on résumés refuse to hire the offending applicants, even if that means withdrawing formal job offers.[27] And even if you do sneak past these filters and get hired, you'll probably be exposed on the job when you can't live up to your own résumé. Résumé fabrications have been known to catch up to people many years into their careers, with embarrassing consequences. Given the networked nature of today's job market, lying on a résumé could haunt you for the rest of your career.[28]

If you're not sure whether to include or exclude a particular point, ask yourself this: Would you be willing to say the same thing to an interviewer in person? If you wouldn't be comfortable saying it in person, don't say it in your résumé. Keep your résumé honest so that it represents who you really are and leads you toward jobs that are truly right for you.

Adapting Your Résumé to Your Audience

Never let the target audience out of your sight while you're composing your résumé. The single most important concept to keep in mind as you write your résumé is to translate your past accomplishments into perceived future potential. In other words, employers are certainly interested in what you've done for other organizations in the past, but they're more interested in what you can do for them in the future. If necessary, customize your résumé for individual companies, too.

Keep in mind that you may need to "translate" your skills and experiences into the terminology of the hiring organization. For instance, military experience can help you develop a number of skills that are valuable in business, but military terminology can sound like a foreign language to people who aren't familiar with it. Isolate the important general concepts and present them in common business language. Similarly, educational achievements in other countries might not align with the standard U.S. definitions of high schools, community colleges, technical and trade schools, and universities. If necessary, include a brief statement explaining how your degree or certificate relates to U.S. expectations—or how your U.S. degree relates to expectations in other countries, if you're applying for work abroad.

Regardless of your background, it's up to you to combine your experiences into a straightforward message that communicates what you can do for your potential employer.[29] Think in terms of an image or a theme you'd like to project. Are you academically gifted? An effective leader? A well-rounded person? A creative genius? A technical wizard? By knowing yourself and your audience, you'll be able to focus on the strengths that potential employers want.

Although your résumé is a highly factual document, it should still tell the "story of you," giving readers a clear picture of the sort of employee you are.

Composing Your Résumé

Write your résumé using a simple and direct style. Use short, crisp phrases instead of whole sentences and focus on what your reader needs to know. Avoid using the word *I*, which can sound both self-involved and repetitious by the time you outline all your skills and accomplishments. Instead, start your phrases with strong action verbs such as these:[30]

Draft your résumé using short, crisp phrases built around strong verbs and nouns.

accomplished	coordinated	initiated	participated	set up
achieved	created	installed	performed	simplified
administered	demonstrated	introduced	planned	sparked
approved	developed	investigated	presented	streamlined
arranged	directed	launched	proposed	strengthened
assisted	established	maintained	raised	succeeded
assumed	explored	managed	recommended	supervised
budgeted	forecasted	motivated	reduced	systematized
chaired	generated	negotiated	reorganized	targeted
changed	identified	operated	resolved	trained
compiled	implemented	organized	saved	transformed
completed	improved	oversaw	served	upgraded

Whenever you can, quantify the results and offer proof so that your claims don't come across as empty puffery.[31] For instance, you might say, "Implemented a new patient-tracking system that reduced errors by 80 percent" or "Managed a fast-food restaurant and four employees." Here are some additional examples of how to phrase your accomplishments using active statements that show results:

Instead of This	Write Active Statements That Show Results
Responsible for developing a new filing system	Developed a new filing system that reduced paperwork by 50 percent
I was in charge of customer complaints and all ordering problems	Handled all customer complaints and resolved all product order discrepancies
I won a trip to Europe for opening the most new customer accounts in my department	Generated the highest number of new customer accounts in my department
Member of special campus task force to resolve student problems with existing cafeteria assignments	Assisted in implementing new campus dining program that balances student wishes with cafeteria capacity

Providing specific supporting evidence is vital but make sure you don't go overboard with small details.[32]

Name and Contact Information Employers obviously need to know who you are and where you can be reached. Your name and contact information constitute the heading of your résumé, so include the following:

Be sure to provide complete and accurate contact information; mistakes in this section of the résumé are surprisingly common.

- Name
- Physical address (both permanent and temporary if you're likely to move during the job search process)
- E-mail address
- Phone number(s)
- The URL of your personal webpage or e-portfolio (if you have one)

If the only e-mail address you have is through your current employer, get a free personal e-mail address from one of the many services that offer them. Using company resources for a job search is not fair to your current employer, and it sends a bad signal to potential employers. Also, if your personal e-mail address is anything like precious.princess@something.com or PsychoDawg@something.com, get a new e-mail address for your business correspondence.

Get a professional-sounding e-mail address for business correspondence (such as firstname.lastname@something.com), if you don't already have one.

Introductory Statement Of all the parts of a résumé, the brief introductory statement that follows your name and contact information probably generates the most disagreement. You can put one of three things here:[33]

- **Career objective.** A career objective identifies either a specific job you want to land or a general career track you would like to pursue. Some experts advise against including a career objective because it can categorize you so narrowly that you miss out on interesting opportunities, and it is essentially about fulfilling your desires, not about meeting the employer's needs. In the past, most résumés included a career objective, but in recent years more job seekers are using a qualifications summary or a career summary. However, if you have little or no work experience in your target profession, a career objective might be your best option. If you do opt for an objective, word it in a way that relates your qualifications to employer needs (see Figure 13.6 on page 347).

You can choose to open with a career objective, a qualifications summary, or a career summary.

- **Qualifications summary.** A qualifications summary offers a brief capsule view of your key qualifications. The goal is to let a reader know within a few seconds what you can deliver. You can title this section generically as "Qualifications Summary" or "Summary of Qualifications," or if you have one dominant qualification, you can use that as the title (see the career summary in Figure 13.5 on page 346 for an example). Consider using a qualifications summary if you have one or more important qualifications but don't yet have a long career history. Also, if you haven't been working long but your college education has given you a dominant professional "theme," such as multimedia design or taxation, you can craft a qualifications summary that highlights your educational preparedness.

If you have a reasonably focused skill set but don't yet have a long career history, a qualifications summary is probably the best type of introductory statement for you.

- **Career summary.** A career summary offers a brief recap of your career with the goal of presenting increasing levels of responsibility and performance. A career summary can be particularly useful for executives who have demonstrated the ability to manage increasingly larger and more complicated business operations—a key consideration when companies look to hire upper-level managers.

Education If you're still in school, education is probably your strongest selling point. Present your educational background in depth, choosing facts that support your "theme." Give this section a heading such as "Education," "Technical Training," or "Academic Preparation," as appropriate. Then, starting with the most recent, list the name and location of each school you have attended, the month and year of your graduation (say "anticipated graduation in" if you haven't graduated yet), your major and minor fields of study, significant skills and abilities you've developed in your course work, and the degrees or certificates you've earned. If you're still working toward a degree, include in parentheses the expected date of completion. Showcase your qualifications by listing courses that have directly equipped you for the job you are seeking and indicate any scholarships, awards, or academic honors you've received.

If you are early in your career, your education is probably your strongest selling point.

The education section should also include relevant training sponsored by business or government organizations. Mention high school or military training only if the associated achievements are pertinent to your career goals.

Whether you list your grade point average depends on the job you want and the quality of your grades. If you don't show your GPA on your résumé—and there's no rule saying you have to—be prepared to answer questions about it during the interview process because many employers will assume that your GPA is not spectacular if you didn't show it on your résumé. If you choose to show a grade point average, be sure to mention the scale, especially if it isn't a four-point scale. If your grades are better within your major than in other courses, you can also list your GPA as "Major GPA" and include only those courses within your major.

Work Experience, Skills, and Accomplishments   Like the education section, the work experience section should focus on your overall theme. Align your past with the employer's future. Call attention to the skills you've developed on the job and to your ability to handle increasing responsibility.

When you describe past job responsibilities, identify the skills and knowledge that you can apply to a future job.

List your jobs in reverse chronological order (starting with the most recent). Include military service and any internships and part-time or temporary jobs related to your career objective. Include the name and location of the employer, and if readers are unlikely to recognize the organization, briefly describe what it does. When you want to keep the name of your current employer confidential, you can identify the firm by industry only ("a large video game developer"). If an organization's name or location has changed since you worked there, state the current name and location and include the old information preceded by "formerly . . ." Before or after each job listing, state your job title and give the years you worked in the job; use the phrase "to present" to denote current employment. Indicate whether a job was part time.

Devote the most space to the jobs that are related to your target position. If you were personally responsible for something significant, be sure to mention it. Facts about your skills and accomplishments are the most important information you can give a prospective employer, so quantify them whenever possible.

Devote the most space to jobs that are related to your target position.

One helpful exercise is to write a 30-second "commercial" for each major skill you want to highlight. The commercial should offer proof that you really do possess the skill. For your résumé, distill the commercials down to brief phrases; you can use the more detailed proof statements in cover letters and as answers to interview questions.[34]

If you have a number of part-time, temporary, or entry-level jobs that don't relate to your career objective, you have to use your best judgment when it comes to including or excluding them. On the one hand, employers will be impressed by the fact that you can land and keep jobs while you're progressing toward your career goals. On the other hand, too many minor and irrelevant work details can clutter your résumé, particularly if you've been in the professional workforce for a few years. Generally speaking, if you don't have a long employment history, use these jobs to show your ability and willingness to work.

You can also include information describing other aspects of your background that pertain to your career objective, such as fluency in multiple languages. If samples of your work might increase your chances of getting the job, insert a line at the end of your résumé, offering to supply them on request or indicating that they're available in your e-portfolio.

Activities and Achievements   Include activities and achievements outside of a work context only if they make you a more attractive job candidate. For example, membership in the Toastmasters public-speaking organization shows an interest in becoming a better communicator, which is something every smart employer values. Similarly, artistic awards could weigh in your favor if you are applying for work at a web design company or an advertising agency. However, unless you are applying to a running-shoe company such as Nike or New Balance, the fact that you are a long-distance runner is irrelevant. Also consider mentioning publications and other accomplishments that required relevant business skills.

You can include personal accomplishments that indicate special skills or qualities that are relevant to the jobs you're seeking.

Because many employers are involved in their local communities, they tend to look positively on applicants who are active and concerned members of their communities as well. Consider including community service activities that suggest leadership, teamwork, communication skills, technical aptitude, or other valuable attributes.

You should generally avoid indicating membership or significant activity in religious or political organizations (unless, of course, you're applying to such an organization) because doing so might raise concerns for people with differing beliefs or affiliations. However, if you want to highlight skills you developed while involved with such a group, you can refer to it generically as a "not-for-profit organization."

Finally, if you have little or no job experience and not much to discuss outside your education, indicating involvement in athletics or other organized student activities lets employers know that you don't spend all your free time hanging around your apartment playing video games. However, this information becomes increasingly irrelevant the longer you have been out of school.

Personal Data and References   In nearly all instances, your résumé should not include any personal data beyond the information described in the previous sections. When applying to U.S. companies, never include any of the following: physical characteristics, age, gender, marital status, sexual orientation, religious or political affiliations, race, national origin, salary history, reasons for leaving jobs, names of previous supervisors, names of references, Social Security number, or student ID number. Also, never include a photo on or with your résumé—some employers won't even look at résumés with photos for fear of being accused of discrimination based on personal characteristics.[35]

Note that standards can vary in other countries. For example, you might be expected to include your citizenship, nationality, or marital status.[36] However, verify such requirements before including any personal data.

The availability of references is usually assumed, so you don't need to put "References available upon request" at the end of your résumé. However, be sure to have a list of several references ready when you begin applying for jobs; you will probably be asked for it at some point in the selection process. Prepare your reference sheet with your name and contact information at the top. For a finished look, use the same design and layout you use for your résumé. Then list three or four people who have agreed to serve as references. (Don't list anyone who hasn't agreed to be listed.) Include each person's name, job title, organization, address, telephone number, and e-mail address (if the reference prefers to be contacted by e-mail).

Completing Your Résumé

As with any other business message, completing your résumé involves revising it for quality, producing it in an appropriate form, and proofreading it for any errors before distributing it to your target employers.

The ideal length of your résumé depends on the depth of your experience and the level of the positions for which you are applying. As a general guideline, if you have fewer than 10 years of professional experience, try to keep your résumé to one page. If you have more experience and are applying for a higher-level position, you may need to prepare a somewhat longer résumé.[37] For highly technical positions, longer résumés are often the norm as well because the qualifications for such jobs can require more description.

Revising Your Résumé

Ask professional recruiters to list the most common mistakes they see on résumés, and you'll hear the same things over and over again. Keep your résumé out of the recycling bin by avoiding these flaws:

- Too long or too wordy
- Too short or sketchy
- Difficult to read
- Poorly written
- Displaying weak understanding of the business world or of a particular industry
- Poor-quality printing or cheap paper
- Full of spelling and grammar errors
- Boastful
- Gimmicky design

Producing Your Résumé

Good design is a must, and it's not difficult to achieve. As you can see in Figures 13.4, 13.5, and 13.6, good designs feature simplicity, order, plenty of white space, and easy-to-read typefaces. (Keep in mind that many of the fancier fonts on your computer are not appropriate for a résumé.) Make your subheadings easy to find and easy to read, placing them either above

Introducing: Erica Vorkamp

Address
993 Church Street, Barrington, Illinois 60010

Phone
847/884/2153

E-mail
live2party@mailsystem.net

1. OBJECTIVE
An event coordinator position in which my broad mix of skills in planning, supervision, and communication will benefit a growing, customer-oriented company

2. SKILLS AND CAPABILITIES
Plan and coordinate large-scale public events
   Develop community support for concerts, festivals, and the arts
      Manage publicity for major events
         Coordinate activities of diverse community groups
      Establish and maintain financial controls for public events
   Create and update website content, blogs, and podcasts
Negotiate contracts with performers, carpenters, electricians, and suppliers

3. SPECIAL EVENT EXPERIENCE
Arranged the 2009 week-long Arts and Entertainment Festival for the Barrington Public Library, involving performances by nearly three dozen musicians, dancers, actors, magicians, and artists
Supervised the 2008 PTA Halloween Carnival, an all-day festival with game booths, live bands, contests, and food service that raised $7,600 for the PTA
Organized the 2007 Midwestern convention for 800 members of the League of Women Voters, which extended over a three-day period and required arrangements for hotels, meals, speakers, and special tours
Chaired the Children's Home Society Fashion Show (2005-2007), an annual luncheon for 400-500 that raised $15,000-$17,000 for orphans and abused children

4. EDUCATION
Associate of Applied Science, Administrative Assistant program with specialization in General Business, Hamilton College–Lincoln (Lincoln, Nebraska), June 2005

5. EMPLOYMENT HISTORY
First National Bank of Chicago, 2005 to present, operations processor; processed checks with a lost/stolen status, contacted customers by phone, inspected checks to determine risk characteristics, processed payment amounts, verified receipt reports, researched check authenticity, managed orientation program for entry-level trainees
Hamilton College–Lincoln, 2004 to 2005, part-time administrative assistant for admissions (Business Department)

Annotations:

Uses inappropriate design elements in an attempt to grab the reader's attention; name and contact information should not be "decorated" in any way

Uses an unconventional format for the phone number, which only looks amateurish

Distracts the reader with large background images (the E and V initials)

Uses unconventional indentations, which force the reader to try to figure out the meaning of the different levels

Fails to use bullet point symbols and white space to separate list items

Uses far too much space for contact information, which then crowds the rest of the document

Includes an inappropriate e-mail address

Fails to use adequate white space between headings and text sections, making reading more difficult

Crams too much information into too little space; the lack of white space makes the body of the résumé extremely difficult to read

Uses a font that some readers will consider too casual for an important business document

Figure 13.7   Ineffective Résumé Design
This résumé tries too hard to be creative and eye-catching, resulting in a document that is difficult to read—and that probably won't get read. Recruiters have seen every conceivable design gimmick, so don't try to stand out from the crowd with unusual design. Instead, provide compelling, employer-focused information that is easy to find.

each section or in the left margin. Use lists to itemize your most important qualifications and leave plenty of white space, even if doing so forces you to use two pages rather than one. Color is not necessary by any means, but if you add color, make it subtle and sophisticated, such as for a thin horizontal line under your name and address. The most common way to get into trouble with résumé design is going overboard (see Figure 13.7).

Depending on the companies you apply to, you might want to produce your résumé in as many as six formats (all are explained in the following sections):

- Printed traditional résumé
- Printed scannable résumé
- Electronic plain-text file
- Microsoft Word file
- HTML format
- PDF file

Some applicants also create PowerPoint presentations or videos to supplement a conventional résumé. Two key advantages of a PowerPoint supplement are flexibility and

Start with a traditional printed résumé but realize that you may need to create several other versions during your job search.

Consider creating multimedia supplements such as a PowerPoint presentation or a video, but don't use them to replace your conventional résumé.

multimedia capabilities. For instance, you can present a menu of choices on the opening screen and allow viewers to click through to such items as a brief biography or photos that document important accomplishments (such as screen shots of websites you designed).

A video résumé can be a compelling supplement as well, but videos are not without controversy. Some employment law experts advise employers not to view videos, at least not until after candidates have been evaluated solely on their credentials. The reason for this caution is the same as with photographs: Seeing visual cues of the age, ethnicity, and gender of candidates early in the selection process exposes employers to complaints of discriminatory hiring practices. In addition, videos are more cumbersome to evaluate than paper or electronic résumés.[38]

Producing a Traditional Résumé   The traditional paper résumé still has a place in this world of electronic job searches, if only to have a few copies ready whenever one of your networking contacts asks for a one. Avoid basic, low-cost white bond paper intended for general office use and gimmicky papers with borders and backgrounds. Choose a heavier, higher-quality paper designed specifically for résumés and other important documents. White or slightly off-white is the best color choice. This paper is more expensive than general office paper, but you don't need much, and it's a worthwhile investment. Make sure the printer you use is well maintained and has adequate toner or ink.

> Strive for a clean, classy look in your printed résumé, using professional-grade paper and a clean, high-quality printer.

Printing a Scannable Résumé   To cope with the flood of unsolicited paper résumés in recent years, many companies now optically scan paper résumés into their applicant tracking systems. Nearly all large companies now use these systems, as do many midsized companies and even some smaller firms.[39]

The emergence of these systems has important implications for your résumé. First, the *optical character recognition (OCR)* software used in these systems doesn't actually "read" anything; it merely looks for shapes that match stored profiles of characters. If the OCR software can't make sense of your fancy fonts or creative page layout, it will enter gibberish into the database. To create a scannable résumé, follow these guidelines (see Figure 13.8):[40]

> Converting your résumé to scannable format is easy to do—and extremely important.

- Use a clean, common sans serif font such as Optima or Arial and size it between 10 and 14 points.
- Avoid italics and underlining.
- Make sure that characters do not touch one another, including the slash (/).
- Don't use side-by-side columns.
- Don't use ampersands (&), percent signs (%), accented characters (such as é and ö), or bullet symbols (use a hyphen—not a lowercase *o*—in place of a bullet symbol).
- Put each phone number and e-mail address on its own line.
- Print on plain white paper.
- Don't fold or staple your pages.

Your scannable résumé will probably be longer than your traditional résumé because you can't compress text into columns and because you need plenty of white space between headings and sections. If your scannable résumé runs more than one page, make sure your name appears on every subsequent page (in case the pages become separated). Before sending a scannable résumé, check the company's website or call the human resources department to see whether it has any specific requirements other than those discussed here.

> A scannable résumé includes a keyword summary of terms that appeal to recruiters and reflect your qualities accurately.

Figure 13.8 shows an important feature of a scannable résumé, the *keyword summary*. This is a list of 20 to 30 words and phrases that define your skills, experience, education, professional affiliations, and so on. Employers generally search for nouns (because verbs tend to be generic rather than specific to a particular position or skill), so make your keywords nouns as well. Use abbreviations sparingly and only when they are well known and unambiguous, such as *MBA*. You can review job descriptions and industry publications to find words most relevant to a given position. Place this list right after your name and address. (Note that you can also use your keywords as tags on your blog, social networking profile, or other elements of your online presence.[41])

Puts each contact element on its own line →

Adds a summary of keywords taken from job descriptions and industry publications →

Removes slashes, bullet points, ampersands (&), and other characters that might confuse the OCR software →

Uses enough white space to ensure successful scanning, without worrying about a pleasing visual design ←

Uses a clean, scanner-friendly font ←

Simplifies layout by removing multiple-column format ←

ROBERTO CORTEZ
5687 Crosswoods Drive
Falls Church, Virginia 22046
Home: (703) 987-0086
Office: (703) 549-6624
E-mail: RCortez@silvernet.com

KEYWORDS

Financial executive, accounting management, international finance, financial analyst, accounting reports, financial audit, exchange rates, Sarbanes-Oxley, joint-venture agreements, budgets, billing, credit processing, MBA, fluent Spanish, fluent German, Microsoft Dynamics, SAP Business One, leadership, planning, negotiating, Latin America

INTERNATIONAL ACCOUNTING MANAGEMENT

Experienced international accountant and financial analyst with proven leadership, planning, negotiating, and intercultural communication skills. Demonstrated ability to improve process efficiency and reduce operating costs.

EXPERIENCE

Staff Accountant Financial Analyst, Inter-American Imports, Alexandria, Virginia, March 2005 to present
- Prepare accounting reports for wholesale giftware importer ($15 million annual sales)
- Audit financial transactions with suppliers in 12 Latin American countries
- Verify Sarbanes-Oxley process and reporting standards
- Serve as project and team leader
- Created a computerized model to adjust accounts for fluctuations in currency exchange rates
- Negotiated joint-venture agreements with major suppliers in Mexico and Colombia
- Implemented electronic funds transfer for vendor disbursements, improving cash flow
  and eliminating payables clerk position

Staff Accountant, Monsanto Agricultural Chemicals, Mexico City, Mexico, October 2001 to March 2005
 - Handled budgeting, billing, and credit-processing functions for the Mexico City branch
- Audited travel and entertainment expenses for Monsanto's 30-member Latin American sales force
- Helped launch an online system to automate all accounting functions, improving reporting accuracy by 65 percent

EDUCATION

Master of Business Administration with emphasis in international business, George Mason University, Fairfax, Virginia, June 2001
Bachelor of Business Administration, Accounting, University of Texas, Austin, Texas, May 1999

CULTURAL SKILLS

- Fluent in Spanish and German
- Extensive business contacts in Latin America

TECHNICAL SKILLS

Proficient with a wide range of financial software and systems, including Excel, Access, Microsoft Dynamics, and SAP Business One

Figure 13.8   Scannable Résumé
This version of the chronological résumé from Figure 13.5 shows the changes necessary to ensure successful scanning. Notice that the résumé doesn't have any special characters, formatting, or design elements that are likely to confuse the scanning software.

One good way to identify which keywords to include in your summary is to underline all the skills listed in ads for the types of jobs you're interested in. (Another advantage of staying current by reading periodicals, networking, and so on is that you'll develop a good ear for current terminology.) Be sure to include only those keywords that correspond with your skills and experience.

Resist the temptation to toss in impressive keywords that don't really apply to you. Increasingly sophisticated résumé analysis systems can now detect whether your keywords truly relate to the job descriptions and other information on your résumé. If a system suspects that you've padded your keyword list, it could move you to the bottom of the ranking or delete your résumé.[42]

Creating a Plain-Text File of Your Résumé   Many employers now prefer to enter résumé information directly into their databases through the use of *plain-text* versions (sometimes referred to as *ASCII text versions*). This approach has the same goal as a scannable résumé, but it's faster, easier, and less prone to errors than the scanning process. If you have the option of

A plain-text version of your résumé is a computer file with a keyword summary without any of the formatting that you typically apply using a word processor.

mailing a scannable résumé or submitting plain text online, go with plain text. Note that a plain-text version should include a keyword summary (see the previous section).

Plain text is just what it sounds like: no font formatting, no bullet symbols, no colors, no lines or boxes, and so on. A plain-text version is easy to create with your word processor. Start with the file you used to create your scannable résumé, use the "Save As" choice to save it as "plain text" or whichever similarly labeled option your software has, and verify the result by using a basic text editor (such as Microsoft Notepad). If necessary, reformat the page manually, moving text and inserting space as needed. For simplicity's sake, left-justify all your headings rather than try to center them manually.

Creating a Word File of Your Résumé   In some cases, an employer or job-posting website will let you upload a Microsoft Word file directly. (Although there are certainly other word processors on the market, Microsoft Word is the de facto standard in business these days.) This method of transferring information preserves the design and layout of your traditional printed résumé and saves you the trouble of creating a plain-text version. However, read the instructions carefully. For instance, you can upload a Word résumé to Monster.com, but the site asks you to follow some specific formatting instructions to make sure your file doesn't become garbled.[43]

Before you submit a Word file to anyone, make sure your system is free of viruses. Infecting a potential employer's PC will not make a good first impression.

Creating an HTML Version of Your Résumé   You can probably find several uses for an HTML (webpage) version of your résumé, including sending it as a fully formatted e-mail message, posting it on your personal webpage, and including it in your e-portfolio. Even if you don't have HTML experience, you can save your résumé as a webpage from within Word. This method won't necessarily create the most spectacularly beautiful webpage, but it should at least be functional.

A major benefit of using an HTML résumé is that you can provide links to supporting details and other materials from within the résumé. You can link to papers you've written, recommendations you've received, and sound or video clips that directly support your résumé.

Creating a PDF Version of Your Résumé   Creating a PDF version of your résumé is a simple procedure, but you need the right software. Adobe Acrobat (not the free Adobe Reader) is the best-known program, but many others are available, including some free versions. You can also use Adobe's online service, at http://createpdf.adobe.com, to create PDFs without buying software.

Proofreading Your Résumé

Employers view your résumé as a concrete example of your attention to quality and detail. Your résumé doesn't need to be good or pretty good—it needs to be *perfect*. In a recent survey, an overwhelming majority of executives said that just one or two errors in the job application package are enough to doom a candidate's chances.[44] Job seekers have committed every conceivable error, from forgetting to put their own names on their résumés to misspelling "Education."[45] Your résumé is one of the most important documents you'll ever write, so don't cut corners when it comes to proofreading. Check all headings and lists for clarity and parallelism and be sure that your grammar, spelling, and punctuation are correct. Ask at least three other people to read it, too. As the creator of the material, you could stare at a mistake for weeks and not see it.

Distributing Your Résumé

How you distribute your résumé depends on the number of employers you target and their preferences for receiving résumés. Employers usually list their preferences on their websites, so verify this information to make sure your résumé ends up in the right format and in the right channel. Beyond that, here are some general distribution tips:

- **Mailing your traditional and scannable résumés.** Take some care with the packaging. Spend a few extra cents to mail these documents in a flat 9 × 12 envelope, or better yet, use a Priority Mail flat-rate envelope, which gives you a sturdy cardboard mailer and

---

Make sure you verify the plain-text file that you create with your word processor; it might need a few manual adjustments using a text editor such as Notepad.

Some employers and websites want your résumé in Microsoft Word format; make sure your computer is thoroughly scanned for viruses before sending Word files.

An HTML version of your résumé can be used as an e-mail attachment, as part of your e-portfolio, or as a page on your personal website.

Your résumé can't be "pretty good" or "almost perfect"; it needs to be *perfect*, so proofread it thoroughly and ask several other people to verify it, too.

When distributing your résumé, pay close attention to the specific instructions provided by each employer, job board, or other recipient.

faster delivery for just a few more dollars. Consider sending both standard and scannable versions to each employer. In your cover letter, explain that for the employer's convenience, you're sending both formats. However, if an employer provides the means to submit a résumé electronically, go with that option, as it increases the chances that your information will get into the applicant tracking system quickly and correctly.

- **Faxing your traditional and scannable résumés.** If you know that an employer prefers résumés via fax, be sure to include a standard fax cover sheet, along with your cover letter, followed by your résumé. Set the fax machine to "fine" mode to help ensure a high-quality printout on the receiving end. Note that a faxed résumé is probably the least desired format for many employers, so choose this route only if the employer requests faxes.

- **E-mailing your résumé.** Unless someone specifically asks for a Word document as an e-mail attachment, chances are a Word file won't get opened (because of virus concerns). Instead, insert plain text into the body of the e-mail message, attach a PDF file, or include a hyperlink in the e-mail that links to a résumé on your website or in your e-portfolio. If you have a reference number or a job ad number, include it in your e-mail subject line.

- **Posting your résumé online.** The range of options for posting résumés online seems to grow every year, particularly with the emergence of social networks and specialized job search websites. Consider all the following in your job search: (1) create an e-portfolio (see the Prologue for an example); (2) create a personal website, which can include your e-portfolio; (3) create a profile on one or more social networking sites; (4) post your résumé on "general-purpose" job websites, such as Monster and CareerBuilder; (5) post your résumé on specialized websites, such as Jobster or Jobfox (note that some specialized sites focus on higher-level positions, so they might not be available to you early in your career); (6) post your résumé with a staffing service, such as Volt, www.jobs.volt .com; and (7) keep an eye out for any new channels that emerge in the coming years. In every case, pay close attention to the instructions. For instance, some sites let you upload a Word file, whereas others want you to copy and paste individual sections of résumé into an online application form.

> You have many options for posting your résumé online; explore them all and keep an eye out for new possibilities.

Before you upload your résumé to any site, learn about its confidentiality protection. Some sites allow you to specify levels of confidentiality, such as letting employers search your qualifications without seeing your personal contact information or preventing your current employer from seeing your résumé. In any case, carefully limit the amount of personal information you provide online. Never put your Social Security number, student ID number, or driver's license number online, and don't post your résumé to any website that doesn't give you the option of restricting the display of your contact information. (Only employers that are registered clients of the service should be able to see your contact information.)[46]

For the latest information on résumé writing and distribution, visit http://real-timeupdates .com/bce and click on Chapter 13. ■

DOCUMENT MAKEOVER

Improve This Résumé

To practice correcting drafts of actual documents, visit the "Document Makeovers" section in either MyBCommLab.com or the Companion Website for this text.

If MyBCommLab.com is being used in your class, see your User Guide for specific instructions on how to access the content for this chapter.

If you are accessing this feature through the Companion Website, click on "Document Makeovers" and then select Chapter 13. You will find a résumé that contains problems and errors related to what you've learned in this chapter about writing effective résumés. Use the "Final Draft" decision tool to create an improved version of this document. Check the résumé for spelling and grammatical errors, effective use of verbs and pronouns, inclusion of unnecessary information, or omission of important facts. ●

❝ CHAPTER REVIEW AND ACTIVITIES

Chapter Summary

Every employer's preferred source of prospects to fill job openings is its own workforce, followed by recommendations from employees or other trusted professionals. If these sources don't yield enough of the right candidates, employers will consider hiring an employment agency or a search firm, begin to review unsolicited résumés, and finally move on to placing advertisements. Networking is vital in today's job market because many job opportunities are never advertised to the public, or at least not until an employer has exhausted other opportunities.

Each approach to organizing a résumé emphasizes different strengths. A chronological résumé helps employers easily locate necessary information, highlights your professional growth and career progress, and emphasizes continuity and stability. If you can use the chronological format, you should because it is the approach employers tend to prefer. A functional résumé helps employers easily see what you can do for them, allows you to emphasize earlier job experience, and lets you downplay any lengthy periods of unemployment or a lack of career progress. However, many employers are suspicious of functional résumés for this very reason. The combination approach uses the best features of the other two, but it tends to be longer, and it can be repetitive.

Perhaps half of all résumés now contain inaccurate information, and some desperate job seekers even go so far as inventing college degrees they never earned or job experiences they never had. However, employers are fighting back with increasingly detailed background checks, so the chances of getting caught could be increasing as well.

Your résumé must include three sections: (1) your contact information (including name, address, telephone number, and e-mail address), (2) your education background (with related skills and accomplishments), and (3) your work experience (with related skills and accomplishments). Options include listing your career objective, qualifications summary, or career summary and describing activities and achievements that are professionally relevant. The six common résumé formats are traditional printed résumé, scannable, electronic plain text, Word file, HTML, and PDF. A scannable résumé requires two significant changes to the traditional printed format: removing all formatting and adding a list of keywords that identify your skills, experience, and education.

Test Your Knowledge

1. Why is networking an essential part of your lifelong career planning?

2. What is a résumé, and why is it important to adopt a "you" attitude when preparing one?

3. Why do most employers prefer chronological résumés over functional résumés?

4. What are some of the most common problems with résumés?

5. Why is it important to provide a keyword summary in a scannable or plain-text résumé?

Apply Your Knowledge

1. How should you present a past job that is unrelated to your current career plans?

2. One of the disadvantages of computerized résumé scanning is that some qualified applicants will be missed because the technology isn't perfect. However, more

companies are using this approach to deal with the flood of résumés they receive. Do you think that scanning is a good idea? Please explain.

3. Can you use a qualifications summary if you don't yet have extensive professional experience in your desired career? Why or why not?

4. Some people don't have a clear career path when they enter the job market. If you're in this situation, how would your uncertainty affect the way your write your résumé?

5. **Ethical Choices** Between your sophomore and junior years, you quit school for a year to earn the money to finish college. You worked as a loan-processing assistant in a finance company, checking references on loan applications, typing, and filing. Your manager made a lot of the fact that he had never attended college. He seemed to resent you for pursuing your education, but he never criticized your work, so you thought you were doing okay. After you'd been working there for six months, he fired you, saying that you had failed to be thorough enough in your credit checks. You were actually glad to leave, and you found another job right away, at a bank doing similar duties. Now that you've graduated from college, you're writing your résumé. Will you include the finance company job in your work history? Explain.

Practice Your Knowledge

Activities

Active links for all websites in this chapter can be found online. If MyBCommLab.com is being used in your class, see your User Guide for instructions on accessing the content for this chapter. Otherwise, visit www.pearsonhighered.com/bovee, locate *Business Communication Essentials*, Fourth Edition, click the Companion Website link, select Chapter 13, and then click on "Featured Websites." Please note that links to sites that become inactive after publication of the book will be removed from the Featured Websites section.

1. **Analyze This Message** Read the following résumé information. (1) Analyze the strengths or weaknesses of the information and (2) create a résumé that follows the guidelines presented in this chapter.

Sylvia Manchester
765 Belle Fleur Blvd.
New Orleans, LA 70113
(504) 312-9504
smanchester@rcnmail.com

PERSONAL: Single, excellent health, 5'8", 136 lbs.; hobbies include cooking, dancing, and reading.

JOB OBJECTIVE: To obtain a responsible position in marketing or sales with a good company.

EDUCATION: BA degree in biology, University of Louisiana, 1998. Graduated with a 3.0 average. Member of the varsity cheerleading squad. President of Panhellenic League. Homecoming queen.

WORK EXPERIENCE

Fisher Scientific Instruments, 2004 to now, field sales representative. Responsible for calling on customers and explaining the features of Fisher's line of laboratory instruments. Also responsible for writing sales letters, attending trade shows, and preparing weekly sales reports.

Fisher Scientific Instruments, 2001–2003, customer service representative. Was responsible for handling incoming phone calls from customers who had questions about delivery, quality, or operation of Fisher's line of laboratory instruments. Also handled miscellaneous correspondence with customers.

Medical Electronics, Inc., 1998–2001, administrative assistant to the vice president of marketing. In addition to handling typical secretarial chores for the vice president of marketing, I was in charge of compiling the monthly sales reports, using figures provided by members of the field sales force. I also was given responsibility for doing various market research activities.

New Orleans Convention and Visitors Bureau, 1995–1998, summers, tour guide. During the summers of my college years, I led tours of New Orleans for tourists visiting the city. My duties included greeting conventioneers and their spouses at hotels, explaining the history and features of the city during an all-day sightseeing tour, and answering questions about New Orleans and its attractions. During my fourth summer with the bureau, I was asked to help train the new tour guides. I prepared a handbook that provided interesting facts about the various tourist attractions, as well as answers to the most commonly asked tourist questions. The Bureau was so impressed with the handbook they had it printed up so that it could be given as a gift to visitors.

University of Louisiana, 1995–1998, part-time clerk in admissions office. While I was a student in college, I worked 15 hours a week in the admissions office. My duties included filing, processing applications, and handling correspondence with high school students and administrators.

2. **Internet**   Based on the preferences you identified in the self-assessment (see page P-4) and the academic, professional, and personal qualities you have to offer, perform an online search for a career opportunity that matches your interests and qualifications (starting with any of the websites listed in Table 13.1). Draft a one-page report indicating how the career you select and the job openings you find match your strengths and preferences.

3. **Teamwork**   Working with another student, change the following statements to make them more effective for a résumé by using action verbs.

   a. Have some experience with database design.

   b. Assigned to a project to analyze the cost accounting methods for a large manufacturer.

   c. I was part of a team that developed a new inventory control system.

   d. Am responsible for preparing the quarterly department budget.

   e. Was a manager of a department with seven employees working for me.

   f. Was responsible for developing a spreadsheet to analyze monthly sales by department.

   g. Put in place a new program for ordering supplies.

4. **Résumé Preparation: Work Accomplishments**   Using your team's answers to Activity 3, make the statements stronger by quantifying them (make up any numbers you need).

5. **Ethical Choices**   Assume that you achieved all the tasks shown in Activity 3 not as an individual employee but as part of a work team. In your résumé, must you mention other team members? Explain your answer.

6. **Résumé Preparation: Electronic Plain-Text Version**   Using your revised version of the résumé from Activity 1, create a plain-text version that includes a keyword summary based on Manchester's qualifications and career objective (make up any information you need).

7. **Résumé Preparation: HTML Version**   Using your revised version of the résumé from Activity 1, create an HTML version. Your instructor may direct you to a particular HTML editing tool, or you can use the "Save as Web Page" function in Microsoft Word. Word also lets you insert hyperlinks, so somewhere in the Work Experience section, create a hyperlink that takes the reader to a secondary page in order to show a work sample. For this new page, you can either use one of your own assignments from this course or simply create a blank page titled "Work Sample for Sylvia Manchester." On this page, create a hyperlink that takes the reader back to the main résumé page.

   Be sure to test your finished files using a web browser. Adjust your formatting as necessary to ensure a clean, professional design. When your files are complete, submit as your instructor indicates.

Expand Your Knowledge

Exploring the Best of the Web

Post an Online Résumé   At CareerBuilder, www.career builder.com, you'll find sample résumés, tips on preparing different types of résumés (including scannable ones), links to additional articles, and expert advice on creating résumés that bring positive results. After you've polished your résumé-writing skills, you can search for jobs online, using the site's numerous links to national and international industry-specific websites. You can access the information at CareerBuilder to develop your résumé and then post it with prospective employers—all free of charge. Take advantage of what this site offers and get ideas for writing or improving a résumé.

Exercises

1. Before writing a new résumé, make a list of action verbs you can use to describe your skills and experience.

2. Describe the advantages and disadvantages of chronological and functional résumé formats. Do you think a combination résumé would be an appropriate format for your résumé? Explain why or why not.

3. List some of the tips you learned at CareerBuilder for preparing an electronic résumé.

Surfing Your Way to Career Success

Bovée and Thill's Business Communication Headline News offers links to hundreds of online resources that can help you with this course, your other college courses, and your career. Visit http://businesscommunicationblog.com and click on "Web Directory." The Employment section connects you to a variety of articles and websites covering such key topics as career planning, résumé writing, employment portfolios, background checks, and salary information. Identify three websites from this section that could be useful in your business career. For each site, write a two-sentence summary of what the site offers and how it could help you launch and build your career.

MyBCommLab.com

Use MyBCommLab.com to test your understanding of the concepts presented in this chapter and explore additional materials that will bring the ideas to life in video, activities, and an online multimedia e-book. Additionally, you can continue to improve your skill with vocabulary by using the "Peak Performance Grammar and Mechanics" module. Click "Vocabulary" and then "Vocabulary 1." Take the Pretest to assess your ability to recognize correct word choices. Review the list of frequently misused words in the Refresher Course and then take the Follow-Up Test to verify your grasp of these essential words.

CASES

▼ *Apply the three-step writing process to the following cases, as assigned by your instructor.*

1. The Right Job, Right Now   Think about yourself. What are some things that come easily to you? What do you enjoy doing? In what part of the country would you like to live? Do you like to work indoors? Outdoors? A combination of the two? How much do you like to travel? Would you like to spend considerable time on the road? Do you like to work closely with others or more independently? What conditions make a job unpleasant? Do you delegate responsibility easily, or do you like to do things yourself? Are you better with words or numbers? Better at speaking or writing? Do you like to work under fixed deadlines? How important is job security to you? Do you want your supervisor to state clearly what is expected of you, or do you like having the freedom to make many of your own decisions?

Your task   After answering these questions, gather information about possible jobs that suit your current qualifications by consulting reference materials (from your college library or placement center) and by searching online. Next, choose a location, a company, and a job that interests you. Write a résumé that matches your qualifications and the job description; use whatever format your instructor specifies.

E-MAIL SKILLS

2. The Dream Job in the Future: What Will It Take to Get There?   Chances are you won't be able to land your dream job right out of college, but that doesn't mean you shouldn't start planning right now to make that dream come true.

Your task   Using online job search tools, find a job that sounds just about perfect for you, even if you're not yet qualified for it. It might even be something that would take 10 or 20 years to reach. Don't settle for something that's not quite right; find a job that is so "you" and so exciting that you would jump out of bed every morning, eager to go to work (such jobs really do exist!). Start with the job description you found online and then supplement it with additional research so that you get a good picture of what this job and career path are all about. Compile a list of all the qualifications you would need to have a reasonable chance of landing such a job. Now compare this list with your current résumé. Write a brief e-mail to your instructor that identifies all the areas in which you would need to improve your skills, work experience, education, and other qualifications in order to land your dream job.

[PRESENTATION SKILLS] **[PORTFOLIO BUILDER]**

3. The Multimedia Me: Creating a PowerPoint Presentation for Your E-Portfolio Using PowerPoint presentations and other multimedia supplements can be a great way to expand on the brief overview that a résumé provides.

Your task Starting with any version of a résumé that you've created for yourself, create a PowerPoint presentation that expands on your résumé information to give potential employers a more complete picture of what you can contribute. Include samples of your work, testimonials from current or past employers and colleagues, videos of speeches you've made, and anything else that tells the story of the professional "you." If you have a specific job or type of job in mind, focus on that. Otherwise, present a more general picture that shows why you would be a great employee for any company to consider. Be sure to review the information from Chapter 12 about creating professional-quality presentations.

Improve Your Grammar, Mechanics, and Usage

Level 1: Self-Assessment—Numbers

Review Section 3.4 in the Handbook of Grammar, Mechanics, and Usage and then complete the following 15 items.

For items 1–15, correct number style wherever necessary.

1. We need to hire one office manager, four bookkeepers, and twelve clerk-typists.

2. The market for this product is nearly six million people in our region alone.

3. Make sure that all 1835 pages are on my desk no later than nine o'clock a.m.

4. 2004 was the year that José Guiterez sold more than $50 thousand dollars worth of stock.

5. Our deadline is 4/7, but we won't be ready before 4/11.

6. 95 percent of our customers are men.

7. More than ½ the U.S. population is female.

8. Cecile Simmons, thirty-eight, is the first woman in this company to be promoted to management.

9. Last year, I wrote 20 15-page reports, and Michelle wrote 24 three-page reports.

10. Of the 15 applicants, seven are qualified.

11. Our blinds should measure 38 inches wide by 64 and one-half inches long by 7/16 inches deep.

12. Deliver the couch to seven eighty-three Fountain Rd., Suite three, Procter Valley, CA 92074.

13. Here are the corrected figures: 42.7% agree, 23.25% disagree, 34% are undecided, and the error is .05%

14. You have to agree that 50,000,000 U.S. citizens cannot be wrong.

15. We need a set of shelves 10 feet, eight inches long.

Level 2: Workplace Applications

The following items contain numerous errors in grammar, capitalization, punctuation, abbreviation, number style, word division, and vocabulary. Rewrite each sentence, correcting all errors. Write *C* for any sentence that is already correct.

1. Speaking at a recent software conference Alan Nichols; ceo of Tekco Systems; said the companys' goal is to reduce response time to 2 to 4 hrs., using software as an enabler.

2. Selling stocks short are the latest rage on wall street, where lately things have just gone from bad to worst.

3. As Electronic Commerce grows people are trying to find new ways to make money off of it.

4. We give a notification not only to the customer but also our salespeople that the product has been shipped because they will want to follow up.

5. When deciding between these various suppliers, we found that each of them offer both advantages and also disadvantages.

6. I found the book, "Marketing is Easy, Selling is Hard," for three different prices on the Internet: $14, $13.25, and $12.00.

7. United Agra Products, a distributor of fertilizers and seeds, in transmission of customer orders over it's private network faced the possibility of serious bottlenecks.

8. The answers you receive on your questionnaire, are influenced by the types of question you ask, the way they are asked, and your subjects cultural and language background.

9. The creation of hazardous by products, like silver in film processing, require us to collect our used chemicals for disposal at a hazardous-waste-facility.

10. As a source of ingredients for our products, we try to establish relationships with small cooperative or farming communities - often in developing countries – because, we believe that the best way to improve peoples' lives is to give them a chance at self reliance.

11. A entrepreneur really should never be in any organization that get's so big that it looses intimacy.

12. Racecar Driver Eddie Cheever, is founder of Aleanza Marketing Group, a seven-person company that handles $10 million dollars in sponsorship campaigns for Cheevers' team Red Bull Cheever Racing.

13. Over the last six years, Business Cluster Development have started 13 technology related incubators, that they call 'business clusters.'

14. In an interview, Gary Hoover said "When I dreamed up Bookstop, we asked people, "If there was a bookstore that carried a huge selection of books and had them all at discount prices, would you go there"? and we got a lot of yawns".

15. The chief attraction of vending machines are their convenience, they are open 24 hours a day, on the other hand, vending machine prices are no bargain.

Level 3: Document Critique

The following document may contain errors in grammar, capitalization, punctuation, abbreviation, number style, vocabulary, and spelling. You may also find problems with organization, format, and word use. Correct all errors using standard proofreading marks (see Appendix C).

THE EXECUTVE SUMMARY
(EXCERPT)

Purpose of the Proposal

This document will acquaint the reader with 3 principle topics by

- Showing what the San Diego State University (SDSU) *Suntrakker* project is

- Showing that the team-oriented, inerdepartmental diciplines at SDSU possesses the tenacity and knowhow to build and race a solar-powered vehical in the World solar Challenge Race in Austrailia next year;

- Define and articulate how this business team expect to promote and generate the neccesary support; funds, and materials from the student body, alumni, community and local businesses to sieze and executive this opportunity;

Project Profile

The *Suntrakker* Solar Car project was conceived by a small group of San Diego State university engineering students motivated by the successof of the General motors "Sunrayce," committed itself to designing and building a superior solar-powered vehicle to compete in the world Solar Challenge.

From modest Beginnings, the *Suntrakker* project quickly revolved into a cross-disciplinary educational effort encompassing students from many colleges of San Diego State University. The project has provides students participants and volunteers with valuable real life experiences and has brought them together in an effort that benefits not only the students and the university but also the environment.

Sponsors of this project are not only contributing to the successful achievment of the overall *Suntrakker* project but will also enhance their goodwill, advertising, and name promotion by association with the project. In addition, the *Suntrakker* offers a unique opportunity for the companies who can donate parts and accessories to showcase their name and test field their products in public in this highly publicized international contest.

Applying and Interviewing for Employment

LEARNING OBJECTIVES

After studying this chapter, you will be able to

1. Explain the purposes of application letters and how to apply the AIDA organizational model to them
2. Describe the typical sequence of job interviews
3. Explain what a behavioral interview is and why many employers use this technique
4. Describe briefly what employers look for during an employment interview and preemployment testing
5. List six tasks you need to complete to prepare for a successful job interview
6. Explain the three stages of an employment interview
7. Identify the most common employment messages that follow an interview and explain when you would use each one

Max Messmer's observation about employment interviewing highlights an important point that is too easy to forget during the often-stressful process of looking for a job: An interview should be approached as a business conversation in which both parties get to know each other better. Don't view it as a test in which you try to guess the "right" answers or as an interrogation in which you have to defend your background and skills. Treat interviews as opportunities to share information. After all, you need to determine which company is the right employer for you, just as those companies need to determine whether you are the right employee for them. You'll learn more this way, and you'll lower the stress level, too.

This chapter will give you a foundation for successful interviewing, along with tips on writing effective application letters and other important employment-related messages.

WRITING APPLICATION LETTERS AND OTHER EMPLOYMENT MESSAGES

Your résumé (see Chapter 13) is the centerpiece of your job search package, but it needs support from several other employment messages, including application letters, job-inquiry letters, application forms, and follow-up notes.

Application Letters

Whenever you mail, e-mail, or hand-deliver your résumé, you should include an **application letter**, also known as a *cover letter*, to let readers know what you're sending, why you're sending it, and how they can benefit from reading it. Take the same care with your application letter that you took with your résumé. Feedback from some hiring professionals suggests that the vast majority of application letters are so carelessly written that they negate the strengths of even the best résumés.[2] Write a great application letter, and you'll stand out from the crowd.

Always accompany your résumé with an application message (letter or e-mail) that motivates the recipient to read the résumé.

The three-step process of planning, writing, and completing an application letter involves the same tasks you've used throughout this course. Start by researching the organization and then focus on your audience so that you can show you've done your homework. During your research, try to find out the name, title, and department of the person you're writing to. If you can't find a specific name, use something like "Dear Hiring Manager."[3] If you're applying for work in another country, be sure to research the hiring practices prevalent in that culture and adjust your letter format as needed.

Resist the temptation to stand out with gimmicky application letters; they almost never work. Impress with knowledge and professionalism instead.

Respect your reader's time. Avoid gimmicks and don't repeat information that already appears in your résumé. Keep your letter straightforward, fact based, short, upbeat, and professional. Here are some quick tips to help you write effective cover letters:[4]

- Be as clear as possible about the kind of opportunity you seek.
- Show that you understand the company and the position.
- Never volunteer salary information unless an employer asks for it.
- Keep it short—and keep e-mail cover letters even shorter; in just two or three paragraphs, convey how your strengths and character would fit the position.
- Show some personality (while maintaining a business-appropriate tone); doing so will help balance the choppy, shorthand style of your résumé.
- Meticulously check your spelling, mechanics, and grammar; errors will send your message directly to the recycling bin. And be aware that potential employers will treat your e-mail messages every bit as seriously as formal, printed letters.[5]

If you're sending a **solicited application letter** in response to an announced job opening, you'll usually know what qualifications the organization is seeking (see Figure 14.1). In contrast, if you're sending an **unsolicited application letter** to an organization that has not announced an opening, you'll need to do some research to identify the requirements the position is likely to have (see Figure 14.2). (Note that even though these documents are referred to as *letters*, they can be e-mail messages as well.)

Getting Attention

Like your résumé, your application letter is a form of advertising, so organize it as you would a sales letter: Use the AIDA approach, focus on your audience, and emphasize reader benefits (as discussed in Chapter 9). Make sure your style projects confidence without being arrogant. To sell a potential employer on your merits, you must believe in yourself and sound as though you do.

The opening paragraph of your application letter needs to clearly convey the reason you're writing and give the recipient a compelling reason to keep reading.

The opening paragraph of your application letter has two important tasks to accomplish: (1) clearly stating your reason for writing and (2) giving the recipient a reason to keep reading by demonstrating that you have some immediate potential for meeting the company's needs. Consider this opening:

> With the recent slowdown in corporate purchasing, I can certainly appreciate the challenge of new fleet sales in this business environment. With my high energy level and 16 months of new-car sales experience, I believe I can produce the results you listed as vital in the job posting on your website.

This applicant does a smooth job of mirroring the company's stated needs while highlighting his personal qualifications along with evidence that he understands the broader market. He balances his relative lack of experience with enthusiasm and knowledge of the industry. Table 14.1 suggests some other ways that you can spark interest and grab attention in your opening paragraph.

Building Interest and Increasing Desire

Use the middle section of your application letter to expand on your opening and present a more complete picture of your strengths.

The middle section of your letter presents your strongest selling points in terms of their potential benefit to the organization, thereby building interest in you and creating a desire to interview you. Be specific and back up your assertions with convincing evidence:

> **Poor:** I completed three college courses in business communication, earning an A in each course, and have worked for the past year at Imperial Construction.

Position			Supply Chain Pricing Analyst		Apply
Position code	T23-6678	Location	Tacoma, WA	Status	Full-time

Sea-Air Global Transport has an immediate opening for a supply chain pricing analyst in our Tacoma, WA, headquarters. This challenging position requires excellent communication skills in a variety of media, a polished customer service presence both in person and over the phone, and proven aptitude in statistical analysis and business mathematics.

The minimum educational requirement for this position is a Bachelors degree or equivalent, preferably in business, statistical methods, or applied mathematics. Experience in customer service is highly desirable, and experience in transportation or logistics is a major plus.

Click here to learn more about Sea-Air or click here to explore the attractive compensation and benefits packages we offer all employees.

Smith's application mirrors the language [of] the job posting

---

27225 Eucalyptus Avenue
Long Beach, CA 90806
March 12, 2009

Sea-Air Global Transport
5467 Port of Tacoma Rd., Suite 230
Tacoma, WA 98421

Dear Hiring Manager:

Sea-Air Global Transport consistently appeared as a top transportation firm in the research I did for my senior project in global supply chain management, so imagine my delight when I discovered the opening for an export pricing analyst in your Tacoma headquarters (Position Code: T23-6678). With a major in business and a minor in statistical methods, my education has been ideal preparation for the challenges of this position.

In fact, my senior project demonstrates most of the skills listed in your job description, including written communication skills, analytical abilities, and math aptitude. I enjoyed the opportunity to put my math skills to the test as part of the statistical comparison of various freight modes.

As you can see from my résumé, I also have more than three years of part-time experience working with customers in both retail and commercial settings. This experience taught me the importance of customer service, and I want to start my professional career with a company that truly values the customer. In reviewing your website and reading several articles on Lloyd's List and other trade websites, I am impressed by Sea-Air's constant attention to customer service in this highly competitive industry.

My verbal communication skills would be best demonstrated in an interview, of course. I would be happy to meet with a representative of your company at the earliest convenience. I can be reached at dalton.k.smith@gmail.com or by phone at (562) 555-3737.

Sincerely,

Dalton Smith

Immediately grabs attention by indicating knowledge of the company and its industry

Emphasizes his customer service orientation and also shows he has done his homework by researching the company

Doesn't include a handwritten signature because the letter was uploaded to a website along with his résumé

Identifies the specific job to which he is applying

Echoes qualifications stated in the job posting

Politely asks for an interview in a way that emphasizes yet another job-related skill

Figure 14.1 Effective Solicited Application Message
In this response to an online job posting, Dalton Smith highlights his qualifications while mirroring the requirements specified in the posting. Following the AIDA model, he grabs attention immediately by letting the reader know that he is familiar with the company and the global transportation business.

Improved: Using the skills gained from three semesters of college training in business communication, I developed a collection system for Imperial Construction that reduced annual bad-debt losses by 25 percent.

When writing a solicited letter in response to an advertisement, be sure to discuss each requirement specified in the ad. If you are deficient in any of these requirements, stress other solid selling points to help strengthen your overall presentation. Don't restrict your message to just core job duties, either. Also highlight personal characteristics that apply to the targeted position, such as your ability to work hard or handle responsibility:

While attending college full time, I worked part-time during the school year and up to 60 hours a week each summer in order to be totally self-supporting while in college. I can offer your organization the same level of effort and perseverance.

457 Mountain View Rd.
Clear Lake, IA 50428
June 16, 2009

Ms. Patricia Downings, Store Manager
Wal-Mart
840 South Oak
Iowa Falls, IA 50126

Dear Ms. Downing:

You want retail clerks and managers who are accurate, enthusiastic, and experienced. You want someone who cares about customer service, who understands merchandising, and who can work with others to get the job done. When you're ready to hire a manager trainee or a clerk who is willing to work toward promotion, please consider me for the job.

Working as a clerk and then as an assistant manager in a large department store has taught me how to anticipate customer problems and deliver the type of service that keeps customers coming back. Moreover, my recent BA degree in retailing, which encompassed such courses as retailing, marketing, management, and business information systems, will provide your store with a well-rounded associate. (Please refer to my enclosed résumé for more information.) You'll find that I'm interested in every facet of retailing, eager to take on responsibility, and willing to continue learning throughout my career.

I understand that Wal-Mart prefers to promote its managers from within the company, and I would be pleased to start out with an entry-level position until I gain the necessary experience. Do you have any associate positions opening up soon? Could we discuss my qualifications? I will phone you early next Wednesday to arrange a meeting at your convenience.

Sincerely,

Glenda Johns

Glenda Johns

Enclosure

Gains attention in the first paragraph by speaking directly to the reader's needs

Builds the reader's interest by demonstrating knowledge of the company's policy regarding promotion

Points out personal qualities that aren't specifically stated in her résumé

Focuses on the reader and displays the "you" attitude, even though the last paragraph uses the word "I"

Figure 14.2 Effective Unsolicited Application Letter
Glenda Johns's experience as a clerk and an assistant manager gives her a good idea of the qualities that Wal-Mart is likely to be looking for in future managers. She uses these insights to craft the opening of her letter.

Don't bring up salary in your application letter unless the recipient has asked you to include your salary requirements.

Mention your salary requirements *only* if the organization has asked you to state them. If you don't know the salary that's appropriate for the position and someone with your qualifications, you can find typical salary ranges at the Bureau of Labor Statistics website, www.bls.gov, or a number of commercial websites. If you do state a target salary, tie it to the value you would offer:

> For the past two years, I have been helping a company similar to yours organize its database marketing efforts. I would therefore like to receive a salary in the same range (the mid-60s) for helping your company set up a more efficient customer database.

Toward the end of this section, refer the reader to your résumé by citing a specific fact or general point covered there:

> As you can see in the attached résumé, I've been working part time with a local publisher since my sophomore year. During that time, I've used client interactions as an opportunity to build strong customer service skills.

TABLE 14.1   Tips for Getting Attention in Application Letters

Tip	Example
Unsolicited Application Letters	
• Show how your strongest skills will benefit the organization	If you need a regional sales specialist who consistently meets sales targets while fostering strong customer relationships, please consider my qualifications.
• Describe your understanding of the job's requirements and then show how well your qualifications fit them	Your annual report stated that improving manufacturing efficiency is one of the company's top priorities for next year. Through my postgraduate research in systems engineering and consulting work for several companies in the industry, I've developed reliable methods for quickly identifying ways to cut production time while reducing resource usage.
• Mention the name of a person known to and highly regarded by the reader	When Janice McHugh of your franchise sales division spoke to our business communication class last week, she said you often need promising new marketing graduates at this time of year.
• Refer to publicized company activities, achievements, changes, or new procedures	Today's issue of the *Detroit News* reports that you may need the expertise of computer programmers versed in robotics when your Lansing tire plant automates this spring.
• Use a question to demonstrate your understanding of the organization's needs	Can your fast-growing market research division use an interviewer with two years of field survey experience, a B.A. in public relations, and a real desire to succeed? If so, please consider me for the position.
• Use a catchphrase opening if the job requires ingenuity and imagination	*Haut monde*—whether said in French, Italian, or Arabic, it still means "high society." As an interior designer for your Beverly Hills showroom, not only could I serve and sell to your distinguished clientele, but I could do it in all these languages. I speak, read, and write them fluently.
Solicited Application Letters	
• Identify where you discovered the job opening; describe what you have to offer	Your ad in the April issue of *Travel & Leisure* for a cruise-line social director caught my eye. My eight years of experience as a social director in the travel industry would allow me to serve your new Caribbean cruise division well.

Motivating Action

The final paragraph of your application letter has two important functions: to ask the reader for a specific action (usually an interview) and to facilitate a reply. Offer to come to the employer's office at a convenient time or, if the firm is some distance away, to meet with its nearest representative or arrange a telephone interview. Include your e-mail address and phone number, as well as the best time to reach you. Alternatively, you can take the initiative and say that you will follow up with a phone call. Refer again to your strongest selling point and, if desired, your date of availability:

> After you have reviewed my qualifications, could we discuss the possibility of putting my marketing skills to work for your company? Because I will be on spring break the week of March 8, I would like to arrange a time to talk then. I will call in late February to schedule a convenient time when we could discuss employment opportunities at your company.

In the final paragraph of your application letter, respectfully ask for specific action and make it easy for the reader to respond.

Application Follow-Ups

If your application letter and résumé fail to bring a response within a month or so, follow up with a second message to let the company know you are still interested. Use this opportunity to share any new information that is relevant to the position:

> Since applying to you on May 3 for a position in your management training program, I have completed three courses in business and management at South River Community College and received straight A's.

> Please keep my application in your active file and let me know when you need a skilled executive assistant.

Even if you've received an acknowledgment that says your application will be kept on file, don't hesitate to send a follow-up message three months later to show that you are still interested:

> Three months have elapsed since I applied to you for an underwriting position, but I want to let you know that I am still very interested in joining your company.
>
> I recently completed a four-week temporary work assignment at a large local insurance agency. I learned several new verification techniques that could increase my value to your underwriting department.
>
> Please keep my application in your active file, and let me know when a position opens for a capable underwriter.

Whatever the circumstances, a follow-up message can demonstrate that you're sincerely interested in working for the organization, persistent in pursuing your goals, and committed to upgrading your skills. If you don't land a job at your dream company on the first attempt, don't give up. Many leading employers take note of applicants who came close but didn't quite make it and may extend offers when positions open up in the future.[6]

Think creatively about a follow-up letter; show that you've continued to add to your skills or that you've learned more about the company or the industry.

UNDERSTANDING THE INTERVIEWING PROCESS

An **employment interview** is a formal meeting during which both you and the prospective employer ask questions and exchange information. The employer's objective is to find the best talent to fill available job openings, and your objective is to find the right match for your goals and capabilities.

As you get ready to begin interviewing, keep two vital points in mind. First, recognize that the process takes time. Start your preparation and research early; the best job offers usually go to the best-prepared candidates. Second, don't limit your options by looking at only a few companies. By exploring a wide range of firms and positions, you might uncover great opportunities that you would not have found otherwise. You'll increase the odds of getting more job offers, too.

Start preparing early for your interviews and be sure to consider a wide range of options.

The Typical Sequence of Interviews

Most employers interview an applicant multiple times before deciding to make a job offer. At the most selective companies, you might have a dozen or more individual interviews across several stages.[7] Depending on the company and the position, the process may stretch out over many weeks, or it may be completed in a matter of days.[8]

Employers start with the *screening stage*, in which they filter out applicants who are unqualified or otherwise not a good fit for the position. Screening can take place on your school's campus, at company offices, or via telephone or computer. Time is limited in screening interviews, so keep your answers short while providing a few key points that differentiate you from other candidates. If your screening interview will take place by phone, try to schedule it for a time when you can be focused and free from interruptions.[9] Also, don't make the mistake of treating the phone call as a casual conversation; you are being interviewed just as seriously as you would be if you were meeting in person.

During the screening stage of interviews, use the limited time available to differentiate yourself from other candidates.

The next stage of interviews, the *selection stage*, helps the organization identify the top candidates from all those who qualify. During these interviews, show keen interest in the job, relate your skills and experience to the organization's needs, listen attentively, and ask insightful questions that show you've done your research.

During the selection stage, continue to show how your skills and attributes can help the company.

If the interviewers agree that you're a good candidate, you may receive a job offer, either on the spot or a few days later by phone, mail, or e-mail. In other cases, you may be invited back for a final evaluation, often by a higher-ranking executive. The objective of the *final stage* is often to sell you on the advantages of joining the organization.

During the final stage, the interviewer may try to sell you on working for the firm.

Common Types of Interviews

Employers can use a variety of interviewing methods, and you need to recognize the different types and be prepared for each one. These methods can be distinguished by the way they are structured, the number of people involved, and the purpose of the interview.

Structured Versus Unstructured Interviews

In a **structured interview**, the interviewer (or a computer) asks a series of prepared questions in a set order. Structured interviews help employers identify candidates who don't meet basic job criteria, and they allow the interview team to compare answers from multiple candidates.[10]

In contrast, in an **open-ended interview**, the interviewer adapts his or her line of questioning based on the answers you give and any questions you ask. Even though it may feel like a conversation, remember that it's still an interview, so keep your answers focused and professional.

A structured interview follows a set sequence of questions, allowing the interview team to compare answers from all candidates.

In an open-ended interview, the interviewer adapts the line of questioning based on your responses and questions.

Panel and Group Interviews

Although one-on-one interviews are the most common format, some employers use panel or group interviews as well. In a **panel interview**, you meet with several interviewers at once. (Some companies have up to 50 employees on the panel, but that is unusual.)[11] Try to make a connection with each person on the panel and keep in mind that each person has a different perspective, so tailor your responses accordingly.[12] For example, an upper-level manager is likely to be interested in your overall business sense and strategic perspective, whereas a potential colleague might be more interested in your technical skills and ability to work in a team. In **group interviews**, one or more interviewers meet with several candidates simultaneously. A key purpose of a group interview is to observe how the candidates interact.[13]

In a panel interview, you meet with several interviewers at once; in a group interview, you and several other candidates meet with one or more interviewers at once.

Behavioral, Situational, Working, and Stress Interviews

Perhaps the most common type of interview these days is the **behavioral interview**, in which you are asked to relate specific incidents and experiences from your past.[14] Traditional, generic interview questions can often be answered with "canned" responses, but behavioral questions require candidates to use their own experiences and attributes to craft answers. Employers use these questions to assess applicants' job-related technical skills and ability to work under pressure, coordinate with others, and resolve conflict.[15] To prepare for a behavioral interview, review your work history or experience on school projects to recall several instances in which you demonstrated an important job-related skill or attribute.

In a behavioral interview, you are asked to describe how you handled situations from your past.

A **situational interview** is similar to a behavioral interview except that the questions focus on how you would handle various hypothetical situations on the job. The situations will likely relate to the job you're applying for, so the more you know about the position, the better prepared you'll be.

In situational interviews, you're asked to explain how you would handle various hypothetical situations.

A **working interview** is the most realistic type of interview: You actually perform a job-related activity during the interview. You may be asked to lead a brainstorming session, solve a business problem, engage in role playing, or even make a presentation.[16]

In a working interview, you actually perform work-related tasks.

The most unnerving type of interview is the **stress interview**, during which you might be asked questions designed to unsettle you or be subjected to long periods of silence, criticism, interruptions, and or even hostile reactions by the interviewer. The theory behind this approach is that you'll reveal how well you handle stressful situations, although some experts find the technique of dubious value.[17] If you find yourself in a stress interview, recognize what is happening and collect your thoughts for a few seconds before you respond.

Stress interviews help recruiters see how you handle yourself under pressure.

Interview Media

In addition to encountering a variety of interview formats, expect to be interviewed through a variety of media. Employers trying to cut travel costs and demands on staff time often interview candidates via telephone, e-mail, instant messaging, videoconferencing systems, webcams, and online interviewing systems. Even virtual worlds such as Second Life (http://secondlife.com) are being used to conduct both job fairs and individual interviews.[18]

Expect to use a variety of media when you interview, from in-person conversations to virtual meetings.

To succeed at a telephone interview, make sure you treat it as seriously as an in-person interview. Be prepared with a copy of all the materials you have sent the employer, including your résumé and any correspondence. In addition, prepare some note cards with key message points you'd like to make and questions you'd like to ask. If possible, arrange to speak on a landline so you don't have to worry about mobile phone reception problems. And remember that you won't be able to use a pleasant smile, a firm handshake, and other nonverbal signals to create a good impression. A positive, alert tone of voice is therefore vital.[19]

Treat a telephone interview as seriously as you would an in-person interview.

When interviewing via e-mail or IM, be sure to take a moment to review your responses before sending them.

E-mail and IM are also sometimes used in the screening stage. While you have almost no opportunity to send and receive nonverbal signals with these formats, you do have the major advantage of being able to review and edit each response before you send it. Maintain a professional style in your responses and be sure to ask questions that demonstrate your knowledge of the company and the position.[20]

In a video interview, speak to the camera as though you are addressing the interviewer in person.

Many employers use video technology for both live and recorded interviews. Live video interviews can involve either a videoconferencing facility or simply a webcam attached to your personal computer. (Some companies will arrange to send you a webcam if you don't have one.) With recorded video interviews, an online system asks a set of questions and records the respondent's answers. Recruiters then watch the videos as part of the screening process. Some systems also include online questionnaires in which you type your answers.[21] Prepare for a video interview as you would for an in-person interview and take the extra steps needed to become familiar with the equipment and the process. If you're interviewing from home, arrange your space so that the webcam doesn't pick up anything distracting or embarrassing in the background. During any video interview, remember to sit up straight and focus on the camera.

Computer-based virtual interviews range from simple structured interviews to realistic job simulations to meetings in virtual worlds.

Virtual online interviews can range from simple structured questionnaires and tests to sophisticated job simulations that are similar to working interviews. People applying for teller positions at SunTrust, a regional bank based in Atlanta, interact with video game–like characters while performing job-related tasks. These job simulations not only identify good candidates but also reduce the risk of employment discrimination lawsuits because they closely mimic actual job skills.[22]

What Employers Look For in an Interview

Interviews give employers the chance to go beyond the basic data of your résumé to get to know you and to answer two essential questions. The first is whether you can handle the responsibilities of the position. You'll probably be asked to describe your education, previous job experiences, and skill set. You may also be asked how you would apply those skills to hypothetical situations on the job. By learning as much as you can about the company, the industry, and the specific job, you have a great opportunity to stand apart from the competition.

Suitability for a specific job is judged on the basis of such factors as

■ Academic preparation
■ Work experience
■ Job-related personality traits

The second essential question is whether you will be a good fit with the organization and the target position. This line of inquiry includes both a general and a specific aspect. The general aspect concerns your overall personality and approach to work. All good employers want people who are confident, dedicated, positive, curious, courteous, ethical, and willing to commit to something larger than their own individual goals. You could have superstar qualifications, but if an employer suspects that you might be a negative presence in the workplace, you probably won't get a job offer.

Compatibility with an organization and a position is judged on the basis of personal background, attitudes, and style.

The specific aspect involves the fit with a particular company and position. Just like people, companies have different "personalities." Some are intense; others are more laid back. Some emphasize teamwork; others expect employees to forge their own way and even to compete with one another. Expectations also vary from job to job within a company and from industry to industry. An outgoing personality is essential for sales but less so for research, for instance. Numerous candidates might have the technical qualifications for a particular job, but not all will have the right mix of personal attributes.

Preemployment Testing and Background Checks

Preemployment tests attempt to provide objective, quantitative information about a candidate's skills, attitudes, and habits.

In an effort to improve the predictability of the selection process and reduce the reliance on the brief interaction that an interview allows, many employers now conduct a variety of preemployment tests.[23] Here is an overview of the most common types of tests:

■ **Integrity tests.** You might not think that a test could identify job candidates who are likely to steal from their employers or commit other ethical or legal infractions, but employers have had some success in using integrity tests.[24]

■ **Personality tests.** Some employers use personality tests to profile overall intellectual ability, attitudes toward work, interests, managerial potential, dependability, commitment, honesty, and motivation.[25] The use of personality tests in hiring is controversial, however; recent research suggests that current tests are not a reliable predictor of job success.[26]

- **Job skills tests.** The most common type of preemployment tests are those designed to assess the competency or specific abilities needed to perform a job.[27] Some larger employers, including Google and Capital One, have created custom evaluation systems that test applicants and continue to track employees after they're hired.[28]

- **Substance tests.** Drug and alcohol testing is one of the most controversial issues in business today. Some employers believe such testing is absolutely necessary to maintain workplace safety and protect companies from lawsuits, whereas others view it as an invasion of employee privacy and a sign of disrespect. In recent years, as many as 80 percent of U.S. employers have conducted drug testing, but that percentage appears to be declining.[29]

- **Background checks.** In addition to testing, most companies conduct some sort of *background check* on job candidates.[30] Such checks can include reviewing your credit record, checking to see whether you have a criminal history, and verifying your education. To help prevent a background check from tripping you up, make sure your college transcript and credit record are correct and up to date.[31] And if you have anything posted online at MySpace, Facebook, or anywhere else that might be potentially embarrassing, take it down now. Recruiters routinely search for information about candidates online.[32] Employers can also find "unscripted references" from online social networks—that is, people who know you in some capacity but whom you haven't listed as references.[33]

PREPARING FOR A JOB INTERVIEW

Preparation will help you feel more confident and perform better under pressure, and preparation starts with learning about the organization.

Learning About the Organization

Today's companies expect serious candidates to demonstrate an understanding of the company's operations, its markets, and its strategic and tactical challenges.[34] You've already done some initial research to identify companies of interest, but when you're invited to interview, it's time to dig a little deeper (see Table 14.2). Making this effort demonstrates your interest in the company, and it identifies you as a business professional who knows the importance of investigation and analysis.

Interviewers expect you to know some basic information about the company and its industry.

Thinking Ahead About Questions

Planning ahead for the interviewer's questions will help you handle them more confidently and successfully. In addition, you will want to prepare insightful questions of your own.

Planning for the Employer's Questions

Throughout the interview process, you can expect to get a mix of questions that are specific to you and the particular job opening and questions that are of a more general nature. Many of these general questions are "stock" queries that you can expect to hear again and again during your interviews. Get ready to face these five at the very least:

- **What is the hardest decision you've ever had to make?** Be prepared with a good example (that isn't too personal), explaining why the decision was difficult and how you made the choice you made.

- **What are your greatest weaknesses?** This question seems to be a favorite of some interviewers, although it probably rarely yields useful information. The standard ways to reply are to describe a weakness so that it sounds like a virtue—such as driving yourself too hard—or to describe a relatively minor shortcoming and explain how you're working to improve.

- **Where do you want to be five years from now?** This question tests (1) whether you're merely using this job as a stopover until something better comes along and (2) whether you've given thought to your long-term goals. Your answer should reflect your desire to contribute to the employer's long-term goals, not just your own goals. Whether this question often yields useful information is also a matter of debate, but be prepared to answer it.[35]

You can expect to face a number of common questions in your interviews, so be sure to prepare for them.

TABLE 4.2　Investigating an Organization and a Job Opportunity

Where to Look and What You Can Learn

- **Company website:** Overall information about the company, including key executives, products and services, locations and divisions, employee benefits, and job descriptions
- **Competitors' websites:** Similar information from competitors, including the strengths those companies claim to have
- **Industry-related websites:** Objective analysis and criticism of the company, its products, its reputation, and its management
- **Marketing materials (brochures, catalogs, etc.):** The company's marketing strategy and customer communication style
- **Company publications (both print and electronic):** Key events, stories about employees, and new products
- **Blogs:** Analysis and criticism (not always fair or unbiased) of the company, its products and services, its reputation, and its management
- **Social networks:** Names and job titles of potential contacts within a company
- **Periodicals (newspapers and trade journals, both print and online):** In-depth stories about the company and its strategies, products, successes, and failures; you may find profiles of top executives
- **Career center at your college:** A wide array of information about companies that hire graduates
- **Current and former employees:** Insights into the work environment

Points to Learn About the Organization

- Full name
- Location (headquarters and divisions, branches, subsidiaries, or other units)
- Ownership (public or private; whether it is owned by another company)
- Age and brief history
- Products and services
- Industry position (whether the company is a leader or a minor player; whether it is an innovator or more of a follower)
- Key financial points (such as stock price and trend, if a public company)
- Growth prospects (whether the company is investing in its future through research and development; whether it is in a thriving industry)

Points to Learn About the Position

- Title
- Functions and responsibilities
- Qualifications and expectations
- Possible career paths
- Salary range
- Travel expectations and opportunities
- Relocation expectations and opportunities

- **What didn't you like about previous jobs you've held?** Answer this one carefully: The interviewer is trying to predict whether you'll be an unhappy or difficult employee.[36] Describe something that you didn't like in a way that puts you in a positive light, such as having limited opportunities to apply your skills or education. Avoid making negative comments about former employers or colleagues.

- **Tell me something about yourself.** Ask if the interviewer would like to know about your specific skills or attributes. If this point is clarified, respond accordingly. If it isn't, explain how your skills can contribute to the job and the organization.

Continue your preparation by jotting down a brief answer to each question in Table 14.3 You can also find typical interview questions at websites such as InterviewUp, www.interviewup .com, where candidates share actual questions they have faced in recent interviews.[37]

Look for ways to frame your responses as brief stories (30 to 90 seconds) rather than simple declarative answers.[38] Instead of just saying you are good at finding ways to reduce costs, tell a story of a time you did just that. Cohesive stories tend to stick in the listener's mind more effectively than disconnected facts and statements.

Look for ways to frame your responses as brief stories rather than as dry facts or statements.

Planning Questions of Your Own

Preparing questions of your own helps you understand the company and the position, and it sends an important signal that you are truly interested.

Remember that an interview is a two-way street: The questions you ask are just as important as the answers you provide. By asking insightful questions, you can demonstrate your understanding of the organization, you can steer the discussion into areas that allow you to present your qualifications to best advantage, and you can verify for yourself whether this is a good

TABLE 14.3 Twenty-Five Common Interview Questions

Questions About College

1. What courses in college did you like most? Least? Why?
2. Do you think your extracurricular activities in college were worth the time you spent on them? Why or why not?
3. When did you choose your college major? Did you ever change your major? If so, why?
4. Do you feel you did the best scholastic work you are capable of?
5. How has your college education prepared you for this position?

Questions About Employers and Jobs

6. What jobs have you held? Why did you leave?
7. What percentage of your college expenses did you earn? How?
8. Why did you choose your particular field of work?
9. What are the disadvantages of your chosen field?
10. Have you served in the military? What rank did you achieve? What jobs did you perform?
11. What do you think about how this industry operates today?
12. Why do you think you would like this particular type of job?

Questions About Personal Attitudes and Preferences

13. Do you prefer to work in any specific geographic location? If so, why?
14. How much money do you hope to be earning in 5 years? In 10 years?
15. What do you think determines a person's progress in a good organization?
16. What personal characteristics do you feel are necessary for success in your chosen field?
17. Tell me a story.
18. Do you like to travel?
19. Why should I hire you?

Questions About Work Habits

20. Do you prefer working with others or by yourself?
21. What type of boss do you prefer?
22. Have you ever had any difficulty getting along with colleagues or supervisors? With instructors? With other students?
23. What would you do if you were given an unrealistic deadline for a task or project?
24. How do you feel about overtime work?
25. What have you done that shows initiative and willingness to work?

opportunity. Plus, interviewers expect you to ask questions, so you must be prepared for that. Here's a list of some things you might want to find out:

- **Are these my kind of people?** Observe the interviewers, and if you can, arrange to talk with other employees.
- **Can I do this work?** Compare your qualifications with the requirements described by the interviewer.
- **Will I enjoy the work?** Will the work give you real feelings of accomplishment and satisfaction?
- **Is the job what I want?** Will it make use of your best capabilities? Does it offer a career path to the long-term goals you've set?
- **Does the job pay what I'm worth?** By comparing jobs and salaries before you're interviewed, you'll know what's reasonable for someone with your skills in your industry.
- **What kind of person would I be working for?** If the interviewer is your prospective boss, watch how others interact with that person, tactfully query other employees, or pose a careful question or two during the interview. If your prospective boss is someone else, discretely ask about that person's name, job title, and responsibilities as a way to learn more.
- **What sort of future can I expect with this organization?** Is this organization in healthy financial shape? Will it grow enough to offer you opportunities to advance?

For a list of good questions that you might use as a starting point, see Table 14.4.

TABLE 14.4   Ten Questions to Ask an Interviewer

Question	Reason for Asking
1. What are the job's major responsibilities?	A vague answer could mean that the responsibilities have not been clearly defined, which is almost guaranteed to cause frustration if you take the job.
2. What qualities do you want in the person who fills this position?	This will help you go beyond the job description to understand what the company really wants.
3. How do you measure success for someone in this position?	A vague or incomplete answer could mean that the expectations you will face are unrealistic or ill defined.
4. What is the first problem that needs the attention of the person you hire?	Not only will this help you prepare, but it can signal whether you're about to jump into a problematic situation.
5. Would relocation be required now or in the future?	If you're not willing to move often or at all, you need to know those expectations now.
6. Why is this job now vacant?	If the previous employee got promoted, that's a good sign. If the person quit, that might not be such a good sign.
7. What makes your organization different from others in the industry?	The answer will help you assess whether the company has a clear strategy to succeed in its industry and whether top managers communicate this to lower-level employees.
8. How would you define your organization's managerial philosophy?	You want to know whether the managerial philosophy is consistent with your own working values.
9. What is a typical workday like for you?	The interviewer's response can give you clues about daily life at the company.
10. What systems and policies are in place to help employees stay up to date in their professions and continue to expand their skills?	If the company doesn't have a strong commitment to employee development, chances are it isn't going to stay competitive very long.

Bolstering Your Confidence

The best way to build your confidence is to prepare thoroughly and address shortcomings as best you can—in other words, take action.

Interviewing is stressful for everyone, so some nervousness is natural. However, you can take steps to feel more confident. Start by reminding yourself that you have value to offer the employer, and the employer already thinks highly enough of you to invite you to an interview.

If some aspect of your appearance or background makes you uneasy, correct it if possible or offset it by emphasizing positive traits such as warmth, wit, intelligence, or charm. Instead of dwelling on your weaknesses, focus on your strengths. Instead of worrying about how you will perform in the interview, focus on how you can help the organization succeed. As with public speaking, the more prepared you are, the more confident you'll be.

Polishing Your Interview Style

Staging mock interviews with a friend is a good way to hone your style.

Competence and confidence are the foundation of your interviewing style, and you can enhance them by giving the interviewer an impression of poise, good manners, and good judgment. You can develop an adept style by staging mock interviews with a friend or using an interview simulator. Record these mock interviews so you can evaluate yourself. Your college's career center may have computer-based systems for practicing interviews as well (see Figure 14.3).

Evaluate the length and clarity of your answers, your nonverbal behavior, and the quality of your voice.

After each practice session, look for opportunities to improve. Have your mock interview partner critique your performance or critique yourself if you're able to record your practice interviews, using the list of warning signs shown in Table 14.5. Pay close attention to the length of your planned answers as well. Interviewers want you to give complete answers, but they don't want you to take up valuable time or test their patience by chatting about minor or irrelevant details.[39]

Evaluate your nonverbal behavior as well. In the United States and most other Western cultures, you are more likely to have a successful interview if you maintain eye contact, smile frequently, sit in an attentive position, and use frequent hand gestures. These nonverbal

Figure 14.3 **Interview Simulators**
Experts recommend practicing your interview skills as much as possible. You can use a friend or classmate as a practice partner, or you might be able to use one of the interview simulators now available, such as this system from Perfect Interview. Ask at your career center, or search online for "practice interviews" or "interview simulators."

signals convince the interviewer that you're alert, assertive, dependable, confident, responsible, and energetic.[40]

The sound of your voice can also have a major impact on your success in a job interview.[41] Recording your voice can help you overcome voice problems. If you tend to speak too rapidly, practice speaking more slowly. If your voice sounds too loud or too soft, practice adjusting it. Work on eliminating speech mannerisms such as *you know*, *like*, and *um*, which make you sound hesitant or inarticulate.

Planning to Look Good

Clothing and grooming are important elements of preparation because they reveal something about a candidate's personality, professionalism, and ability to sense the unspoken "rules" of a situation. Your research into various industries and professions should give you insight into expectations for business attire. If you're not sure what to wear, ask someone who works in the same industry—and don't be afraid to call the company for advice. You don't need to spend a

Dress conservatively and be well groomed for every interview.

TABLE 14.5 Warning Signs: 25 Attributes That Interviewers Don't Like to See	
1. Poor personal appearance	13. Poor scholastic record; just got by
2. Overbearing, overaggressive, or conceited demeanor; a "superiority complex"; a know-it-all attitude	14. Unwillingness to start at the bottom; expecting too much too soon
3. Inability to express ideas clearly; poor voice, diction, or grammar	15. Tendency to make excuses
4. Lack of knowledge or experience	16. Evasive answers; hedging on unfavorable factors in record
5. Poor preparation for the interview	17. Lack of tact
6. Lack of interest in the job	18. Lack of maturity
7. Lack of planning for career; lack of purpose or goals	19. Lack of courtesy; poorly mannered
8. Lack of enthusiasm; passive and indifferent demeanor	20. Condemnation of past employers
9. Lack of confidence and poise; appearance of being nervous and ill at ease	21. Lack of social skills
10. Insufficient evidence of achievement	22. Marked dislike for schoolwork
11. Failure to participate in extracurricular activities	23. Lack of vitality
12. Overemphasis on money; interest only in the best dollar offer	24. Failure to look interviewer in the eye
	25. Limp, weak handshake

fortune on interview clothes, but your clothes must be clean, pressed, and appropriate. The following look will serve you well in just about any interview situation:[42]

- Neat, "adult" hairstyle
- Conservative business suit (for women, that means no exposed midriffs, short skirts, or plunging necklines), in dark solid color or a subtle pattern such as pinstripes
- White shirt for men; coordinated blouse for women
- Conservative tie (classic stripes or subtle patterns) for men
- Limited jewelry (men, especially, should wear very little jewelry)
- No visible piercings other than one or two earrings (for women only)
- No visible tattoos
- Stylish but professional-looking shoes (no high heels or casual shoes)
- Clean hands and nicely trimmed fingernails
- Little or no perfume or cologne (some people are allergic and many people are put off by strong smells)
- Subtle makeup (for women)
- Exemplary personal hygiene

If you want to be taken seriously, dress and act seriously.

Remember that an interview is not the place to express your individuality or to let your inner rebel run wild. Send a clear signal that you understand the business world and know how to adapt to it. You won't be taken seriously otherwise.

Being Ready When You Arrive

Be ready to go the minute you arrive at the interviewing site; don't fumble around for your résumé or your list of questions.

When you go to your interview, take a small notebook, a pen, a list of the questions you want to ask, several copies of your résumé (protected in a folder), an outline of what you have learned about the organization, and any past correspondence about the position. You may also want to take a small calendar, a transcript of your college grades, a list of references, and a portfolio containing samples of your work, performance reviews, and certificates of achievement.[43] Carry all these items in a good-quality briefcase.

Be sure you know when and where the interview will be held. The worst way to start any interview is to be late. Verify the route and time required to get there, even if that means traveling there ahead of time. Plan to arrive early.

When you arrive, you may have to wait for a while. Use this time to review the key messages about yourself you want to get across in the interview. Conduct yourself professionally while waiting. Show respect for everyone you encounter and avoid chewing gum, eating, or drinking. Anything you do or say at this stage may get back to the interviewer, so make sure your best qualities show from the moment you enter the premises.

INTERVIEWING FOR SUCCESS

At this point, you have a good sense of the overall process and know how to prepare for your interviews. The next step is to get familiar with the three stages of every interview: the warm-up, the question-and-answer session, and the close.

The Warm-Up

The first minute of the interview is crucial, so stay alert and be on your best business behavior.

Of the three stages, the warm-up is the most important, even though it may account for only a small fraction of the time you spend in the interview. Studies suggest that many interviewers, particularly those who are poorly trained in interviewing techniques, make up their minds within the first 20 seconds of contact with a candidate.[44] Don't let your guard down if it appears that the interviewer wants to engage in what feels like small talk; these exchanges are every bit as important as structured questions.

Body language is crucial at this point. Stand or sit up straight, maintain regular but natural eye contact, and don't fidget. When the interviewer extends a hand, respond with a firm but not overpowering handshake. Repeat the interviewer's name when you're introduced

("It's a pleasure to meet you, Ms. Litton"). Wait until you're asked to be seated or the interviewer has taken a seat. Let the interviewer start the discussion, and be ready to answer one or two substantial questions right away. The following are some common openers:[45]

- Why do you want to work here?
- What do you know about us?
- Tell me a little about yourself.

Recognize that you could face substantial questions as soon as your interview starts, so make sure you are prepared and ready to go.

The Question-and-Answer Stage

Questions and answers usually consume the greatest part of the interview. The interviewer will ask about your qualifications and discuss many of the points mentioned in your résumé. You'll also be asking questions of your own.

Answering and Asking Questions

Let the interviewer lead the conversation and never answer a question before he or she has finished asking it. Not only is this type of interruption rude, but the last few words of the question might alter how you respond. As much as possible, avoid one-word yes-or-no answers. Use the opportunity to expand on a positive response or explain a negative response. If you're asked a difficult question, pause before responding. Think through the implications of the question; for instance, the recruiter may know that you can't answer a question and only wants to know how you'll respond.

Listen carefully to questions before you answer.

Whenever you're asked if you have any questions, or whenever doing so naturally fits the flow of the conversation, ask a question from the list you've prepared. Probe for what the company is looking for in its new employees so that you can show how you meet the firm's needs. Also try to zero in on any reservations the interviewer might have about you so that you can dispel them.

Listening to the Interviewer

Paying attention when the interviewer speaks can be as important as giving good answers or asking good questions. Review the tips on listening offered in Chapter 2.

The interviewer's facial expressions, eye movements, gestures, and posture may tell you the real meaning of what is being said. Be especially aware of how your comments are received. Does the interviewer nod in agreement or smile to show approval? If so, you're making progress. If not, you might want to introduce another topic or modify your approach.

Paying attention to both verbal and nonverbal messages can help you turn the question-and-answer stage to your advantage.

Handling Discriminatory Questions

A variety of federal, state, and local laws prohibit employment discrimination on the basis of race, ethnicity, gender, age (at least if you're between 40 and 70), marital status, religion, national origin, or disability. Interview questions designed to elicit information on these topics are potentially illegal.[46] Table 14.6 compares some specific questions that employers are and are not allowed to ask during an employment interview.

Federal, state, and local laws prohibit a wide variety of interview questions.

If your interviewer asks these personal questions, how you respond depends on how you feel about revealing the information asked for, what you think the interviewer will do with the information, and whether you want to work for a company that asks such questions. Remember that you always have the option of simply refusing to answer or of telling the interviewer that you think a particular question is unethical—although either of these responses is likely to leave an unfavorable impression.[47] If you do want the job, you might (1) ask how the question is related to your qualifications, (2) explain that the information is personal, (3) respond to what you think is the interviewer's real concern, or (4) answer both the question and the concern.

Think about how you might respond if you were asked a potentially unlawful question.

If you do answer an unethical or unlawful question, you run the risk that your answer may hurt your chances, so think carefully before answering.[48] In any event, don't forget the two-way nature of the interview process: The organization is learning about you, and you're learning about the organization. Would you want to work for an organization that

TABLE 14.6   Interview Questions That Employers Are and Are Not Allowed to Ask

Interviewers May Ask This . . .	But Not This . . .
What is your name?	What was your maiden name?
Are you over 18?	When were you born?
Did you graduate from high school?	When did you graduate from high school?
[No questions about race are allowed.]	What is your race?
Can you perform [specific tasks]?	Do you have physical or mental disabilities?
	Do you have a drug or alcohol problem?
	Are you taking any prescription drugs?
Would you be able to meet the job's requirement to frequently work weekends?	Would working on weekends conflict with your religion?
Do you have the legal right to work in the United States?	What country are you a citizen of?
Have you ever been convicted of a felony?	Have you ever been arrested?
This job requires that you speak Spanish. Do you?	What language did you speak in your home when you were growing up?

condones illegal or discriminatory questions or that doesn't train its employees enough to avoid them?

If you believe an interviewer's questions are unreasonable, unrelated to the job, or an attempt to discriminate, you may complain to the nearest field office of the Equal Employment Opportunity Commission (find offices online at www.eeoc.gov) or to the agency in your state that regulates fair employment practices.

The Close

Like the warm-up, the end of the interview is more important than its brief duration would indicate. These last few minutes are your last opportunity to emphasize your value to the organization and to correct any misconceptions the interviewer might have. Be aware that many interviewers will ask if you have any more questions at this point, so save one or two from your list.

Concluding Gracefully

Conclude an interview with courtesy and enthusiasm.

You can usually tell when the interviewer is trying to conclude the session. He or she may ask whether you have any more questions, check the time, sum up the discussion, or simply tell you that the allotted time for the interview is up. When you get the signal, be sure to thank the interviewer for the opportunity and express your interest in the organization. If you can do so comfortably, try to pin down what will happen next, but don't press for an immediate decision.

If this is your second or third visit to the organization, the interview may end with an offer of employment. If you have other offers or need time to think about this offer, it's perfectly acceptable to thank the interviewer for the offer and ask for some time to consider it. If no job offer is made, the interview team may not have reached a decision yet, but you may tactfully ask when you can expect to know the decision.

Discussing Salary

Research salary ranges in your job, industry, and geographic region before you try to negotiate salary.

If you receive an offer during the interview, you'll naturally want to discuss salary. However, let the interviewer raise the subject. If asked your salary requirements during the interview or on a job application, you can say that your requirements are open or negotiable or that you would expect a competitive compensation package.[49]

If you don't like the offer, you can ask whether there is any room for negotiation. How far you can negotiate depends on several factors, including market demand for your particular skills, the overall strength of the job market, the company's compensation policies, the company's financial health, and whether you currently have other job offers. Remember that you're negotiating a business deal, not asking for personal favors, so focus on the unique value you can bring to the job. The more information you have, the stronger your position will be.

If salary isn't negotiable, look at the overall compensation and benefits package. You may find flexibility in a signing bonus, profit sharing, pension and other retirement benefits, health coverage, vacation time, and other valuable elements.[50]

> Negotiating benefits may be one way to get more value from an employment package.

Interview Notes

If yours is a typical job search, you'll have many interviews before you accept an offer. For that reason, keeping clear, well-organized notes is essential. As soon as you leave the interview facility, jot down the names and titles of the people you met. Briefly summarize the interviewer's answers to your questions. Then quickly evaluate your performance during the interview, listing what you handled well and what you didn't. Going over these notes can help you improve your performance in the future.[51] In addition to improving your performance during interviews, interview notes help you keep track of any follow-up messages you'll need to send.

> Keeping a careful record of your job interviews is essential.

For the latest information on interviewing strategies, visit http://real-timeupdates.com/bce and click on Chapter 14.

FOLLOWING UP AFTER AN INTERVIEW

Staying in contact with a prospective employer after an interview shows that you really want the job and are determined to get it. Doing so also gives you another chance to demonstrate your communication skills and sense of business etiquette. Following up brings your name to the interviewer's attention once again and reminds him or her that you're actively looking and waiting for the decision.

Thank-You Message

Write a thank-you message within two days of the interview, even if you feel you have little chance of getting the job. Not only is this good etiquette, but it can be an essential step in promoting yourself to the employer. The thank-you message gives you the opportunity to reinforce the reasons you are a good choice for the position, and it lets you respond to any negatives that might've arisen in the interview.[52] Acknowledge the interviewer's time and courtesy, convey your continued interest, reinforce the reasons that you are a good fit for the position, and ask politely for a decision (see Figure 14.4).

> A thank-you message is more than a professional courtesy; it's another chance to promote yourself to an employer.

Depending on the company and the relationship you've established with the interviewer, the thank-you message can be handled via letter or e-mail. Keep your thank-you message brief and organize it like a routine message. Demonstrate the "you" attitude and sound positive without sounding overconfident.

Message of Inquiry

If you're not advised of the interviewer's decision by the promised date or within two weeks, you might make an inquiry. A message of inquiry (which can be handled by e-mail if the interviewer has given you his or her e-mail address) is particularly appropriate if you've received a job offer from a second firm and don't want to accept it before you have an answer from the first. The following message illustrates the general model for a direct request:

> Use the model for a direct request when you write an inquiry about a hiring decision.

> When we talked on April 7 about the fashion coordinator position in your Park Avenue showroom, you indicated that a decision would be made by May 1. I am still enthusiastic about the position and eager to know what conclusion you've reached.

● Identifies the position and introduces the main idea

> To complicate matters, another firm has now offered me a position and has asked that I reply within the next two weeks.

● Places the reason for the request second

> Because your company seems to offer a greater challenge, I would appreciate knowing about your decision by Thursday, May 12. If you need more information before then, please let me know.

● Makes a courteous request for specific action last, while clearly stating a preference for this organization

Indicates the writer's flexibility and commitment to the job if hired

Closes on a confident, "you"-oriented note with a request for a decision

Reminds the interviewer of the reasons for meeting and graciously acknowledges the consideration shown to the applicant

Reminds the recruiter of special qualifications

Figure 14.4   E-Mail Thank-You Message
In three brief paragraphs, Michael Espinosa acknowledges the interviewer's time and consideration, expresses his continued interest in the position, explains a crucial discussion point that he has reconsidered, and asks for a decision.

Request for a Time Extension

If you receive a job offer while other interviews are still pending, you can ask the employer for a time extension. Open with a strong statement of your continued interest in the job, ask for more time to consider the offer, provide specific reasons for the request, and assure the reader that you will respond by a specific date (see Figure 14.5).

Letter of Acceptance

Use the model for positive messages when you write a letter of acceptance.

When you receive a job offer that you want to accept, reply within five days. Begin by accepting the position and expressing thanks. Identify the job that you're accepting. In the next paragraph, cover any necessary details. Conclude by saying that you look forward to reporting for work. As always, a positive letter should convey your enthusiasm and eagerness to cooperate:

Confirms the specific terms of the offer with a good-news statement at the beginning

I'm delighted to accept the graphic design position in your advertising department at the salary of $2,875 per month.

Covers miscellaneous details in the middle

Enclosed are the health insurance forms you asked me to complete and sign. I've already given notice to my current employer and will be able to start work on Monday, January 18.

Closes with another reference to the good news and a look toward the future

The prospect of joining your firm is exciting. Thank you for giving me this opportunity for what I'm sure will be a challenging future.

Written acceptance of a job offer can be considered a legally binding contract.

Be aware that a job offer and a written acceptance of that offer can constitute a legally binding contract, for both you and the employer. Before you write an acceptance letter, be sure you want the job.

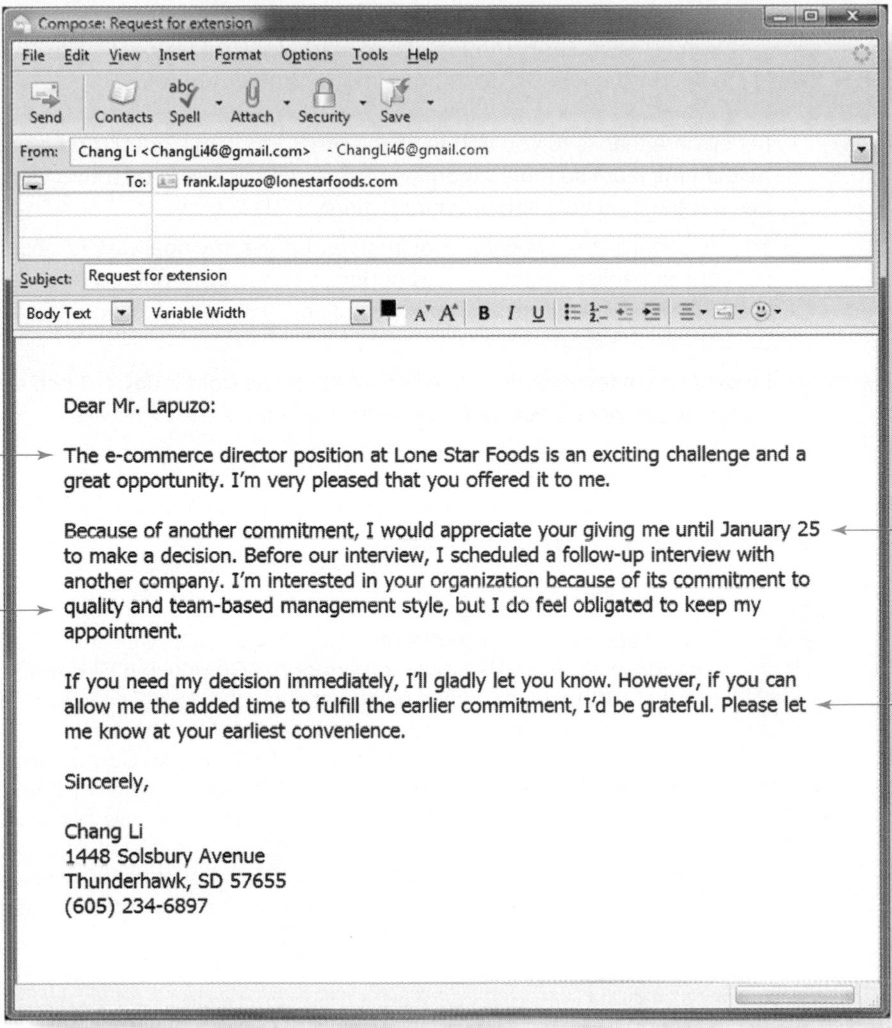

Compose: Request for extension

File Edit View Insert Format Options Tools Help

Send   Contacts   Spell   Attach   Security   Save

From: Chang Li <ChangLi46@gmail.com> - ChangLi46@gmail.com

To: frank.lapuzo@lonestarfoods.com

Subject: Request for extension

Body Text | Variable Width | A⁻ A⁺ B I U

Begins with a strong statement of interest in the job →

Dear Mr. Lapuzo:

The e-commerce director position at Lone Star Foods is an exciting challenge and a great opportunity. I'm very pleased that you offered it to me.

Because of another commitment, I would appreciate your giving me until January 25 to make a decision. Before our interview, I scheduled a follow-up interview with another company. I'm interested in your organization because of its commitment to quality and team-based management style, but I do feel obligated to keep my appointment.

← *Stresses a professional obligation as the reason for the request, rather than the desire to learn what the other company may offer*

Emphasizes specific reasons for preferring the first job offer to help reassure the reader of sincerity →

If you need my decision immediately, I'll gladly let you know. However, if you can allow me the added time to fulfill the earlier commitment, I'd be grateful. Please let me know at your earliest convenience.

← *Closes with an expression of willingness to yield or compromise, while conveying continued interest in the position*

Sincerely,

Chang Li
1448 Solsbury Avenue
Thunderhawk, SD 57655
(605) 234-6897

Figure 14.5 Effective Request for a Time Extension
If you need to request more time to make a decision about a job offer, make sure to reaffirm that you are still interested in the job.

Letter Declining a Job Offer

After all your interviews, you may find that you need to write a letter declining a job offer. Use the techniques for negative messages (see Chapter 8): Open warmly, state the reasons for refusing the offer, decline the offer explicitly, and close on a pleasant note that expresses gratitude. By taking the time to write a sincere, tactful letter, you leave the door open for future contact:

If you decide to decline a job offer, do so tactfully, using the model for negative messages.

One of the most interesting interviews I have ever had was the one last month at your Durham facility. I'm flattered that you would offer me the computer analyst position that we talked about.

• *Uses a buffer in the opening paragraph*

I was fortunate to receive two job offers during my search. Because my desire to work abroad can more readily be satisfied by another company, I have accepted that job offer.

• *Precedes the bad news with tactfully phrased reasons for the applicant's unfavorable decision and then delivers the negative news*

I deeply appreciate the time you spent talking with me. Thank you again for your consideration and kindness.

• *Lets the reader down gently with a sincere and cordial ending*

Letter of Resignation

If you get a job offer while currently employed, you can maintain good relations with your current employer by writing a thoughtful letter of resignation to your immediate supervisor. Follow the advice for negative messages and make the letter sound positive, regardless

Letters of resignation should always be written in a gracious and professional style that avoids criticism of your employer or your colleagues.

of how you feel. Say something favorable about the organization, the people you work with, or what you've learned on the job. Then state your intention to leave and give the date of your last day on the job. Be sure you give your current employer at least two weeks' notice.

Uses an appreciative opening that serves as a buffer	My sincere thanks to you and to all the other Emblem Corporation employees for helping me learn so much about serving the public these past two years. You have given me untold help and encouragement.
States reasons before the bad news itself, using tactful phrasing to help keep the relationship friendly, should the writer later want letters of recommendation	You may recall that when you first interviewed me, my goal was to become a customer relations supervisor. Because that opportunity has been offered to me by another organization, I am submitting my resignation. I will miss all of you, but I want to take advantage of this opportunity.
Discusses necessary details in an extra paragraph	I would like to terminate my work here two weeks from today but can arrange to work an additional week if you want me to train a replacement.
Tempers any disappointment with a cordial close	My sincere thanks and best wishes to all of you.

DOCUMENT MAKEOVER

Improve This Letter

To practice correcting drafts of actual documents, visit the "Document Makeovers" section in either MyBCommLab.com or the Companion Website for this text.

If MyBCommLab.com is being used in your class, see your User Guide for specific instructions on how to access the content for this chapter.

If you are accessing this feature through the Companion Website, click on "Document Makeovers" and then select Chapter 14. You will find a letter that contains problems and errors related to what you've learned in this chapter about applying and interviewing for employment. Use the "Final Draft" decision tool to create an improved version of this request for a time extension. Check the letter for all the elements necessary to reassure the potential employer, ask for the extension, explain the reasons for the request, offer to compromise, and facilitate a quick reply. ●

" CHAPTER REVIEW AND ACTIVITIES

Chapter Summary

The purposes of an application letter are to introduce your résumé, persuade an employer to read it, and request an interview. With the AIDA model, get attention in the opening paragraph by explaining how you can benefit the organization. Build interest and desire by showing how you can meet the job requirements. Finally, motivate action by asking for an interview.

The typical sequence of interviews involves three stages. During the screening stage, employers filter out unqualified applicants and identify promising candidates. During the selection stage, the pool of applicants is narrowed through a variety of structured and unstructured interviewing methods. In the final stage, employers select the candidates who will receive offers and, if necessary, promote the benefits of joining the company.

Employers favor behavioral interviews because traditional, generic interview questions can often be answered with "canned" responses. Behavioral questions require candidates to use their own experiences and attributes to craft answers.

Employers look for two things during an employment interview. First, they seek evidence that an applicant is qualified for the position. Second, they seek reassurance that an applicant will be a good fit with the "personality" of the organization and the position.

To prepare for a successful job interview, (1) complete the research you started when planning your résumé, (2) think ahead about questions you'll need to answer and questions you'll want to ask, (3) bolster your confidence by focusing on your strengths and preparing thoroughly, (4) polish your interviewing style, (5) plan to look your best with businesslike clothing and good grooming, and (6) arrive on time and ready to begin.

All employment interviews have three stages. The warm-up stage is the most important because first impressions greatly influence an interviewer's decision. The question-and-answer stage, during which you will answer and ask questions, is the longest. The close is your final opportunity to promote your value to the organization and counter any misconceptions the interviewer may have.

Following an interview, send a thank-you message to show appreciation, emphasize your strengths, and politely ask for a decision. Send an inquiry if you haven't received the interviewer's decision by the date promised or within two weeks of the interview—especially if you've received a job offer from another firm. You can request a time extension if you need more time to consider an offer. Send a letter of acceptance within five days of receiving a job offer that you want to take. Send a letter declining a job offer when you want to refuse an offer tactfully. Finally, if you are currently employed, send a letter of resignation after you have accepted the offer of another job.

Test Your Knowledge

1. Why do many employers now use situational or behavioral interviews?

2. What should your objective be during a selection interview?

3. How does a structured interview differ from an open-ended interview?

4. Why are the questions you ask during an interview as important as the answers you give to the interviewer's questions?

5. What are the three stages of every interview, and which is the most important?

Apply Your Knowledge

1. How can you distinguish yourself from other candidates in a screening interview and still keep your responses short and to the point? Explain.

2. How can you prepare for a situational or behavioral interview if you have no experience with the job for which you are interviewing?

3. If you want to switch jobs because you can't work with your supervisor, how can you explain this situation to a prospective employer?

4. During a group interview, you notice that one of the other candidates is trying to monopolize the conversation. He's always the first to answer, his answers are the longest, and he interrupts the other candidates while they are talking. The interviewer doesn't seem to be concerned about his behavior, but you are. You would like to have more time to speak so that the interviewer can get to know you better. What should you do?

5. **Ethical Choices**   Why is it important to distinguish unethical or illegal interview questions from acceptable questions? Explain.

Practice Your Knowledge

Activities

Active links for all websites in this chapter can be found online. If MyBCommLab.com is being used in your class, see your User Guide for instructions on accessing the content for this chapter. Otherwise, visit www.pearsonhighered.com/bovee, locate *Business Communication Essentials*, Fourth Edition, click the Companion Website link, select Chapter 14, and then click on "Featured Websites." Please note that links to sites that become inactive after publication of the book will be removed from the Featured Websites section.

1. **Analyze This Message**   Read the following letter. (1) Analyze its strengths or weaknesses and (2) revise it so that it follows this chapter's guidelines.

   I'm writing to let you know about my availability for the brand manager job you advertised. As you can see from my enclosed résumé, my background is perfect for the position. Even though I don't have any real job experience, my grades have been outstanding considering that I went to a top-ranked business school.

   I did many things during my undergraduate years to prepare me for this job:

   - Earned a 3.4 out of a 4.0 with a 3.8 in my business courses
   - Elected representative to the student governing association
   - Selected to receive the Lamar Franklin Award
   - Worked to earn a portion of my tuition

   I am sending my résumé to all the top firms, but I like yours better than any of the rest. Your reputation is tops in the industry, and I want to be associated with a business that can pridefully say it's the best.

   If you wish for me to come in for an interview, I can come on a Friday afternoon or anytime on weekends when I don't have classes. Again, thanks for considering me for your brand manager position.

2. **Analyze This Message**   Read the following letter. (1) Analyze its strengths or weaknesses and (2) revise it so that it follows this chapter's guidelines.

   Did you receive my résumé? I sent it to you at least two months ago and haven't heard anything. I know you keep résumés on file, but I just want to be sure that you keep me in mind. I heard you are hiring health-care managers and certainly would like to be considered for one of those positions.

   Since I last wrote you, I've worked in a variety of positions that have helped prepare me for management. To wit, I've become lunch manager at the restaurant where I work, which involved a raise in pay. I now manage a waitstaff of 12 girls and take the lunch receipts to the bank every day.

   Of course, I'd much rather be working at a real job, and that's why I'm writing again. Is there anything else you would like to know about me or my background? I would really like to know more about your company. Is there any literature you could send me? If so, I would really appreciate it.

   I think one reason I haven't been hired yet is that I don't want to leave Atlanta. So I hope when you think of me, it's for a position that wouldn't require moving. Thanks again for considering my application.

3. **Analyze This Message**   Read the following letter. (1) Analyze its strengths or weaknesses and (2) revise it so that it follows this chapter's guidelines.

   Thank you for the really marvelous opportunity to meet you and your colleagues at Starret Engine Company. I really enjoyed touring your facilities and talking with all the people there. You have quite a crew! Some of the other companies I have visited have been so rigid and uptight that I can't imagine how I would fit in. It's a relief to run into a group of people who seem to enjoy their work as much as all of you do.

   I know that you must be looking at many other candidates for this job, and I know that some of them will probably be more experienced than I am. But I do want to emphasize that my two-year hitch in the Navy involved a good deal of engineering work. I don't think I mentioned all my shipboard responsibilities during the interview.

Please give me a call within the next week to let me know your decision. You can usually find me at my dormitory in the evening after dinner (phone: 877-9080).

4. **Analyze This Message**   Read the following letter. (1) Analyze its strengths or weaknesses and (2) revise it so that it follows this chapter's guidelines.

I have recently received a very attractive job offer from the Warrington Company. But before I let them know one way or another, I would like to consider any offer that your firm may extend. I was quite impressed with your company during my recent interview, and I am still very interested in a career there.

I don't mean to pressure you, but Warrington has asked for my decision within 10 days. Could you let me know by Tuesday whether you plan to offer me a position? That would give me enough time to compare the two offers.

5. **Analyze This Message**   Read the following letter. (1) Analyze its strengths or weaknesses and (2) revise it so that it follows this chapter's guidelines.

I'm writing to say that I must decline your job offer. Another company has made me a more generous offer, and I have decided to accept. However, if things don't work out for me there, I will let you know. I sincerely appreciate your interest in me.

6. **Teamwork**   Divide the class into two groups. Half the class will be recruiters for a large chain of national department stores, looking to fill 15 manager-trainee positions. The other half of the class will be candidates for the job. The company is specifically looking for candidates who demonstrate these three qualities: initiative, dependability, and willingness to assume responsibility.

   a. Have each recruiter select and interview an applicant for 10 minutes.

   b. Have all the recruiters discuss how they assessed the applicant in each of the three desired qualities. What questions did they ask or what did they use as an indicator to determine whether the candidate possessed the quality?

   c. Have all the applicants discuss what they said to convince the recruiters that they possessed each of the three desired qualities.

7. **Internet**   Select a large company (one on which you can easily find information) where you might like to work. Use Internet sources to gather some preliminary research on the company; don't limit your search to the company's own website.

   a. What did you learn about this organization that would help you during an interview there?

   b. What Internet sources did you use to obtain this information?

   c. Armed with this information, what aspects of your background do you think might appeal to this company's recruiters?

   d. If you choose to apply for a job with this company, what keywords would you include on your résumé? Why?

8. **Interviews: Being Prepared**   Prepare written answers to 10 of the questions listed in Table 14.3 on page 375.

9. **Interviews: Understanding Qualifications**   Write a short e-mail to your instructor, discussing what you believe are your greatest strengths and weaknesses from an employment perspective. Next, explain how these strengths and weaknesses would be viewed by interviewers evaluating your qualifications.

10. **Ethical Choices**   You have decided to accept a new position with a competitor of your company. Write a letter of resignation to your supervisor, announcing your decision.

   a. Will you notify your employer that you are joining a competing firm? Explain.

   b. Will you use the direct or indirect approach? Explain.

   c. Will you send your letter by e-mail, send it by regular mail, or place it on your supervisor's desk?

Expand Your Knowledge

Exploring the Best of the Web

Prepare and Practice Before the First Interview   How can you practice for a job interview? What are some questions that you might be asked and how should you respond? What questions are you not obligated to answer? Job-interview.net, www. job-interview.net, provides mock interviews based on actual job openings. It provides job descriptions, questions and answers for specific careers and jobs, and links to company guides and annual reports. You'll find a step-by-step plan that outlines key job requirements, lists practice interview questions, and helps you put together practice interviews. The site offers tips on the keywords to look for in a job description, which will help you narrow your search and anticipate the questions you might be asked on your first or next job interview.

Exercises

1. What are some problem questions you might be asked during a job interview? How would you handle these questions?

2. Choose a job title from the list and read more about that job. What did you learn that could help during an actual interview for the job you selected?

3. Developing an "interview game plan" ahead of time helps you make a strong positive impression during an interview. What are some of the things you can practice to help make everything you do during an interview seem to come naturally?

Surfing Your Way to Career Success

Bovée and Thill's Business Communication Headline News offers links to hundreds of online resources that can help you with this course, your other college courses, and your career. Visit http://businesscommunicationblog.com and click on "Web Directory." The Reference section connects you to a variety of websites that can help in all aspects of business communication, from writing centers and online libraries to dictionaries, encyclopedias, and more. Identify three websites from this section that could be useful in your business career. For each site, write a two-sentence summary of what the site offers and how it could help you launch and build your career.

MyBCommLab.com   ·

Use MyBCommLab.com to test your understanding of the concepts presented in this chapter and explore additional materials that will bring the ideas to life in video, activities, and an online multimedia e-book. Additionally, you can improve your skill with frequently confused, misused, and misspelled words by using the "Peak Performance Grammar and Mechanics" module within the lab. Take the Pretest to determine whether you have any weak areas. Then review those areas in the Refresher Course. Take the Follow-Up Test to check your grasp of handling these tricky words. For an extra challenge, take the Advanced Test. Finally, for even more reinforcement, go to the "Improve Your Grammar, Mechanics, and Usage" section that follows the cases, and complete the "Level 1: Self-Assessment" exercises.

Cases

▼ *Apply the three-step writing process to the following cases, as assigned by your instructor.*

Preparing Other Types of Employment Messages

1. Online Application: Electronic Cover Letter Introducing a Résumé   While researching a digital camera purchase, you stumble on the webzine *Megapixel* (www.megapixel.net), which offers product reviews on a wide array of camera models. The quality of the reviews and the stunning examples of photography on the site inspire you to a new part-time business idea: You'd like to write a regular column for *Megapixel*. The webzine does a great job addressing the information needs of experienced camera users, but you see an opportunity to write for "newbies," people who are new to digital photography and need a more basic level of information.[53]

Your task   Write an e-mail message that will serve as your cover letter and address your message to Denys Bouton, who edits the English edition of *Megapixel*. (It is also published in French.) Try to limit your message to one screen (generally 20–25 lines). You'll need a creative "hook" and a reassuring approach that identifies you as the right person to launch this new feature in the webzine. (Make up any details about your background that you may need to complete the message.)

2. All Over the Map: Application Letter to Google Earth   You've applied yourself with vigor and resolve for four years, and you're just about to graduate with your business degree. While cruising the web to relax one night, you stumble on something called Google Earth. You're hooked instantly by the ability to zoom all around the globe and look at detailed satellite photos of places you've been to or dreamed of visiting. You can even type in the address of your apartment and get an aerial view of your neighborhood. You're amazed at the three-dimensional renderings of major U.S. cities. Plus, the photographs and maps are linked to Google's other search technologies, allowing you to locate everything from ATMs to coffee shops in your neighborhood.

You've loved maps since you were a kid, and discovering Google Earth is making you wish you had majored in geography. Knowing how important it is to follow your heart, you decide to apply to Google anyway, even though you don't have a strong background in geographic information systems. What you do have is a ton of passion for maps and a good head for business.[54]

Your task   Visit http://earth.google.com and explore the system's capabilities. (You can download a free copy of the software.) In particular, look at the business and government applications of the technology, such as customized aerial photos and maps for real estate sales, land use and environmental impact analysis, and emergency planning for homeland security agencies. Be sure to visit the Community pages, where you can learn more about the many interesting applications of this technology. Draft an application e-mail to Google (address it to jobs@google.com), asking to be considered for the Google Earth team. Think about how you could help the company develop the commercial potential of this product line and make sure your enthusiasm shines through in the message.

Interviewing with Potential Employers

3. Interviewers and Interviewees: Classroom Exercise in Interviewing   Interviewing is an interactive process involving at least two people. The best way to practice for interviews is to work with others.

Your task   You and all other members of your class are to write letters of application for an entry-level or management-trainee position that requires a pleasant personality and intelligence but a minimum of specialized education or experience. Sign your letter with a fictitious name that conceals your identity. Next, polish (or create) a résumé that accurately identifies you and your educational and professional accomplishments.

Now, three members of the class who volunteer as interviewers divide up all the anonymously written application letters. Then each interviewer selects a candidate who seems the most pleasant and convincing in his or her letter. At this time, the selected candidates identify themselves and give the interviewers their résumés.

Each interviewer then interviews his or her chosen candidate in front of the class, seeking to understand how the items on the résumé qualify the candidate for the job. At the end of the interviews, the class decides who gets the job and discusses why this candidate was successful. Afterward, retrieve your letter, sign it with the right name, and submit it to the instructor for credit.

4. Internet Interview: Exercise in Interviewing   Locate the website of a company in an industry in which you might like to work and then identify an interesting position within the company. Study the company, using the research process described in Chapter 10, and prepare for an interview with that company.

Your task   Working with a classmate, take turns interviewing each other for your chosen positions. Interviewers should take notes during the interview. When the interview is complete, critique each other's performance. (Interviewers should critique how well candidates prepared for the interview and answered the questions; interviewees should critique the quality of the questions asked.) Write a follow-up letter thanking your interviewer and submit the letter to your instructor.

Following Up After an Interview

5. A Slight Error in Timing: Letter Asking for Delay of an Employment Decision   Due to a mix-up in your job application scheduling, you accidentally applied for your third-choice job before going after what you really wanted. What you want to do is work in retail marketing with the upscale department store Neiman Marcus in Dallas; what you have been offered is a similar job with Longhorn Leather and Lumber, 55 dry and dusty miles away in Commerce, just south of the Oklahoma panhandle.

You review your notes. Your Longhorn interview was three weeks ago with the human resources manager, R. P. Bronson, who has just written to offer you the position. The store's address is 27 Sam Rayburn Drive, Commerce, TX 75428. Mr. Bronson notes that he can hold the position open for 10 days. You have an interview scheduled with Neiman Marcus next week, but it is unlikely that you will know the store's decision within this 10-day period.

Your task   Write to R. P. Bronson, requesting a reasonable delay in your consideration of his job offer.

6. Job Hunt: Set of Employment-Related Letters to a Single Company   Where would you like to work? Choose one of your favorite products, find out which company either manufactures it or sells it in the United States (if it's manufactured in another country). Assume that a month ago you sent your résumé and application letter to this company. Not long afterward, you were invited to come for an interview, which seemed to go very well.

Your task   Use your imagination to write the following: (a) a thank you letter for the interview, (b) a note of inquiry, (c) a request for more time to decide, (d) a letter of acceptance, and (e) a letter declining the job offer.

Improve Your Grammar, Mechanics, and Usage

Level 1: Self-Assessment—Vocabulary

Review Sections 4.1, 4.2, and 4.3 in the Handbook of Grammar, Mechanics, and Usage and then complete the following 15 items.

In items 1–7, circle the correct word provided in parentheses.

1. Everyone (*accept/except*) _____ Barbara King has registered for the company competition.

2. We need to find a new security (*device/devise*) _____.

3. The Jennings are (*loath/loathe*) _____ to admit that they are wrong.

4. The judge has ruled that this town cannot enforce such a local (*ordinance/ordnance*) _____.

5. To stay on schedule, we must give (*precedence/precedents*) _____ to the Marley project.

6. This month's balance is greater (*than/then*) _____ last month's.

7. That decision lies with the director, (*who's/whose*) _____ in charge of this department.

In items 8–15, underline errors and write corrections in the space provided:

8. _____ In this department, we see alot of mistakes like that.

9. _____ In my judgement, you'll need to redo the cover.

10. _____ He decided to reveal the information, irregardless of the consequences.

11. _____ Why not go along when it is so easy to accomodate his demands?

12. _____ When you say that, do you mean to infer that I'm being unfair?

13. _____ She says that she finds this sort of ceremony embarassing.

14. _____ All we have to do is try and get along with him for a few more days.

15. _____ A friendly handshake should always preceed negotiations.

Level 2: Workplace Applications

The following items contain numerous errors in grammar, capitalization, punctuation, abbreviation, number style, word division, and vocabulary. Rewrite each sentence, correcting all errors. Write *C* for any sentence that is already correct.

1. An entrepreneur and their business, are so closely tied together that a bank will want to see how they handle their personal affairs, before granting a small business line of credit.

2. The companys' annual meeting will be held from 2–4 PM on May 3d in the Santa Fe room at the Marriott hotel.

3. Well over four hundred outstanding students from coast-to-coast, have realized their dreams of a college education thanks to the NASE Scholarship program.

4. If you're home is you're principle place of business you can deduct generally the cost of traveling from you're home, to any business destination.

5. Companies like McLeod USA sprung into being in the 1990's to provide cut rate phone services to small- and medium-size businesses in competition with the established baby bells.

6. Some question whether a 'new economy' exists and if so how it differs from the old economy?

7. When the music industry claimed by stealing intellectual property Napster were committing piracy - Napster argued that it was'nt doing anything illegal or un-ethical.

8. The World Bank plays an important roll in todays fast changing closely-meshed global economy.

9. When it comes to consumer rights the F.D.A., F.T.C., and Agriculture department are concerned not only with safety but also accurate information.

10. Fujitsu, a $50 billion company with 190,000 employees, dominates the Japanese computer industry.

11. The fortune 500 ranks not only corporations by size but also offers brief company descriptions; along with industry statistics, and additional measures of corporate performance.

12. Having bought 55 companies over the past decade, plans to make ten to 15 new acquisitions each year are being made by Cisco Systems.

13. In 1984 Michael Dell decided to sell P.C.'s direct and built to order, now everybody in the industry are trying to imitate Dells' strategy.

14. Resulting in large cost savings for the company, American Express have reduced the number of field office's from 85 to 7 by using virtual teams.

15. In Europe and Asia, people are using mobile phones to send text messages to other users; exchange e-mail; read the morning news; surfing certain websites; and to make purchases such as movie tickets and charge it to they're monthly phone bill.

Level 3: Document Critique

The following document may contain errors in grammar, capitalization, punctuation, abbreviation, number style, vocabulary, and spelling. You may also find problems with organization, format, and word use. Correct all errors using standard proofreading marks (see Appendix C).

Morgan Mitras

2397 Glencrest ridge, Fort Worth, TEX 76119

(817/ 226-1804

February 2 2009:

Norton Acctg. Group

Ms Nancy Remington, Human Resources

3778 Parkway North

Indianapolis, Indiana 46205

Dear Ms. Remington—

With your companys' reputation for quality, customer service, employee empowerment, you'll will want to hire someone who is not only accurrate and efficient but also self motivated and results-oriented—someone who is able to make decisions as well as coperate with team members and clients. The ad you placed in the February 1st issue of *The Wall Street Journal* for someone to fill a financial management position really has me very excited and eager.

During my 3 years at Tandy corporation -see attached résumé- I've conducted internal auditing for accounts valued at $450 million dollars. Some of my many, countless accomplishments include

- Increasing both internal and client support for the auditing process
- I save the company over 2.5 million dollars when I discovered billing errors
- Suggest ways accounts receivable processes could be streamlined

In addition it might be that Norton Accounting may appreciate my ability to complete projects on time as well as keeping them under budget. One of my priorities is a position in which my expereince will be broaden: so any opportunity to travel would be welcomed by me!

I'll be in your area during the weak of February 20; I'll call your office on Feb. 8 to see whether we can arrange to meet. I hope you'll give me a chance, please.

Sincerely,

Morgan Mitras,

Applicant

Appendix A

FORMAT AND LAYOUT OF BUSINESS DOCUMENTS

The format and layout of business documents vary from country to country; they even vary within regions of the United States. In addition, many organizations develop their own variations of standard styles, adapting documents to the types of messages they send and the kinds of audiences they communicate with. The formats described here are more common than others.

First Impressions

Your documents tell readers a lot about you and about your company's professionalism. So all your documents must look neat, present a professional image, and be easy to read. Your audience's first impression of a document comes from the quality of its paper, the way it is customized, and its general appearance.

Paper

To give a quality impression, businesspeople consider carefully the paper they use. Several aspects of paper contribute to the overall impression:

- **Weight.** Paper quality is judged by the weight of four reams (each a 500-sheet package) of letter-size paper. The weight most commonly used by U.S. business organizations is 20-pound paper, but 16- and 24-pound versions are also used.

- **Cotton content.** Paper quality is also judged by the percentage of cotton in the paper. Cotton doesn't yellow over time the way wood pulp does, plus it's both strong and soft. For letters and outside reports, use paper with a 25 percent cotton content. For memos and other internal documents, you can use a lighter-weight paper with lower cotton content. Airmail-weight paper may save money for international correspondence, but make sure it isn't too flimsy.[1]

- **Size.** In the United States, the standard paper size for business documents is $8\frac{1}{2}$ by 11 inches. Standard legal documents are $8\frac{1}{2}$ by 14 inches. Executives sometimes have heavier 7-by-10-inch paper on hand (with matching envelopes) for personal messages such as congratulations.[2] They may also have a box of note cards imprinted with their initials and a box of plain folded notes for condolences or for acknowledging formal invitations.

- **Color.** White is the standard color for business purposes, although neutral colors such as gray and ivory are sometimes used. Memos can be produced on pastel-colored paper to distinguish them from external correspondence. In addition, memos are sometimes produced on various colors of paper for routing to separate departments. Light-colored papers are appropriate, but bright or dark colors make reading difficult and may appear too frivolous.

Customization

For letters to outsiders, U.S. businesses commonly use letterhead stationery, which may be either professionally printed or designed in-house using word processing templates and graphics. The letterhead includes the company's name and address, usually at the top of the page but sometimes along the left side or even at the bottom. Other information may be included in the letterhead as well: the company's telephone number, fax number, cable address, website address, product lines, date of establishment, officers and directors, slogan, and symbol (logo). Well-designed letterhead gives readers[3]

- Pertinent reference data
- A favorable image of the company
- A good idea of what the company does

For as much as it's meant to accomplish, the letterhead should be as simple as possible. Too much information makes the page look cluttered, occupies space needed for the message, and might become outdated before all the stationery can be used. If you correspond frequently with people abroad, your letterhead must be intelligible to foreigners. It must include the name of your country in addition to your cable, telex, e-mail, or fax information.

In the United States, businesses always use letterhead for the first page of a letter. Successive pages are usually plain sheets of paper that match the letterhead in color and quality. Some companies use a specially printed second-page letterhead that bears only the company's name. Other countries have other conventions.

Many companies also design and print standardized forms for memos and frequently written reports that always require the same sort of information (such as sales reports and expense reports). These forms may be printed in sets for use with carbon paper or in carbonless-copy sets that produce multiple copies automatically. More and more organizations use computers to generate their standardized forms, which can save them both money and time.[4]

Appearance

Nearly all business documents are produced using an inkjet or laser printer; make sure to use a clean, high-quality printer. Certain documents, however, should be handwritten (such as a short informal memo or a note of condolence). Be sure to handwrite, print, or type the envelope to match the document. However, even a letter on the best-quality paper with the best-designed letterhead may look unprofessional if it's poorly produced. So pay close attention to all the factors affecting appearance, including the following:

- **Margins.** Companies in the United States make sure that documents (especially external ones) are centered on the page, with margins of at least 1 inch all around. Using word processing software, you can achieve this balance simply by defining the format parameters.

- **Line length.** Lines are rarely justified, because the resulting text looks too much like a form letter and can be hard to read (even with proportional spacing). Varying line length makes the document look more personal and interesting.

- **Line spacing.** You can adjust the number of blank lines between elements (such as between the date and the inside address) to ensure that a short document fills the page vertically or that a longer document extends at least two lines of the body onto the last page.

- **Character spacing.** Use proper spacing between characters and after punctuation. For example, U.S. conventions include leaving one space after commas, semicolons, colons, and sentence-ending periods. Each letter in a person's initials is followed by a period and a single space. However, abbreviations such as U.S.A. or MBA may or may not have periods, but they never have internal spaces.

- **Special symbols.** Take advantage of the many special symbols available with your computer's selection of fonts. (In Microsoft Word, click on the Insert menu, then select Symbol.) Table A.1 shows some of the more common symbols used in business documents. In addition, see if your company has a style guide for documents, which may include other symbols you are expected to use.

- **Corrections.** Messy corrections are unacceptable in business documents. If you notice an error after printing a document with your word processor, correct the mistake and reprint. (With informal memos to members of your own team or department, the occasional small correction in pen or pencil is acceptable, but never in formal documents.)

Letters

All business letters have certain elements in common. Several of these elements appear in every letter; others appear only when desirable or appropriate. In addition, these letter parts are usually arranged in one of three basic formats.

Standard Letter Parts

The letter in Figure A.1 shows the placement of standard letter parts. The writer of this business letter had no letterhead available but correctly included a heading. All business letters typically include these seven elements.

Heading

Most companies have preprinted *letterhead* sheets that show the company name, address, telephone number, website URL, and a general e-mail address. Executive letterhead also bears the name

TABLE A.1 Special Symbols on a Computer	
	Computer symbol
Case fractions	$\frac{1}{2}$
Copyright	©
Registered trademark	®
Cents	¢
British pound	£
Paragraph	¶
Bullets	●,♦,■,□,✓,☑,⊗
Em dash	—
En dash	–

of an individual within the organization. Computers allow you to design your own letterhead (either one to use for all correspondence or a new one for each piece of correspondence). If letterhead stationery is not available, the heading includes a return address (but no name) and starts 13 lines from the top of the page, which leaves a 2-inch top margin.

Date

If you're using letterhead, place the date at least one blank line beneath the lowest part of the letterhead. Without letterhead, place the date immediately below the return address. The standard method of writing the date in the United States uses the full name of the month (no abbreviations), followed by the day (in numerals, without *st, nd, rd,* or *th*), a comma, and then the year: July 14, 2009 (7/14/09). Some organizations follow other conventions (see Table A.2). To maintain the utmost clarity in international correspondence, always spell out the name of the month in dates.[5]

When communicating internationally, you may also experience some confusion over time. Some companies in the United States refer to morning (A.M.) and afternoon (P.M.), dividing a 24-hour day into 12-hour blocks so that they refer to four o'clock in the morning (4:00 A.M.) or four o'clock in the afternoon (4:00 P.M.). The U.S. military and European companies refer to one 24-hour period so that 0400 hours (4:00 A.M.) is always in the morning and 1600 hours (4:00 P.M.) is always in the afternoon.[6] Make sure your references to time are as clear as possible, and be sure you clearly understand your audience's time references.

Inside Address

The inside address identifies the recipient of the letter. For U.S. correspondence, begin the inside address at least one line below the date. Precede the addressee's name with a courtesy title, such as *Dr., Mr.,* or *Ms.* The accepted courtesy title for women in business is *Ms.,* although a woman known to prefer the title *Miss* or *Mrs.* is always accommodated. If you don't know whether a person is a man or a woman (and you have no way of finding out), omit the courtesy title. For example, *Terry Smith* could be either a man or a woman. The first line of the inside address would be just *Terry Smith,* and the salutation would be *Dear Terry Smith.* The same is true if you know only a person's initials, as in *S. J. Adams.*

Spell out and capitalize titles that precede a person's name, such as *Professor* or *General* (see Table A.3 for the proper forms of address). The person's organizational title, such as *Director,* may be included on this first line (if it is short) or on the line below; the name of a department may follow. In addresses and signature lines, don't forget to capitalize any professional title that follows a person's name:

Mr. Ray Johnson, Dean

Ms. Patricia T. Higgins

Assistant Vice President

However, professional titles not appearing in an address or signature line are capitalized only when they directly precede the name:

President Kenneth Johanson will deliver the speech.

Maria Morales, president of ABC Enterprises, will deliver the speech.

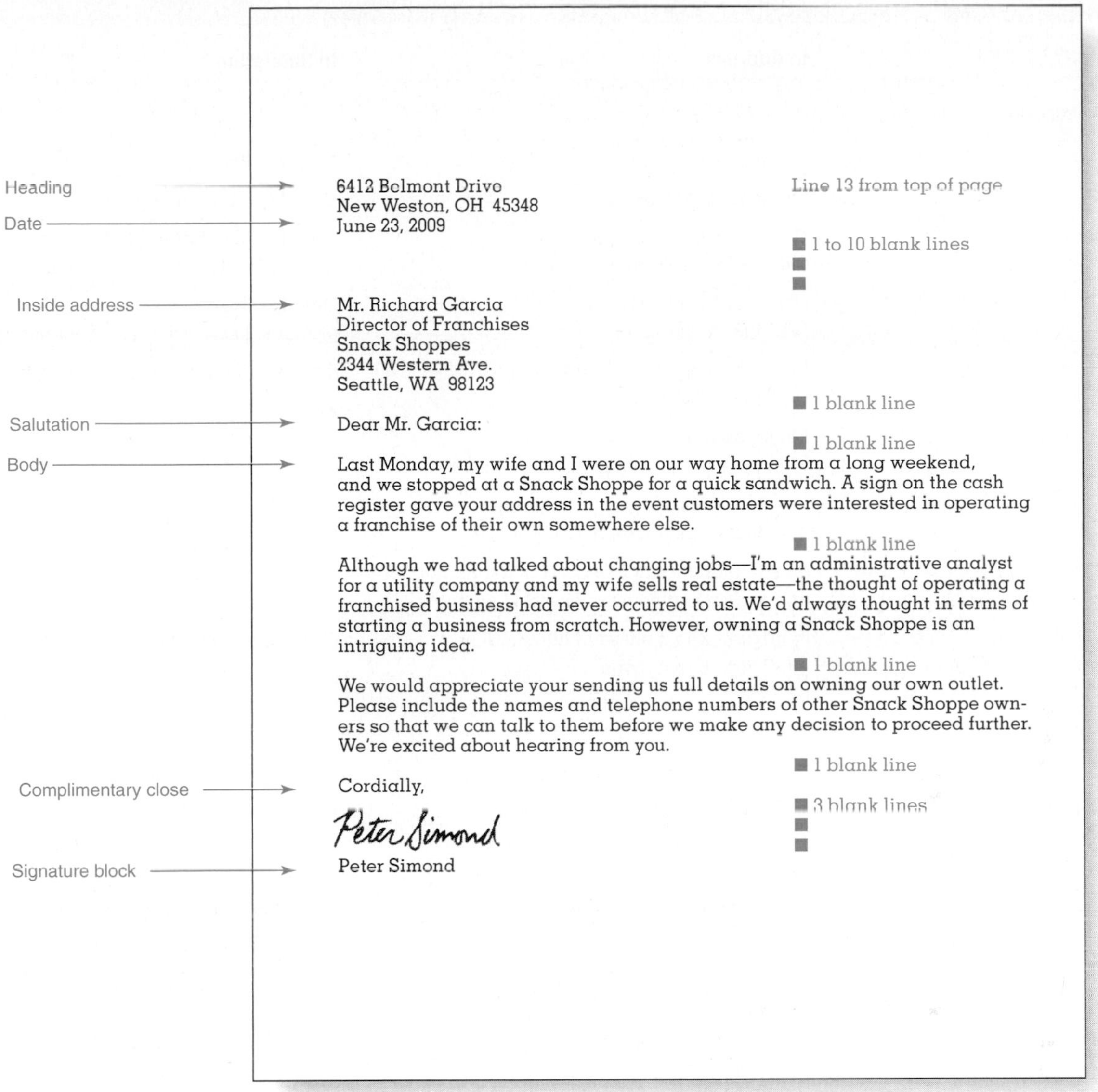

Heading → 6412 Belmont Drive
New Weston, OH 45348
Date → June 23, 2009

Line 13 from top of page

■ 1 to 10 blank lines
■
■

Inside address → Mr. Richard Garcia
Director of Franchises
Snack Shoppes
2344 Western Ave.
Seattle, WA 98123

■ 1 blank line

Salutation → Dear Mr. Garcia:

■ 1 blank line

Body → Last Monday, my wife and I were on our way home from a long weekend, and we stopped at a Snack Shoppe for a quick sandwich. A sign on the cash register gave your address in the event customers were interested in operating a franchise of their own somewhere else.

■ 1 blank line

Although we had talked about changing jobs—I'm an administrative analyst for a utility company and my wife sells real estate—the thought of operating a franchised business had never occurred to us. We'd always thought in terms of starting a business from scratch. However, owning a Snack Shoppe is an intriguing idea.

■ 1 blank line

We would appreciate your sending us full details on owning our own outlet. Please include the names and telephone numbers of other Snack Shoppe owners so that we can talk to them before we make any decision to proceed further. We're excited about hearing from you.

■ 1 blank line

Complimentary close → Cordially,

■ 3 blank lines
■
■

Peter Simond

Signature block → Peter Simond

Figure A.1 Standard Letter Parts

The Honorable Helen Masters, senator from Arizona, will deliver the speech.

If the name of a specific person is unavailable, you may address the letter to the department or to a specific position within the department. Also, be sure to spell out company names in full, unless the company itself uses abbreviations in its official name.

Other address information includes the treatment of buildings, house numbers, and compass directions (see Table A.4).

TABLE A.2 Common Date Forms			
Convention	**Description**	**Date—Mixed**	**Date—All Numerals**
U.S. standard	Month (spelled out) day, year	July 14, 2009	7/14/09
U.S. government and some U.S. industries	Day (in numerals) month (spelled out) year	14 July 2009	14/7/09
European	Replace U.S. solidus (diagonal line) with periods	14 July 2009	14.7.2009
International standard	Year month day	2009 July 14	2009,7,14

TABLE A.3 Forms of Address

Person	In Address	In Salutation
PERSONAL TITLES		
Man	Mr. [first & last name]	Dear Mr. [last name]:
Woman[1]	Ms. [first & last name]	Dear Ms. [last name]:
Two men (or more)	Mr. [first & last name] and Mr. [first & last name]	Dear Mr. [last name] and Mr. [last name] *or* Messrs. [last name] and [last name]:
Two women (or more)	Ms. [first & last name] and Ms. [first & last name]	Dear Ms. [last name] and Ms. [last name] *or* Mses. [last name] and [last name]:
One woman and one man	Ms. [first & last name] and Mr. [first & last name]	Dear Ms. [last name] and Mr. [last name]:
Couple (married)	Mr. [husband's first name] and Mrs. [wife's first name] [couple's last name]	Dear Mr. and Mrs. [last name]:
Couple (married with different last names)	Mr. [first & last name of husband] Ms. [first & last name of wife]	Dear Mr. [husband's last name] and Ms. [wife's last name]:
Couple (married professionals with same title and same last name)	[title in plural form] [husband's first name] and [wife's first name] [couple's last name]	Dear [title in plural form] [last name]:
Couple (married professionals with different titles and same last name)	[title] [first & last name of husband] and [title] [first & last name of wife]	Dear [title] and [title] [last name]:
PROFESSIONAL TITLES		
President of a college or university	[title] [first & last name], President	Dear [title] [last name]:
Dean of a school of college	Dean [first & last name] *or* Dr., Mr., *or* Ms. [first & last name], Dean of [title]	Dear Dean [last name]: *or* Dear Dr., Mr., *or* Ms. [last name]:
Professor	Professor *or* Dr. [first & last name]	Dear Professor *or* Dr. [last name]:
Physician	[first & last name], M.D.	Dear Dr. [last name]:
Lawyer	Mr. *or* Ms. [first & last name] Attorney at Law	Dear Mr. *or* Ms. [last name]:
Military personnel	[full rank, first & last name, abbreviation of service designation] (add *Retired* if applicable)	Dear [rank][last name]:
Company or corporation	[name of organization]	Ladies and Gentlemen: *or* Gentlemen and Ladies:
GOVERNMENTAL TITLES		
President of the United States	The president	Dear Mr. *or* Madam President:
Senator of the United States	Honorable [first & last name]	Dear Senator [last name]:
Cabinet member Postmaster General Attorney General	Honorable [first & last name]	Dear Mr. *or* Madam Secretary: Dear Mr. *or* Madam Postmaster General: Dear Mr. *or* Madam Attorney General:
Mayor	Honorable [first & last name], Mayor of [name of city]	Dear Mayor [last name]:
Judge	The Honorable [first & last name]	Dear Judge [last name]:

[1]Use *Mrs.* or *Miss* only if the recipient has specifically requested that you use one of these titles; otherwise *always* use *Ms.* in business correspondence. Also, never refer to a married woman by her husband's name (e.g., Mrs. Robert Washington) unless she specifically requests that you do so.

TABLE A.4 Inside Address Information

Description	Example
Capitalize building names.	Empire State Building
Capitalize locations within buildings (apartments, suites, rooms).	Suite 1073
Use numerals for all house or building numbers, except the number *one*.	One Trinity Lane; 637 Adams Ave., Apt. 7
Spell out compass directions that fall within a street address	1074 West Connover St.
Abbreviate compass directions that follow the street address	783 Main St., N.E., Apt. 27

The following example shows all the information that may be included in the inside address and its proper order for U.S. correspondence:

Ms. Linda Coolidge, Vice President
Corporate Planning Department
Midwest Airlines
Kowalski Building, Suite 21-A
7279 Bristol Ave.
Toledo, OH 43617

Canadian addresses are similar, except that the name of the province is usually spelled out:

Dr. H. C. Armstrong
Research and Development
Commonwealth Mining Consortium
The Chelton Building, Suite 301
585 Second St. SW
Calgary, Alberta T2P 2P5

The order and layout of address information vary from country to country. So when addressing correspondence for other countries, carefully follow the format and information that appear in the company's letterhead. However, when you're sending mail from the United States, be sure that the name of the destination country appears on the last line of the address in capital letters. Use the English version of the country name so that your mail is routed from the United States to the right country. Then, to be sure your mail is routed correctly within the destination country, use the foreign spelling of the city name (using the characters and diacritical marks that would be commonly used in the region). For example, the following address uses *Köln* instead of *Cologne*:

H. R. Veith, Director	Addressee
Eisfieren Glaswerk	Company name
Blaubachstrasse 13	Street address
Postfach 10 80 07	Post office box
D-5000 Köln I	District, city
GERMANY	Country

For additional examples of international addresses, see Table A.5.

Be sure to use organizational titles correctly when addressing international correspondence. Job designations vary around the world. In England, for example, a managing director is often what a U.S. company would call its chief executive officer or president, and a British deputy is the equivalent of a vice president. In France, responsibilities are assigned to individuals without regard to title or organizational structure, and in China the title *project manager* has meaning, but the title *sales manager* may not.

To make matters worse, businesspeople in some countries sign correspondence without their names typed below. In Germany, for example, the belief is that employees represent the company, so it's inappropriate to emphasize personal names.[7] Use the examples in Table A.5 as guidelines when addressing correspondence to countries outside the United States.

Salutation

In the salutation of your letter, follow the style of the first line of the inside address. If the first line is a person's name, the salutation is *Dear Mr.* or *Ms. Name*. The formality of the salutation depends on your relationship with the addressee. If in conversation you would say "Mary," your letter's salutation should be *Dear Mary*, followed by a colon. Otherwise, include the courtesy title and last name, followed by a colon. Presuming to write *Dear Lewis* instead of *Dear Professor Chang* demonstrates a disrespectful familiarity that the recipient will probably resent.

If the first line of the inside address is a position title such as *Director of Personnel*, then use *Dear Director*. If the addressee is unknown, use a polite description, such as *Dear Alumnus, Dear SPCA Supporter*, or *Dear Voter*. If the first line is plural (a department or company), then use *Ladies and Gentlemen* (look again at Table A.3). When you do not know whether you're writing to an individual or a group (for example, when writing a reference or a letter of recommendation), use *To whom it may concern*.

In the United States some letter writers use a "salutopening" on the salutation line. A salutopening omits *Dear* but includes the first few words of the opening paragraph along

TABLE A.5 International Addresses and Salutations

Country	Postal Address	Address Elements	Salutations
Argentina	Sr. Juan Pérez Editorial Internacional S.A. Av. Sarmiento 1337, 8° P. C. C1035AAB BUENOS AIRES–CF ARGENTINA	S.A. = Sociedad Anónima (corporation) Av. Sarmiento (name of street) 1337 (building number) 8° = 8th. P = Piso (floor) C (room or suite) C1035AAB (postcode + city) CF = Capital Federal (federal capital)	Sr. = Señor (Mr.) Sra. = Señora (Mrs.) Srta. = Señorita (Miss) Don't use given names except with people you know well.
Australia	Mr. Roger Lewis International Publishing Pty. Ltd. 166 Kent Street, Level 9 GPO Box 3542 SYDNEY NSW 2001 AUSTRALIA	Pty. Ltd. = Proprietory Limited (corp.) 166 (building number) Kent Street (name of street) Level (floor) GPO Box (P.O. box) city + state (abbrev.) + postcode	Mr. and Mrs. used on first contact. Ms. not common (avoid use). Business is informal—use given name freely.
Austria	Herrn Dipl.-Ing.J.Gerdenitsch International Verlag Ges.m.b.H. Glockengasse 159 1010 WIEN AUSTRIA	Herrn = To Mr. (separate line) Dipl.-Ing. (engineering degree) Ges.m.b.H. (a corporation) Glockengasse (street name) 159 (building number) 1010 (postcode + city) WIEN (Vienna)	Herr (Mr.) Frau (Mrs.) Fräulein (Miss) obsolete in business, so do not use. Given names are almost never used in business.
Brazil	Ilmo. Sr. Gilberto Rabello Ribeiro Editores Internacionais S.A. Rua da Ajuda, 228 – 6° Andar Caixa Postal 2574 20040–000 RIO DE JANEIRO–RJ BRAZIL	Ilmo. = Ilustrissimo (honorific) Ilma. = Ilustrissima (hon. female) S.A. = Sociedade Anônima (corporation) Rua = street, da Ajuda (street name) 228 (building number) 6° = 6th. Andar (floor) Caixa Postal (P.O. box) 20040–000 (postcode + city)–RJ (state abbrev.)	Sr. = Senhor (Mr.) Sra. = Senhora (Mrs.) Srta. = Senhorita (Miss) Family name at end, e.g., Senhor Ribeiro (Rabello is mother's famlly name) Given names readily used in business.
China	Xia Zhiyi International Publishing Ltd. 14 Jianguolu Chaoyangqu BEIJING 100025 CHINA	Ltd. (limited liability corporation) 14 (building number) Jianguolu (street name), lu (street) Chaoyangqu (district name) (city + postcode)	Family name (single syllable) first. Given name (2 syllables) second, sometimes reversed. Use Mr. or Ms. at all times (Mr. Xia).
France	Monsieur LEFÈVRE Alain Éditions Internationales S.A. Siège Social Immeuble Le Bonaparte 64–68, av. Galliéni B.P. 154 75942 PARIS CEDEX 19 FRANCE	S.A. = Société Anonyme (corporation) Siège Social (head office) Immeuble (building + name) 64–68 (building occupies 64, 66, 68) av. = avenue (no initial capital) B.P. = Boîte Postale (P.O. box) 75942 (postcode + city) CEDEX (postcode for P.O. box)	Monsieur (Mr.) Madame (Mrs.) Mademoiselle (Miss) Best not to abbreviate. Family name is sometimes in all caps with given name following.
Germany	Herrn Gerhardt Schneider International Verlag GmbH Schillerstraße 159 44147 DORTMUND GERMANY	Herrn = To Mr. (on a separate line) GmbH (inc.—incorporated) –straße (street—'ß' often written 'ss') 159 (building number) 44147 (postcode + city)	Herr (Mr.) Frau (Mrs.) Fräulein (Miss) obsolete in business. Business is formal: (1) do not use given names unless invited, and (2) use academic titles precisely.
India	Sr. Shyam Lal Gupta International Publishing (Pvt.) Ltd. 1820 Rehaja Centre 214, Darussalam Road Andheri East BOMBAY–400049 INDIA	(Pvt.) (privately owned) Ltd. (limited liability corporation) 1820 (possibly office #20 on 18th floor) Rehaja Centre (building name) 214 (building number) Andheri East (suburb name) (city + hyphen + postcode)	Shri (Mr.), Shrimati (Mrs.) but English is common business language, so use Mr., Mrs., Miss. Given names are used only by family and close friends.

TABLE A.5 *Continued*

Country	Postal Address	Address Elements	Salutations
Italy	Egr. Sig. Giacomo Mariotti Edizioni Internazionali S.p.A. Via Terenzio, 21 20138 MILANO ITALY	Egr. = Egregio (honorific) Sig. = Signor (not nec. a separate line) S.p.A. = Società per Azioni (corp.) Via (street) 21 (building number) 20138 (postcode + city)	Sig. = Signore (Mr.) Sig.ra = Signora (Mrs.) Sig.a (Ms.) Women in business are addressed as Signora. Use given name only when invited.
Japan	Mr. Taro Tanaka Kokusai Shuppan K.K. 10–23, 5-chome, Minamiazabu Minato-ku TOKYO 106 JAPAN	K.K. = Kabushiki Kaisha (corporation) 10 (lot number) 23 (building number) 5-chome (area #5) Minamiazabu (neighborhood name) Minato-ku (city district) (city + postcode)	Given names not used in business. Use family name + job title. Or use family name + "-san" (Tanaka-san) or more respectfully, add "-sama" or "-dono."
Korea	Mr. Kim Chang-ik International Publishers Ltd. Room 206, Korea Building 33–4 Nonhyon-dong Kangnam-ku SEOUL 135–010 KOREA	English company names common Ltd. (a corporation) 206 (office number inside the building) 33–4 (area 4 of subdivision 33) -dong (city neighborhood name) -ku (subdivision of city) (city + postcode)	Family name is normally first but sometimes placed after given name. A two-part name is the given name. Use Mr. or Mrs. in letters, but use job title in speech.
Mexico	Sr. Francisco Pérez Martínez Editores Internacionales S.A. Indopondonoia No.322 Col. Juárez 06050 MEXICO D.F.	S.A. = Sociedad Anónima (corporation) Independencia (street name) No. = Número (number) 322 (building number) Col. = Colonia (city district) Juárez (locality name) 06050 (postcode + city) D.F. = Distrito Federal (federal capital)	Sr. = Señor (Mr.) Sra. = Señora (Mrs.) Srta. = Señorita (Miss) Family name in middle: e.g., Sr. Pérez (Martínez is mother's family). Given names are used in business.
South Africa	Mr. Mandla Ntuli International Publishing (Pty.) Ltd. Private Bag X2581 JOHANNESBURG 2000 SOUTH AFRICA	Pty. = Proprietory (privately owned) Ltd. (a corporation) Private Bag (P.O. Box) (city + postcode) or (postcode + city)	Mnr = Meneer (Mr.) Mev. = Mevrou (Mrs.) Mejuffrou (Miss) is not used in business. Business is becoming less formal, so the use of given names is possible.
United Kingdom	Mr. N. J. Lancaster International Publishing Ltd. Kingsbury House 12 Kingsbury Road EDGEWARE Middlesex HA8 9XG ENGLAND	N. J. (initials of given names) Ltd. (limited liability corporation) Kingsbury House (building name) 12 (building number) Kingsbury Road (name of street/road) EDGEWARE (city—all caps) Middlesex (county—not all caps) HA8 9XG	Mr. and Ms. used mostly. Mrs. and Miss sometimes used in North and by older women. Given names—called Christian names—are used in business after some time. Wait to be invited.

with the recipient's name. After this line, the sentence continues a double space below as part of the body of the letter, as in these examples:

> Thank you, Mr. Brown,   *Salutopening Body*
> for your prompt payment of your bill.
>
> Congratulations, Ms. Lake!   *Salutopening Body*
> Your promotion is well deserved.

Whether your salutation is informal or formal, be especially careful that names are spelled right. A misspelled name is glaring evidence of carelessness, and it belies the personal interest you're trying to express.

Body

The body of the letter is your message. Almost all letters are single-spaced, with one blank line before and after the salutation or salutopening, between paragraphs, and before the complimentary close. The body may include indented lists, entire paragraphs indented for emphasis, and even subheadings. If it does, all similar elements should be treated in the same way.

Your department or company may select a format to use for all letters.

Complimentary Close

The complimentary close begins on the second line below the body of the letter. Alternatives for wording are available, but currently the trend seems to be toward using one-word closes, such as *Sincerely* and *Cordially*. In any case, the complimentary close reflects the relationship between you and the person you're writing to. Avoid cute closes, such as *Yours for bigger profits*. If your audience doesn't know you well, your sense of humor may be misunderstood.

Signature Block

Leave three blank lines for a written signature below the complimentary close, and then include the sender's name (unless it appears in the letterhead). The person's title may appear on the same line as the name or on the line below:

Cordially,

Raymond Dunnigan
Director of Personnel

Your letterhead indicates that you're representing your company. However, if your letter is on plain paper or runs to a second page, you may want to emphasize that you're speaking legally for the company. The accepted way of doing that is to place the company's name in capital letters a double space below the complimentary close and then include the sender's name and title four lines below that:

Sincerely,
WENTWORTH INDUSTRIES

(Ms.) Helen B. Taylor
President

If your name could be taken for either a man's or a woman's, a courtesy title indicating gender should be included, with or without parentheses. Also, women who prefer a particular courtesy title should include it:

Mrs. Nancy Winters
(Ms.) Juana Flores
Ms. Pat Li
(Mr.) Jamie Saunders

Additional Letter Parts

Letters vary greatly in subject matter and thus in the identifying information they need and the format they adopt. The letter in Figure A.2 shows how these additional parts should be arranged. The following elements may be used in any combination, depending on the requirements of the particular letter:

- **Addressee notation.** Letters that have a restricted readership or that must be handled in a special way should include such addressee notations as *Personal, Confidential,* or *Please Forward*. This sort of notation appears a double space above the inside address, in all-capital letters.

- **Attention line.** Although not commonly used today, an attention line can be used if you know only the last name of the person you're writing to. It can also direct a letter to a position title or department. Place the attention line on the first line of the inside address and put the company name on the second.[8] Match the address on the envelope with the style of the inside address. An attention line may take any of the following forms or variants of them:

Attention Dr. McHenry
Attention Director of Marketing
Attention Marketing Department

- **Subject line.** The subject line tells recipients at a glance what the letter is about (and indicates where to file the letter for future reference). It usually appears below the salutation, either against the left margin, indented (as a paragraph in the body), or centered. It can be placed above the salutation or at the very top of the page, and it can be underscored. Some businesses omit the word *Subject*, and some organizations replace it with *Re:* or *In re:* (meaning "concerning" or "in the matter of"). The subject line may take a variety of forms, including the following:

Subject: RainMaster Sprinklers
About your February 2, 2009, order
FALL 2009 SALES MEETING
Reference Order No. 27920

- **Second-page heading.** Use a second-page heading whenever an additional page is required. Some companies have second-page letterhead (with the company name and address on one line and in a smaller typeface). The heading bears the name (person or organization) from the first line of the inside address, the page number, the date, and perhaps a reference number. Leave two blank lines before the body. Make sure that at least two lines of a continued paragraph appear on the first and second pages. Never allow the closing lines to appear alone on a continued page. Precede the complimentary close or signature lines with at least two lines of the body. Also, don't hyphenate the last word on a page. All the following are acceptable forms for second-page headings:

Ms. Melissa Baker
May 10, 2009
Page 2
Ms. Melissa Baker, May 10, 2009, Page 2
Ms. Melissa Baker -2- May 10, 2009

- **Company name.** If you include the company's name in the signature block, put it all in capital letters a double space below the complimentary close. You usually include the company's name in the signature block only when the writer is serving as the company's official spokesperson or when letterhead has not been used.

- **Reference initials.** When businesspeople keyboard their own letters, reference initials are unnecessary, so they are becoming rare. When one person dictates a letter and another person produces it, reference initials show who

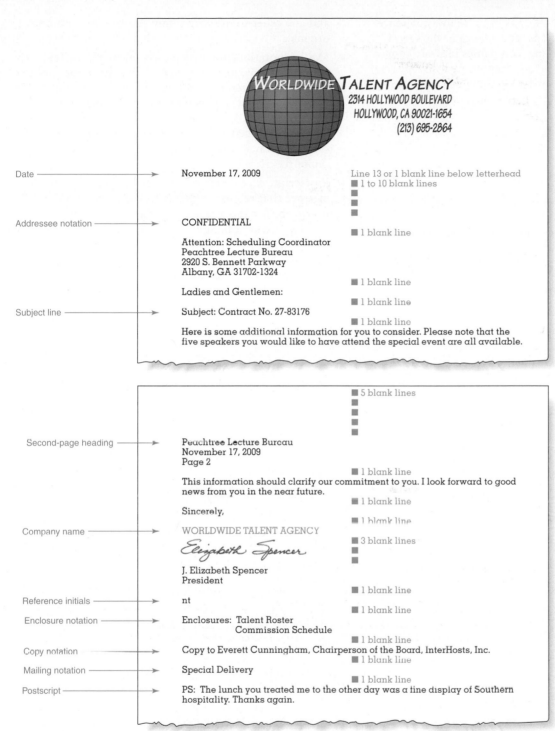

Figure A.2   Additional Letter Parts

helped prepare it. Place initials at the left margin, a double space below the signature block. When the signature block includes the writer's name, use only the preparer's initials. If the signature block includes only the department, use both sets of initials, usually in one of the following forms: *RSR/sm, RSR:sm,* or *RSR:SM* (writer/preparer). When the writer and the signer are different people, at least the file copy should bear both their initials as well as the typist's: *JFS/RSR/sm* (signer/writer/preparer).

- **Enclosure notation.** Enclosure notations appear at the bottom of a letter, one or two lines below the reference initials. Some common forms include the following:

  Enclosure

  Enclosures (2)

  Enclosures: Résumé
       Photograph
       Attachment

- **Copy notation.** Copy notations may follow reference initials or enclosure notations. They indicate who's receiving a *courtesy copy* (*cc*). Some companies indicate copies made on a photocopier (*pc*), or they simply use *copy* (*c*). Recipients are listed in order of rank or (rank being equal) in alphabetical order. Among the forms used are the following:

  cc: David Wentworth, Vice President

  pc: Dr. Martha Littlefield

  Copy to Hans Vogel

  748 Chesterton Road

  Snohomish, WA 98290

  c: Joseph Martinez with brochure and technical sheet

  When sending copies to readers without other recipients knowing, place *bc*, *bcc*, or *bpc* ("blind copy," "blind courtesy copy," or "blind photocopy") along with the name and any other information only on the copy, not on the original.

- **Mailing notation.** You may place a mailing notation (such as *Special Delivery* or *Registered Mail*) at the bottom of the letter, after reference initials or enclosure notations (whichever is last) and before copy notations. Or you may place it at the top of the letter, either above the inside address on the left side or just below the date on the right side. For greater visibility, mailing notations may appear in capital letters.

- **Postscript.** A postscript is an afterthought to the letter, a message that requires emphasis, or a personal note. It is usually the last thing on any letter and may be preceded by *P.S.*, *PS.*, *PS:*, or nothing at all. A second afterthought would be designated *P.P.S.* (post postscript). Since postscripts usually indicate poor planning, generally avoid them. However, they're common in sales letters as a punch line to remind readers of a benefit for taking advantage of the offer.

Figure A.3 Block Letter Format

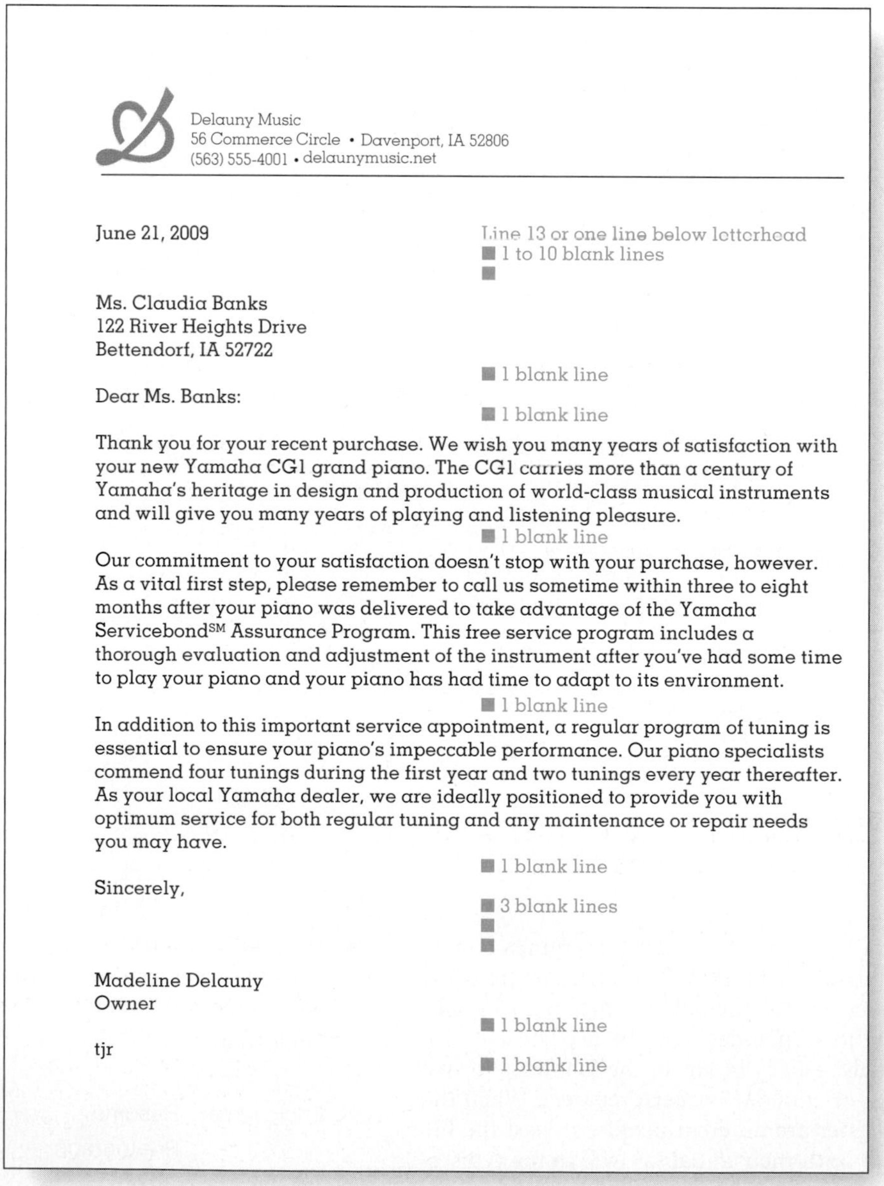

Delauny Music
56 Commerce Circle • Davenport, IA 52806
(563) 555-4001 • delaunymusic.net

June 21, 2009 — Line 13 or one line below letterhead; 1 to 10 blank lines

Ms. Claudia Banks
122 River Heights Drive
Bettendorf, IA 52722

■ 1 blank line

Dear Ms. Banks:

■ 1 blank line

Thank you for your recent purchase. We wish you many years of satisfaction with your new Yamaha CG1 grand piano. The CG1 carries more than a century of Yamaha's heritage in design and production of world-class musical instruments and will give you many years of playing and listening pleasure.

■ 1 blank line

Our commitment to your satisfaction doesn't stop with your purchase, however. As a vital first step, please remember to call us sometime within three to eight months after your piano was delivered to take advantage of the Yamaha Servicebond℠ Assurance Program. This free service program includes a thorough evaluation and adjustment of the instrument after you've had some time to play your piano and your piano has had time to adapt to its environment.

■ 1 blank line

In addition to this important service appointment, a regular program of tuning is essential to ensure your piano's impeccable performance. Our piano specialists commend four tunings during the first year and two tunings every year thereafter. As your local Yamaha dealer, we are ideally positioned to provide you with optimum service for both regular tuning and any maintenance or repair needs you may have.

■ 1 blank line

Sincerely,

■ 3 blank lines

Madeline Delauny
Owner

■ 1 blank line

tjr

■ 1 blank line

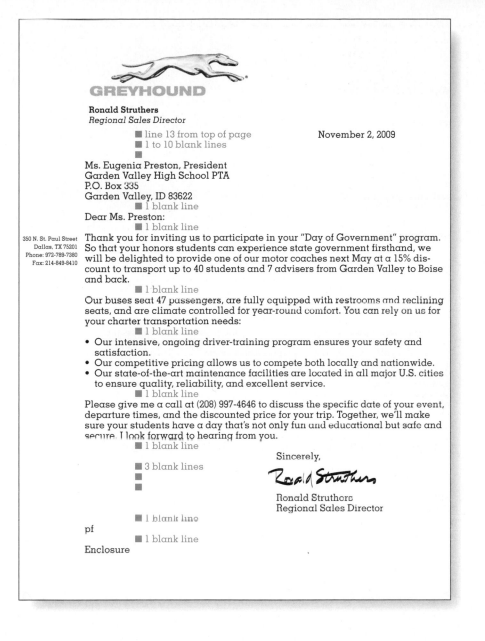

Letter Formats

A letter format is the way of arranging all the basic letter parts. Sometimes a company adopts a certain format as its policy; sometimes the individual letter writer or preparer is allowed to choose the most appropriate format. In the United States, three major letter formats are commonly used:

- **Block format.** Each letter part begins at the left margin. The main advantage is quick and efficient preparation (see Figure A.3).

- **Modified block format.** Same as block format, except that the date, complimentary close, and signature block start near the center of the page (see Figure A.4). The modified block format does permit indentions as an option. This format mixes preparation speed with traditional placement of some letter parts. It also looks more balanced on the page than the block format does.

- **Simplified format.** Instead of using a salutation, this format often weaves the reader's name into the first line or two of the body and often includes a subject line in capital letters (see Figure A.5). With no complimentary close, your signature appears after the body, followed by your printed (or typewritten) name (usually in all capital letters). This format is convenient when you don't know the reader's name; however, some people object to it as mechanical and impersonal (a drawback you can overcome with a warm writing style). Because certain letter parts are eliminated, some line spacing is changed.

These three formats differ in the way paragraphs are indented, in the way letter parts are placed, and in some punctuation. However, the elements are always separated by at least one blank line, and the printed (or typewritten) name is always separated from the line above by at least three blank lines to allow space for a signature. If paragraphs are indented, the indention is normally five spaces. The most common formats for intercultural business letters are the block style and the modified block style.

In addition to these three letter formats, letters may also be classified according to their style of punctuation. *Standard,* or

Figure A.5 Simplified Letter Format

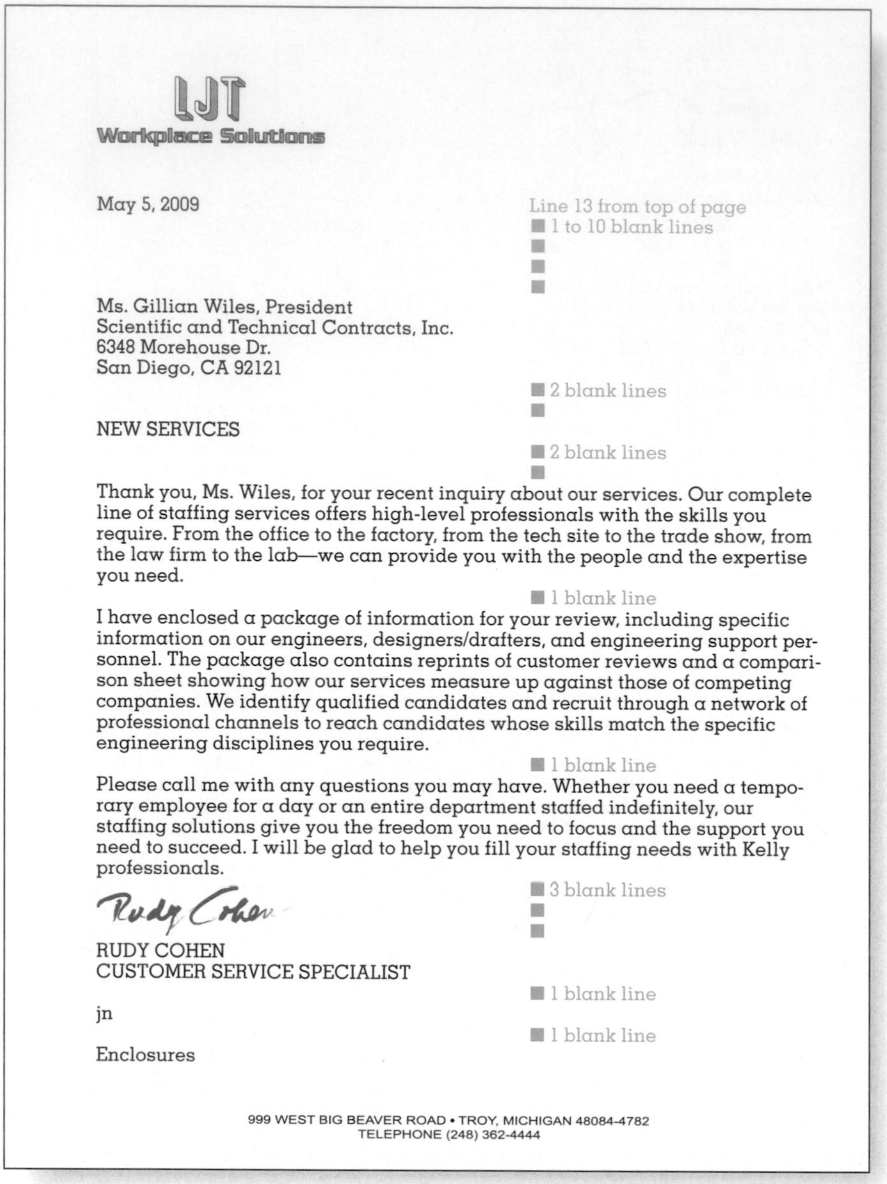

LJT
Workplace Solutions

May 5, 2009
Line 13 from top of page
■ 1 to 10 blank lines
■
■
■

Ms. Gillian Wiles, President
Scientific and Technical Contracts, Inc.
6348 Morehouse Dr.
San Diego, CA 92121
■ 2 blank lines
■

NEW SERVICES
■ 2 blank lines
■

Thank you, Ms. Wiles, for your recent inquiry about our services. Our complete line of staffing services offers high-level professionals with the skills you require. From the office to the factory, from the tech site to the trade show, from the law firm to the lab—we can provide you with the people and the expertise you need.
■ 1 blank line

I have enclosed a package of information for your review, including specific information on our engineers, designers/drafters, and engineering support personnel. The package also contains reprints of customer reviews and a comparison sheet showing how our services measure up against those of competing companies. We identify qualified candidates and recruit through a network of professional channels to reach candidates whose skills match the specific engineering disciplines you require.
■ 1 blank line

Please call me with any questions you may have. Whether you need a temporary employee for a day or an entire department staffed indefinitely, our staffing solutions give you the freedom you need to focus and the support you need to succeed. I will be glad to help you fill your staffing needs with Kelly professionals.
■ 3 blank lines
■
■

Rudy Cohen

RUDY COHEN
CUSTOMER SERVICE SPECIALIST
■ 1 blank line

jn
■ 1 blank line

Enclosures

999 WEST BIG BEAVER ROAD • TROY, MICHIGAN 48084-4782
TELEPHONE (248) 362-4444

mixed, punctuation uses a colon after the salutation (a comma if the letter is social or personal) and a comma after the complimentary close. *Open punctuation* uses no colon or comma after the salutation or the complimentary close. Although the most popular style in business communication is mixed punctuation, either style of punctuation may be used with block or modified block letter formats. Because the simplified letter format has no salutation or complimentary close, the style of punctuation is irrelevant.

Envelopes

For a first impression, the quality of the envelope is just as important as the quality of the stationery. Letterhead and envelopes should be of the same paper stock, have the same color ink, and be imprinted with the same address and logo. Most envelopes used by U.S. businesses are No. 10 envelopes (9½ inches long), which are sized for an 8½-by-11-inch piece of paper folded in thirds. Some occasions call for a smaller, No. 6¾,

envelope or for envelopes proportioned to fit special stationery. Figure A.6 shows the two most common sizes.

Addressing the Envelope

No matter what size the envelope, the address is always single-spaced with all lines aligned on the left. The address on the envelope is in the same style as the inside address and presents the same information. The order to follow is from the smallest division to the largest:

1. Name and title of recipient
2. Name of department or subgroup
3. Name of organization
4. Name of building
5. Street address and suite number, or post office box number
6. City, state, or province, and zip code or postal code
7. Name of country (if the letter is being sent abroad)

Because the U.S. Postal Service uses optical scanners to sort mail, envelopes for quantity mailings, in particular, should be

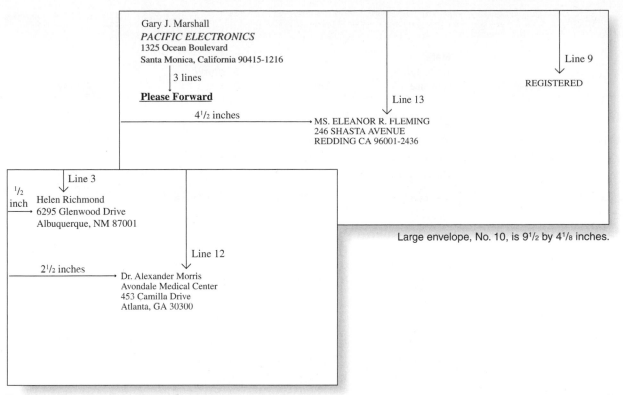

Figure A.6   **Prescribed Envelope Format**

addressed in the prescribed format. Everything is in capital letters, no punctuation is included, and all mailing instructions of interest to the post office are placed above the address area (see Figure A.6). Canada Post requires a similar format, except that only the city is all in capitals, and the postal code is placed on the line below the name of the city. The post office scanners read addresses from the bottom up, so if a letter is to be sent to a post office box rather than to a street address, the street address should appear on the line above the box number. Figure A.6 also shows the proper spacing for addresses and return addresses.

The U.S. Postal Service and the Canada Post Corporation have published lists of two-letter mailing abbreviations for states, provinces, and territories (see Table A.6). Postal authorities prefer no punctuation with these abbreviations, but some executives prefer to have state and province names spelled out in full and set off from city names by a comma. The issue is unresolved, although the comma is most often included. Quantity mailings follow post office requirements. For other letters, a reasonable compromise is to use traditional punctuation, uppercase and lowercase letters for names and street addresses, but two-letter state or province abbreviations, as shown here:

Mr. Kevin Kennedy

2107 E. Packer Dr.

Amarillo, TX 79108

For all out-of-office correspondence, use zip and postal codes that have been assigned to speed mail delivery. The U.S. Postal Service has divided the United States and its territories into 10 zones (0 to 9); this digit comes first in the zip code. The second and third digits represent smaller geographical areas within a state, and the last two digits identify a "local delivery area." Canadian postal codes are alphanumeric, with a three-character "area code" and a three-character "local code" separated by a single space (K2P 5A5). Zip and postal codes should be separated from state and province names by one space. Canadian postal codes may be treated the same or may be put in the bottom line of the address all by itself.

The U.S. Postal Service has added zip + 4 codes, which add a hyphen and four more numbers to the standard zip codes. The first two of the new numbers may identify an area as small as a single large building, and the last two digits may identify one floor in a large building or even a specific department of an organization. The zip + 4 codes are especially useful for business correspondence. The Canada Post Corporation achieves the same result with special postal codes assigned to buildings and organizations that receive a large volume of mail.

Folding to Fit

The way a letter is folded also contributes to the recipient's overall impression of your organization's professionalism. When sending a standard-size piece of paper in a No. 10 envelope, fold it in thirds, with the bottom folded up first and the top folded down over it (see Figure A.7); the open end should be at the top of the envelope and facing out. Fit smaller stationery neatly into the appropriate envelope simply by folding it in half or in thirds. When sending a standard-size letterhead in a No. 6¾ envelope, fold it in half from top to bottom and then in thirds from side to side.

TABLE A.6 Two-Letter Mailing Abbreviations for the United States and Canada

State/Territory/Province	Abbreviation	State/Territory/Province	Abbreviation	State/Territory/Province	Abbreviation
UNITED STATES		Massachusetts	MA	Texas	TX
Alabama	AL	Michigan	MI	Utah	UT
Alaska	AK	Minnesota	MN	Vermont	VT
American Samoa	AS	Mississippi	MS	Virginia	VA
Arizona	AZ	Missouri	MO	Virgin Islands	VI
Arkansas	AR	Montana	MT	Washington	WA
California	CA	Nebraska	NE	West Virginia	WV
Canal Zone	CZ	Nevada	NV	Wisconsin	WI
Colorado	CO	New Hampshire	NH	Wyoming	WY
Connecticut	CT	New Jersey	NJ	**CANADA**	
Delaware	DE	New Mexico	NM	Alberta	AB
District of Columbia	DC	New York	NY	British Columbia	BC
Florida	FL	North Carolina	NC	Labrador	NL
Georgia	GA	North Dakota	ND	Manitoba	MB
Guam	GU	Northern Mariana	MP	New Brunswick	NB
Hawaii	HI	Ohio	OH	Newfoundland	NL
Idaho	ID	Oklahoma	OK	Northwest Territories	NT
Illinois	IL	Oregon	OR	Nova Scotia	NS
Indiana	IN	Pennsylvania	PA	Nunavur	NU
Iowa	IA	Puerto Rico	PR	Ontario	ON
Kansas	KS	Rhode Island	RI	Prince Edward Island	PE
Kentucky	KY	South Carolina	SC	Quebec	PQ
Louisiana	LA	South Dakota	SD	Saskatchewan	SK
Maine	ME	Tennessee	TN	Yukon Territory	YT
Maryland	MD	Trust Territories	TT		

International Mail

Postal service differs from country to country, so it's always a good idea to investigate the quality and availability of various services before sending messages and packages internationally. Also, compare the services offered by delivery companies such as UPS, FedEx, and DHL to find the best rates and options for each destination and type of shipment. No matter which service you choose, be aware that international mail requires more planning than domestic mail. For example, for anything beyond simple letters, you generally need to prepare *customs forms* and possibly other documents, depending on the country of destination and the type of shipment. You are responsible for following the laws of the United States and any countries to which you send mail and packages.

The U.S. Postal Service currently offers four classes of international delivery, listed here from the fastest (and most expensive) to the slowest (and least expensive):

- **Global Express Guaranteed** is the fastest option. This service, offered in conjunction with FedEx, provides delivery in one to three business days to more than 190 countries and territories.

- **Express Mail International** guarantees delivery in three to five business days to a limited number of countries, including Australia, China, Hong Kong, Japan, and South Korea.

- **Priority Mail International** offers delivery guarantees of 6 to 10 business days to more than 190 countries and territories.

- **First Class Mail International** is an economical way to send correspondence and packages weighing up to four pounds to virtually any destination worldwide.

To prepare your mail for international delivery, follow the instructions provided at www.usps.com/business/international. There you'll find complete information on the

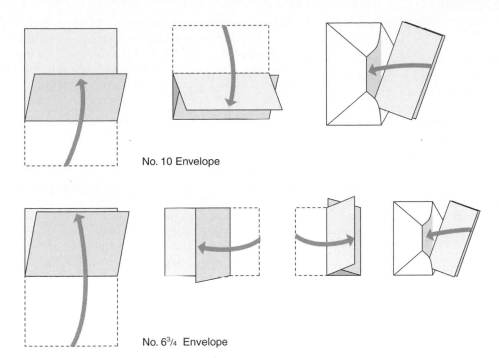

No. 10 Envelope

No. 6³/₄ Envelope

international services available through the U.S. Postal Service, along with advice on addressing and packaging mail, completing customs forms, and calculating postage rates and fees. The *International Mail Manual*, also available on this website, offers the latest information and regulations for both outbound and inbound international mail. For instance, you can click on individual country names to see current information about restricted or prohibited items and materials, required customs forms, and rates for various classes of service.[9] Various countries have specific and often extensive lists of items that may not be sent by mail at all or that must be sent using particular postal service options.

Memos

Many organizations have memo forms preprinted, with labeled spaces for the recipient's name (or sometimes a checklist of all departments in an organization or all persons in a department), the sender's name, the date, and the subject (see Figure A.8). If such forms don't exist, you can use a memo template (which comes with word processing software and provides margin settings, headings, and special formats), or you can use plain paper.

On your document, include a title such as MEMO or INTEROFFICE CORRESPONDENCE (all in capitals) centered at the top of the page or aligned with the left margin. Also at the top, include the words *To, From, Date,* and *Subject*—followed by the appropriate information—with a blank line between as shown here:

MEMO

TO:

FROM:

DATE:

SUBJECT:

Sometimes the heading is organized like this:

MEMO

TO:	DATE:
FROM:	SUBJECT:

You can arrange these four pieces of information in almost any order. The date sometimes appears without the heading *Date.* The subject may be presented with the letters *Re:* (in place of *SUBJECT:*) or may even be presented without any heading (but in capital letters so that it stands out clearly). You may want to include a file or reference number, introduced by the word *File.*

MEMO

TO: _____

DEPT: _____ FROM: _____

DATE: _____ TELEPHONE: _____

SUBJECT: _____ *For your* ☐ APPROVAL ☐ INFORMATION ☐ COMMENT

Figure A.8   **Preprinted Memo Form**

The following guidelines will help you effectively format specific memo elements:

- **Addressees.** When sending a memo to a long list of people, include the notation *See distribution list* or *See below* in the *To* position at the top; then list the names at the end of the memo. Arrange this list alphabetically, except when high-ranking officials deserve more prominent placement. You can also address memos to groups of people—*All Sales Representatives, Production Group, New Product Team.*
- **Courtesy titles.** You need not use courtesy titles anywhere in a memo; first initials and last names, first names, or even initials alone are often sufficient. However, use a courtesy title if you would use one in a face-to-face encounter with the person.
- **Subject line.** The subject line of a memo helps busy colleagues quickly find out what your memo is about. Although the subject "line" may overflow onto a second line, it's most helpful when it's short (but still informative).
- **Body.** Start the body of the memo on the second or third line below the heading. Like the body of a letter, it's usually single-spaced with blank lines between paragraphs. Indenting paragraphs is optional. Handle lists, important passages, and subheadings as you do in letters. If the memo is very short, you may double-space it.
- **Second page.** If the memo carries over to a second page, head the second page just as you head the second page of a letter.
- **Writer's initials.** Unlike a letter, a memo doesn't require a complimentary close or a signature, because your name is already prominent at the top. However, you may initial the memo—either beside the name appearing at the top of the memo or at the bottom of the memo—or you may even sign your name at the bottom, particularly if the memo deals with money or confidential matters.
- **Other elements.** Treat elements such as reference initials, enclosure notations, and copy notations just as you would in a letter.

Figure A.9 A Typical E-Mail Message

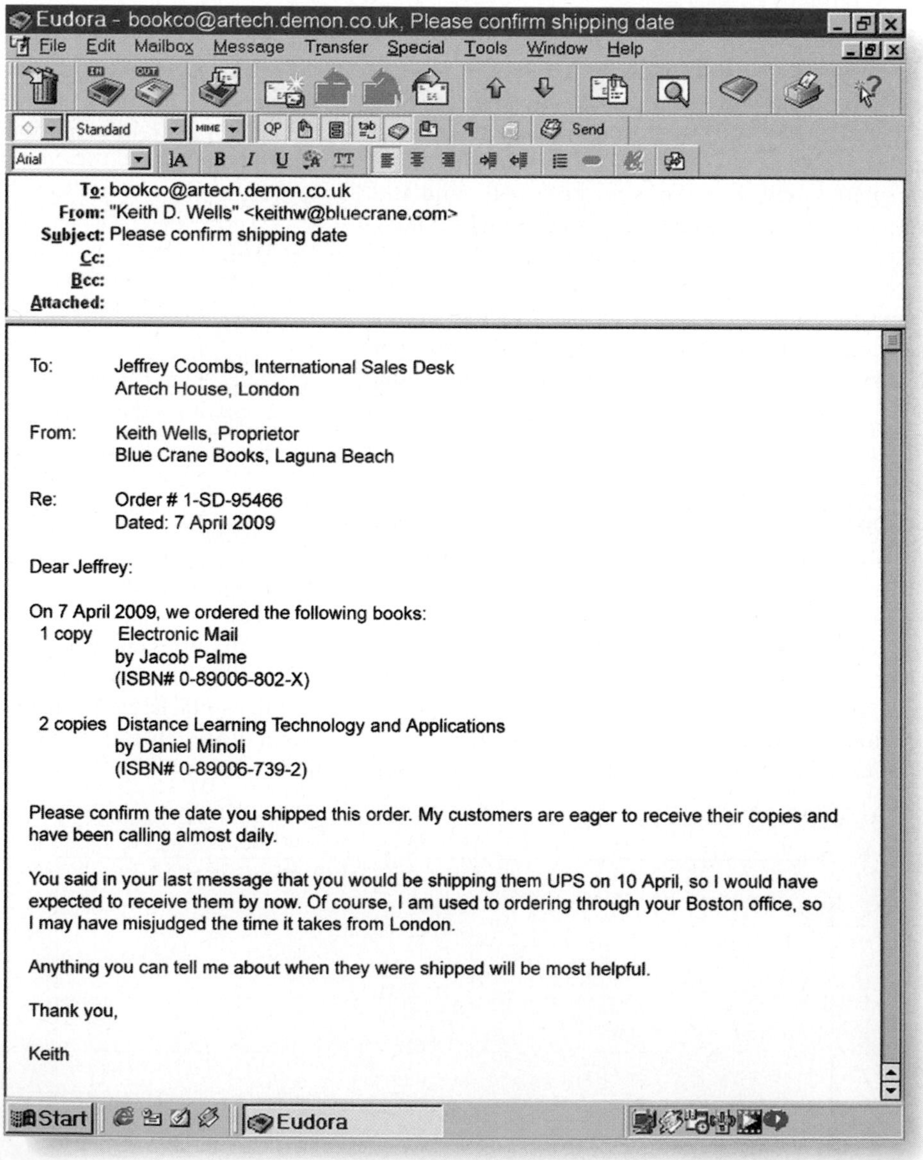

To: bookco@artech.demon.co.uk
From: "Keith D. Wells" <keithw@bluecrane.com>
Subject: Please confirm shipping date
Cc:
Bcc:
Attached:

To: Jeffrey Coombs, International Sales Desk
Artech House, London

From: Keith Wells, Proprietor
Blue Crane Books, Laguna Beach

Re: Order # 1-SD-95466
Dated: 7 April 2009

Dear Jeffrey:

On 7 April 2009, we ordered the following books:

1 copy Electronic Mail
by Jacob Palme
(ISBN# 0-89006-802-X)

2 copies Distance Learning Technology and Applications
by Daniel Minoli
(ISBN# 0-89006-739-2)

Please confirm the date you shipped this order. My customers are eager to receive their copies and have been calling almost daily.

You said in your last message that you would be shipping them UPS on 10 April, so I would have expected to receive them by now. Of course, I am used to ordering through your Boston office, so I may have misjudged the time it takes from London.

Anything you can tell me about when they were shipped will be most helpful.

Thank you,

Keith

Memos may be delivered by hand, by the post office (when the recipient works at a different location), or through interoffice mail. Interoffice mail may require the use of special reusable envelopes that have spaces for the recipient's name and department or room number; the name of the previous recipient is simply crossed out. If a regular envelope is used, the words *Interoffice Mail* appear where the stamp normally goes, so that it won't accidentally be stamped and mailed with the rest of the office correspondence.

Informal, routine, or brief reports for distribution within a company are often presented in memo form. Don't include report parts such as a table of contents and appendixes, but write the body of the memo report just as carefully as you'd write a formal report.

E-Mail

Because e-mail messages can act both as memos (carrying information within your company) and as letters (carrying information outside your company and around the world), their format depends on your audience and purpose. You may choose to have your e-mail resemble a formal letter or a detailed report, or you may decide to keep things as simple as an interoffice memo. A modified memo format is appropriate for most e-mail messages.[10] All e-mail programs include two major elements: the header and the body (see Figure A.9).

Header

The e-mail header depends on the particular program you use. Some programs even allow you to choose between a shorter and a longer version. However, most headers contain similar information:

- **To:** Contains the audience's e-mail address (see Figure A.10). Most e-mail programs also allow you to send mail to an entire group of people all at once. First, you create a distribution list.

Then you type the name of the list in the *To:* line instead of typing the addresses of every person in the group.[11] The most common e-mail addresses are addresses such as

nmaa.betsy@c.si.edu (Smithsonian Institute's National Museum of American Art)

webwsj@dowjones.com (*Wall Street Journal*)

relpubli@mairie-toulouse.mipnet.fr (Municipal Services, Toulouse, France)

- **From:** Contains your e-mail address.
- **Date:** Contains the day of the week, date (day, month, year), time, and time zone.
- **Subject:** Describes the content of the message and presents an opportunity for you to build interest in your message.
- **Cc:** Allows you to send copies of a message to more than one person at a time. It also allows everyone on the list to see who else received the same message.
- **Bcc:** Lets you send copies to people without the other recipients knowing—a practice considered unethical by some.[12]
- **Attachments:** Contains the name(s) of the file(s) you attach to your e-mail message. The file can be a word processing document, a digital image, an audio or video message, a spreadsheet, or a software program.[13]

Most e-mail programs now allow you the choice of hiding or revealing other lines that contain more detailed information, including

- **Message-Id:** The exact location of this e-mail message on the sender's system
- **X-mailer:** The version of the e-mail program being used

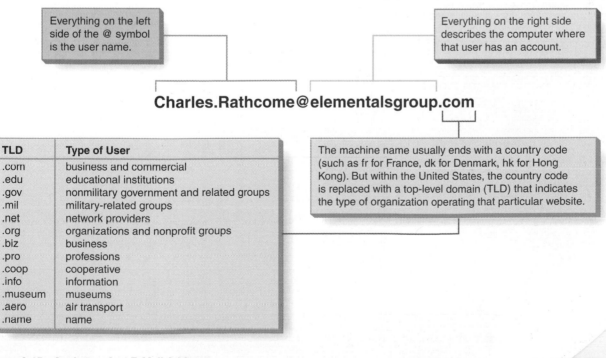

Everything on the left side of the @ symbol is the user name.

Everything on the right side describes the computer where that user has an account.

Charles.Rathcome@elementalsgroup.com

TLD	Type of User
.com	business and commercial
.edu	educational institutions
.gov	nonmilitary government and related groups
.mil	military-related groups
.net	network providers
.org	organizations and nonprofit groups
.biz	business
.pro	professions
.coop	cooperative
.info	information
.museum	museums
.aero	air transport
.name	name

The machine name usually ends with a country code (such as fr for France, dk for Denmark, hk for Hong Kong). But within the United States, the country code is replaced with a top-level domain (TLD) that indicates the type of organization operating that particular website.

Figure A.10   Anatomy of an E-Mail Address

- **Content type:** A description of the text and character set that is contained in the message
- **Received:** Information about each of the systems your e-mail passed through en route to your mailbox[14]

Body

The rest of the space below the header is for the body of your message. In the *To:* and *From:* lines, some headers actually print out the names of the sender and receiver (in addition to their e-mail addresses). Other headers do not. If your mail program includes only the e-mail addresses, you might consider including your own memo-type header in the body of your message, as in Figure A.9. The writer even included a second, more specific subject line in his memo-type header. Some recipients may applaud the clarity of such second headers; however, others will criticize the space it takes. Your decision depends on how formal you want to be.

Do include a greeting in your e-mail. As pointed out in Chapter 7, greetings personalize your message. Leave one line space above and below your greeting to set it off from the rest of your message. You may end your greeting with a colon (formal), a comma (conversational), or even two hyphens (informal)—depending on the level of formality you want.

Your message begins one blank line space below your greeting. Just as in memos and letters, skip one line space between paragraphs and include headings, numbered lists, bulleted lists, and embedded lists when appropriate.

One blank line space below your message, include a simple closing, often just one word. A blank line space below

that, include your signature. Whether you type your name or use a signature file, including your signature personalizes your message.

Reports

Enhance your report's effectiveness by paying careful attention to its appearance and layout. Follow whatever guidelines your organization prefers, always being neat and consistent throughout. If it's up to you to decide formatting questions, the following conventions may help you decide how to handle margins, headings, and page numbers.

Margins

All margins on a report page are at least 1 inch wide. For double-spaced pages, use 1-inch margins; for single-spaced pages, set margins between 1¼ and 1½ inches. The top, left, and right margins are usually the same, but the bottom margins can be 1½ times deeper. Some special pages also have deeper top margins. Set top margins as deep as 2 inches for pages that contain major titles: prefatory parts (such as the table of contents or the executive summary), supplementary parts (such as the reference notes or bibliography), and textual parts (such as the first page of the text or the first page of each chapter).

If you're going to bind your report at the left or at the top, add half an inch to the margin on the bound edge (see Figure A.11): The space taken by the binding on left-bound reports makes the center point of the text a quarter inch to the right of the center of the paper. Be sure to center headings between the margins, not between the edges of the paper. The "center"

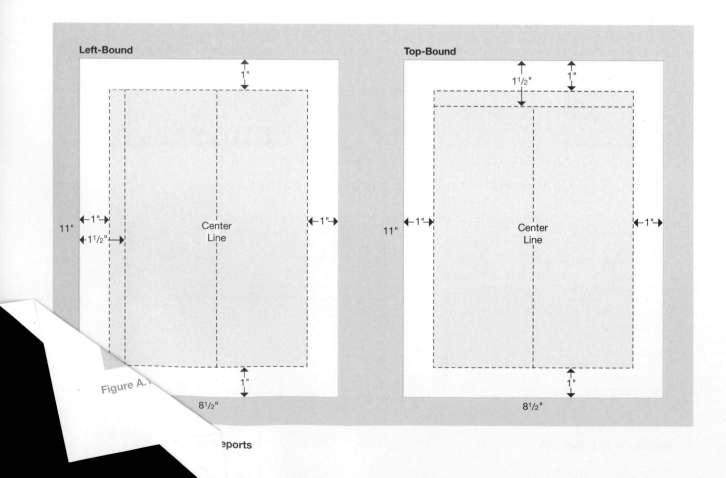

Figure A.

eports

paragraph format setting in your word processor does this automatically.

Headings

Headings of various levels provide visual clues to a report's organization. Figure 12.3, on page 315, illustrates one good system for showing these levels, but many variations exist. No matter which system you use, be sure to be consistent.

Page Numbers

Remember that every page in the report is counted; however, not all pages show numbers. The first page of the report, normally the title page, is unnumbered. All other pages in the prefatory section are numbered with a lowercase roman numeral, beginning with *ii* and continuing with *iii, iv, v,* and so on. The unadorned (no dashes, no period) page number is centered at the bottom margin.

Number the first page of the text of the report with the unadorned arabic numeral 1, centered at the bottom margin (double- or triple-spaced below the text). In left-bound reports, number the following pages (including the supplementary parts) consecutively with unadorned arabic numerals (2, 3, and so on), placed at the top right-hand margin (double- or triple-spaced above the text). For top-bound reports and for special pages having 2-inch top margins, center the page numbers at the bottom margin.

DOCUMENTATION OF REPORT SOURCES

By providing information about your sources, you improve your own credibility as well as the credibility of the facts and opinions you present. Documentation gives readers the means for checking your findings and pursuing the subject further. Also, documenting your report is the accepted way to give credit to the people whose work you have drawn from.

What style should you use to document your report? Experts recommend various forms, depending on your field or discipline. Moreover, your employer or client may use a form different from those the experts suggest. Don't let this discrepancy confuse you. If your employer specifies a form, use it; the standardized form is easier for colleagues to understand. However, if the choice of form is left to you, adopt one of the styles described here. Whatever style you choose, be consistent within any given report, using the same order, punctuation, and format from one reference citation or bibliography entry to the next.

A wide variety of style manuals provide detailed information on documentation. These publications explain the three most commonly used styles:

- American Psychological Association, *Publication Manual of the American Psychological Association*, 5th ed. (Washington, D.C.: American Psychological Association, 2001). Details the author–date system, which is preferred in the social sciences and often in the natural sciences as well.

- *The Chicago Manual of Style*, 15th ed. (Chicago: University of Chicago Press, 2003). Often referred to only as "*Chicago*" and widely used in the publishing industry; provides detailed treatment of source documentation and many other aspects of document preparation.

- Joseph Gibaldi, *MLA Style Manual and Guide to Scholarly Publishing*, 3rd ed. (New York: Modern Language Association, 2008). Serves as the basis for the note and bibliography style used in much academic writing and is recommended in many college textbooks on writing term papers; provides a lot of examples in the humanities.

For more information on these three guides, visit http://real-timeupdates.com/bce and click on Appendix B. Although many schemes have been proposed for organizing the information in source notes, all of them break the information into parts: (1) information about the author (name), (2) information about the work (title, edition, volume number), (3) information about the publication (place, publisher), (4) information about the date, and (5) information on page ranges.

In the following sections, we summarize the major conventions for documenting sources in three styles: *The Chicago Manual of Style* (Chicago), the *Publication Manual of the American Psychological Association* (APA), and the *MLA Style*

Chicago Humanities Style

The Chicago Manual of Style recommends two types of documentation systems. The *documentary-note*, or *humanities*, style gives bibliographic citations in notes—either footnotes (when printed at the bottom of a page) or endnotes (when printed at the end of the report). The humanities system is often used in literature, history, and the arts. The other system strongly recommended by *Chicago* is the *author-date* system, which cites the author's last name and the date of publication in the text, usually in parentheses, reserving full documentation for the reference list (or bibliography). For the purpose of comparing styles, we will concentrate on the humanities system, which is described in detail in *Chicago*.

In-Text Citation—Chicago Humanities Style

To document report sources in text, the humanities system relies on superscripts—arabic numerals placed just above the line of type at the end of the reference:

> Toward the end of his speech, Myers sounded a note of caution, saying that even though the economy is expected to grow, it could easily slow a bit.[10]

The superscript lets the reader know how to look for source information in either a footnote or an endnote (see Figure B.1). Some readers prefer footnotes so that they can simply glance at the bottom of the page for information. Others prefer endnotes so that they can read the text without a clutter of notes on the page. Also, endnotes relieve the writer from worrying about how long each note will be and how much space it will take away from the page. Both footnotes and endnotes are handled automatically by today's word processing software.

For the reader's convenience, you can use footnotes for **content notes** (which may supplement your main text with asides about a particular issue or event, provide a cross-reference to another section of your report, or direct the reader to a related source). Then you can use endnotes for **source notes** (which document direct quotations, paraphrased passages, and visual aids). Consider which type of note is most common in your report, and then choose whether to present these notes all as endnotes or all as footnotes. Regardless of the method you choose for referencing textual information in your report, notes for visual aids (both content notes and source notes) are placed on the same page as the visual.

Bibliography—Chicago Humanities Style

The humanities system may or may not be accompanied by a bibliography (because the notes give all the necessary bibliographic information). However, endnotes are arranged in order of appearance in the text, so an alphabetical bibliography can be valuable to your readers. The bibliography may be titled *Bibliography, Reference List, Sources, Works Cited* (if you include only those sources you actually cited in your report), or *Works Consulted* (if you include uncited sources as well). This list of

NOTES

Journal article with volume and issue numbers

1. James Assira, "Are They Speaking English in Japan?" *Journal of Business Communication* 36, no. 4 (Fall 2002): 72.

Brochure

2. BestTemp Staffing Services, *An Employer's Guide to Staffing Services,* 2d ed. (Denver: BestTemp Information Center, 2000), 31.

Newspaper article, no author

3. "Buying Asian Supplies on the Net," *Los Angeles Times,* 12 February 2000, sec. D, p. 3.

Annual report

4. The Walt Disney Company, *2007 Annual Report* (Burbank, Calif.: The Walt Disney Company, 2008), 48.

Magazine article

5. Kerry A. Dolan, "A Whole New Crop" *Forbes,* 2 June 2008, 72–75.

Television broadcast

6. Daniel Han, "Trade Wars Heating Up Around the Globe," *CNN Headline News* (Atlanta: CNN, 5 March 2002).

Internet, World Wide Web

7. "Intel—Company Capsule," Hoover's Online [cited 19 June 2008], 3 screens; available from www.hoovers.com/intel/-ID_13787-/free-co-factsheet.xhtml.

Book, component parts

8. Sonja Kuntz, "Moving Beyond Benefits," in *Our Changing Workforce,* ed. Randolf Jacobson (New York: Citadel Press, 2001), 213–27.

Unpublished dissertation or thesis

9. George H. Morales, "The Economic Pressures on Industrialized Nations in a Global Economy" (Ph.D. diss., University of San Diego, 2001), 32–47.

Paper presented at a meeting

10. Charles Myers, "HMOs in Today's Environment" (paper presented at the Conference on Medical Insurance Solution, Chicago, Ill., August 2001), 16–17.

Online magazine article

11. Leo Babauta, "17 Tips to Be Productive with Instant Messaging," in *Web Worker Daily* [online] (San Francisco, 2007 [updated 14 November 2007; cited 14 February 2008]); available from http://webworkerdaily.com.

CD-ROM encyclopedia article, one author

12. Robert Parkings, "George Eastman," *The Concise Columbia Encyclopedia* (New York: Columbia University Press, 1998) [CD-ROM].

Interview

13. Georgia Stainer, general manager, Day Cable and Communications, interview by author, Topeka, Kan., 2 March 2000.

Newspaper article, one author

14. Evelyn Standish, "Global Market Crushes OPEC's Delicate Balance of Interests," *Wall Street Journal,* 19 January 2002, sec. A, p. 1.

Book, two authors

15. Miriam Toller and Jay Fielding, *Global Business for Smaller Companies* (Rocklin, Calif.: Prima Publishing, 2001), 102–3.

Government publication

16. U.S. Department of Defense, *Stretching Research Dollars: Survival Advice for Universities and Government Labs* (Washington, D.C.: GPO, 2002), 126.

Figure B.1 Sample Endnotes—Chicago Humanities Style

sources may also serve as a reading list for those who want to pursue the subject of your report further, so you may want to annotate each entry—that is, comment on the subject matter and viewpoint of the source, as well as on its usefulness to readers. Annotations may be written in either complete or incomplete sentences. (See the annotated list of style manuals early in this appendix.) A bibliography may also be more manageable if you subdivide it into categories (a classified bibliography), either by type of reference (such as books, articles, and unpublished material) or by subject matter (such as government regulation, market forces, and so on). Following are the major conventions for developing a bibliography according to Chicago style (see Figure B.2):

- Exclude any page numbers that may be cited in source notes, except for journals, periodicals, and newspapers.

- Alphabetize entries by the last name of the lead author (listing last name first). The names of second and succeeding authors are listed in normal order. Entries without an author name are alphabetized by the first important word in the title.

- Format entries as hanging indents (indent second and succeeding lines three to five spaces).

- Arrange entries in the following general order: (1) author name, (2) title information, (3) publication information, (4) date, (5) periodical page range.

- Use quotation marks around the titles of magazines, newspapers, and journals. C and last words, as well as all other imp prepositions, articles, and coordin

BIBLIOGRAPHY

Assira, James. "Are They Speaking English in Japan?" *Journal of Business Communication* 36, no. 4 (Fall 2002): 72.

Babauta, Leo. "17 Tips to Be Productive with Instant Messaging," In *Web Worker Daily* [online], San Francisco, 2007 [updated 14 November 2007, cited 14 February 2008]. Available from http://webworkerdaily.com.

BestTemp Staffing Services. *An Employer's Guide to Staffing Services.* 2d ed. Denver: BestTemp Information Center, 2000.

"Buying Asian Supplies on the Net." *Los Angeles Times,* 12 February 2000, sec. D, p. 3.

Dolan, Kerry A. "A Whole New Crop," *Forbes,* 2 June 2008, 72–75.

Han, Daniel. "Trade Wars Heating Up Around the Globe." *CNN Headline News.* Atlanta: CNN, 5 March 2002.

"Intel—Company Capsule." *Hoover's Online* [cited 19 June 2008]. 3 screens; Available from www.hoovers.com/intel/-ID_13787-/free-co-factsheet.xhtml.

Kuntz, Sonja. "Moving Beyond Benefits." In *Our Changing Workforce*, edited by Randolf Jacobson. New York: Citadel Press, 2001.

Morales, George H. "The Economic Pressures on Industrialized Nations in a Global Economy." Ph.D. diss., University of San Diego, 2001.

Myers, Charles. "HMOs in Today's Environment." Paper presented at the Conference on Medical Insurance Solutions, Chicago, Ill., August 2001.

Parkings, Robert. "George Eastman." *The Concise Columbia Encyclopedia.* New York: Columbia University Press, 1998. [CD-ROM].

Stainer, Georgia, general manager, Day Cable and Communications. Interview by author. Topeka, Kan., 2 March 2000.

Standish, Evelyn. "Global Market Crushes OPEC's Delicate Balance of Interests." *Wall Street Journal,* 19 January 2002, sec. A, p. 1.

Toller, Miriam, and Jay Fielding. *Global Business for Smaller Companies.* Rocklin, Calif.: Prima Publishing, 2001.

U.S. Department of Defense. *Stretching Research Dollars: Survival Advice for Universities and Government Labs.* Washington, D.C.: GPO, 2002.

The Walt Disney Company, *2007 Annual Report,* Burbank, Calif.: The Walt Disney Company, 2008.

The labels in the left margin of the figure identify the source types:

- Journal article with volume and issue numbers
- Online magazine article
- Brochure
- Newspaper article, no author
- Magazine article
- Television broadcast
- Internet, World Wide Web
- Book, component parts
- Unpublished dissertation or thesis
- Paper presented at a meeting
- CD-ROM encyclopedia article, one author
- Interview
- Newspaper article, one author
- Book, two authors
- Government publication
- Annual report

Figure B.2   Sample Bibliography—Chicago Humanities Style

- Use italics to set off the names of books, newspapers, journals, and other complete publications. Capitalize the first and last words, as well as all other important words.

- For journal articles, include the volume number and the issue number (if necessary). Include the year of publication ~~inside~~ parentheses and follow with a colon and the page ~~of~~ the article: *Journal of Business Communication* 36, ~~no.~~ 72. (In this source, the volume is 36, the number ~~4,~~ page is 72.)

- Exp~~lain~~ from ~~...~~

- ~~Iden~~tify all electronic references: [Online ~~...~~]

- ~~...referen~~ces can be reached: Available ~~...~~ WWVL.

- Give the citation date for online references: Cited 23 August 2007.

APA Style

The American Psychological Association (APA) recommends the author–date system of documentation, which is popular in the physical, natural, and social sciences. When using this system, you simply insert the author's last name and the year of publication within parentheses following the text discussion of the material cited. Include a page number if you use a direct quote. This approach briefly identifies the source so that readers can locate complete information in the alphabetical reference list at the end of the report. The author–date system is both brief and clear, saving readers time and effort.

In-Text Citation—APA Style

To document report sources in text using APA style, insert the author's surname and the date of publication at the end of a statement. Enclose this information in parentheses. If the author's name is referred to in the text itself, then the name can be omitted from parenthetical material.

> Some experts recommend both translation and back-translation when dealing with any non-English-speaking culture (Assira, 2001).
>
> Toller and Fielding (2000) make a strong case for small companies succeeding in global business.

Personal communications and interviews conducted by the author would not be listed in the reference list at all. Such citations would appear in the text only.

> Increasing the role of cable companies is high on the list of Georgia Stainer, general manager at Day Cable and Communications (personal communication, March 2, 2007).

List of References—APA Style

For APA style, list only those works actually cited in the text (so you would not include works for background or for further reading). Report writers must choose their references judiciously. Following are the major conventions for developing a reference list according to APA style (see Figure B.3):

- Format entries as hanging indents.
- List all author names in reversed order (last name first), and use only initials for the first and middle names.
- Arrange entries in the following general order: (1) author name, (2) date, (3) title information, (4) publication information, (5) periodical page range.
- Follow the author name with the date of publication in parentheses.

Figure B.3 Sample References—APA Style

REFERENCES

Journal article with volume and issue numbers	Assira, J. (2002). Are they speaking English in Japan? *Journal of Business Communication, 36*(4), 72.
Online magazine article	Babauta, L. (2007, November 14), 17 tips to be productive with instant messaging. *Web Worker Daily*. Retrieved February 14, 2008, from http://webworkerdaily.com.
Brochure	BestTemp Staffing Services. (2000). *An employer's guide to staffing services* (2d ed.) [Brochure]. Denver: BestTemp Information Center.
Newspaper article, no author	Buying Asian supplies on the net. (2000, February 12). *Los Angeles Times*, p. D3.
Magazine article	Dolan, K. A. (2008, June 2). A whole new crop. *Forbes*, 72–75.
Television broadcast	Han, D. (2002, March 5). Trade wars heating up around the globe. *CNN Headline News*. [Television broadcast]. Atlanta, GA: CNN.
Internet, World Wide Web	Hoover's Online. (2003). *Intel—Company Capsule*. Retrieved June 19, 2008, from http://www.hoovers.com/intel/-ID_13787-/free-co-factsheet.xhtml.
Book, component parts	Kuntz, S. (2001). Moving beyond benefits. In Randolph Jacobson (Ed.), *Our changing workforce* (pp. 213–227). New York: Citadel Press.
Unpublished dissertation or thesis	Morales, G. H. (2001). *The economic pressures on industrialized nations in a global economy*. Unpublished doctoral dissertation, University of San Diego.
Paper presented at a meeting	Myers, C. (2001, August). *HMOs in today's environment*. Paper presented at the Conference on Medical Insurance Solutions, Chicago, IL.
CD-ROM encyclopedia article, one author	Parkings, R. (1998). George Eastman. On *The concise Columbia encyclopedia*. [CD-ROM]. New York: Columbia University Press.
Interview	*Cited in text only, not in the list of references.*
Newspaper article, one author	Standish, E. (2002, January 19). Global market crushes OPEC's delicate balance of interests. *Wall Street Journal*, p. A1.
Book, two authors	Toller, M., & Fielding, J. (2001). *Global business for smaller companies*. Rocklin, CA: Prima Publishing.
Government publication	U.S. Department of Defense. (2002). *Stretching research dollars: Survival advice for universities and government labs*. Washington, DC: U.S. Government Printing Office.
Annual report	The Walt Disney Company. (2008). *2007 Annual Report*. Burbank, Calif.: The Walt Disney Company.

- List titles of articles from magazines, newspapers, and journals without underlines or quotation marks. Capitalize only the first word of the title, any proper nouns, and the first word to follow an internal colon.

- Italicize titles of books, capitalizing only the first word, any proper nouns, and the first word to follow a colon.

- Italicize names of magazines, newspapers, journals, and other complete publications. Capitalize all the important words.

- For journal articles, include the volume number (in italics) and, if necessary, the issue number (in parentheses). Finally, include the page range of the article: *Journal of Business Communication, 36*(4), 72. (In this example, the volume is 36, the number is 4, and the page number is 72.)

- Include personal communications (such as letters, memos, e-mail, and conversations) only in text, not in reference lists.

- Electronic references include author, date of publication, title of article, name of publication (if one), volume, date of retrieval (month, day, year), and the source.

- For electronic references, indicate the actual year of publication and the exact date of retrieval.

- For electronic references, specify the URL; leave periods off the ends of URLs.

MLA Style

The style recommended by the Modern Language Association of America is used widely in the humanities, especially in the study of language and literature. Like APA style, MLA style uses brief parenthetical citations in the text. However, instead of including author name and year, MLA citations include author name and page reference.

Figure B.4 Sample Works Cited—MLA Style

Journal article with volume and issue numbers	Assira, James. "Are They Speaking English in Japan?" *Journal of Business Communication* 36, 4 (2002): 72.
Online magazine article	Babauta, Leo. "17 Tips to Be Productive with Instant Messaging," *Web Worker Daily* 14 Nov. 2007. 14 Feb. 2008. <http://webworkerdaily.com>.
Brochure	BestTemp Staffing Services. *An Employer's Guide to Staffing Services.* 2d ed. Denver: BestTemp Information Center, 2000.
Newspaper article, no author	"Buying Asian Supplies on the Net." *Los Angeles Times* 12 Feb. 2000: D3.
Magazine article	Dolan, Kerry A. "A Whole New Crop" *Forbes*, 2 June 2008: 72–75.
Television broadcast	Han, Daniel. "Trade Wars Heating Up Around the Globe." *CNN Headline News*. CNN, Atlanta. 5 Mar. 2002.
Internet, World Wide Web	"Intel—Company Capsule." *Hoover's Online.* 2008. Hoover's Company Information. 19 June 2008 <http://www.hoovers.com/intel/-ID_13787/free-co-factsheet.xhtml.
Book, component parts	Kuntz, Sonja. "Moving Beyond Benefits." *Our Changing Workforce*. Ed. Randolf Jacobson. New York: Citadel Press, 2001. 213–27.
Unpublished dissertation or thesis	Morales, George H. "The Economic Pressures on Industrialized Nations in a Global Economy." Diss. U of San Diego, 2001.
Paper presented at a meeting	Myers, Charles. "HMOs in Today's Environment." Conference on Medical Insurance Solutions. Chicago. 13 Aug. 2001.
CD-ROM encyclopedia article, one author	Parkings, Robert. "George Eastman." *The Concise Columbia Encyclopedia*. CD-ROM. New York: Columbia UP, 1998.
Interview	Stainer, Georgia, general manager, Day Cable and Communications. Telephone interview. 2 Mar. 2000.
Newspaper article, one author	Standish, Evelyn. "Global Market Crushes OPEC's Delicate Balance of Interests." *Wall Street Journal* 19 Jan. 2002: A1.
Book, two authors	Toller, Miriam, and Jay Fielding. *Global Business for Smaller Companies*. Rocklin, CA: Prima Publishing, 2001.
Government publication	United States. Department of Defense. *Stretching Research Dollars: Survival Advice for Universities and Government Labs*. Washington: GPO, 2002.
Annual report	The Walt Disney Company, *2007 Annual Report*. Calif.: The Walt Disney Company, 2008.

WORKS CITED

In-Text Citation—MLA Style

To document report sources in text using MLA style, insert the author's last name and a page reference inside parentheses following the cited material: (Matthews 63). If the author's name is mentioned in the text reference, the name can be omitted from the parenthetical citation: (63). The citation indicates that the reference came from page 63 of a work by Matthews. With the author's name, readers can find complete publication information in the alphabetically arranged list of works cited that comes at the end of the report.

> Some experts recommend both translation and back-translation when dealing with any non-English-speaking culture (Assira 72).

> Toller and Fielding make a strong case for small companies succeeding in global business (102–03).

List of Works Cited—MLA Style

The *MLA Style Manual* recommends preparing the list of works cited first so that you will know what information to give in the parenthetical citation (for example, whether to add a short title if you're citing more than one work by the same author, or whether to give an initial or first name if you're citing two authors who have the same last name). The list of works cited appears at the end of your report, contains all the works that you cite in your text, and lists them in alphabetical order. Following are the major conventions for developing a reference list according to MLA style (see Figure B.4):

- Format entries as hanging indents.
- Arrange entries in the following general order: (1) author name, (2) title information, (3) publication information, (4) date, (5) periodical page range.

- List the lead author's name in reverse order (last name first), using either full first names or initials. List second and succeeding author names in normal order.

- Use quotation marks around the titles of articles from magazines, newspapers, and journals. Capitalize all important words.

- Italicize the names of books, newspapers, journals, and other complete publications, capitalizing all main words in the title.

- For journal articles, include the volume number and the issue number (if necessary). Include the year of publication inside parentheses and follow with a colon and the page range of the article: *Journal of Business Communication* 36, 4 (2001): 72. (In this source, the volume is 36, the number is 4, and the page is 72.)

- Electronic sources are less fixed than print sources, and they may not be readily accessible to readers. So citations for electronic sources must provide more information. Always try to be as comprehensive as possible, citing whatever information is available (however, see the note below about extremely long URLs).

- The date for electronic sources should contain both the date assigned in the source and the date accessed by the researcher.

- The URL for electronic sources must be as accurate and complete as possible, from access-mode identifier (such as http or ftp) to all relevant directory and file names. If the URL is extremely long, use the URL of the website's home page or the URL of the site's search page if you used the site's search function to find the article. Be sure to enclose this path inside angle brackets: <http://www.hoovers.com/capsules/13787.html>.

Appendix C

CORRECTION SYMBOLS

Instructors often use these short, easy-to-remember correction symbols and abbreviations when evaluating students' writing. You can use them too, to understand your instructor's suggestions and to revise and proofread your own letters, memos, and reports. Refer to the Handbook of Grammar, Mechanics, and Usage (pp. H-1–H-30) for further information.

Content and Style

Acc	Accuracy. Check to be sure information is correct.
ACE	Avoid copying examples.
ACP	Avoid copying problems.
Adp	Adapt. Tailor message to reader.
App	Follow proper organization approach. (Refer to Chapter 4.)
Assign	Assignment. Review instructions for assignment.
AV	Active verb. Substitute active for passive.
Awk	Awkward phrasing. Rewrite.
BC	Be consistent.
BMS	Be more sincere.
Chop	Choppy sentences. Use longer sentences and more transitional phrases.
Con	Condense. Use fewer words.
CT	Conversational tone. Avoid using overly formal language.
Depers	Depersonalize. Avoid attributing credit or blame to any individual or group.
Dev	Develop. Provide greater detail.
Dir	Direct. Use direct approach; get to the point.
Emph	Emphasize. Develop this point more fully.
EW	Explanation weak. Check logic; provide more proof.
Fl	Flattery. Avoid compliments that are insincere.
FS	Figure of speech. Find a more accurate expression.
GNF	Good news first. Use direct order.
GRF	Give reasons first. Use indirect order.
GW	Goodwill. Put more emphasis on expressions of goodwill.
	Honesty/ethics. Revise statement to reflect good business practices.
Jar	usiness practices.
Log	Avoid being direct.
	Develop further.
	pecialized language.
	...ment of argument.

A-26

Neg	Negative. Use more positive approach or expression.
Obv	Obvious. Do not state point in such detail.
OC	Overconfident. Adopt humbler language.
OM	Omission.
Org	Organization. Strengthen outline.
OS	Off the subject. Close with point on main subject.
Par	Parallel. Use same structure.
Pom	Pompous. Rephrase in down-to-earth terms.
PV	Point of view. Make statement from reader's perspective rather than your own.
RB	Reader benefit. Explain what reader stands to gain.
Red	Redundant. Reduce number of times this point is made.
Ref	Reference. Cite source of information.
Rep	Repetitive. Provide different expression.
RS	Resale. Reassure reader that he or she has made a good choice.
SA	Service attitude. Put more emphasis on helping reader.
Sin	Sincerity. Avoid sounding glib or uncaring.
SL	Stereotyped language. Focus on individual's characteristics instead of on false generalizations.
Spec	Specific. Provide more specific statement.
SPM	Sales promotion material. Tell reader about related goods or services.
Stet	Let stand in original form.
Sub	Subordinate. Make this point less important.
SX	Sexist. Avoid language that contributes to gender stereotypes.
Tone	Tone needs improvement.
Trans	Transition. Show connection between points.
UAE	Use action ending. Close by stating what reader should do next.
UAS	Use appropriate salutation.
UAV	Use active voice.
Unc	Unclear. Rewrite to clarify meaning.
UPV	Use passive voice.
USS	Use shorter sentences.
V	Variety. Use different expression or sentence pattern.
W	Wordy. Eliminate unnecessary words.
WC	Word choice. Find a more appropriate word.
YA	"You" attitude. Rewrite to emphasize reader's needs.

Grammar, Mechanics, and Usage

Ab	Abbreviation. Avoid abbreviations in most cases; use correct abbreviation.
Adj	Adjective. Use adjective instead.
Adv	Adverb. Use adverb instead.
Agr	Agreement. Make subject and verb or noun and pronoun agree.
Ap	Appearance. Improve appearance.
Apos	Apostrophe. Check use of apostrophe.
Art	Article. Use correct article.
BC	Be consistent.
Cap	Capitalize.
Case	Use cases correctly.
CoAdj	Coordinate adjective. Insert comma between coordinate adjectives; delete comma between adjective and compound noun.
CS	Comma splice. Use period or semicolon to separate clauses.
DM	Dangling modifier. Rewrite so that modifier clearly relates to subject of sentence.
Exp	Expletive. Avoid expletive beginnings, such as it is, there are, there is, this is, and these are.
F	Format. Improve layout of document.
Frag	Fragment. Rewrite as complete sentence.
Gram	Grammar. Correct grammatical error.
HCA	Hyphenate compound adjective.
lc	Lowercase. Do not use capital letter.
M	Margins. Improve frame around document.
MM	Misplaced modifier. Place modifier close to word it modifies.
NRC	Nonrestrictive clause (or phrase). Separate from rest of sentence with commas.
P	Punctuation. Use correct punctuation.
Par	Parallel. Use same structure.
PH	Place higher. Move document up on page.
PL	Place lower. Move document down on page.
Prep	Preposition. Use correct preposition.
RC	Restrictive clause (or phrase). Remove commas that separate clause from rest of sentence.
RO	Run-on sentence. Separate two sentences with comma and coordinating conjunction or with semicolon.
SC	Series comma. Add comma before *and*.
SI	Split infinitive. Do not separate *to* from rest of verb.
Sp	Spelling error. Consult dictionary.
S-V	Subject-verb pair. Do not separate with comma.
Syl	Syllabification. Divide word between syllables.
WD	Word division. Check dictionary for proper end-of-line hyphenation.
WW	Wrong word. Replace with another word.

Proofreading Marks

Symbol	Meaning	Symbol Used in Context	Corrected Copy
═	Align horizontally	meaningful result	meaningful result
‖	Align vertically	1. Power cable 2. Keyboard	1. Power cable 2. Keyboard
bf	Boldface	Recommendations bf	**Recommendations**
≡	Capitalize	Pepsico, Inc.	PepsiCo, Inc.
⌐ ¬	Center	Awards Banquet	Awards Banquet
⌒	Close up space	self- confidence	self-confidence
e	Delete	harassment and abuse	harassment
ds	Double-space	text in first line text in second line ds	text in first line text in second line
∧	Insert	turquoise shirts (u, and white)	turquoise and white shirts
∨	Insert apostrophe	our teams goals	our team's goals
∧	Insert comma	a, b and c	a, b, and c
⹀	Insert hyphen	third quarter sales	third-quarter sales
⊙	Insert period	Harrigan et al	Harrigan et al.
∨ ∨	Insert quotation marks	This team isn't cooperating.	This "team" isn't cooperating.
#	Insert space	real estate testcase	real estate test case
ital	Italics	Quarterly Report ital	*Quarterly Report*
/	Lowercase	TULSA, South of here	Tulsa, south of here
⎣ ⎦	Move down	Sincerely,	Sincerely,
⌐	Move left	Attention: Security	Attention: Security
¬	Move right	February 2, 2009	February 2, 2009
⌐ ¬	Move up	THIRD-QUARTER SALES	THIRD-QUARTER SALES
STET	Restore	staff talked openly and frankly STET	staff talked openly
∽	Run lines together	Manager, Distribution	Manager, Distribution
ss	Single space	text in first line text in second line	text in first line text in second line
◯	Spell out	COD	cash on delivery
sp	Spell out	sp Assn. of Biochem. Engrs.	Association of Biochemical Engineers
⌐	Start new line	Marla Fenton, Manager, Distribution	Marla Fenton, Manager, Distribution
⁋	Start new paragraph	The solution is easy to determine but difficult to implement in a competitive environment like the one we now face.	The solution is easy to determine but difficult to implement in a competitive environment like the one we now face.
		airy, light, casual tone	light, airy, casual tone

Video Guide

Your instructor may elect to show you one or more of the videos described on the following pages. These programs supplement course concepts with real-life examples of businesspeople meeting important communication challenges. This video guide includes several review and analysis questions as well as exercises for each video. Be sure to review the appropriate page ahead of time so that you'll know what to look for when you watch the video.

Effective Ineffective Communication

Learning Objectives

After viewing this video, you will be able to

1. Recognize the importance of communication in the business environment
2. Recognize the elements that distinguish effective from ineffective communication
3. Understand why brevity is an important part of effective communication

Background Information

Effective communication delivers a number of business benefits, including stronger decision making and faster problem solving, earlier warning of potential problems, increased productivity and steadier workflow, stronger business relationships, clearer and more persuasive marketing messages, enhanced professional images for both employers and companies, lower employee turnover and higher employee satisfaction, better financial results, and higher return for investors. To be considered effective, communication efforts need to provide practical information, give facts rather than vague impressions, present information concisely, clarify expectations and responsibilities, and offer persuasive arguments and recommendations.

The Video

This video portrays a new employee at an advertising agency as he learns the importance of effective communication—and learns how to improve his communication efforts. As he goes through a typical day accompanied by a "message mentor," he observes the results of both effective and ineffective communication.

Discussion Questions

1. Why might new hires fresh out of college face challenges in learning how to communicate in the workplace?
2. How should you handle situations in which you are asked to provide solid information but the only information available to you is imprecise and potentially unreliable?
3. How can effective communication improve employee morale?
4. How can you judge how much information to provide your audience in any given situation?

5. Can communication efforts be both effective and unethical? For example, what about a marketing campaign that uses compelling information to persuade people to buy an inferior product when a better product is available from the competition?

Follow-up Assignment

Most companies make an effort to define external communication strategies, but many don't have a formal strategy for internal communication—which is every bit as essential to their success. Read the article, "Internal Communication Strategies—The Neglected Strategic Element," at http://workhelp.org/content/view/171/46/ and then answer the following questions:

1. What are the advantages of effective internal communication?
2. How does communication help align the efforts of everyone in the organization toward common goals?
3. Why is it important to have a companywide strategy for internal communication?

For Further Research

The *HR Magazine* article "Great Communicators, Great Communication," at www.shrm.org/hrmagazine/articles/0706/0706gptw_pomeroy.asp (or go to www.shrm.org and search for the article title), emphasizes the role communication plays in creating great workplaces. After reading the article, summarize the steps companies have taken to be included among the magazine's list of the 50 best small and medium companies to work for in the United States.

Ethical Communication

Learning Objectives

After viewing this video, you will be able to

1. Describe a process for deciding what is ethical or unethical
2. Explain the importance of meeting your personal and professional responsibilities in an ethical manner
3. Discuss the possible consequences of ethical and unethical choices and talk about the impact of these choices on direct and related audiences

Background Information

Communication is ethical when it includes all relevant information, when it's true in every sense, and when it isn't deceptive in any way. In contrast, communication is unethical when it includes false information, fails to include important information, or otherwise misleads an audience. To avoid unethical choices in your communication efforts, you m[ust] consider not only legal issues but also the needs of your [audi]ence and the expectations of society and your emp[loyer. In] turn, companies that demonstrate high standar[ds] maintain credibility with employees, custo[mers, and] stakeholders.

The Video

This video identifies two important tools in a communicator's toolbox: honesty and objectivity. These tools help businesspeople resolve ethical dilemmas and avoid ethical lapses, both within the company and during interactions with outside audiences. Poor ethical choices can damage a company's credibility and put employees, customers, and the surrounding community at risk. Unfortunately, some ethical choices are neither clear nor simple, and you may face situations in which the needs of one group or individual must be weighed against the needs of another.

Discussion Questions

1. Would you ever consider compromising your ethics for self-gain? If so, under what circumstance? If not, why?
2. The video mentions the role of misrepresentations in the collapse of Enron. If you were the head of communications at Enron and had some knowledge of the true nature of the company's financial condition, what would you have done?
3. Identify risks involved when you choose to act in an unethical manner.
4. How can you be an effective business communicator without credibility?
5. Is it ethical to call in sick to work, even though you are not ill? What happens to your credibility if someone finds out you were not sick?

Follow-up Assignment

Many businesses, from small companies to large corporations, formulate codes of ethics that outline ethical standards for employees. Review IBM's guidelines, which are posted on its website, at www.ibm.com/ibm/responsibility/policy2.shtml. Now answer the following questions:

1. What does IBM want employees to do if they are aware of unethical situations within the organization?
2. How does IBM view misleading statements or innuendos about competitors?
3. What advice does IBM give employees on the subject of receiving gifts from people outside the company?

For Further Research

Advertising communications, particularly advertising aimed at children, can present a variety of ethical concerns. Visit the American Psychological Association's website at www.apa.org and search for the article "Advertising to children: Is it ethical?" After reading this article, do you believe it is unethical for psychologists to advise companies on how to target children more effectively through advertising? Why or why not?

ss Etiquette

2. ljectives

seek leo, you will be able to

impact that poor etiquette can have

ry bad-news message should

3. Identify situations in which the indirect approach is likely to be more effective than the direct approach

Background Information

Etiquette strikes some people as a fine idea for tea parties but something that has little relevance in the contemporary workplace. However, the stresses and strains of today's business environment make etiquette more important than ever. Poor etiquette harms relationships, hinders communication, lowers morale and productivity, and limits career potential. Successful professionals know that taking the time and effort to treat others with respect—through their words and their actions—pays off for everyone in the long run.

The Video

This video shows a young employee learning firsthand the value of business etiquette. A business associate whom he has offended through clumsy communication turns the tables and helps him understand the negative effect that poor etiquette has on people in the workplace. She then helps him grasp the steps needed to present himself respectably and to communicate in ways that get his point across without unnecessarily stirring up negative emotions.

Discussion Questions

1. Is paying attention to standards of etiquette likely to save time or cost time in the workplace? Why?
2. If you need to deliver bad news to a person with whom you will probably never interact again, how can you justify taking extra time and effort to communicate carefully and respectfully? Are you wasting your company's money by spending time on such efforts?
3. How does a well-written buffer in an indirect negative message help the receiver accept the bad news?
4. Can a buffer also make the task of delivering negative messages less stressful? Why or why not?
5. Is the indirect approach to negative messages deceptive? Shouldn't communication always be straightforward and direct? Be prepared to explain your answer.

Follow-up Assignment

Visit www.executiveplanet.com and click on any country that interests you. Explore the Public Behaviour section(s) for that country and identify three tips that would help anyone from the United States who is preparing to do business there.

For Further Research

Take the brief business etiquette quiz at www.gradview.com/careers/etiquette.html. Were you able to figure out answers to these situations? Do you agree with the responses that the website identifies as being correct?

Learning to Listen and Creativity at Second City

Learning Objectives

After viewing this video, you will be able to

1. Understand the functions of interpersonal communication in the workplace

2. Identify the ways to overcome barriers to effective communication
3. Discuss the importance of active listening both socially and professionally

Background Information

Chicago's Second City Improv is more than the world's best-known comedy theater. Second City now brings its famous brand of humor to corporate giants such as Coca-Cola, Motorola, and Microsoft. With over 40 years of experience in corporate services, Second City's teachers help business professionals develop communication skills through lessons in improvisational theater. Business Communications Training is Second City's fastest-growing practice, fueled by the demands of more than two hundred Fortune 500 companies. Workshops are tailored to client's needs in such areas as listening and giving presentations, collaborative leadership and team skills, interviewing, breaking down barriers to successful communication, and using humor to convey important messages. The next time you watch improvisational sketch comedy, ask yourself how a lesson in the art of "improv" might give your career a boost.

The Video

In these two video segments, you'll see Second City's training techniques in action. The first segment addresses the need to listen actively, and the second explores techniques for encouraging innovation. The second clip is less focused on communication, but you can see how the techniques for stimulating innovation work equally well for fostering meaningful, two-way conversation that encourages people to open up rather than shut down.

Discussion Questions

1. How do the exercises featured in this video address the contrasting needs of the trial lawyer, the divorce lawyer, and the media buyer?
2. Would ABC's talkative guest Kay Jarman, the 47-year-old award-winning salesperson, be a good candidate for Second City's training workshop?
3. What other workshops might Tom Yorton want to offer companies in response to the current economic and political climate?
4. How might the "Yes and" rule of improvisation be used to train customer service representatives at an L.L. Bean or a Dell computer call center? Without physical cues, such as facial expression and body language, is the "Yes and" rule still effective?
5. As president and managing director of Second City Communications, Tom Yorton says the following: "You have to be willing to fail to be able to get the results you want . . . to connect with an audience." Do you agree that this statement is as true in business as it is in comedy? Support your chosen position.

Follow-up Assignment

Enjoy Second City Communications's website at www.secondcity.com. If you are a loyal fan, you might want to check out the book titles offered and read more about the group's history. Now explore Second City's Corporate Services: Scan the client roster, read the testimonials, and then select a case study

that you find compelling. If you are currently employed, which workshop would be most beneficial to you and to your work team? Explain your choice. If you are not currently employed, how might you and your fellow business students benefit from a Second City workshop? Which workshop would you most like to participate in? Explain how you think it might help you in terms of your social life, your career planning, and your interviewing skills.

For Further Research

The importance of active listening is at the core of *consultative selling*, an approach that emphasizes posing questions to the potential buyer in order to identify needs and expectations—rather than rattling off a prepared sales speech. PublicSpeakingSkills.com (www.publicspeakingskills.com) is one of many companies that offer training in consultative selling. Review the description of the company's Consultative Selling and Negotiating Skills course. Do the principles espoused match the concept of the "you" attitude and the elements of ethical communication that you've learned so far?

Communicating in the Global Workplace

Learning Objectives

After viewing this video, you will be able to

1. Discuss the challenges of communicating in the global workplace
2. Identify barriers to effective communication across borders
3. Explain the critical role of time in global communication efforts

Background Information

Many businesses are crossing national boundaries to engage in international business. However, operating in a global environment presents a variety of challenges related to culture and communication. Understanding and respecting these challenges can mean the difference between success and failure, so executives must make sure that employees are educated on cultural issues before attempting to do business in other countries.

The Video

This video identifies the challenges to effective communication in the global marketplace, including the barriers posed by language, culture, time, and technology. You will see that a significant amount of research needs to be conducted before a company can engage in successful global business ventures. For instance, if communicators are unaware of differences in gestures, expressions, and dialect, they can inadvertently offend or confuse their audiences. In addition, time zone differences require organizations to plan carefully in advance so that they can develop, translate, and deliver information in a timely manner.

Discussion Questions

1. Language can be a barrier to effective comm What steps can a company take to minimize riers across borders?
2. What characteristics of a country's researched to ensure business suc

3. How does a company ensure that a message is properly translated into the local language and dialect of the people it conducts business with?
4. What challenges does a company face when trying to hold a conference call or video meeting with affiliates and employees around the world?
5. The video mentions that some companies have trusted contacts in a country they wish to do business with, while other companies rely on a significant amount of research to learn more about culture and other local characteristics. What method do you feel is most effective for gathering useful, accurate, and up-to-date information regarding cultural issues?

Follow-up Assignment

The Coca-Cola Company has local operations in more than 200 countries throughout the world. Visit www.coca-cola.com to learn more about the company's business activities in a variety of countries. What steps does Coke take to communicate through its website with customers around the world? Does the company strive to develop products that meet local tastes and needs? If so, how and why?

For Further Research

Choose a country other than the United States and research your selection using both online and library resources to identify important cultural characteristics specific to that country. For example, you may want to gather information about gestures and other nonverbal communication that would be considered offensive, about work habits, or about laws related to conducting business in that country. The characteristics you identify should be useful and accurate.

Based on what you've learned about this country and your personal beliefs, values, and life experiences, is there any risk that you might have a prejudiced or ethnocentric viewpoint regarding people from this country? Why or why not?

Impact of Culture on Business: Spotlight on Latin America

Learning Objectives

After viewing this video, you will be able to

1. List key aspects of Latin American cultures and indicate the influences on their development
2. Identify factors that might lead to cultural change in Latin America
3. Explain some of the major cultural contrasts within Latin America and their impact on international business operations

...ound Information

...gree, culture defines the way all human beings ...bound ...ond to life's changing circumstances. When ...and the ...ple from your own culture, your shared ...tions usually enhance the communica- ...ommon language and frame of ref- ...communicate across cultural ...your audience's culture— ...r own culture shapes your

perceptions—can result in partial or even total failure of the communication process. Moreover, culture is rarely static, so impressions you may have gathered at one point in your life may need to be revisited and revised over time.

The Video

This video takes a broad look at Latin America's various countries and cultures and explores the business implications of cultural similarities and differences. You'll learn how cultural groups that may appear identical on the surface can in fact have subtle but profound differences. Although communication is just one of many topics discussed in the video, you will get a sense of just how important—and challenging—communication can be when conducting business across cultural boundaries.

Discussion Questions

1. Explain what the video means when it says that your own culture can "sneak up on you."
2. How is business influencing the economic gulf between urban and rural populations in Latin America?
3. How have imperial conquests and slavery affected the populations and cultures of Latin America?
4. How do many outsiders view the issue of business and government corruption in Latin America?
5. Is business etiquette in most of Latin America considered relatively formal or relatively informal?

Follow-up Assignment

The World Bank plays an important role in today's fast-changing, closely meshed global economy. Visit the bank's website, at www.worldbank.org, and explore the programs and initiatives under way in the Latin American region. How is the bank using this website to foster better communication between Latin America and the rest of the world?

For Further Research

In today's global marketplace, knowing as much as possible about your international customers' business practices and customs could give you a strategic advantage. To help you successfully conduct business around the globe, navigate the resources at the U.S. Government Export portal. Start at www.export .gov, then click on "Market Research" and then on "Country Information—Quick Reference (TIC)." Click anywhere on the world map to learn more about each country.

How can resources such as this website help U.S. businesses communicate more successfully with customers, employees, and other groups in Latin America?

Technology and the Tools of Communication

Learning Objectives

After viewing this video, you will be able to

1. Identify technology-related issues to consider when developing communication strategies
2. Identify advantages of using technology as a tool for effective communication
3. Differentiate between "push" and "pull" communication

Background Information

From instant messaging to online meetings, technology has become an integral element of business communication. When used with care, technological tools can help you reach more people in less time with more effective messages. However, when technology is misused or misunderstood, it can cause more problems than it solves. Knowing which technologies to use in every situation—and knowing how to use each one—are vital to your success.

The Video

This video discusses how the Internet, e-mail, voicemail, and other devices have revolutionized the way people communicate. These technological tools increase the speed, frequency, and range of business communication. The video also discusses factors to consider when choosing the most appropriate vehicle for your communication, including the all-important challenge of getting and keeping your audience's attention. The advantages of using technological communication tools are presented throughout the video.

Discussion Questions

1. Identify six questions you need to consider when choosing a technology vehicle for your messages.
2. List the advantages of communicating via e-mail within an organization.
3. What role does technology play in ensuring effective communication within an organization?
4. What are some of the more common challenges that business communicators can encounter when they use technology for communication purposes?
5. Identify the difference between "push" and "pull" communications, and provide an example of each method.

Follow-up Assignment

VolResource (at www.volresource.org.uk/samples/olcomms .htm) provides practical and informative resources for volunteer organizations that are trying to develop online communication strategies. The VolResource website further details questions that need to be addressed in the process of developing an effective communication strategy for any organization. What issues do you think are the most important to consider? Why?

For Further Exploration

Visit the Yellow Transportation website, at www.myyellow .com, and explore the various e-commerce tools this company utilizes to communicate effectively with its customers. Examine these tools and consider their effectiveness. What are some of the advantages of these online communication tools? How do they benefit the client? How do they benefit Yellow Transportation?

Giving an Oral Presentations

Learning Objectives

After viewing this video, you will be able to

1. Reiterate the importance of knowing your audience before creating and delivering oral presentations

2. Discuss the role of teamwork in preparing and delivering complex presentations
3. Explain the importance of anticipating objections likely to be raised during a presentation

Background Information

Oral presentations are a vital communication medium in most companies. In particular, important decisions often involve one or more presentations, either in person or online, in which people advocating a specific choice present their case to the people responsible for making the decision. Such presentations usually combine informational and analytical reporting, along with the persuasive aspects of a proposal. Beyond the mere delivery of information, however, presentations also involve an element of performance. Audiences search for both verbal and nonverbal clues to help them assess presenters' knowledge, confidence, and credibility.

The Video

This video follows three colleagues as they create and deliver a presentation that seeks to convince the audience to approve the purchase of a particular software system that will be used to manage the company's sales force. The presenters explain the importance of understanding the expectations of their audience, from the types of visuals they prefer to the objections they are likely to raise. The team also explains how they took advantage of each member's individual strengths to create a more effective presentation.

Discussion Questions

1. How did the presenters demonstrate their knowledge of the audience?
2. Why did one presenter use a $100 bill as a prop?
3. What are the risks of using props such as the $100 bill?
4. How did the presenters prepare for objections raised by the audience?
5. How would the team need to modify its presentation for an online webcast instead of an in-person oral presentation?

Follow-up Assignment

Podcasts (audio only) and vidcasts (podcasts with video) are quickly catching on as a medium for business presentations. Visit www.technorati.com and click on the Business category. Select any three podcasts. Listen to them while taking careful notes so that you can compare the three selections in terms of grabbing your attention, keeping your attention, and effectively communicating the podcast's information. Which of the three podcasts is the most effective? Why?

For Further Research

Musicians, actors, jugglers—virtually everyone who performs in public experiences *performance anxiety*, or *stage fright*, as it is commonly known. This anxiety is simply the natural outcome of caring about how well you do. After all, if you didn't care, wouldn't feel anxious. Seasoned performers not only re that anxiety is natural but they also have learned how emotion to their advantage by giving them extr www.petethomas.co.uk/performance-nerve .jugglingdb.com (search for "stage frigh "Collective wisdom on stage fright")

accomplished performers handle the anxiety of performing in public. How can you adapt their techniques to business presentations?

Interviewing Skills

Learning Objectives

After viewing this video, you will be able to

1. Explain how the AIDA approach helps create effective application letters
2. Identify mistakes that can cause an otherwise qualified candidate to lose out on a job opportunity
3. Explain why planning for tough questions is such an important part of your interviewing strategy

Background Information

Most companies would admit that the employment interview is an imperfect test of a candidate's skills and personality fit with the organization. In response, some are beginning to add testing, job simulations, and other evaluation tools to the selection process. However, the classic face-to-face interview remains the dominant decision-making tool in the hiring process, so developing your interviewing skills will be vital to your success at every stage in your career.

The Video

This video follows the progress of two candidates applying and interviewing for a technical writing position. One candidate has more experience in this area, but his approach to the interview process ends up costing him the job opportunity. In contrast, a candidate with less experience takes a confident and creative approach that nets her the job.

Discussion Questions

1. Why are multiple StayCom managers involved in this interviewing process? Couldn't one manager handle it?
2. Why does one of the managers compare an application letter to a news story?
3. What steps did Cheryl Yung take to overcome a potential shortcoming in her qualifications?
4. What mistakes did candidate Buddy McCoy make in his interview?
5. Why would the interviewers care about the interpersonal skills of someone who will be writing for a living?

Follow-up Assignment

Nonverbal cues are important in every communication scenario, but perhaps never more important than in job interviews. Not only are interviewers looking for any clues they can find that will guide their decisions but they tend to make up their minds quickly—perhaps even before the candidate has said anything at all. Use the Web Search feature at http://businesscommunicationblog.com/websearch to find advice on nonverbal communication in interviews. Distill this information down to a half dozen or so key points that you can write on a note card to study before you step into your next job interview.

For Further Research

You look great in your new interview outfit, your hair is perfect but not too perfect, your smile radiates positive energy, and you're ready to dazzle the interviewer. Then, oops—you discover that your first interview will be held over the telephone, so none of your visual cues will help you at this stage. Don't fret; read the telephone interviewing advice at www.collegegrad.com/jobsearch/phone-Interviewing-Success/, and you'll be ready to dazzle the interviewer long distance.

Handbook of Grammar, Mechanics, and Usage

The rules of grammar, mechanics, and usage provide the guidance every professional needs in order to communicate successfully with colleagues, customers, and other audiences. Understanding and following these rules helps you in two important ways. First, the rules determine how meaning is encoded and decoded in the communication process. If you don't encode your messages using the same rules your readers or listeners use to decode them, chances are your audiences will not extract your intended meaning from your messages. Without a firm grasp of the basics of grammar, mechanics, and usage, you risk being misunderstood, damaging your company's image, losing money for your company, and possibly even losing your job. In other words, if you want to get your point across, you need to follow the rules of grammar, mechanics, and usage. Second, apart from transferring meaning successfully, following the rules tells your audience that you respect the conventions and expectations of the business community.

You can think of *grammar* as the agreed-upon structure of a language, the way that individual words are formed and the manner in which those words are then combined to form meaningful sentences. *Mechanics* are style and formatting issues such as capitalization, spelling, and the use of numbers and symbols. *Usage* involves the accepted and expected way in which specific words are used by a particular community of people—in this case, the community of businesspeople who use English. This handbook can help you improve your knowledge and awareness in all three areas. It is divided into the following sections:

- **Diagnostic Test of English Skills.** Testing your current knowledge of grammar, mechanics, and usage helps you find out where your strengths and weaknesses lie. This test offers 50 items taken from the topics included in this handbook.

- **Assessment of English Skills.** After completing the diagnostic test, use the assessment form to highlight the areas you most need to review.

- **Essentials of Grammar, Mechanics, and Usage with Practice Sessions.** This section helps you quickly review the basics. You can study the things you've probably already learned but may have forgotten about grammar, punctuation, mechanics (including capitalization, abbreviation, number style, and word division), and vocabulary (including frequently confused words, frequently misused words, frequently misspelled words, and transitional words and phrases). Practice sessions throughout this section help you test yourself and reinforce what you learn. Use this essential review not only to study and improve your English skills but also as a reference for any questions you may have during this course.

Diagnostic Test of English Skills

Use this test to determine whether you need more practice with grammar, punctuation, mechanics, or vocabulary. When you've answered all the questions, ask your instructor for an answer sheet so that you can score the test. On the Assessment of English Skills form (page H-3), record the number of questions you answered incorrectly in each section.

The following choices apply to items 1–5. Write in each blank the letter of the choice that best describes the part of speech that is underlined.

- **A.** noun
- **B.** pronoun
- **C.** verb
- **D.** adjective
- **E.** adverb
- **F.** preposition
- **G.** conjunction
- **H.** article

_____ 1. The new branch location will be decided <u>by</u> next week.

_____ 2. We must hire only <u>qualified</u>, ambitious graduates.

_____ 3. After their <u>presentation</u>, I was still undecided.

_____ 4. See <u>me</u> after the meeting.

_____ 5. Margaret, pressed for time, turned in <u>unusually</u> sloppy work.

In the blanks for items 6–15, write the letter of the word or phrase that best completes each sentence.

_____ 6. (A. Russ's, B. Russ') laptop was stolen last week.

_____ 7. Speaking only for (A. me, B. myself), I think the new policy is discriminatory.

_____ 8. Of the five candidates we interviewed yesterday, (A. who, B. whom) do you believe is the best choice?

_____ 9. India has increased (A. it's, B. its) imports of corn and rice.

_____ 10. Anyone who wants to be (A. their, B. his or her) own boss should think about owning a franchise.

_____ 11. If the IT department can't (A. lie, B. lay) the fiber-optic cable by March 1, the plant will not open on schedule.

_____ 12. Starbucks (A. is, B. are) opening five new stores in San Diego in the next year.

_____ 13. The number of women-owned small businesses (A. has, B. have) increased sharply in the past two decades.

_____ 14. Greg and Bernyce worked (A. good, B. well) together.

_____ 15. They distributed the supplies (A. among, B. between) the six staff members.

The following choices apply to items 16–20. Write in blank the letter of the choice that best describes the structure problem with each item.

- **A.** sentence fragment
- **B.** comma splice
- **C.** misplaced modifier

D. fused sentence
E. lack of parallelism
F. unclear antecedent

_____ **16.** The number of employees who took the buyout offer was much higher than expected, now the entire company is understaffed.

_____ **17.** The leader in Internet-only banking.

_____ **18.** Diamond doesn't actually sell financial products rather it acts as an intermediary.

_____ **19.** Helen's proposal is for not only the present but also for the future.

_____ **20.** When purchasing luxury products, quality is more important than price for consumers.

For items 21–30, circle the letter of the preferred choice in each of the following groups of sentences.

21. A. What do you think of the ad slogan "Have it your way?"
B. What do you think of the ad slogan "Have it your way"?

22. A. Send copies to Jackie Cross, Uniline, Brad Nardi, Peale & Associates, and Tom Griesbaum, MatchMakers.
B. Send copies to Jackie Cross, Uniline; Brad Nardi, Peale & Associates; and Tom Griesbaum, MatchMakers.

23. A. They've recorded 22 complaints since yesterday, all of them from long-time employees.
B. They've recorded 22 complaints since yesterday; all of them from long-time employees.

24. A. We are looking for two qualities in applicants: experience with computers and an interest in people.
B. We are looking for two qualities in applicants; experience with computers and an interest in people.

25. A. At the Center for the Blind the clients we serve have lost vision, due to a wide variety of causes.
B. At the Center for the Blind, the clients we serve have lost vision due to a wide variety of causes.

26. A. Replace your standard light bulbs with new, compact fluorescent bulbs.
B. Replace your standard light bulbs with new, compact, fluorescent bulbs.
C. Replace your standard light bulbs with new compact fluorescent bulbs.

27. A. Blue Cross of California may have changed its name to Anthem Blue Cross but the company still has the same commitment to California.
B. Blue Cross of California may have changed its name to Anthem Blue Cross, but the company still has the same commitment to California.

...ks in this country—maybe nine can han-
...this magnitude.
...his country—maybe nine—can
...magnitude.

29. A. Instead of focusing on high-growth companies, we targeted mature businesses with only one or two people handling the decision making.
B. Instead of focusing on high growth companies, we targeted mature businesses with only one or two people handling the decision-making.

30. A. According to board president Damian Cabaza "having a crisis communication plan is a high priority."
B. According to board president Damian Cabaza, "Having a crisis communication plan is a high priority."

For items 31–40, select the best choice from among those provided.

31. A. At her previous employer, Mary-Anne worked in Marketing Communications and Human Resources.
B. At her previous employer, Mary-Anne worked in marketing communications and human resources.

32. A. By fall, we'll have a dozen locations between the Mississippi and Missouri rivers.
B. By Fall, we'll have a dozen locations between the Mississippi and Missouri Rivers.

33. A. The Board applauded President Donlan upon her reelection for a fifth term.
B. The board applauded president Donlan upon her reelection for a fifth term.
C. The board applauded President Donlan upon her reelection for a fifth term.

34. A. If you want to travel to France, you need to be au courant with the business practices.
B. If you want to travel to France, you need to be "au courant" with the business practices.

35. A. As the company's CEO, Thomas Spurgeon handles all dealings with the FDA.
B. As the company's C.E.O., Thomas Spurgeon handles all dealings with the F.D.A.

36. A. The maximum speed limit in most states is 65 mph.
B. The maximum speed limit in most states is 65 m.p.h.

37. A. Sales of graphic novels increased nine percent between 2008 and 2009.
B. Sales of graphic novels increased 9 percent between 2008 and 2009.

38. A. Our store is open daily from nine A.M. to seven P.M.
B. Our store is open daily from 9:00 A.M. to 7:00 P.M.

39. A. The organizing meeting is scheduled for July 27, and the event will be held in January 2010.
B. The organizing meeting is scheduled for July 27th, and the event will be held in January, 2010.

40. A. We need six desks, eight file cabinets, and 12 trashcans.
B. We need 6 desks, 8 file cabinets, and 12 trashcans.

For items 41–50, write in each blank the letter of the word that best completes each sentence.

_____ 41. Will having a degree (A. affect, B. effect) my chances for promotion?

_____ 42. Try not to (A. loose, B. lose) this key; we will charge you a fee to replace it.

_____ 43. I don't want to discuss my (A. personal, B. personnel) problems in front of anyone.

_____ 44. Let us help you choose the right tie to (A. complement, B. compliment) your look.

_____ 45. The repairman's whistling (A. aggravated, B. irritated) all of us in accounting.

_____ 46. The bank agreed to (A. loan, B. lend) the Smiths $20,000 for their start-up.

_____ 47. The credit card company is (A. liable, B. likely) to increase your interest rate if you miss a payment.

_____ 48. The airline tries to (A. accommodate, B. accomodate) disabled passengers.

_____ 49. Every company needs a policy regarding sexual (A. harrassment, B. harassment).

_____ 50. Use your best (A. judgment, B. judgement) in selecting a service provider.

Assessment of English Skills

In the space provided, record the number of questions you answered incorrectly.

Questions	Skills Area	Number of Incorrect Answers
1–5	Parts of speech	_____
6–15	Usage	_____
16–20	Sentence structure	_____
21–30	Punctuation	_____
31–40	Mechanics	_____
41–50	Vocabulary	_____

If you had more than two incorrect answers in any of the skills areas, focus on those areas in the appropriate sections of this handbook.

Essentials of Grammar, Mechanics, and Usage

The following sentence looks innocent, but is it really?

We sell tuxedos as well as rent.

You sell tuxedos, but it's highly unlikely that you sell rent—which is what this sentence says. Whatever you're selling, some people will ignore your message because of a blunder like this. The following sentence has a similar problem:

Vice President Eldon Neale told his chief engineer that he would no longer be with Avix, Inc., as of June 30.

Is Eldon or the engineer leaving? No matter which side the facts are on, the sentence can be read the other way. Now look at this sentence:

The year before we budgeted more for advertising sales were up.

Confused? Perhaps this is what the writer meant:

The year before, we budgeted more for advertising. Sales were up.

Or maybe the writer meant this:

The year before we budgeted more for advertising, sales were up.

These examples show that even short, simple sentences can be misunderstood because of errors on the part of the writer. As you've learned in numerous courses over your schooling, an English sentence consists of the parts of speech being combined with punctuation, mechanics, and vocabulary to convey meaning. Making a point of brushing up on your grammar, punctuation, mechanics, and vocabulary skills will help ensure that you create clear, effective business messages.

1.0 Grammar

Grammar is the study of how words come together to form sentences. Categorized by meaning, form, and function, English words fall into various parts of speech: nouns, pronouns, verbs, adjectives, adverbs, prepositions, conjunctions, articles, and interjections. You will communicate more clearly if you understand how each of these parts of speech operates in a sentence.

1.1 Nouns

A **noun** names a person, a place, a thing, or an idea. Anything you can see or detect with one of your senses has a noun to name it. Some things you can't see or sense are also nouns—ions, for example, or space. So are things that exist as ideas, such as accuracy and height. (You can see that something is accurate or that a building is tall, but you can't see the idea of accuracy or the idea of height.) These names for ideas are known as **abstract nouns**. The simplest nouns are the names of things you can see or touch: *car, building, cloud, brick;* these are termed **concrete nouns**. A few nouns, such as *algorithm, software,* and *code,* are difficult to categorize as either abstract or concrete but can reasonably be considered concrete even though they don't have a physical presence.

1.1.1 Proper Nouns and Common Nouns

So far, all the examples of nouns have been **common nouns**, referring to general classes of things. The word *building* refers a whole class of structures. Common nouns such as *buil* not capitalized.

If you want to talk about one particular buil you might refer to the Glazier Building. The na indicating that *Glazier Building* is a **proper**

Here are three sets of common and proper nouns for comparison:

Common	Proper
city	Kansas City
company	Blaisden Company
store	Books Galore

1.1.2 Nouns as Subject and Object

Nouns may be used in sentences as subjects or objects. That is, the person, place, thing, or idea that is being or doing (subject) is represented by a noun. So is the person, place, idea, or thing that is being acted on (object). In the following sentence, the nouns are underlined:

The web designer created the homepage.

The web designer (subject) is acting in a way that affects the home page (object). The following sentence is more complicated:

The installer delivered the carpet to the customer.

Installer is the subject. *Carpet* is the object of the main part of the sentence (acted on by the installer), and *customer* is the object of the phrase *to the customer*. Nevertheless, both *carpet* and *customer* are objects.

1.1.3 Plural Nouns

Nouns can be either singular or plural. The usual way to make a plural noun is to add *s* or *es* to the singular form of the word:

Singular	Plural
file	files
tax	taxes
cargo	cargoes

Many nouns have other ways of forming the plural. Some plurals involve a change in a vowel (*mouse/mice, goose/geese, woman/women*), the addition of *en* or *ren* (*ox/oxen, child/children*), the change from *y* to *ies* (*city/cities, specialty/specialties*), or the change from *f* to *v* (*knife/knives, half/halves;* some exceptions: *fifes, roofs*). Some words of Latin origin offer a choice of plurals (*phenomena/phenomenons, indexes/indices, appendixes/appendices*). It's always a good idea to consult a dictionary if you are unsure of the correct or preferred plural spelling of a word.

The plurals of compound nouns are usually formed by _____ *s* or *es* to the main word of the compound (*fathers-in-_____, -in-chief, attorneys-at-law*).

_____ ns are the same whether singular or plural (*sleep,* _____ He _____ nouns are plural in form but singular in use apost_____ me nouns are used in the plural only DVDs). _____

_____ ords used as words are sometimes _____ rophe and an *s* (*A's, Ph.D.'s, I's*). _____ created by leaving off the _____ just add the *s* (*1990s, RFPs,*

1.1.4 Possessive Nouns

A noun becomes possessive when it's used to show the ownership of something. Then you add *'s* to the word:

the man's car   the woman's apartment

However, ownership does not need to be legal:

the secretary's desk   the company's assets

Also, ownership may be nothing more than an automatic association:

a day's work   the job's prestige

An exception to the rule about adding *'s* to make a noun possessive occurs when the word is singular and already has two "s" sounds at the end. In cases like the following, an apostrophe is all that's needed:

crisis' dimensions   Mr. Moses' application

When the noun has only one "s" sound at the end, however, retain the *'s:*

Chris's book   Carolyn Nuss's office

With compound (hyphenated) nouns, add *'s* to the last word:

Compound Noun	Possessive Noun
mother-in-law	mother-in-law's
mayor-elect	mayor-elect's

To form the possessive of plural nouns, just begin by following the same rule as with singular nouns: add *'s*. However, if the plural noun already ends in an *s* (as most do), drop the one you've added, leaving only the apostrophe:

the clients' complaints   employees' benefits

To denote joint possession by two or more proper nouns, add the *'s* to the last name only (*Moody, Nation,* and *Smith's* ad agency). To denote individual possession by two or more persons, add an *'s* to each proper noun (*Moody's, Nation's,* and *Smith's* ad agencies).

1.1.5 Collective Nouns

Collective nouns encompass a group of people or objects: *crowd, jury, committee, team, audience, family, couple, herd, class.* They are often treated as singular nouns. (For more on collective nouns, see Section 1.3.4, Subject–Verb Agreement.)

Practice Session: Nouns

Underline the preferred choice within each set of parentheses in the following sentences.

1. We are moving company headquarters to New York (*City, city*).
2. The historic Bradbury (*Building, building*) is the site of the press conference; the (*Building, building*) is located in downtown Los Angeles.
3. During the conference, our staff will be staying at the Hyatt, Hilton, and Marriott (*hotels', hotels*).

4. Accuracy requires that you cross your (*ts, t's*) and dot your (*is, i's*).
5. The industry has been on a downward spiral since the early (*1990's, 1990s*).
6. The new (*shelfs, shelves*) will be installed on Friday.
7. Our (*specialtys, specialties*) are unparalleled service and premium brands.
8. As a result of several Internet-related (*cases, case's*), the copyright laws are under scrutiny.
9. Before a job interview, you should learn about the (*company's, companies'*) mission statement.
10. Sending the newsletter to the printer is the (*editor's-in-chief, editor-in-chief 's*) responsibility.
11. All the downtown (*business', businesses', businesses's*) signs must be repainted.
12. Because the (*passenger's, passengers'*) luggage had been damaged, they had to file claims with the airline.
13. Dealing with angry customers is all in a (*days, day's, days'*) work for Mr. Jemas.
14. Its large airport is one of (*Dallases, Dallas', Dallas's*) main appeals for industrial firms.
15. We were skeptical of (*Jone's, Jones', Jones's*) plan.

1.2 Pronouns

A **pronoun** is a word that stands for a noun; it saves repeating the noun:

> Employees have some choice of weeks for vacation, but *they* must notify the HR office of *their* preference by March 1.

The pronouns *they* and *their* stand in for the noun *employees*. The noun that a pronoun stands for is called the **antecedent** of the pronoun; *employees* is the antecedent of *they* and *their*.

When the antecedent is plural, the pronoun that stands in for it has to be plural; *they* and *their* are plural pronouns because *employees* is plural. Likewise, when the antecedent is singular, the pronoun has to be singular:

> We thought the contract had expired, but we soon learned that *it* had not.

1.2.1 Multiple Antecedents

Sometimes a pronoun has a double (or even a triple) antecedent:

> Kathryn Boettcher and Luis Gutierrez went beyond *their* sales quotas for January.

If taken alone, *Kathryn Boettcher* is a singular antecedent. So is *Luis Gutierrez*. However, when together they are the plural antecedent of a pronoun, so the pronoun has to be plural. Thus the pronoun is *their* instead of *her* or *his*.

1.2.2 Unclear Antecedents

In some sentences the pronoun's antecedent is unclear:

> Sandy Wright sent Jane Brougham *her* production figures for the previous year. *She* thought they were too low.

To which person does the pronoun *her* refer? Someone who knew Sandy and Jane and knew their business relationship might be able to figure out the antecedent for *her*. Even with such an advantage, however, a reader might receive the wrong

meaning. Also, it would be nearly impossible for any reader to know which name is the antecedent of *she*.

The best way to clarify an ambiguous pronoun is usually to rewrite the sentence, repeating nouns when needed for clarity:

> Sandy Wright sent her production figures for the previous year to Jane Brougham. Jane thought they were too low.

The noun needs to be repeated only when the antecedent is unclear.

1.2.3 Pronoun Classes

Personal pronouns consist of *I, you, we/us, he/him, she/her, it,* and *they/them.*

Compound personal pronouns are created by adding *self* or *selves* to simple personal pronouns: *myself, ourselves, yourself, yourselves, himself, herself, itself, themselves.* Compound personal pronouns are used either *intensively*, to emphasize the identity of the noun or pronoun (I *myself* have seen the demonstration), or *reflexively*, to indicate that the subject is the receiver of his or her own action (I promised *myself* I'd finish by noon). Compound personal pronouns are used incorrectly if they appear in a sentence without their antecedent:

> Walter, Virginia, and *I* (not *myself*) are the top salespeople.
>
> You need to tell *her* (not *herself*) about the mixup.

Relative pronouns refer to nouns (or groups of words used as nouns) in the main clause and are used to introduce clauses:

> Purina is the brand *that* most dog owners purchase.

The relative pronouns are *which, who, whom, whose,* and *what.* Other words used as relative pronouns include *that, whoever, whomever, whatever,* and *whichever.*

Interrogative pronouns are those used for asking questions: *who, whom, whose, which,* and *what.*

Demonstrative pronouns point out particular persons, places, or things:

> *That* is my desk.   *This* can't be correct.

The demonstrative pronouns are *this, these, that,* and *those.*

Indefinite pronouns refer to persons or things not specifically identified. They include *anyone, someone, everyone, everybody, somebody, either, neither, one, none, all, both, each, another, any, many,* and similar words.

1.2.4 Case of Pronouns

The case of a pronoun tells whether it's acting or acted upon:

> *She* sells an average of five packages each week.

In this sentence, *she* is doing the selling. Because *she* is ac[...] *she* is said to be in the **nominative case**. Now consid[...] happens when the pronoun is acted upon:

> After six months, Ms. Browning promote[...]

In this sentence, the pronoun *her* is acted[...] to be in the **objective case**.

Contrast the nominative and objective pronouns in this list:

Nominative	Objective
I	me
we	us
he	him
she	her
they	them
who	whom
whoever	whomever

Objective pronouns may be used as either the object of a verb (such as *promoted*) or the object of a preposition (such as *with*):

> Rob worked with *them* until the order was filled.

In this example, *them* is the object of the preposition *with* because Rob acted upon—worked with—them. Here's a sentence with three pronouns, the first one nominative, the second the object of a verb, and the third the object of a preposition:

> He paid *us* as soon as the check came from *them*.

He is nominative; *us* is objective because it's the object of the verb *paid*; *them* is objective because it's the object of the preposition *from*.

Every writer sometimes wonders whether to use *who* or *whom*:

> (*Who, Whom*) will you hire?

Because this sentence is a question, it's difficult to see that *whom* is the object of the verb *hire*. You can figure out which pronoun to use if you rearrange the question and temporarily try *she* and *her* in place of *who* and *whom*: "Will you hire *she*?" or "Will you hire *her*?" *Her* and *whom* are both objective, so the correct choice is "Whom will you hire?" Here's a different example:

> (*Who, Whom*) logged so much travel time?

Turning the question into a statement, you get:

> He logged so much travel time.

Therefore, the correct statement is:

> Who logged so much travel time?

1.2.5 Possessive Pronouns

Possessive pronouns work like possessive nouns—they show automatic association:

> their preferences
> its equipment

...are different from possessive ... Possessive pronouns never

Possessive Noun	Possessive Pronoun
the woman's estate	her estate
Roger Franklin's plans	his plans
the shareholders' feelings	their feelings
the vacuum cleaner's attachments	its attachments

The word *its* is the possessive of *it*. Like all other possessive pronouns, *its* has no apostrophe. Some people confuse *its* with *it's*, the contraction of *it is*. (Contractions are discussed in Section 2.9, Apostrophes.)

1.2.6 Pronoun–Antecedent Agreement

Like nouns, pronouns can be singular or plural. Pronouns must agree in number with their antecedents—a singular antecedent requires a singular pronoun:

> The president of the board tendered *his* resignation.

Multiple antecedents require a plural pronoun:

> The members of the board tendered *their* resignations.

A pronoun referring to singular antecedents connected by *or* or *nor* should be singular:

> Neither Sean nor Terry made his quota.

But a pronoun referring to a plural and a singular antecedent connected by *or* or *nor* should be plural:

> Neither Sean nor the twins made *their* quotas.

Formal English prefers the nominative case after the linking verb *to be*:

> It is *I*.   That is *he*.

However, for general usage it's perfectly acceptable to use the more natural "It's me" and "That's him."

Practice Session: Pronouns

Underline the preferred choice within each set of parentheses in the following sentences.

1. Just between you and (*I, me*), I don't think we will make the deadline.
2. The final speaker at the luncheon was (*she, her*).
3. When you are finished, give the report to (*he, him*).
4. (*We, Us*) telemarketers have a tarnished reputation.
5. The company is sending the marketing communications staff—Mary-Ann, Alan, and (*I, me, myself*)—to the conference.
6. The company will issue (*their, its*) annual report next month.
7. Anyone who hasn't yet turned in (*their, his or her*) questionnaire should do so by tomorrow.
8. (*Who, Whom*) shall I say called?
9. To (*who, whom*) should I address the letter?
10. (*Who, Whom*) will they hire?
11. We need more people in our department like (*she, her*).
12. When dealing with an angry customer, try to calm (*him, him or her, them*) down.

13. It was either Sarah or Charlene who left (*her, their*) briefcase on the train.
14. The company needs to update (*its, it's*) website.
15. (*Who, Whom*) do you think will be given the promotion?
16. Be sure to include (*your, you're*) e-mail address on the form.
17. Each brand should have (*its, their*) own trademark.
18. The "dynamic duo"—Bruce and (*I, me*)—are in charge of next week's office party.
19. The supervisor thanked the team members for (*their, they're*) support.
20. The pharmaceutical giant agreed to take (*their, its*) diet drug off the market.

1.3 Verbs

A **verb** describes an action or acts as a link between a subject and words that define or describe that subject:

> They all *quit* in disgust.
>
> Working conditions *were* substandard.

The English language is full of **action verbs**. Here are a few you'll often run across in the business world:

verify	perform	fulfill
hire	succeed	send
leave	improve	receive
accept	develop	pay

You could undoubtedly list many more.

The most common linking verbs are all the forms of *to be*: I *am, was,* or *will be*; you *are, were,* or *will be*. Other words that can serve as linking verbs include *seem, become, appear, prove, look, remain, feel, taste, smell, sound, resemble, turn,* and *grow*:

> It *seemed* a good plan at the time.
>
> She *sounds* impressive at a meeting.
>
> The time *grows* near for us to make a decision.

These verbs link what comes before them in the sentence with what comes after; no action is involved. (See Section 1.7.5 for a fuller discussion of linking verbs.)

An **auxiliary verb** is one that helps another verb and is used for showing tense, voice, and so on. A verb with its helpers is called a **verb phrase**. Verbs used as auxiliaries include *do, did, have, may, can, must, shall, might, could, would,* and *should*.

1.3.1 Verb Tenses

English has three simple verb tenses: present, past, and future.

Present:	Our branches in Hawaii *stock* other items.
Past:	We *stocked* Purquil pens for a short time.
Future:	Rotex Tire Stores *will stock* your line of tires when you begin a program of effective national advertising.

With most verbs (the regular ones), the past tense ends in *ed*, and the future tense always has *will* or *shall* in front of it. But the present tense is more complex, depending on the subject:

	First Person	Second Person	Third Person
Singular	I stock	you stock	he/she/it stocks
Plural	we stock	you stock	they stock

The basic form, *stock*, takes an additional *s* when *he, she,* or *it* precedes it. (See Section 1.3.4 for more on subject–verb agreement.)

In addition to the three simple tenses, the three **perfect tenses** are created by adding forms of the auxiliary verb *have*. The present perfect tense uses the past participle (regularly the past tense) of the main verb, *stocked*, and adds the present-tense *have* or *has* to the front of it:

> (I, we, you, they) *have stocked*.
>
> (He, she, it) *has stocked*.

The past perfect tense uses the past participle of the main verb, *stocked*, and adds the past-tense *had* to the front of it:

> (I, you, he, she, it, we, they) *had stocked*.

The future perfect tense also uses the past participle of the main verb, *stocked*, but adds the future-tense *will have*:

> (I, you, he, she, it, we, they) *will have stocked*.

Verbs should be kept in the same tense when the actions occur at the same time:

> When the payroll checks *came in*, everyone *showed up* for work.
>
> We *have found* that everyone *has pitched* in to help.

When the actions occur at different times, you may change tense accordingly:

> The shipment *came* last Wednesday, so if another one *comes* in today, please return it.
>
> The new employee *had been* ill at ease, but now she *has become* a full-fledged member of the team.

1.3.2 Irregular Verbs

Many verbs don't follow some of the standard patterns for verb tenses. The most irregular of these verbs is *to be*:

Tense	Singular	Plural
Present:	I *am* you *are* he, she, it *is*	we *are* you *are* they *are*
Past:	I *was* you *were* he, she, it *was*	we *were* you *were* they *were*

The future tense of *to be* is formed in the same way that the future tense of a regular verb is formed.

The perfect tenses of *to be* are also formed as they would for a regular verb, except that the past participle is a form, *been*, instead of just the past tense:

Present perfect:	you have been
Past perfect:	you had been
Future perfect:	you will

Here's a sampling of other irregular verbs:

Present	Past	Past Participle
begin	began	begun
shrink	shrank	shrunk
know	knew	known
rise	rose	risen
become	became	become
go	went	gone
do	did	done

Dictionaries list the various forms of other irregular verbs.

1.3.3 Transitive and Intransitive Verbs

Many people are confused by three particular sets of verbs:

lie/lay   sit/set   rise/raise

Using these verbs correctly is much easier when you learn the difference between transitive and intransitive verbs.

Transitive verbs require a receiver; they "transfer" their action to an object. Intransitive verbs do not have a receiver for their action. Some intransitive verbs are complete in themselves and need no help from other words (prices *dropped*; we *won*). Other intransitive words must be "completed" by a noun or adjective called a **complement**. Complements occur with linking verbs.

Here are some sample uses of transitive and intransitive verbs:

Intransitive	Transitive
We should include in our new offices a place to *lie* down for a nap.	The workers will be here on Monday to *lay* new carpeting.
Even the way an interviewee *sits* is important.	That crate is full of stemware, so *set* it down carefully.
Salaries at Compu-Link, Inc., *rise* swiftly.	They *raise* their level of production every year.

The workers *lay* carpeting, you *set down* the crate, they *raise* production; each action is transferred to something. In the intransitive sentences, a person *lies down*, an interviewee *sits*, and salaries *rise* without affecting anything else. Intransitive sentences are complete with only a subject and a verb; transitive senten̲ces are not complete unless they also include an object; or ̲̲̲̲̲ to transfer the action to.

̲̲̲̲̲ a confusing element of the lie/lay problem:

The̲̲ Past	Past Participle
alike, ̲	I *have lain*
̲me-	I *have laid* (something down)

̲ense of *lay* look and sound ̲rbs.

1.3.4 Subject–Verb Agreement

Whether regular or irregular, every verb must agree with its subject, both in person (first, second, or third) and in number (single or plural).

	First Person	Second Person	Third Person
Singular	I *am*	you *are*	he/she/it *is*
	I *write*	you *write*	he/she/it *writes*
Plural	we *are*	you *are*	they *are*
	we *write*	you *write*	they *write*

In a simple sentence, making a verb agree with its subject is a straightforward task:

Hector Ruiz *is* a strong competitor. (third-person singular)

We *write* to you every month. (first-person plural)

Confusion sometimes arises when sentences are a bit more complicated. For example, be sure to avoid agreement problems when words come between the subject and verb. In the following examples, the verb appears in italics, and its subject is underlined:

The <u>analysis</u> of existing documents *takes* a full week.

Even though *documents* is a plural, the verb is in the singular form. That's because the subject of the sentence is *analysis*, a singular noun. The phrase *of existing documents* can be disregarded. Here is another example:

The <u>answers</u> for this exercise *are* in the study guide.

Take away the phrase *for this exercise* and you are left with the plural subject *answers*. Therefore, the verb takes the plural form.

Verb agreement is also complicated when the subject is a collective noun or pronoun or when the subject may be considered either singular or plural. In such cases, you often have to analyze the surrounding sentence to determine which verb form to use:

The <u>staff</u> *is* quartered in the warehouse.

The <u>staff</u> *are* at their desks in the warehouse.

The <u>computers</u> and the <u>staff</u> *are* in the warehouse.

Neither the staff nor the <u>computers</u> *are* in the warehouse.

<u>Every</u> computer *is* in the warehouse.

Many a <u>computer</u> *is* in the warehouse.

Did you notice that words such as *every* use the singular verb form? In addition, when an *either/or* or a *neither/nor* phrase combines singular and plural nouns, the verb takes the form that matches the noun closest to it.

In the business world, some subjects require extra attention. Company names, for example, are considered singular and therefore take a singular verb in most cases—even if they contain plural words:

Stater Brothers *offers* convenient grocery shopping.

In addition, quantities are sometimes considered singular and sometimes plural. If a quantity refers to a total amount, it takes a singular verb; if a quantity refers to individual, countable units, it takes a plural verb:

> Three hours *is* a long time.
>
> The eight dollars we collected for the fund *are* tacked on the bulletin board.

Fractions may also be singular or plural, depending on the noun that accompanies them:

> One-third of the warehouse *is* devoted to this product line.
>
> One-third of the products *are* defective.

To decide whether to use a singular or plural verb with subjects such as *number* and *variety*, follow this simple rule: If the subject is preceded by *a*, use a plural verb:

> A number of products *are* being displayed at the trade show.

If the subject is preceded by *the*, use a singular verb:

> *The* variety of products on display *is* mind-boggling.

For a related discussion, see Section 1.7.1, Longer Sentences.

1.3.5 Voice of Verbs

Verbs have two voices, active and passive. When the subject comes first, the verb is in **active voice**; when the object comes first, the verb is in **passive voice**:

> **Active:**   The buyer *paid* a large amount.
>
> **Passive:**   A large amount *was paid* by the buyer.

The passive voice uses a form of the verb *to be*, which adds words to a sentence. In the example, the passive-voice sentence uses eight words, whereas the active-voice sentence uses only six to say the same thing. The words *was* and *by* are unnecessary to convey the meaning of the sentence. In fact, extra words usually clog meaning. So be sure to opt for the active voice when you have a choice.

At times, however, you have no choice:

> Several items *have been taken*, but so far we don't know who took them.

The passive voice becomes necessary when you don't know (or don't want to say) who performed the action; the active voice is bolder and more direct.

1.3.6 Mood of Verbs

Verbs can express one of three moods: indicative, imperative, or subjunctive. The **indicative mood** is used to make a statement or to ask a question:

> The secretary mailed a letter to each supplier.
>
> Did the secretary mail a letter to each supplier?

Use the **imperative mood** when you wish to command or request:

> Please mail a letter to each supplier.

With the imperative mood, the subject is the understood *you*.

The **subjunctive mood** is used to express doubt or a wish or a condition contrary to fact:

> If I *were* you, I wouldn't send that e-mail.

The subjunctive is also used to express a suggestion or a request:

> I asked that Rosario *be* [not *is*] present at the meeting.

1.3.7 Verbals

Verbals are verbs that are modified to function as other parts of speech. They include infinitives, gerunds, and participles.

Infinitives are formed by placing a *to* in front of the verb (*to go, to purchase, to work*). They function as nouns. Although many of us were taught that it is "incorrect" to split an infinitive—that is, to place an adverb between the *to* and the verb—that rule is not a hard and fast one. In some cases, the adverb is best placed in the middle of the infinitive to avoid awkward constructions or ambiguous meaning:

> Production of steel is expected to *moderately exceed* domestic use.

Gerunds are verbals formed by adding *ing* to a verb (*going, having, working*). Like infinitives, they function as nouns. Gerunds and gerund phrases take a singular verb:

> *Borrowing* from banks *is* preferable to getting venture capital.

Participles are verb forms used as adjectives. The present participle ends in *ing* and generally describes action going on at the same time as other action:

> *Checking* the schedule, the contractor was pleased with progress on the project.

The past participle is usually the same form as the past tense and generally indicates completed action:

> When *completed*, the project will occupy six city blocks.

The **perfect participle** is formed by adding *having* to the past participle:

> *Having completed* the project, the contractor submitted his last invoice.

Practice Session: Verbs

Underline the preferred choice within each set of parentheses in the following sentences.

1. When Hastings (*come, comes, came*) in, tell him I (*want, wanted*) to see him.
2. Even though Sheila (*knowed, knew*) the right password, she typed it incorrectly.
3. The presentation had not yet (*began, begun*) when Charles arrived.
4. What I always say is, let sleeping dogs (*lay, lie*).
5. The workers (*lay, laid*) the tile in the executive bathroom yesterday.
6. This is where the president of the board (*sits, sets*) during meetings.
7. Just (*sit, set*) the boxes down over there.
8. Do you think management will (*raise, rise*) prices across the board next week?
9. A list of promotions (*was, were*) posted on the company intranet.

10. The supervisor of the assembly-line workers (*is, are*) being replaced.
11. The committee (*is, are*) considering the proposal today.
12. The board and the committee (*is, are*) having a joint meeting on June 25.
13. Neither the board nor the committee (*is, are*) expected to approve the proposal.
14. Every member of the board (*is, are*) going to make a statement.
15. Katten and Associates (*represent, represents*) clients in the entertainment industry.
16. Five hours (*is, are*) all I can give you to get the project done.
17. Half of the vacant lots (*is, are*) already sold.
18. Half of the hall (*is, are*) reserved for the luncheon.
19. Mario suggested that the public relations department (*send, sends*) out a news release about the merger.
20. If I (*was, were*) CEO, I'd fire the whole accounting staff.

1.4 Adjectives

An **adjective** modifies (tells something about) a noun or pronoun. Each of the following phrases says more about the noun or pronoun than the noun or pronoun would say alone:

an *efficient* staff	a *heavy* price
brisk trade	*light* web traffic

Adjectives modify nouns more often than they modify pronouns. When adjectives do modify pronouns, however, the sentence usually has a linking verb:

They were *attentive*.	It looked *appropriate*.
He seems *interested*.	You are *skillful*.

1.4.1 Types of Adjectives

Adjectives serve a variety of purposes. **Descriptive adjectives** express some quality belonging to the modified item (*tall, successful, green*). **Limiting** or **definitive adjectives**, on the other hand, point out the modified item or limit its meaning without expressing a quality. Types include:

- Numeral adjectives (*one, fifty, second*)
- Articles (*a, an, the*)
- Pronominal adjectives: pronouns used as adjectives (*his* desk, *each* employee)
- Demonstrative adjectives: *this, these, that, those* (*these* tires, *that* invoice)

Proper adjectives are derived from proper nouns:

Chinese customs	*Orwellian* overtones

Predicate adjectives complete the meaning of the predicate and are introduced by linking verbs:

The location is *perfect*.	Prices are *high*.

1.4.2 Comparative Degree

Most adjectives can take three forms: simple, comparative, and superlative. The simple form modifies a single noun or pronoun. Use the comparative form when comparing two items. When comparing three or more items, use the superlative form:

Simple	Comparative	Superlative
hard	harder	hardest
safe	safer	safest
dry	drier	driest

The comparative form adds *er* to the simple form, and the superlative form adds *est*. (The *y* at the end of a word changes to *i* before the *er* or *est* is added.)

A small number of adjectives are irregular, including these:

Simple	Comparative	Superlative
good	better	best
bad	worse	worst
little	less	least

When the simple form of an adjective has two or more syllables, you usually add *more* to form the comparative and *most* to form the superlative:

Simple	Comparative	Superlative
useful	more useful	most useful
exhausting	more exhausting	most exhausting
expensive	more expensive	most expensive

The most common exceptions are two-syllable adjectives that end in *y*:

Simple	Comparative	Superlative
happy	happier	happiest
costly	costlier	costliest

If you choose this option, change the *y* to *i* and tack *er* or *est* onto the end.

Some adjectives cannot be used to make comparisons because they themselves indicate the extreme. For example, if something is perfect, nothing can be more perfect. If something is unique or ultimate, nothing can be more unique or more ultimate.

1.4.3 Hyphenated Adjectives

Many adjectives used in the business world are actually combinations of words: *up-to-date* report, *last-minute* effort, *fifth-floor* suite, *well-built* engine. As you can see, they are hyphenated when they come before the noun they modify. However, when such word combinations come after the noun they modify, they are not hyphenated. In the following example, the adjectives appear in italics and the nouns they modify are underlined:

The <u>report</u> is *up to date* because of our team's *last-minute* <u>efforts</u>.

Hyphens are not used when part of the combination is a word ending in *ly* (because that word is usually not an adjective). Hyphens are also omitted from word combinations that are used so frequently that readers are used to seeing the words together:

We live in a *rapidly shrinking* world.

Our *highly motivated* employees will be well paid.

Please consider renewing your *credit card* account.

Send those figures to our *data processing* department.

Our new intern is a *high school* student.

1.5 Adverbs

An **adverb** modifies a verb, an adjective, or another adverb:

Modifying a verb:	Our marketing department works *efficiently*.
Modifying an adjective:	She was not dependable, although she was *highly* intelligent.
Modifying another adverb:	When signing new clients, he moved *extremely* cautiously.

An adverb can be a single word (*clearly*), a phrase (*very clearly*), or a clause (*because it was clear*).

1.5.1 Types of Adverbs

Simple adverbs are simple modifiers:

The door opened *automatically*.

The order arrived *yesterday*.

Top companies were *there*.

Interrogative adverbs ask a question:

Where have you been?

Conjunctive adverbs connect clauses:

We can't start *until* Maria gets here.

Jorge tried to explain *how* the new software works.

Words frequently used as conjunctive adverbs include *where, wherever, when, whenever, while, as, how, why, before, after, until,* and *since*.

    Negative adverbs include *not, never, seldom, rarely, scarcely, hardly,* and similar words. Negative adverbs are powerful words and therefore do not need any help in conveying a negative thought. Avoid using double negatives like these:

I don't want no mistakes.
(Correct: "I don't want any mistakes," or "I want no mistakes.")

They couldn't hardly read the report.
(Correct: "They could hardly read the report," or "They couldn't read the report.")

They scarcely noticed neither one.
(Correct: "They scarcely noticed either one," or "They noticed neither one.")

1.5.2 Adverb–Adjective Confusion

Many adverbs are adjectives turned into adverbs by adding *ly*: *highly, extremely, officially, closely, really*. In addition, many words can be adjectives or adverbs, depending on their usage in a particular sentence:

The *early* bird gets the worm. [adjective]	We arrived *early*. [adverb]
It was a *hard* decision. [adjective]	He hit the wall *hard*. [adverb]

Because of this situation, some adverbs are difficult to distinguish from adjectives. For example, in the following sentences, is the underlined word an adverb or an adjective?

They worked <u>well</u>.

The baby is <u>well</u>.

In the first sentence, *well* is an adverb modifying the verb *worked*. In the second sentence, *well* is an adjective modifying the noun *baby*. To choose correctly between adverbs and adjectives, remember that linking verbs are used to connect an adjective to describe a noun. In contrast, you would use an adverb to describe an action verb:

Adjective	**Adverb**
He is *good* worker. (What kind of worker is he?)	He works *well*. (How does he work?)
It is a *real* computer. (What kind of computer is it?)	It *really* is a computer. (To what extent is it a computer?)
The traffic is *slow*. (What quality does the traffic have?)	The traffic moves *slowly*. (How does the traffic move?)
This food tastes *bad* without salt. (What quality does the food have?)	This food *badly* needs salt. (How much is it needed?)

1.5.3 Comparative Degree

Like adjectives, adverbs can be used to compare items. Generally, the basic adverb is combined with *more* or *most*, just as long adjectives are. However, some adverbs have one-word comparative forms:

One Item	**Two Items**	**Three Items**
quickly	more quickly	most quickly
sincerely	less sincerely	least sincerely
fast	faster	fastest
well	better	best

Practice Session: Adjectives and Adverbs

Underline the preferred choice within each set of parentheses in the following sentences.

1. I always choose the (*less, least*) expensive brand.
2. Which would be (*better, best*), the store brand or the generic brand?
3. This audit couldn't have come at a (*worse, worst*) time.
4. When it comes to data analysis, Claire is (*more competent, competenter*) than Alexander.
5. The ad agency's campaign for our new vitamin supplement is (*unique, very unique, most unique*), to say the least.
6. A corporation can benefit from a (*well written, well-written*) annual report.
7. The chairman's introductory message to the annual report was (*well written, well-written*).

8. Even a (*beautifully written, beautifully-written*) report can be hampered by poor design and production.
9. According to Bank of America, the number of mortgage applications from (*lower-income, lower income*) consumers has tripled in the past year.
10. Angela wasn't feeling (*good, well*), so she went home early.
11. Harrison and Martinez work (*good, well*) together.
12. We are (*real, really*) excited about next week's product launch.
13. Could this project be moving any more (*slow, slowly*) through the bureaucratic system?
14. We (*could hardly, couldn't hardly*) wait to see how the brochure had turned out.
15. Today TeKTech is (*more heavy, more heavily, most heavily*) involved in nanotechnology, compared to five years ago.

1.6 Other Parts of Speech

Nouns, pronouns, verbs, adjectives, and adverbs carry most of the meaning in a sentence. Four other parts of speech link them together in sentences: prepositions, conjunctions, articles, and interjections.

1.6.1 Prepositions

A **preposition** is a word or group of words that describes a relationship between other words in a sentence. A simple preposition is made up of one word: *of, in, by, above, below*. A *compound preposition* is made up of two prepositions: *out of, from among, except for, because of*.

A **prepositional phrase** is a group of words introduced by a preposition that functions as an adjective (an adjectival phrase) or as an adverb (adverbial phrase) by telling more about a pronoun, noun, or verb:

The shipment will be here *by next Friday*.

Put the mail *in the out-bin*.

Prepositional phrases should be placed as close as possible to the element they are modifying:

Shopping *on the Internet* can be confusing for the uninitiated. (*not* Shopping can be confusing for the uninitiated *on the Internet*.)

Some prepositions are closely linked with a verb. When using phrases such as *look up* and *wipe out*, keep them intact and do not insert anything between the verb and the preposition.

You may have been told that it is unacceptable to put a preposition at the end of a sentence. However, that is not a hard-and-fast rule, and trying to follow it can sometimes be a challenge. You can end a sentence with a preposition as along as the sentence sounds natural and as long as rewording the sentence would create awkward wording:

I couldn't tell what they were interested in.

What did she attribute it to?

What are you looking for?

Avoid using unnecessary prepositions. In the following examples, the prepositions in parentheses should be omitted:

All (of) the staff members were present.

I almost fell off (of) my chair with surprise.

Where was Mr. Steuben going (to)?

They couldn't help (from) wondering.

The opposite problem is failing to include a preposition when you should. Consider these two sentences:

Sales were over $100,000 for Linda and Bill.

Sales were over $100,000 for Linda and for Bill.

The first sentence indicates that Linda and Bill had combined sales over $100,000; the second, that Linda and Bill each had sales over $100,000, for a combined total in excess of $200,000. The preposition *for* is critical here.

When the same preposition can be used for two or more words in a sentence without affecting the meaning, only the last preposition is required:

We are familiar (with) and satisfied with your company's products.

But when different prepositions are normally used with the words, all the prepositions must be included:

We are familiar with and interested in your company's products.

Some prepositions have come to be used in a particular way with certain other parts of speech. Here is a partial list of some prepositions that have come to be used with certain words:

according to	independent of
agree to (a proposal)	inferior to
agree with (a person)	plan to
buy from	prefer to
capable of	prior to
comply with	reason with
conform to	responsible for
differ from (things)	similar to
differ with (person)	talk to (without interaction)
different from	talk with (with interaction)
get from (receive)	wait for (person or thing)
get off (dismount)	wait on (like a waiter)

If you are unsure of the correct idiomatic expression, check a dictionary.

Some verb–preposition idioms vary depending on the situation: You agree *to* a proposal but *with* a person, *on* a price, or *in* principle. You argue *about* something, *with* a person, and *for* or *against* a proposition. You compare one item *to* another to show their similarities; you compare one item *with* another to show differences.

Here are some other examples of preposition usage that have given writers trouble:

among/between: *Among* is used to refer to three or more (Circulate the memo *among* the staff); *between* is used to refer to two (Put the copy machine *between* Judy and Dan).

as if/like: *As if* is used before a clause (It seems *as if* we should be doing something); *like* is used before a noun or pronoun (He seems *like* a nice guy).

have/of: *Have* is a verb used in verb phrases (They should *have* checked first); *of* is a preposition and is never used in such cases.

in/into: *In* is used to refer to a static position (The file is *in* the cabinet); *into* is used to refer to movement toward a position (Put the file *into* the cabinet).

1.6.2 Conjunctions

Conjunctions connect the parts of a sentence: words, phrases, and clauses. A **coordinating conjunction** connects two words, phrases, or clauses of equal rank. The simple coordinating conjunctions include *and, but, or, nor, for, yet,* and *so.* **Correlative conjunctions** are coordinating conjunctions used in pairs: *both/and, either/or, neither/nor, not only/but also.* Constructions with correlative conjunctions should be parallel, with the same part of speech following each element of the conjunction:

> The purchase was *not only* expensive *but also* unnecessary.
>
> The purchase *not only* was expensive *but also was* unnecessary.

Conjunctive adverbs are adverbs used to connect or show relationships between clauses. They include *however, nevertheless, consequently, moreover,* and *as a result.*

A **subordinate conjunction** connects two clauses of unequal rank; it joins a dependent (subordinate) clause to the independent clause on which it depends (for more on dependent and independent clauses, see Section 1.7.1). Subordinate conjunctions include *as, if, because, although, while, before, since, that, until, unless, when, where,* and *whether.*

1.6.3 Articles and Interjections

Only three **articles** exist in English: *the, a,* and *an.* These words are used, like adjectives, to specify which item you are talking about. *The* is called the *definite article* because it indicates a specific noun; *a* and *an* are called the *indefinite articles* because they are less specific about what they are referring to.

If a word begins with a vowel (soft) sound, use *an;* otherwise, use *a.* It's *a history,* not *an history, a hypothesis,* not *an hypothesis.* Use *an* with an "h" word only if it is a soft "h," as in *honor* and *hour.* Use *an* with words that are pronounced with a soft vowel sound even if they are spelled beginning with a consonant (usually in the case of abbreviations): *an SEC application, an MP3 file.* Use *a* with words that begin with vowels if they are pronounced with a hard sound: *a university, a Usenet account.*

Repeat an article if adjectives modify different nouns: *The red house and the white house are mine.* Do not repeat an article if all adjectives modify the same noun: *The red and white house is mine.*

Interjections are words that express no solid information, only emotion:

Wow!	Well, well!
Oh, no!	Good!

Such purely emotional language has its place in private life and advertising copy, but it only weakens the effect of most business writing.

Practice Session: Prepositions, Conjunctions, Articles, and Interjections

Circle the letter of the preferred choice in each pair of sentences.

1. **A.** If we want to have the project done next week, we'll need those balance sheets by Wednesday.
   B. If we want to have the project done next week, by Wednesday we'll need those balance sheets.

2. **A.** From where did that information come?
   B. Where did that information come from?

3. **A.** Please look up the shipping rates for packages to France.
   B. Please look the shipping rates up for packages to France.

4. **A.** You need to indicate the type job you're seeking.
   B. You need to indicate the type of job you're seeking.

5. **A.** Michael got the actuarial data off of the Internet.
   B. Michael got the actuarial data off the Internet.

6. **A.** When the meeting is over, Michelle will prepare the minutes.
   B. When the meeting is over with, Michelle will prepare the minutes.

7. **A.** Sharon is familiar and knowledgeable about HTML coding.
   B. Sharon is familiar with and knowledgeable about HTML coding.

8. **A.** We'll be deciding among the four applicants this afternoon.
   B. We'll be deciding between the four applicants this afternoon.

9. **A.** Because Marshall isn't here, it looks like the conference call will have to be canceled.
   B. Because Marshall isn't here, it looks as if the conference call will have to be canceled.

10. **A.** I would have had the memo done sooner, but my computer crashed.
    B. I would of had the memo done sooner, but my computer crashed.

11. **A.** When we have the survey results, we can put them in the report.
    B. When we have the survey results, we can put them into the report.

12. **A.** If you agree with the settlement, I can prepare the final papers.
    B. If you agree to the settlement, I can prepare the final papers.

13. **A.** It is important that you provide not only your name but also your address and telephone number.
    B. It is important that you provide not only your name but also address and telephone number.

14. **A.** The conference will be held in either March or July.
   B. The conference will be held either in March or July.

15. **A.** Please prepare an RFP for the construction job.
   B. Please prepare a RFP for the construction job.

1.7 Sentences

Sentences are constructed with the major building blocks, the parts of speech. Take, for example, this simple two-word sentence:

> Money talks.

It consists of a noun (*money*) and a verb (*talks*). When used in this way, the noun works as the first requirement for a sentence, the **subject**, and the verb works as the second requirement, the **predicate**. Without a subject (who or what does something) and a predicate (the doing of it), you have merely a collection of words, not a sentence.

1.7.1 Longer Sentences

More complicated sentences have more complicated subjects and predicates, but they still have a simple subject and a predicate verb. In the following examples, the subject is underlined once, the predicate verb twice:

> <u>Marex</u> and <u>Contron</u> <u><u>enjoy</u></u> higher earnings each quarter.

Marex [and] *Contron* do something; *enjoy* is what they do.

> My <u>interview</u>, coming minutes after my freeway accident, <u><u>did</u></u> not <u><u>impress</u></u> or <u><u>move</u></u> anyone.

Interview is what did something. What did it do? It *did* [not] *impress* [or] *move*.

> In terms of usable space, a steel <u>warehouse</u>, with its extremely long span of roof unsupported by pillars, <u><u>makes</u></u> more sense.

Warehouse is what *makes*.

These three sentences demonstrate several things. First, in all three sentences, the simple subject and predicate verb are the "bare bones" of the sentence, the parts that carry the core idea of the sentence. When trying to find the subject and predicate verb, disregard all prepositional phrases, modifiers, conjunctions, and articles.

Second, in the third sentence, the verb is singular (*makes*) because the subject is singular (*warehouse*). Even though the plural noun *pillars* is closer to the verb, *warehouse* is the subject. So *warehouse* determines whether the verb is singular or plural. Subject and predicate must agree.

Third, the subject in the first sentence is compound (*Marex* [and] *Contron*). A compound subject, when connected by *and*, requires a plural verb (*enjoy*). Also, the second sentence shows how compound predicates can occur (*did* [not] *impress* [or] *move*).

Fourth, the second sentence incorporates a group of words—*coming minutes after my freeway accident*—containing a form of a verb (*coming*) and a noun (*accident*). Yet, this group of words is not a complete sentence for two reasons:

- Not all nouns are subjects: *Accident* is not the subject of *coming*.
- Not all verbs are predicates: A verb that ends in *ing* can never be the predicate of a sentence (unless preceded by a form of *to be*, as in *was coming*).

Because they don't contain a subject and a predicate, the words *coming minutes after my freeway accident* (called a **phrase**) can't be written as a sentence. That is, the phrase cannot stand alone; it cannot begin with a capital letter and end with a period. So a phrase must always be just one part of a sentence.

Sometimes a sentence incorporates two or more groups of words that do contain a subject and a predicate; these word groups are called **clauses**:

> My <u>interview</u>, because it <u>came</u> minutes after my freeway accident, <u>did</u> not <u>impress</u> or <u>move</u> anyone.

The **independent clause** is the portion of the sentence that could stand alone without revision:

> My *interview* <u>did</u> not <u>impress</u> or <u>move</u> anyone.

The other part of the sentence could stand alone only by removing *because*.

> (because) It <u>came</u> minutes after my freeway accident.

This part of the sentence is known as a **dependent clause**; although it has a subject and a predicate (just as an independent clause does), it's linked to the main part of the sentence by a word (*because*) showing its dependence.

In summary, the two types of clauses—dependent and independent—both have a subject and a predicate. Dependent clauses, however, do not bear the main meaning of the sentence and are therefore linked to an independent clause. Nor can phrases stand alone, because they lack both a subject and a predicate. Only independent clauses can be written as sentences without revision.

1.7.2 Types of Sentences

Sentences come in four main types, depending on the extent to which they contain clauses. A **simple sentence** has one subject and one predicate; in short, it has one main independent clause:

> Boeing is the world's largest aerospace company.

A **compound sentence** consists of two independent clauses connected by a coordinating conjunction (*and*, *or*, *but*, etc.) or a semicolon:

> Airbus outsold Boeing for several years, but Boeing has recently regained the lead.

A **complex sentence** consists of an independent clause and one or more dependent clauses:

> Boeing is betting [independent clause] that airlines will begin using moderately smaller planes to fly passengers between smaller cities [dependent clause introduced by *that*].

A **compound-complex sentence** has two main clauses, at least one of which contains a subordinate (dependent clause):

> Boeing is betting [independent clause] that airlines will begin using moderately smaller planes to fly passengers between smaller cities [dependent clause], and it anticipates that new airports will be developed to meet passenger needs [independent clause].

1.7.3 Sentence Fragments

An incomplete sentence (a phrase or a dependent clause) that is written as though it were a complete sentence is called a **fragment**. Consider the following sentence fragments:

> Marilyn Sanders, having had pilferage problems in her store for the past year. Refuses to accept the results of our investigation.

This serious error can easily be corrected by putting the two fragments together:

> Marilyn Sanders, having had pilferage problems in her store for the past year, refuses to accept the results of our investigation.

The actual details of a situation will determine the best way for you to remedy a fragment problem.

The ban on fragments has one exception. Some advertising copy contains sentence fragments, written knowingly to convey a certain rhythm. However, advertising is the only area of business in which fragments are acceptable.

1.7.4 Fused Sentences and Comma Splices

Just as there can be too little in a group of words to make it a sentence, there can also be too much:

> All our mail is run through a postage meter every afternoon someone picks it up.

This example contains two sentences, not one, but the two have been blended so that it's hard to tell where one ends and the next begins. Is the mail run through a meter every afternoon? If so, the sentences should read:

> All our mail is run through a postage meter every afternoon. Someone picks it up.

Perhaps the mail is run through a meter at some other time (morning, for example) and is picked up every afternoon;

> All our mail is run through a postage meter. Every afternoon someone picks it up.

The order of words is the same in all three cases; sentence division makes all the difference. Either of the last two cases is grammatically correct. The choice depends on the facts of the situation.

Sometimes these so-called **fused sentences** have a more obvious point of separation:

> Several large orders arrived within a few days of one another, too many came in for us to process by the end of the month.

Here, the comma has been put between two independent clauses in an attempt to link them. When a lowly comma separates two complete sentences, the result is called a **comma splice**. A comma splice can be remedied in one of three ways:

- Replace the comma with a period and capitalize the next word: ". . . one another. Too many ". . ."
- Replace the comma with a semicolon and do not capitalize the next word: ". . . one another; too many . . ." This remedy works only when the two sentences have closely related meanings.

- Change one of the sentences so that it becomes a phrase or a dependent clause. This remedy often produces the best writing, but it takes more work.

The third alternative can be carried out in several ways. One is to begin the sentence with a subordinating conjunction:

> Whenever several large orders arrived within a few days of one another, too many came in for us to process by the end of the month.

Another way is to remove part of the subject or the predicate verb from one of the independent clauses, thereby creating a phrase:

> Several large orders arrived within a few days of one another, too many for us to process by the end of the month.

Finally, you can change one of the predicate verbs to its *ing* form:

> Several large orders arrived within a few days of one another, too many coming in for us to process by the end of the month.

In many cases, simply adding a coordinating conjunction can separate fused sentences or remedy a comma splice:

> You can fire them, or you can make better use of their abilities.

> Margaret drew up the designs, and Matt carried them out.

> We will have three strong months, but after that sales will taper off.

Be careful with coordinating conjunctions: Use them only to join simple sentences that express similar ideas.

Also, because they say relatively little about the relationship between the two clauses they join, avoid using coordinating conjunctions too often: *and* is merely an addition sign; *but* is just a turn signal; *or* only points to an alternative. Subordinating conjunctions such as *because* and *whenever* tell the reader a lot more.

1.7.5 Sentences with Linking Verbs

Linking verbs were discussed briefly in the section on verbs (Section 1.3). Here, you can see more fully the way they function in a sentence. The following is a model of any sentence with a linking verb:

> A *(verb)* B.

Although words such as *seems* and *feels* can also be linking verbs, let's assume that the verb is a form of *to be*:

> A *is* B.

In such a sentence, A and B are always nouns, pronouns, or adjectives. When one is a noun and the other is a pronoun, or when both are nouns, the sentence says that one is the same as the other:

> She is president.

> Rachel is president.

> She is forceful.

Recall from Section 1.3.3 that the noun or adjective that follows the linking verb is called a *complement*. When it is a noun or noun phrase, the complement is called a *predicate nominative*, when the complement is an adjective, it is referred to as a *predicate adjective*.

1.7.6 Misplaced Modifiers

The position of a modifier in a sentence is important. The movement of *only* changes the meaning in the following sentences:

Only we are obliged to supply those items specified in your contract.

We are obliged only to supply those items specified in your contract.

We are obliged to supply only those items specified in your contract.

We are obliged to supply those items specified only in your contract.

In any particular set of circumstances, only one of those sentences would be accurate. The others would very likely cause problems. To prevent misunderstanding, place such modifiers as close as possible to the noun or verb they modify.

For similar reasons, whole phrases that are modifiers must be placed near the right noun or verb. Mistakes in placement create ludicrous meanings:

Antia Information Systems bought new computer chairs for the programmers with more comfortable seats.

The anatomy of programmers is not normally a concern of business writers. Obviously, the comfort of the chairs was the issue:

Antia Information Systems bought programmers the new computer chairs with more comfortable seats.

Here is another example:

I asked him to file all the letters in the cabinet that had been answered.

In this ridiculous sentence, the cabinet has been answered, even though no cabinet in history is known to have asked a question. *That had been answered* is too far from *letters* and too close to *cabinet*. Here's an improvement:

I asked him to file in the cabinet all the letters that had been answered.

The term **dangling modifier** is often used to refer to a clause or phrase that because of its position in the sentence seems to modify a word that it is not meant to modify. For instance:

Lying motionless, co-workers rushed to Barry's aid.

Readers expect an introductory phrase to modify the subject of the main clause. But in this case it wasn't the *co-workers* who were lying motionless but rather *Barry* who was in this situation. Like this example, most instances of dangling modifiers occur at the beginning of sentences. The source of some danglers is a passive construction:

To find the needed information, the whole book had to be read.

In such cases, switching to the active voice can usually remedy the problem:

To find the needed information, you will need to read the whole book.

1.7.7 Parallelism

Two or more sentence elements that have the same relation to another element should be in the same form. Otherwise, the reader is forced to work harder to understand the meaning of the sentence. When a series consists of phrases or clauses, the same part of speech (preposition, gerund, etc.) should introduce them. Do not mix infinitives with participles or adjectives with nouns. Here are some examples of nonparallel elements:

Andersen is hiring managers, programmers, and people who work in accounting. [nouns not parallel]

Andersen earns income by auditing, consulting, and by bookkeeping. [prepositional phrases not parallel]

Andersen's goals are to win new clients, keeping old clients happy, and finding new enterprises. [infinitive mixed with gerunds]

Practice Session: Sentences

Circle the letter of the preferred choice in each group of sentences.

1. **A.** Cyberterrorism—orchestrated attacks on a company's information systems for political or economic purposes—is a very real threat.
   B. Cyberterrorism—orchestrated attacks on a company's information systems for political or economic purposes—are a very real threat.

2. **A.** E-mail, phone calls, and IM messages, each one a distraction, interrupts employees when they work.
   B. E-mail, phone calls, and IM messages, each one a distraction, interrupt employees when they work.

3. **A.** About 35 percent of major U.S. companies keep tabs on workers. Because they want to protect valuable company information.
   B. About 35 percent of major U.S. companies keep tabs on workers because they want to protect valuable company information.
   C. About 35 percent of major U.S. companies keep tabs on workers; because they want to protect valuable company information.

4. **A.** Despite its small size and relative isolation in the Arctic Circle. Finland leads the pack in mobile phone technology and its applications.
   B. Despite its small size and relative isolation in the Arctic Circle; Finland leads the pack in mobile phone technology and its applications.

C. Despite its small size and relative isolation in the Arctic Circle, Finland leads the pack in mobile phone technology and its applications.

5. A. Many employees erroneously believe that their e-mail and voice mail messages are private they're surprised when e-mail ends up in places where they did not intend it to go.
   B. Many employees erroneously believe that their e-mail and voice mail messages are private, they're surprised when e-mail ends up in places where they did not intend it to go.
   C. Many employees erroneously believe that their e-mail and voice mail messages are private, so they're surprised when e-mail ends up in places where they did not intend it to go.

6. A. Each day people in the United States treat themselves to more than 3 million Krispy Kreme doughnuts, they buy more than 11,000 dozen of those doughnuts every hour.
   B. Each day people in the United States treat themselves to more than 3 million Krispy Kreme doughnuts, buying more than 11,000 dozen of those doughnuts every hour.

7. A. The procedure for making Krispy Kreme doughnuts takes about an hour, the manufacturing process begins long before local stores crank up their production lines.
   B. The procedure for making Krispy Kreme doughnuts takes about an hour; the manufacturing process begins long before local stores crank up their production lines.
   C. The procedure for making Krispy Kreme doughnuts takes about an hour. But the manufacturing process begins long before local stores crank up their production lines.

8 A. After blending the ingredients, the doughnut mix is stored in Krispy Kreme's warehouse for a week.
   B. After blending the ingredients, Krispy Kreme's warehouse is used to store the doughnut mix for a week.
   C. After the ingredients have been blended, the doughnut mix is stored in Krispy Kreme's warehouse for a week.

9. A. Using computer-aided design, our engineers customize every bike to meet the rider's size and component preferences.
   B. Our engineers customize every bike with computer-aided design to meet the rider's size and component preferences

10. A. Catering to its customers, about 2,000 bikes are built annually by Green Gear Cycling.
    B. Catering to its customers, about 2,000 bikes are built by Green Gear Cycling annually.
    C. Catering to its customers, Green Gear Cycling builds about 2,000 bikes annually.

2.0 Punctuation

On the highway, signs tell you when to slow down or stop, where to turn, and when to merge. In similar fashion, punctuation helps readers negotiate your prose. The proper use of punctuation keeps readers from losing track of your meaning.

2.1 Periods

Use a period (1) to end any sentence that is not a question, (2) with certain abbreviations, and (3) between dollars and cents in an amount of money.

2.2 Question Marks

Use a question mark after any direct question that requests an answer:

> Are you planning to enclose a check, or shall we bill you?

Don't use a question mark with commands phrased as questions for the sake of politeness:

> Will you send us a check today.

A question mark should precede quotation marks, parentheses, and brackets if it is part of the quoted or parenthetical material; otherwise, it should follow:

> This issue of *Inc.* has an article titled "What's Your Entrepreneurial IQ?"

> Have you read the article "Five Principles of Guerrilla Marketing"?

Do not use the question mark with indirect questions or with requests:

> Mr. Antonelli asked whether anyone had seen Nathalia lately.

Do not use a comma or a period with a question mark; the question mark takes the place of these punctuation marks.

2.3 Exclamation Points

Use exclamation points after highly emotional language. Because business writing almost never calls for emotional language, you will seldom use exclamation points.

2.4 Semicolons

Semicolons have three main uses. One is to separate two closely related independent clauses:

> The outline for the report is due within a week; the report itself is due at the end of the month.

A semicolon should also be used instead of a comma when the items in a series have commas within them:

> Our previous meetings were on November 11, 2004; February 20, 2005; and April 28, 2006.

Finally, a semicolon should be used to separate independent clauses when the second one begins with a conjunctive adverb such as *however*, *therefore*, or *nevertheless* or a phrase such as *for example* or *in that case*:

> Our supplier has been out of part D712 for 10 weeks; however, we have found another source that can ship the part right away.

> His test scores were quite low; on the other hand, he has a lot of relevant experience.

Section 4.4 provides more information on using transitional words and phrases.

Semicolons should always be placed outside parentheses.

> Events Northwest has the contract for this year's convention (August 23–28); we haven't awarded the contract for next year yet.

2.5 Colons

Use a colon after the salutation in a business letter. You should also use a colon at the end of a sentence or phrase introducing a list or (sometimes) a quotation:

> Our study included the three most critical problems: insufficient capital, incompetent management, and inappropriate location.

A colon should not be used when the list, quotation, or idea is a direct object of the verb or preposition. This rule applies whether the list is set off or run in:

> We are able to supply
>
> staples
>
> wood screws
>
> nails
>
> toggle bolts

> This shipment includes 9 DVDs, 12 CDs, and 4 USB flash drives.

Another way you can use a colon is to separate the main clause and another sentence element when the second explains, illustrates, or amplifies the first:

> Management was unprepared for the union representatives' demands: this fact alone accounts for their arguing well into the night.

However, in contemporary usage, such clauses are frequently separated by a semicolon.

Like semicolons, colons should always be placed outside parentheses.

> He has an expensive list of new demands (none of which is covered in the purchase agreement): new carpeting, network cabling, and a new security system.

Practice Session: Punctuation 1

Circle the letter of the preferred choice in the following groups of sentences.

1. **A.** She asked me whether we should increase our insurance coverage?
   B. She asked me whether we should increase our insurance coverage.

2. **A.** Would you please let me know when the copier is free.
   B. Would you please let me know when the copier is free?

3. **A.** You won't want to miss this exciting seminar!
   B. You won't want to miss this exciting seminar.

4. **A.** The officers of the board of directors are John Rogers, president, Robin Doug Donlan, vice president for programming, Bill Pittman, vice president for operations, and Mary Sturhann, secretary.
   B. The officers of the board of directors are John Rogers, president; Robin Doug Donlan, vice president for programming; Bill Pittman, vice president for operations; and Mary Sturhann, secretary.

   C. The officers of the board of directors are John Rogers, president; Robin Doug Donlan, vice president for programming; Bill Pittman, vice president for operations, and Mary Sturhann, secretary.

5. **A.** Edward Jones is the best brokerage house in America; it has more offices than any other brokerage house.
   B. Edward Jones is the best brokerage house in America, it has more offices than any other brokerage house.

6. **A.** One of the SEC's top priorities is to crack down on insider trading, however it readily admits that it has not been very successful to date.
   B. One of the SEC's top priorities is to crack down on insider trading; however, it readily admits that it has not been very successful to date.

7. **A.** To keep on top of financial news, you should consult three newspapers aimed specifically at investors: *The Wall Street Journal, Investor's Business Daily,* and *Barron's*.
   B. To keep on top of financial news, you should consult three newspapers aimed specifically at investors; such as, *The Wall Street Journal, Investor's Business Daily,* and *Barron's*.
   C. To keep on top of financial news, you should consult three newspapers aimed specifically at investors; such as *The Wall Street Journal, Investor's Business Daily,* and *Barron's*.

8. **A.** I wonder if it is appropriate to call John's clients while he is on vacation.
   B. I wonder if it is appropriate to call John's clients while he is on vacation?

9. **A.** The three basic concepts that guide accountants are: the fundamental accounting equation, double-entry bookkeeping, and the matching principle.
   B. The three basic concepts that guide accountants are the fundamental accounting equation, double-entry bookkeeping, and the matching principle.
   C. The three basic concepts that guide accountants are the fundamental accounting equation; double-entry bookkeeping; and the matching principle.

10. **A.** Accountants are guided by three basic concepts, the fundamental accounting equation, double-entry bookkeeping, and the matching principle.
    B. Accountants are guided by three basic concepts: the fundamental accounting equation; double-entry bookkeeping; and the matching principle.
    C. Accountants are guided by three basic concepts: the fundamental accounting equation, double-entry bookkeeping, and the matching principle.

2.6 Commas

Commas have many uses; the most common is to separate items in a series:

> He took the job, learned it well, worked hard, and succeeded.

> Put paper, pencils, and paper clips on the requisition list.

Company style may dictate omitting the final comma in a series. However, if you have a choice, use the final comma; it's often necessary to prevent misunderstanding.

A second place to use a comma is between independent clauses that are joined by a coordinating conjunction (*and, but,* or *or*).

> She spoke to the sales staff, and he spoke to the production staff.
>
> I was advised to proceed, and I did.

A third use for the comma is to separate a dependent clause at the beginning of a sentence from an independent clause:

> Because of our lead in the market, we may be able to risk introducing a new product.

However, a dependent clause at the end of a sentence is separated from the independent clause by a comma only when the dependent clause is unnecessary to the main meaning of the sentence:

> We may be able to introduce a new product, although it may involve some risk.

A fourth use for the comma is after an introductory phrase or word:

> Starting with this amount of capital, we can survive in the red for one year.
>
> Through more careful planning, we may be able to serve more people.
>
> Yes, you may proceed as originally planned.

However, with short introductory prepositional phrases and some one-syllable words (such as *hence* and *thus*), the comma is often omitted:

> Before January 1 we must complete the inventory.
>
> Thus we may not need to hire anyone.
>
> In July we will complete the move to Tulsa.

Fifth, paired commas are used to set off nonrestrictive clauses and phrases. A **restrictive clause** is one that cannot be omitted without altering the meaning of the main clause, whereas a **nonrestrictive clause** can be:

> The *Time Magazine* website, which is produced by Steve Conley, has won several design awards. [nonrestrictive: the material set off by commas could be omitted]
>
> The website that is produced by Steve Conley has won several design awards. [restrictive: no commas are used before and after *that is produced by Steve Conley* because this information is necessary to the meaning of the sentence—it specifies which website]

A sixth use for commas is to set off appositive words and phrases. (An **appositive** has the same meaning as the word it is in apposition to.) Like nonrestrictive clauses, appositives can be dropped without changing or obscuring the meaning of the sentence:

> Conley, a freelance designer, also produces the websites for several nonprofit corporations.

Seventh, commas are used between adjectives modifying the same noun (coordinate adjectives):

> She left Monday for a long, difficult recruiting trip.

To test the appropriateness of such a comma, try reversing the order of the adjectives: *a difficult, long recruiting trip.* If the order cannot be reversed, leave out the comma (a *good old friend* isn't the same as an *old good friend*). A comma should not be used when one of the adjectives is part of the noun. Compare these two phrases:

> a distinguished, well-known figure
>
> a distinguished public figure

The adjective–noun combination of *public* and *figure* has been used together so often that it has come to be considered a single thing: *public figure.* So no comma is required.

Eighth, commas are used both before and after the year in sentences that include month, day, and year:

> It will be sent by December 15, 2007, from our Cincinnati plant.

Some companies write dates in another form: 15 December 2007. No commas should be used in that case. Nor is a comma needed when only the month and year are present (December 2007).

Ninth, commas are used to set off a variety of parenthetical words and phrases within sentences, including state names, dates, abbreviations, transitional expressions, and contrasted elements:

> They were, in fact, prepared to submit a bid.
>
> Habermacher, Inc., went public in 1999.
>
> Our goal was increased profits, not increased market share.
>
> Service, then, is our main concern.
>
> The factory was completed in Chattanooga, Tennessee, just three weeks ago.
>
> Joanne Dubiik, M.D., has applied for a loan from First Savings.
>
> I started work here on March 1, 2003, and soon received my first promotion.

Tenth, a comma is used to separate a quotation from the rest of the sentence:

> Your warranty reads, "These conditions remain in effect for one year from date of purchase."

However, the comma is left out when the quotation as a whole is built into the structure of the sentence:

> He hurried off with an angry "Look where you're going."

Finally, a comma should be used whenever it's needed to avoid confusion or an unintended meaning. Compare the following:

> Ever since they have planned new ventures more carefully.
>
> Ever since, they have planned new ventures more carefully.

2.7 Dashes

Use dashes to surround a comment that is a sudden turn in thought:

> Membership in the IBSA—it's expensive but worth it—may be obtained by applying to our New York office.

A dash can also be used to emphasize a parenthetical word or phrase:

> Third-quarter profits—in excess of $2 million—are up sharply.

Finally, use dashes to set off a phrase that contains commas:

> All our offices—Milwaukee, New Orleans, and Phoenix—have sent representatives.

Don't confuse a dash with a hyphen. A dash separates and emphasizes words, phrases, and clauses more strongly than commas or parentheses can; a hyphen ties two words so tightly that they almost become one word.

When using a computer, use the em dash symbol. When typing a dash in e-mail, type two hyphens with no space before, between, or after.

A second type of dash, the en dash, can be produced with computer word processing and page-layout programs. This kind of dash is shorter than the regular dash and longer than a hyphen. It is reserved almost exclusively for indicating "to" or "through" with numbers such as dates and pages: *2001–2002, pages 30–44*.

2.8 Hyphens

Hyphens are mainly used in three ways. The first is to separate the parts of compound words beginning with such prefixes as *self-*, *ex-*, *quasi-*, and *all-*:

self-assured	quasi-official
ex-wife	all-important

However, do not use hyphens in words that have prefixes such as *pro, anti, non, re, pre, un, inter*, and *extra*:

prolabor	nonunion
antifascist	interdepartmental

Exceptions occur when (1) the prefix occurs before a proper noun or (2) the vowel at the end of the prefix is the same as the first letter of the root word:

pro-Republican	anti-American
anti-inflammatory	extra-atmospheric

When in doubt, consult your dictionary.

Hyphens are used in some types of spelled-out numbers. For instance, they are used to separate the parts of a spelled-out number from *twenty-one* to *ninety-nine* and for spelled-out fractions: *two-thirds, one-sixth* (although some style guides say not to hyphenate fractions used as nouns).

Certain compound nouns are formed by using hyphens: *secretary-treasurer, city-state*. Check your dictionary for compounds you're unsure about.

Hyphens are also used in some compound adjectives, which are adjectives made up of two or more words. Specifically, you should use hyphens in compound adjectives that come before the noun:

an interest-bearing account	well-informed executives

However, you need not hyphenate when the adjective follows a linking verb:

> This account is interest bearing.
> Their executives are well informed.

You can shorten sentences that list similar hyphenated words by dropping the common part from all but the last word:

> Check the costs of first-, second-, and third-class postage.

Finally, hyphens may be used to divide words at the end of a typed line. Such hyphenation is best avoided, but when you have to divide words at the end of a line, do so correctly (see Section 3.5). Dictionaries show how words are divided into syllables.

2.9 Apostrophes

Use an apostrophe in the possessive form of noun (but not in a pronoun):

> On his desk was a reply to Bette *Ainsley's* application for the *manager's* position.

Apostrophes are also used in place of the missing letter(s) of a contraction:

Whole Words	Contraction
we will	we'll
do not	don't
they are	they're

2.10 Quotation Marks

Use quotation marks to surround words that are repeated exactly as they were said or written:

> The collection letter ended by saying, "This is your third and final notice."

Remember: (1) When the quoted material is a complete sentence, the first word is capitalized. (2) The final comma or period goes inside the closing quotation marks.

Quotation marks are also used to set off the title of a newspaper story, magazine article, or book chapter:

> You should read "Legal Aspects of the Collection Letter" in *Today's Credit*.

Quotation marks may also be used to indicate special treatment for words or phrases, such as terms that you're using in an unusual or ironic way:

> Our management "team" spends more time squabbling than working to solve company problems.

When you are defining a word, put the definition in quotation marks:

> The abbreviation *etc.* means "and so forth."

When using quotation marks, take care to insert the closing marks as well as the opening ones.

Although periods and commas go inside any quotation marks, colons and semicolons generally go outside them.

A question mark goes inside the quotation marks only if the quotation is a question:

> All that day we wondered, "Is he with us?"

If the quotation is not a question but the entire sentence is, the question mark goes outside:

> What did she mean by "You will hear from me"?

For quotes within quotes, use single quotation marks within double:

> As David Pottruck, former co-CEO of Charles Schwab, told it, "I assembled about 100 managers at the base of the Golden Gate Bridge and gave them jackets emblazoned with the phrase 'Crossing the Chasm' and then led them across the bridge."

Otherwise, do not use single quotation marks for anything, including titles of works—that's British style.

2.11 Parentheses and Brackets

Use parentheses to surround comments that are entirely incidental or to supply additional information:

> Our figures do not match yours, although (if my calculations are correct) they are closer than we thought.

> These kinds of supplements do not require FDA (Food and Drug Administration) approval.

Parentheses are used in legal documents to surround figures in arabic numerals that follow the same amount in words:

> Remittance will be One Thousand Two Hundred Dollars ($1,200).

Be careful to put punctuation marks (period, comma, and so on) outside the parentheses unless they are part of the statement in parentheses. And keep in mind that parentheses have both an opening and a closing mark; both should always be used, even when setting off listed items within text: *(1)*, not *1)*.

Brackets are used for notation, comment, explanation, or correction within quoted material:

> In the interview, multimillionaire Bob Buford said, "One of my major influences was Peter [Drucker], who encourages people and helps them believe in themselves."

Brackets are also used for parenthetical material that falls within parentheses:

> Drucker's magnum opus *(Management: Tasks, Responsibilities, Practices* [Harper & Row, 1979]) has influenced generations of entrepreneurs.

2.12 Ellipses

Use ellipsis points, or three evenly spaced periods, to indicate that material has been left out of a direct quotation. Use them only in direct quotations and only at the point where material was left out. In the following example, the first sentence is quoted in the second:

> The Dow Jones Industrial Average fell 276.39 points, or 2.6%, during the week to 10292.31.

> According to the *Wall Street Journal*, "The Dow Jones Industrial Average fell 276.39 points . . . to 10,292.31."

The number of dots in ellipses is not optional; always use three. Occasionally, the points of an ellipsis come at the end of a sentence, where they seem to grow a fourth dot. Don't be fooled: One of the dots is a period. Ellipsis points should always be preceded and followed by a space.

Avoid using ellipses to represent a pause in your writing; use a dash for that purpose:

> At first we had planned to leave for the conference on Wednesday—but then we changed our minds. [not *on Wednesday . . . but then*]

2.12.1 Practice Session: Punctuation 2

Circle the letter of the preferred choice in each group of sentences.

1. **A.** Capital One uses data mining to predict what customers might buy, and how the company can sell those products to them.
   B. Capital One uses data mining to predict what customers might buy and how the company can sell those products to them.

2. **A.** During the three-year lawsuit, pressure built to settle out of court.
   B. During the three-year lawsuit pressure built to settle out of court.

3. **A.** The music store, which had been in the Harper family for three generations, was finally sold to a conglomerate.
   B. The music store which had been in the Harper family for three generations was finally sold to a conglomerate.

4. **A.** After the fire, Hanson resolved to build a bigger better bottling plant.
   B. After the fire, Hanson resolved to build a bigger, better bottling plant.

5. **A.** Wild Oats, a chain of natural food grocery stores, uses kiosks to deliver nutrition information to customers.
   B. Wild Oats; a chain of natural food grocery stores; uses kiosks to deliver nutrition information to customers.

6. **A.** Management consultant Peter Drucker said "The aim of marketing is to know the customer so well that the product or service sells itself.
   B. Management consultant Peter Drucker said, "The aim of marketing is to know the customer so well that the product or service sells itself."

7. **A.** Companies use a wide variety of techniques-contests, displays, and giveaways, to name a few-to sell you things.
   B. Companies use a wide variety of techniques—contests, displays, and giveaways, to name a few—to sell you things.
   C. Companies use a wide variety of techniques—contests, displays, and giveaways to name a few—to sell you things.

8. A. Self-insurance plans are not subject to state regulation or premium taxes.

   B. Self insurance plans are not subject to state regulation or premium taxes.

   C. Selfinsurance plans are not subject to state regulation or premium taxes.

9. A. Because ours is a non-profit corporation, we don't pay federal taxes.

   B. Because ours is a nonprofit corporation, we don't pay federal taxes.

10. A. The decision-making process depends on a buyer's culture, social class, and self-image.

   B. The decision-making process depends on a buyer's culture, social class, and self image.

   C. The decision making process depends on a buyer's culture, social class, and self-image.

11. A. Situation factors also play a role in consumer decision-making.

   B. Situation factors also play a role in consumer decision making.

12. A. Did you read the article "Citi Will Return $7 Billion to Investors"?

   B. Did you read the article "Citi Will Return $7 Billion to Investors?"

   C. Did you read the article "Citi Will Return $7 Billion to Investors?".

13. A. An insider at Arthur Andersen said that "the fall of the accounting giant stemmed from a series of poor management decisions made over decades."

   B. An insider at Arthur Andersen said that, "The fall of the accounting giant stemmed from a series of poor management decisions made over decades."

14. A. Have you read Jason Zein's article "Measuring the Internet?"

   B. Have you read Jason Zein's article "Measuring the Internet"?

15. A. According to Jamba Juice founder Kirk Peron, "jamba" is a West African word meaning *to celebrate.*

   B. According to Jamba Juice founder Kirk Peron, *jamba* is a West African word meaning "to celebrate."

   C. According to Jamba Juice founder Kirk Peron, "jamba" is a West African word meaning to celebrate.

3.0 Mechanics

The most obvious and least tolerable mistakes that a business writer makes are probably those related to grammar and punctuation. However, a number of small details, known as writing mechanics, demonstrate the writer's polish and reflect on the company's professionalism.

When it comes to mechanics, also called *style*, many of the "rules" are not hard and fast. Publications and organizations vary in their preferred styles for capitalization, abbreviations, numbers, italics, and so on. Here, we'll try to differentiate

between practices that are generally accepted and those that can vary. When you are writing materials for a specific company or organization, find out the preferred style (such as *The Chicago Manual of Style* or Webster's *Style Manual*). Otherwise, choose a respected style guide. The key to style is consistency: If you spell out the word *percent* in one part of a document, don't use the percent sign in a similar context elsewhere in the same document.

3.1 Capitalization

With capitalization, you can follow either an "up" style (when in doubt, capitalize: *Federal Government, Board of Directors*) or a "down" style (when in doubt, use lowercase: *federal government, board of directors*). The trend over the last few decades has been toward the down style. Your best bet is to get a good style manual and consult it when you have a capitalization question. Following are some rules that most style guides agree on.

Capital letters are used at the beginning of certain word groups:

- **Complete sentence:** Before hanging up, he said, "We'll meet here on Wednesday at noon."

- **Formal statement following a colon:** She has a favorite motto: Where there's a will, there's a way.

- **Phrase used as sentence:** Absolutely not!

- **Quoted sentence embedded in another sentence:** Scott said, "Nobody was here during lunch hour except me."

- **List of items set off from text:** Three preliminary steps are involved:
  > Design review
  > Budgeting
  > Scheduling

Capitalize proper adjectives and proper nouns (the names of particular persons, places, and things):

> Darrell Greene lived in a Victorian mansion.

> We sent Ms. Larson an application form, informing her that not all applicants are interviewed.

> Let's consider opening a branch in the West, perhaps at the west end of Tucson, Arizona.

> As office buildings go, the Kinney Building is a pleasant setting for TDG Office Equipment.

> We are going to have to cancel our plans for hiring French and German sales reps.

Larson's name is capitalized because she is a particular applicant, whereas the general term *applicant* is left uncapitalized. Likewise, *West* is capitalized when it refers to a particular place but not when it means a direction. In the same way, *office* and *building* are not capitalized when they are general terms (common nouns), but they are capitalized when they are part of the title of a particular office or building (proper nouns). Some proper adjectives are lowercased when they are part of terms that have come into common use, such as *french fries* and *roman numerals*.

Titles within families or companies as well as professional titles may also be capitalized:

> I turned down Uncle David when he offered me a job.
> I wouldn't be comfortable working for one of my relatives.

We've never had a president quite like President Sweeney.

People's titles are capitalized when they are used in addressing a person, especially in a formal context. They are not usually capitalized, however, when they are used merely to identify the person:

Address the letter to Chairperson Anna Palmer.

I wish to thank Chairperson Anna Palmer for her assistance.

Anna Palmer, chairperson of the board, took the podium.

Also capitalize titles if they are used by themselves in addressing a person:

Thank you, Doctor, for your donation.

Always capitalize the first word of the salutation and complimentary close of a letter:

Dear Mr. Andrews: *Yours* very truly,

The names of organizations are capitalized, of course; so are the official names of their departments and divisions. However, do not use capitals when referring in general terms to a department or division, especially one in another organization:

Route this memo to Personnel.

Larry Tien was transferred to the Microchip Division.

Will you be enrolled in the Psychology Department?

Someone from the personnel department at EnerTech stopped by the booth.

Capitalization is unnecessary when using a word like *company*, *corporation*, or *university* alone:

The corporation plans to issue 50,000 shares of common stock.

Likewise, the names of specific products are capitalized, although the names of general product types are not:

Apple Inc.   Xerox machine
Tide laundry detergent

When it comes to government terminology, here are some guides to capitalization: (1) Lowercase *federal* unless it is part of an agency name; (2) capitalize names of courts, departments, bureaus, offices, and agencies but lowercase such references as *the bureau* and *the department* when the full name is not used; (3) lowercase the titles of government officers unless they precede a specific person's name: *the secretary of state, the senator, the ambassador, the governor, and the mayor* but *Mayor Gonzalez* (Note: style guides vary on whether to capitalize *president* when referring to the president of the United States without including the person's name); capitalize the names of laws and acts: *the Sherman Antitrust Act, the Civil Rights Act*; (5) capitalize the names of political parties but lowercase the word *party: Democratic party, Libertarian party*.

One problem that often arises in writing about places is the treatment of two or more proper nouns of the same type. When the common word comes before the specific names, it is capitalized; when it comes after the specific names, it is not:

Lakes Ontario and Huron

Allegheny and Monongahela rivers

The names of languages, races, and ethnic groups are capitalized: Japanese, Caucasian, Hispanic. But racial terms that denote only skin color are not capitalized: black, white.

When referring to the titles of books, articles, magazines, newspapers, reports, movies, and so on, you should capitalize the first and last words and all nouns, pronouns, adjectives, verbs, and adverbs, and capitalize prepositions and conjunctions with five letters or more. Except for the first and last words, do not capitalize articles:

Economics During the Great War

"An Investigation into the Market for Long-Distance Services"

"What Successes Are Made Of"

When *the* is part of the official name of a newspaper or magazine, it should be treated this way too:

The Wall Street Journal

Style guides vary in their recommendations regarding capitalization of hyphenated words in titles. A general guide is to capitalize the second word in a temporary compound (a compound that is hyphenated for grammatical reasons and not spelling reasons), such as *Law-Abiding Citizen*, but to lowercase the word if the term is always hyphenated, such as *Son-in-law*).

References to specific pages, paragraphs, lines, and the like are not capitalized: *page 73, line 3*. However, in most other numbered or lettered references, the identifying term is capitalized:

Chapter 4   *Serial No. 382-2203*   *Item B-11*

Finally, the names of academic degrees are capitalized when they follow a person's name but are not capitalized when used in a general sense:

I received a bachelor of science degree.

Thomas Whitelaw, Doctor of Philosophy, will attend.

Similarly, general courses of study are not capitalized, but the names of specific classes are:

She studied accounting as an undergraduate.

She is enrolled in Accounting 201.

3.2 Underscores and Italics

Usually a line typed underneath a word or phrase either provides emphasis or indicates the title of a book, magazine, or newspaper. If possible, use italics instead of an underscore. Italics (or underlining) should also be used for defining terms and for discussing words as words:

In this report, *net sales* refers to after-tax sales dollars.

The word *building* is a common noun and should not be capitalized.

Also use italics to set off foreign words, unless the words have become a common part of English:

Top Shelf is considered the *sine qua non* of comic book publishers.

Chris uses a laissez-faire [no italic] management style.

3.3 Abbreviations

Abbreviations are used heavily in tables, charts, lists, and forms. They're used sparingly in prose. Here are some abbreviation situations to watch for:

- In most cases do not use periods with acronyms (words formed from the initial letter or letters of parts of a term): *CEO, CD-ROM, DOS, YWCA, FDA;* but *Ph.D., M.A., M. D.*

- Use periods with abbreviations such as *Mr., Ms., Sr., Jr., a.m., p.m., B.C.,* and *A.D.*

- The trend is away from using periods with such units of measure as *mph, mm,* and *lb.*

- Use periods with such Latin abbreviations as *e.g., i.e., et al.,* and *etc.* However, style guides recommend that you avoid using these Latin forms and instead use their English equivalents (*for example, that is,* and *others,* and *and so on,* respectively). If you must use these abbreviations, such as in parenthetical expressions or footnotes, do not put them in italics.

- Some companies have abbreviations as part of their names (*&, Co., Inc., Ltd.*). When you refer to such firms by name, be sure to double-check the preferred spelling, including spacing: *AT&T; Barnes & Noble; Carson Pirie Scott & Company; PepsiCo; Kate Spade, Inc.; National Data Corporation; Siemens Corp.; Glaxo Wellcome PLC; US Airways; U.S. Business Reporter.*

- Most style guides recommend that you spell out *United States* as a noun and reserve *U.S.* as an adjective preceding the noun modified.

One way to handle an abbreviation that you want to use throughout a document is to spell it out the first time you use it, follow it with the abbreviation in parentheses, and then use the abbreviation in the remainder of the document.

3.4 Numbers

Numbers may be correctly handled many ways in business writing, so follow company style. In the absence of a set style, however, generally spell out all numbers from one to nine and use arabic numerals for the rest.

There are some exceptions to this general rule. For example, never begin a sentence with a numeral:

> Twenty of us produced 641 units per week in the first 12 weeks of the year.

Use numerals for the numbers one through nine if they're in the same list as larger numbers:

> Our weekly quota rose from 9 to 15 to 27.

Use numerals for percentages, time of day (except with o'clock), dates, and (in general) dollar amounts:

> Our division is responsible for 7 percent of total sales.

> The meeting is scheduled for 8:30 a.m. on August 2.

> Add $3 for postage and handling.

When using numerals for time, be consistent: It should be *between 10:00 a.m. and 4:30 p.m.,* not *between 10 a.m. and 4:30 p.m.* Expressions such as *4:00 o'clock* and *7 a.m. in the morning* are redundant.

Use a comma in numbers expressing thousands (1,257), unless your company specifies another style. When dealing with numbers in the millions and billions, combine words and figures: 7.3 million, 2 billion.

When writing dollar amounts, use a decimal point only if cents are included. In lists of two or more dollar amounts, use the decimal point either for all or for none:

> He sent two checks, one for $67.92 and one for $90.00.

When two numbers fall next to each other in a sentence, use figures for the number that is largest, most difficult to spell, or part of a physical measurement; use words for the other:

> I have learned to manage a classroom of 30 twelve-year-olds.

> She won a bonus for selling 24 thirty-volume sets.

> You'll need twenty 3-inch bolts.

In addresses, all street numbers except One are in numerals. So are suite and room numbers and zip codes. For street names that are numbered, practice varies so widely that you should use the form specified on an organization's letterhead or in a reliable directory. All the following examples are correct:

Telephone numbers are always expressed in numerals. Parentheses may separate the area code from the rest of the

One Fifth Avenue	297 Ninth Street
1839 44th Street	11026 West 78 Place

number, but a slash or a hyphen may be used instead, especially if the entire phone number is enclosed in parentheses:

382-8329	(602/382-8329)	602-382-8329

Percentages are always expressed in numerals. The word *percent* is used in most cases, but % may be used in tables, forms, and statistical writing.

Ages are usually expressed in words—except when a parenthetical reference to age follows someone's name:

> Mrs. Margaret Sanderson is seventy-two.

> Mrs. Margaret Sanderson, 72, swims daily.

Also, ages expressed in years and months are treated like physical measurements that combine two units of measure: *5 years 6 months.*

Physical measurements such as distance, weight, and volume are also often expressed in numerals: *9 kilometers, 5 feet 3 inches, 7 pounds 10 ounces.*

Decimal numbers are always written in numerals. In most cases, add a zero to the left of the decimal point if the number is less than one and does not already start with a zero:

1.38	.07	0.2

In a series of related decimal numbers with at least one number greater than one, make sure that all numbers smaller than one have a zero to the left of the decimal point: 1.20, 0.21, 0.09.

Simple fractions are written in words, but more complicated fractions are expressed in figures or, if easier to read, in figures and words:

two-thirds	9/32	2 hundredths

Most style guides recommend that you use a comma with numbers consisting of four digits: *2,345,* not *2345.*

When typing ordinal numbers, such as *3rd edition* or *21st century,* your word processing program may automatically make the letters *rd* (or *st, th,* or *nd*) into a superscript. Do yourself a favor and turn that formatting function off in your "Preferences," as superscripts should not be used in regular prose or even in bibliographies.

3.5 Word Division

In general, avoid dividing words at the end of lines. When you must do so, follow these rules:

- Don't divide one-syllable words (such as *since, walked,* and *thought*), abbreviations (*mgr.*), contractions (*isn't*), or numbers expressed in numerals (*117,500*).

- Divide words between syllables, as specified in a dictionary or word-division manual.

- Make sure that at least three letters of the divided words are moved to the second line: *sin-cerely* instead of *sincere-ly*.

- Do not end a page or more than three consecutive lines with hyphens.

- Leave syllables consisting of a single vowel at the end of the first line (*impedi-ment* instead of *imped-iment*), except when the single vowel is part of a suffix such as *-able, -ible, -ical,* or *-ity* (*re-spons-ible* instead of *re-sponsi-ble*).

- Divide between double letters (*tomor-row*), except when the root word ends in double letters (*call-ing* instead of *cal-ling*).

- Wherever possible, divide hyphenated words at the hyphen only: instead of *anti-inde-pendence,* use *anti-independence.*

- Whenever possible, do not break URLs or e-mail addresses. If you have to break a long URL or e-mail address, do not insert a hyphen at the end of the first line.

Practice Session: Mechanics

Circle the letter of the preferred choice in each of the following groups of sentences.

1. **A.** When you are in New York City for the sales meeting, be sure to visit the art deco Chrysler Building.
   B. When you are in New York city for the sales meeting, be sure to visit the Art Deco Chrysler building.
   C. When you are in New York City for the sales meeting, be sure to visit the Art Deco Chrysler Building.

2. **A.** We plan to expand our national operations to the west as well as the south.
   B. We plan to expand our national operations to the West as well as the South.
   C. We plan to expand our national operations to the west as well as the South.

3. **A.** Lee Marrs, who is President of Lee Marrs Designs, has been chosen to revamp our website.
   B. Lee Marrs, who is president of Lee Marrs Designs, has been chosen to revamp our website.
   C. Lee Marrs, who is President of Lee Marrs Designs, has been chosen to revamp our Website.

4. **A.** There's one thing we know for sure: Having a good idea doesn't guarantee success.
   B. There's one thing we know for sure: having a good idea doesn't guarantee success.

5. **A.** Be sure to order manila envelopes in all sizes: 9", 12", 11", 14", etc.
   B. Be sure to order manila envelopes in all sizes: 9", 12", 11", 14" and etc.

6. **A.** The traditional trading period for U.S. stock exchanges is 9:30 A.M. to 4 o'clock P.M.

7. **B.** The traditional trading period for U.S. stock exchanges is 9:30 A.M. to 4 P.M.
   C. The traditional trading period for U.S. stock exchanges is 9:30 A.M to 4:00 P.M.

7. **A.** The number of members on the board of directors has been reduced from 13 to nine.
   B. The number of members on the board of directors has been reduced from 13 to 9.

8. **A.** The CDs are priced at $15, $12.95, and $11.00.
   B. The CDs are priced at $15.00, $12.95, and $11.00.
   C. The CDs are priced at $15, $12.95, and $11.

9. **A.** Twenty people have signed up for the spreadsheet software class, but there is room for 25.
   B. 20 people have signed up for the spreadsheet software class, but there is room for 25.

10. **A.** The best way to divide the word *sincerely* is "sin-cerely."
    B. The best way to divide the word *sincerely* is "sincere-ly."

4.0 Vocabulary

Using the right word in the right place is a crucial skill in business communication. However, many pitfalls await the unwary.

4.1 Frequently Confused Words

Because the following sets of words sound similar, be careful not to use one when you mean to use the other:

Word	Meaning
accede	to comply with
exceed	to go beyond
accept	to take
except	to exclude
access	admittance
excess	too much
advice	suggestion
advise	to suggest
affect	to influence
effect	the result
allot	to distribute
a lot	much or many
all ready	completely prepared
already	completed earlier
born	given birth to
borne	carried
capital	money; chief city
capitol	a government building
cite	to quote
sight	a view
site	a location
complement	complete amount; to go well with
compliment	expression of esteem; to flatter
corespondent	party in a divorce suit
correspondent	letter writer

Word	Meaning
council	a panel of people
counsel	advice; a lawyer
defer	to put off until later
differ	to be different
device	a mechanism
devise	to plan
die	to stop living; a tool
dye	to color
discreet	careful
discrete	separate
envelop	to surround
envelope	a covering for a letter
forth	forward
fourth	number four
holey	full of holes
holy	sacred
wholly	completely
human	of people
humane	kindly
incidence	frequency
incidents	events
instance	example
instants	moments
interstate	between states
intrastate	within a state
later	afterward
latter	the second of two
lead	a metal; to guide
led	guided
lean	to rest at an angle
lien	a claim
levee	embankment
levy	tax
loath	reluctant
loathe	to hate
loose	free; not tight
lose	to mislay
material	substance
materiel	equipment
miner	mineworker
minor	underage person
moral	virtuous; a lesson
morale	sense of well-being
ordinance	law
ordnance	weapons
overdo	to do in excess
overdue	past due

Word	Meaning
peace	lack of conflict
piece	a fragment
pedal	a foot lever
peddle	to sell
persecute	to torment
prosecute	to sue
personal	private
personnel	employees
precedence	priority
precedents	previous events
principal	sum of money; chief; main
principle	general rule
rap	to knock
wrap	to cover
residence	home
residents	inhabitants
right	correct
rite	ceremony
write	to form words on a surface
role	a part to play
roll	to tumble; a list
root	part of a plant
rout	to defeat
route	a traveler's way
shear	to cut
sheer	thin, steep
stationary	immovable
stationery	paper
than	as compared with
then	at that time
their	belonging to them
there	in that place
they're	they are
to	a preposition
too	excessively; also
two	the number
waive	to set aside
wave	a swell of water; a gesture
weather	atmospheric conditions
whether	if
who's	contraction of "who is" or "who has"
whose	possessive form of who

In the preceding list, only enough of each word's meaning is given to help you distinguish between the words in each group. Several meanings are left out entirely. For more complete definitions, consult a dictionary.

Practice Session: Confused Words

In the following sentences, underline the preferred choice within each set of parentheses.

1. If our bid is (*accepted, excepted*), we will begin the project in November.
2. This website offers some great (*advice, advise*) on setting up a new business.
3. How will the accounting scandal (*affect, effect*) Arthur Andersen's future?
4. Most of the costs of the project will be (*born, borne*) by the contractor.
5. In preparing the budget, we have to decide where best to invest our (*capital, capitol*).
6. Be sure to (*cite, site*) the sources for your data when you prepare your report.
7. The acquisition of LPC Group should (*compliment/complement*) our other holdings.
8. Leo sought the (*council, counsel*) of his attorney before signing the contract.
9. I didn't have to be told to be (*discrete, discreet*) about the sexual harassment case.
10. When Jennings Hardware got behind in its debts, one of the creditors placed a (*lean, lien*) on its building.
11. Mr. Hathaway was (*loath, loathe*) to fire Elizabeth, but he had no choice.
12. To comply with local zoning (*ordinances, ordnances*), we had to replace our sign.
13. As a teenager, Gary Sassaman used to (*pedal, peddle*) newspapers in downtown Pittsburgh.
14. Business owners along El Cajon Boulevard have vowed to (*persecute, prosecute*) anyone caught painting graffiti on their buildings.
15. We don't know of any (*precedence, precedents*) for the exponential growth of sales for this kind of product.
16. The (*principle, principal*) reason for closing down operations was obsolete production equipment that was too expensive to replace.
17. It's hard to say what (*role, roll*) the downturn in the economy played in the failure of Seven Hills Distribution.
18. Sunbeam employees were shocked by new CEO Al Dunlap's (*shear, sheer*) ruthlessness in axing jobs and slashing costs.
19. Now that our area code has changed, we will need to order new (*stationary, stationery*).
20. The Rodriguez brothers couldn't decide (*weather, whether*) to form a partnership or establish a corporation.

4.2 Frequently Misused Words

The following words tend to be misused for reasons other than their sound. Reference books (including the *Random House College Dictionary*, revised edition; Follett's *Modern American Usage*; and Fowler's *Modern English Usage*) can help you with similar questions of usage:

a lot: When the writer means "many," *a lot* is always two separate words, never one.

aggravate/irritate: *Aggravate* means "to make things worse." Sitting in the smoke-filled room *aggravated* his sinus condition. *Irritate* means "to annoy." Her constant questions *irritated* [not *aggravated*] me.

anticipate/expect: *Anticipate* means "to prepare for": Macy's *anticipated* increased demand for athletic shoes in spring by ordering in November. In formal usage, it is incorrect to use *anticipate* for *expect*: I *expected* (not *anticipated*) a better response to our presentation than we actually got.

compose/comprise: The whole comprises the parts:

The company's distribution division *comprises* four departments.

It would be incorrect usage to say

The company's distribution division *is comprised of* four departments.

In that construction, *is composed of* or *consists of* would be preferable. It might be helpful to think of *comprise* as meaning "encompasses" or "contains."

continual/continuous: *Continual* refers to ongoing actions that have breaks:

Her *continual* complaining will accomplish little in the long run.

Continuous refers to ongoing actions without interruptions or breaks:

A *continuous* stream of paper came out of the fax machine.

convince/persuade: One is *convinced* of a fact or that something is true; one is *persuaded* by someone else to do something. The use of *to* with *convince* is unidiomatic—you don't convince someone to do something, you persuade them to do it.

correspond with: Use this phrase when you are talking about exchanging letters. Use *correspond to* when you mean "similar to." Use either *correspond with* or *correspond to* when you mean "relate to."

dilemma/problem: Technically, a *dilemma* is a situation in which one must choose between two undesirable alternatives. It shouldn't be used when no choice is actually involved.

disinterested: This word means "fair, unbiased, having no favorites, impartial." If you mean "bored" or "not interested," use *uninterested*.

etc.: This abbreviated form of the Latin phrase *et cetera* means "and so on" or "and so forth," so it is never correct to write *and etc.* The current tendency among business writers is to use English rather than Latin.

flaunt/flout: To *flaunt* is to be ostentatious or boastful; to *flout* is to mock or scoff at.

impact: Avoid using *impact* as a verb when *influence* or *affect* is meant.

imply/infer: Both refer to hints. Their great difference lies in who is acting. The writer *implies*, the reader *infers*, sees between the lines.

lay: This word is a transitive verb. Never use it for the intransitive *lie*. (See Section 1.3.3.)

lend/loan: *Lend* is a verb; *loan* is a noun. Usage such as "Can you loan me $5?" is therefore incorrect.

less/fewer: Use *less* for uncountable quantities (such as amounts of water, air, sugar, and oil). Use *fewer* for countable quantities (such as numbers of jars, saws, words, page, and humans). The same distinction applies to *much* and *little* (uncountable) versus *many* and *few* (countable).

liable/likely: *Liable* means "responsible for": I will hold you *liable* if this deal doesn't go through. It is incorrect to use *liable* for "possible": Anything is *likely* (not *liable*) to happen.

literally: *Literally* means "actually" or "precisely"; it is often misused to mean "almost" or "virtually." It is usually best left out entirely or replaced with *figuratively*.

many/much: See *less/fewer*.

regardless: The *less* suffix is the negative part. No word needs two negative parts, so don't add *ir* (a negative prefix) to the beginning. There is no such word as *irregardless*.

try: The *less* suffix is the negative part. No word needs two negative parts, so don't add *ir* (a negative prefix) to the beginning. There is no such word as *irregardless*.

try: Always follow with *to*, never *and*.

verbal: People in the business community who are careful with language frown on those who use *verbal* to mean "spoken" or "oral." Many others do say "verbal agreement." Strictly speaking, *verbal* means "of words" and therefore includes both spoken and written words. Follow company usage in this matter.

Practice Session: Misused Words

In the following sentences, underline the preferred choice within each set of parentheses.

1. My boss told me that I still have (*a lot, alot*) to learn.
2. The U.S. Congress corresponds (*to, with*) the British Parliament.
3. I tried to convince my co-workers to sign up for the stress reduction program, but they all seemed (*uninterested, disinterested*).
4. When you say that the books have some discrepancies, are you (*inferring, implying*) that our accountant is embezzling from us?
5. From the auditor's silent stare, Margaret (*implied, inferred*) that the man was not amused by her jokes.
6. The report came out to (*less, fewer*) pages than we had originally anticipated.
7. Mr. Martens was treating Heather (*like, as if*) she had done something wrong.
8. You have to finish the job, (*irregardless, regardless*) of your loathing for it.
9. When talking to customers on the phone, try (*and, to*) be as pleasant as possible.
10. When making (*an oral, a verbal*) presentation, it's a good idea to make eye contact with your audience.

4.3 Frequently Misspelled Words

All of us, even the world's best spellers, sometimes have to check a dictionary for the spelling of some words. People who have never memorized the spelling of commonly used words must look up so many that they grow exasperated and give up on spelling words correctly.

Don't expect perfection and don't surrender. If you can memorize the spelling of just the words listed here, you'll need the dictionary far less often and you'll write with more confidence:

absence	achieve	aluminum	gesture
absorption	advantageous	ambience	grievous
accessible	affiliated	analyze	
accommodate	aggressive	apparent	haphazard
accumulate	alignment	appropriate	harassment
		argument	holiday
		asphalt	
		assistant	illegible
		asterisk	immigrant
		auditor	incidentally
			indelible
		bankruptcy	independent
		believable	indispensable
		brilliant	insistent
		bulletin	intermediary
			irresistible
		calendar	
		campaign	jewelry
		category	judgment
		ceiling	judicial
		changeable	
		clientele	labeling
		collateral	legitimate
		committee	leisure
		comparative	license
		competitor	litigation
		concede	
		congratulations	maintenance
		connoisseur	mathematics
		consensus	mediocre
		convenient	minimum
		convertible	
		corroborate	necessary
		criticism	negligence
			negotiable
		definitely	newsstand
		description	noticeable
		desirable	
		dilemma	occurrence
		disappear	omission
		disappoint	
		disbursement	parallel
		discrepancy	pastime
		dissatisfied	peaceable
		dissipate	permanent
			perseverance
		eligible	persistent
		embarrassing	personnel
		endorsement	persuade
		exaggerate	possesses
		exceed	precede
		exhaust	predictable
		existence	preferred
		extraordinary	privilege
			procedure
		fallacy	proceed
		familiar	pronunciation
		flexible	psychology
		fluctuation	pursue
		forty	

questionnaire	superintendent
	supersede
receive	surprise
recommend	
repetition	tangible
rescind	tariff
rhythmical	technique
ridiculous	tenant
	truly
salable	
secretary	unanimous
seize	until
separate	
sincerely	vacillate
succeed	vacuum
suddenness	vicious

Practice Session: Misspelled Words

In the following sentences, underline the preferred choice within each set of parentheses.

1. We try to (*accomodate, accommodate*) any reasonable request from our customers.
2. You will need to (*analyse, analyze*) the sales data to determine which products to phase out.
3. Because the weather in Chicago is so (*changable, changeable*), the conference reception has a backup indoor venue.
4. The board reached a (*concencus, consensus*) on the new CEO.
5. It will be (*embarassing, embarrassing*) for the company if this information leaks out.
6. The auditors discovered the (*existance, existence*) of hidden accounts in foreign banks.
7. Every company should have a written sexual (*harassment, harrassment*) policy.
8. In today's book business, (*independant, independent*) publishers are having a tough time finding distribution.
9. Use your best (*judgment, judgement*) when choosing the paper for our new stationery.
10. The cost of a business (*licence, license, liscence*) varies from city to city.
11. With all the turmoil (*occuring, occurring*) in the stock market, we've decided to shift our investments toward real estate.
12. The marketing survey found that consumers (*prefered, preferred*) brand-name dog food over generic brands.
13. Because her cost-cutting measures saved the company millions of dollars, Carolyn Kelly (*received, recieved*) a raise and a promotion.
14. Please send (*separate, seperate*) invoices for the two projects.
15. My supervisor didn't need to be so (*vicious, viscious*) in his critique of my performance.

4.4 Transitional Words and Phrases

The following sentences don't communicate as well as they could because they lack a transitional word or phrase:

> Production delays are inevitable. Our current lag time in filling orders is one month.

A semicolon between the two sentences would signal a close relationship between their meanings, but it wouldn't even hint at what that relationship is. Here are the sentences again, now linked by means of a semicolon, with a space for a transitional word or phrase:

> Production delays are inevitable; _____, our current lag time in filling orders is one month.

Now read the sentence with *nevertheless* in the blank space. Then try *therefore, incidentally, in fact,* and *at any rate* in the blank. Each substitution changes the meaning of the sentence.

Here are some transitional words (conjunctive adverbs) that will help you write more clearly:

accordingly	furthermore	moreover
anyway	however	otherwise
besides	incidentally	still
consequently	likewise	therefore
finally	meanwhile	

The following transitional phrases are used in the same way:

as a result	in other words
at any rate	in the second place
for example	on the other hand
in fact	to the contrary

When one of these words or phrases joins two independent clauses, it should be preceded by a semicolon and followed by a comma:

> The consultant recommended a complete reorganization; moreover, she suggested that we drop several products.

Practice Session Answers

Answers for Nouns: 1. City 2. Building / building 3. hotels 4. *t*'s / *i*'s 5. 1990s 6. shelves 7. specialties 8. cases 9. company's 10. editor-in-chief's 11. businesses' 12. passengers' 13. day's 14. Dallas's 15. Jones's

Answers for Pronouns: 1. me 2. she 3. him 4. We 5. me 6. its 7. his or her 8. Who 9. whom 10. Whom 11. her 12. him or her 13. her 14. its 15. Who 16. your 17. its 18. I 19. their 20. its

Answers for Verbs: 1. comes, want 2. knew 3. begun 4. lie 5. laid 6. sits 7. set 8. raise 9. was 10. is 11. is 12. are 13. is 14. is 15. represents 16. is 17. are 18. is 19. send 20. were

Answers for Adjectives and Adverbs: 1. least 2. better 3. worse 4. more competent 5. unique 6. well-written 7. well written 8. beautifully written 9. lower-income 10. well 11. well 12. really 13. slowly 14. could hardly 15. more heavily

Answers for Prepositions, Conjunctions, Articles, and Interjections: 1. a 2. b 3. a 4. b 5. b 6. a 7. b 8. a 9. b 10. a 11. b 12. b 13. a 14. a 15. a

Answers for Sentences: 1. a 2. b 3. b 4. c 5. c 6. b 7. c 8. c 9. a 10. c

Answers for Punctuation 1:   1. b 2. a 3. b 4. b 5. a 6. b 7. a 8. a 9. b 10. c

Answers for Punctuation 2:   1. b 2. a 3. a 4. b 5. a 6. b 7. b 8. a 9. b 10. a 11. b 12. a 13. a 14. b 15. b

Answers for Mechanics: 1. c 2. b 3. b 4. a 5. a 6. c 7. b 8. b 9. a 10. a

Answers for Confused Words: 1. accepted 2. advice 3. affect 4. borne 5. capital 6. cite 7. complement 8. counsel 9. discreet 10. lien 11. loath 12. ordinances 13. peddle 14. prosecute 15. precedents 16. principal 17. role 18. sheer 19. stationery 20. whether

Answers for Misused Words: 1. a lot 2. to 3. uninterested 4. implying 5. inferred 6. fewer 7. as if 8. regardless 9. to 10. an oral

Answers for Misspelled Words: 1. accommodate 2. analyze 3. changeable 4. consensus 5. embarrassing 6. existence 7. harassment 8. independent 9. judgment 10. license 11. occurring 12. preferred 13. received 14. separate 15. vicious

Answer Key

ANSWER KEY TO THE LEVEL 1 SELF-ASSESSMENT EXERCISES

CHAPTER 1: Self-Assessment—Nouns

1. Give the <u>balance sheet</u> to ⬛Melissa⬛. (1.1.1)
2. We'd like to order <u>50</u> more <u>satchels</u> for ⬛Craigmont Stores⬛ and <u>3</u> each for the other <u>stores</u> on our <u>list</u>. (1.1.1)
3. ⬛Tarnower Corporation⬛ donates a <u>portion</u> of its <u>profits</u> to <u>charity</u> every <u>year</u>. (1.1.1)
4. Which aluminum <u>bolts</u> are packaged? (1.1.1)
5. Please send the ⬛Joneses⬛ a <u>dozen</u> of each of the <u>following</u>: <u>stopwatches</u>, <u>canteens</u>, <u>headbands</u>, and <u>wristbands</u>. (1.1.1)
6. The <u>technician</u> has already repaired the ⬛machine⬛ for the ⬛client⬛. (1.1.2)
7. An <u>attorney</u> will talk to the ⬛group⬛ about ⬛incorporation⬛. (1.1.2)
8. After her ⬛vacation⬛, the <u>buyer</u> prepared a third-quarter ⬛budget⬛. (1.1.2)
9. The new flat <u>monitors</u> are serving our ⬛department⬛ very well. (1.1.2)
10. <u>Accuracy</u> overrides ⬛speed⬛ in ⬛importance⬛. (1.1.2)
11. <u>copies</u>_____ Make sure that all <u>copys</u> include the new addresses. (1.1.2)
12. <u>employees'</u>_____ Ask Jennings to collect all <u>employee's</u> donations for the Red Cross drive. (1.1.4)
13. <u>sons-in-law / businesses</u> Charlie now has two <u>son-in-laws</u> to help him with his two online <u>business's</u>. (1.1.3, 1.1.4)
14. <u>parentheses</u> Avoid using too many <u>parenthesises</u> when writing your reports. (1.1.3)
15. <u>Ness's / week's</u> Follow President <u>Nesses</u> rules about what constitutes a <u>weeks</u> work. (1.1.4)

CHAPTER 2: Self-Assessment—Pronouns

1. whom (1.2)
2. them (1.2)
3. them (1.2)
4. its (1.2)
5. whose (1.2)
6. The sales staff is preparing guidelines for (*their*, ⬛*its*⬛) clients. (1.2.5)
7. Few of the sales representatives turn in (⬛*their*⬛, *its*) reports on time. (1.2.5)
8. The board of directors has chosen (*their*, ⬛*its*⬛) officers. (1.2.5)
9. Gomez and Archer have told (*his*, ⬛*their*⬛) clients about the new program. (1.2.1)
10. Each manager plans to expand (*his*, *their*, ⬛*his or her*⬛) sphere of control next year. (1.2.3)
11. Has everyone supplied (*his*, *their*, ⬛*his or her*⬛) Social Security number? (1.2.3)
12. After giving every employee (*his*, *their*, ⬛*a*⬛) raise, George told (⬛*them*⬛, *they*, *all*) about the increased work load. (1.2.3, 1.2.4)

13. Bob and Tim have opposite ideas about how to achieve company goals. (⬛*Who*⬛, *Whom*) do you think will win the debate? (1.2.4)
14. City Securities has just announced (*who*, ⬛*whom*⬛) it will hire as CEO. (1.2.4)
15. Either of the new products would readily find (*their*, ⬛*its*⬛) niche in the marketplace. (1.2.5)

CHAPTER 3: Self-Assessment—Verbs

1. have become (1.3.1)
2. knew (1.3.1)
3. has moved (1.3.1)
4. will do (1.3.1)
5. will have returned (1.3.1)
6. Leslie Cartwright will write the report. (1.3.5)
7. I failed to record the transaction. (1.3.5)
8. Has the claims department notified you of your rights? (1.3.5)
9. We depend on their services for our operation. (1.3.5)
10. The customer returned the damaged equipment before we even located a repair facility. (1.3.5)
11. Everyone upstairs (*receive*, ⬛*receives*⬛) mail before we do. (1.3.4)
12. Neither the main office nor the branches (*is*, ⬛*are*⬛) blameless. (1.3.4)
13. C&B Sales (⬛*is*⬛, *are*) listed in the directory. (1.3.4)
14. When measuring shelves, 7 inches (⬛*is*⬛, *are*) significant. (1.3.4)
15. About 90 percent of the employees (⬛*plan*⬛, *plans*) to come to the company picnic. (1.3.4)

CHAPTER 4: Self-Assessment—Adjectives

1. greater (1.4.1)
2. most perfect (1.4.1)
3. most interesting (1.4.1)
4. better (1.4.1)
5. hardest (1.4.1)
6. A highly placed source revealed Dotson's last-ditch efforts to cover up the mistake. (1.4.2)
7. Please send an extra-large dust cover for my photocopier. (1.4.2)
8. A top-secret document was taken from the president's office last night. (1.4.2)
9. A 30-year-old person should know better. (1.4.2)
10. If I write a large-scale report, I want to know that it will be read by upper-level management. (1.4.2)
11. The two companies are engaged in an all-out, no-holds-barred struggle for dominance. (1.4)
12. A tiny metal shaving is responsible for the problem. (1.4)
13. She came to the office with a bruised, swollen knee. (1.4)
14. A chipped, cracked sheet of glass is useless to us. (1.4)
15. You'll receive our usual cheerful, prompt service. (1.4)

CHAPTER 5: Self-Assessment—Adverbs

1. good (1.5)
2. surely (1.5)
3. sick (1.5)
4. well (1.5)
5. good (1.5)
6. faster (1.5.2)
7. most recently (1.5.2)
8. more happily (1.5.2)
9. better (1.5.2)
10. most logically (1.5.2)
11. He doesn't seem to have any. *OR* He seems to have none. (1.5.1)
12. That machine is scarcely used. *OR* That machine is never used. (1.5.1)
13. They can't get any replacement parts until Thursday. *OR* They can get no replacement parts until Thursday. (1.5.1)
14. It wasn't any different from the first event we promoted. *OR* It was no different from the first event we promoted. (1.5.1)
15. We've looked for it, and it doesn't seem to be anywhere. *OR* We've looked for it, and it seems to be nowhere. (1.5.1)

CHAPTER 6: Self-Assessment— Prepositions and Conjunctions

1. Where was your argument leading ~~to~~? (1.6.1)
2. I wish he would get off ~~of~~ the phone. (1.6.1)
3. This is a project ~~into which~~ you can sink your teeth into. (1.6.1)
4. U.S. Mercantile must become aware of and sensitive to its customers' concerns. (1.6.1)
5. We are responsible for aircraft safety in the air, in the hangars, and on the runways. (1.6.1)
6. to (1.6.1)
7. among (1.6.1)
8. for (1.6.1)
9. to (1.6.1)
10. from (1.6.1)
11. She is active ~~in~~ not only in a civic group but also in an athletic organization. *OR* She is active in not only a civic group but ~~in~~ also an athletic organization. (1.6.2)
12. That is either a mistake or ~~was~~ an intentional omission. (1.6.2)
13. The question is whether to set up a booth at the convention or ~~be~~ to host a hospitality suite. (1.6.2)
14. We are doing better ~~in~~ both in overall sales and in profits. *OR* We are doing better in both overall sales and ~~in~~ profits. (1.6.2)
15. She had neither the preferred educational background, nor ~~did she have~~ the suitable experience. (1.6.2)

CHAPTER 7: Self-Assessment—Periods, Question Marks, and Exclamation Points

1. Dr. Eleanor H. Hutton has requested information on TaskMasters, Inc. (2.1)
2. That qualifies us as a rapidly growing new company, don't you think? (2.2)
3. Our president, Daniel Gruber, is a CPA. On your behalf, I asked him why he started the company. (2.1)

4. In the past three years, we have experienced phenomenal growth of 800 percent. *OR* In the past three years, we have experienced phenomenal growth of 800 percent! (2.1, 2.3)
5. Contact me at 1358 N. Parsons Avenue, Tulsa, OK 74204. (2.1)
6. Jack asked, "Why does he want to know? Maybe he plans to become a competitor." *OR* Jack asked, "Why does he want to know? Maybe he plans to become a competitor!" (2.1, 2.2, 2.3)
7. The debt load fluctuates with the movement of the U.S. prime rate. (2.1)
8. I can't believe we could have missed such a promising opportunity! (2.3)
9. Is consumer loyalty extinct? Yes and No. (2.2, 2.1)
10. Johnson and Kane, Inc., has gone out of business. What a surprise. *OR* Johnson and Kane, Inc., has gone out of business. What a surprise! (2.1, 2.3)
11. Will you please send us a check today so that we can settle your account. (2.1)
12. Mr. James R. Capp will be our new CEO, beginning January 20, 2009. (2.1)
13. The rag doll originally sold for $1,098, but we have lowered the price to a mere $599. (2.1)
14. Will you be able to make the presentation at the conference, or should we find someone else? (2.2)
15. So I ask you, "When will we admit defeat?" Never! (2.2, 2.3)

CHAPTER 8: Self-Assessment—Semicolons and Colons

1. This letter looks good; that one doesn't. (2.4)
2. I want to make one thing perfectly clear: neither of you will be promoted if sales figures don't improve. (2.5)
3. The Zurich airport has been snowed in; therefore, I won't be able to meet with you before January 4. (2.4)
4. His motivation was obvious: to get Meg fired. (2.5)
5. Only two firms have responded to our survey: J. J. Perkins and Tucker & Tucker. (2.5)
6. Send a copy to Mary Kent, Marketing Director; Robert Bache, Comptroller; and Dennis Mann, Sales Director. (2.4)
7. Please be sure to interview these employees next week: Henry Gold, Doris Hatch, and George Iosupovich. (2.5)
8. We have observed your hard work; because of it, we are promoting you to manager of your department. (2.4)
9. You shipped three items on June 7; however, we received only one of them. (2.4)
10. The convention kit includes the following response cards: giveaways, brochures, and a display rack. (2.5)
11. The workers wanted an immediate wage increase; they had not had a raise in nearly two years. (2.4)
12. This, then, is our goal for 2009: to increase sales 35 percent. (2.5)
13. His writing skills are excellent; however, he still needs to polish his management style. (2.4)
14. We would like to address three issues: efficiency, profitability, and market penetration. (2.5)
15. Remember this rule: When in doubt, leave it out. (2.5)

CHAPTER 9: Self-Assessment—Commas

1. Please send us four cases of filters, two cases of wing nuts, and a bale of rags. (2.6)
2. Your analysis, however, does not account for returns. (2.6)
3. As a matter of fact, she has seen the figures. (2.6)
4. Before May 7, 1999, they wouldn't have minded either. (2.6)
5. After Martha has gone, talk to me about promoting her. (2.6)
6. Stoneridge, Inc., went public on September 9, 2009. (2.6)
7. We want the new copier, not the old model. (2.6)
8. "Talk to me," Sandra said, "before you change a thing." (2.6)
9. Because of a previous engagement, Dr. Stoeve will not be able to attend. (2.6)
10. The company started attracting attention during the long, hard recession of the mid-1970s. (2.6)
11. You can reach me at this address: 717 Darby Place, Scottsdale, Arizona 85251. (2.6)
12. Transfer the documents from Fargo, North Dakota, to Boise, Idaho. (2.6)
13. Sam O'Neill, the designated representative, is gone today. (2.6)
14. With your help, we will soon begin. (2.6)
15. She may hire two new representatives, or she may postpone filling those territories until spring. (2.6)

CHAPTER 10: Self-Assessment—Dashes and Hyphens

1. Three qualities—speed, accuracy, and reliability—are desirable in any applicant to the data entry department. (2.7)
2. A highly placed source explained the top-secret negotiations. (2.8)
3. The file on Marian Gephardt—yes, we finally found it— reveals a history of late payments. (2.7)
4. They're selling a well-designed machine. (2.8)
5. A bottle-green sports jacket is hard to find. (2.8)
6. Argentina, Brazil, Mexico—these are the countries we hope to concentrate on. (2.7)
7. Only two sites—maybe three—offer the things we need. (2.7)
8. How many owner-operators are in the industry? (2.8)
9. Your ever-faithful assistant deserves—without a doubt—a substantial raise. (2.8, 2.7)
10. Myrna Talefiero is this organization's president-elect. (2.8)
11. Stealth, secrecy, and surprise—those are the elements that will give us a competitive edge. (2.7)
12. The charts are well placed on each page—unlike the running heads and footers. (2.8, 2.7)
13. We got our small-business loan—an enormous advantage. (2.8, 2.7)
14. Ron Franklin—do you remember him?—will be in town Monday. (2.7)
15. Your devil-may-care attitude affects everyone involved in the decision-making process (2.8)

CHAPTER 11: Self-Assessment—Quotation Marks, Parentheses, Ellipses, Underscores, and Italics

1. Be sure to read "How to Sell by Listening" in this month's issue of Fortune. (2.10, 3.2)
2. Her response (see the attached memo) is disturbing. (2.11)
3. Contact is an overused word. (3.2)
4. We will operate with a skeleton staff during the holiday break (December 21 through January 2). (2.11)
5. "The SBP's next conference," the bulletin noted, "will be held in Minneapolis." (2.10)
6. Sara O'Rourke (a reporter from The Wall Street Journal) will be here on Thursday. (2.11, 3.2)
7. I don't care why you didn't fill my order; I want to know when you'll fill it. (3.2)
8. The term up in the air means "undecided" (2.10, 3.2)
9. Her assistant (the one who just had the baby) won't be back for four weeks. (2.11)
10. "Ask not what your country can do for you . . ." is the beginning of a famous quotation from John F. Kennedy. (2.10, 2.12)
11. Whom do you think Time magazine will select as its Person of the Year? (3.2)
12. Do you remember who said "And away we go"? (2.10)
13. Refinements in robotics may prove profitable. (More detail about this technology appears in Appendix A.) (2.11)
14. The resignation letter begins, "Since I'll never regain your respect . . ." and goes on to explain why that's true. (2.10, 2.12)
15. You must help her distinguish between i.e. (which means "that is") and e.g. (which means "for example"). (2.10, 3.2)

CHAPTER 12: Self-Assessment—Capitals and Abbreviations

1. Dr. Paul Hansen is joining our staff. (3.1)
2. New Caressa skin cream should be in a position to dominate that market. (3.1)
3. Send this report to ~~MR~~ Mr. H. K. Danforth, ~~rural route~~ RR 1, Warrensburg, ~~new york~~NY 12885. (3.1, 3.3)
4. You are responsible for training my new assistant to operate the Xerox machine. (3.1)
5. She received her ~~master of business administration~~MBA degree from the University of Michigan. (3.1, 3.3)
6. The building is located on the corner of Madison and Center streets. (3.1)
7. Call me tomorrow at 8 a.m. ~~morning~~, ~~pacific standard time~~PST, and I'll have the information you need. (3.3)
8. When Jones becomes CEO next month, we'll need your input ASAP. (3.1, 3.3)
9. Address it to Art Bowers, Chief of Production. (3.1)
10. Please RSVP to Sony ~~corp.~~Corporation just as soon as you know your schedule. (3.1, 3.3)
11. The data processing department will begin work on ~~feb.~~February 2, just one ~~wk.~~week from today. (3.3)
12. You are to meet him on Friday at the UN building in NYC. (3.3)
13. Whenever you can come, Professor, our employees will greatly enjoy your presentation. (3.1)
14. At 50 per box, our ~~std.~~standard contract forms are $9 a box, and our warranty forms are $7.95 a box. (3.3)
15. We plan to establish a sales office on the West Coast. (3.1)

CHAPTER 13: Self-Assessment—Numbers

1. We need to hire ~~one~~1 office manager, ~~four~~4 bookkeepers, and ~~twelve~~12 clerk-typists. (3.4)
2. The market for this product is nearly ~~six~~6 million people in our region alone. (3.4)

3. Make sure that all 1,835 pages are on my desk no later than ~~nine o'clock~~9:00 a.m. *OR* Make sure that all 1,835 pages are on my desk no later than nine o'clock in the morning. (3.4)

4. In 2004, ~~was the year that~~ José Guiterez sold more than $50,<u>000</u> ~~thousand dollars~~ worth of stock. (3.4)

5. Our deadline is ~~4/7~~April 7, but we won't be ready before ~~4/11~~April 11. (3.4)

6. ~~95~~Ninety-five percent of our customers are men. (*OR* Of our customers, 95 percent are men.) (3.4)

7. More than ~~1/2~~ half the U.S. population is female. (3.4)

8. Cecile Simmons, 38, is the first woman in this company to be promoted to management. (3.4)

9. Last year, I wrote 20 ~~15~~fifteen-page reports, and Michelle wrote 24 three-page reports. (3.4)

10. Of the 15 applicants, ~~seven~~7 are qualified. (3.4)

11. Our blinds should measure 38 inches wide by 64-<u>1/2</u> ~~and one half~~ inches long by 7/16 inches deep. (3.4)

12. Deliver the couch to ~~seven eighty-three~~783 Fountain Road, Suite ~~three~~3, Procter Valley, CA 92074. (3.4)

13. Here are the corrected figures: 42.70% agree, 23.25% disagree, 34.<u>00</u>% are undecided, and the error is 0.05%. (3.4)

14. You have to agree that 50,~~000,000~~ million U.S. citizens cannot be wrong. (3.4)

15. We need a set of shelves 10 feet, ~~eight~~8 inches long. (3.4)

CHAPTER 14: Self-Assessment— Vocabulary

1. Everyone (*accept,* *except*) Barbara King has registered for the company competition. (4.1)

2. We need to find a new security (*device* *devise*). (4.1)

3. The Jennings are (*loath* *loathe*) to admit that they are wrong. (4.1)

4. The judge has ruled that this town cannot enforce such a local (*ordinance* *ordnance*). (4.1)

5. To stay on schedule, we must give (*precedence* *precedents*) to the Marley project. (4.1)

6. This month's balance is greater (*than* *then*) last month's. (4.1)

7. That decision lies with the director, (*who's* *whose*) in charge of this department. (4.1)

8. <u>a lot</u>_____ In this department, we see <u>alot</u> of mistakes like that. (4.2)

9. <u>judgment</u>_____ In my <u>judgement</u>, you'll need to redo the cover. (4.3)

10. <u>regardless</u>_____ He decided to reveal the information <u>irregardless</u> of the consequences. (4.2)

11. <u>accommodate</u>_____ Why not go along when it is so easy to <u>accomodate</u> his demands? (4.3)

12. <u>imply</u>_____ When you say that, do you mean to <u>infer</u> that I'm being unfair? (4.2)

13. <u>embarrassing</u>_____ She says that she finds this sort of ceremony <u>embarassing</u>. (4.3)

14. <u>to</u>_____ All we have to do is try <u>and</u> get along with him for a few more days. (4.2)

15. precede_____ A friendly handshake should always <u>preceed</u> negotiations. (4.3)

References

PROLOGUE

1. "Advocacy Small Business Statistics and Research," U.S. Small Business Administration [accessed 3 July 2007] www.sba.gov; Malik Singleton, "Same Markets, New Marketplaces," *Black Enterprise*, September 2004, 34; Edmund L. Andrews, "Where Do the Jobs Come From?" *New York Times*, 21 September 2004, E1, E11; Maureen Jenkins, "Yours for the Taking," *Boeing Frontiers* online, June 2004 [accessed 25 September 2005] www.boeing .com; "Firm Predicts Top 10 Workforce/Workplace Trends for 2004, *Enterprise*, 8–14 December 2003, 1–2; Scott Hudson, "Keeping Employees Happy," *Community Banker*, September 2003, 34+; Marvin J. Cetron and Owen Davies, "Trends Now Changing the World: Technology, the Workplace, Management, and Institutions," *Futurist* 35, no. 2 (March/April 2001): 27–42.
2. "Career Planning: Do It Directionally," Leadership Now blog, 27 June 2007 [accessed 7 July 2008] www.leadershipnow.com.
3. Vivian Yeo, "India Still Top Choice for Offshoring," *BusinessWeek*, 27 June 2008 [accessed 7 July 2008] www.businessweek.com; Jim Puzzanghera, "Coalition of High-Tech Firms to Urge Officials to Help Keep U.S. Competitive," *San Jose Mercury News*, 8 January 2004 [accessed 14 February 2004] www.ebscohost.com.
4. Amanda Bennett, "GE Redesigns Rungs of Career Ladder," *Wall Street Journal*, 15 March 1993, B1, B3.
5. Robin White Goode, "International and Foreign Language Skills Have an Edge," *Black Enterprise*, May 1995, 53.
6. Nancy M. Somerick, "Managing a Communication Internship Program," *Bulletin of the Association for Business Communication* 56, no. 3 (1993): 10–20.
7. Fellowforce website [accessed 7 July 2008] www .fellowforce.com.
8. Joan Lloyd, "Changing Workplace Requires You to Alter Your Career Outlook," *Milwaukee Journal Sentinel*, 4 July 1999, 1; Camille DeBell, "Ninety Years in the World of Work in America," *Career Development Quarterly* 50, no.1 (September 2001): 77–88.
9. Jeffrey R. Young, "'E-Portfolios' Could Give Students a New Sense of Their Accomplishments," *The Chronicle of Higher Education*, 8 March 2002, A31.
10. Brian Carcione, e-portfolio [accessed 20 December 2006] http://eportfolio.psu.edu.

CHAPTER 1

1. Paul Gillin, *The New Influencers* (Sanger, Calif.: Quill Driver Books, 2007), xi.
2. "Watson Wyatt Study Reveals Six Communication 'Secrets' of Top-Performing Employers," CNNMoney.com, 4 December 2007 [accessed 26 January 2008] www.moncy .cnn.com.
3. "US Comms Efforts Aren't Keeping Employees Satisfied, Study Says," Internal Comms Hub, 27 February 2007 [accessed 26 January 2008] www.internalcommshub.com.
4. Lee Woods, "War of the Words," Smart People Write blog, 10 August 2006 [accessed 26 January 2008] http:// smartpeoplewrite1.blogspot.com.
5. Jeff Davidson, "Fighting Information Overload," *Canadian Manager*, Spring 2005, 16+.
6. "Do-It-Yourself Skills Enhancement: CFOs Value Communication Skills, but Few Firms Provide Training, Survey Shows," press release, Accountemps, 28 July 2006 [accessed 8 August 2006] www.accountemps.com.
7. A. Thomas Young, "Ethics in Business: Business of Ethics," *Vital Speeches*, 15 September 1992, 725–730.
8. Nate Anderson, "FTC Says Stealth Marketing Unethical," Ars Technica, 13 December 2006 [accessed 27 January 2008] http://arstechnica.com; "Undercover Marketing Uncovered," CBSnews.com, 25 July 2004 [accessed 11 April 2005] www.cbsnews.com; Stephanie Dunnewind, "Teen Recruits Create Word-of-Mouth 'Buzz' to Hook Peers on Products," *Seattle Times*, 20 November 2004 [accessed 11 April 2005] www.seattletimes.com.
9. Alli McConnon, "An Uptick in Untruths," *BusinessWeek*, 17 December 2007, 17.
10. Philip C. Kolin, *Successful Writing at Work*, 6th ed. (Boston: Houghton Mifflin, 2001), 17–23.
11. "8 Mass. Auto Dealers Fined for Misleading Advertising," *Boston Globe*, 3 January 2008 [accessed 27 January 2008] www.boston.com.
12. "Less Than Half of Companies Encourage Discussion of Ethical Issues at the Workplace," press release, International Association of Business Communicators Research Foundation, 23 May 2006 [accessed 12 August 2006] www.iabc.com.
13. Richard L. Daft, *Management*, 6th ed. (Cincinnati: Thomson South-Western, 2003), 155.
14. "Work–Life Balance Affects Ethics, Survey Says," Internal Comms Hub, 23 April 2007 [accessed 25 January 2008] www.internalcommshub.com.
15. Based in part on Robert Kreitner, *Management*, 9th ed. (Boston: Houghton Mifflin, 2004), 163.
16. Tracy Novinger, *Intercultural Communication, A Practical Guide* (Austin, Tex.: University of Texas Press, 2001), 15.
17. Jensen J. Zhao and Calvin Parks, "Self-Assessment of Communication Behavior: An Experiential Learning Exercise for Intercultural Business Success," *Business Communication Quarterly* 58, no. 1 (1995): 20–26; Charley H. Dodd, *Dynamics of Intercultural Communication*, 3rd ed. (Dubuque, Iowa: Brown, 1991), 142–143, 297–299; Stephen P. Robbins, *Organizational Behavior*, 6th ed. (Paramus, N.J.: Prentice Hall, 1993), 345.
18. Geneviève Hilton, "Becoming Culturally Fluent," *Communication World*, November/December 2007, 34–35.

19. Linda Beamer, "Teaching English Business Writing to Chinese- Speaking Business Students," *Bulletin of the Association for Business Communication* 57, no. 1 (1994): 12–18.

20. Edward T. Hall, "Context and Meaning," in *Intercultural Communication: A Reader*, 6th ed., edited by Larry A. Samovar and Richard E. Porter (Belmont, Calif: Wadsworth, 1991), 34–42.

21. Daft, *Management*, 459.

22. Shital Kakkar Mehra, "Understanding Cultures," *The Economic Times* (India), 21 September 2007 [accessed 27 January 2008] http://economictimes.indiatimes.com.

23. Beamer, "Teaching English Business Writing to Chinese-Speaking Business Students."

24. Dodd, *Dynamics of Intercultural Communication*, 69–70.

25. Daft, *Management*, 459.

26. "Different Personalities Can Create Culture Clashes, Study Warns," Internal Comms Hub 27 February 2007 [accessed 25 January 2008] www.internalcommshub.com.

27. James Wilfong and Toni Seger, *Taking Your Business Global* (Franklin Lakes, N.J.: Career Press, 1997), 277–278.

28. Philip R. Harris and Robert T. Moran, *Managing Cultural Differences*, 3rd ed. (Houston: Gulf, 1991), 260.

29. Guo-Ming Chen and William J. Starosta, *Foundations of Intercultural Communication* (Boston: Allyn & Bacon, 1998), 288–289.

30. Jonathan Katz, "Workforce Management—Worlds of Difference," *IndustryWeek*, 1 December 2007 [accessed 27 January 2008] www.industryweek.com.

31. Mark Landler and Michael Barbaro, "Wal-Mart Finds That Its Formula Doesn't Fit Every Culture," *New York Times*, 2 August 2006 [accessed 23 August 2006] www.nytimes.com.

32. Lillian H. Chaney and Jeanette S. Martin, *Intercultural Business Communication*, 4th ed. (Upper Saddle River, N.J.: Pearson Prentice Hall, 2007), 9.

33. Daft, *Management*, 455.

34. Chaney and Martin, *Intercultural Business Communication*, 53.

35. Mona Casady and Lynn Wasson, "Written Communication Skills of International Business Persons," *Bulletin of the Association for Business Communication* 57, no. 4 (1994): 36–40.

36. Chuck Williams, *Management*, 2nd ed. (Cincinnati: Thomson South-Western, 2002), 706–707.

37. "Many Senior Managers Communicate Badly, Survey Says," Internal Comms Hub, 6 August 2007 [accessed 25 January 2008] www.internalcommshub.com.

CHAPTER 2

1. The Container Store website [accessed 12 March 2008] www.containerstore.com; "2005: Best Companies to Work For," *Fortune*, 24 January 2005 [accessed 11 March 2005] www.fortune.com; Bob Nelson, "Can't Contain Excitement at The Container Store," BizJournals.com [accessed 11 March 2005] www.bizjournals.com; Mike Duff, "Top-Shelf Employees Keep Container Store on Track," *DSN Retailing Today*, 8 March 2004, 7, 49; Bob Nelson, "The Buzz at The Container Store," *Corporate Meetings & Incentives*, June 2003, 32; Jennifer Saba, "Balancing Act," *Potentials*, 1 October 2003 [accessed 15 April 2004] www.highbeam.com; Peter S. Cohan, "Corporate Heroes," *Financial Executive*, 1 March 2003 [accessed 15 April 2004] www.highbeam.com; David Lipke, "Container Store's CEO: People Are Most Valued Asset," 13 January 2003, *HFN* [accessed 9 March 2003] www.highbeam.com; Lorrie Grant, "Container Store's Workers Huddle Up to Help You Out," 30 April 2002, *USA Today*, B1.

2. Courtland L. Bovée, and John V. Thill, *Business in Action*, 3rd ed. (Upper Saddle River, N.J.: Pearson Prentice Hall, 2005), 175.

3. "Five Case Studies on Successful Teams," *HR Focus*, April 2002, 18+.

4. "Communication Plays Important Part in Determining Success for Today's Organizational Teams," Internal Comms Hub, 5 May 2006 [accessed 29 January 2008] www.internalcommshub.com.

5. Lynda McDermott, Bill Waite, and Nolan Brawley, "Executive Teamwork," *Executive Excellence*, May 1999, 15.

6. Nicola A. Nelson, "Leading Teams," *Defense AT&L*, July–August 2006, 26–29; Larry Cole and Michael Cole, "Why Is the Teamwork Buzz Word Not Working?" *Communication World*, February–March 1999, 29; Patricia Buhler, "Managing in the 90s: Creating Flexibility in Today's Workplace," *Supervision*, January 1997, 24+; Allison W. Amason, Allen C. Hochwarter, Wayne A. Thompson, and Kenneth R. Harrison, "Conflict: An Important Dimension in Successful Management Teams," *Organizational Dynamics*, Autumn 1995, 20+.

7. Richard L. Daft, *Management*, 6th ed. (Cincinnati: Thomson South-Western, 2003), 614.

8. Geoffrey Colvin, "Why Dream Teams Fail," *Fortune*, 12 June 2006, 87–92.

9. Vijay Govindarajan and Anil K. Gupta, "Building an Effective Global Business Team," *MIT Sloan Management Review*, Summer 2001, 63+.

10. Louise Rehling, "Improving Teamwork Through Awareness of Conversational Styles," *Business Communication Quarterly*, December 2004, 475–482.

11. Stephen R. Robbins, *Essentials of Organizational Behavior*, 6th ed. (Upper Saddle River, N.J.: Prentice Hall, 2000), 98.

12. Max Landsberg and Madeline Pfau, "Developing Diversity: Lessons from Top Teams," *Strategy + Business*, Winter 2005, 10–12.

13. "Groups Best at Complex Problems," *Industrial Engineer*, June 2006, 14.

14. Mary Beth Debs, "Recent Research on Collaborative Writing in Industry," *Technical Communication*, November 1991, 476–484.

15. "TWiki Success Stories," TWiki website [accessed 18 August 2006] www.twiki.org.

16. Tony Kontzer, "Learning to Share," *InformationWeek*, 5 May 2003, 28; Jon Udell, "Uniting Under Groove," *InfoWorld*, 17 February 2003 [accessed 9 September 2003] www.elibrary.com; Alison Overholt, "Virtually There?" *Fast Company*, 14 February 2002, 108.

17. John Hollon, "No Tolerance for Jerks," *Workforce Management*, 12 February 2007, 34.

18. Dana May Casperson, *Power Etiquette: What You Don't Know Can Kill Your Career* (New York: AMACOM, 1999), 9.

19. Marilyn Pincus, *Everyday Business Etiquette* (Hauppauge, N.Y.: Barron's Educational Series, 1996), 7, 133.

20. Pincus, *Everyday Business Etiquette*, 136.

21. Gerald H. Graham, Jeanne Unrue, and Paul Jennings, "The Impact of Nonverbal Communication in Organizations: A Survey of Perceptions," *Journal of Business Communication* 28, no. 1 (Winter 1991): 45–62.

22. Pincus, *Everyday Business Etiquette*, 100–101.

23. Maggie Jackson, "Turn Off That Cellphone. It's Meeting Time," *New York Times*, 2 March 2003, sec. 3, 12.

24. "Practice Courtesy When Using Cellular Phones," *Cumberland (Maryland) Times-News*, 26 July 2007 [accessed 29 January 2008] www.times-news.com.

25. Casperson, *Power Etiquette: What You Don't Know Can Kill Your Career*, 10–14; Ellyn Spragins, "Introducing Politeness," *Fortune Small Business*, November 2001, 30.

26. Tanya Mohn, "The Social Graces As a Business Tool," *New York Times*, 10 November 2002, 3.12.

27. Casperson, *Power Etiquette: What You Don't Know Can Kill Your Career*, 19; Pincus, *Everyday Business Etiquette*, 7–8.

28. Casperson, *Power Etiquette: What You Don't Know Can Kill Your Career*, 44–46.

29. Casperson, *Power Etiquette: What You Don't Know Can Kill Your Career*, 109–110.

30. "Better Meetings Benefit Everyone: How to Make Yours More Productive," *Working Communicator Bonus Report*, July 1998, 1.

31. "Better Meetings Benefit Everyone."

32. Roger O. Crockett, "The 21st Century Meeting," *Business Week*, 26 February 2007, 72–79.

33. "Unlock the Full Power of the Web Conferencing," CEOworld.biz, 20 November 2007 [accessed 30 January 2008] www.ceoworld.biz.

34. IBM InnovationJam website [accessed 30 January 2008] www.globalinnovationjam.com; "Big Blue Brainstorm," *BusinessWeek*, 7 August 2006 [accessed 15 August 2006] www.businessweek.com.

35. Mitch Wagner, "Using Second Life as a Business-to-Business Tool," *InformationWeek*, 26 April 2007 [accessed 30 January 2008] www.informationweek.com; Linda Zimmer, "Second Life: What Is It Good For?" Business Communicators of Second Life blog, 24 January 2007 [accessed 7 February 2007] http://freshtakes.typepad.com/sl_communicators; Robert D. Hof, "My Virtual Life," *BusinessWeek*, 1 May 2006 [accessed 7 February 2007] www.businessweek.com; David Needle, "Sun Finds a Home in Second Life," Internetnews.com, 11 October 2006 [accessed 7 February 2007] www.internetnews.com.

36. "17 Tips for More Productive Conference Calls," AccuConference [accessed 30 January 2008] www.accuconference.com.

37. Judi Brownell, *Listening*, 2nd ed. (Boston: Allyn & Bacon, 2002), 9, 10.

38. Carmine Gallo, "Why Leadership Means Listening," *BusinessWeek*, 31 January 2007 [accessed 29 January 2008] www.businessweek.com.

39. Augusta M. Simon, "Effective Listening: Barriers to Listening in a Diverse Business Environment," *Bulletin of the Association for Business Communication* 54, no. 3 (September 1991): 73–74.

40. Robyn D. Clarke, "Do You Hear What I Hear?" *Black Enterprise*, May 1998, 129.

41. Dennis M. Kratz and Abby Robinson Kratz, *Effective Listening Skills* (New York: McGraw-Hill, 1995), 45–53; J. Michael Sproule, *Communication Today* (Glenview, Ill.: Scott Foresman, 1981), 69.

42. Brownell, *Listening*, 230–231.

43. Kratz and Kratz, *Effective Listening Skills*, 78–79; Sproule, *Communication Today*.

44. Tyner Blaine, "Ten Supercharged Active Listening Skills to Make You More Successful," Tyner Blain blog, 15 March 2007 [accessed 16 April 2007] http://tynerblain.com/blog; Bill Brooks, "The Power of Active Listening," *American Salesman*, June 2003, 12; "Active Listening," Study Guides and Strategies [accessed 5 February 2005] www.studygs.net.

45. Bob Lamons, "Good Listeners Are Better Communicators," *Marketing News*, 11 September 1995, 13+; Phillip Morgan and H. Kent Baker, "Building a Professional Image: Improving Listening Behavior," *Supervisory Management*, November 1985, 35–36.

46. Clarke, "Do You Hear What I Hear?"; Dot Yandle, "Listening to Understand," *Pryor Report Management Newsletter Supplement* 15, no. 8 (August 1998): 13.

47. Brownell, *Listening*, 14; Kratz and Kratz, *Effective Listening Skills*, 8–9; Sherwyn P. Morreale and Courtland L. Bovée, *Excellence in Public Speaking* (Orlando, Fla.: Harcourt Brace, 1998), 72–76; Lyman K. Steil, Larry L. Barker, and Kittie W. Watson, *Effective Listening: Key to Your Success* (Reading, Mass.: Addison-Wesley, 1983), 21–22.

48. Patrick J. Collins, *Say It with Power and Confidence* (Upper Saddle River, N.J.: Prentice Hall, 1997), 40–45.

49. Morreale and Bovée, *Excellence in Public Speaking*, 296.

50. Judee K. Burgoon, David B. Butler, and W. Gill Woodall, *Nonverbal Communication: The Unspoken Dialog* (New York: McGraw-Hill, 1996), 137.

51. "Study: Human Lie Detectors Rarely Wrong," *CNN.com*, 14 October 2004 [accessed 14 October 2004] www.cnn.com.

52. Dale G. Leathers, *Successful Nonverbal Communication: Principles and Applications* (New York: Macmillan, 1986), 19.

53. Gerald H. Graham, Jeanne Unrue, and Paul Jennings, "The Impact of Nonverbal Communication in Organizations: A Survey of Perceptions," *Journal of Business Communication* 28, no. 1 (Winter 1991): 45–62.

54. Bremer Communications website [accessed 28 January 2008] www.bremercommunications.com.

55. Virginia P. Richmond and James C. McCroskey, *Nonverbal Behavior in Interpersonal Relations* (Boston: Allyn & Bacon, 2000), 2–3.

CHAPTER 3

1. IBM website [accessed 13 March 2008] www.ibm.com; Toby Ward, "Podcasting the Intranet at IBM," *Intranet Blog*, 11 December 2005 [accessed 9 April 2006] http://intranetblog.blogware.com; Stacy Cowley, "IBM Employees Play with Podcasting," *InfoWorld*, 23 November 2005 [accessed 9 April 2006] www.infoworld.com.
2. Sanford Kaye, "Writing Under Pressure," *Soundview Executive Book Summaries* 10, no. 12, part 2 (December 1988): 1–8.
3. Laurey Berk and Phillip G. Clampitt, "Finding the Right Path in the Communication Maze," *IABC Communication World*, October 1991, 28–32.
4. Linda Duyle, "Get Out of Your Office," *HR Magazine*, July 2006, 99–101.
5. Jim Courtney, "Skype News Roundup: Crossing 11 Million Online; PlayStation Portable Update," *Skype Journal* blog, 1 February 2008 [accessed 1 February 2008] http://skypejournal.com.
6. Kris Maher, "The Jungle," *Wall Street Journal*, 5 October 2004, B10.
7. Kevin Maney, "Surge in Text Messaging Makes Cell Operators :-)," *USA Today*, 28 July 2005, B1–B2.
8. David Kirkpatrick, "It's Hard to Manage if You Don't Blog," *Fortune*, 4 October 2004, 46; Lee Gomes, "How the Next Big Thing in Technology Morphed into a Really Big Thing," *Wall Street Journal*, 4 October 2004, B1; Jeff Meisner, "Cutting Through the Blah, Blah, Blah," *Puget Sound Business Journal*, 19–25 November 2004, 27–28; Lauren Gard, "The Business of Blogging," *BusinessWeek*, 13 December 2004, 117–119; Heather Green, "Online Video: The Sequel," *BusinessWeek*, 10 January 2005, 40; Michelle Conlin and Andrew Park, "Blogging with the Boss's Blessing," *BusinessWeek*, 28 June 2004, 100–102.
9. Berk and Clampitt, "Finding the Right Path in the Communication Maze."
10. Berk and Clampitt, "Finding the Right Path in the Communication Maze."
11. Raymond M. Olderman, *10 Minute Guide to Business Communication* (New York: Alpha Books, 1997), 19–20.
12. Mind Mapping Software Weblog [accessed 1 February 2008] http://mindmapping.typepad.com; bubbl.us website [accessed 1 February 2008] http://bubbl.us.

CHAPTER 4

1. Dice.com advertisement retrieved from adverlicio.us [accessed 6 February 2008] http://adverlicio.us.
2. Elizabeth Blackburn and Kelly Belanger, "You-Attitude and Positive Emphasis: Testing Received Wisdom in Business Communication," *Bulletin of the Association for Business Communication* 56, no. 2 (June 1993): 1–9.
3. Placard at Alaska Airlines ticket counters, Seattle-Tacoma International Airport, 3 October 2003.
4. Annette N. Shelby and N. Lamar Reinsch, Jr., "Positive Emphasis and You Attitude: An Empirical Study," *Journal of Business Communication* 32, no. 4 (1995): 303–322.

5. Sherryl Kleinman, "Why Sexist Language Matters," *Qualitative Sociology* 25, no. 2 (Summer 2002): 299–304.
6. Judy E. Pickens, "Terms of Equality: A Guide to Bias-Free Language," *Personnel Journal*, August 1985, 24.
7. Lisa Taylor, "Communicating About People with Disabilities: Does the Language We Use Make a Difference?" *Bulletin of the Association for Business Communication* 53, no. 3 (September 1990): 65–67.
8. Susan Benjamin, *Words at Work* (Reading, Mass.: Addison-Wesley, 1997), 136–137.
9. Stuart Crainer and Des Dearlove, "Making Yourself Understood," *Across the Board*, May/June 2004, 23–27.
10. Plain Language.gov website [accessed 6 February 2008] www.plainlanguage.gov.
11. Plain English Campaign website [accessed 12 March 2008] www.plainenglish.co.uk.
12. Susan Jaderstrom and Joanne Miller, "Active Writing," *Office Pro*, November/December 2003, 29.
13. Portions of this section are adapted from Courtland L. Bovée, *Techniques of Writing Business Letters, Memos, and Reports* (Sherman Oaks, Calif.: Banner Books International, 1978), 13–90.
14. Catherine Quinn, "Lose the Office Jargon; It May Sunset Your Career," *The Age* (Australia), 1 September 2007 [accessed 5 February 2008] www.theage.com.au.
15. Robert Hartwell Fiske, *The Dimwit's Dictionary* (Oak Park, Ill.: Marion Street Press, 2002), 16–20.
16. Visuwords website [accessed 5 February 2008] www.visuwords.com.
17. David A. Fryxell, "Lost in Transition?" *Writer's Digest*, January 2005, 24–26.
18. Food Allergy Initiative website [accessed 23 September 2006] www.foodallergyinitiative.org; Diana Keough, "Snacks That Can Kill; Schools Take Steps to Protect Kids Who Have Severe Allergies to Nuts," *Plain Dealer*, 15 July 2003, E1; "Dawdling Over Food Labels," *New York Times*, 2 June 2003, A16; Sheila McNulty, "A Matter of Life and Death, *Financial Times*, 10 September 2003, 14.
19. Inspired by Inglesina website [accessed 14 March 2008] www.inglesina.com and BestBabyGear website [accessed 14 March 2008] www.bestbabygear.com.
20. Adapted from a mailer received from Evolution Benefits, 10 January 2008. (None of the errors shown in this exercise exist in the original.)

CHAPTER 5

1. Robert Hartwell Fiske, *The Dictionary of Concise Writing: 10,000 Alternatives to Wordy Phrases* (Oak Park, Ill.: Marion Street Press, 2002), 17.
2. Natalie Canavor and Claire Meirowitz, "Good Corporate Writing: Why It Matters, and What to Do," *Communication World*, July–August 2005, 30–33.
3. "Revision in Business Writing," Purdue OWL website [accessed 8 February 2008] http://owl.english.purdue.edu.
4. Holly Weeks, "The Best Memo You'll Ever Write," *Harvard Management Communication Letter*, Spring 2005, 3–5.

5. Lynn Gaertner-Johnston, "Best Practices for Bullet Points," Business Writing blog, 17 December 2005 [accessed 8 February 2008] www.businesswritingblog.com.

6. William Zinsser, *On Writing Well*, 5th ed. (New York: HarperCollins, 1994), 7, 17.

7. Mary A. DeVries, *Internationally Yours* (Boston: Houghton Mifflin, 1994), 160.

8. Zinsser, *On Writing Well*, 126.

9. Deborah Gunn, "Looking Good on Paper," *Office Pro*, March 2004, 10–11.

10. Jacci Howard Bear, "Desktop Publishing Rules of Page Layout," About.com [accessed 22 August 2005] www .about.com.

11. Robin Williams, *The Non-Designer's Type Book* (Berkeley, Calif.: Peachpit Press, 2006), 123.

12. Jacci Howard Bear, "Desktop Publishing Rules for How Many Fonts to Use," About.com [accessed 22 August 2005] www.about.com.

CHAPTER 6

1. Bill Owens, "Why Can't I Make Reservations Further in Advance?" Nuts About Southwest blog, 24 January 2007 [accessed 15 May 2007] www.blogsouthwest.com; Bill Owens, "I Blogged. You Flamed. We Changed." Nuts About Southwest blog, 18 April 2007 [accessed 10 May 2007] www.blogsouthwest.com; "Welcome to the Nuts About Southwest Blog—A User's Guide," Nuts About Southwest blog, [accessed 15 May 2007] www. blogsouthwest.com; "Southwest Airlines Is Nuts About Blogging," Southwest Airlines press release, 27 April 2007 [accessed 15 May 2007] www.prnewswire.com.

2. Dave Carpenter, "Companies Discover Marketing Power of Text Messaging," *Seattle Times*, 25 September 2006 [accessed 25 September 2006] www.seattletimes.com.

3. "A Definition of Social Media," *Technology in Translation* blog, 6 April 2007 [accessed 11 June 2007] http:// technologyintranslation.blockwork.org; Robert Scoble, "What Is Social Media?" Scobleizer blog, 16 February 2007 [accessed 11 June 2007] www.scobleizer.com; Paul Gillin, *The New Influencers* (Sanger, Calif.: Quill Driver Books, 2007), xi–xii.

4. Angelo Fernando, "Social Media Change the Rules," *Communication World*, January February 2007, 9–10; Geoff Livingston and Brian Solis, *Now Is Gone: A Primer on New Media for Executives and Entrepreneurs* (Laurel, Md.: Bartleby Press, 2007), 60.

5. Don Tapscott and Anthony D. Williams, *Wikinomics: How Mass Collaboration Changes Everything* (London: Portfolio, 2006), 216–217; Dan Schawbel, "Why Social Media Makes It Possible for Gen-Y to Succeed," Personal Branding Blog, 12 December 2007 [accessed 14 February 2008] http://personalbrandingblog.wordpress.com.

6. Hilary Potkewitz and Rachel Brown, "Spread of E-Mail Has Altered Communication Habits at Work," *Los Angeles Business Journal*, 18 April 2005 [accessed 30 April 2006] www.findarticles.com; Nancy Flynn, *Instant Messaging Rules* (New York: AMACOM, 2004), 47–54.

7. Hannah Clark, "How to (Legally) Spy on Employees," *Forbes*, 25 October 2006 [accessed 12 February 2008] www.forbes.com; Greg Burns, "For Some, Benefits of E-Mail Not Worth Risk," *San Diego Union-Tribune*, 16 August 2005, A1, A8; Pui-Wing Tam, Erin White, Nick Wingfield, and Kris Maher, "Snooping E-Mail by Software Is Now a Workplace Norm," *Wall Street Journal*, 9 March 2005, B1+; "Employee Communication Is Cause for Concern," Duane Morris LLP website, 23 August 2006 [accessed 4 October 2006] www.duanemorris .com.

8. Matt Cain, "Managing E-Mail Hygiene," ZD Net Tech Update, 5 February 2004 [accessed 19 March 2004] www.techupdate.zdnet.com.

9. Lizette Alvarez, "Got 2 Extra Hours for Your E-Mail?" *New York Times*, 10 November 2005 [accessed 10 November 2005] www.nytimes.com.

10. Jack Trout, "Beware of 'Infomania,'" *Forbes*, 11 August 2006 [accessed 5 October 2006] www.forbes.com.

11. Reid Goldsborough, "'Creeping Informality' Can Be Big Mistake in Business E-Mails," *New Orleans City Business*, 14 March 2005, 18; Jack E. Appleman, "Bad Writing Can Cost Insurers Time & Money," *National Underwriter*, 27 September 2004, 34; Adina Genn, "RE: This Is an Important Message, Really," *Long Island Business News*, 5–11 December 2003, 21A; Lynn Lofton, "Regardless of What You Thought, Grammar Rules *Do* Apply to E-Mail," *Mississippi Business Journal*, 23–29 May 2005, 1.

12. Mary Munter, Priscilla S. Rogers, and Jone Rymer, "Business E-Mail: Guidelines for Users," *Business Communication Quarterly*, March 2003, 26+; Renee B. Horowitz and Marian G. Barchilon, "Stylistic Guidelines for E-Mail," *IEEE Transactions on Professional Communication* 37, no. 4 (December 1994): 207–212.

13. Daniel Goleman, "E-Mail Is Easy to Write (and to Misread)," *New York Times*, 7 October 2007 [accessed 14 February 2008] www.nytimes.com.

14. "E-Mail Is So Five Minutes Ago," *BusinessWeek* online, 28 November 2005 [accessed 3 May 2006] www.businessweek .com.

15. Robert J. Holland, "Connected—More or Less," Richmond .com, 8 August 2006 [accessed 5 October 2006] www .richmond.com.

16. Vayusphere website [accessed 22 January 2006] www .vayusphere.com; Christa C. Ayer, "Presence Awareness: Instant Messaging's Killer App," *Mobile Business Advisor*, 1 July 2004 [accessed 22 January 2006] www.highbeam.com; Jefferson Graham, "Instant Messaging Programs Are No Longer Just for Messages," *USA Today*, 20 October 2003, 5D; Todd R. Weiss, "Microsoft Targets Corporate Instant Messaging Customers," *Computerworld*, 18 November 2002, 12; "Banks Adopt Instant Messaging to Create a Global Business Network," *Computer Weekly*, 25 April 2002, 40; Michael D. Osterman, "Instant Messaging in the Enterprise," *Business Communications Review*, January 2003, 59–62; John Pallato, "Instant Messaging Unites Work Groups and Inspires Collaboration," *Internet World*, December 2002, 14+.

17. Angelo Fernando, "Social Media Change the Rules," *Communication World*, July/August 2007, 11–12; "E-Mail and Text Us, Consumers Say," eMarketer.com, 16 November 2007 [accessed 14 February 2008] www. emarketer.com; Paul Kedrosky, "Why We Don't Get the (Text) Message," *Business 2.0*, 2 October 2006 [accessed 4 October 2006] www .business2.com; Carpenter, "Companies Discover Marketing Power of Text Messaging."

18. Mark Gibbs, "Racing to Instant Messaging," *NetworkWorld*, 17 February 2003, 74.

19. "E-Mail Is So Five Minutes Ago."

20. Elizabeth Millard, "Instant Messaging Threats Still Rising," Newsfactor.com, 6 July 2005 [accessed 5 October 2006] www.newsfactor.com.

21. Walaika K. Haskins, "New Virus Spreads by Chatting with You," Newsfactor.com, 9 December 2005 [accessed 5 October 2006] www.newsfactor.com.

22. Clint Boulton, "IDC: IM Use Is Booming in Business," InstantMessagingPlanet.com, 5 October 2005 [accessed 22 January 2006] www.instantmessagingplanet.com; Jenny Goodbody, "Critical Success Factors for Global Virtual Teams," *Strategic Communication Management*, February/March 2005, 18–21; Ann Majchrzak, Arvind Malhotra, Jeffrey Stamps, and Jessica Lipnack, "Can Absence Make a Team Grow Stronger?" *Harvard Business Review*, May 2004, 131–137; Christine Y. Chen, "The IM Invasion," *Fortune*, 26 May 2003, 135–138; Yudhijit Bhattacharjee, "A Swarm of Little Notes," *Time*, September 2002, A3–A8; Mark Bruno, "Taming the Wild Frontiers of Instant Messaging," *Bank Technology News*, December 2002, 30–31; Richard Grigonis, "Enterprise-Strength Instant Messaging," Convergence.com, 10–15 [accessed March 2003] www.convergence.com.

23. Leo Babauta, "17 Tips to Be Productive with Instant Messaging," Web Worker Daily, 14 November 2007 [accessed 14 February 2008] http://webworkerdaily.com; Pallato, "Instant Messaging Unites Work Groups and Inspires Collaboration."

24. Anita Hamilton, "You've Got Spim!" *Time*, 2 February 2004 [accessed 1 March 2004] www.time.com.

25. Robert Scoble and Shel Israel, *Naked Conversations* (Hoboken, N.J.: Wiley, 2006), 15–18.

26. GM FastLane blog [accessed 4 May 2006] http:// fastlane.gmblogs.com.

27. Fredrik Wackå, "Six Types of Blogs—A Classification," CorporateBloggingInfo website, 10 August 10 2004 [accessed 5 October 2006] www.corporatebblogginginfo.com; Stephen Baker, "The Inside Story on Company Blogs," *BusinessWeek* 14 February 2006 [accessed 15 February 2006] www .businessweek.com; Jeremy Wright, *Blog Marketing* (New York: McGraw-Hill, 2006), 45–56; Paul Chaney, "Blogs: Beyond the Hype!" 26 May 2005 [accessed 4 May 2006] http://radiantmarketinggroup.com.

28. Michael Barbaro, "Wal-Mart Tastemakers Write Unfiltered Blog," *New York Times*, 3 March 2008 [accessed 1 June 2008] www.nytimes.com.

29. Evolve24 website [accessed 12 February 2008] www.evolve24.com.

30. Dianne Culhane, "Blog Logs a Culture Change, *Communication World*, January/February 2008, 40–41.

31. Stephen Baker and Heather Green, "Blogs Will Change Your Business," *BusinessWeek*, 2 May 2005, 57–67.

32. Joel Falconer, "Six Rules for Writing Great Web Content," Blog News Watch, 9 November 2007 [accessed 14 February 2008] www.blognewswatch.com.

33. Julie Moran Alterio, "Podcasts a Hit Inside and Outside IBM," *The (White Plains, N.Y.) Journal News*, 9 January 2006 [accessed 5 May 2006] www.thejournalnews.com.

34. "Turn Your Feed into a Podcast," Lifehacker blog, 12 January 2006 [accessed 6 May 2006] www.lifehacker.com.

35. "Set Up Your Podcast for Success," FeedForAll website [accessed 4 October 2006] www.feedforall.com.

36. Shel Holtz, "Ten Guidelines for B2B Podcasts," Webpronews .com, 12 October 2005 [accessed 9 March 2006] www .webpronews.com.

37. Todd Cochrane, *Podcasting: The Do-It-Yourself Guide* (Indianapolis, Ind.: Wiley, 2005), 107–109.

38. Michael W. Goeghegan and Dan Klass, *Podcast Solutions: The Complete Guide to Podcasting* (Berkeley, Calif.: Friends of Ed, 2005), 57–86; Cochrane, *Podcasting: The Do-It-Yourself Guide*, 87–136.

39. Mark Choate, "What Makes an Enterprise Wiki?" CMS Watch website, 28 April 2006 [accessed 18 August 2006] www.cmswatch.com.

40. "Codex: Guidelines," WordPress website [accessed 16 February 2008] http://wordpress.com; Michael Shanks, "Wiki Guidelines," Traumwerk website [accessed 18 August 2006] http://metamedia.stanford.edu/projects/ traumwerk/home; Joe Moxley, MC Morgan, Matt Barton, and Donna Hanak, "For Teachers New to Wikis," Writing Wiki [accessed 18 August 2006] http://writingwiki.org; "Wiki Guidelines," PsiWiki [accessed 18 August 2006] http://psi-im.org.

41. Rachael King, "No Rest for the Wiki," *BusinessWeek*, 12 March 2007 [accessed 14 February 2008] www .businessweek.com.

42. "Codex: Guidelines," WordPress website [accessed 14 February 2008] http://wordpress.com.

43. "Wikipedia: Edit War," Wikipedia.com [accessed 14 February 2008] http://en.wikipedia.org.

44. Adapted from Comic-Con website [accessed 16 January 2007] www.comic-con.org; Tom Spurgeon, "Welcome to Nerd Vegas: A Guide to Visiting and Enjoying Comic-Con International in San Diego, 2006!" The Comics Reporter .com, 11 July 2006 [accessed 16 January 2007] www .comicsreporter.com; Rebecca Winters Keegan, "Boys Who Like Toys," *Time*, 19 April 2007 [accessed 15 May 2007] www.time.com.

45. Adapted from Tom Lowry, "ESPN.COM: Guys and Dollars," *BusinessWeek*, 17 October 2005 [accessed 16 January 2007] www.businessweek.com.

46. Adapted from Seymour Powell website [accessed 16 January 2007] www.seymourpowell.com; Sam Roberts, "51% of Women Now Living Without a Spouse," *New York Times*, 16 January 2007 [accessed 16 January 2007] www.nytimes.com.

47. Adapted from Sharon Terlep, "UAW: Expect Sacrifice," *Detroit News*, 16 January 2007 [accessed 17 January 2007] www.detnews.com; Ford Motor Company website [accessed 17 January 2007] www.ford.com.

48. Adapted from Bruce Einhorn and Ben Elgin, "Helping Big Brother Go High Tech," *BusinessWeek*, 18 September 2006, 47–52.

49. Adapted from Crutchfield website [accessed 17 January 2007] www.crutchfield.com.

50. Adapted from *Logan* website [accessed 16 January 2007] www.loganmagazine.com.

51. Adapted from job description for Global Marketing Manager–Apparel, New Balance website [accessed 24 August 2005] www.newbalance.com.

CHAPTER 7

1. Warren E. Buffett, *Preface* to *A Plain English Handbook*, Plain English website [accessed 12 May 2006] www.plainlanguage.gov.

2. Pat Cataldo, "Op-Ed: Saying 'Thank You'; Can Open More Doors Than You Think," Penn State University Smeal College of Business website [accessed 19 February 2008] www.smeal.psu.edu.

3. Jackie Huba, "Five Must-Haves for Thank-You Notes," Church of the Customer Blog, 16 November 2007 [accessed 19 February 2008] www.churchofthecustomer.com.

4. Mary Mitchell, "The Circle of Life—Condolence Letters," ULiveandLearn.com [accessed 18 July 2005] www.liveandlearn.com; Donna Larcen, "Authors Share the Words of Condolence," *Los Angeles Times*, 20 December 1991, E11.

5. Adapted from Bruce Frankel and Alex Tresniowski, "Stormy Skies," *People Weekly*, 31 July 2000, 112–115.

6. Adapted from Keith H. Hammonds, "Difference Is Power," *Fast Company*, 36, 258 [accessed 11 July 2000] www.fastcompany.com; Terri Morrison, Wayne Conaway, and George A. Borden, *Kiss, Bow, or Shake Hands* (Avon, Mass.: Adams Media Corp., 1994, 1–5.

7. Adapted from Tom Abate, "Need to Preserve Cash Generates Wave of Layoffs in Biotech Industry," *San Francisco Chronicle*, 10 February 2003 [accessed 18 July 2005] www.sfgate.com.

8. Adapted from Lisa DiCarlo, "IBM Gets the Message—Instantly," Forbes.com, 7 July 2002 [accessed 22 July 2003] www.forbes.com; "IBM Introduces Breakthrough Messaging Technology for Customers and Business Partners," *M2 Presswire*, 19 February 2003 [accessed 24 July 2003] www.proquest.com; "IBM and America Online Team for Instant Messaging Pilot," *M2 Presswire*, 4 February 2003 [accessed 24 July 2003] www.proquest.com.

9. Adapted from CES website [accessed 18 July 2005] www.cesweb.org.

10. Adapted from Michael Mandel, "What's Really Propping Up the Economy," *BusinessWeek*, 25 September 2006 [accessed 16 January 2007] www.businessweek.com.

11. Adapted from SitePoint website [accessed 20 February 2008] www.sitepoint.com; Dylan Tweney, "The Defogger: Slim Down That Homepage," *Business 2.0*, 13 July 2001 [accessed 1 August 2001] www.business2.com.

12. Adapted from Public Relations Society of America website [accessed 18 June 2005] www.prsa.org.

13. Adapted from Mitchell, "The Circle of Life—Condolence Letters"; Larcen, "Authors Share the Words of Condolence."

14. Adapted from Burt Helm, "Wal-Mart, Please Don't Leave Me," *BusinessWeek*, 9 October 2006, 84–89.

15. Adapted from Jeff Nachtigal, "It's Easy and Cheap Being Green," *Fortune*, 16 October 2006, 53; Adobe Wins Platinum Certification Awarded by U.S. Green Building Council," press release, 3 July 2006 [accessed 15 October 2006] www.adobe.com.

CHAPTER 8

1. "Taurus and Homer Simpson—Separated at Birth?" CNN.com, 29 January 2008 [accessed 26 February 2008] www.cnn.com.

2. Katie Grasso, "Deliver Bad News to Worker Face-to-Face, with Empathy," *(Camden, New Jersey) Courier-Post*, 8 February 2006 [accessed 14 May 2006] www.courierpostonline.com.

3. Ian McDonald, "Marsh Can Do $600 Million, but Apologize?" *Wall Street Journal*, 14 January 2005, C1, C3; Adrienne Carter and Amy Borrus, "What if Companies Fessed Up?" *BusinessWeek*, 24 January 2005, 59–60; Patrick J. Kiger, "The Art of the Apology," *Workforce Management*, October 2004, 57–62.

4. "The Power of Apology: Removing the Legal Barriers," A Special Report by the Ombudsman of the Province of British Columbia, February 2006 [accessed 14 May 2006] www.ombud.gov.bc.ca; Ameeta Patel and Lamar Reinsch, "Companies Can Apologize: Corporate Apologies and Legal Liability," *Business Communication Quarterly*, March 2003 [accessed 1 December 2003] www.elibrary.com.

5. Maura Dolan and Stuart Silverstein, "Court Broadens Liability for Job References," *Los Angeles Times*, 28 January 1997, A1, A11; Frances A. McMorris, "Ex-Bosses Face Less Peril Giving Honest Job References," *Wall Street Journal*, 8 July 1996, B1, B8.

6. "HR Manners," *Workforce Week Management*, January 29–February 4, 2006.

7. Thomas S. Brice and Marie Waung, "Applicant Rejection Letters: Are Businesses Sending the Wrong Message?" *Business Horizons*, March–April 1995, 59–62.

8. Gwendolyn N. Smith, Rebecca F. Nolan, and Yong Dai, "Job-Refusal Letters: Readers' Affective Responses to Direct and Indirect Organizational Plans," *Business Communication Quarterly* 59, no. 1 (1996): 67–73; Brice and Waung, "Applicant Rejection Letters."

9. Judi Brownell, "The Performance Appraisal Interviews: A Multipurpose Communication Assignment," *Bulletin of the Association for Business Communication* 57, no. 2 (1994): 11–21.

10. Brownell, "The Performance Appraisal Interviews."

11. Howard M. Bloom, "Performance Evaluations," *New England Business*, December 1991, 14.

12. David I. Rosen, "Appraisals Can Make—or Break—Your Court Case," *Personnel Journal*, November 1992, 113.

13. Patricia A. McLagan, "Advice for Bad-News Bearers: How to Tell Employees They're Not Hacking It and Get Results," *IndustryWeek*, 15 February 1993, 42; Michael Lee Smith, "Give Feedback, Not Criticism," *Supervisory Management*, 1993, 4; "A Checklist for Conducting Problem Performer Appraisals," *Supervisory Management*, December 1993, 7–9.

14. Carrie Brodzinski, "Avoiding Wrongful Termination Suits," *National Underwriter Property & Casualty—Risk & Benefits Management*, 13 October 2003 [accessed 2 December 2003] www.elibrary.com.

15. Jane R. Goodson, Gail W. McGee, and Anson Seers, "Giving Appropriate Performance Feedback to Managers: An Empirical Test of Content and Outcomes," *Journal of Business Communication* 29, no. 4 (1992): 329–342.

16. Craig Cox, "On the Firing Line," *Business Ethics*, May–June 1992, 33–34.

17. Cox, "On the Firing Line."

18. Michelle Conlin, "Web Attack," *BusinessWeek*, 16 April 2007 [accessed 27 February 2008] www.businessweek .com; Melissa Allison, "Corporations Seek to Clean Up Online Rumors," *Seattle Times*, 4 March 2007 [accessed 4 March 2007] www.seattletimes.com; Charles Wolrich, "Top Corporate Hate Web Sites," *Forbes*, 8 March 2005 [accessed 16 August 2005] www.forbes.com; PlanetFeedback.com website [accessed 27 February 2008] www.planetfeedback.com; "Health Related Hoaxes and Rumors," Centers for Disease Control and Prevention website [accessed 16 August 2005] www.cdc.gov; Snopes.com [accessed 16 August 2005] www.snopes.com; "Pranksters, Activists and Rogues: Know Your Adversaries and Where They Surf," *PR News*, 26 June 2000 [accessed 3 December 2003] www.elibrary.com.

19. Adapted from Sylvia Ann Hewlett and Carolyn Buck Luce, "Off-Ramps and On-Ramps," *Harvard Business Review*, March 2005, 43–54.

20. Adapted from Stanton website [accessed 18 August 2005] www.stanton.com.

21. Adapted from "Bathtub Curve," *Engineering Statistics Handbook*, National Institute of Standards and Technology website [accessed 16 April 2005] www.nist.gov; Robert Berner, "The Warranty Windfall," *BusinessWeek*, 20 December 2004, 84–86; Larry Armstrong, "When Service Contracts Make Sense," *BusinessWeek*, 20 December 2004, 86.

22. Adapted from "FDA Notifies Public That Vail Products, Inc., Issues Nationwide Recall of Enclosed Bed Systems," FDA press release, 30 June 2005 [accessed 18 August 2005] www.fda.gov.

23. Adapted from Pui-Wing Tam, Erin White, Nick Wingfield, and Kris Maher, "Snooping E-Mail by Software Is Now a Workplace Norm," *Wall Street Journal*, 9 March 2005, B1+.

24. Adapted from Alion website [accessed 19 August 2005] www.alionscience.com.

25. Adapted from United Airlines website [accessed 31 December 2003] www.united.com; "United Airlines First to Offer Inflight Email on Domestic Flights: Verizon Airfone Outfits UAL's Fleet with JetConnect^{sm}," United Airlines press release [accessed 21 July 2003] www .united.com; "Laptops Sprout Wings with Verizon Airfone JetConnect Service," *PR Newswire*, 24 September 2002 [accessed 21 July 2003] www.proquest.com; "Verizon Hopes Data Flies with Airfone JetConnect," *Wireless Data News*, 7 May 2003 [accessed 24 July 2003] www.proquest .com.

26. Adapted from Sean Doherty, "Dynamic Communications," *Network Computing*, 3 April 2003, 26 [accessed 24 July 2003] http://search.epnet.com; Todd Wasserman, "Post-Merger HP Invents New Image to Challenge Tech Foes IBM and Dell," *Brandweek*, 18 November 2002, 9 [accessed 24 July 2003] http://search.epnet.com; R. P. Srikanth, "IM Tools Are Latest Tech Toys for Corporate Users," *Express Computer*, 1 July 2002 [accessed 21 July 2003] www .expresscomputeronline.com.

27. "Viral Effect of E-Mail Promotion," Alka Dwivedi blog [accessed 19 October 2006] www.alkadwivedi.net; Teresa Valdez Klein, "Starbucks Makes a Viral Marketing Misstep," Blog Business Summit website [accessed 19 October 2006] www.blogbusinesssummit.com.

28. Adapted from EQ Company press releases [accessed 27 October 2006] www.eqonline.com; "N.C. Residents to Return After Fire," *ScienceDaily*, 6 October 2006 [accessed 27 October 2006] www.sciencedaily.com; "Hazardous Waste Plant Fire in N.C. Forces 17,000 to Evacuate," FOXNews.com, 6 October 2006 [accessed 27 October 2006] www.foxnews.com.

CHAPTER 9

1. Brian Clark, "The Two Most Important Words in Blogging," Copyblogger blog [accessed 1 March 2008] www.copyblogger.com.

2. Jay A. Conger, "The Necessary Art of Persuasion," *Harvard Business Review*, May–June 1998, 84–95; Jeanette W. Gilsdorf, "Write Me Your Best Case for . . ." *Bulletin of the Association for Business Communication* 54, no. 1 (March 1991): 7–12.

3. "Vital Skill for Today's Managers: Persuading, Not Ordering, Others," *Soundview Executive Book Summaries*, September 1998, 1.

4. Mary Cross, "Aristotle and Business Writing: Why We Need to Teach Persuasion," *Bulletin of the Association for Business Communication* 54, no. 1 (March 1991): 3–6.

5. IKEA website [accessed 3 March 2008] www.ikea.com; Liz C. Wang, Julie Baker, Judy A. Wagner, and Kirk Wakefield, "Can a Retail Web Site Be Social?" *Journal of Marketing* 71, no. 3 (July 2007), 143–157.

6. Stephen Bayley and Roger Mavity, "How to Pitch," *Management Today*, March 2007, 48–53.

7. Robert B. Cialdini, "Harnessing the Science of Persuasion," *BusinessWeek*, 4 December 2007 [accessed 4 March 2008] www.businessweek.com.

8. Wesley Clark, "The Potency of Persuasion," *Fortune*, 12 November 2007, 48; W. H. Weiss, "Using Persuasion Successfully," *Supervision*, October 2006, 13–16.

9. Tom Chandler, "The Copywriter's Best Friend," The Copywriter Underground blog, 20 December 2006 [accessed 4 March 2008] http://copywriterunderground.com.

10. John D. Ramage and John C. Bean, *Writing Arguments: A Rhetoric with Readings*, 3rd ed. (Boston: Allyn & Bacon, 1995), 430–442.

11. Philip Vassallo, "Persuading Powerfully: Tips for Writing Persuasive Documents," *et Cetera*, Spring 2002, 65–71.

12. Dianna Booher, *Communicate with Confidence* (New York: McGraw-Hill, 1994), 102.

13. Conger, "The Necessary Art of Persuasion."

14. Paul Endress, "The Art of Persuasion: Get the Edge You Need to Reach Your Goals," *American Salesman*, April 2007, 7–10.

15. iPod nano main product page, Apple website [accessed 4 March 2008] www.apple.com/ipodnano.

16. "HealthGrades Reveals America's Best Hospitals," 27 February 2008 [accessed 4 March 2008] www.ivanhoe.com.

17. Saturn VUE product page, Saturn website [accessed 14 May 2006] www.saturn.com.

18. Lancôme website [accessed 4 March 2008] www.lancome-usa.com.

19. *Living in France* product page, Insider Paris Guides website [accessed 4 March 2008] www.insiderparisguides.com.

20. U.S. Department of Energy, Energy Efficiency and Renewable Energy website [accessed 4 March 2008] www.eere.energy.gov.

21. Microsoft Office website [accessed 4 March 2008] http://office.microsoft.com.

22. Fast Break Backpack product page, Lands End website [accessed 8 December 2003], www.landsend.com.

23. iPod nano main product page, Apple website [accessed 4 March 2008] www.apple.com/ipodnano.

24. "Technical Specifications," iPod nano, Apple website [accessed 4 March 2008] www.apple.com/ipodnano.

25. Larry Weber, *Marketing to the Social Web* (Hoboken, N.J.: Wiley, 2007), 12–14; David Meerman Scott, *The New Rules of Marketing and PR* (Hoboken, N.J.: Wiley, 2007), 62; Paul Gillin, *The New Influencers* (Sanger, Calif.: Quill Driver Books, 2007), 34–35; Jeremy Wright, *Blog Marketing: The Revolutionary Way to Increase Sales, Build Your Brand, and Get Exceptional Results* (New York: McGraw-Hill, 2006), 263–365.

26. Gilsdorf, "Write Me Your Best Case for . . ."

27. *Frequently Asked Advertising Questions: A Guide for Small Business*, U.S. Federal Trade Commission website [accessed 9 December 2003] www.ftc.gov.

28. *Milwaukee Journal Sentinel* website [accessed 4 March 2008] http://blogs.jsonline.com.

29. Adapted from Samsung website [accessed 22 October 2006] www.samsung.com.

30. Adapted from GM FastLane blog [accessed 23 August 2005] http://fastlane.gmblogs.com.

31. Adapted from Podcast Bunker website [accessed 25 August 2005] www.podcastbunker.com.

32. Adapted from Time Inc. website [accessed 25 August 2005] www.timewarner.com.

33. Adapted from Starbucks website [accessed 23 August 2005] www.starbucks.com.

34. Adapted from Kelly Services website [accessed 9 January 2004], www.kellyservices.com.

35. Adapted from Give Life website [accessed 23 August 2005] www.givelife.org; American Red Cross website [accessed 3 October 2001] www.redcross.org; American Red Cross San Diego Chapter website [accessed 3 October 2001] www.sdarc.org/blood.htm.

36. Adapted from Sarah Plaskitt, "Case Study: Hilton Uses SMS with Success," *B&T Marketing & Media*, 27 June 2002 [accessed 22 July 2003] www.bandt.com.au; "Wireless Messaging Briefs," *Instant Messaging Planet*, 4 October 2002 [accessed 22 July 2003] www.instantmessagingplanet.com; Hilton Hotels Corporation, *Hoover's Company Capsules*, 1 July 2003 [accessed 24 July 2003] www.proquest.com; Matthew G. Nelson, "Hilton Takes Reservations Wireless," *InformationWeek*, 25 June 2001, 99 [accessed 24 July 2003] www.web22.cpnet.com; Hilton Hotels website [accessed 15 January 2004] www.hilton.com.

37. Adapted from "Community Relations," IBM website [accessed 15 January 2004] www.ibm.com; "DAS Faces an Assured Future with IBM," IBM website [accessed 16 January 2004] www.ibm.com; IBM website, "Sametime" [accessed 16 January 2004] www.ibm.com.

38. Adapted from Andrew Ferguson, "Supermarket of the Vanities," *Fortune*, 10 June 1996, 30, 32; Whole Foods Market website [accessed 9 January 2004] www.wholefoodsmarket.com.

39. Adapted from Web Accessibility Initiative website [accessed 8 March 2008] www.w3.org/wai.

40. Adapted from American Beefalo International website [accessed 8 March 2008] www.ababeefalo.org.

CHAPTER 10

1. Molly Selvin, "No Gobbledygook; Company Handbook Is in Plain English," *Seattle Times*, 27 January 2008 [accessed 8 March 2008] www.seattletimes.com.

2. Courtland L. Bovée, Michael J. Houston, and John V. Thill, *Marketing*, 2nd ed. (New York: McGraw-Hill, 1995), 194–196.

3. Legal-Definitions.com [accessed 17 December 2003] www.legal-definitions.com.

4. AllTheWeb.com advanced search page [accessed 27 August 2005] www.alltheweb.com; Google advanced search page [accessed 27 August 2005] www.google.com; Yahoo! advanced search page [accessed 27 August 2005] www.yahoo.com.

5. NewsGator website [accessed 8 March 2008] www.newsgator.com; Google website [accessed 8 March 2008] www.google.com.

6. "About Google Desktop," Google website [accessed 3 November 2006] www.google.com; "Desktop Search Tools Matrix," Goebel Group website [accessed 3 November 2006] www.goebelgroup.com.

7. "Top 10 Benefits of OneNote 2007," Microsoft website [accessed 8 March 2008] www.microsoft.com; "Welcome

to Google Notebook," Google website [accessed 8 March 2008] www.google.com.

8. Naresh K. Malhotra, *Basic Marketing Research* (Upper Saddle River, N.J.: Prentice Hall, 2002), 314–317; "How to Design and Conduct a Study," *Credit Union Magazine*, October 1983, 36–46.

9. American Marketing Association website [accessed 14 December 2003] www.marketingpower.com.

10. Karen J. Bannan, "Companies Save Time, Money with Online Surveys," *B to B*, 9 June 2003, 1+; Allen Hogg, "Online Research Overview," American Marketing Association website [accessed 15 December 2003] www.marketingpower.com.

11. Sherwyn P. Morreale and Courtland L. Bovée, *Excellence in Public Speaking* (Fort Worth, Tex.: Harcourt Brace College Publishers, 1998), 182.

12. Lynn Quitman Troyka, *Simon & Schuster Handbook for Writers*, 6th ed. (Upper Saddle River, N.J.: Prentice Hall, 2002), 481.

13. Jakob Nielsen, "How Users Read on the Web" [accessed 11 November 2004] www.useit.com/alertbox/9710a.html.

14. Reid Goldsborough, "Words for the Wise," *Link-Up*, September–October 1999, 25–26.

15. Julie Rohovit, "Computer Eye Strain: The Dilbert Syndrome," Virtual Hospital website [accessed 9 November 2004] www.vh.org.

16. Nick Usborne, "Two Pillars of a Successful Site," *Excess Voice*, May 2004 [accessed 8 November 2004] www.excessvoice.com.

17. Shel Holtz, "Writing for the Wired World," (San Francisco: International Association of Business Communicators, 1999), 6–9.

18. Holtz, "Writing for the Wired World," 28–29.

19. Adapted from Catherine Holahan and Spencer E. Ante, "SXSW: Where Tech Mingles with Music," *BusinessWeek*, 7 March 2008 [accessed 9 March 2008] www.businessweek.com; SXSW website [accessed 9 March 2008] http://sxsw.com.

20. Adapted from Air-Trak website [accessed 9 March 2008] www.air-trak.com.

CHAPTER 11

1. Martin Couzins, "Expert's View: Tania Menegatti on How to Improve Your Communication Skills," *Personnel Today*, 30 August 2005 [accessed 22 May 2006] www.epnet.com.

2. A. S. C. Ehrenberg, "Report Writing—Six Simple Rules for Better Business Documents," *Admap*, June 1992, 39–42.

3. Michael Netzley and Craig Snow, *Guide to Report Writing* (Upper Saddle River, N.J.: Prentice Hall, 2001), 15.

4. Philip C. Kolin, *Successful Writing at Work*, 6th ed. (Boston: Houghton Mifflin, 2001), 552–555.

5. "Web Writing: How to Avoid Pitfalls," *Investor Relations Business*, 1 November 1999, 15.

6. Sant Corporation website [accessed 11 March 2008] www.santcorp.com; Kadient website [accessed 11 March 2008] www.kadient.com.

7. Alexis Gerard and Bob Goldstein, *Going Visual* (Hoboken, N.J.: Wiley, 2005), 18.

8. Gerard and Goldstein, *Going Visual*, 103–106.

9. Edward R. Tufte, *Visual Explanations: Images and Quantities, Evidence and Narrative* (Cheshire, Conn.: Graphics Press, 1997), 82.

10. Joshua David McClurg-Genevese, "The Principles of Design," *Digital Web Magazine*, 13 June 2005 [accessed 23 November 2006] www.digital-web.com.

11. Charles Kostelnick and Michael Hassett, *Shaping Information: The Rhetoric of Visual Conventions* (Carbondale, Ill.: Southern Illinois University Press, 2003), 17.

12. Edward R. Tufte, *The Visual Display of Quantitative Information* (Cheshire, Conn.: Graphic Press, 1983), 113.

13. "Data Visualization: Modern Approaches," Smashing Magazine website, 2 August 2007 [accessed 15 March 2008] www.smashingmagazine.com; "7 Things You Should Know About Data Visualization," Educause Learning Initiative [accessed 15 March 2008] www.educause.edu; TagCrowd website [accessed 15 March 2008] www.tagcrowd.com.

14. John Morkes and Jakob Nielsen, "Concise, Scannable, and Objective: How to Write for the Web," UseIt.com [accessed 13 November 2006] www.useit.com.

15. Netzley and Snow, *Guide to Report Writing*, 57.

16. Toby B. Gooley, "Ocean Shipping: RFPs that Get Results," *Logistics Management*, July 2003, 47–52.

17. Adapted from Ieva M. Augstumes, "Buyers Take the Driver's Seat," *Dallas Morning News*, 20 February 2004 [accessed 30 June 2004] www.highbeam.com; Jill Amadio, "A Click Away: Automotive Web Sites Are Revved Up and Ready to Help You Buy," *Entrepreneur*, 1 August 2003 [accessed 30 June 2004] www.highbeam.com; Dawn C. Chmielewski, "Car Sites Lend Feel-Good Info for Haggling," *San Jose Mercury News*, 1 August 2003 [accessed 30 June 2004] www.highbeam.com; Cromwell Schubarth, "Autoheroes Handle Hassle of Haggling," *Boston Herald*, 24 July 2003 [accessed 30 June 2004] www.highbeam.com; Rick Popely, "Internet Doesn't Change Basic Shopping Rules," *Chicago Tribune*, 28 February 2004 [accessed 30 June 2004] www.highbeam.com; Matt Nauman, "Walnut Creek, Calif., Firm Prospers as Online Car Buying Becomes More Popular," *San Jose Mercury News*, 21 June 2004 [accessed 30 June 2004] www.highbeam.com; Cliff Banks, "e-Dealer 100," *Ward's Dealer Business*, 1 April 2004 [accessed 30 June 2004] www.highbeam.com; Cars.com website [accessed 30 June 2004] www.cars.com; CarsDirect.com website [accessed 30 June 2004] www.carsdirect.com.

CHAPTER 12

1. EZspeech website [accessed 19 March 2008] www.ez-speech.com; Marc S. Friedman, "Use Visual Aids, Not

Visual Crutches," *Training*, 24 December 2007 [accessed 19 March 2008] www.presentations.com.

2. Carmine Gallo, "Loaded for Bore," *BusinessWeek*, 5 August 2005 [accessed 19 September 2005] www.businessweek.com.

3. Sarah Lary and Karen Pruente, "Powerless Point: Common PowerPoint Mistakes to Avoid," *Public Relations Tactics*, February 2004, 28.

4. Cliff Atkinson, *Beyond Bullet Points: Using Microsoft PowerPoint to Create Presentations That Inform, Motivate, and Inspire* (Redmond, Wash.: Microsoft Press, 2005), 29, 55, 65.

5. Sherwyn P. Morreale and Courtland L. Bovée, *Excellence in Public Speaking* (Fort Worth, Tex.: Harcourt Brace College Publishers, 1998), 234–237.

6. John Windsor, "Presenting Smart: Keeping the Goal in Sight," *Presentations*, 6 March 2008 [accessed 19 March 2008] www.presentations.com.

7. Morreale and Bovée, *Excellence in Public Speaking*, 241–243.

8. Carmine Gallo, "Grab Your Audience Fast," *BusinessWeek*, 13 September 2006, 19.

9. Walter Kiechel III, "How to Give a Speech," *Fortune*, 8 June 1987, 180.

10. *Communication and Leadership Program* (Santa Ana, Calif.: Toastmasters International, 1980), 44, 45.

11. "Polishing Your Presentation," 3M Meeting Network [accessed 8 June 2001] www.mmm.com/meetingnetwork/readingroom/meetingguide_pres.html.

12. "Now Presenting: Text-Heavy Slides a Real Snooze," *Presentations*, 18 February 2008 [accessed 20 March 2008] www.presentations.com.

13. Margo Halverson, "Choosing the Right Colors for Your Next Presentation," 3M Meeting Network [accessed 8 June 2001] www.mmm.com/meetingnetwork.

14. Jon Hanke, "Five Tips for Better Visuals," 3M Meeting Network [accessed 8 June 2001] www.mmm.com/meetingnetwork.

15. Lary and Pruente, "Powerless Point: Common PowerPoint Mistakes to Avoid."

16. Jeff Yocom, "TechRepublic Survey Yields Advice on Streaming Video," TechRepublic website [accessed 16 February 2004] www.techrepublic.com.

17. TechWeb website [accessed 20 March 2008] www.techweb.com; "Webcasting Tips & Advice," Spider Eye Studios [accessed 13 February 2004] www.spidereye.com.

18. Jerry Weissman, *Presenting to Win: The Art of Telling Your Story* (Upper Saddle River, N.J.: Pearson Prentice Hall, 2006), 162–163.

19. Ted Simons, "Handouts That Won't Get Trashed," *Presentations*, February 1999, 47–50.

20. Morreale and Bovée, *Excellence in Public Speaking*, 24–25.

21. Jennifer Rotondo and Mike Rotondo, Jr., *Presentation Skills for Managers* (New York: McGraw-Hill, 2002), 9.

22. Rick Gilbert, "Presentation Advice for Boardroom Success," *Financial Executive*, September 2005, 12.

23. Rotondo and Rotondo, *Presentation Skills for Managers*, 151.

24. Teresa Brady, "Fielding Abrasive Questions During Presentations," *Supervisory Management*, February 1993, 6.

25. Robert L. Montgomery, "Listening on Your Feet," *The Toastmaster*, July 1987, 14–15.

26. Adapted from Loopt website [accessed 9 December 2006] www.loopt.com; Boost Mobile website [accessed 9 December 2006] www.boostmobile.com.

27. Adapted from Robert D. Hof, "There's Not Enough 'Me' in MySpace," *BusinessWeek*, 4 December 2006, 40.

CHAPTER 13

1. Ed Tazzia, "Wanted: A Résumé That Really Works," *Brandweek*, 15 May 2006, 26.

2. Anne Fisher, "How to Get Hired by a 'Best' Company," *Fortune*, 4 February 2008, 96.

3. Caroline A. Drakeley, "Viral Networking: Tactics in Today's Job Market," *Intercom*, September–October 2003, 4–7.

4. "CareerXroads 6th Annual Sources of Hire Study, 2006," CareerXroads website [accessed 30 March 2008] www.careerxroads.com.

5. Jobfox website [accessed 24 August 2007] www.jobfox.com; Olga Kharif, "The Job of Challenging Monster," *BusinessWeek*, 6 September 2005 [accessed 25 September 2005] www.businessweek.com; "Job Sites: The 'Second Generation,'" *BusinessWeek*, 7 September 2005 [accessed 25 September 2005] www.businessweek.com.

6. Jeanette Borzo, "Taking on the Recruiting Monster," *FSB*, May 2007, 89–90.

7. Douglas MacMillan, "The Art of the Online Résumé," *BusinessWeek*, 7 May 2007, 86.

8. Fisher, "How to Get Hired by a 'Best' Company."

9. Drakeley, "Viral Networking: Tactics in Today's Job Market," 5.

10. Erik Sherman, "The New Way to Network for Jobs," *Advertising Age*, 17 March 2008, 6–7.

11. Anne Fisher, "Greener Pastures in a New Field," *Fortune*, 26 January 2004, 48.

12. Liz Ryan, "Etiquette for Online Outreach," Yahoo! Hotjobs website [accessed 26 March 2008] http://hotjobs.yahoo.com.

13. Career and Employment Services, Danville Area Community College website [accessed 23 March 2008] www.dacc.edu/career; Career Counseling, Sarah Lawrence College website [accessed 23 March 2008] www.slc.edu/occ; Cheryl L. Noll, "Collaborating with the Career Planning and Placement Center in the Job-Search Project," *Business Communication Quarterly* 58, no. 3 (1995): 53–55.

14. Rockport Institute, "How to Write a Masterpiece of a Résumé" [accessed 24 March 2008] www.rockportinstitute.com.

15. Pam Stanley-Weigand, "Organizing the Writing of Your Resume," *Bulletin of the Association for Business Communication* 54, no. 3 (September 1991): 11–12.

16. Kim Isaacs, "Resume Dilemma: Criminal Record," Monster.com [accessed 23 May 2006] www.monster.com; Kim Isaacs, "Resume Dilemma: Employment Gaps and

Job-Hopping," Monster.com [accessed 23 May 2006] www.monster.com; Susan Vaughn, "Answer the Hard Questions Before Asked," *Los Angeles Times*, 29 July 2001, W1–W2.

17. John Steven Niznik, "Landing a Job with a Criminal Record," About.com [accessed 12 December 2006] http://jobsearchtech.about.com.

18. Richard H. Beatty and Nicholas C. Burkholder, *The Executive Career Guide for MBAs* (New York: Wiley, 1996), 133.

19. Adapted from Burdette E. Bostwick, *How to Find the Job You've Always Wanted* (New York: Wiley, 1982), 69–70.

20. Norma Mushkat Gaffin, "Recruiters' Top 10 Resume Pet Peeves," Monster.com [accessed 19 February 2004] www.monster.com; Beatty and Burkholder, *The Executive Career Guide for MBAs*, 151.

21. Katharine Hansen, "Should You Consider a Functional Format for Your Resume?" QuintCareers.com [accessed 24 March 2008] www.quintcareers.com.

22. Rockport Institute, "How to Write a Masterpiece of a Résumé."

23. "How to Ferret Out Instances of Résumé Padding and Fraud," *Compensation & Benefits for Law Offices*, June 2006, 1+.

24. "Resume Fraud Gets Slicker and Easier," CNN.com [accessed 11 March 2004] www.cnn.com.

25. Lisa Takeuchi Cullen, "Getting Wise to Lies," *Time*, 1 May 2006, 59; "Resume Fraud Gets Slicker and Easier"; Employment Research Services website [accessed 18 March 2004] www.erscheck.com.

26. "How to Ferret Out Instances of Résumé Padding and Fraud."

27. Jacqueline Durett, "Redoing Your Résumé? Leave Off the Lies," *Training*, December 2006, 9; "Employers Turn Their Fire on Untruthful CVs," *Supply Management*, 23 June 2005, 13.

28. Marilyn Moats Kennedy, "Don't Get Burned by Résumé Inflation," *Marketing News*, 37–38.

29. Sal Divita, "If You're Thinking Résumé, Think Creatively," *Marketing News*, 14 September 1992, 29.

30. Rockport Institute, "How to Write a Masterpiece of a Résumé."

31. Lora Morsch, "25 Words That Hurt Your Resume," CNN.com, 20 January 2006 [accessed 20 January 2006] www.cnn.com.

32. Liz Ryan, "The Reengineered Résumé," *BusinessWeek*, 3 December 2007, SC12.

33. Anthony Balderrama, "Resume Blunders That Will Keep You from Getting Hired," CNN.com, 19 March 2008 [accessed 26 March 2008] www.cnn.com; Michelle Dumas, "5 Resume Writing Myths," Distinctive Documents blog, 17 July 2007 [accessed 26 March 2008] http://blog.distinctiveweb.com; Kim Isaacs, "Resume Dilemma: Recent Graduate," Monster.com [accessed 26 March 2008] http://career-advice.monster.com.

34. Karl L. Smart, "Articulating Skills in the Job Search," *Business Communication Quarterly* 67, no. 2 (June 2004): 198–205.

35. "25 Things You Should Never Include on a Resume," HR World website 18 December 2007 [accessed 25 March 2008] www.hrworld.com.

36. "When to Include Personal Data," ResumeEdge.com [accessed 25 March 2008] www.resumeedge.com.

37. "Résumé Length: What It Should Be and Why It Matters to Recruiters," *HR Focus*, June 2007, 9.

38. John Sullivan, "Résumés: Paper, Please," *Workforce Management*, 22 October 2007, 50; "Video Résumés Offer Both Pros and Cons During Recruiting," *HR Focus*, July 2007, 8.

39. "Scannable Resume Design," ResumeEdge.com [accessed 19 February 2004] www.resumeedge.com.

40. "Career Opportunities: Submit Your Résumé," Western Digital website [accessed 25 March 2008] www.wdc.com; Kim Isaacs, "Tips for Creating a Scannable Resume," Monster.com [accessed 19 February 2004] www.monster.com.

41. Christian Anderson, "New Year's Resolutions—Jobster Style," Jobster blog, 21 December 2007 [accessed 28 March 2008] www.jobster.blogs.com.

42. Sarah E. Needleman, "Why Sneaky Tactics May Not Help Resume; Recruiters Use New Search Technologies to Ferret Out Bogus Keywords," *Wall Street Journal*, 6 March 2007, B8.

43. Kim Isaacs, "Enhance Your Resume for Monster Upload," Monster.com [accessed 19 February 2004] www.monster.com.

44. "10 Reasons Why You Are Not Getting Any Interviews," *Miami Times*, 7–13 November 2007, 6D.

45. "The Rogue's Gallery of 25 Awful Résumé Mistakes," CareerExplorer.net [accessed 19 February 2004] www.careerexplorer.net.

46. "Protect Yourself From Identity Theft When Hunting for a Job Online," *Office Pro*, May 2007, 6.

CHAPTER 14

1. Max Messmer, "Five Common Interview Mistakes and How to Avoid Them," *Strategic Finance*, April 2005, 12–14.

2. Joann Lublin, "Cover Letters Get You in the Door, So Be Sure Not to Dash Them Off," *Wall Street Journal*, 6 April 2004, B1.

3. "The Writer Approach," *Los Angeles Times*, 17 November 2002, W1.

4. Toni Logan, "The Perfect Cover Story," *Kinko's Impress* 2 (2000): 32, 34.

5. James Gonyea, "Money Talks: Salary History Versus Salary Requirements," Monster.com [accessed 19 October 2004] www.monster.com; Marguerite Higgins, "Tech-Savvy Job Hunters Not So Suave in Writing; E-Mail Résumés Appall Employers," *Washington Times*, 17 December 2002 [accessed 22 February 2004] www.highbeam.com; "Keep Goal in Mind When Crafting a Résumé," *(Eugene, Ore.) Register-Guard*, 3 August 2003 [accessed 22 February 2004] www.highbeam.com; Anis F. McClin, "Effects of Spelling Errors on the Perception of Writers," *Journal of*

General Psychology, January 2002 [accessed 22 February 2004] www.highbeam.com.

6. Anne Fisher, "How to Get Hired by a 'Best' Company," *Fortune*, 4 February 2008, 96.

7. Fisher, "How to Get Hired by a 'Best' Company."

8. Sarah E. Needleman, "Speed Interviewing Grows as Skills Shortage Looms; Strategy May Help Lock in Top Picks; Some Drawbacks," *Wall Street Journal*, 6 November 2007, B15.

9. Scott Beagrie, "How to Handle a Telephone Job Interview," *Personnel Today*, 26 June 2007, 29.

10. John Olmstead, "Predict Future Success with Structured Interviews," *Nursing Management*, March 2007, 52–53.

11. Fisher, "How to Get Hired by a 'Best' Company."

12. Erinn R. Johnson, "Pressure Sessions," *Black Enterprise*, October 2007, 72.

13. "What's a Group Interview?" About.com Tech Careers [accessed 5 April 2008] http://jobsearchtech.about.com.

14. Fisher, "How to Get Hired by a 'Best' Company."

15. "FAQs About Behavioral Based Interviewing," University of Wisconsin–Eau Clair website [accessed 5 April 2008] www.uwec.edu; "Advice on Mastering the 'Behavioral' Interview," *Financial Executive*, November 2007, 11.

16. Chris Pentilla, "Testing the Waters," *Entrepreneur*, January 2004 [accessed 27 May 2006] www.entrepreneur.com; Terry McKenna, "Behavior-Based Interviewing," *National Petroleum News*, January 2004, 16; Nancy K. Austin, "Goodbye Gimmicks," *Incentive*, May 1996, 241.

17. William Poundstone, "Beware the Interview Inquisition," *Harvard Business Review*, May 2003, 18+.

18. Anjali Athavaley, "A Job Interview You Don't Have to Show Up For; Microsoft, Verizon, Others Use Virtual Worlds to Recruit; Dressing Avatars for Success," *Wall Street Journal*, 20 June 2007, D1.

19. Peter Vogt, "Mastering the Phone Interview," Monster.com [accessed 13 December 2006] www.monster.com; Nina Segal, "The Global Interview: Tips for Successful, Unconventional Interview Techniques," Monster.com [accessed 13 December 2006] www.monster.com.

20. Segal, "The Global Interview: Tips for Successful, Unconventional Interview Techniques."

21. HireVue website [accessed 4 April 2008] www.hirevue.com; in2View website [accessed 4 April 2008] www.in2view.biz; Victoria Reitz, "Interview Without Leaving Home," *Machine Design*, 1 April 2004, 66.

22. Connie Winkler, "Job Tryouts Go Virtual," *HR Magazine*, September 2006, 131–134.

23. Dino di Mattia, "Testing Methods and Effectiveness of Tests," *Supervision*, August 2005, 4–5.

24. David W. Arnold and John W. Jones, "Who the Devil's Applying Now?" *Security Management*, March 2002, 85–88.

25. Arnold and Jones, "Who the Devil's Applying Now?" 86.

26. Frederick P. Morgeson, Michael A. Campion, Robert L. Dipboye, John R. Hollenbeck, Kevin Murphy, and Neil Schmitt, "Are We Getting Fooled Again? Coming to Terms with Limitations in the Use of Personality Tests in Personnel Selection," *Personnel Psychology* 60, no. 4 (Winter 2007): 1029–1049.

27. Adam Agard, "Preemployment Skills Testing: An Important Step in the Hiring Process," *Supervision*, June 2003, 7+.

28. Ashlea Ebeling, "Corporate Moneyball," *Forbes*, 23 April 2007, 102+.

29. "Drug Test Company Official Disputes Report Pre-employment Tests Falling," *Drug Detection Report*, 23 March 2006, 43.

30. Matthew J. Heller, "Digging Deeper," *Workforce Management*, 3 March 2008, 35–39.

31. "Check Yourself Before Employer Does," *CA Magazine*, June/July 2005, 12.

32. Scott Medintz, "Talkin' 'Bout MySpace Generation," *Money*, February 2006, 27.

33. Michael Kaplan, "Job Interview Brainteasers," *Business 2.0*, September 2007, 35–37.

34. Austin, "Goodbye Gimmicks."

35. Nick Corcodilos, "How to Answer a Misguided Interview Question," *Seattle Times*, 30 March 2008 [accessed 5 April 2008] www.seattletimes.com.

36. Katherine Spencer Lee, "Tackling Tough Interview Questions," *Certification Magazine*, May 2005, 35.

37. InterviewUp website [accessed 5 April 2008] www.interviewup.com.

38. Joe Turner, "An Interview Strategy: Telling Stories," Yahoo! HotJobs [accessed 5 April 2008] http://hotjobs.yahoo.com.

39. "A Word of Caution for Chatty Job Candidates," *Public Relations Tactics*, January 2008, 4.

40. Robert Gifford, Cheuk Fan Ng, and Margaret Wilkinson, "Nonverbal Cues in the Employment Interview: Links Between Applicant Qualities and Interviewer Judgments," *Journal of Applied Psychology* 70, no. 4 (1985): 729.

41. Dale G. Leathers, *Successful Nonverbal Communication* (New York: Macmillan, 1986), 225.

42. Randall S. Hansen, "When Job-Hunting: Dress for Success," QuintCareers.com [accessed 5 April 2008] www.quintcareers.com; Alison Doyle, "Dressing for Success," About.com [accessed 5 April 2008] http://jobsearch.about.com.

43. William S. Frank, "Job Interview: Pre-Flight Checklist," *The Career Advisor* [accessed 28 September 2005] http://careerplanning.about.com.

44. T. Shawn Taylor, "Most Managers Have No Idea How to Hire the Right Person for the Job," *Chicago Tribune*, 23 July 2002 [accessed 29 September 2005] www.ebsco.com.

45. "10 Minutes to Impress," *Journal of Accountancy*, July 2007, 13.

46. Steven Mitchell Sack, "The Working Woman's Legal Survival Guide: Testing," FindLaw.com [accessed 22 February 2004] www.findlaw.com.

47. Gerald L. Wilson, "Preparing Students for Responding to Illegal Selection Interview Questions," *Bulletin of the Association for Business Communication* 54, no. 2 (1991): 44–49.

48. Jeff Springston and Joann Keyton, "Interview Response Training," *Bulletin of the Association for Business*

Communication 54, no. 3 (1991): 28–30; Gerald L. Wilson, "An Analysis of Instructional Strategies for Responding to Illegal Selection Interview Questions," *Bulletin of the Association for Business Communication* 54, no. 3 (1991): 31–35.

49. "Negotiating Salary: An Introduction," *InformationWeek* online [accessed 22 February 2004] www.informationweek .com.

50. "Negotiating Salary: An Introduction."

51. Harold H. Hellwig, "Job Interviewing: Process and Practice," *Bulletin of the Association for Business Communication* 55, no. 2 (1992): 8–14.

52. Joan S. Lublin, "Notes to Interviewers Should Go Beyond a Simple Thank You," *Wall Street Journal,* 5 February 2008, B1.

53. Adapted from Megapixel.net website [accessed 6 April 2008] www.megapixel.net.

54. Adapted from Google Earth website [accessed 6 April 2008] http://earth.google.com.

APPENDIX A

1. Mary A. De Vries, *Internationally Yours* (Boston: Houghton Mifflin, 1194), 9.

2. Patricia A. Dreyfus, "Paper That's Letter Perfect," *Money,* May 1985, 184.

3. "When Image Counts, Letterhead Says It All," *Stamford* (Conn.) *Advocate and Greenwich Times,* 10 January 1993, F4.

4. Mel Mandell, "Electronic Forms are Cheap and Speedy," *D&B Reports,* July–August 1993, 44–45.

5. Linda Driskill, *Business and Managerial Communication: New Perspectives* (Orlando, Fla.: Harcourt Brace Jovanovich, 1992), 470.

6. Driskill, *Business and Managerial Communication,* 470.

7. Lennie Copeland and Lewis Griggs, *Going International: How to Make Friends and Deal Effectively in the Global Marketplace,* 2d ed. (New York: Random House, 1985), 24–27.

8. De Vries, *Internationally Yours,* 8.

9. U.S. Postal Service, *International Mail Manual,* Issue 34, 14 May 2007 [accessed 23 October 2007] www.usps.gov.

10. Renee B. Horowitz and Marian G. Barchilon, "Stylistic Guidelines for E-Mail," *IEEE: Transactions on Professional Communications,* 37, no. 4 (1994): 207–212.

11. Jill H. Ellsworth and Matthew V. Ellsworth, *The Internet Business Book* (New York: Wiley, 1994), 93.

12. William Eager, *Using the Internet* (Indianapolis: Que Corporation, 1994), 11.

13. Eager, *Using the Internet,* 10.

14. William Eager, Larry Donahue, David Forsyth, Kenneth Mitton, and Martin Waterhouse, *Net.Search* (Indianapolis: Que Corporation, 1995), 221.

Acknowledgments

(Prologue, page P-2) David Mager/Pearson Learning Photo Studio. (Figure 1.2) Mary O'Hara-Devereaux and Robert Johansen, *Global Work: Bridging Distance, Culture, and Time* (San Francisco: Jossey Bass, 1994), 55, 59. (Chapter 1: Photo Essay pp. 16–19) Belkin International, Inc. Getty Images—Digital Division; Lance Davies Photography/Polyvision, A Steelcase Company; Ethan Hill Photography; Ethan Hill Photography; Studio M/Stock Connection; Peter Christopher/ Masterfile Corporation; United Parcel Service; Photolibrary .com; Cranial Tap, Inc.; Marcio Jose Sanchez/AP Wide World Photos; Staples, Inc.; (Figure 2.4) Adapted from Roger Axtell, *Gestures: The Do's and Taboos of Body Language Around the World,* (New York: Wiley, 1991), 117–119. (Table 2.1) Alf Nucifora, "Voice Mail Demands Good Etiquette from Both Sides," *Puget Sound Business Journal,* 5–11 September 2003, 24; Ruth Davidhizar and Ruth Shearer, "The Effective Voice Mail Message," *Hospital Material Management Quarterly,* November 2000, 45–49; "How to Get the Most Out of Voice Mail," *The CPA Journal,* February 2000, 11; Jo Ind, "Hanging on the Telephone," *Birmingham Post,* 28 July 1999, PS10; Larry Barker and Kittie Watson, *Listen Up* (New York: St.Martin's Press, 2000), 64–65; Lin Walker, *Telephone Techniques,* (New York: Amacom, 1998), 46–47; Dorothy Neal, *Telephone Techniques,* 2nd ed. (New York: Glencoe McGraw-Hill, 1998), 31; Jeannie Davis, *Beyond "Hello"* (Aurora, Colo.: Now Hear This, Inc., 2000), 2–3; "Ten Steps to Caller-Friendly Voice Mail," *Managing Office Technology,* January 1995, 25; Rhonda Finniss, "Voice Mail: Tips for a Positive Impression," *Administrative Assistant's Update,* August 2001, 5. (Figure 2.3) Cranial Tap, Inc. (Table 2.2) Madelyn Burley-Allen, *Listening: The Forgotten Skill* (New York: Wiley, 1995), 70–71, 119–120; Judi Brownell, *Listening: Attitudes, Principles, and Skills* (Boston: Allyn and Bacon, 2002); 3, 9, 83, 89, 125; Larry Barker and Kittie Watson, *Listen Up* (New York: St. Martin's, 2000), 8, 9, 64, 77. (Figure 3.1) Adapted from Kevin J. Harty and John Keenan, *Writing for Business and Industry: Process and Product* (New York: Macmillan, 1987), 3–4; Richard Hatch, *Business Writing* (Chicago, Ill.: Science Research Associates, 1983), 88–89; Richard Hatch, *Business Communication Theory and Technique* (Chicage, Ill.: Science Research Associates, 1983), 74–75; Center for Humanities, *Writing as a Process: A Step-by-Step Guide* (four filmstrips and cassettes). Mount Kisco, N.Y., 1987; Michael L. Keene, *Effective Professional Writing* (New York: D.C. Heath, 1987), 28–34. (Table 6.2) Robert Scoble and Shel Israel, *Naked Conversations* (Hoboken, New Jersey: John Wiley & Sons, 2006), 78–81, 190–194; Paul McFedries, *The Complete Idiot's Guide to Creating a Web Page & Blog,* 6th ed. (New York: Alpha, 2004), 206–208, 272–276; Shel Holtz and Te Demopoulos, *Blogging for Business* (Chicago: Kaplan, 2006), 54–59, 113–114; Denise Wakeman, "Top 10 Blog Writing Tips," Blogarooni.com [accessed 1 February 2006] www.blogarooni.com; Dennis A. Mahoney, "How to Write a Better Weblog," 22 February 2002, A List Apart [accessed 1 February 2006] www.alistapart.com. (Figure 7.1) Google blog screenshot © Google Inc. and is used with permission. (Figure 7.6) Courtesy Herman Miller. (Figure 9.1) Courtesy ClubMom.com. (Figure 9.4) BGF Industries, Inc., Gladiator is a registered trademark of Whirlpool, U.S.A. (Figure 9.5) Courtesy of Conversation Marketing, http://www.conversationmarketing .com. (Figure 11.9) Courtesy Tag Crowd. (Figure 11.12) Alan Gough/Alan Gough Photography. (Figure 12.6) Microsoft PowerPoint 2007 software. (Table 12.2) Adapted from Carmen Matthews, "Speaker's Notes," *Presentations,* April 2005, 42; Eric J. Adams, "Management Focus: User-Friendly Presentation Software," *World Trade,* March 1995, 92. (Table 12.3) Adapted from Claudyne Wilder and David Fine, *Point, Click & Wow* (San Francisco: Jossey-Bass Pfeiffer, 1996), 63, 527. (Figure 13.2) Adapted from Richard Nelson Bolles, *What Color Is Your Parachute?* (Berkeley, Calif.: Ten Speed Press, 1997), 67. (Table 13.1) The Riley Guide [accessed 30 March 2008] www. rileyguide.com; SimplyHired website [accessed 30 March 2008] www.simplyhired.com; Indeed website [accessed 30 March 2008] www.indeed.com; CollegeRecruiter.com [accessed 30 March 2008] www.collegerecruiter.com; Jobster website [accessed 30 March 2008] www.jobster.com; InternshipPrograms.com [accessed 30 March 2008] http://internshipprograms.com. (Figure 14.3) Courtesy of PerfectInterview.com/Contexxa Corporation (Table 14.3) Adapted from InterviewUp website [accessed 6 April 2008] www.interviewup.com; *The Northwestern Endicott Report* (Evanston, Ill.: Northwestern University Placement Center). (Table 14.4) Joe Conklin, "Turning the Tables: Six Questions to Ask Your Interviewer," *Quality Progress,* November 2007, 55; Andrea N. Browne, "Keeping the Momentum at the Interview; Ask Questions, Do Your Research, and Be a Team Player," *Washington Post,* 29 July 2007, K1; Marilyn Sherman, "Questions R Us: What to Ask at a Job Interview," *Career World,* January 2004, 20; H. Lee Rust, *Job Search: The Complete Manual for Jobseekers* (New York: American Management Association, 1979), 56. (Table 14.5) Adapted from *The Northwestern Endicott Report* (Evanston: Ill.: Northwestern University Placement Center). (Table 14.6) Deanna G. Kucler, "Interview Questions: Legal or Illegal?" *Workforce Management* [accessed 28 September 2005] www.workforce.com; "Illegal Interview Questions," *USA Today,* 29 January 2001 [accessed 28 September 2005] www.usatoday.com; "Dangerous Questions," *Nation's Business,* May 1999, 22. (Figure A.4) With permission of Greyhound Lines, Inc.

Index

A

a lot, H-27
abbreviations, H-24
    for states A-14
abbreviations, punctuation with, A-2
abstract words, 77–78, H-3
abstracts, in reports, 293
abusive language, 183
acceptance letters, 382
accidents, drug abuse and, 373
accuracy
    of information, 52
    in reports, 261
    of visuals, 277
achievement, congratulating people
        on, 156
achievements section, on résumés, 351
Acrobat, 101, 269
acronyms, H-24
    in e-mail messages, 119
action
    messages requesting, 145–146
    persuasive requests for, 207
action buttons, in PowerPoint, 324
action items, in oral presentations, 319
action phase, of AIDA model, 204, 213, 369
action verbs, 287, H-7
    on résumés, 349
active voice, 76, 77, H-9
address, proper forms of, A-3–A-4
addressee notation, A-8
addresses
    for envelopes, A-12–A-13
    for international correspondence, 14
adjectives, 96, H-10–H-11
adjustments
    granting, 150–154
    persuasive requests for, 207–208
    refusing, 181–183
    requesting, 148, 149
Adobe Acrobat, 101, 269
Adobe InDesign, 105
Adobe Photoshop, 276
Adobe Systems, 168
adverbs, 96, H-11, H-29
advertising
    deception in, 9
    of job openings, 338
    online, 223
    truth in, 215
age bias, 72, 73
age discrimination, 352, 379
agenda, for meetings, 33
agenda slides, 326
agendas, hidden, 29
aggravate/irritate, H-27
agreement, subject-verb, H-8–H-9
aggregator, 18, 124
AIDA model, 204
    for job application letters, 366–369
    for persuasive requests, 207, 208
    for sales messages, 210–212
    for social media, 213

Air-Trak, 256
Alaska Airlines, 70
alcohol testing, 373
Alcon Laboratories, 340
Alion Science and Technology, 194
Allen, Sharon, 9
almanacs, 238
American Psychological Association
        (APA), 292, A-20, A-22
among/between, H-12
analogies, faulty, 206
analogy, arguing by, 205
analytical reports, 232, 233
    direct approach for, 244, 245,
        263
    example of, 279–293
    indirect approach for, 245–246, 263
    memo format for, 262–263
    organization of, 244–246
    planning of, 244–246
    types of, 244
    2 + 2 approach to, 245
    yardstick approach to, 245
animation, 55, 269
    for reports, 276
    functional vs. decorative,
        323–324
    in slide shows, 320, 323–324
announcements, company, 186
annual reports, 251
antecedents, H-5
anticipate/expect, H-27
anxiety, speech, 328
APA style, 292, A-2–A-24
apologies, 175, 179
    exaggerated, 152
apostrophes, H-20
    with possessives, H-4, H-6
appeals, emotional vs. logical, 204–206,
        211, 212
appearance, 30
    as nonverbal communication, 40
    for job interviews, 377
appendixes, in reports, 293
Apple, 211
Apple Keynote, 320
applicant tracking systems, 340
application letters, 365–370
appositives, H-19
appreciation, messages of, 156
area charts, 271
Argentina, A-6
arguments
    framing, 204
    logical, 206
Arial, 104, 105, 323
articles, 98, H-13
as if/like, H-12
ASCII text, for résumés, 355
AT&T, 195
attachments, 108, A-17
    résumés as, 357
attacking of opponents, 206

attention
    in job interviews, 379
    listening and, 38
    to nonverbal cues, 40
attention-getters, 210–211
    for job application letters, 366, 369
    for oral presentations, 317
attention line, A-8
attention phase, of AIDA model, 204,
        210–211, 366
attitudes, changing, 207
audience
    adapting to, 68–76
    analyzing, 50–51, 201, 311
    arousing interest of, 317–318
    building relationship with, 72–74
    for business blogs, 124
    composition of, 50
    for e-mail messages, 118
    emotional vs. logical appeals to,
        204–206
    expectations of, 51
    experience of, 312
    global, 268
    holding attention of, 318–319
    hostile, 206–207, 329
    information needs of, 52
    input from, 52
    level of understanding of, 50–51
    media preferences of, 55, 235
    needs of, 201
    offending, 70
    for persuasive messages, 201
    primary, 50
    probable reaction of, 51, 59–60, 202, 312
    questions from, 328–329
    for reports, 260
    for résumés, 342
    sensitivity to needs of, 69–72
    size of, 50, 312, 361
    for websites, 268
audience-centered approach, 9, 10
Australia, A-6
Austria, A-6
author-date system, A-20, A-21
authorization letter, 278
autocompletion, 84
autocorrection, 84
automated reputation analysis, 124
Autor, David, 122
autoresponders, 166
avatars, 35, 54, 202
awkward references, 96

B

back orders, 181
background checks, by employers, 344,
        340, 373
bad news, presenting, 70, 174, 177
    see also negative messages
balance
    as design element, 104, 269
    in reports, 261

bar charts, 270, 272–273
bcc (blind courtesy copy), 120, A-17
beefalo, 226
behavioral interviews, 371
benefits
    to audience, 70, 209, 210
    employment, 381
Berkshire Hathaway, 143
bias, of sources, 238
bias-free language, 72, 73
bibliography, 292, 293
    APA style for, 292, A-23–A-24
    Chicago style for, A-20–A-21, A-22
    compiling, 239
    MLA style for, 292, A-24, A-25
Black & Decker, 191
blaming, 151–152, 181
block format, for letters, A-10, A-11
blogging systems, 105
blogs/blogging, 54, 55, 65, 116, 123–126
    business applications of, 123–124
    comment function for, 10, 123
    corporate, 19
    community building with, 213
    directories for, 340
    for employment research, 340
    microblogs, 117
    model documents of, 10, 34, 125, 144, 214
    multiauthor, 30
    newsfeeds from, 215
    podcasts on, 128
    three-step process for, 124–126
    tips for, 127
    tone of, 123
    topics for, 123
Blue Mountain, 161
blueprint slides, 326
body, 59
    of e-mail, A-18
    of job application letters, 366–368
    of negative messages, 175, 176–178
    of oral presentations, 314, 318–319
    of reports, 261, 263, 267
    of routine requests, 145
    of positive messages, 149–150
    of proposals, 264–265, 267, 294
    of reports, 293
    of sales messages, 211–213
body language, 39–40
    of audience, 329
    in intercultural communication, 15
    in job interviews, 378–379
body movements, 39
boilerplate, 84, 268
boldface type, 105
bookmarking sites, 18
Boolean search, 239
Boone, Garrett, 28
bots, 19, 121, 166
brackets, H-21
bragging, 75
Brainbench, 138
brainstorming, 58, 168, 320
    online, 35
    using blogs for, 124
Brazil, A-6
buffers, in negative messages, 176, 177
Buffet, Warren, 143
builds, in slide shows, 324

bulleted lists, 94, 106, 286, 288
    in slides, 321
bumper slides, 326
Bureau of Labor Statistics, 368
business/financial news, keeping up with, 340
Business Owners Toolkit, 192
business plans, 242
Business Writer's Free Library, 25
buzzwords, 79

C

Canada Post, A-11
capitalization, H-22–H-23
captions, 277
career counseling, 342
career objective, on résumés, 350
career planning, P-1–P-5; 338–357
CareerBuilder, 339, 341, 361
cars, purchasing online, 305
CarsDirect.com, 305
case, of pronouns, H-5–H-6
categories, report organization based on, 242
cause and effect, 206
    as way to develop paragraphs, 83
cc (courtesy copy) function, 118, 120, A-10,
    A-17
CD-ROM, résumés on, 344
Cell Genesys, 164
cell phones. *See* mobile phones
centered type, 104
chain of command, e-mail and, 118
chalkboards, 320
champions, 213
Channel 9 (video blog), 123
channels, communication, 7
character spacing, A-2
charts. *See* bar charts; line charts
chatterbots, 166
Chicago Manual of Style, The, A-20
China, 11, A-6
chronological résumés, 345, 346
chronology, report organization based on, 242
circular reasoning, 206
Cisco, 137
citations
    APA style for, A-23
    Chicago style for, A-20–A-21
    MLA style for, A-25
claims
    granting, 150–154
    making, 148, 149
    persuasive, 207–208
    refusing, 152, 181–183
clarity, editing for, 95–97
Clark, Brian, 200
classification, as way to develop paragraphs, 83
clauses, 80, H-14, H-15
    restrictive vs. nonrestrictive, H-19
clichés, 79
clip art, 102, 322
close
    complimentary, A-8
    importance of, 93
    of job application letters, 369
    of meetings, 34
    of messages, 59
    of negative messages, 175,
    of oral presentations, 314, 319
    of positive messages, 150

of proposals, 267, 267, 294
of routine requests, 145
of reports, 261, 263–264, 267, 293
of sales messages, 213
closed questions, 240
clothing
    as nonverbal communication, 40
    for job interviews, 377
    work, 30
ClubMom, 201
Coca-Cola, 124
codes of ethics, 9
collaborating
    dynamic, 168
    as purpose of message, 50
collaborative writing, 29–30
    wikis for, 17, 128–129
collective nouns, H-4
CollegeRecruiter.com, 341
colons, H-18
color
    emotions and, 322
    in slides, 322
    use of, 269
column formatting, 105
Comic-Con International, 136
comma splices, H-15
commands, H-14
commas, H-18–H-19
commenting
    on blogs, 10, 123
    in word processors, 101
common nouns, H-3
communication
    defined, 4
    effective, 4–5
    ethical, 8–9
    external vs. internal, 4
    unified, 16
    see also nonverbal communication
communication process, 7–8
communication skills, benefits of, 4–5
community building, 213
companies
    negative news about, 186–187
    researching, 340–341, 373
company documents, as source of information,
    51–52
company image, projecting, 74
company news, using blogs for, 123
company policy, hiding behind, 177
comparative degree
    of adjectives, H-10
    of adverbs, H-11
comparison, report organization based on,
    242
comparison/contrast, as way to develop
    paragraphs, 83
competition, analyzing, 209
complaints, customer, 148, 149, 186–187,
    207–208
completing stage, 49, 92–107
    for business blogs, 126
    for negative messages, 173
    for oral presentations, 325–329
    for persuasive messages, 203–207
    for reports and proposals, 277–296
    for résumés, 352–357
    for routine and positive messages, 143

complex sentences, 80, H-14
compliance reports, 242
complimentary close, A-8
compliments, in goodwill messages, 155
compose/comprise, H-27
compound-complex sentences, 80, H-14
compound sentences, 80, H-14
compound words, H-20
compromise, 207
computer
    creating visuals with, 276–277
    symbols on, A-2
conciseness, editing for, 97–99
conclusions, 291, 293
    drawing, 241
    focusing on, 244, 245
    placement of, 263
concrete words, 77–78
condolence, messages of, 156–157
confidence, 74, 376
confidentiality
    e-mail and, 117
    on job boards, 357
congratulations, 156
conjunctions, 80, H-13, H-15
conjunctive adverbs, H-29
consistency, as design element, 104, 269, 322
Consumer Electronics Show, 165
Container Store, The, 28
content, evaluating, 92–93
content listening, 36
content management systems, 30, 129, 296
content managers, 239
content notes, A-20
context, cultural, 11–12
continual/continuous, H-27
contractions, H-20
contracts, 12
contrast, as design principle, 269
conversation marketing, 4, 210, 213, 214
conversational tone, 74–75
convince/persuade, H-27
coordinating conjunctions, H-15
copy notation, A-10
corporate blogs, 19
correction symbols, A-26–A-27
corrections, on business documents, A-2
correspond with, H-27
correspondence, international, 13–14, A-6–A-7,
    A-14–A-15
courtesy, in business messages, 70
courtesy copy (cc), 118, 120, A-10, A-17
courtesy titles, A-2
cover, for reports, 278
cover letters, for résumés, 365–370
Cranial Tap, 16, 35
credibility
    establishing, 73–74, 173
    in oral presentations, 318
    in persuasive messages, 203, 206
    proofreading and, 106, 294
    of sources, 238
criminal record, résumés and, 344
crisis communication, 186
    using blogs for, 124
critical listening, 36
criticism
    in performance reviews, 184
    in recommendation letters, 154

Crutchfield, 137
cultural context, 11–12
cultural differences, 11–13
    in audience needs, 201
    in nonverbal communication, 13, 39
    persuasive messages and, 203
    reports and, 261
cultural pluralism, 13
culture
    defined, 10
    ethics and, 12
    law and, 12
    oral communication and, 15
curriculum vitae (CV), 342
Curves, 226
customer relationship management, 54
customer satisfaction, 150
customer support
    online, 19
    using blogs for, 123–124
customers
    anticipating objections of, 210
    communication with, 19, 150
    complaints from, 148, 149, 186–187,
        207–208
    denying claims by, 181–183
    needs of, 209
    negative messages to, 179, 181
    social media and, 213
cut and paste, 99
Cycle Computers, 166

D

dangling modifiers, 95–96, H-16
dashes, H-19–H-20
data
    analyzing, 241–242
    finding, 236, 237–242
    processing, 237
    using visuals to present, 270
data security, 215
data visualization, 273m 274
databases
    electronic, 238
    online, 239
    for résumés, 354
dates, format for, A-2, A-3
deception
    in advertising, 9
    in sales messages, 215
decimal numbers, H-24
decision making, in teams, 29
decision-making meetings, 32
decoding, 7
decorative animation, 324
deductive reasoning, 206
defamation, 182–183
definitions, in report introduction, 262
Delicious.com, 18, 239
delivery, of oral presentations, 327–374
delivery cues, in speaking outline, 316
Dell, 251
Deloitte LLP, 9
demographics, 201
dependent clauses, 80, 81, H-14, H-19
descriptive headings, 94, 286
design
    of documents, 102–105
    principles of, 104, 269, 322

proofing of, 106
    of résumés, 352–353
    of slides, 321–324
    of visuals, 276–277
desire phase, of AIDA model, 204, 211–213, 367
desktop publishing software, 105
desktop search engines, 239
detail
    amount of, 59
    as design element, 104
    in reports, 263
diagrams, 270, 275
Dice.com, 68, 341
dictionaries, visual, 79
Dictionary of Concise Writing, The (Fiske), 92
digg.com, 239
digital image manipulation, 276
dilemma/problem, H-27
dining etiquette, 31
diplomacy, in business messages, 70
direct approach 59–60
    for analytical reports, 244, 245
    for claims/adjustment requests, 150
    for informational reports, 242
    for negative messages, 174–175
    for oral presentations, 313–314
    for persuasive messages, 202
    for positive messages, 148
    for refusing requests, 179
    for rejecting job applicants, 184
    for reports, 236, 263
    for routine replies, 148
    for routine requests, 145
directories, as resources, 238
disability bias, 72, 73
discrimination, in hiring, 352
discriminatory questions, in job interviews,
    379–380
dishonesty, detecting, 38
disinterested, H-27
distribution
    of messages, 107–108
    of reports and proposals, 296
distribution list, for e-mail, A-17
documentation, of sources, 239, A-20–A-25
documents
    distribution of, 296
    embedded, 268
    formatting of, 268, A-1–A-19
    linked, 268
    multimedia, 269
    production of, 102–106
Documentum eRoom, 30
downloadable files, 296
drawings, 270, 275
drug testing, 373
due diligence reports, 244
dynamic collaboration, 168

E

editing
    of messages, 95–97
    of others' work, 98
    see also revision
education section, on résumés, 350–351
Edwards, Ben, 48
eFax, 55
electronic databases, 238
electronic documents, 269

electronic forms, 268
electronic media, 53–55, 116–129
   advantages of, 56
   disadvantages of, 56
   tact in, 70
electronic presentations, 16, 55, 105, 320–324
electronic résumé production, 354–356
electronic whiteboards. *See* whiteboards,
   electronic
Electrovision, 233–234, 277, 279–293
ellipses, H-21
e-mail, 53, 116, 117–120
   company policy for, 117
   effective use of, 6
   for interviews, 240
   for job interviews, 371
   for positive replies to requests, 152
   overflow of, 118
   personal use of company, 117
   using blogs instead of, 124
e-mail address, personal, 398–350
e-mail addresses, A-17
e-mail hygiene, 118
e-mail messages
   audience analysis for, 118
   carelessness in, 117, 119
   company monitoring of, 117
   design of, 103
   etiquette for, 118, 119
   formality of, 119
   formatting of, 119, A-17–A-18
   greetings in, A-18
   headers in, A-17
   legal aspects of, 117
   length of, 119
   planning of, 118
   subject lines for, 119–120, A-17
   three-step process for, 117–119
   tips for, 119
   writing of, 119–120
e-mail newsletters, opt-in, 215
e-portfolio, P-6, 357
em dash, H-20
embedded documents, 268
emotional appeals, 204–206, 211, 212
emotions
   in e-mail messages, 120
   in negative messages, 183
   venting of, 36
empathic listening, 36
emphasis
   as design principle, 269
   using lists for, 94
   in sentences, 80–81
   type styles for, 105
employee engagement, using blogs for, 124
employee handbooks, 232
employees
   blogging by, 125
   communication skills of, 5–6
   e-mail messages of, 117–118
   ethics codes for, 9
   performance reviews of, 184–186
   podcasts for, 126
   termination of, 186
employers
   attributes sought in job candidates, 371
   background checks by, 344, 348, 373
   performance reviews by, 184–186

   preemployment testing by, 371–372
   preferences for finding new employees,
      338–339
   recruiting by, 370–372
   refusal to write recommendations, 183
employment, negative messages about, 183–187
employment interviews. *See* job interviews
employment messages
   application letters, 365–370
   follow-up, 369–370, 381–382
   résumés, 342–357
en dash, H-20
enclosure notation, A-9
encoding, 7
endnotes, 84, 239, A-20
endorsements, to establish credibility, 74
England, A-7
English, plain, 76
enterprise instant messaging (EIM), 121
enterprise search engines, 239
enthusiasm, moderating, 97
envelopes, A-12–A-13, A–15
EQ Industrial Services, 196
Equal Employment Opportunity Commission
   (EEOC), 380
Ernst & Young, 193
eRoom, 30
ESPN.com, 136
etc., H-24, H-27
ethical aspects
   of buffers in negative messages, 176
   of creating visuals, 277
   of euphemisms, 72
   of message content, 52
   of intercultural communication, 12
   of job interview questions, 379–380
   of marketing and sales messages, 214–215
   of quoting from sources, 241
ethical communication, 8–9
ethical choices, 12
ethical dilemmas, 9
ethical lapses, 9
ethics, 8–9
   codes of, 9
   in conducting research, 237
   culture and, 12
ethnic bias, 72, 73
ethnocentrism, 13
etiquette
   business, 20, 30–32
   in business messages, 70
   in conducting research, 237
   cultural differences in, 12
   e-mail, 118, 119
   in job interviews, 378
   for negative messages, 173
   of mobile phone usage, 31
   of sales messages, 215
euphemisms, 72
evidence, in outlining, 60–61
Evolve24, 124
exclamation points, H-17
executive dashboard, 235
Executive Planet, 44
executive summary, 282, 293, 294
expectations, of audience, 51
experience, of audience, 312
expertise, 74
Express Mail International, A-14

extranets, 18
eye contact, 39
   in job interviews, 376
   in oral presentations, 327, 328

F

face-to-face communication, 55
facial expressions, 39, 39
facts
   double checking, 261
   sources for, 238
failure analysis reports, 244
FastLane blog, 123
faxes, 54–55
faxing, of résumés, 357
feasibility reports, 244, 359
features, of products, 209, 210
Federal Trade Commission, 215, 218
feedback
   from audience, 70
   in communication process, 7–8
   constructive, 15, 20
   destructive, 15, 20
   giving, 15, 20
   in intercultural communication, 15
   in oral presentations, 319
   in performance reviews, 184
   on reports and proposals, 235
Fellowforce.com, P-5
file merge, 84
files
   sending, 108
   uploading, 296, 357
FinalScratch, 193
firewalls, 324
First Class Mail International, A-14
first draft, 76, 92
first impressions,
   of business documents, A-1
   in job interviews, 378
Fiske, Robert Hartwell, 92
flaming, in e-mail, 120
flaunt/flout, H-27
flipcharts, 320
flowcharts, 270, 274, 275
follow-me phone service, 16
following up
   on job application letters, 369–370
   after job interviews, 381–382
fonts, 104
   for OCR scanning, 354
   for slides, 322, 323
   symbols in, A-2
footers, 105
footnotes, 84, 239, A-20
Forbes, 65
Ford Motor Company, 137, 172
form responses, 150
form tools, 268
formality, 74–75
   medium and, 55
   of oral presentations, 317
   of reports and proposals, 260–261
formatting
   of business documents, 105, A-1–A-19
   of e-mail messages, 119
forms
   electronic, 268
   standardized, A-1

forms-based searches, 239
fractions, H-24
France, 39, A-6
franchises, 302–303
free riders, 29
Friedman, Marc, 310
functional animation, 323–324
fused sentences, H-15

G

gender bias, 72, 73
gender-neutral pronouns, H-6
General Motors, 123, 222
generalizations, hasty, 206
geographic information systems, 275
geography, report organization based on, 242
Germany, 13, 39, A-6
gestures, 39
Gibaldi, Joseph, A-20
Gillin, Paul, 4
Gladiator GarageWorks, 212
Global Express Guaranteed, A-14
Global Positioning System (GPS), 18
Google, 144
Google Earth, 388
Google Notebook, 239
government publications, 238
government terms, capitalization of, H-23
grade point average (GPA), on résumés,
        350–351
grammar, 77, H-3–H-16
grammar checkers, 102
grant proposals, 246
graphics, business, 269–277
graphics software, 102
graphs, 270, 271–273
greetings, in e-mail, A-18
grooming
        for job interviews, 377
        as nonverbal communication, 40
        for workplace, 30
group interviews, 371
groupthink, 29
groupware, 30, 101, 324
guilt, admitting, 175
Gunderson Partners, 338

H

handouts, 327
handshake, 30, 39
        in job interviews, 378
hard-sell approach, 203, 206
have/of, H-13
headers, 105
headhunters, 339
headings, 94
        in reports, 268, 286, A-19
        in table of contents, 281
        typefaces for, 104
hedging sentences, 95
help lines, 19
Helvetica, 104, 105
Herman Miller, Inc., 152
Hewlett-Packard, 195
hidden agendas, 29
high-context cultures, 11–12
Highway Bytes, 166
Hilton Hotels, 225
hiring practices, 370–372

Home Depot, 191
honesty, 12, 73
        on résumés, 348
        testing for, 371
        in visuals, 277
HTML, 102
HTML format, for résumés, 356
humanities style, A-20–A-23
humor
        in business messages, 76
        in business reports, 261
        in business settings, 31
hyperlinks, 102
        in blogs, 126
        in reports, 268
        in résumés, 356
        in slide shows, 324
hyphenated adjectives, H-10–H-11
hyphenated nouns, H-4
hyphens, H-20, H-25

I

IBM, 35, 48, 54, 126, 225
IBM Lotus Sametime, 164
IBM Lotus Team Workspace, 30
ideas, generating, 58
IKEA, 202
illustration, as way to develop paragraphs, 83
illustrations, list of, 281, 293
IM. *See* instant messaging
IM systems, business-grade, 121, 122
IMDiversity, 341
impact, H-27
imperative mood, H-9
impersonal style, for reports, 261
imply/infer, H-27
importance, report organization based
        on, 242
impressions, first, 30–31
in/into, H-13
Indeed.com, 341
independent clauses, H-14, H-15, H-17, H-19
InDesign, 105
indexes, 84, 293
India, A-7
indicative mood, H-9
indirect approach, 59–60
        for analytical reports, 245–246
        for employment messages, 183
        for negative messages, 176–178
        for oral presentations, 314
        for persuasive messages, 202, 204
        for refusing requests, 179
        for rejecting job applicants, 184
        for reports, 236, 263
inductive reasoning, 206
infinitives, 98
information
        accuracy of, 52, 261
        completeness of, 52
        ethical, 52
        finding, 236, 237–242
        gathering, 51–52, 202, 234–235
        organization of, 56–61
        pertinence of, 52
        verification of, 238
        see also negative information
information architecture, of websites, 243–244
information overload, 118

information requests, 150
        replying to, 150, 151, 152
informational meetings, 32
informational reports, 232, 233
        direct approach for, 242
        organization of, 242
        planning of, 242–244
        types of, 242
informative headings, 94, 286
informing, as purpose of message, 50
Infotech, 180
inquiry letters, 381
inside address, A-2–A-5
instant messaging (IM), 54, 71, 116, 120–122
        business benefits of, 121
        for customer service, 152
        for job interviews, 371
        security of, 121
        three-step process for, 121–122
        tips for using, 122–123
        workplace use of, 121–122
integrity tests, 371
intellectual property, 237
interactive surveys, 240
interactivity, of electronic media, 117
intercultural communication
        oral, 15
        oral presentations for, 322, 328
        see also cultural differences; culture
interest phase, of AIDA model, 204, 211,
        366–367
interjections, H-13
International Association of Business
        Communicators, 9
international communication, dates in, A-2, A-3
international correspondence, 13–14, A-6–A-7,
        A-14–A-15
International Mail Manual, A-15
Internet
        business news on, 340
        for conducting surveys, 240
        finding information on, 238–239
        hidden, 239
        job boards on, 339, 341
        meeting via, 35
        researching companies on, 339
        see also websites
Internet-based phone service, 54
Internet Public Library, 253
Internship-Programs.com, 341
interpreters, 328
interruption, of speaker, 38
interview simulators, 377
interviews, research, 240
        see also job interviews
intimacy, in business messages, 76
intranets, 18, 235
intransitive verbs, H-8
introducing oneself, 31
introducing people to each other, 31
introduction
        for oral presentations, 314, 317–318
        for proposals, 264, 267, 294
        for reports, 261–263, 267, 283, 293
introduction slides, 326
inverted pyramid style, 268
investment proposals, 246
iPod, 211–212
iPod Touch, 10

iPhone, 10
irregular verbs, H-7
It is, 98–99
italic type, 105, H-23
Italy, A-7

J

Japan, 39, A-7
jargon, 14, 79
job applicants
    background checks on, 344, 348
    employment process for, 338–339
    interviewing of, 370–381
    networking by, 341–342
    recommendation requests from, 146–148
    refusing recommendation requests from, 183
    rejecting, 184, 185
    responding to requests for
        recommendations from, 154, 155
    what employers look for in, 371
job application letters, 365–370
    follow-ups to, 369–370
    three-step process for, 366
job boards, online, 339, 341, 357
job counseling, 342
job interview(s), 370–381
    appearance in, 377
    arrival for, 378
    candidate's questions in, 374–375, 376
    close of, 380–381
    confidence in, 376
    employer's questions in, 373–374, 375
    following up after, 381–382
    media for, 371–372
    mock, 376
    note-taking after, 381
    practicing for, 376–377
    preparing for, 373–378
    question-and-answer stage of, 379–434
    requesting, 369
    sequence of, 370
    simulators for, 377
    stages of, 378–381
    telephone, 370, 371
    things to take to, 378
    types of, 370–371
    warm-up period in, 378–379
    warning signs in, 377
job-interview.net, 388
job market, hidden, 338
job offers, 370, 380, 382
    declining, 383
job search, 338–357
    interview process in, 370–372
Jobfox, 339
jobs skills tests, 373
Jobster, 339
journalistic approach, 58
journalistic style, 261
journals, as resources, 238
justification, of type, 104
justification reports, 244
JWS Remodeling Solutions, 265

K

Keirsey Temperament Sorter, 342
Kelly Services, 224
Kentucky Cabinet for Economic
    Development, 223

keyword search, 239
keyword summary, on résumés, 354–355
kiosks, in-store, 19
knowledge management systems, 52, 237
Korea, A-7

L

La Cristallerie, 14
language
    abusive, 183
    bias-free, 72, 73
    euphemistic, 72
    obsolete, 75
    pompous, 75
Lay/lie, H-27
layout
    page, 106, 123
    of slides, 322–323
legal aspects
    of apologizing, 175–175
    of defamation, 182–183
    of e-mail messages, 117
    of hiring, 352
    of job interviews, 379–380
    of job offer acceptance, 382
    of negative messages, 183
    of negative organizational news, 186
    of performance reviews, 184
    of recommendation letters, 183
    of sales messages, 215
    of termination letters, 186
    of using copyrighted material, 239
legal systems, 12
legends, for visuals, 277
lend/loan, H-27
length, of messages, 58–59
less/fewer, H-27
letterhead, A-1, A-2
letters, 53
    of acceptance, 382
    additional parts for, A-8–A-10
    application, 365–370
    of authorization, 278
    declining job offer, 383
    folding of, A-13, A-15
    follow-up, 369–370
    formats for, A-10, A-11–A-12
    of inquiry, 381
    international, 13–14, A-6–A-7, A-14–A-15
    recommendation, 154, 155, 183
    of resignation, 383–384
    requesting information or action, 145–146
    requesting recommendation, 146–148
    standard parts for, A-2–A-18
    termination, 186
    of transmittal, 278
liable/likely, H-28
libel, 182–183
library, finding information at, 238
Library of Congress, 222
lie/lay, H-8
limitations, of reports, 262
line charts, 270, 271
line length, A-1
    in e-mails, A-18
line spacing, A-1
LinkedIn.com, 341
linking verbs, H-7, H-15–H-16, H-20
links, in reports, 268

list of illustrations, 281, 293
listening
    effective, 37
    in intercultural communication, 15
    in job interviews, 379
    in meetings, 34
    for nonverbal cues, 40
    overcoming barriers to, 37–38
    process of, 36–37
    selective, 37–38
    types of, 36
    value of, 36
listening skills, 36–38
    self-assessment of, 43–44
lists, 94, 106, 286, 288, H-22
literally, H-27
location and tracking technologies, 18
Logan magazine, 138
logical appeals, 204–206
logical arguments, in reports, 245
logical flaws, 206
long-term memory, 38
Loopt, 334
low-context cultures, 11–12
Lurie, Ian, 214
Lutz, Bob, 222
lying, 38
    on résumés, 348

M

Macromedia Flash, 276
mail merge, 84, 150
mailing notation, A-10
mailings, quantity, A-11
main idea
    defining, 58
    for oral presentations, 313
    in outlining, 60
    for persuasive messages, 202
    in routine replies and positive messages,
        148–149
    in summaries, 241
major points
    number of, 58–59
    for oral presentations, 315
    in outlining, 60
manipulation
    buffers as, 176
    in sales messages, 215
manners, 12
many/much, H-28
maps, 270, 275
margins, 104, A-1, A-18, A-19
market analysis reports, 244
market research, using blogs for, 124
Marketer's Guide to Social Media,
    A (Gillin), 4
marketing, stealth, 8
marketing messages, 208–215
materialism, 10
meals, business, 31
measurements, H-24
mechanics, H-22–H-25
media (medium)
    audience preferences for, 55
    communication, 7
    costs of, 55
    electronic, 53–55, 116–129
    formality and, 55

for job interviews, 371–372
for negative messages, 173
oral, 53, 56
for oral presentations, 312–313
for persuasive messages, 202
for reports, 235
for résumés, 344
selecting, 52–56
urgency and, 55
visual, 53, 56
written, 53, 56
see also specific media
media richness, 55
media specialists, 202
meeting people, 30–31
meetings, 32–36
formal, 33
leading, 33–34
making arrangements for, 32
minutes of, 34–35
preparing for, 32–33
purpose of, 32
selecting participants for, 32
technology for, 35–36
types of, 32
virtual, 17, 35
web-based, 17, 35–36
Megapixel, 388
memo of transmittal, 278, 280
memorization, 38, 327
memory, listening and, 37, 38
memos, 53
format for, A-15–A-17
Menegatti, Tania, 260
messages
of appreciation, 156
composing, 76–83
of condolence, 156–157
of congratulations, 156
decoding of, 7
distribution of, 107–108
efficiency of, 58
encoding of, 7
follow-up, 381–382
goodwill, 154–157
informative, 154
main idea of, 58
marketing, 208–215
negative, 172–187, 384
persuasive, 200–215
positive, 148–157
producing, 102–106
proofreading of, 106
purpose of, 50
revising, 92–102
routine, 143–157
sales, 208–215
scope of, 58–59
tact in, 70
topic of, 58
whether worth sending, 50
Messmer, Max, 365
metacrawlers, 239
metasearch engines, 239
Mexico, 12, A-7
Michaels, Randy, 232
microblogs, 117
Microsoft, 123
Microsoft Office, 268

Microsoft OneNote, 239
Microsoft PowerPoint. *See* PowerPoint
Microsoft Producer, 105
Microsoft Publisher, 105
Microsoft SharePoint, 30
Microsoft Word, 84, 100, 101, 239
for résumés, 356
symbols in, A-2
military service, on résumés, 350
Milwaukee Journal Sentinel, 215
mind mapping, 58
minutes, of meetings, 34–35
misquoting, 8
misunderstanding
cultural differences and, 11
listening and, 38
MLA style, 292, A-24–A-25
*MLA Style Manual and Guide to Scholarly
Publishing,* A-20, A-25
mnemonics, 38
mobile blogs (moblogs), 55, 123
mobile phones
in public, 31
in workplace, 30
Modern Language Association (MLA), 292,
A-20, A-24
modifiers, H-10–H-11
dangling, 95–96
misplaced, H-17
placement of, 96
Monster Trak, 341
Monster.com, 339, 341, 342, 356
mood, of verbs, H-9
Moreno, Linda, 233–234, 277, 279–293
motivation, of audience, 201
moving blueprint, 326
Mulally, Alan, 172
multimedia, 55
for résumés, 354
in reports, 276
multimedia documents, 269
multimedia presentations, 320, 324
multimedia production, 105
Music99, 193
MySpace, 334

N

Napoleonic Code, 12
natural language searches, 239
navigational flow, of websites, 243–244
navigational slides, 326
needs
of audience, 69, 201
of customers, 209
negative adverbs, H-11
negative information
in positive messages, 150
in recommendation letters, 154
negative messages, 70
buffers in, 176, 177
completing, 173
direct approach for, 174–175
about employment, 183–187
indirect approach for, 176–178
about organizations, 186–187
organizing, 173–178
planning, 172–173
refusing requests, 179, 180
three-step process for, 172–173

about transactions, 179, 181
writing, 173
negotiation, of job benefits, 380–381
nervousness
in job interviews, 376
in oral presentations, 310, 328
Nesbit, Robert, 345
Net-Temps, 341
networking, by job hunters, 341–342
New Balance, 139
new media, 213
newsfeed aggregators, 239, 340
newsfeed subscriptions, 239
newsfeeds, for business blogs, 126, 215
newspapers, as resources, 238
newsreaders, 18
noise, as communication barrier, 7
nominative pronouns, H-6
nonrestrictive clauses, H-19
Non-Stop Messenger Service, 166
nonverbal communication, 38–40
culture and, 13, 39
in job interviews, 376–377
Nooyi, Indra, 169
note cards, for oral presentations, 316
note-taking tools, 239
Notebook, 239
notes, speaking from, 327
noun sequences, long, 96
nouns, H-3–H-4
numbers
handling of, 14
misrepresenting, 8
style for, H-24

O

O'Donnell & Associates, 295
objections, anticipating, 206–207, 210
objective pronouns, H-6
objectivity, 74, 261
objects, in word-processing documents, 106
obsolete language, 75
Oceana Pacific Airways, 208
OCR software, 354
office, virtual, 30
office technology, 16
OK sign, 39
Olson, Logan, 138
OneNote, 239
online brainstorming systems, 35
online research, 238–239
online surveys, 240
online video, 324
Online Writing Lab (OWL), 89
*Online! A Reference Guide to Using Internet
Sources,* A-20
Opal Pools and Patios, 195
open-ended interviews, 371
open-ended questions, 240
opening
for routine requests, 145
importance of, 93
of job application letters, 366
of messages, 59
for negative messages, 174, 176
for persuasive messages, 204, 207, 210–211
of positive messages, 148–149
for reports, 261–263, 267
see also introduction

operating reports, 242
opt-in e-mail, 215
oral communication, feedback in, 70
oral media, 52–53, 56
oral presentations, 310–329
    audience size for, 312
    composing, 317–319
    creating slides for, 320–324
    delivery of, 327–328
    direct vs. indirect approach for, 313–314
    editing, 325–326
    estimating time for, 313
    formality of, 317
    length of, 314
    organizing, 313–316
    planning, 311–316
    practicing, 313, 327–328
    purpose of, 311
    question period in, 328–329
    self-assessment for, 333
    three-step process for, 311
    writing, 316–319
organization
    good, 56–58
    evaluating, 93
    of negative messages, 173–178
    of persuasive messages, 202
organization charts, 274, 275
Organizers Unlimited, 167
outline
    for oral presentations, 314–315
    preliminary, 245
outlining, 60–61
outsourcing, 207, 224
overhead transparencies, 320
Owens, Bill, 116

P
page numbering, in reports, 281, 282, 283, 284,
    A-19
page setup, 105
panel interviews, 371
paper
    for business documents, A-1
    for résumés, 354
Paradigm Online Writing Assistant (POWA),
    112
paragraph formatting, 105
paragraphs, 81–82
    developing, 83
    in international correspondence, 14
    length of, 94
parallelism, 95, H-16
paraphrasing, 241
parentheses, H-21
parliamentary procedure, 33
parts of speech, H-3–H-13
passive voice, 76, 77, H-9
PDFs, 54, 108, 269
    editing in, 101
    for reports, 296
    for résumés, 356
Pechanga Casino Entertainment Center, 224
PepsiCo, 169
percentages, H-24
perception, selective, 38
Perfect Interview, 377
performance, in teams, 29
performance reviews, negative, 184–186

periodicals
    as resources, 238
    as source of business/financial news, 340
periods, H-17
    with abbreviations, H-24
permission-based marketing, 215
personal activity reports, 242, 243
personal appearance, 30
    for job interviews, 377
    as nonverbal communication, 40
personal data, on résumés, 352
personal digital assistant (PDA), 16
personal space, 40
personality tests, 371
persuasion, 200
    as purpose of message, 50
    negative connotations of, 214
persuasive messages, 70, 200–215
    direct approach for, 202
    ethics of, 214–215
    indirect approach for, 202, 204
    mistakes in, 206–207
    organization of, 202
    in social media, 213
    strategies for, 203–207
    three-step process for, 200–203
phone calls, 54
phone service
    follow-me, 16
    Internet-based, 54
phone skills, 30, 31
photo-sharing sites, 117
photographs, 270, 276
Photoshop, 276
phrases, H-14
    transitional, 82, H-29
    wordy, 97, 98
PictureMate Personal Photo Lab, 167
pictures, insertion of, 106
pie charts, 270, 273, 274
placement offices, college, 342
plagiarism, 8, 241
plain English, 14, 76
plain text, for résumés, 355
planning
    of analytical reports, 244–246
    of business blogs, 124–125
    of e-mail messages, 118
    of informational reports, 242-244
    of interviews, 240
    of job application letters, 366
    of oral presentations, 311–316
    of proposals, 246–249
    of research, 236, 237
    of résumés, 342–347
planning outline, 315–316
planning stage, 48–61
    for negative messages, 172–173
    for persuasive messages, 200–202
    for reports and proposals, 233–249
    for routine and positive messages, 143
plans, 242
plural nouns, H-4
plurals, agreement with, H-8–H-9
Podcast Alley, 340
podcasting channels, 126
podcasts/podcasting, 19, 48, 117, 126–128, 340
    equipment needed for, 128
    three-step process for, 126–127

Point 1 Promotions, 155
policy reports, 242
policy statements, 154
pompous language, 75
portable document format. *See* PDFs
position papers, 242
positive, emphasizing, 70–71
positive close, 319
positive language
    in negative messages, 173
    in persuasive messages, 202
positive messages
    granting claims, 150–154
    providing recommendations, 154, 155
    responding to requests, 148–150
possessive nouns, H-20, H-4
possessive pronouns, H-6
postal codes, Canadian, A-13
postscripts, A-10
    in sales letters, 213
posture, 39
PowerPoint, 105, 276, 320–324
    for résumés, 353–354
preaching, 75
predicate, 96, H-14
preemployment testing, 371–372
prefatory parts
    for proposals, 293
    for reports, 277, 278, 279–282, 293, A-19
prefixes, hyphenation of, H-20
prejudgment, 38
Premier Building Systems, 212
prepositional phrases, 96
prepositions, H-12–H-13
presence awareness, 121
presentation software, 102
presentations
    electronic, 16, 55 105, 320–324
    multimedia, 55
    online, 324–325
    see also oral presentations
Presenters Online, 333
preview sections, in reports, 268
previewing, in oral presentations, 318
price, in sales messages, 210
Priority Mail International, A-14
privacy
    invasion of, 215
    of messages, 108
    of research participants, 237
    preemployment testing and, 373
problem/solution, as way to develop
        paragraphs, 83
problem-solving reports, 244, 262–263
problem statement, 237, 264
procedural changes, messages about, 154
production, of messages, 102–106
products
    bad news about, 179
    benefits of, 209, 210
    features of, 209, 210
professional titles, H-23
progress reports, 242
project management, using blogs for, 123
pronouns, H-5–H-6
    relative, 97
proofreading, 106, 107
    of job-related messages, 366
    of reports and proposals, 295–295

proofreading symbols, 99, A-28
proper nouns, H-3, H-22
property, intellectual, 237
proposals, 232, 233
    components of, 293
    drafting content for, 264–265
    examples of, 246–249, 295–298
    format for 265–266
    internal vs. external, 246
    planning of, 246–249
    producing, 293–296
    proofreading, 294–295
    revising, 277
    solicited vs. unsolicited, 264
    statement of purpose for, 235
    three-step process for, 232–233, 234
    types of, 246–249
provinces, abbreviations for, A-14
psychographics, 201
public relations, 213
    using blogs for, 124
public speaking, 310
Publication Manual of the American
    Psychological Association, A-20
punctuality, 40
punctuation, H-17–H-21
    letter format and, A-11
    spacing and, A-2
Purdue University, 89
purpose
    of business blogs, 124–125
    defining, 50
    general, 50
    of meetings, 32
    of oral presentations, 311
    for persuasive messages, 201
    for reports and proposals, 233–234
    specific, 50
    statement of, 233–234

Q

qualifications, in proposals, 266
Quark XPress, 105
question-and-answer chain, 58
question-and-answer period, 328–329
question marks, H-17
questionnaires, 240
questions
    discriminatory, 379–380
    in job interviews, 371, 373–375, 376
    in request letters, 145
    for research interviews, 240
    for surveys, 240
quotation marks, H-19, H-20–H-21
quoting, from sources, 241

R

racial bias, 72, 73
radio frequency identification (RFID)
    tags, 18
raise/rise, H-8
readability
    designing for, 102–105
    revising for, 93–95
reading, online, 243
reasoning
    in analytical reports, 245
    in logical appeals, 205–206
    circular, 206

receiver, of message, 7, 37
recommendations
    focusing on, 244–245, 262–263
    in reports, 287, 288, 291, 293
    making, 241–242
    placement of, 263
    providing, 154
    refusing requests for, 183
    requesting, 146–148
recording software, 128
recruiting, by employers, 124, 339, 370–372
Red Cross, 224
redundancy, 98
reference initials, A-8–A-9
References, 292, A-20, A-23, A-24
regardless, H-28
reinforcing, of position, 206
reliability, of surveys, 240
"replace all" option, 99
replies, routine, 148–157
"Reply All" function, 120
reports, 53
    amount of detail to include in, 263
    body of, 293
    close of, 293
    completing stage for, 277–296
    components of, 277, 278
    composing, 261–269
    cover for, 278
    distribution of, 296
    documentation of, A-20–A-25
    drafting content for, 261–264
    formal, 277–293
    format for, A-18–A-19
    length of, 236
    online, 268
    organization of, 236
    prefatory parts for, 277, 278, 279–282, 293
    producing, 277–293
    proofreading of, 294–295
    research for, 236–242
    revision of, 277
    statement of purpose for, 233–234
    supplementary parts of, 293
    three-step process for, 232–233, 234
    title for, 278, 279
    types of, 232, 233, 242
    see also analytical reports; informational
      reports
reputation analysis, 124
request for proposals (RFP), 247, 264, 293
requests,
    via e-mail, 119
    making, 144–148
    persuasive, 207
    refusing, 179, 180
    responding to, 119
    three-step writing process for, 144–145, 146
resale information, 178
research managers, 239
research
    ethical aspects of, 271–237
    of potential employers, 340–341
    planning, 236, 237
    primary, 237, 239–240
    for reports, 236–242
    secondary, 237, 238–239
    summarizing results of, 240–241
    using results of, 240–242

resignation, letters of, 383–384
restrictive clauses, H-19
résumés, 342–357
    activities/achievements section
      on, 351
    adapting to audience, 348
    career objective on, 350
    chronological, 345, 346
    combination, 347
    common problems with, 344
    contact information on, 349–350
    cover letters for, 365–370
    deception on, 348
    design of, 352–353
    distributing, 356–357
    education section on, 350–351
    e-mailing, 356, 357
    faxing, 357
    formats for, 353–356
    functional, 345, 347
    mailing, 356–357
    media for, 344
    misperceptions about, 343
    mistakes on, 338
    multimedia, 354
    online, 356
    online samples of, 348
    organization of, 344–347
    personal data on, 352
    plain text file for, 355
    planning, 342–347
    producing, 352–357
    proofreading, 356
    purpose of, 342
    revising, 352
    scannable, 354–355
    three-step process for, 342, 343, 346
    work experience on, 350
    writing, 348–352
review sections, in reports, 268
revision, 92–111
    of others' work, 98
revision control, 30
revision marks, 101
RFP, 247, 264, 293
Richter Office Solutions, 161
Riley Guide, 341
Robert Hall International, 365
Roberts Rules of Order, 33
routine messages, 143–157
    asking for information or action,
      145–146
    direct approach for, 144
    making claims, 148, 149
    making requests, 144–148
    requesting adjustments, 148, 149
    requesting recommendation, 146–148
routine requests, 144–148
    direct approach for, 145
    replying to, 150
RSS newsfeeds, 18, 126, 239, 340
Ryze.com, 341

S

salary requirements, 366, 368, 380–381
sales messages, 208–215
    AIDA model for, 210–213
sales promotion, 178
sales proposals, 249

salutations, A-4–A-6, H-23
    international, A-6–A-7
salutopening, A-5
sampling bias, 240
sandbox, for wikis, 129
sans serif typefaces, 104, 322, 323
scannable résumés, 354–355
scope
    of business blogs, 125
    of messages, 58–59
    of oral presentations, 313
    of persuasive messages, 202
screening interviews, 370, 373
search and replace, 99
search engines, 238–239
Second Life, 16, 35, 371
second-page heading, A-8
Securities and Exchange Commission, 251
security
    of e-mail, 117–118
    of instant messages, 121
    of messages, 108
selection interviews, 370
self-consciousness, 376
selling points, 209–210
    in job application letters, 366
semicolons, H-15, H-17, H-29
sender, of message, 7
sensitivity, intercultural, 10–15
sentence fragments, H-15
sentences, 80–81, H-3
sentences, grammar of, H-14–H-16
    length of, 80, 93–94
    overly long, 95
    topic, 81
    types of, 80–81, H-14
sequence, report organization based on, 242
serif typefaces, 104, 105, 322, 323
Seymour Powell, 137
shared workspace, 17, 30
SharePoint, 30
shopping, online, 19
short messaging service (SMS), 121
short-term memory, 38
sign language interpreters, 328
signature block, A-8
signature file, for e-mails, 118, 119, 120
simple sentences, 80
simplicity
    as design element, 104, 269
    in designing slides, 320
SimplyHired.com, 341
sincerity, 74, 155
sit/set, H-8
situation, analyzing, 49–52, 201, 233–234,
    311–312
situational interviews, 371
skills résumé, 345
Skype, 54
slander, 182–183
slang, 14
slide master, 322–323
slide shows, 320–324
    finalizing, 325–326
slide sorter view, 325–326
slides
    background designs for, 322
    content for, 320, 321
    creating, 320–324

design elements for, 322
designing, 321–324
templates for, 324
text, 320
smiling, 39, 376
    culture and, 13
    in workplace, 30
Snowdrift Winter Sports, 125
social bookmarking, 126, 239
social commerce, 213
social customs, 12–13
social mapping, 334
social media, 4, 8, 55, 117
    negative company information and, 186–187
    persuasive messages in, 213
social networks/networking
    background checks and, P-6, 373
    for job referrals, 339, 341
    for posting résumés, 357
    with persuasive messages, 213
social tagging, 18
solicited application letters, 366, 367
solicited proposals, 247, 264, 295–298
sound bites, in documents, 102
source notes, A-20
sources
    documenting, 239, A-20–A-25
    evaluating, 237–238
    finding, 238–239
South Africa, A-7
South by Southwest, 251–252
Southwest Airlines, 116
spacing, in reports, A-19
spam blocking, 118
speaking notes, 316, 327
speaking outline, 315
speaking
    in intercultural communication, 15
    rate of, 38, 39, 313
special effects, in slide shows, 323–324
speech anxiety, 328
speech mannerisms, 377
speeches. See oral presentations
spell checkers, 101–102
spelling, H-28–H-29
spim, 122
Spoke.com, 341
spreadsheets, 268
standardized forms, A-1
Stanton, 193
Staples, 19
Starbucks, 196, 223
states, abbreviations for, A-14
stationery, letterhead, A-1, A-2
Statistical Abstract of the United States, 238
statistics, sources for, 238
stealth marketing, 8
Stewart, Potter, 8
storyteller's tour, 58
streaming video, 324
stress interviews, 371
structured interviews, 371
style, 74–76
    for business blogs, 123, 126
    evaluating, 93
    in formal reports, 282, 293
    impersonal, 261
    for reports and proposals, 260
    sentence, 80–81

style checkers, 102
style manuals, A-20
style sheets, 84, 105
subheadings, 94, 268
    typefaces for, 104
subject, of sentence, 96
subject line
    attention-getting, 204
    in e-mails, 119–120, A-17
    in letters, A-8
    in memos, A-15, A-16
subject-verb agreement, H-8–H-9
subjunctive mood, H-9
subordinating conjunctions, H-15
summarizing, 241
summary, in reports, 293
summary of qualifications, on résumés, 350
Sun Microsystems, 16, 35
SunTrust, 371
supplementary parts, of reports, 293
supply chain management, 18
surface charts, 271
surveys, 240
symbols, in word processors, A-2
sympathy, apologies and, 175
sympathy messages, 1156–157
synopsis
    in proposals, 294
    in reports, 293

T
table of contents, 84, 281, 293
tables, 273–274, 290
    production of, 106
    standard parts of, 271
tact, 70, 156
tag cloud, 273, 274
tagging, 18, 117, 126
Tazzia, Ed, 338
Team Workspace, 30
teams, 28–30
    advantages of, 29
    disadvantages of, 29
    effective communication in, 28–29
    performance of, 29
    technology for, 17
    virtual, 35
technology
    for business communication, 16–19, 20–21
    for composing messages, 84
    for producing messages, 105–106
    for producing reports, 268–269
    for revision, 99–102
    keeping in perspective, 20
    using productively, 21
Technorati, 340
telephone, 54
telephone etiquette, 30, 31
telephony, Internet, 54
telepresence, 17
templates, 84, 105, 268, 276
tense, of verbs, H-7
termination, job, 344
termination letters, 186
testing, preemployment, 371–372
text boxes, 106, 268
text messaging, 54, 116, 121
text slides, 320
thank-you messages, 381, 382

There are, 98–99
thesaurus, computer, 102
Thomas site, 222
three-step writing process, 48–49
    for business blogs, 124–126
    for creating podcasts, 126–127
    for e-mail messages, 117–119
    for instant messages, 121–122
    for job application letters, 366
    for negative messages, 172–173
    for oral presentations, 311
    for persuasive messages, 200–203
    for proposals, 232–233, 234
    for recommendation requests, 146–148
    for refusing a claim, 182
    for reports, 232–233, 234
    for responding to claims, 153
    for résumés, 342, 343, 346
    for routine and positive messages, 143–144,
        146, 147
    for wikis, 129
time allotment, for writing, 49
time and space, as nonverbal communication, 40
time extension, request for, 382, 383
time limits, for oral presentations, 313
Time, Inc., 223
Times New Roman, 323
Times Roman, 104, 105
Tindell, Kip, 28
title
    italics for, H-23
    capitalization of, H-23
    for reports, 278, 279
    for visuals, 277
title fly, 278
title page, 278, 278, 279
title slides, 326
titles, professional, A-2, A-4
tone
    for business blogs, 123
    of claims/adjustment requests, 150
    of condolences, 156
    controlling, 74–75
    evaluating, 93
    of formal reports, 282
    formality of, 74–75
    for negative messages, 173, 175, 179, 181
    of positive messages, 150
    for reports and proposals, 260–261
    in responding to claims requests, 151–152
    of routine requests, 145
    in sales and marketing messages, 213
topic, of message, 58
topic sentence, 81
topical organization, 242
touch, as nonverbal communication, 40
trade journals, as resources, 238
training, 9
    using podcasts for, 126
transactions, bad news about, 179, 181
transitions, 82, H-29
    in international correspondence, 14
    in oral presentations, 318
    in reports, 268, 289
    in slide shows, 324
transitive verbs, H-8
translation, 14, 93, 268
transmittal letter, 278
transmittal memo, 278, 280

transparencies, overhead, 320
trends, visuals showing, 271
Tribune Company, 232
troubleshooting reports, 244, 357,
    246–247
truth, detecting, 38
try, H-28
Turkey, 12
Twitter, 117
2 + 2 approach, to organizing reports, 245
type
    justified, 104
    legibility of, 322
    size of, 105
type styles, 105
    for e-mail messages, 119
    for slides, 322
typefaces, 104
TypePad, 10
typographical errors, 106, 107

U

underlining, 105, H-23
unified communications, 16
United Airlines, 195
United Kingdom, A-7
unsolicited application letters, 366, 368
unsolicited proposals, 248–249, 264
uploading of files, 296, 357
uppercase letters, 105
U.S. Federal Trade Commission, 8
U.S. Postal Service, A-11, A-14, A-15
USA Jobs, 341
usage, 77, H-25–H-27
user authentication, with IM, 121
user-generated content, 117

V

Vail Products, 194
validity, of surveys, 240
value networks, 117
Vehix.com, 305
verbs, H-7–H-9
    action, 349
    camouflaged, 96
    voice of, 76, 77, H-9
very, 97
vidcasts, 55
video, 55
    in documents, 102, 276
    for résumés, 354
    in slide shows, 324
video blogs (vlogs), 55
video interviews, 371
video podcasts. *See* vidcasts
video-sharing sites, 117
videoconferences, 17, 35
video résumés, 354
viral marketing, using blogs for, 124
virtual agents, 19
virtual meeting spaces, 16
virtual meetings, 35
virtual office, 16, 30
virtual reality. *See* virtual worlds
virtual whiteboards, 35
virtual worlds, 35, 371
viruses, spread by bots, 121
virus protection, 118, 119
visual media, 53, 56

visuals
    benefits of, 320
    deciding where to use, 269
    designing, 276–277
    distortion of, 8
    integrating into text, 277
    introducing, 285
    numbering of, 284, 285
    for oral presentations, 320–324
    placement of, 284
    proofing of, 277
    purpose of, 269
    for reports, 269–277
    titles for, 284
    types of, 269–273
Visuwords, 79
Vital Speeches of the Day, 331
vlogs, 123
vocabulary, H-25–H-29
vocal characteristics
    as nonverbal communication, 39
    in job interviews, 377
voice mail, 31
voice recognition, 17
voice synthesis, 17
voice technologies, 17
voice, of verbs, 76, 77, H-9
VoIP. *See* Internet-based phone service
Volt, 357

W

W. R. Grace, 13
Wal-Mart, 13, 124, 168
"walk-arounds," 53
want ads, 338
    responding to, 366, 367
wardrobe, business, 30
warranties, extended, 193
Web 2.0, 117
Web Accessibility Initiative (WAI), 226
web-based meetings, 17, 35–36
web-based seminars, 320
web content management systems. *See* content
        management systems
web directories, 239
web publishing systems, 105
webcasts, 32, 312, 320, 324
Webcor Builders, 194
webinars, 320
webpages, search engines and, 238–239
websites
    company, 339
    complaint, 186–187
    job, 339
    organizing content for, 242–244
    posting résumés to, 356
    résumés on, 356
    see also Internet
white space, 104, 286
whiteboards, 320
    electronic, 16
    virtual, 35
Whole Foods Market, 225
wikis, 17, 30, 117, 128–129
    collaborating on, 128–129
Winnebago Industry, 165
wireless networking, 16
wizards, 84
Word. *See* Microsoft Word

word choice, 77–79
word division, H-20, H-25
Word of Mouth Marketing Association, 8
word processing
    features of, 99, 101–102
    source documentation tools in, 239
    for document production, 105
    for producing reports, 268
word processing tools, 84
words
    abstract, 77–78, H-3
    correct use of, 77
    effective, 77, 78
    familiar, 78, 79
    frequently confused, H-25–H-26
    frequently misspelled, H-28–H-29
    frequently misused, H-27–H-28
    long, 98
    positive, 173

    powerful, 78, 79
    strong vs. weak, 77, 79
    transitional, 82, H-29
    unnecessary, 97
work experience, on résumés, 350
work plan, 234, 265
working interviews, 371
workplace, etiquette in, 30
Works Cited, 292, A-20, A-25, A-26
Works Consulted, A-20
workspace, shared, 17, 30
WorldConnect Language Services, 226
writing, collaborative, 29–30, 101
writing stage, 49, 68–84
    for business blogs, 126
    for negative messages, 173
    for oral presentations, 316–319
    for persuasive messages, 202–203
    for reports and proposals, 260–269

    for résumés, 348–352
    for routine and positive messages, 143
written media, 53, 56

XYZ

xenophobia, 13
XtremityPlus, 196
Yahoo!, 30
Yahoo! Hotjobs, 341, 406
yardstick approach, to organizing
    reports, 245
you, when not to use, 69
"you" attitude, 9, 69–70
    in oral presentations, 313
    in persuasive messages, 202
    plain English and, 76
    in reports, 260
    in sales messages, 214–215
ZIP codes, A-13